THE PENGUIN BOOK OF

MODERN CANADIAN
DRAMA

MODERN CANADIAN DRAMA

EDITED BY
RICHARD PLANT

PREFACE BY HERBERT WHITTAKER

Penguin Books

Penguin Books Canada Ltd., 2801 John Street, Markham, Ontario, Canada
  L3R 1B4
Penguin Books Ltd., Harmondsworth, Middlesex, England
Penguin Books, 40 West 23rd Street, New York
Penguin Books Australia Ltd., Ringwood, Victoria, Australia
Penguin Books (N.Z.) Ltd., 182-190 Wairau Road, Auckland 10, New Zealand

Published in Penguin Books, 1984

Manufactured in Canada by Webcom
DESIGN: Brant Cowie Art-Plus Ltd
TYPESETTING: Jay Tee Graphics Ltd.

CANADIAN CATALOGUING IN PUBLICATION DATA

Main entry under title:
Penguin book of modern Canadian drama

ISBN 0-14-048188-5 (v. 1)

1. Canadian drama (English) – 20th century.*
I. Plant, Richard.

PS8307.P46 1984   C812'.5'08   C84-098581-9
PR9196.6.P46 1984

ACKNOWLEDGEMENTS

"Riel" (page 27) by John Coulter reprinted by permission of Clare Coulter and Primrose Coulter Pemberton. Copyright © The Estate of John Coulter. All rights, including performing rights, must be obtained from Mrs. John Pemberton, 17 Cornish Road, Toronto, Ontario, Canada M4T 2E3.

"Indian" (page 152) by George Ryga reprinted by permission of the author. Copyright © 1962 by George Ryga. All rights, including performing rights, must be obtained from Ryga & Associates, P.O. Box 430, Summerland, B.C., Canada V0H 1Z0.

"Fortune and Men's Eyes" (page 175) by John Herbert reprinted by permission of Grove Press, Inc., New York. Copyright © 1967 by John Herbert. All rights, including performing rights (except amateur and stock), must be obtained from Ellen Neuwald Inc., 905 West End Avenue, New York, N.Y., U.S.A. 10025. Amateur and stock performing rights must be obtained from Samuel French Ltd.

"Wedding in White" (page 246) by William Fruet © Dermet Productions, 1974. Reprinted by permission of Simon & Pierre Publishing Co. Ltd. Production rights are controlled exclusively by Simon & Pierre, Box 280 Adelaide Street Post Office, Toronto, Ontario, Canada M5C 2J4. No performances may be given without obtaining written permission in advance and payment of the requisite fee.

"Creeps" (page 333) by David E. Freeman reprinted by permission of the author and University of Toronto Press. Copyright © 1972 by David E. Freeman. All performing rights must be obtained from Ellen Neuwald Inc., 905 West End Avenue, New York, N.Y., U.S.A. 10025.

"Of the Fields, Lately" (page 380) by David French reprinted by permission of the author and General Publishing Co. Limited, Toronto, Canada. Copyright © 1975 by David French. The play may not be performed except by permission of the author.

"Handcuffs" (page 452) by James Reaney reprinted from *The Donnellys* by permission of the author and Press Porcepic Ltd., Victoria and Toronto. All performing rights of "Handcuffs", reprinted here from *The Donnellys* © 1983 by James Reaney, are fully protected, and permission to perform it, whether by amateurs or professionals, on stage, in motion pictures, public reading, radio, television, or any other means, in whole or in part, must be obtained in advance from Sybil Hutchinson, Apt. 409 Ramsden Place, 50 Hillsboro Avenue, Toronto, Canada M5R 1S8, agent for James Reaney and authorized to negotiate terms.

"Blood Relations" (page 562) by Sharon Pollock reprinted by permission of NeWest Publishers Ltd., Edmonton, Alberta. All publication rights must be obtained from NeWest Publishers Ltd. All other rights, including performing rights, must be obtained from Sharon Pollock, 319 Manora Drive N.E., Calgary, Alberta, Canada T2A 4P2.

"Ever Loving" (page 636) by Margaret Hollingsworth reprinted by permission of Margaret Hollingsworth. All rights, including performing rights, must be obtained from Margaret Hollingsworth c/o Playwrights Union of Canada, Toronto, Ontario, Canada.

"Rexy!" (page 740) by Allan Stratton reprinted by permission of Allan Stratton. First published by Playwrights Canada in 1981. Copyright © 1981 by Allan Stratton. All rights, including performing rights, must be obtained from Allan Stratton, c/o Penguin Books Canada Limited, 2801 John Street, Markham, Ontario, Canada L3R 1B4.

"Garage Sale" (page 804) by Gwen Pharis Ringwood reprinted by permission of Borealis Press Ltd. Copyright © Gwen Pharis Ringwood and Borealis Press Ltd. All rights, including professional, amateur, and motion picture performance or production; recitation; public reading; radio and television broadcasting are reserved. For permission write to Borealis Press Limited, 9 Ashburn Drive, Ottawa, Ontario, Canada K2E 6N4.

"The Art of War" (page 838) by George Walker reprinted by permission of George F. Walker. "The Art of War" was commissioned by Simon Fraser University as the keynote address to the Conference on Art and Reality, August, 1982. It was first produced professionally by Factory Theatre Lab, Toronto Workshop Productions, in February 1983. Copyright © George F. Walker. All rights, including performing rights, must be obtained from Great North Artists Management Inc., 345 Adelaide Street West, Suite 500, Toronto, Ontario, Canada M5V 1R5.

Contents

Preface

A DREAM OF NATIONAL THEATRE for Canada inspired John Coulter to invite the British director Tyrone Guthrie, who had worked with the CBC in the '30s, back to this country in 1942, a decade before he actually returned to launch the Stratford Shakespearean Festival. According to Coulter a rival effort by Roly Young, who preceded me as drama critic at *The Globe and Mail*, sabotaged this plan. Coulter was angry: being a poet, a playwright, and an Irishman he understood that you can't have a national theatre without a national drama.

He wasn't the only person who had noticed that, of course. There were many of us. I had directed my first original script, Janet McPhee's *Divinity*, in Montreal as far back as 1939. The Montreal Repertory Theatre, to which I became attached, worked hard for new scripts. But Canadian writers favoured other outlets and, to tell the truth, the directors of the "little theatres" seemed to prefer Samuel French's acting editions.

"At the Arts and Letters Club," said Coulter, speaking of the influential Toronto institution, "we did a series of plays not because they were good but because they were by Canadians about Canadians." His own were included. He told me that when he asked the members for suggestions about Canadian subjects the consensus was that Louis Riel, the Métis who had brought Manitoba into Confederation, would supply excellent theatrical material. So Coulter wrote *Riel*.

This 1950 success strikes me as an excellent choice by Professor Richard Plant to lead off this selection of modern Canadian drama. I would be remiss, however, if I did not remind readers that modern drama in this country did not start with Coulter, and warn them of our Canadian trick of labelling every milestone the first one. About a decade before Coulter extended his invitation to Guthrie, the Dominion Drama Festival showed the same concern by instituting the Sir Barry Jackson Challenge Trophy "for the best presentation of a play written by a Canadian." Martha Allan of the Montreal Repertory won it first with her own *All on a Summer's Day* in 1936, although the young Festival had already welcomed Mazo de la Roche's *Low Life* and Lillian Thomas' *Jim Barber's Spite Fence*, from Montreal and Winnipeg respectively. But it was London, Ontario "little theatre" which scored both a Barry Jackson and a Bessborough top production award with W. Eric Harris' *Twenty-Five Cents*. Personally, I had actively campaigned for an all-Canadian play festival as far back as 1950, but it didn't happen until 1967. It took our centennial to bring it about.

The easy abundance of plays from Britain, France, the United States, and the bookshelves have at times made it look as if Canadians had decided that playwrights were, like wine, best imported. But this attitude has rarely gone uncontested. We have had playwrights like W. A. Tremayne (in Montreal we called him Billy Tremayne), Merrill Denison, and the visionary from Sarnia, Herman Voaden; Michel Tremblay, Rick Salutin, Carol Bolt, Jacques Languirand, Len Peterson, and Marcel Dubé in our more recent history; but if we pursue the subject we can go back to the days of political burlesques, garrison japes, explorer's masques, and native rituals. (It no longer seems so important that Brian Doherty, Joanna M. Glass, and Bernard Slade could make the Broadway scene, but for too long it was the seal of approval we needed.)

Riel is an excellent choice if you put it in such perspective. It also salutes a determined pioneer, Dora Mavor Moore, whose New Play Society proclaimed a preference for new works. In 1949, when I arrived at Toronto's *Globe and Mail* from *The Montreal Gazette* to pursue my career as drama critic, I was most encouraged by a New Play Society season which matched five new plays against five classics. Though I missed the NPS showing of Morley Callaghan's *To Tell the Truth* at the city's proud road-house, the Royal Alexandra, I was on hand to review the premiere of *Riel*, directed by Donald Harron and starring Mavor Moore. I wrote: "Where the Coulter drama shines out as worthy of the stage is in the sharply-explored characterizations, the unfailing humour, the economy of historical exposition, the swiftness and colour of the action, all of which are more marked in the first half than the second."

Riel took off and Coulter brought that second half up to scratch. "Changes prompted by what actual production revealed," the dramatist noted in the text he sent me. There have been changes, too, for the radio and television versions and others to come, but I am glad that Professor Plant has chosen the first revised text, a genuine milestone along the rugged road of Canadian self-expression on stage.

Like *Riel*, George Ryga's *The Ecstacy of Rita Joe* brought a native shame to national attention. Its first production, in 1967 by director George Bloomfield of the Vancouver Playhouse, a champion of playwrights from its start, also helped open the National Arts Centre two years later. I caught the last NAC performance, sharing my seats with Gratien Gélinas, who had created another milestone with *Tit-Coq* in 1949. Deeply moved, we went backstage to compliment Frances Hyland, the original Rita, and Chief Dan George. Then we went home, each to stage our own productions of *Rita Joe*; his for Montreal's Comédie Canadienne, mine for the University Alumnae at Toronto's Central Library. That's how impressed we both were by *The Ecstacy of Rita Joe*. *Indian*, an earlier work, is included in this collection.

I saw John Herbert's sensational *Fortune and Men's Eyes* in 1963 off-Broadway after it had been nurtured by *The Toronto Star* drama critic Nathan Cohen, columnist Lotta Dempsey, and a Stratford Festival workshop. The Actor's Playhouse in New York had honed it to a point which demanded a Canadian production of this vivid indictment of our penal system. It was to get many showings here, including one at Montreal's Centaur Theatre in 1969, before Maurice Podbrey discovered David Fennario, Centaur's own controversial dramatist. In 1975, the play won a Chalmers Award for Toronto's Phoenix Theatre, having taken a long time to reach the city's professional stage.

Like *Fortune and Men's Eyes*, William Fruet's *Wedding in White* was to become a motion picture, but the difference was that this film was made in Canada, though with British actor Donald Pleasance replacing Anthony Parr, the original father in this unflattering view of Canada at war. The first showing of the play took place at The Poor Alex, a small space which the Royal Alexandra's new owner, Edwin Mirvish, helped establish for experimental work in what we then called "the alternate theatre." *Wedding* was one of the first "alternate" successes.

David Freeman's *Creeps* was marked by two Toronto openings no less, both directed by Bill Glassco. His 1971 success at the dedicated Factory Lab with this bitingly comic script about disadvantaged Canadians led him to open his own Tarragon Theatre with it the very next year. It was the mood of the times which gave Toronto greater attention for its thrust towards indigenous drama than had been accorded the West Coast outburst in the '60s or the explosion in Quebec in the '50s and earlier. As a native Montrealer I'm more inclined than Professor Plant to celebrate this latter expression of a nation, but I must remember that this volume includes only English-Canadian plays.

9

It was at Tarragon that David French made his debut as a playwright with *Leaving Home* in 1972. It ran there in both spring and fall of that year. But an even greater satisfaction for me came when I saw it in Vancouver, going from Tarragon's modest space to main-stage production at the Playhouse, with that uncontested Canadian star, Kate Reid, succeeding to the role Florence Patterson had played so well. The Playhouse program reported French's new success with *Of The Fields, Lately* back at Tarragon with Florence Patterson in the role of Mary.

Tarragon, to which French brought his experience as a displaced Newfoundlander, later explored modern Quebec for Ontario through the sharp eyes of Michel Tremblay. It also explored Ontario with the three Donnelly plays by James Reaney, vividly staged by Keith Turnbull in collaboration with the Stratford-born poet and teacher. Each play in the trilogy achieved high critical approval and hence three nominations for Chalmers Awards in 1973, 1974, and 1975. Professor Plant's selection of *Handcuffs*, the third winner, honours the whole Donnelly trilogy. It also traces a change in attitude to wrong-doers. The view of the Donnellys as rejects from our culture opened the field to more vulnerable heroes on our stage.

It is a relief to encounter Sharon Pollock's *Blood Relations* (1975) and Margaret Hollingsworth's *Ever Loving* (1980) at this point in the collection, for the presence of these two Western-based writers helps redress any threat of regional imbalances. The inclusion of veteran Gwen Pharis Ringwood's 1981 work, *Garage Sale*, makes us feel easier still.

Blood Relations brings a Canadian perspective to a cherished American crime in an original way that reminds me that, among her many other accomplishments in theatre, the author won a Best Actress Award from the DDF in 1966. *Ever Loving* examines our colonization by war brides after the Second World War. It makes a welcome partner to *Waiting for the Parade*, in which another gifted Western playwright, John Murrell, looks at the war through the eyes of the women waiting at home. I saw *Ever Loving* at Toronto's Adelaide Court, but its premiere took place at Victoria's Belfry Theatre, where I had once shown five Australian critics Linda Griffith's *Maggie and Pierre*. It astonished them that we took such a public peek at our Prime Minister's private life.

Would they be equally astonished at Allan Stratton's view of a previous Prime Minister in the 1981 play *Rexy!*? The fun of this was enhanced significantly by Larry Reynolds' impersonation of William Lyon Mackenzie King at the Phoenix Theatre. No comment on our drama can ignore the actors — drama is, above all, a collaborative art.

From Mavor Moore, Bruno Gerussi, and Albert Millaire, who all played Riel, through the capable casts of *Fortune and Men's Eyes* and *Creeps* (one especially remembers Victor Sutton) to Florence Patterson and Kate Reid in the French plays, to Patricia Ludwig, Jerry Franken, and Michael Hogan as Donnellys, to Shirley Douglas, Clare Coulter, and Marti Maraden in *Blood Relations* and on to David Bolt and David Fox in George Walker's work, we now recognize that our actors can win livelihood and reputation without leaving the country, that our playwrights have accumulated a splendid body of collaborators.

Walker and the late Mrs Ringwood, two representative but sharply contrasted writers, conclude this collection. The latter's *Garage Sale* comes a half century after she won, as a student, national notice with *Still Stands the House*. This later play, first staged at Pam Hawthorne's New Play Centre in Vancouver, gives us the opportunity to salute both a beloved, sensitive playwright and a great source of support on our Western scene.

Walker won acclaim before *The Art of War* was first seen in a Factory Lab production at George Luscombe's Toronto Workshop Productions theatre, home of such collective creations as *Mr Bones*, *Ten Lost Years*, and *Ain't Lookin'*, as important to our drama's development as Theatre Passe Muraille's *The Farm Show* and *Doukhobors* under Paul Thompson's direction. Walker is very much his own man, even directing his own successes, such as *Zastrozzi* (1977) and *Theatre of Film Noir* (1981), and this lively satire in 1983.

Between Coulter and Walker lies a whole parade of playwrights, appropriately celebrated here. Within a scant three decades we have reached a point at which we are looking back for our Lost Plays, being already confident that the plays to come will be well looked after by the newly-arrived Playwrights Union of Canada. Time indeed for a *Penguin Book of Modern Canadian Drama, Volume One*.

HERBERT WHITTAKER
Toronto, June 1984

Introduction

This anthology brings together twelve plays that are eminently worth performing or reading, as well as representative of recent developments in English-Canadian theatre and drama. They offer not only a view of the stylistic and thematic range of English-Canadian drama over approximately the past two decades, but also a sense of our theatre's enormous geographical distribution. At the same time they demonstrate the generally recognized quality of recent years: among the twelve are six Chalmers Award nominees (four of them winners), the winner of the first Governor General's Award for published drama (*Blood Relations*, 1981), and four nominees for the Dora Mavor Moore Awards (one winner). The fact that this is the first anthology of contemporary Canadian drama in English brought out by a major publishing house is in itself worthy of note. A mere twenty years ago Canadian drama did not have even a small publisher willing and able to provide such an anthology. At the time many people would have complained that Canadian plays did not warrant such attention. Now, the abundance of good Canadian drama is sufficient to support a number of different collections.

Since the audience for this book is likely to include a number of people unfamiliar with Canadian theatre and drama, this introduction is intended, along with the preface, the short biographical sketch of each playwright, and the note on each play's production history, to place the drama in a meaningful perspective.

Riel is an appropriate place to begin, for it offers a link with Canadian theatre of the past at the same time it foreshadows the plays that follow it. Written by John Coulter, an Irish-immigrant playwright whose early Irish works (e.g., *The House in the Quiet Glen*) were very popular with Canadian "little theatres" in the '30s and '40s, *Riel* opened on 17 February 1950 in a Toronto production by the New Play Society. Run by the indomitable Dora Mavor Moore, the NPS staged 47 new Canadian plays between 1946 and 1956. These were years of great ferment in the Canadian arts. More than a dozen professionally-oriented theatre companies had emerged by 1954 across a Canada that had previously been entertained largely by foreign plays put on by local amateur groups and their umbrella organization, the Dominion Drama Festival. Most professional productions at the time were by visiting foreign companies, predominantly from the United States. No wonder, then, that despite the limitations of its performance (Nathan Cohen was later to remark, "an enthusiastic but lamentable rendering on the matchbox stage of the Royal Ontario Museum concert hall"(*The Toronto Star*, 29 March 1962), *Riel* was seen as highly significant. Elizabeth Hay Trott spoke of the "general exaltation" over *Riel*, commenting, "It is not often, unfortunately, that good plays are written with a Canadian background, or that Canadian audiences will throng to see a drama by one of their own countrymen" (Verdon *Empire Advance*, 5 April 1950).

Here, people seemed to feel, was a Canadian play worthy of their serious attention, centred on a Canadian hero, performed by a Canadian company, and starring Canadian actors. Moreover, it was written by a Canadian playwright. (Like numerous other immigrant authors, including Margaret Hollingsworth, Coulter quickly became "Canadian." His adoption was no doubt aided by his energetic work on behalf of indigenous theatre almost from the moment he arrived in 1936.) Built on a dramatic action that involved age-old Canadian hostilities — French vs. English vs. Irish, natives vs. interlopers, ancestral vs. conqueror's land rights, Catholics vs. Protestants, industrial advance vs. Nature, to name a few — the play caught on.

Following the NPS staging, Canadians enjoyed a radio adaptation (1951), a two-part CBC television production (1961), the publication of an improved text (1962; 1972), and a lavish performance in a further revised script at Ottawa's National Arts Centre (1975). In addition there have been several spin-offs: the Harry Somers-Mavor Moore opera in 1970 dedicated to John Coulter; George Woodcock's *The Defender of the Past* (1967) and *Six Dry Cakes for the Hunted* (1975); Rod Langley's *Tales of a Prairie Drifter* (1972); Claude Dorge's *Le Roitelet* (1976). Whether, as some claim, Coulter started what Geoffrey James in *Time* (3 February 1975) called the "Riel industry" is a debatable point, for as early as 1886 the Riel rebellion had engendered Bayer and Parage's melodramatic *Riel: drame historique en quatre actes et un prologue* and Elzéar Paquin's polemical *Riel: tragédie en quatre actes*, as well as an inconsequential "military extravaganza," George Broughall's *The 90th on Active Service* (1885), and Sergeant L. Dixon's burlesque, *Our Boys in the Riel Rebellion* (1886).

Whatever the case, one of the strengths of Coulter's play is the inherently charismatic Riel, the kind of figure of which myth is made: an enigmatic madman/traitor/visionary/patriot/martyr. In 1950, however, not everyone agreed that Coulter's ambiguous treatment of his hero was laudable. Vincent Tovell was an example: "In the end Mr Coulter leaves us with the questions that stimulated him, the puzzle of Riel's personality and the problem of placing and evaluating him in history, but without the author's own opinions. Had he been willing to adopt a point of view and

15

set out the story from that perspective, its significance, and the drama inherent in it, might perhaps have been fixed more vividly in our minds" (University of Toronto *Quarterly*, v. 20, p. 274). Surely, however, what would have resulted from that approach is a narrower drama avoiding the complexity of issues inherent in the character and action.

When Coulter revised the script for its first publication in 1962, he did so with the advantage of the staging and broadcasts the play had received. The text was improved, and it is that 1962 version, the best of all his versions, which is printed here. Among the changes, Coulter removed a melodramatic subplot — the ill-fated love story of a young Indian woman — and dropped the subtitle, "Patriot or Traitor," without answering the implied question. Yet, he moved a little in Tovell's direction in the 1975 Ottawa revisions where Riel (played admirably by Quebec's Albert Millaire) and the Métis appeared victims more of national politics and an intractable judicial process than of the balance of forces in the script published here. Coulter also tightened up the often-criticized, talky second act (scenes 8, 10, 12, 14, and 16 were cut as was the embarrassing Trooper in 17). He had Riel's mother and the Métis speak French, and ended Act One with a confrontation between Taché and Wolseley which revealed the abuse of the Métis by Wolseley's soldiers. The trial proceedings were re-worked, giving the Defence and Crown long addresses: the former argued that government failures to correct injustices against the Métis forced an essentially pacifist Riel to act and that the extreme circumstances drove him mad; the Crown replied, with less success, that Riel was sane, his actions deliberate. Then, as he does in the present scenes 7 and 9, Riel spoke movingly on his own behalf. These addresses possess more rhetorical than dramatic power, but combine with the other changes to strengthen the Métis' case.

One is tempted to see in the 1975 revisions a connection with changes occurring in Canada at the time: the evolution of a national policy on bilingualism and governmental willingness to listen to claims for native rights. We likely also see the influence on the text of the bilingual cast available to the National Arts Centre. In those respects, as well as in obvious aspects of its dramaturgy, the text we have published reflects more clearly than the Ottawa version the 1950s and early 1960s, which is one of the reasons it appears in this anthology. It allows a window on the development of modern Canadian drama.

From *Riel* and its antecedents (see Anton Wagner, ed., *Canada's Lost Plays*, v. 1-4), English-Canadian drama evolved in quantity and quality through plays such as George Ryga's *Indian* (1962), heavily influenced by radio and television, to an explosion of often self-consciously nationalistic activity in the later '60s and early '70s. The impact of programs celebrating the nation's centennial in 1967, a year marked by the appearance in Vancouver of George Ryga's memorable *The Ecstasy of Rita Joe*, of *Fortune and Men's Eyes* (ironically, in New York), and at the Stratford Festival of James Reaney's innovative *Colours in the Dark*, obviously had something to do with the evolution. But the largest push came when a number of small professional theatre companies appeared on the scene and chose as their mandate the development and production of Canadian plays. *Of the Fields, Lately*, *Wedding in White*, and *Creeps* date from that period. In recent years — from the late '70s on — this exclusivity has been tempered by the inclusion of non-Canadian plays in the seasons of some of the nationally-oriented theatres (the most notable might be Toronto's Tarragon Theatre). Many people see this as a maturing of vision in Canadian theatre, paralleled by Canadian playwrights looking beyond Canada for subjects and settings: *Blood Relations* is a case in point.

Another sign of increasing maturity in Canadian drama after *Riel* is the willingness of playwrights to probe Canadian life and character in a highly critical way. Throughout the first half of the twentieth century, English-Canadian drama was dominated by light comedies, farces, domestic melodramas, historical pageants, and the like, very few of which questioned anything seriously. Most of them exhibited little dramatic excellence. A few important plays of

17

the time stand out, of course: Merrill Denison's *Marsh Hay* (1923), Herman Voaden's daring experiments in his "symphonic expressionism" (1930s), Gwen Pharis Ringwood's *Still Stands the House* (1937), Len Peterson's *Burlap Bags* (1946), and, among his other satirical works, Robertson Davies' *Fortune, My Foe* (1949), as well as the plays of the left-wing Workers' Theatres in the '30s. But the playwrights in this collection, like their colleagues, see significant upheaval in Canadian life. Most of this upheaval is common to universal situations, but all of it has a particular Canadian application.

When he argued that Riel's actions were defensible in light of English-Canadian persecution of the French-Indian Métis, John Coulter upset conventional English-Canadian history, which had firmly established Louis Riel as a villain. Then in 1962, on national television, only a year after *Riel* appeared on the same medium, George Ryga's *Indian* repeated the indictment against white Canada. In a country which prided itself on the absence of American-style wild-west Indian massacres, and whose self-perception was one of a beneficent friend to native peoples, the revelation of multi-level racial prejudice was cause for reflection. *Indian* was soon followed by Ryga's *The Ecstasy of Rita Joe* (1967), which brought the native/white clash into even higher profile, as did Herschel Hardin's Inuit drama, *Esker Mike and his Wife Agiluk* (1969).

At about the same time, drawing on his own personal experience, John Herbert in *Fortune and Men's Eyes* (1967) graphically dramatized the corruption of young prison inmates and Canadian society's belligerent intolerance of those outside the norm. David E. Freeman, also drawing on personal experience for his hard-hitting *Creeps* (1971), depicted a more subtle bias against those who are different. Ostensibly about cerebral palsy victims, the play can also be seen to operate somewhat metaphorically representing individuals whose physical and/or psychological handicaps doom them to the washrooms of the world, society's lower depths, as it were. In one way there seems little difference between the prison of *Fortune and Men's Eyes* and the sheltered workshop of *Creeps*, or among the self-perpetuating ghetto conditions reflected in *Indian*, *Fortune and Men's Eyes*, and *Creeps*.

The same fierce attacks on Canadian society continue in William Fruet's *Wedding in White*. The focus here, however, is the simple-minded puritanism, often associated, rightly or wrongly, with the Scots-Canadian heritage, that is unable to deal effectively with an apparent conflict between purity and worldly experience. The resulting distorted and repressive code of behaviour, largely concerning sexual roles in *Wedding in White*, also fosters the psychological tensions in David French's *Of the Fields, Lately*. Incapable of revealing intimate thoughts and emotions freely, and in an "acceptable" way, French's characters repress their reactions until they explode in psychological or physical attacks on other people.

Recent years have seen a move toward subtler criticism in a skilfully crafted comic vein. That is the fashion of *Rexy!* where Allan Stratton gently reveals shortcomings in the achievements and quirky aspirations of the late Prime Minister Mackenzie King. Through him we see Canadians themselves. George Walker's *The Art of War* is equally comic and skilful, but explores larger questions. The play implies that in the ongoing war between philistinism and civilization, the latter has lost, at least temporarily, to the largely philistine modern world's quest for political and economic power. While Walker's battle is fought in an international arena, the same war has been especially evident in Canada where utilitarianism and puritanical restraint from pleasure (including cultural pleasure) hold a high place in our consciousness. We find the same warring cultural and anti-cultural forces reflected in James Reaney's Donnelly trilogy.

In fact Reaney brings all the previously mentioned areas of Canadian life under attack in his broadly conceived view of the Canadian consciousness at work in the Donnelly massacre of 1880. The plays imply that this consciousness still exists. Before going on with my comments, however, I should provide a brief note on the substance of the two

Donnelly plays, *Sticks and Stones* and *The St Nicholas Hotel*, which precede *Handcuffs*, and which many readers may not know.

Sticks and Stones opens after James and Johanna Donnelly (Mrs Donnelly in *Handcuffs*) have emigrated from Ireland and established a homestead with a family of seven boys in Biddulph Township. But the Irish Blackfoot-Whitefoot feud, which has also emigrated, catches them in its fearful bigotry and persecution. The play dramatizes events around James Donnelly's provoked killing of Patrick Farl at a logging bee. Donnelly is jailed; Johanna successfully petitions for his release; but their troubles have only begun. Terrorists in the community try unsuccessfully to drive them out, and the play ends with James and Johanna vowing to remain. Yet we are aware at that moment, as we have been throughout the play, that they are "handcuffed" as it were, to Biddulph, their only escape a spiritual one through the death their resolve brings about. *The St Nicholas Hotel*, with its recurrent images of toll gates guarding the boundaries of Biddulph and of a railway on which an unstoppable death train runs, focuses on three incidents: the wars of the "Opposition Stage" which the Donnelly boys operate, the fated love between Maggie Donovan and Will Donnelly (the crippled, artistic son), and the murder, instigated by James Carroll, of Michael Donnelly, a railway brakeman living outside Biddulph. (There is no escape for the Donnellys.) As *Handcuffs* begins, we have witnessed a chain of persecution which the Donnellys have faced with heroic courage and integrity, held together by bonds of love and trust within their family. *Handcuffs* opens years after the massacre in 1880.

Like Louis Riel, the Donnellys live in many Canadian minds as historic villains. They cut the tongues out of horses, burned people's barns, and their ghoulish spirits have stalked the earth for over a century. In short, they are the very personification of evil, an idea picked up in William Donnelly's crippled foot and fiddle playing. Much of this character has been created by malignant fiction such as Thomas Kelley's *The Black Donnellys* and *Vengeance of the Black Donnellys* or by word-of-mouth exaggeration — "If you don't go to sleep, child, the Donnellys'll getcha." But like Coulter in his history play, Reaney wants to look at the other side of the story, at what drove a community to murder the Donnellys and let the murderers go unpunished. In doing so he greatly surpasses the limited success of Coulter's *Riel*. He turns folk tale and factual history into poetic legend, tipping the balance in favour of the martyred family and revealing the warped sensibility of a Canadian society governed by fear.

Among the forces behind the Donnelly murders are puritanical repression, hypocrisy, and prejudice against a minority of individuals who are different, hence threatening, to the rest of society. These are the tools of a terrified people against their apparent enemies — in this case, somewhat figuratively speaking, heroes on a romantic quest in search of truth and freedom. It is a recurrent theme in Canadian drama, reflecting actual experience. As in the Donnelly trilogy, the migrant heroes may come from outside the country — we see this repeated in *Ever Loving* and *Wedding in White*; as in *Of the Fields, Lately*, they may move from one part of Canada to another. Without stretching the framework too much, one may also be able to see the ineffectual T.M. Power in *The Art of War*, in his bumbling, parodic fashion, unconsciously travelling on a similar mission. These dramatic visions of peaceable kingdoms continually thwarted on social, cultural or metaphysical levels are indeed condemning ones.

Sharon Pollock's *Blood Relations* presents another attack on puritanical repressiveness and hypocrisy, for those are the forces which shape Lizzie Borden's feelings for her parents. The play offers the same rather simple but intense psychological realism of *Wedding in White* and *Of the Fields, Lately* with the same accompanying social and moral criticism. On another level Pollock's drama centres around a character closer in size to the mythical Donnellys, for Lizzie is more than psychologically trapped by social and moral restrictions. In fact, as long as she remains the Lizzie Borden of murder-trial notoriety, she has no existence at all. That is

21

where the play is especially sophisticated: the idea is the form. We are never allowed to see the real Lizzie. She is either an actress playing Lizzie Borden in 1902 when the action opens; that Lizzie in turn playing Bridget, the maid, in 1892; or an actress playing Lizzie's actress/lover playing Lizzie in the "psychodramatic game" (to borrow Ann Saddlemyer's aptly chosen term) at the core of the drama. The multi-level impersonations, slightly reminiscent of Genet's monumental works, raise questions about the fundamental nature of human character, action, and identity. As graphically illustrated in the unresolved parricide scene, Lizzie as we know her is denied action — after all she has been acquitted — and as a result of that denial, she exists only as the spirit of freedom seeking physical embodiment or identity.

Garage Sale, Gwen Ringwood's play, also asks large questions about human character at the same time it explores some of the same territory covered by other plays in this collection. As well, it focuses on biases and discrimination against individuals whom society sees as different. Ringwood's method, however, is subtler than that of most other Canadian playwrights. At a distance — the same distance or level of ignorance that so often breeds prejudice — the Crangs appear socially and morally aberrant, even to the point of selling their baby. That possibility, however, is a frightening, humorous figment of Reb's imagination, as is his Quixotic mission to rectify the situation. The sense of isolation which Reb and Rachel project onto the Crangs is obviously their own. This projection reflects their geographical isolation from a world they would like to know, a traditional Canadian experience brought on as much by a fear of the unknown as by great land distances. It also reflects Reb and Rachel's relationship with their children and the typical loneliness of old age. On another level the isolation is a manifestation of their relationship with each other and with themselves. A deftly maintained undercurrent in the play suggests that Rachel and Reb have always had desires that remained unfulfilled, both by each other and by themselves. To some extent the characters are two sides of one human being: simply stated, the romantic or imaginative and the realist. The play dramatizes the gap between the two and implies that where they cannot be brought together in equal fulfilment — and perhaps they cannot be at all — only compassion, tolerance, and understanding will allow survival. It is a play with a profound sense of human existence.

Garage Sale appears in this collection for reasons other than its skilful playwriting and the subtle strength of its thematic expression. Its author, Gwen Pharis Ringwood, was a western Canadian theatre pioneer writing for the stage and radio fifty years ago. Her presence in the modern day theatre, possibly even more than John Coulter's, links the past with the present; for instance, George Ryga studied under her at the Banff School of Fine Arts. It may be more than a coincidence, then, that his one-act play, *Indian*, shares its topic of the Indians' confrontation with white society, with an earlier one-act by Ringwood, *Maya* (*Lament for Harmonica* in a later version). As well, *Garage Sale* leans back to the '30s and '40s, the beginning of Ringwood's career, when the one-act play in a realistic mode dominated Canadian playwriting. Her own *Still Stands the House* (1937) is now a Canadian classic in the form. During those early years the one-act was established, at least in part, by the Dominion Drama Festival. Half-hour drama broadcasts on national radio were also a strong influence. Joined by television drama in the '50s, these short programs have helped maintain the one-act form up to the present, as *Indian* illustrates.

The traditional realistic mode has played an enormous role in Canadian drama throughout the twentieth century, reaching a moment of special significance during the late '60s and early '70s when plays like *Creeps*, *Wedding In White*, and *Of the Fields, Lately* were performed. The social and psychological realism of the period drew attention to questions about Canadian identity with the proliferation of realistic detail on the stage confirming for audiences the authenticity — the "Canadian-ness" — of their own lives.

23

Nonetheless, throughout the twentieth-century, in Canada as elsewhere, playwrights have persistently sought to break the confines of realism. Gwen Ringwood's plays have always been touched by elements of the poetic and fantastic, and although John Coulter's early works, such as *The Family Portrait*, were often in a conventional realistic mode, one senses throughout his career a desire to try other possibilities. No wonder then the appeal of the imaginative freedom of radio. Ringwood wrote extensively for radio; Coulter worked for both the BBC and CBC. Coulter also learned from the experiments in modern staging he became acquainted with through Tyrone Guthrie from the '20s on. The neo-Elizabethan style and episodic, chronological structure of *Riel*, which were much commented on in 1950, owe something to these influences. Oddly, however, despite the impact of the Stratford Festival (established after Coulter wrote *Riel*), the neo-Elizabethan style he calls for has appeared in few, if any, successful Canadian plays. On the other hand an episodic, chronological structure (essentially the form of *Rexy!*), in conjunction with a documentary approach, has become firmly established among the many Canadian companies using an improvisational, collective creation method. The mode has resulted in highly popular plays such as *The Farm Show* and *The West Show* by Theatre Passe Muraille and *Paper Wheat* by Twenty-Fifth Street Theatre. This style, only indirectly represented here in James Reaney's *Handcuffs*, which requires a great deal of improvisation in its performance, is a subject for an anthology unto itself in conjunction with other innovative work from recent years, for more radical experiments than those represented here have taken place in English-Canadian theatre. A few examples might hint at the range. Environmental theatre has found fascinating expression in John Juliani's Savage God company and in John Krizanc's *Tamara*, a meaningful tale of political intrigue, espionage, and romance which was staged in an old mansion where perambulating audiences followed individual characters from room to room, "spying" on their activities. An Artaudian-Grotowski inspired approach has been the core of Richard Nieoczym's work at the Actor's Lab Theatre. Surrealism flourished in elements of Lawrence Russell's *The Mystery of the Pig Killer's Daughter*, and among Hrant Alianak's non-realistic, often satirical plays is *Mathematics*, in total 190 seconds during which six groups of carefully selected, highly associative objects are thrown one by one onto the stage at precisely timed intervals. In a wholly different vein Michael Ondaatje adapted his award-winning fiction, *The Collected Works of Billy the Kid*, into an often-produced stage piece built on fragmentary scenes containing the poetic reflections and evocative prose vignettes of the original. To the extent that he continues to work with the Factory Theatre Lab, George Walker has a connection with the experimental theatre. We can see a glimpse of it in his lightly irreverent use of the conventions of murder-detective mysteries as the vehicle for a more serious comment on life than the form would normally express.

In many ways James Reaney's Donnelly trilogy is as innovative as any Canadian play. The trilogy form itself is unusual. Although the plays have normally been performed singly on separate occasions, at least once all three were staged in one day, much to the pleasure of the tenacious audience. As one would expect, the cumulative effect of the trilogy, particularly its dramatic irony, deepened the significance of the tragic events it portrays.

As the reader can judge from *Handcuffs*, the Donnelly plays consist of an arrangement of incidents that, while maintaining a loose chronology overall, folds back and forth on itself: *Handcuffs*, for instance, brings 1880 together with the present day and the years in between. This melding of one time and action into another is complemented by a similar fluency of place. Unusual in early Canadian drama, this manipulation of time, place, and action has now become commonplace. *Blood Relations* capitalizes on the three interwoven time frames that accompany the multi-level impersonations of its characters. Pollock is thus able to shift our attention away from a simple perception of what is going on, literally, to the implications of the action and layers of character. *Ever Loving* offers an equally intricate structure in which Margaret Hollingsworth places more than one time, place, and action on stage at once. The result, as in *Blood Relations*, is a sophisticated dramatic tension, often ironic, that plays one apparent reality against another, an effect similar to that achieved by Reaney's choral parts.

The tension that really ties Reaney's play together, as has often been pointed out, is that in the resonant poetic imagery. The recurrent word patterns in the dialogue are obvious in the printed text. But the reader will need to be attentive to the stage directions and read with a fertile imagination to obtain the full potential of the script. Reaney's plays are above all pieces for performance where we find the imagery in the dialogue extended into a reverberation between the spoken language and the visual picture made up of character presence and stage objects. The style of performance involves a lot of character doubling and the actors' use of props and setting in a way that sees objects taking on many different identities. The air of easy transformation facilitates the resonant echoing of the barrage of images from different sources.

One last aspect of these plays bears brief mention. Modern Canadian drama, particularly that with a documentary force behind it, often offers a different dramatic tension from that created by the traditional protagonist-antagonist opposition. In the Donnelly trilogy, *Blood Relations*, *Rexy!*, and *Riel* — plays in which the main characters are familiar historical figures — we become caught up in the tension engendered by the reality of the characters being revealed on stage bouncing off the reality of the audience's preconceptions of them. The result is our involvement in a third reality, the "real" identities of the characters and their implications. This too seems a sophisticated dramatic tension, and another indication that Canadian drama has come of age.

RICHARD PLANT
Queen's University, June 1984

THE PENGUIN BOOK OF

MODERN CANADIAN DRAMA

John Coulter

Riel

John Coulter
Riel

EDITOR'S NOTE: John Coulter was born in Belfast, Northern Ireland in 1888. By the time he emigrated to Canada in 1936, where he married Olive Clare Primrose, he was already an active playwright. His first professionally-produced play, "Sally's Chance", was directed by Tyrone Guthrie for BBC radio (Belfast) in 1924. Later re-titled *The House in the Quiet Glen*, this Ulster folk comedy won Canada's Dominion Drama Festival final in 1937 and remained a favourite with amateur theatre groups over the next two decades. From his arrival in Canada, Coulter worked tirelessly for the establishment of an indigenous Canadian theatre, and on behalf of the arts in general. Among his writings are over two dozen plays and opera libretti, a dozen pieces of short fiction, a novel, a volume of verse, an autobiography, and numerous essays. He died 1 December 1980.

Riel was first performed by the New Play Society, opening 17 February 1950 on the tiny stage of the Royal Ontario Museum theatre in Toronto. The play was broadcast on CBC radio in 1951 and on CBC television in 1961, but had its first major professional stage production only in 1975 at Ottawa's National Arts Centre. It was published by Ryerson Press in 1962 and again in 1972 by Cromlech.

For my daughter Clare whose passion is the theatre and for that enlivening master who has been an inspiration to theatre in this young country, mon ami Michel Saint-Denis.

This play in two parts is designed for presentation in the Elizabethan manner: a continuous flow of scenes on a bare stage with the aid of no more than indicative settings and properties and modern stage lighting.

Of the numerous persons who appear, few of those in Part One are seen again in Part Two, and some of those appearances are brief and do not recur. Hence, with actors doubling their roles, a cast of twenty-five is sufficient for all speaking parts. Non-speaking parts for crowd scenes may be cast to whatever extent the resources of a production allow.

The action takes place in the North-West Territories, now part of Canada, during the seventies and eighties of the last century.

PART ONE 1869-1870
1. Riel's Living Room
2. River Meadows near Fort Garry
3. Room in Fort Garry
4. Fort Garry Precincts
5. Cell in Fort Garry
6. Room in Fort Garry
7. An Open Place in Ontario
8. Fort Garry Precincts
9. Prime Minister's Room, Ottawa
10. Fort Garry Precincts
11. Room in Fort Garry
12. Room in Fort Garry

PART TWO 1885-1886
1. Porch of Riel's House, Montana
2. An Open Place in Saskatchewan
3. Another Open Place in Saskatchewan
4. Church at Batoche
5. Outside Riel's House, Batoche
6. Tent of General Middleton
7. Courtroom, Regina
8. Vicinity of Courtroom, Regina
9. Courtroom, Regina
10. Vicinity of Courtroom, Regina

11. Courtroom, Regina
12. Corridor to Cells in Police Barracks, Regina
13. Cell in Police Barracks, Regina
14. Precincts of Parliament, Ottawa
15. Prime Minister's Room, Ottawa
16. Precinct's of Police Barracks, Regina
17. Cell and Precincts in Police Barracks, Regina
18. A Place of Prayer and Mourning

The Persons: In Part One and Part Two

RIEL	Louis Riel, leader of the Métis, the half-breeds
MOTHER	His mother, a white woman
MACDONALD	Sir John A. Macdonald, Prime Minister of Canada

In Part One Only

PRIEST	A local curé
RABBIE	Scots settler
XAVIER	Half-breed
FRANÇOIS	Half-breed
SCOTT	Thomas Scott, navvy, Orangeman from Ontario
DENNIS	Colonel Stoughton Dennis, surveyor
O'DONOGHUE	One of the Council, a Fenian
YOUNG	Methodist minister
SMITH	Donald A. Smith, later Lord Strathcona
TACHE	Bishop of St. Boniface
WOLSELEY	Colonel Garnet Wolseley
CARTIER	Sir Georges Etienne Cartier
SERGEANT	British Regular
SURVEYORS,	
VOLUNTEER SETTLERS,	
HALF-BREEDS,	
INDIANS	

In Part Two Only

MARGUERITE	Indian wife of Riel
INDIAN	Riel partisan
HALF-BREED	Riel partisan

29

PRIEST	A local curé
WOMAN	Half-breed
ARMSTRONG	Scout, with Middleton's forces
MIDDLETON	General Frederick Middleton
CLERK	Clerk of the Court
JUDGE	His Honour Judge Richardson
CROWN	Counsel for the Crown
DEFENCE	Counsel for the Defence
NOLIN	Charles Nolin, cousin of Riel
ANDRE	Father Alexis André
ROY	Dr. Francis Roy
JUKES	Dr. Jukes, police surgeon
POLICEMAN	North-West Mounted Police Officer
SHERIFF	Deputy Sheriff Gibson
MARC	Newspaperman
BILL	Newspaperman
FOREMAN	Foreman of the jury
CHAPLEAU	Hon. J. A. Chapleau
TROOPER	Another North-West Mounted Police Officer

FATHER MCWILLIAMS,
HANGMAN,
PEOPLE

PART ONE SCENE ONE

Riel's Living Room

A table. Some chairs. Lamplight. The living-room of Riel's house near Fort Garry. PRIEST and O'DONOGHUE are waiting with the half-breeds FRANÇOIS and XAVIER. Except for the PRIEST, they are wearing bandoliers and have Enfield rifles. Riel's MOTHER, a brooding, watchful, raw-boned woman of the frontier, is also present.

FRANÇOIS: We wait. We wait. He does not come.

XAVIER: Always it is like this. But if he does not come soon . . . .

MOTHER: He will come when it is time to come.

O'DONOGHUE: The time to come was an hour ago. What right has he to keep us waiting here twirling our thumbs?

MOTHER: Always when he must decide something, he goes riding on the plains. . . .

O'DONOGHUE: His solitary pow-wows with the Almighty! So he can blame his unpunctuality on the Almighty — who's always punctual himself or what a divil of a smash-up there'd be in his universe!

PRIEST: Mr. O'Donoghue, in my presence at least if you would refrain from trifling with the attributes of the Almighty.

O'DONOGHUE: Is it trifling, to wish that a touch of the divine attribute of absolute punctuality should be acquired by Riel . . . ?

He is interrupted by the entrance of RABBIE, a Scots settler, who also has bandolier and rifle.

MOTHER: Rabbie, Rabbie, he comes, my Louis? He comes now?

RABBIE: Naw, not yet. No sign o' him yet. The laddies are gathering at the rendezvous frae all airts and pairts, but no sign of him. Ambroise Lepine is there. *Adjutant* Lepine, beg pardon.

FRANÇOIS: Ambroise! *(Hurriedly rising.)* It is time we go.

XAVIER: Ya! *He* gets mad always if *we* are late!

MOTHER: Go then, François. Go Xavier.

RABBIE: Aye, it'll be "Fall in!" by the time we get the length. Are you coming with us or biding, Mr. O'Donoghue?

O'DONOGHUE: I'll be after you.

MOTHER: I will go where I think Louis is. I will bring him.

MOTHER goes out with RABBIE, FRANÇOIS and XAVIER.

31

PRIEST: Mr. O'Donoghue. You're one of the few men of education here. I must appeal to you. If you would help to restrain this madness. . . .

O'DONOGHUE: But father, I'm the maddest of the mad myself — if any of us *are* mad! I disagree with Riel. But chiefly because his madness isn't mad enough. He's for holding the North-West — but under protection of the British flag. I'm for holding it under the protection of our own flag, our own arms!

PRIEST: I had hoped that even at this last moment common sense and Christian teaching might prevail.

O'DONOGHUE: It's common sense and Christian teaching to fight off any attempt by an invader to march in. . . . Or what do you want us to do? Run out and welcome the invader? Fire a salute! Send an escort!

PRIEST: It's ridiculous to speak of the survey-party sent here by the Canadian government as invaders.

O'DONOGHUE: They're the vanguard of the invasion.

PRIEST: Nonsense.

O'DONOGHUE: If we tolerate them Canadians will swarm in after them in thousands. They'll grab both us and ours. They'll lay us under tribute. Tax us! Bleed us white! For what? To help them build great buildings and roads and bridges and railways and canals — but not here! Not for us in the North-West. No, but for themselves, in Canada! To make their own big cities bigger and richer still! But no, oh no! We won't let Canada do to us what England did to Ireland. . . .

PRIEST: There we go! There we go! The thorn in the flesh for ever!

O'DONOGHUE: What any big over-blown nation in history does to a small neighbour — grab it! Gobble it up!

PRIEST: Your Irish eloquence runs away with you.

O'DONOGHUE: Irish eloquence is the flame leaping out of the fire — the passion for the rights of small peoples.

PRIEST: Yes, yes, but as well as flame there is also much smoke. It may blind you to the long perspectives, the larger purpose of Providence for *all* peoples.

O'DONOGHUE: Meaning what?

PRIEST: Meaning that history must unfold according to the divine plan in the mind of God. Whoever or whatever tries to stop it will be broken.

O'DONOGHUE: Meaning Riel and the rest of us here, the Council, will be broken?

PRIEST: Yes. If what you persist in doing is contrary to the divine plan.

O'DONOGHUE: As God won't take us into his confidence about his plan we must go on and risk being broken, if necessary, for what we think is right.

PRIEST: And who will decide what is to be thought right?

O'DONOGHUE: Ah! Now *that's* a question! But here's the oracle. Ask him.

RIEL has come in with his MOTHER. RIEL is an intense young man in his mid-twenties. He has some Indian blood. He has a moustache and sideburns. He wears a tweed jacket with dark trousers and moccasins. He does not carry arms, nor consequently does he wear a bandolier. He has on a woollen toque. He bows deeply to the PRIEST and nods to O'DONOGHUE.

PRIEST: Monsieur Riel!

O'DONOGHUE: If you'll excuse me, I'll join my comrades-in-arms.

O'DONOGHUE goes out.

33

PRIEST: An unbeliever.

RIEL: But a good accountant. We will use him in our Provisional Government.

PRIEST: Louis Riel, I am your friend as well as your priest. As your friend I warn you: this step you and the Council are taking — it is bound to have the most serious consequences.

RIEL: We have weighed the consequences, father. We must go on.

PRIEST: And if you fail?

RIEL: We will not fail.

PRIEST: But suppose — *suppose* you do?

RIEL: Suppose? No. It is no good to suppose what must not be.

PRIEST: In any case, passions will be let loose. There's bound to be killing: much bloodshed and great misery.

RIEL: We will do all we can to avoid bloodshed.

PRIEST: You won't succeed. You can't.

RIEL: I think we may.

PRIEST: No.

RIEL: Well, that is your opinion.

PRIEST: My opinion. Having given it, as emphatically and plainly as I can, I don't feel I can do more. It is a matter outside my province as a priest.

RIEL: Yes, father, yes. Outside your province. (*With point.*) It is good that you see this.

PRIEST: (*Nettled.*) You tell me what is good!

RIEL: I think it is God's will that we . . . .

PRIEST: *You* tell *me* what is God's will!

RIEL: I have prayed much. I have asked God. I think God is with us.

PRIEST: I've heard you speak in this manner before. Presuming to know the mind of God. This grows on you. I have warned you it is a fearful presumption, particularly in a layman.

RIEL: God has made his will known to laymen before.

PRIEST: God speaks through Holy Church.

RIEL: But father, I am a member of Holy Church, humble and obedient.

PRIEST: In some things about as humble and obedient as Lucifer.

MOTHER: No father, no, do not say this. . . .

RIEL: That will do, that will do! *(To PRIEST, rising to end the discussion.)* I think there is nothing more to say.

PRIEST: *(Not accepting it.)* Even that is for you to decide!

RIEL: Father I have heard your opinion.

PRIEST: Only to disregard it. A whole community is to be plunged in bloodshed simply because you say so.

RIEL: The people and the Council say so.

PRIEST: Persuaded by you. What will they say when precious lives have been lost and we are mourning our dead?

RIEL: God will give us the victory.

PRIEST: So that you may set yourself up to lord it over everyone with the high hand!

RIEL: You must not say this!

Exclamation from MOTHER.

PRIEST: But if instead you find yourself before a firing squad . . . .

MOTHER: O father!

PRIEST: Do not blame it on God or the people. It will be your own fault.

RIEL: My fault, my fault.

PRIEST: For the last time I must admonish you. . . .

RIEL: Not again please. You will not.

PRIEST: I am not asking your permission.

RIEL: Father, I will continue to make my confession to you as my priest, humbly and penitently. But you will not over-rule me in what as you say is outside your province. That is all. Now shall we leave this? I will pray for you, father. Will you please pray for me?

PRIEST: As I pray for all the insolent and erring.

RIEL: Pray that I may be kept humble and faithful.

PRIEST: Oh Louis, Louis, if only you could acquire a little, even a little genuine humility.

RIEL: I will try, father.

The tramping of men not properly trained to march is heard, coming nearer.

MOTHER: There! They are riding!

RIEL: The volunteers.

PRIEST: Then it is too late, for anything but prayer . . . *(Voice of command, off. The troop halts.)* and pained disapproval of — mock soldiering.

RIEL: Mock soldiering!

MOTHER: They have Enfield rifles, father, every man. And fifty rounds.

PRIEST: You seem well-versed in the particulars.

RIEL: From tonight they will enforce our authority here, our Provisional Government. . . .

PRIEST: *(Preparing to leave.)* My coming has been a waste of time.

RIEL: Not altogether. I wanted to see you, to ask you something. *(The PRIEST waits to hear.)* We have appointed you chaplain.

PRIEST: Chaplain?

RIEL: To our Catholic volunteers.

PRIEST: Your Catholic volunteers! Do you mean my parishioners?

RIEL: Most of them, yes. You will be chaplain?

PRIEST: Chaplain nonsense! They're my parishioners. Whatever folly you and the Council may lead them into I will still attend to their spiritual needs.

RIEL: That is all we ask.

PRIEST: Your asking has nothing to do with it.

RIEL: No, father, no. I thank you. *(The PRIEST is again turning to leave.)* Before you go, father. Will you bless me now? *(Kneels.)*

MOTHER: *(Also kneeling.)* And me, father.

PRIEST: *(To RIEL.)* Certainly not as leader of this — insurrection.

RIEL: No, father, only as the most humble, most unworthy of your parishioners.

PRIEST: May God in his mercy help you to become truly humble and less unworthy. *(Signing them with the cross as he gives the blessing.)* Benedictio Dei omnipotentis patris et filii et spiritus sancti descendat super vos et maneat semper. Amen.

37

RIEL and MOTHER: Amen.

PRIEST: *(Quietly, in paternal affection.)* Oh Louis, Louis Riel, what *am* I to make of you?

SCENE 2

River Meadows near Fort Garry

The river meadows near Fort Garry. Bright morning. A hullabaloo of angry, protesting voices is heard approaching from the right. Presently the incensed people, half-breeds, settlers, an Indian — come in, gesticulating and looking off left towards the occasion of the trouble. Most of the men are volunteers. They are armed with rifles and wear bandoliers, but they are in their working clothes and farm boots or moccasins. Among them are: RABBIE, the Scots settler who, for this occasion, may be wearing his kilts and tam-o-shanter; FRANÇOIS and XAVIER, the two French-Indian half-breeds or Métis. Riel's MOTHER.

RABBIE: *(In Scots accent.)* Grabbers! Land grabbers! That's what they are!

Cast: ad lib: "Oui Oui! Aye! Grabbers! Land Grabbers."

RABBIE: Surveyors they call themselves. But they're here to grab our lands! Look at them! Measuring!

XAVIER: *(Very agitated.)* That is my field they measure now! First, André Nault's. Now, mine! They go there. They measure! They do not ask! *(Putting up rifle and sighting as if to fire.)* Ah, they will not! they will not!

MOTHER: *(Pulling down the rifle.)* Wait, Xavier. Wait for Louis.

RABBIE: Aye, dinna fash yoursels, lads. You'll laugh when you see them scootin' back hame to the East wi' their tails atween their legs — an' a pickle or two o' lead in their behinds for auld lang syne.

XAVIER: We take them prisoners.

FRANÇOIS: Ya, ya, prisoners.

Other approving "ya ya's." A move in the direction off left is checked by Riel's MOTHER.

MOTHER: Wait for Louis. Let Louis deal with them.

From up left, a road-navvy has come in and witnessed the action. He carries a shovel or some other implement indicative of his trade. He wears working clothes, and is a surly, aggressive, fanatical-looking man. This is THOMAS SCOTT.

SCOTT: What's up here, folks, yous wi' your guns an' all? *(Catching at one of the rifles and then at one of the bandoliers in a contemptuous, inquisitive way.)* Enfields, no less! And cartridges! Who might yous be for shootin' at?

RABBIE: Maybe yoursel'.

SCOTT: Eh!

RABBIE: If you dinna march on an' quit pokin' your long Ulster snout in what dinna concern you.

SCOTT: *(With slow provocativeness.)* Frae Scotlan', eh! *(If RABBIE is wearing kilts.)* Kilts an' all, eh!

RABBIE: *(Very angry.)* March on, Ah tell you.

SCOTT: Man oh man oh man! And who do you think you're givin' orders to, you funny wee kiltie you!

RABBIE: *(Cocking the rifle.)* Mind yoursel' now or I'll gie you what you're workin' for.

SCOTT: You would would you! *(Grabs at the rifle.)* Gimme that gun here.

RABBIE: If you dare lay hand on it!

MOTHER: No, Rabbie, no, it is enough. *(Turning on SCOTT.)* And you. Go on you. Go. *(She pushes him.)*

SCOTT: Mind who you're pushin' missus.

FRANÇOIS: We know.

XAVIER: Ya.

FRANÇOIS: Thomas Scott.

SCOTT: That's right.

FRANÇOIS: Orangeman. From Ontario.

SCOTT: Right again. Yous is all Catholics I suppose.

MOTHER: We do not want Orangemen here. Go on. Go!

Others join in with: "Go on. Go!"

SCOTT: I'll go when I'm ready to go and not till then. And I'm takin' no orders from a pack o' mongrel Papishes.

This provokes an outraged chorus of: "Mongrel! Papishes!" The half-breeds and the Indian move threateningly on SCOTT with: "Kill him! Kill him!"

SCOTT: *(Throwing away his shovel or implement and circling away from them with his fists raised.)* Try it on, then, try it on, till I beat the gizzards out o' yous. Come on. *(Throws off his coat.)* Who's first for the massacree? I'll beat the best man o' the lot o' yous so come on the first o' yous that wants a lump o' his death. *(Selects FRANÇOIS.)* You there, Frenchie. I'll fight you first. Come on, if you're a proper fightin' man and not a Papish mongrel and a coward born. *(Strikes him.)* There's your cowardy.

FRANÇOIS: *(Leaping at him.)* Coward! He calls me coward!

XAVIER: *(And others.)* Kill him! Kill him, François!

MOTHER: *(Trying to get him away.)* No no, François. The mad Orange dog . . . . *(Turning to the right as she fails to stop them.)* Oh where is Louis! Come, Louis, come! *(Hurries off down right to fetch him.)*

SCOTT: One of yous at a time. One of yous at a time and I'll beat the gizzards out o' the whole jing-bang o' yous.

While the scuffle is at its height, with SCOTT and FRANÇOIS flailing at each other, and the others encouraging FRANÇOIS excitedly, two members of a survey party hurry in from up left. Although they resemble English sportsmen, they are, in fact, from Ontario. They are COLONEL STOUGHTON DENNIS and MR. WEBB. They vigorously intervene.

DENNIS: Look here, look here you people you can't do this. *(Between them.)* Drop it. Drop it I say. *(Pushing FRANÇOIS towards his friends to the right.)* Keep that man back. *(With WEBB's help pushing SCOTT to the left.)* Keep away you. Calm yourself. Control yourself.

SCOTT: Papish mongrels! Cowards born!

DENNIS: Calm down. Restrain yourself.

SCOTT: I'll smoflicate the whole jing-bang o' them, aye be Jasus will I and with one hand tied behind my back. Let me at them. Let me at them.

DENNIS: Be on your way. Go on. Take yourself off!

SCOTT: Holy kripes! So *yous* is for givin' me orders next!

DENNIS: Go on. You're making yourself obnoxious to the people here.

SCOTT: And what about yous — land grabbers!

DENNIS: Land grabbers! Balderdash!

SCOTT: It's what *they* called yous. *(Shouts at group round FRANÇOIS over to the right.)* Hi! Did yous call these ones *(Jerks his thumb at DENNIS and WEBB.)* land grabbers or did yous not?

DENNIS: *(Advancing to placate them.)* Please, please, never mind this man. I'm Colonel Dennis. Colonel Stoughton Dennis. Mr. Webb with me. Our party came out here from Ontario with full authority to make a survey. . . .

From the right. RIEL has come in quickly with his MOTHER and two armed half-breed guards. He has no rifle or bandolier. He at once intervenes.

RIEL: I beg your pardon Colonel Dennis. I am Louis Riel. I speak for the people here.

DENNIS: Indeed!

RIEL: You are not permitted to trespass any longer here.

DENNIS: Did you say trespass?

RIEL: These plains of the North-West are not for sale. Your survey will not be tolerated.

DENNIS: My dear man may I just say . . . .

RIEL: No.

DENNIS: I have a right to speak.

RIEL: Pardon, you have no rights whatever here.

DENNIS: These are the Queen's domains. We're British subjects. Canadian citizens.

SCOTT: *(Slapping DENNIS heartily on the back and being pushed angrily off by DENNIS.)* Bully Stoughty!

RIEL: Canadians have no rights whatever in these Territories.

SCOTT: Ach don't heed the Papish mongrel.

Outcries at this.

RIEL: *(To guards, sternly.)* If that man interrupts again, arrest him.

SCOTT advances menacingly on RIEL, and Riel's MOTHER and others move forward to intercept him. But RIEL holds up his hand to stop them. In tense silence, he stands quite still and eyes SCOTT.

SCOTT: Who do *you* think you are?

He suddenly strikes RIEL. In the same fraction of time the GUARDS pounce on him, and there are exclamations of shock and anger from all except RIEL, who stands rigid.

MOTHER: He is the devil. He is the devil!

RIEL: Take him away.

SCOTT is being subdued and dragged off to the left by the GUARDS with the assistance of FRANÇOIS and XAVIER, who will return later.

SCOTT: *(As they struggle with him.)* Lemme go. Lemme go. Lemme go till I knock the stuffin' out o' yous.

DENNIS: Unforgivable. An obnoxious fanatic.

RIEL: He will be punished.

MOTHER: He is the devil, the devil. For this he should be shot.

RIEL: *(To DENNIS.)* As for you, please. You go back to Canada. At once. I order this.

DENNIS: Would you mind enlightening us — by what authority . . . .

RIEL: By authority of the Provisional Government we set up today.

DENNIS: I think you must be mad.

Exclamation from MOTHER: "Louis!"

RIEL: You are speaking to the representative of the Provisional Government.

DENNIS: The Hudson's Bay Company are the legal government here under charter from her Majesty.

RIEL: Not now. They traded or tried to trade these Territories and us that live on them to Canada — without consulting us. But we will not be bought and sold. Three hundred thousand pounds from Canada — to fill the pockets of the *(Bitterly contemptuous.)* Honourable Company of Gentlemen Adventurers. . . . A pretty mess of pottage for *our* birthright! *(RIEL shouts and he shakes his clenched fist.)* The Honourable Adventurers will not sit on their honourable backsides in London and sell *us* — to Canada, or any other bidder. Twelve thousand of us. . . .

DENNIS: *(Bored.)* I hate to interrupt but if you'll allow me . . . .

RIEL: Twelve thousand loyal subjects of her Majesty. We own these lands, these plains of the North-West are ours. We had them from our mothers who had them from God, our country since the beginning of the world. *(Again there are shouts.)* Are they such fools in London and Ottawa — to think we can be pushed about and spat upon — sold, like we were sheep — twelve thousand head of sheep!

There are cries of delighted approval from RIEL's supporters: "Bravo!" "Vive!"

MOTHER: Good, Louis! Good, good!

RABBIE: *(Simultaneously.)* Fine, Mister Riel, fine! Rub their noses in it man!

DENNIS: *(Wearily patient.)* Is it my turn now to say just a word?

RIEL: It is not a discussion. I tell what is happening here and I am trying to be patient to tell it. . . .

DENNIS: Oh the dickens with it!

RIEL: Because it is important. It is a great important principle. The people of a country *(His voice rises towards a pas-
sionate climax.)* can not be taken over and incorporated
into some other country without their own consent. To
try to do that to a people is an outrage. A violation of the
rights and dignities of free men. We will fight against it.
God has directed me. . . .

DENNIS: Suppose we leave God out of it.

MOTHER: To leave God out of it!

RIEL: In London and Ottawa you may leave God out of it
but we are Christians here *(He adds, with venom.)* not
savages.

DENNIS: Yes, yes, yes, but about your rights and dignities of
course they'll be respected by Canada.

RIEL: Of course for I will make sure, very sure — if I agree
to treat with Canada. . . .

DENNIS: If *you* agree.

RIEL: And if Canada accepts my terms. . . .

DENNIS: Your terms.

RIEL: To enter Confederation.

DENNIS: I think you're a preposterous, presumptuous fool,
fit only to be certified.

*Bystanders are incensed. There are shouts of: "Strike him." "Slap
his mouth." "Shoot him."*

MOTHER: He will not say this. Do not take this Louis.

RIEL: *(With some irritation, quelling her and the others.)* Please I
will deal with it.

*As this is happening, another Scots SETTLER comes in, right — a
farmer, carrying a rake or pitchfork. He halts and watches but
takes no side. Meanwhile DENNIS and WEBB have turned away
to go off to the left.*

45

DENNIS: Come on, Webb, enough of this tomfoolery.

But at a sign from RIEL, XAVIER and FRANÇOIS bar the way with their rifles cocked.

DENNIS: Out of our way you scallywags.

RIEL: *(To their backs, with cool politeness.)* Pardon, gentlemen. If you please.

DENNIS: *(Disregarding him.)* How dare you try to stop us. Stand aside.

MOTHER: *(Peremptorily.)* When Louis speaks, turn round!

RIEL: *(To her, sharply.)* I can deal with it. *(To his back.)* Colonel Dennis I wait.

DENNIS and WEBB turn around from the levelled rifles reluctantly.

DENNIS: Well, as you have the coward's advantage of us . . . .

RIEL: You and your party will leave the settlement at once. I give you twenty-four hours to be across the border. After that if I catch any of you here . . . .

DENNIS: Well, go on?

RIEL: I think I will not catch you. But if I do you will be put in irons and locked up. *(Pointing off, up left.)* There in Fort Garry.

DENNIS: *(Surprised.)* Fort Garry?

RIEL: By noon we will have marched in. Some of us have already entered the gates.

DENNIS: Then I can only say if ever a dangerous irresponsible madman was at large I'm talking to him now. *(Turning to the others and stopping them as they begin to protest.)* As for you, you can't know what this means. I beg you don't let him lead you on, or you'll be parties to his criminal folly and you'll be crushed with him for crushed he'll surely be. There's still time to save yourselves. Which of you'll be the first?

The Scots SETTLER, who entered earlier, moves across to DENNIS who looks at RIEL.

DENNIS: Here's one who doesn't side with you. Any others? *(Singling them out.)* What about you? And you? *(They stare stonily back at him without moving.)*

RIEL: *(After a moment; smiling, ironic.)* What! No others! *(To DENNIS.)* You see. And everywhere it is the same. With all the people — all are with me but a few *(Glaring at SETTLER.)* traitors.

DENNIS: Whoever doesn't side with you's a traitor.

RIEL: Yes traitor — to the folks they made their home with here. *(His voice rises to a frenzy.)* But God's my witness if our traitors organize against us I will strike them down — without warning or mercy. I will seize their homes and fields and stock and arms and stores. I will batter them down — *(In a paroxysm.)* sweep them from this soil they desecrate.

A shocked silence. There is a shout, off to the left. THOMAS SCOTT rushes in wildly excited.

SCOTT: *(To DENNIS and WEBB.)* Hi, hi! What are yous waitin' for! Don't yous know what's afoot?

DENNIS: *(With distaste.)* Back again. You.

SCOTT: The heathen mongrels is marchin' down the road. They're headin' for the Fort. Most o' them's half-roads there already and some o' them's right inside the gates. Come on, Colonel, give us our marchin' orders!

RIEL: *(To XAVIER and FRANÇOIS who are still ready to bar the way.)* Let them go on. *(To DENNIS as he turns to go.)* Twenty-four hours. No more.

47

DENNIS: *(Moves to the left. Pauses. Turns and, with deliberation, calls.)* Riel, you'll hang for this! *(Goes out with WEBB and THOMAS SCOTT, to the left.)*

RIEL: *(Struck by the remark.)* Hang for this.

His supporters are around him, chattering excitely and congratulating him: "Bravo! Riel! Vive! Monsieur Riel!"

MOTHER: Oh Louis. Louis son!

RABBIE: Aye, for a man that's no a Scot you argued it fine.

RIEL: God is with us friends. We will go on in his strength for without him we are nothing. Join your comrades in Fort Garry, and do all you do for the honour of religion and the salvation of your souls.

They all move off, up left, chattering: "Fort Garry." "Riel!" "Thomas Scott." "Dennis." "Our friends."

SCENE 3

Room in Fort Garry

A table. A bench or form. At the back a frame over which hangs the Union Jack. This is a room in Fort Garry. Daylight. Lounging are RABBIE, FRANÇOIS, XAVIER, other half-breeds and Indians. All are armed. Their rifles, not necessarily in sight, have been stacked — but their bandoliers are over their shoulders. They have jugs of liquor. Some are smoking cigars.

RABBIE: Here's tae us, lads. To sittin' snug wi' all the best to eat and drink — pemmican, brandy, baccy — ours wi'out a shot! *(He raises his drink.)*

FRANÇOIS: Victoire!

XAVIER: Brava!

They drink the toast. As they are doing so, O'DONOGHUE enters briskly from the left, carrying a rolled-up flag of green-and-white cloth. O'DONOGHUE wears a tweed knickerbocker suit, and a tie, with belt and pistol.

O'DONOGHUE: *(Sharply, sarcastically.)* Victoire! Brava! Without a shot! That's something to be whooping about!

RABBIE: An' what would please you? If some o' us had been killt!

O'DONOGHUE: *(Unfolding the flag.)* You'll have lots of chances to get killed. So save you breath to blow your porridge — in the other place.

RABBIE: Mister O'Donoghue, you pass wi' some folks for an eddicated man *(O'DONOGHUE smiles to himself and grunts.)* so would you favour us wi' your opeenion: Why did McTavish let us march in wi'out a shot?

O'DONOGHUE: Presumably because he wanted us in.

RABBIE: But why, man, why?

O'DONOGHUE: I didn't ask him and he didn't say.

FRANÇOIS: *(Very slightly tipsy.)* Monsieur Riel — he prays — he prays. And something happens. They do not close the gates. They do not shoot. We march in.

XAVIER: Like when he prays he makes a miracle.

RABBIE: I hae a strong suspeecion the miracle didna work on Mister McTavish wi'out some sort o' a cash consideration. Suppose, now, suppose, the bosses in London didna gie him his fair whack o' the pig's cheek — the three-hundred-thousand-pounds. What does McTavish do? He tells them to stick it you know where, and just tae spite them he lets us march in wi'out a shot.

FRANÇOIS: Ya, ya.

XAVIER: Rabbie is right.

RABBIE: Am I right Mister O'Donoghue?

O'DONOGHUE: I don't know.

RABBIE: Gie a guess man, gie a guess.

O'DONOGHUE: I'm not a guesser.

RABBIE: Och but you're thrawn the day. What's vexin' you sae sore?

FRANÇOIS: The Irish — always they are sore.

O'DONOGHUE: *(After unfolding the green-and-white flag, he points to the Union Jack.)* Pull down that rag.

RABBIE: The flag?

O'DONOGHUE: Down with it. Pull it down.

RABBIE: Is he gone daft or what?

FRANÇOIS: Monsieur Riel said it will stay, the flag.

O'DONOGHUE: Riel! Riel! *(Pulling the Union Jack down roughly and bundling it.)* There's for Riel and his kowtowing to the *(Kicking the Union Jack under the table.)* English.

RABBIE: Aye, daft. Clean daft.

O'DONOGHUE: *(Preparing to place the green-and-white flag where the Union Jack was.)* Who owns this country anyway? Us? Or the English?

XAVIER: Not the English.

RABBIE: *(Tartly.)* No, nor the Fenian Irish.

O'DONOGHUE: The Fenian Irish would come across the border and help us.

RABBIE: They'd tether us to the tail o' the U.S.A.

O'DONOGHUE: They'd help us to kick the English out and keep out Canada and fly our own flag — fleur-de-lis and shamrock. . . .

The green-and-white flag is now in the Union Jack's place. During the last speech, RIEL has come in from the left, attended by two armed Métis guards. He carries some papers in his hand, and takes in what has been going on.

RIEL: *(Sternly.)* O'Donoghue! I turn my back and you are at this — nonsense.

O'DONOGHUE: *(Belligerently.)* It isn't nonsense.

RIEL: I told you it is not a time to make trouble about flags. Where is the flag that was there? I said it was not to be disturbed. *(RIEL waits for an answer; O'DONOGHUE stares defiantly but does not speak.)* I asked, where is it?

O'DONOGHUE: *(Pointing.)* Where it belongs — among the spits and sawdust.

RIEL: *(His voice small and constricted with rage.)* For this, I should have you put in irons. You do not obey. If you will not obey I will make you an example. It is impossible to be in arms and not have discipline. *(Indicating the green-and-white flag.)* Look at this thing! At the moment when everything for the North-West is touch and go you play at schoolboy nonsense about flags.

O'DONOGHUE: It is not schoolboy nonsense.

RIEL: *(Loudly.)* I say it is.

O'DONOGHUE: *(Contemptuously.)* You say!

RIEL: *(He regards O'DONOGHUE a moment, his eyes blazing. But he controls himself.)* Give me the flag. *(He indicates the Union Jack under the table.)* Pick up the flag and give it to me. *(Pause, O'DONOGHUE makes no move.)* You heard me. *(O'DONOGHUE still does not respond.)* O'Donoghue it is an order. I wait. *(Reluctantly O'DONOGHUE obeys, picking up the Union Jack and handing it to RIEL.)* Thank you. *(He unfolds the Union Jack and drapes it over and along his extended arm, speaking.)* Do you think it is for nothing I say always we in the North-West are loyal subjects of her Majesty? Do you know why, you Irishman? I am only one little drop Irish. One little drop of Limerick Irish blood. It is

51

not enough to make me lose my senses and to jump and scream and tear down the flag and kick it in the — spits and sawdust. How many men have we? Seven hundred. How many British? Three million. Seven hundred to fight three million. For what? To say *(The Union Jack.)* we do not like this flag. *(The green-and-white flag.)* This one — it is much prettier!

O'DONOGHUE: To talk like that's insulting. You know as well as I do the flag's a symbol. . . .

RIEL: A symbol.

O'DONOGHUE: Of our independence and integrity as a people. I say we should fly it openly and honestly and fight for it to the death and never compromise.

RIEL: *(Keeping his patience with difficulty.)* Mister O'Donoghue — it is very noble to have such sentiments. Fight, for a symbol. Never compromise. And it gets you what? Only to fight. Ah, you Irishmen, up in the sky. But here we are not in Ireland. Here we must stand on the ground and it is sometimes muck below our feet. And you will learn — you have been professor of mathematics and you will learn that in politics also two-and-two sometimes do — except in Ireland — make four.

O'DONOGHUE: It isn't a question of politics but of principle. We're a new people, a nation in the making. We are not British.

RIEL: But we *are* British subjects.

O'DONOGHUE: We shouldn't be.

RIEL: We choose to be.

O'DONOGHUE: If we do it's to our shame.

RIEL: Because we *must* be. Do you know why? So three million British will have the honour of protecting us when we can not protect ourselves.

O'DONOGHUE: Protect us against whom?

52

RIEL: You ask this! It is too — naive. I think sometimes: to be a scholar is it also to be a child? To protect us against whoever would march in to grab and conquer even if the would-be grabber is Canada — or the U.S.A. That is why we call England — Mother Country.

O'DONOGHUE: (Bitterly.) And go on letting ourselves be strangled by the blessed old umbilical!

RIEL: (Hurt, shouting.) We are not yet strong enough to stand on our own legs without her.

RABBIE: A sound argument, Mister Riel.

O'DONOGHUE: Contemptible.

RABBIE: (Raising his drink.) Here's tae you, man. (Drinks.)

RIEL: So, Mister O'Donoghue, we will try first to secure the substance of independence — our own self-government here — and after that, perhaps, to think a little about the — symbol. (Lightly, turning to the green-and-white flag.) I am sorry. It is a pretty flag. Pretty shamrock. Pretty fleurs-de-lis. Green and white. Very pretty. But . . . . (Shakes his head sadly.) Take it down, please. (Waits. No response.) I ask please, take down that flag.

O'DONOGHUE: (Furious.) It isn't for you to say which flag. It's for the Council and the Council hasn't decided.

RIEL: (Also furious.) It is decided. I am the Council.

O'DONOGHUE: Riel — you dare say that — openly!

RIEL: I order you at once to take it down or I will tear it down with my own hands. (In a tense pause O'DONOGHUE does not move. RIEL turns from him and speaks quietly.) Some of you, please.

At once FRANÇOIS and XAVIER scramble to take it down.

O'DONOGHUE: (Starting forward to prevent them.) No. No. Don't touch it. If you dare . . . . (They have pulled it down.)

Oh you — unprincipled, contemptible, cowardly scum! *(He wheels and stalks off, right.)*

RIEL: *(The green-and-white flag.)* Fold it carefully. *(FRANÇOIS and XAVIER do so.)* Put this back. *(He gives the Union Jack to the guards who put it up again. A moment later.)* God save the Queen. Say it with me — all — please. *(He says it louder, but not all say it with him.)* God save the Queen. Not all said it. Some are sitting down. *(Anger rising.)* Stand up!

Reluctantly, all rise.

RABBIE: *(Embarrassed.)* Now, now, Mister Riel, it isna wise to push a good thing sae far it makes us look rideeculous.

RIEL: All say it now.

This time it is spoken by all, in an awkward embarrassed way.

ALL: God save the Queen.

RIEL: *(Quietly.)* Thank you. *(To one of the older Métis guards.)* André Nault. *(ANDRE stands forward a pace.)* No one will tamper with the flag again, here or on the flagpost in the yard. If anyone tries — you will place a sentry to shoot down anyone who tries, at sight. That is an order, André.

ANDRE acknowledges with a nod, and moves towards the flag. RIEL turns to go, left. There is general relaxing. RABBIE and others sit down again and start to drink. RIEL meets the PRIEST who enters, left, and bows to him. The PRIEST nods acknowledgement and whispers a word to RIEL which may be "drinking." RIEL turns back. All of this takes only an instant.

RIEL: *(To the men.)* I am still here. And the good father. You will please not sit down. *(They stand again.)* There is one other thing. It is what I came at first to say but this flag business . . . . When folks take on themselves to run their own government it is not a soiree — a little pic-nic. It is instead a serious thing to make it work. I asked from everyone sacrifice, discipline. Instead — you have a good time, you laugh, you *drink*!

RABBIE: If you'll pardon me. . . .

RIEL: *(Loudly.)* Why not bring in the girls and dance, dance, have music, make whoopee!

RABBIE: What ails you the day man?

RIEL: *(At RABBIE.)* You have already drunk too much.

RABBIE: You're like a body half-demented.

RIEL: *(Reacting slightly to the last remark.)* Now you will please be quiet. *(To the others.)* I must order — till our position is established — no more drinking.

The PRIEST nods approval but others exclaim against it: "Monsieur Riel!" "No drinking!" "But please . . . ." "We do not get drunk!"

RIEL: No more liquor will be bought or sold or taken.

RABBIE: Startin' from when?

RIEL: From now. I will thank you each to leave your drinks here, and go.

Reluctantly they file past RIEL and place their unfinished drinks on the table before him and the PRIEST. RABBIE is last. He halts at the table, gazes ruefully into his drink, shakes his head and, deciding he cannot leave it, raises it to drain it. As he does, he speaks.

RABBIE: Naw. It would break my heart. *(He drains it, and planks the pot upside down on the table.)* There you are. Mister Riel. I hae a great respect for your abeelity — but man, man, you're in sore need o' a wee touch o' a sense o' humour!

He follows the others out.

PRIEST: *(Smiling in spite of himself.)* So insubordinate.

RIEL: The Scots, they are *born* insubordinate.

A hullabaloo, off right. Armed guards force THOMAS SCOTT in before them, manacled. They prod him on.

RIEL: This man again.

SCOTT: Aye, you won't get rid of me so easy. I'll fix you yet! I swore an oath on my holy Bible! I'll fix you yet!

GUARD: We caught him. He had a gun. He said it was for Monsieur Riel. To shoot Monsieur Riel.

SCOTT: That's right, that's right.

GUARD: We took the gun.

SCOTT: Gun or no gun I'll fix you yet.

RIEL: Take him away. Keep him in chains this time. This time he must not escape.

SCOTT: See if I don't. You're a dead man as sure as God. Aye be Jasus are you, and I'm the boy will send you tumblin' to hell, you Papish ghet.

He is forcibly prodded off left.

RIEL: Evil. Evil. He is evil that man. I feel the evil coming out of him. At me. And at religion. He would destroy religion. He would destroy — everything here. He goes about plotting. Shouting against us. Stirring up strife. Already — he has had his chance. I sent him across the border, but he comes back. He is sent back, to kill me. That is what they would have him do. Kill me. Assassinate. . . . Many have urged me to have him marched before a firing squad. I do not wish this. No! No! I would not! But — it may have to be.

PRIEST: If he could first be tried.

RIEL: Yes, yes, he will be tried.

PRIEST: And may I suggest by a properly constituted court.

RIEL: By a Court Martial. Adjutant Ambroise Lépine will summon a Court Martial. Ambroise, with André Nault, Elzéar Lagimodière, Bapiste Lépine, Joseph Delorme. . . .

SCENE 4

Fort Garry Precincts

RABBIE and FRANÇOIS, wearing bandoliers but without rifles, are off duty. They are standing before a posted notice, down left. Throughout this Scene, FRANÇOIS speaks rapidly and excitedly; RABBIE, by contrast, is grave and slow.

RABBIE: *(Looking up at notice.)* Man-oh-man-oh-man.

FRANÇOIS: Six are to shoot him.

RABBIE: Aye, thank God I'm no one o' them.

FRANÇOIS: It is near the time. Already I have the jumps.

RABBIE: Three o' the carbines is loaded with blanks. But all the same . . . . *(He shakes his head.)*

FRANÇOIS: They had rum. He served the rum himself.

RABBIE: I could do wi' the rum. But naw — not even for the rum. *(He reads from the notice.)* ". . . Court Martial . . . this day tried Thomas Scott, labourer . . . having broken an oath not to take arms against . . . Provisional Government . . . and that also . . . having struck his guards. . . ."

FRANÇOIS: Ya, ya, he struck Monsieur Riel. Always he shouts, I will kill Riel, I will kill him. . . . He starts much trouble.

RABBIE: *(Not having taken his eyes from the notice.)* "Verdict of the Court — guilty."

FRANÇOIS: Sure he was guilty.

RABBIE: "Sentence of the Court — majority — death."

FRANÇOIS: *(Under his breath, crossing himself.)* Death.

RABBIE: ". . . To be executed by a Firing Squad . . . at noon."

He turns slowly away from notice.

FRANÇOIS: Rabbie. We will be late. Come, Rabbie, quick.

RABBIE: Naw.

FRANÇOIS: We can see.

RABBIE: Naw, naw.

FRANÇOIS: You do not come?

RABBIE: *(Shaking his head.)* Naw, naw, naw. He brought it on himsel', but I hae no great grah tae see him or any ither poor misguided fool blasted into the presence o' his Maker.

FRANÇOIS: *(Eager to be off.)* Ya, ya. . . .

RABBIE: I canna help but think it might sae easy 'a' been mysel'.

FRANÇOIS: Ya sure. . . .

RABBIE: What!

FRANÇOIS: I can not wait.

Hurries off, up right.

RABBIE: How any decent Christian can relish sich a sight. . . .

He shakes his head and goes off, slowly, left.

SCENE 5

Cell in Fort Garry

The "condemned cell." A spot comes up on corner down right. It picks out SCOTT, kneeling, manacled. Beside him kneels a Methodist clergyman, the Reverend MR. YOUNG. Scott is in distress.

YOUNG: *(Gravely.)* It's a solemn thing to be passing out of life into eternity. But if you've now truly repented of your sins and taken Jesus into your heart as your Lord and Saviour . . . . *(SCOTT sobs.)* Then, my brother, do not fear or grieve. He won't fail you. He'll be with you, to go hand-in-hand with you through this brief shadow into the eternal glory beyond.

A knocking, as on the cell door. SCOTT, fearing the execution call, whimpers and sinks low to the floor.

SCOTT: No. No. Oh no.

VOICE: The President.

An armed half-breed GUARD appears behind SCOTT. RIEL follows. The Reverend MR. YOUNG stands up and bows. RIEL returns the bow.

YOUNG: *(Gently, bending over SCOTT.)* Can you stand up, brother. It's Monsieur Riel, the President. Rise if you can.

He tries to help SCOTT up but he remains crouched down in his misery.

RIEL: No matter no matter, if he can hear what I come to say.

YOUNG: Thomas Scott, can you hear? Can you?

SCOTT: *(Out of his sobs.)* What, what, oh what?

RIEL: I come myself to ask, even at this last minute, are you prepared to make an end of stirring up revolt, against me and the government here? *(Pause. No answer.)* Thomas Scott, have you heard me?

YOUNG: *(For SCOTT to hear.)* You would spare his life?

RIEL: Is he now ready to swear an oath of full loyalty to us . . . to our Government here? *(Pause. Again no answer.)* Are you? *(Pause. No answer. Sharply and angrily.)* Are you? Thomas Scott. Answer!

SCOTT writhes and whimpers like a tortured animal, clenching and unclenching his fists and hammering them on his knees and his head. This takes place through RIEL's last questioning. At the final "Thomas Scott. Answer!" SCOTT leaps up and shouts hysterically.

SCOTT: No! No! That's your answer. Never! Never! No surrender to Papish ghets!

Simultaneously and masking the end of it.

YOUNG: Thomas Scott, Thomas Scott, oh my brother I beg you. . . .

SCOTT makes a sudden leap at RIEL, swinging his manacled fists.

SCOTT: Let me at him. Let me at him. To hell with him. I'll take him with me. I'll see him roastin'. Roastin' in hell!

RIEL has stepped behind the GUARD who, helped by the Reverend MR. YOUNG, is grappling with SCOTT.

SCENE 6

Room in Fort Garry

Spot comes up on a small table on which stands a little statue of St. Joseph. Seated at the table are the PRIEST and MR. D. A. SMITH, a deputation.

SMITH: Not much hope, father.

PRIEST: If Scott himself would help us! But he won't.

They rise at once as RIEL enters. He is very agitated, but bows to the deputation.

RIEL: I am sorry, father. Sorry Mister Smith. I have seen him. I am very shaken. Nothing will change that man. He is evil. Evil. I tell you *(His voice rises sharply.)* Satan is in him. He *is* Satan. He is Anti-Christ.

SMITH: *(Deprecating.)* Mr. President!

PRIEST: Perhaps having you execute him is Satan's means to wreck your — mission.

RIEL: No. No. *(Gathering himself.)* You have pleaded for him with much eloquence. I thank you. But . . . .

PRIEST: You have shown clemency before. You reprieved Boulton and . . . .

RIEL: Sentence of death is the law's last resort. Clemency always would make it a joke.

SMITH: True, true, but there's the question of expediency. . . .

PRIEST: We think the execution is bound to have very serious consequences in Protestant Ontario. Demands for vengeance. Ottawa would almost certainly be forced to act.

RIEL: Whatever Orange Ontario or Ottawa may do, later, now it is necessary to have acceptance here of our authority. It is my duty as President to compel this, first, before everything. I will not have all we stand for put in jeopardy by endless plotting against us. This execution, now, in a few minutes, of this devil, this, this . . . . *(Controlling himself with difficulty.)* The prisoner, Scott, may bring our trouble-makers to their senses. He has been found guilty by Court Martial. The majority was for death. And he must die. If he did not, something of much importance — more than his life — might perish — our Government and all we hope from it. *(Relaxing his more or less formal tone, to one gentle and most polite.)* So, for the Christian charity that brought you here, my humble thanks. That is all.

He bows in dismissal. The PRIEST and SMITH bow in return.

SMITH: Thank you Mr. President.

PRIEST: There is no more we can say or do?

RIEL: Only what I myself beg leave to do — to pray, for his soul.

They go out, left. As they leave, Riel's MOTHER enters quickly, passing them and bowing to the PRIEST. She is very agitated.

MOTHER: Pardon. Louis. It is the time. They have marched him out. It is noon. In a moment you will hear it strike. I thought if you would let me . . . to be with you, when . . . .

RIEL: No, please. No one with me.

MOTHER: But me? Not me, Louis?

RIEL: No one.

MOTHER: Louis . . . .

Because of something in his manner, she turns reluctantly away and goes, left. As she leaves a large clock off stage begins to strike the four quarters of the hour, and goes on to strike twelve. RIEL, alone now, sits heavily at the little table and clutches the statue of

St. Joseph in his hands. His head drops to the crook of his arm on the table. He stands up, clutching the statue, listens with eyes closed and lips moving as the clock goes on striking. He is very agitated. After the fifth stroke, he speaks.

RIEL:

Lord have mercy on us.

(Sixth stroke)

Christ hear us.

(Seventh stroke)

Christ graciously hear us.

(Eighth stroke)

God the Father in Heaven have mercy on us.

(Ninth stroke)

God the Son, Redeemer of the world, have mercy on us.

(Tenth stroke)

God the Holy Ghost have mercy on us.

(Eleventh stroke)

Holy Trinity One God have mercy on us.

(Twelfth stroke)

Holy Mary pray for us.

RIEL stands rigid, waiting.

VOICE OF COMMAND: *(Off, up right.)*
  Ready!
  Present!
  Fire!

The volley of the Firing Squad shatters the silence.

RIEL: *(Overcome.)* Me too. My life too. My life too it is taken. This will be. This will be. Oh there is blood and blood.

SCENE 7

An Open Place in Ontario

A mob spectacle which may be included or not according to the resources of the production. It may be staged as a night spectacle, with torches and the glow of bonfires. Orange drums are heard somewhere in the background. The clamour of an approaching mob is heard. The mob swarms on the stage, a yelling, gesticulating, fanatical mass of people, farmers, artisans, in working clothes. They are armed with sticks and some have the brass-spiked poles used by sidesmen at Orange processions. They carry flags and boards hoisted on poles with roughly painted legends: "Hang Riel," "Vengeance for Thomas Scott," "March on Red River." Carried high is an effigy hanging from a scaffold and labelled "Riel." The key words that keep recurring in the frenzied shouting are: Riel, Murder, Scott, Orangeman, Revenge. They occur in such phrases as: "Hang Riel!" "Murder in Red River!" "Orangeman Thomas Scott — murdered!" "Who murdered Thomas Scott?" "Riel!" "Revenge for Thomas Scott!" As the mob moves across the stage, the lights rapidly dim and the noise dwindles rapidly to silence and black out.

SCENE 8

Fort Garry Precincts

Light comes up on an outdoor scene. Bright morning. RABBIE stands reading some sensational headlines from a newspaper. FRANÇOIS and XAVIER come along and join him, looking glum.

RABBIE: *(Reading aloud.)* "Hang Riel!" "Revenge for Thomas Scott!" "Orangeman murdered!" "Ontario up in arms!"

FRANÇOIS: Trouble for Louis! Much trouble!

XAVIER: Like you say, "the fat it is in the fire."

RABBIE: Aye, the fat's in the fire now all right! *(Again reading aloud.)* "All Ontario ablaze!" *(Recognizing a jingle in the paper.)* Hi! Look what's here! "We'll hang him up the river, with your yah, yah, yah!" I mind them yelling that one — back in the old country when the blood was up. *(He sings it.)*

We'll hang him up the river / with your yah, yah, yah!
We'll hang him up the river / with your yah, yah, yah!
We'll hang him up the river
And he'll roast in hell for ever / with your yah, yah, yah,
Yah! Yah! Yah!

The PRIEST and SMITH have come along and halted.

SMITH: He'll roast in hell for ever?

RABBIE: Riel. If Ontario has its way.

PRIEST: It's true. Ontario's gone mad. Toronto. Every town big or little. Wherever Orangemen meet — hang Riel! Revenge for Thomas Scott.

SMITH: Nasty situation.

PRIEST: Nasty for Ottawa.

SMITH: Getting out of hand. . . .

PRIEST: Very dangerous.

SMITH: But, I trust John A.

PRIEST: *(Not understanding it.)* John-nie?

SMITH: Macdonald. Sir John A. Prime Minister.

PRIEST: Of course of course.

SMITH: He'll know how to cope with it.

PRIEST: He'll need all his guile.

SMITH: Scots canniness.

PRIEST: Same thing. Commodity he's well endowed with.

SMITH: Aye. And he has good advice. The best. Cartier. Bishop Taché.

PRIEST: The Bishop? In Ottawa? He *was* in Rome. The Ecumenical. . . .

SMITH: Macdonald called him back post-haste.

PRIEST: Then — there may be some hope. First ray of hope!

SMITH: He knows his flock out here.

PRIEST: To him at least, they aren't just — savages.

RABBIE: Macdonald and the Bishop! Man-oh-man-oh-man! I'd gie a siller poun' to hae one keek at *that* set-to!

SCENE 9

Prime Minister's Room, Ottawa

Light comes up on the Prime Minister's room at Ottawa. In conference are MACDONALD, CARTIER, TACHE and WOLSELEY. Somewhere outside a demonstrating mob is roughly singing "We'll hang him up the river." MACDONALD and the others listen for a few moments. The mob's singing dwindles during the speeches that follow.

MACDONALD: Barbarians! Barbarians! Rank barbarians!

CARTIER: *(Slyly.) Orange* barbarians.

MACDONALD: Orange barbarians.

TACHE: Alas, Sir John, that comment cannot be overheard by your Ontario constituencies.

MACDONALD: Your Grace is privileged. Fortunately for you the Church doesn't depend on the whims of an electorate.

WOLSELEY: Ditto the Army.

MACDONALD: However, gentlemen, to turn from these pleasantries to the business before us, let us first get a clear view of the facts. The North-West Territories are still outside Confederation. We need them in. Riel is master there.

The mob's singing outside has now died out.

WOLSELEY: A madman, Riel! Utterly mad!

TACHE: Colonel Wolseley, please!

WOLSELEY: Stark, staring mad!

MACDONALD: Mad he may be, though I've a notion he's merely mad — Nor'-Nor'-West!

TACHE and CARTIER deprecate the pun.

MACDONALD: In any case he runs rings round the pompous blunderers who've acted for us out there: McDougall and Stoughton Dennis.

TACHE: They couldn't have done more to compromise your Government with Riel and my flock. They've opened an abyss. . . .

MACDONALD: Aye, it's a mistake, to send out overwashed would-be Englishmen utterly ignorant of the country and just as full of crochets as all Englishmen are. . . .

WOLSELEY: I take strong exception to that remark!

MACDONALD: I except the army. . . .

WOLSELEY: Crochets! *Crochets!*

MACDONALD: Especially the Officers Corps where crochets, of course, are unknown. However . . . *(He helps himself to snuff.)* by the grace of God and the gumption of this extraordinary person Riel, the Provisional Government headed by him is willing to enter Confederation with us and become a province of Canada — on Riel's terms, of course. *(Sneezes.)* He showed his astuteness in refusing to let our blockhead representative McDougall even cross the border till the terms are signed.

WOLSELEY: Surely he had no right to act in such a dastardly high-handed way!

CARTIER: Perhaps he had.

MACDONALD: There's no doubt of it.

TACHE: You admit this, Sir John?

MACDONALD: *(Pauses. He glances at him, pointedly.)* I do — to you.

TACHE: *(Acknowledging it.)* Of course. I understand.

WOLSELEY: I don't.

MACDONALD: My view is that on the Hudson's Bay Company's withdrawal no legal government existed, leaving a state of anarchy. In such cases the inhabitants may by the law of nations form a government, *ex necessitate*, for the protection of life and property. And such a government has certain sovereign rights by the *jus gentium*. This is laid down by Blackstone. A most important principle. And it is precisely what this — allegedly mad but actually very astute — creature Riel has had the gumption to grasp and act upon.

CARTIER: It makes entirely legal the status of himself and his Provisional Government?

TACHE: And also whatever actions they may have thought necessary to preserve their authority?

WOLSELEY: *(Sarcastically.)* Including the murder of Thomas Scott I daresay!

TACHE: The *execution* . . . .

WOLSELEY: Murder. Murder I said and murder I mean. In my opinion . . . .

MACDONALD: If you'll bear with me Colonel it isn't a matter for military opinion. And meanwhile what we're considering is whether we've any right to enter the territory of Riel's government without their consent. At present I think we have none whatever — no more than we have to enter the U.S.A. at Buffalo or any other port without the U.S.A.'s consent. Riel knows this — and stands us off — till we negotiate specific terms, and sign. He has set out these terms very ably in a Bill of Rights. This Bill — with the anxious approval and blessing of Her Majesty's Imperial Government in London — Fenian and other annexationist forces in the U.S.A. not lost sight of — we shall make the basis of an Act incorporating the North-West with Canada. . . .

CARTIER: Here, here.

MACDONALD: A new Province in Confederation. And I think we may say that Riel has fathered this new Province. He has even proposed to name it — Manitoba.

WOLSELEY: Name of some Red Indian god or bogeyman or something?

MACDONALD: I understand the word is Indian for "the god who speaks."

WOLSELEY: Meaning Riel himself!

MACDONALD: Manitoba — the god who speaks: from Manitou — the Great Spirit. My two Indian words!

TACHE: Congratulations, Prime Minister, on acquiring the native language of your country — to that extent!

MACDONALD: Touché (Smiles and adds.) Taché. (For WOLSELEY's benefit.) Our good friend Taché has interrupted his visit to Rome to help with his wild people out there.

TACHE: With my — people.

MACDONALD: With his people. He takes with him assurances of a general amnesty.

WOLSELEY: Is it supposed to cover the cold-blooded murder of Thomas Scott?

MACDONALD: It is intended to assuage passion by all means — to help the setting-up of the new Province.

WOLSELEY: My orders are to proceed with my forces to Fort Garry. Once there I shall certainly make short work of — assuaging passion.

MACDONALD: We're glad to have given Colonel Wolseley the chance of glory, and the risk of the scalping knife. We shall watch him march off with pride. . . .

WOLSELEY: (Stiffly.) Thank you.

MACDONALD: And perhaps a little amusement. . . .

WOLSELEY: Amusement!

MACDONALD: An engaging, an almost symbolic, British figure, sallying forth clasping an olive branch in one hand and a pistol in the other.

70

WOLSELEY: I resent this tone. I'm a soldier. Unlike politicians we soldiers prefer plain speech and plain dealing. I ask, is the scoundrel who murdered Thomas Scott to escape punishment?

MACDONALD: Colonel Wolseley, I know that, because of this most unfortunate affair of Scott, recruiting for your volunteers is brisk in Ontario. But I remind you that your expedition to Fort Garry was organized long before we had news of Scott. Its purpose hasn't changed. You're going out there not to punish Riel or anyone else but . . . .

WOLSELEY: I am going out there to see that the waves of immigrants you mean to send are not molested.

MACDONALD: You are going out there simply to keep order — till the new Governor arrives and takes over from Riel.

WOLSELEY: I will keep order — but certainly not under this criminal blackguard Riel.

MACDONALD: Riel will formally hand over to Governor Archibald. . . . *(Pauses. With careful point.)* I am making this very clear. . . .

WOLSELEY: For the benefit of an obtuse soldier.

MACDONALD: For the benefit of all whom it may concern, now and hereafter: Till Governor Archibald has taken over we recognize Riel as head of the government out there. . . .

WOLSELEY: When I arrive . . . .

MACDONALD: I've no doubt Riel will receive you with all ceremony and the height of courtesy — for which, I understand, he is remarkable . . . *(With a twinkle at CARTIER and TACHE.)* even among his French compatriots.

TACHE and CARTIER: *(Together, bowing and smiling.)* Merci! Merci!

MACDONALD: H'm. Do you think *that* comment has been overheard by the — Quebec constituencies?

CARTIER: I shall certainly see that it echoes around Quebec.

MACDONALD: I have often been grateful for Quebec's remarkable acoustic properties!

WOLSELEY: *(A grunted aside.)* Politicians! Same everywhere!

MACDONALD rises, the others follow.

MACDONALD: And now with your permission, gentlemen, I'll resume my game of Patience.

They exchange bows. MACDONALD turns to go, left. WOLSELEY marches off right.

WOLSELEY: *(As before.)* Politicians! Pah!

MACDONALD: *(Turning back.)* It might be as well, Monseigneur Taché, if you could reach Fort Garry *before* the Colonel and his — volunteers.

CARTIER: I share Sir John's misgivings. What with Wolseley's unhelpful attitude and this ugly clamour to hang Riel — we have a very explosive situation indeed.

TACHE: I pray to God nothing may go amiss.

MACDONALD and CARTIER: Amen.

SCENE 10

Fort Garry Precincts

RABBIE, sauntering along, is met by O'DONOGHUE, who is hurrying in the opposite direction. RABBIE halts him. Neither has rifle nor bandolier. Outdoors.

RABBIE: You're an eddicated man, Mister O'Donoghue.

O'DONOGHUE: Eddicated?

RABBIE: Aye, eddicated.

O'DONOGHUE: If you call me that again I'll smother you with your own sporran!

RABBIE: Man, man, you're no ashamed o' your superior eddication are you!

O'DONOGHUE: What do you want my opeenion on this time?

RABBIE: What else but the big news.

O'DONOGHUE: (Rapidly.) If you mean do I think Wolseley and his Orange volunteers are coming here with anything in mind but the old, old British game of perfidy — the answer is I don't.

He starts on his way again.

RABBIE: (Detaining him.) Now what kind o' a connotation hae you in mind for the word perfidy?

O'DONOGHUE: Fair promises — then the yoke on the neck and the whip-lash on the back. The same old (Mimics Rabbie.) connotation. Good-day to you.

Again trying to be off.

RABBIE: (Again detaining him.) Bide a bit, Mister O'Donoghue.

O'DONOGHUE: What now?

RABBIE: You have vouchsafed only a sort o' a general answer; but, in parteecular, now . . . .

O'DONOGHUE: If in particular you mean do I think Wolseley and his Orange riff-raff have the least intention of forgetting about Thomas Scott and sitting down instead to smoke the pipe of peace with Ex-Monsieur-le-Président Louis Riel — again the answer is — I don't.

RABBIE: In your considered opeenion, then . . . .

O'DONOGHUE: *(Loudly.)* Riel's a fool!

This time he briskly moves along and goes off.

RABBIE: *(Gazing after him.)* Man-oh-man-oh-man!

He turns and resumes his meditative stroll in the opposite direction.

SCENE 11

Room in Fort Garry

As the light comes up, there is applause from a group of people, Riel's supporters: members of the Council, volunteers — but neither O'DONOGHUE nor FRANÇOIS is among them. They are gathered in a room at Fort Garry, and they stand listening to RIEL, who now wears a formal black frock coat, with a "Gladstone" wide-wing collar. He carries a silk tall-hat in his hands. But he is wearing moccasins. TACHE hovers in the background, listening with anxious attention. Something is affecting RIEL. In his voice there is evidence of feeling controlled only with difficulty. This becomes increasingly noticeable as he proceeds.

RIEL: So, we have prepared a reception. A great reception. To celebrate the setting-up of this new Province . . . in Confederation. And to honour the arrival, here, of the first *(He hesitates.)* Governor . . . with Colonel Wolseley and his troops. We shall fire a salute of cannon, and provide an escort of as many horsemen as we can muster. I have sent forward my . . . personal . . . respects . . . to . . . Governor Archibald. *(This is received with dissenting cries: "No!" "No!" "We want you!" "Riel for Governor!" "Governor Riel!" RIEL cuts in.)* No, no, no. I thank you but it is not my wish. *(With sudden sharp emphasis.)* It is not my wish to be

Governor! *(Pause. He recovers himself. Then, continues quietly.)* I beg you, please. You know I have said always I wish to have power only till I can hand it on. For the best interests of religion and of you my own people here. Now, it is the time to . . . hand on . . . *(He stops abruptly. Sways. Steadies himself.)* That is all. I thank you. Please go now.

They are puzzled and murmur in concern, but they bow and file out. When they have gone, RIEL slumps. TACHE comes to him, very concerned.

TACHE: Monsieur! Monsieur Riel! What is it?

RIEL: Nothing, nothing, I am nothing.

TACHE: But at this moment — of your victory!

RIEL: Victory. *(With sudden vehemence.)* He is a fine man Archibald!

This non sequitur *and the violence of it strikes TACHE, but he is unsure of the import.*

TACHE: Yes, yes.

RIEL: *(Fiercely.)* A fine man!

TACHE: I pray he may prove so.

RIEL crushes his silk hat and tosses it aside. He is very agitated. TACHE is horrified. RIEL drops to his knees.

RIEL: Will you bless me, will you bless me?

TACHE: Yes, my son, yes.

RIEL: I will say a prayer, may I say a prayer?

TACHE: What prayer?

RIEL: *(Crying out.)* Oh my Father, help me! Help me — to — accept — endure — this.

TACHE: *(Gently.)* You may say that prayer.

RIEL: If this be thy will. According to the views of thy Providence — which are beautiful and without measure.

There is a loud scuffling and hullabaloo. O'DONOGHUE is trying to break in and an armed guard is trying to prevent him.

VOICE OF GUARD: You can not. You can not go in. We have orders.

VOICE OF O'DONOGHUE: *(Simultaneously.)* I must! I must go in! Out of my way! It's life or death!

O'DONOGHUE forces his way in, left, standing off the GUARD. The GUARD retires and O'DONOGHUE comes excitedly forward. RIEL rises and with TACHE he turns on O'DONOGHUE with shock and resentment.

RIEL: O'Donoghue!

TACHE: Mr. O'Donoghue!

RIEL: How dare you . . . .

TACHE: What is the meaning . . . .

O'DONOGHUE: Perfidy. In one word — perfidy.

RIEL and TACHE: Perfidy?

O'DONOGHUE: The old, old story. I warned you. Wolseley! The British soldiers! The Orangemen volunteers! They're here. A few hours march. We could have stopped them. Cut them in pieces. But it's too late. . . . There are a dozen strategic points where we could have *(He shouts.)* decimated them! And the Fenians would have helped.

RIEL: They are against the Church the Fenians.

O'DONOGHUE: Nonsense, nonsense, that old idiotic lie.

TACHE: It's neither nonsense nor a lie — the Fenians are a secret society and as such banned by the Church.

O'DONOGHUE: All right, all right, all right, welcome the Orangemen. Welcome Wolseley. He'll spring his steel trap on you while you welcome him.

TACHE: Mr. O'Donoghue, you are grievously mistaken. Colonel Wolseley has precise instructions, from London and Ottawa.

O'DONOGHUE: He's on his own, thousands of miles from London and Ottawa. . . .

TACHE: He must obey instructions.

O'DONOGHUE: He'll do what he wants to do out here and square it after with — instructions.

TACHE: We will not argue. You will please not go further.

O'DONOGHUE: I must.

TACHE: In that case I am not prepared to listen. *(He turns pointedly away.)* Monsieur Riel, you have the assurances of the ministers and my personal assurance. Count on my presence and support when the Colonel and Governor Archibald arrive.

RIEL: Thank you, Monseigneur.

He bows as TACHE goes out, left.

O'DONOGHUE: Oh, Riel, you *are* a fool! *(RIEL merely turns away.)* Listen . . . .

RIEL: *(Listlessly.)* I have the Proclamation of Wolseley, signed by himself. *(He produces it and prepares to read.)*

O'DONOGHUE: *(Regarding it with impatient scepticism.)* Proclamation! That he's coming here to grab the land, and fight to keep it for Macdonald's immigrants.

RIEL: *(Reading.)* "My mission is one of peace. . . ."

O'DONOGHUE: Of course, of course, the old, old trick.

RIEL: "The forces I have the honour of commanding will enter your Province representing no party, either in religion or politics. . . ."

O'DONOGHUE: No party! His Orangemen no party, it makes me laugh!

RIEL: "We will afford equal protection to the lives and property of all races and creeds. . . ."

O'DONOGHUE: Equal protection no protection, nothing equal to nothing. The old perfidious game. Soothe them with syrup. Get their confidence. Then — pounce.

RIEL: *(Without conviction.)* I will not believe this.

The scene begins to darken.

O'DONOGHUE: Riel you *do* believe it. That's what's eating your heart. *(RIEL turns away and sits on the chair.)* Why do you *want* this, to be trapped! *(Sure he has a clue.)* Look at him! Look! The noble patriot, betrayed! The tragic man! *(Their eyes meet. RIEL says nothing. O'DONOGHUE closes in.)* The Orangemen came a thousand miles to have your blood — they'll have your blood and march back with your battered head mounted for trophy on an Orange drum. *(Slight pause. Finally, exasperated past bearing, he shouts.)* Why do you sit there in a daze — waiting for them to strike! Could Wolseley stop his Orangemen even if he wanted to? *(Himself almost hysterical.)* Riel! *(No response. Giving it up.)* All right, you want it and you won't have long to wait.

The GUARD has come in from the left.

GUARD: Monsieur Riel. François is here.

RIEL rises.

RIEL: Bring him. *(The GUARD goes to bring FRANÇOIS. To O'DONOGHUE.)* I sent François to find out.

O'DONOGHUE: To spy.

RIEL: Now I will talk to him — please, alone.

O'DONOGHUE: When Wolseley comes count on my presence too, in support — but with my gun.

O'DONOGHUE goes quickly out, right, as FRANÇOIS enters, left. FRANÇOIS is a little out of breath, dishevelled, wet and mud-bespattered. He is very agitated.

RIEL: You travelled fast.

FRANÇOIS: The news. It could not wait.

RIEL: Tell me.

FRANÇOIS: The Colonel Wolseley, already he takes prisoners.

RIEL: Prisoners?

FRANÇOIS: The folks who went there from Fort Garry. To see him come. To shout Brava.

RIEL: He seized them? *(FRANÇOIS nods in assent.)* He seized these unarmed folk?

FRANÇOIS: Ya. Ya.

A slight pause. RIEL steadies himself.

RIEL: What more, François?

FRANÇOIS: I saw many things. I did not like what I saw. The soldiers. The *volunteers*. They shout. They shake the fist. They say, "There will be some hangings in Fort Garry! Some French will hang."

RIEL: You heard this?

FRANÇOIS: And always they talk of Scott. Revenge for Scott. They say . . . . *(He hesitates.)* Pardon, Monsieur Riel. I tell only what they say. . . .

RIEL: What?

FRANÇOIS: "Monsieur Riel he will be first to hang, tomorrow."

RIEL: François, I was prepared to welcome them.

FRANÇOIS: They sing a song, "We'll hang him up the river. . . ."

RIEL: Please, it is enough. François I have one question. The answer to it will tell, everything. *(Carefully.)* The Governor — Archibald. Is he in camp with Wolseley? Does he come here with Wolseley?

FRANÇOIS: This I know. He is not with them. He does not come for many days.

RIEL: *(A slight pause. Then quietly, as to himself.)* Then it is — perfidy. *(Pause. He reflects. Then suddenly he seizes the Proclamation, tears it in two and flings it on the floor. He shouts.)* Proclamation! Perfidy! *(He makes a gesture of contempt, then turns briskly to FRANÇOIS.)* Where do they camp tonight?

FRANÇOIS: At Grenouillière.

RIEL: I will go there.

FRANÇOIS: Monsieur Riel!

RIEL: Now. At once. I will make sure.

FRANÇOIS: If they take you!

RIEL: *(With pistol.)* They will not take me.

FRANÇOIS: It pours rain. It pours now, everywhere. Much rain! Everywhere it will be dark, dark.

The scene is now almost dark.

RIEL: Dark, dark everywhere! Come, François.

They go, quickly.

SCENE 12

Room in Fort Garry

Room, as before, in Fort Garry. It is daylight, the next morning. The Union Jack is draped at the back. The torn halves of the Proclamation are still on the floor. TACHE and O'DONOGHUE. O'DONOGHUE is armed, and dishevelled. TACHE paces to and fro.

TACHE: Poor man, poor man.

O'DONOGHUE: The rain was from the north. Cold rain. It poured, all night. Downpour. Deluge. The roar of it, pounding down! You could hardly hear your neighbour shouting in your ear. No, nor see him either, it was so dark. Riel says he could hardly see Baptiste Nault nor Pierre Champagne riding beside him, so close, their knees were rubbing his.

TACHE: So they were with him?

O'DONOGHUE: And Colonel Gay and St. Luc, and François. For once Louis was armed like the rest, from head to foot.

TACHE: Thank God they had no chance to use their arms.

O'DONOGHUE: A great relief to Louis. No love for guns.

TACHE: What time did they get back?

O'DONOGHUE: One of the morning. I was back when they came in. Drowned. Like myself. Shivering. Cluttered with mud. Riel threw off his seeping overcoat and shoes, and tumbled on the bed in a couple of heavy blankets.

TACHE: He got *some* sleep?

O'DONOGHUE: Not much. About an hour. He was up. Sorting his papers out. Getting ready to leave.

TACHE: He must be worn out.

O'DONOGHUE: But the way it takes him, he's ready to drop, one minute. Next, he's rushing about, giving orders. Cool and calm one minute, than walking up and down wringing his hands like someone half-demented. His eyes are red and swollen. Last night exhausted him.

TACHE: He took a fearful risk to go near the camp. How near did he go?

O'DONOGHUE: Close enough. He saw the glow of the fires and went on, close. Right up to the sentries and outposts.

TACHE: Fearful risk.

O'DONOGHUE: The horses nearly gave them away. *They* knew something was up. Started to whinney and snort. But Louis had seen all he needed to see. He turned back.

TACHE: Mercifully.

O'DONOGHUE: Just in time. Wolseley's pack was on his heels. Forced march. Through the mud. Knee-deep in mud. They've closed in now, all round the Fort. Some of the Orangemen — wearing their regalia!

TACHE: The British, I trust, will be a steadying influence.

O'DONOGHUE: They won't. They can't. The Orangemen in the pack are panting to get at Riel, slavering for the kill.

TACHE: If only he had left in time! He ordered everyone else to leave.

O'DONOGHUE: He could still leave. They've left us the River Gate. I suppose hoping we'll run for it so they can shoot us down. Why have you stayed, Monseigneur?

TACHE: To receive Wolseley.

O'DONOGHUE: So have I — to receive him — with lead. Ambroise Lépine's still here. Myself. And others. Even the few of us should man the guns and fight.

TACHE: I will fight. Oh I will fight. (*O'DONOGHUE looks surprised and pleased.*) But where my fight may be of use. (*Unobserved, RIEL comes in, left. His appearance agrees with*

O'DONOGHUE's description of him.) I shall go at once, the weary trail again to Ottawa. I will plead . . . .

RIEL: Not for me, Monseigneur. Please no pleading for me.

TACHE: You must allow me. I will communicate at once with London. *(Touched by his dejected appearance.)* Ah, Monsieur, Monsieur. . . . Her Majesty will be grieved, she will. . . .

RIEL: I am not now a — loyal subject of Her Majesty.

O'DONOGHUE: Riel! At last! *(Glances at the flag, alight with his intention.)* Now I can tear it down.

He rushes to Union Jack, seizes it and, as before, rips it down and kicks it below the table. Neither TACHE nor RIEL betray interest in this violent action, nor in what O'DONOGHUE presently says and does.

TACHE: *(To RIEL.)* I beg you — if you can be patient in this evil — all will come right.

RIEL begins laughing, hysterical laughter.

TACHE: Riel!

O'DONOGHUE: My compliments to Colonel Wolseley. . . .

RIEL: Pardon, Monseigneur, pardon, if I laugh now. . . .

O'DONOGHUE: Say I'll be back with friends to greet him, soon. Fenians!

RIEL: What do I do now but laugh. . . .

O'DONOGHUE: Fenians will fight! Fenians at least will fight!

He leaves indignantly, right, neither RIEL nor TACHE paying attention.

RIEL: *(Thrusting the phrases out in an ascending pitch between starts of laughing.)* I know by the Grace of God. . . . I am

83

the founder of Manitoba. . . . But now, already at its birth. . . . Is it not funny, Monseigneur. . . . I am to fly. . . . I am to. . . . Hide! Monsieur le Président to hide. . . . An outlaw. . . . Riel. . . . In exile. . . . *(Laughter now changes to sobs.)* Oh Monseigneur, Monseigneur, this is my victory!

TACHE: *(Distressed by it.)* Yes, yes, Monsieur Riel it is still your victory.

RIEL: My great victory!

TACHE: Yes. Whatever it may seem for the moment my son. Time will prove it. But now. Come, come, brace yourself. Now you must brace yourself to do what is best to do — the most difficult of all — to leave when victory is won — to turn your back on victory and wait — in prayer and patience saving yourself, for whatever work God yet may call on you to do.

Off, at first at some distance, but drawing close as this incident proceeds, a rabble of soldiery is beginning to run amok. A GUARD, armed, comes in, left.

GUARD: Monseigneur! Monsieur Riel! They are in the Fort! Crossing the yard.

Retires again, left.

TACHE: My son, go, go quickly, wait for God's time.

RIEL: God's time!

GUARD again, very agitated.

GUARD: The Colonel Wolseley! He comes here!

TACHE: *(Urging RIEL.)* Go! Go, my son. It is God's will.

RIEL: I will come back. I will come back!

RIEL goes off, right, in a distracted manner.

TACHE: *(To the GUARD.)* Go with him.

The GUARD hurries after RIEL. TACHE turns to receive WOLSELEY. At left, a red-coat SERGEANT enters with his carbine at the ready. He looks around sharply.

SERGEANT: Oh! Excuse me your Reverence. 'Oos 'ere as well as you?

TACHE: No one.

SERGEANT: *(Advancing into the room, but alert.)* Thank you, your Reverence. Excuse me.

He makes a rapid examination.

TACHE: *(Sternly.)* I said there is no one here.

SERGEANT: We likes to make sure — but no offense, your Reverence, no offense. *(Having satisfied himself, he returns to the left, takes his stance and calls through, "O.K., sir." He stands at attention as WOLSELEY comes in.)*

WOLSELEY: *(At once seeing TACHE and advancing to greet him.)* Ah, Your Grace, we meet again!

TACHE: It is not a pleasure.

WOLSELEY: *(Momentarily taken aback.)* What! Oh!

TACHE: You had express instructions that on arrival here . . . .

WOLSELEY: My instructions were *my* instructions. Your Grace will permit me to interpret them according to my own — no doubt inferior — judgment. *(Being infuriating.)* It seems I'm to be spared the painful duty of dealing with this *(Implying "scoundrel.")* . . . with Riel.

Outside the rabble are singing: "We'll hang him up the river."

TACHE: I will make it my business to see that not only the Prime Minister and the Governor General of Canada, but Her Majesty — and her Majesty's minister in Whitehall the Earl of Granville — are fully informed of this, this — I scarcely know how to characterize it — this *creditable* exploit!

TACHE turns and walks indignantly out, right.

WOLSELEY: Look here, Bishop. . . . *(But TACHE goes on.)* Oh confound these interfering clergy. Can't be content with managing men's souls. *(He sees the Union Jack under the table.)* Hullo! *(Picks it up.)* Part of our welcome from Riel no doubt. *(He listens to the rough singing now of: "We'll hang him up the river.")* They'll hang him up the river. H'm! *(To the SERGEANT, referring to the singing and the tipsy hullabaloo now mounting to an ugly climax.)* Bless me, isn't it a rumpus!

SERGEANT: Yessir! Men runnin' a bit wild, sir. Lootin' the liquor, sir.

WOLSELEY: What liquor?

SERGEANT: 'Ee 'ad it all locked up, sir. Strict t't' 'ee was.

WOLSELEY: Yes, yes, mad, quite mad.

SERGEANT: Yessir. Our men don't 'old with no t't' nonsense sir, not after marchin' a thousand miles with their tongues 'angin' out as you might say, sir.

WOLSELEY: Looting the liquor!

He listens.

SERGEANT: Yes, sir. The lucky ones as is off duty, sir. Won't be much left by mornin', sir.

WOLSELEY: Sergeant, are you conveying a subtle hint?

SERGEANT: 'Int, sir! Oh no, sir!

WOLSELEY: Because it would be highly irregular and un-soldierly.

SERGEANT: Yessir.

WOLSELEY: But your tongue *is* hanging out, as you might say?

SERGEANT: Yessir.

WOLSELEY: What!

SERGEANT: Oh no, sir, no sir.

WOLSELEY: Which is it?

SERGEANT: Well sir, if you was to say, "Sergeant, 'ow abat joinin' your comrades-in-arms . . . ."

WOLSELEY: Sergeant, how about joining your comrades-in-arms?

SERGEANT: At the double, sir.

WOLSELEY: At the double, Sergeant.

SERGEANT: Yessir. Thank you, sir. Won't see my 'eels for stour, sir!

He salutes and hurries out, left.

WOLSELEY: *(Amused by the SERGEANT, he smiles. He listens a moment to the uproar, then sees and picks up the torn Proclamation. He snorts.)* My proclamation! Very well, very well, if that's how you'd have it! *(He crushes it and, as he kicks it from him, speaks contemptuously.)* Riel! *(Outside, drunken singing and uproar. If the resources of a particular production warrant it, "Hang him up the river" could now be effectively accompanied by kettle drums, big drum and flute. For the first time shots are heard, desultory shooting. With the shots, loud cries of outrage and protest, pierced by a woman's prolonged scream, are heard.)*

PART TWO SCENE 1

Porch of Riel's House, Montana

RIEL and MARGUERITE. They sit on rickety chairs. Outdoors. RIEL is fifteen years older. His clothes are shabbier. A cross hangs on his breast. He wears a toque. He is sitting a little apart from MARGUERITE, his mind wholly concerned with two letters which he holds in his hands. He considers their contents, giving an occasional glance at the letters. MARGUERITE, his wife, is a half-breed Indian in her early twenties. She is sewing some child's garment. She keeps glancing at RIEL, in growing irritation, and is several times about to speak. Finally she does.

MARGUERITE: Louis. *(RIEL glances at her, not speaking.)* What is it, Louis?

RIEL: What is what?

MARGUERITE: A long time you do not speak. You do not look. You sit there. Sometimes you read the letters. Then you close your eyes. You — think. Your thoughts are not here. It is the same every day.

RIEL: Every day, I think it is a long time I am an exile.

Pause. Neither speaks. Then Riel returns to the letters.

MARGUERITE: Again the letters, the letters.

RIEL: Marguerite, they are of great importance, these letters. There is great need to think much of what they say.

MARGUERITE: What do they say? You have not told me.

RIEL: This one is from my countrymen in the North-West. From Batoche. The Saskatchewan.

MARGUERITE: The North-West. Batoche. Saskatchewan. Ah, Louis it is no good to me to hear those names.

RIEL: This one is from the good Père André. There is no curé in that country so wise and so well-loved. He says I am to come. Come quickly. He says, *(Reading.)* "Dear

Louis Riel. You are the most popular man with all the people here. . . . There will be great disappointment if you do not come. So you see you absolutely must come. . . ."

MARGUERITE: What do they want you for? Why should you go there?

RIEL: Again there is great trouble. Like it was fifteen years ago. My people, again they suffer. They do not get their rights. They wait, they suffer, they send to Ottawa, they beg to have their rights and they get nothing, nothing, only the spittle. . . . *(He illustrates this vigorously.)* And more police, police, police. And now it is enough. They will not take this any more. Now they will fight. They are not — savages. They are not cowards. If to fight is the only way, again they fight they fight . . . and they send for me again to lead them. They send a — deputation.

MARGUERITE: What is it, "deputation"?

RIEL: Some men from my country, my people. They come here today. I look for them. Ah, I have not seen for so long — Gabriel Dumont, Michel Dumas, James Isbister. . . .

MARGUERITE: *(MARGUERITE has been taking in the import of this with growing alarm, she has risen and crossed to him.)* Louis, Louis, men from your country, your people. Your country now is here. Montana, this is your home. And me, our children, *we* are your people. Those men who come — you will not go back with them Louis.

RIEL: God has told me. I have asked God. I have waited fifteen years and now it is God's time. I am to go.

MARGUERITE: You will not go, you will not. Here in Montana you are safe.

RIEL: What is it to be safe? It is not for me. I have known this, always.

MARGUERITE: You have been happy here.

RIEL: Sometimes happy. Now, I am not. Also, to be happy it is not everything.

MARGUERITE: It is everything to me.

RIEL: That is — childish. We are not in this world only to be happy. Marguerite — you know — I told you — I have a mission. I am the Prophet of the New World. God has spoken to me and I must obey.

MARGUERITE: You will not go again to the North-West. You will not. It is trouble for you there — bad trouble. Do you know something, Louis: last night you called out in your sleep. You screamed. Oh Louis it was horrible, that scream. Your hands and face were wet, with sweat. You called out the holy names. I tried to wake you up. I could not. You called out "Cross! a cross! There, on that hill! I am hanging from that cross!" I was scared. I shook you hard. I slapped your hands. The children woke. They cried, to hear you. They were so scared, there in the dark. Poor little Jean Louis. And Marie-Angelique. *(She breaks off, noticing that he is not listening but is gazing off intently, to the left.)* Louis! You do not even listen. What is it, Louis?

RIEL: *(Rising, his face lighting up. He does not avert his gaze from what he is watching off left.)* It is "God's time." Look, they are here.

He begins to move off left.

MARGUERITE: *(Also on her feet, apprehensive.)* The men. The men from your country.

RIEL: *(Calling and waving his hand as he goes off.)* Gabriel! Gabriel Dumont! Gabriel!

GABRIEL'S VOICE: *(Off left.)* Louis. Louis Riel!

RIEL: Michel Dumas!

RIEL goes on, and the names are heard being called as the men meet somewhere, off.

MARGUERITE: *(As he moves off.)* Louis! The children! I will bring the children. *(She turns to hurry off right, calling to the children.)* Jean Louis! Marie-Angelique!

SCENE 2

An Open Place in Saskatchewan

Tom-toms are heard, at first at some little distance, but coming closer and beating ever a little faster as this scene continues. A spot, dimmed, picks out a few men — they are half-breeds, settlers, Indians, excitedly grouped down left. They gather round one who has a paper he is about to read, peering at it, perhaps by a lantern point of light. There is a tense, conspiratorial feeling about everything.

ALL: *(A general whispering.)* Riel. Riel is here, Louis Riel.

THE ONE WITH THE PAPER: It is from him. *(Reads.)* "To the Half-breeds. To the Indians. From Louis David Riel. Exovede. Dear Brothers. Dear Relatives. It is the time. Justice commands us to take up arms. Seize all stores. Stop the police and take their arms. If possible do not kill. Do not molest or ill-treat anyone. But fear not . . . take arms and come . . . quickly."

The dimmed spot on this group fades out as a dimmed spot comes up on a similar small group down right. The undercurrent of the whispers — "Riel. Riel is here." — is maintained continuously between the readings from Riel's messages.

SCENE 3

Another Open Place in Saskatchewan

HALF-BREED WITH THE PAPER: *(Reading.)* "Justice commands us to take up arms. Rise. Face the enemy. Seize all stores, all powder, shot and cartridges. Join us quickly for the sake of God, under the keeping of Jesus Christ, the Holy Virgin, St. Joseph and St. Jean Baptiste. Signed, Louis David Riel. Exovede."

SCENE 4

Church at Batoche

An altar with a monstrance and crucifix. Before the altar RIEL and the PRIEST are in altercation. RIEL now wears an oddly assorted quasi-clerical outfit: a black jacket and a purple waistcoat on which hangs a large cross.

PRIEST: Louis Riel, even at this last moment, before it is too late. I beg you. Lay aside your arms. Do not persist in this blind folly.

RIEL: It is not blind folly.

PRIEST: It is monstrous madness. And evil.

RIEL: It is certainly not evil.

PRIEST: I say it is. It is against the Church. Against religion.

RIEL: No, Father, no.

PRIEST: Armed rebellion! Disobedience to authority!

RIEL: It is obedience, to *the* authority above all authorities — God.

PRIEST: What are you presuming to say?

RIEL: God has told me to fight, and I obey.

PRIEST: That is blasphemy! Rank blasphemy! You cannot understand what you have said.

RIEL: I understand what God has said — to me — directly.

PRIEST: Louis Riel I warn you! You are being deluded. By the enemy of your soul.

RIEL: Deluded?

PRIEST: Yes. Into mistaking the promptings of your own arrogant will and monstrous vanity for the voice of God.

RIEL: *(Coolly.)* This is what they always say. They said it to many Protestants: Protestant martyrs.

PRIEST: Protestants! A Protestant! Possibly a martyr!

RIEL: Father, I wish only to do God's bidding. If for that you call me Protestant *(He shrugs.)* . . . call me Protestant! God bids me lead the people and go forward to this battle without fear.

PRIEST: *(Crying out against it.)* Oh! Oh the pride! the vanity! The blind stubborn will!

RIEL: *(Sharply.)* Father has God ever spoken to you?

PRIEST: What!

RIEL: I mean direct to you, yourself?

PRIEST: I am a priest of the Church. . . .

RIEL: Are you an honest priest?

PRIEST: How dare you!

RIEL: Oh it is not for sarcasm. Honesty is hard, even in religion.

PRIEST: Go on. Instruct me in religion.

RIEL: Or maybe specially hard in religion. For you must know if God speaks direct to anyone there is no mistaking his voice for the promptings of pride or vanity.

PRIEST: When you have quite finished instructing me . . . .

RIEL: No! It is no good! You *will* not see!

PRIEST: What have you come here for? *(Armed half-breeds enter, cross themselves, genuflect and move up toward the altar.)* Why are these men here, carrying arms?

RIEL: To get the Church's blessing on our arms!

PRIEST: There will be no blessing.

RIEL: Today we go into battle.

PRIEST: The Church does not approve.

RIEL: We are facing death.

93

PRIEST: The Church forbids it. Whoever fires a shot commits a sin.

Half-breeds begin to waver. RIEL catches roughly at the PRIEST's cassock and pulls it.

PRIEST: What are you doing?

RIEL: I think beneath your cassock I might see — an angel. One of Satan's brood. Or Satan himself. . . .

The PRIEST cries out and the half-breeds cower and back away. RIEL turns on them in fury.

RIEL: Stay! Come forward here! Why do you fear this man! *(Turning again on the Priest.)* This man's a traitor — traitor-priest! Scourge him from this temple he pollutes!

PRIEST: *(To the half-breeds.)* Be warned, all of you! The sacraments will be refused to any man who fires a shot!

RIEL: Away with him! I will give the sacraments myself! I am God's servant too!

PRIEST: Evil man! Louis Riel — now by the power conferred on me . . . .

RIEL: Conferred by Satan. The Satan that sits in Rome! On the Pope's throne! The Anti-Christ!

PRIEST: I name you heretic, arch-heretic!

RIEL: I name you traitor, arch-traitor to the people here. Oh yes! Hold up your holy hands to heaven! Soiled hands! Soiled by your treachery! *(To the half-breeds.)* My brothers, this is true! This priest conspired against us with the enemy. I have information that he told the enemy what plans we have, what arms, what stores, how many of us! Now he forbids us to go on, to fight. He would withhold the sacraments! But he will not! He will not! You will receive God into your mouths by my own hand! *(An afterthought.)* If God is in the wafer which he is not.

The PRIEST, horrified, takes the monstrance from the altar and carries it off. Some half-breeds move to stop him but RIEL prevents them.

RIEL: Let him go! God is still here with us as well as in that gilded box! *(He seizes the crucifix from the altar and holds it up.)* He will go with us to the battle!

PRIEST: *(Turning to shout a malediction as he leaves.)* God has forsaken you Louis Riel! All now will fail you! You will be humbled now! Your punishment is sure!

RIEL: Listen, my brothers, my dear relatives in Jesus Christ! Do not let that man's words make you afraid. God is with us. It is God's time to strike the enemy. *(Tom-toms are heard again, far off, but coming closer as the scene proceeds.)* God sent the herds of buffalo grazing on the plains to bless our forebears, in abundance never-failing! Marvellous as manna falling from heaven! We failed in gratefulness to God. For this our land was taken from us, a penance for our sins. But now, that is finished! Now, when we ask justice in our poverty and suffering, the Government at Ottawa will no longer put us off with lies. Lies lies lies! And always more police, more police, no answer but police! *(Angry mutterings against the police.)* They are all round our woods. Gathering round us now and closing in. They are well-armed. But do not fear their firearms who can destroy our bodies only. It is appropriate we go to meet them from this Church *(Lifting the crucifix aloft.)* for we will take God with us. Now — to the rifle pits. Make your peace with God. Obey him. Ask him to be among us and to give us victory!

Cries of: "Victoire! Vive Riel! God with us! God with us!" as the rally gathers behind RIEL who, holding the crucifix aloft, is leading them off. In the general stir, the tom-toms are heard again.

SCENE 5

Outside Riel's House, Batoche

MARGUERITE, distracted with anxiety, listens to the firing of volley and counter-volley in the distance. There are sounds of a stir nearby.

MARGUERITE: God is with us. With Louis. We must win. Louis must win. There are many against us but he must win, he must win.

Through the nearby stir rises the sound of lamenting.

MARGUERITE: What is that? What is that now? The women crying? What do they say? *(She listens and what she hears confirms her fears.)* Oh Mary ever blessed! Oh do not forsake him now! Help him now! Help him St. Joseph! Joseph most just, most chaste, most prudent, look to him now! Defend him! Pray for him!

VOICES OF LAMENTING WOMEN: Oi, oi, oi!

MARGUERITE: It is lost.

WOMAN comes in. She does not address herself to MARGUERITE but laments.

WOMAN: Our men they run. They fall down. Maxime. Baptiste. Dead. Many are dead!

MARGUERITE: My Louis?

WOMAN: Gabriel was very brave but he could not! Old man Ouelette, he would not leave the pits, he would not save himself, and he is dead. Pierre, he too! Oh Pierre! Oh Pierriche! The blood poured out! Pierriche, he died! And Jimus! I saw the horse tramp on his face! Oh Jesu!

MARGUERITE: But Louis, Louis, is there no news of Louis?

WOMAN: *(Out of her daze.)* What? What did you say?

MARGUERITE: Louis?

WOMAN: Louis. No. No. He is gone.

Distant rifle-fire and tom-toms have dwindled to nothing.

MARGUERITE: *(In dead silence.)* Gone!

WOMAN: Into the woods. They run after him into the woods to catch him! Many police run after him.

MARGUERITE: Oh Louis! You will be taken! This time you will be taken!

SCENE 6

Tent of General Middleton

A table and chair. A stool nearby. MIDDLETON sits at the table in his uniform greatcoat. Scout ARMSTRONG approaches and salutes.

MIDDLETON: Yes, Armstrong?

ARMSTRONG: Riel is here, General.

MIDDLETON: Ah! Bravo! Got him here safely, eh?

ARMSTRONG: Just managed it, but only just.

MIDDLETON: Deuced clever of you!

ARMSTRONG: Did take some cunning. Lots of the boys rearing to get at him. Calling him, "Son of a bitch. Goddam son of a bitch." *Etcetera!*

MIDDLETON: Did Riel himself give trouble?

ARMSTRONG: Couldn't have been less trouble. Meek as a lamb.

97

MIDDLETON: You don't say! All that noise, but — soft inside?

ARMSTRONG: He's — kinda simple.

MIDDLETON: Foxing?

ARMSTRONG: Couldn't be sure. *Seems* a decent, friendly sort. Got to like him.

MIDDLETON: Well, well. Great thing is you haltered him! Got him here, sound of wind and limb.

ARMSTRONG: Not so sound.

MIDDLETON: What's the matter with him?

ARMSTRONG: Looks miserable. Down in the mouth.

MIDDLETON: Well, in the circumstances — just been thoroughly walloped hasn't he? Hardly expect him to be cock-a-hoop!

ARMSTRONG: No. But as well — pretty cold now here, nights, General! Not much vittals hanging on trees! Poor guy's been drifting around. . . .

MIDDLETON: Ah! Ah, yes, to-be-sure-to-be-sure! Have some hot food brought for him. And, eh . . . fetch one of my greatcoats will you, Armstrong. Must look after him now. After all — eight thousand men, five million dollars out of Canadian pockets to get him here! Prize prisoner!

ARMSTRONG: *Prisoner's* not what he thinks he is.

MIDDLETON: What? What's that?

ARMSTRONG: He thinks he's here to talk.

MIDDLETON: Talk?

ARMSTRONG: Terms — for an armistice.

MIDDLETON: Armistice! Bless me! (*A loud, mirthless ejaculation.*) Hach! Must be right, all we've heard of him. Must be mad! Well-well-well-well! (*Thinks a moment.*) Well, poor fella, bring him in, bring him in.

ARMSTRONG salutes and goes.

MIDDLETON: Armistice? Terms? What's he up to? *(He reflects, takes out and examines his pistol.)* Some funny game? Knows he's walloped, surely? Or can't admit? One of these blokes who can't admit? Tiresome! Tiresome fools! Deuce take them!

ARMSTRONG brings RIEL, who still wears his quasi-clerical outfit — black coat, purple waistcoat with dangling pendant cross. He is bedraggled, dejected, very tired.

ARMSTRONG: General, this is Mr. Riel.

RIEL bows deeply. MIDDLETON rises and shakes hands with him. ARMSTRONG retires.

MIDDLETON: I hoped we might meet.

RIEL: It was also my hope, but not in these circumstances.

MIDDLETON: H'm! Quite! Quite! *(Moves stool near RIEL.)* Pray be seated.

RIEL: *(Gratefully sitting.)* I thank you. You are kind, General.

MIDDLETON: Not at all, not at all. You've been on the stretch — quite an innings!

RIEL: I had hoped we might have a — little talk.

MIDDLETON: Oh! Indeed!

RIEL: I gave myself up, with that hope. I asked for safe conduct to come here, to tell you the just demands and grievances of my people.

MIDDLETON: Why? What on earth for? Why tell *me*?

RIEL: If you would grant an armistice . . . .

MIDDLETON: Look here, you can't be serious.

RIEL: If there is anything serious in life or death it is most serious that my people's just demands be weighed in Ottawa. An armistice would give time. . . .

MIDDLETON: Out of the question. In fact, preposterous!

RIEL: The grievances of my people . . . .

MIDDLETON: Not my concern. Now, Mr. Riel . . . .

RIEL: If you would do me the honour to let me tell what the North-West is fighting for . . . .

MIDDLETON: My dear good man, the North-West isn't fighting for anything, now. The fighting's over. Surely you understand! It's over. And as for you. . . . Forgive me — you are under arrest.

RIEL: *(He begins to rise.)* I came as emissary.

MIDDLETON: Nonsense! Pray remain seated. *(RIEL hesitates, seems bewildered.)* I am not prepared to . . . .

RIEL: General, as emissary I request, I *demand* . . . .

MIDDLETON: You are being insolent. *(Peremptorily.)* Sit down, sir!

RIEL: *(Sitting, reluctantly.)* I was mistaken in coming here.

MIDDLETON: You had no choice.

RIEL: It is not true, no choice.

MIDDLETON: Mr. Riel . . . .

RIEL: There were horses saddled and waiting for me to take me across the border, back to Montana. Gabriel Dumont and Napoleon Nault my cousin had horses and they begged me to go, with them. I could not. I had promised God, and my people, and I could not fail them. I had still to fight for them. I believed you would protect me till my people's wrongs were weighed in Ottawa. . . .

MIDDLETON: Mr. Riel, I have every sympathy. But this is not the place. . . .

RIEL: Then, you will permit me, I will go to Ottawa. . . .

MIDDLETON: No, sir. Certainly not. You stay here. Sorry, but you are my prisoner. I shall be sending you, in custody, to Regina. You will stand trial.

RIEL: Prisoner. Trial.

MIDDLETON: You will be tried for treachery to the legal government.

RIEL: They would not answer our petitions. We had to fight. What else could we do?

MIDDLETON: You thought your half-breeds — a few hundred untrained half-breeds and Indians could defeat the whole of Canada, and Britain herself as well?

RIEL: I thought only if we showed strength of purpose and would fight, even so monstrously unequal and unfair a fight . . . .

MIDDLETON: Steady, my good man, steady. Don't harangue me. I'm not a public meeting.

RIEL: I thought those politicians there in Ottawa at last would have to listen and deal honourably with us. . . . *(Bitterly.)* Not look at each other, oh so sly, and wink and smile, and file our petitions away for ever. I thought . . . .

MIDDLETON: Oh, look here, look here . . . .

RIEL: Pardon. You may not know these men. You are a soldier. Those politicians! Dishonest! The sins of the whole world are on their heads. My people here in the North-West, all, all, and not the Métis only . . . .

MIDDLETON: No doubt, no doubt, but . . . .

RIEL: Métis and whites, all have grievances, foul, festering, suppurating sores of grievance that *smell*, and poison the body of society!

MIDDLETON: Spare me, pray, spare me more. You may tell the Court. All this. Pour it all out in Court. 'Twill do you good, I'm sure — "cleanse your bosom of such perilous stuff."

RIEL: *(Hushed, uplifted and lapsed, as if he has had an illumination.)* Yes! Yes!

MIDDLETON: "Such?" "Much?" *Much* perilous stuff? Oh bother! Comes to the same thing. Bother the Bard!

RIEL: General . . . .

MIDDLETON: What? What now?

RIEL: A light — breaks! God *is* with me! He sent me to you. *This* is his plan! His Divine Providence opens a way for me to tell our story where all Canada, all the world will hear. *(He closes his eyes. Prays.)* Oh my Father I thank thee. . . .

MIDDLETON: H'm! H'm! Well now! Well, if that's all right, if that's agreed.

RIEL: *(Looking around at MIDDLETON, as if still lapsed in vision.)* May I be worthy. St. Joseph, help me to be worthy when I come to that Court.

He suddenly sways and slumps down on the stool.

MIDDLETON: Mr. Riel!

RIEL: *(With an effort.)* Forgive me. I am weary. Very weary.

MIDDLETON: Poor man, no wonder no wonder! *(Brightly.)* But — we can do something about that!

ARMSTRONG has come to the tent with hot rations, with one of Middleton's military greatcoats over his arm. MIDDLETON indicates to him to set down the rations, and winks covertly his half-amused contempt of Riel's condition. Then, quietly, to Armstrong.

MIDDLETON: Rum.

ARMSTRONG: Rum?

MIDDLETON: Rum. *(They exchange looks. ARMSTRONG grimaces and goes out. MIDDLETON puts his hand on Riel's shoulder. Kindly.)* Come now. Come. A little food. A little warmth. Good sleep. Can work wonders. *(He holds his greatcoat for RIEL.)* First, this. Feel better in this.

SCENE 7

Courtroom, Regina

The VOICE OF THE CLERK of the Court is heard.

VOICE OF THE CLERK: Oyez, oyez, oyez!

He enters, down right, gowned and holding papers in his hand. As he enters he is speaking.

CLERK: That the said Louis Riel . . . not regarding the duty of his allegiance to our sovereign Lady the Queen, nor having the fear of God in his heart, but being moved and seduced by the instigation of the Devil as a false traitor against our said Lady the Queen, here stands charged before my lord the Queen's Justice. . . .

While the CLERK has been speaking, four separate areas have been spot-lighted. In Spot One, down left, JUDGE RICHARD-SON is standing before the raised seat which is the "bench." In Spot Two, up left centre, RIEL stands behind a rail which is the dock. Spot Three, down right of centre, and Spot Four, down right, are for the time-being unoccupied. In the unlit area, up right, stand, in separate groups, the SIX JURYMEN, CROWN and DEFENCE COUNSEL, WITNESSES, and the PUBLIC. The CLERK now moves to vicinity of the "bench." An usher's "knock-knock" is heard.

CLERK: Order! Order!

JUDGE RICHARDSON bows deeply to the Court and sits down. All others remain standing.

CLERK: *(Gabbling it off rapidly.)* Oyez oyez oyez all persons having business with my lord the Queen's Justice draw near and give attention and you shall be heard God save the Queen.

All present, except RIEL, sit down.

JUDGE: *(As to himself, consulting his papers.)* Queen versus Riel. High treason. *(Calls.)* Louis Riel. *(RIEL bows deeply and remains standing.)* Counsel for the Crown. *(The COUNSEL for the CROWN steps forward into Spot Three, bows to the JUDGE and retires.)* Counsel for the defence. *(The COUNSEL for the DEFENCE steps forward into Spot Three, bows to the JUDGE and retires.)* Arraign the prisoner.

CLERK: *(Rising from his position below the "bench.")* On this the sixth day of July in the year of our Lord, 1885, at the town of Regina, Louis Riel, you stand charged on oath that with divers other false traitors armed and arrayed in a warlike manner, you did levy and make war against our Lady the Queen, and did maliciously and traitorously attempt by force of arms to destroy the Constitution and Government of the Realm . . . and to depose our said Lady the Queen from the style honour and kingly name of the Imperial Crown of the Realm to the evil example of others in like case offending. Louis Riel, are you guilty or not guilty?

RIEL: I have the honour to answer the Court I am not guilty.

CLERK: You may sit down.

RIEL bows and sits down. The JUDGE nods to the CROWN ATTORNEY, who enters Spot Three.

JUDGE: Proceed.

CROWN: The jury assembled here must pass judgment in the most serious trial that has ever taken place in Canada. In the presence of witnesses the prisoner stated that in one week the Government police would be wiped out of existence. A few days later he told another witness that the rebellion had commenced; that he had been waiting fifteen years to get this opportunity. He wrote and signed an ultimatum to Major Crozier of the North-West Mounted Police in which he stated: "We intend to commence a war of extermination upon all who have shown themselves hostile to our rights." I think you will be satisfied before this case is over that this matter is brought about by the personal vanity of the man on trial. I would like to call as witness Major General Frederick Middleton.

MIDDLETON enters Spot Four. The oath in brief form may be taken by successive witnesses.

CROWN: General Middleton, you commanded the Canadian Militia in its campaign against the rebels at Batoche and Duck Lake?

MIDDLETON: Yes, that is correct.

CROWN: Did you at any time see the prisoner in the field of battle?

MIDDLETON: I did. At Duck Lake. Although he did not appear to be armed, he led a charge on horseback and shouted encouragement to his troops.

CROWN: Tell us what happened at Batoche.

MIDDLETON: There was some severe fighting. Our troops encountered unexpectedly stiff opposition. The enemy were so skilfully concealed in rifle-pits behind thick cover that we could neither see them nor get at them. Their commander, one Gabriel Dumont — who, I understand, was responsible for the actual military operations — showed uncommon skill, as well as a thorough grasp of all the tricks and cunning associated with Indian methods of so-called warfare.

CROWN: Can you say what part in all this, if any, was played by the prisoner.

MIDDLETON: He seems to have been the ringleader. He managed to inspire his men with almost fanatical bravery and tenacity. We were unable to dislodge them until we could bring into play the superior fire-power of our Gatling gun. That made short work of 'em. Got 'em on the run. Soon they dispersed altogether, and I sent out scouts to search the woods as far as Batoche. Scouts Howrie and Armstrong came upon the prisoner wandering in the woods. He asked them for safe conduct. To be brought to me with the purpose, he said, of discussing terms. When he reached my tent he said he had come to ask for an armistice, to have the just demands and grievances of his people seriously weighed by Ottawa. I told him the people's demands and grievances weren't my affair. And that he would be taken in custody to Regina, where he'd have a chance to put his case before a court of law. And — well — here we are.

CROWN: In what capacity did he present himself to you, with this absurd request for an armistice?

MIDDLETON: He said he was leader of the Métis.

CROWN: Did he speak to you on religious subjects?

MIDDLETON: Oh yes. From the first moment. Later, he spoke often of religion. He said the saints had talked to him. That visions had been vouchsafed to him. He told me St. Peter had appeared to him, in the Church of St. James at Washington, District of Columbia. He said St. Peter had ordered him to undertake his mission.

CROWN: His mission?

MIDDLETON: To lead the people of the North-West. He said a Bishop, or Archbishop, called Bourget, I think, had already told him he had a mission. He seemed to have Mission on the brain. It bored me. I remember thinking, Oh confound him, he's always bothering about the saints and his mission and religion. He's anxious I should know about his religion. I noticed that when any conversation reached a point where he wanted to evade or gain time to answer — he immediately turned to religious matters.

CROWN: Ah! He used his ideas on religion in that way?

MIDDLETON: I so regarded it.

CROWN: Tell us any of the views he expressed on religion.

MIDDLETON: He spoke about Rome and the Pope. He wanted the government of the Church to be located not in Rome but here, in the new world, in Canada.

CROWN: The Vatican in Canada?

MIDDLETON: Yes. He told me he thought Rome was all wrong and corrupt, and that the priests were narrow-minded and had interfered too much with the people. And others of his ideas were excessively good.

CROWN: What were they?

MIDDLETON: He thought that religion should be based on humanity and morality and charity. His view of hell was that God's mercy was too great to be sinned away by anyone in the short time he had to live. Also he wanted to purge the Christian Church of its relics of paganism — such as the names of the days of the week.

CROWN: He wanted to give new names to the days of the week?

MIDDLETON: Yes, instead of the present pagan names.

CROWN: During all your interviews with him did you see anything to indicate unsoundness of mind?

MIDDLETON: On the contrary, I should say he was a man of rather acute intellect; in fact, deucedly clever.

CROWN: And the idea of mental aberration never occurred to you?

MIDDLETON: I believe it was put on — for a purpose.

CROWN: Thank you.

107

The CROWN gives place in Spot Three to the DEFENCE.

DEFENCE: What experience have you had in dealing with people of unsound mind?

MIDDLETON: None at all.

DEFENCE: But you think yourself qualified to give an opinion as to sanity?

MIDDLETON: Not a medical opinion. But I think that in living with him several days I would know if I was living with a lunatic.

DEFENCE: Are you aware that medical experts say it takes four months to detect insanity in many cases?

MIDDLETON: Living with him it would be different.

DEFENCE: Have you seen any document signed by the prisoner?

MIDDLETON: Yes.

DEFENCE: Was there anything peculiar in the manner of the signature?

MIDDLETON: The signature was sometimes Louis Riel and sometimes Louis David Riel. I understand he included David to identify himself with the Biblical hero — the boy who slew the giant with a sling shot.

JUDGE: Was this told you by Riel himself?

MIDDLETON: No, your honour.

DEFENCE: Any other peculiarity you observed about his signature?

MIDDLETON: The word exovede.

DEFENCE: Exovede?

MIDDLETON: It frequently appeared after his name. He told me he invented it — from the Latin words, *ex*, from, and *ovile*, flock. From the flock. He said he used it to show he was assuming no authority except as one of the flock, an ordinary member of society. He said that his Council, being composed of exovedes, was to be called, exovedate.

DEFENCE: *(With careful point.)* And in all this — you see no indication whatever of mental aberration?

MIDDLETON: As I said, I think he put it all on — for a purpose.

DEFENCE: Thank you.

MIDDLETON retires. The DEFENCE steps out of Spot Three.

CLERK: Charles Nolin.

NOLIN enters Spot Four. The CROWN enters Spot Three.

CROWN: You know the prisoner?

NOLIN: He is my cousin.

CROWN: You have frequently seen him since he returned from Montana?

NOLIN: When he returned he was a guest in my house for several weeks.

CROWN: Did he talk to you about his ideas and plans?

NOLIN: He never stopped talking about them.

CROWN: Tell us something of what he said.

NOLIN: He said he was sending out messengers all over the country with secret messages to rouse the Indians and half-breeds. Calling them to come and help. He said that together we could defeat the police and militia and bring Canada to her knees. He said he had plans to bring foreign armies here, to drive out Canada and take possession of Manitoba and the North-West for the half-breeds and Indians. He said if we didn't drive out or destroy the white men we would be over-run and driven out or destroyed ourselves. He said the white men from the east would keep on swarming in to grab our lands. And that we would soon be no better than so many hungry, mangy coyotes to be hunted and shot at. We were to go on living our own kind of life, respecting and keeping up our own old customs and laws, and fighting for that to the death; or be despised and pushed aside and go down, down, down till we were lost.

CROWN: He seriously thought that a scattering of half-breeds and Indians had a right, and duty, to fence off these vast empty lands against the spread of population from all the rest of the over-crowded world?

NOLIN: He said what was ours was ours and we should fight and fight to hold it. Any man who wouldn't take up arms and fight to hold it was a traitor. He said we were to rise in arms. He had asked God and God had told him. He had waited fifteen years for God to tell him. And God had told him. It was God's time. We were to rise in arms.

CROWN: Did you believe this?

NOLIN: No.

CROWN: But many did?

NOLIN: They thought he was a prophet. He played on this. He could do what he liked with them. They were ready to die for him.

CROWN: And many of them did?

NOLIN: Yes. There was much bloodshed and great misery.

CROWN: Would it be true to say that prisoner was the chief instigator of this rising in arms?

NOLIN: He was the one that roused the people to get together and fight; but Gabriel Dumont was the one that planned and led the fighting here, like Ambroise Lépine did fifteen years ago at Fort Garry.

CROWN: But prisoner was the one who roused them to fight?

NOLIN: Without him it would not have happened. It might have flared up but it would have fizzled out.

CROWN: One last question. When the fighting started did prisoner himself take any active part in it?

NOLIN: He was the one that went about the rifle-pits giving the order to fire.

The CROWN gives place to the DEFENCE.

DEFENCE: Prisoner, you say, is your cousin?

NOLIN: Yes.

DEFENCE: You have — or had — great affection and admiration for him?

NOLIN: We were on friendly terms.

DEFENCE: But you did admire him?

NOLIN: I thought he was — clever — a cut above the rest of us.

DEFENCE: Were you ever envious or jealous of his cleverness?

NOLIN: No.

DEFENCE: You have mentioned the trouble at Fort Garry. Is it true that there, as here again, you were with your cousin and his cause at first, and later decided to desert them?

NOLIN: I had to be with him at first. It was the only way to save my life. I did not think he would fight. I did not want to fight.

During the examination of this witness, RIEL shows signs of exasperation and resentment.

DEFENCE: When you thought he would not fight you were with him to save your life. When you thought he would

111

fight, and might be defeated, you again decided to save your life?

NOLIN: I did not want to fight, there or here. Here, when I'd had enough, he had me arrested and court-martialled. I was condemned to death, but reprieved. Then I escaped.

DEFENCE: And now you are here to give evidence against him! You have said that at the rifle-pits he gave orders to fire. Did he himself fire?

NOLIN: He had no rifle. He was always afraid of fire-arms. When the shooting started he went about carrying a crucifix.

DEFENCE: What for? What did he do with the crucifix?

NOLIN: When a volley was fired by the police and militia he lifted up the crucifix and gave the order to fire in return. He said: "In the name of God the Father who created us, reply to that!" Next time it would be: "In the name of Jesus Christ who redeemed us, reply to that!" Next it would be: "In the name of the Holy Ghost who sanctifies us, reply to that!" And so on, calling on the saints one after another.

DEFENCE: Did this strike you as in any way unusual or peculiar?

NOLIN: He was always trying to make out there was something out of the ordinary about him. That he was a prophet. Speaking for God. He even dressed up sometimes like a sort of priest — in a black suit with a purple waistcoat and a big cross hanging on his front.

DEFENCE: Did *that* strike you as indicating anything not quite normal in his mentality?

NOLIN: I think he knew what he was doing.

RIEL, unable to restrain himself any longer, suddenly rises.

RIEL: Your Honour, would you permit me a little while to . . . .

112

JUDGE: *(Surprised and a little flustered.)* Eh? What?

RIEL: I have some questions. . . .

JUDGE: At the proper time. You will be given every opportunity.

RIEL: Is there any legal way that I could be allowed to speak? To ask some questions?

JUDGE: You should suggest any questions to your own Counsel.

RIEL: Do you allow me to speak? I have some observations, some questions to ask this witness . . . .

DEFENCE: *(Interrupting.)* I don't think this is the proper time, your Honour.

RIEL: Before this man leaves the witness box. . . .

JUDGE: I agree it is not the proper time.

RIEL reluctantly sits down.

DEFENCE: I think it is necessary that the prisoner should thoroughly understand that anything that is done in his behalf in this case must be done through me.

JUDGE: The statute of High Treason states that the prisoner can defend himself personally or by counsel.

DEFENCE: But after counsel has been accepted . . . .

RIEL: *(Rising again.)* Your Honour, this case comes to be extraordinary. The Crown are trying to show that I am guilty. It is their duty. My Counsel, my good friends and lawyers, whom I respect, are trying to show that I am insane. It is their line of defence. I reject it. I indignantly deny that I am insane. I am not insane! I declare . . . .

JUDGE: Now you must stop.

RIEL: The chance to ask important questions of witness is slipping by. My good Counsel does not know what questions to ask because he does not know this man and because he is from Quebec and does not understand our ways out here. . . .

JUDGE: I have said you must stop. Now stop at once.

RIEL: I will stop and obey your Court.

CROWN: *(Rising, smiling and soothing.)* Your Honour, the prosecution does not object to the prisoner putting questions to witnesses.

DEFENCE: *(Becoming angry.)* Your Honour, the prisoner is actually obstructing the proper management of his case and he must not be allowed to interfere in it.

JUDGE: Isn't that a matter between yourself and your client?

DEFENCE: I don't pretend to argue with the Court, but if I am to continue the case the prisoner must be made to abandon his attitude.

RIEL: *(Again rising.)* I cannot abandon my dignity. Here I have to defend myself against the accusation of high treason. Or I have to allow the plea that I am insane and consent to the animal life of an asylum. I don't care much about animal life if I am not allowed to carry with it the moral existence of an intellectual being.

JUDGE: *(Peremptorily.)* Now stop.

RIEL: *(Beaten. He sits down.)* Yes, your Honour.

JUDGE: *(To the DEFENCE.)* Proceed.

DEFENCE: *(To Nolin.)* You may go. *(To the Clerk.)* Call Father André.

CLERK: Father Alexis André.

FATHER ANDRE enters Spot Four. He is a noticeably unkempt bearded man in a greasy cassock.

DEFENCE: What is your name in religion?

ANDRE: Alexis André, Oblat.

DEFENCE: Since how long have you been in this country?

ANDRE: Since 1865 in The Saskatchewan.

DEFENCE: You know of the political activities of the population?

ANDRE: I do.

DEFENCE: Do you know of petitions and resolutions being sent to the Federal Government?

ANDRE: Yes.

DEFENCE: Did these petitions and resolutions — adopted at public meetings and sent to the Government — have any result?

ANDRE: The continual silence or evasions of the Government produced great dissatisfaction, and drove the people to think their only hope lay in resort to force. And I . . . .

The COUNSEL for the CROWN intervenes, coming into the spot with the DEFENCE.

CROWN: *(To the JUDGE.)* I must object to this class of question. My learned friend has opened a case of treason justified only by the insanity of the prisoner, and he is now seeking to justify armed rebellion for the redress of their grievances.

JUDGE: Which is like trying the Government.

CROWN: And that isn't open to any one on trial for high treason. *(Withdraws.)*

DEFENCE: *(To the JUDGE.)* I don't want to justify the rebellion. I want to show the state of things in the country, and that the prisoner was justified in coming back across the border from Montana.

JUDGE: That, I think, is not questioned.

DEFENCE: *(He bows to the JUDGE, and turns again to the WITNESS.)* You have had occasion to meet the prisoner between July 1884 and the time of the rebellion?

ANDRE: Yes.

DEFENCE: Have you spoken to him on politics and religion?

ANDRE: Frequently.

DEFENCE: Did he speak in a sensible manner?

ANDRE: Not on politics and religion. On these subjects he did not have his intelligence of mind. I want to state a fact to the Court regarding the prisoner. You know the life of that man affected us during a certain time.

DEFENCE: In what way?

ANDRE: He was a fervent Catholic, attending to his religious duties. But he stated things that frightened the priests. And he was subject to violent outbursts in which he would flout the authority and holy office of the priests. It is true that when the rebellious and hot-tempered mood had passed he would appear sad and contrite. He would then outdo himself in being extravagantly apologetic and polite, even abasing himself. Once, all the priests met together to decide if the man could be allowed to continue in his religious duties. They unanimously decided that, on questions of religion and politics, there was no way of explaining his conduct except that he was insane.

DEFENCE: Insane?

ANDRE: Insane.

The CROWN replaces the DEFENCE in Spot Three.

CROWN: You say the prisoner made statements that frightened the priests. What statements?

ANDRE: He wanted to change the Mass and the liturgy, the ceremonies and the symbols. He thought only the first person in the Trinity was God, and he did not admit the doctrine of the Divine Presence. God was not present in the Host according to him, but only an ordinary man six feet high.

CROWN: Do you deny that a man may be a great reformer of religious questions without being a fool?

ANDRE: I do not deny history.

CROWN: Is it not a fact that the half-breeds are extremely religious, and that religion has a great influence on them?

ANDRE: Yes. It was just because he was so religious and appeared so devout that he exercised such a great influence on them.

CROWN: He was at pains to appear devout to the half-breeds?

ANDRE: I did not say "he was at pains."

CROWN: But you do say he appeared devout to the half-breeds?

ANDRE: Yes.

CROWN: You heard the evidence of the previous witnesses?

ANDRE: Yes.

CROWN: You heard them give their opinion that prisoner sometimes used religion for a purpose?

ANDRE: I have said that where religion is concerned I believe the prisoner is of unsound mind.

CROWN: Thank you.

ANDRE and the CROWN withdraw.

CLERK: François Roy, doctor of medicine

DR. ROY enters Spot Four. The DEFENCE enters Spot Three.

DEFENCE: You are a doctor of medicine?

ROY: Yes.

117

DEFENCE: In the City of Quebec?

ROY: Yes. For a great many years I have been medical superintendent, and one of the proprietors, of the lunatic asylum of Beaufort.

DEFENCE: You have made a special study of the diseases of the brain?

ROY: Yes.

DEFENCE: Were you superintendent of the asylum at Beaufort in 1875 and 1876?

ROY: Yes.

DEFENCE: In those years did you see the prisoner?

ROY: Many times.

DEFENCE: Where?

ROY: In the asylum.

DEFENCE: As a patient?

ROY: Yes.

DEFENCE: Was he admitted with all the formalities required by law?

ROY: Yes.

DEFENCE: Did you study the mental disease by which the prisoner was afflicted?

ROY: Yes — megalomania.

DEFENCE: In a case of this kind, could a casual observer, without medical experience, form an estimate as to the state of the man's mind?

ROY: Not usually.

DEFENCE: You were present at the examination of witnesses here today?

ROY: Yes.

DEFENCE: You heard their evidence as to the prisoner's views on religion?

ROY: I did.

DEFENCE: From what you heard can you say whether he was then of sound mind?

ROY: I believe he was of unsound mind.

DEFENCE: Do you believe he was capable or incapable of knowing the nature and quality of the acts which he did?

ROY: I believe he was not master of his acts.

DEFENCE: Will you swear that the man did not know what he was doing, or whether he was contrary to law in reference to his particular delusion?

ROY: That is my belief.

The DEFENCE gives place to the CROWN in Spot Three.

CROWN: Under what name was the prisoner in your asylum?

ROY: Under the name of Larochelle.

CROWN: Did you know that the man was Riel?

ROY: He himself told me so.

CROWN: From what facts in evidence did you say the prisoner was incapable of distinguishing between right and wrong?

ROY: They never could persuade him that his special mission didn't exist.

CROWN: How would you describe his belief in his special mission?

ROY: As an insane delusion.

CROWN: Do you say that any man claiming to be inspired is suffering from an insane delusion, so as not to be able to distinguish between right and wrong?

ROY: It is possible.

DEFENCE: Does not the whole evidence sustain the theory, that prisoner's claim to a special mission was a skilful fraud?

ROY: There is no evidence of fraud.

DEFENCE: Do you say the evidence is inconsistent with fraud?

ROY: When the prisoner was under my care . . . .

DEFENCE: (Sharply.) Will you answer my question?

ROY: Put the question another way.

DEFENCE: (He pauses. Then, with a glance at the JUDGE, he continues.) If you cannot answer my question, I may as well let you go. You may go.

ROY and the CROWN withdraw.

CLERK: Dr. Jukes.

DR. JUKES enters Spot Four. The CROWN re-enters Spot Three.

CROWN: You are at present the medical officer attached to the Mounted Police force?

JUKES: I am the Senior Surgeon of the Mounted Police.

CROWN: In your medical capacity insane persons come under your observation?

JUKES: Yes.

CROWN: You know the prisoner?

JUKES: Yes.

CROWN: Have you formed an opinion as to his sanity or insanity?

JUKES: I have seen nothing to induce me to believe he is insane.

CROWN: Is he capable of knowing the nature and quality of any act which he would commit, so as to distinguish between right and wrong?

JUKES: Very acutely.

CROWN gives place to the DEFENCE.

DEFENCE: You have heard of the mental disease known as megalomania?

JUKES: Yes.

DEFENCE: What are the symptoms?

JUKES: The patient has delusions, grandiose delusions.

DEFENCE: That he is powerful?

JUKES: Yes.

DEFENCE: A great soldier?

JUKES: Yes.

DEFENCE: A great leader and statesman?

JUKES: Yes.

DEFENCE: That he is identified with some heroic Biblical or other character?

JUKES: Yes.

DEFENCE: That he is a great prophet with a mission divinely inspired?

JUKES: He may be a great anything and everything.

DEFENCE: Do such insane persons believe they are in constant intercourse with God and are directed by him?

JUKES: I have known patients of that kind.

DEFENCE: From the evidence and your own observation you have no doubt that prisoner's conduct is compatible with a perfectly sound mind?

JUKES: I've heard nothing that might not be accounted for by other causes, for instance fraud or deception.

DEFENCE: If it can be proved that a man is labouring under an insane delusion that he was in communication with the Holy Ghost and acting under direct inspiration of God, and was bound to do a certain act, and did it, would he be responsible for that act?

JUKES: Views on that subject are so different, even among the sane. . . . There are men who have held very remarkable views on religion and who have always been declared to be insane — until they gathered great numbers of followers in a new sect — then they became great prophets and great men; Mahomet for instance.

DEFENCE: You think the conduct of Mr. Riel compatible with the conduct of a man like Mahomet?

JUKES: (Carefully.) My opinion is, rather, that Mr. Riel is a man of great shrewdness and very great depth, and that he *might* have assumed, for the purpose of maintaining his influence with his followers, more than he really believed.

DEFENCE: That is your impression, doctor?

JUKES: I have thought it *might* be so.

DEFENCE: Are you in a position to say, doctor, on your oath, that this man is not insane?

JUKES: I have never spoken to him on a single subject on which he has spoken irrationally.

DEFENCE: Thank you.

JUKES leaves Spot Four. The DEFENCE steps outside Spot Three.

CLERK: Police officer, Bromley-Witheroe.

The POLICEMAN enters Spot Four. The DEFENCE re-enters Spot Three.

DEFENCE: You are an Englishman?

POLICEMAN: I am.

DEFENCE: And you have had a good education?

POLICEMAN: (With a deprecating smile.) Well, it may not be an answer but I *am* a university graduate.

DEFENCE: The prisoner has been in your charge?

POLICEMAN: Yes.

DEFENCE: So you have had ample opportunity to observe him?

POLICEMAN: I have.

DEFENCE: Tell us what you have observed.

POLICEMAN: He occupies the cell next to the guard room in the barracks. His little statue of St. Joseph stands on the table and when he's telling his beads I've noticed that he holds it in his hand and hugs it. His countenance usually displays a calm composure, and his eyes are nearly always bent on the ground as if he were wrapped in contemplation and study.

DEFENCE: Can you tell us more? Anything in his conduct that seemed to you different from that of the other prisoners?

POLICEMAN: He wrote a great deal in a book which he describes as written with buffalo blood.

DEFENCE: With buffalo blood?

POLICEMAN: Yes. I understand it's about himself and what he calls his people, his mission in the North-West. A sort of *apologia pro vita sua*.

DEFENCE: Have you noticed any other peculiarity of conduct?

POLICEMAN: Sometimes in his cell he talks all night.

DEFENCE: To whom?

123

POLICEMAN: There's no one visible in the cell with him. But he talks as though God were in the cell with him. He speaks intimately, addressing God by name. And sometimes it's one of the Saints. Particularly St. Joseph. He addresses himself frequently as if to the actual presence of St. Joseph.

DEFENCE: And at such times he speaks aloud?

POLICEMAN: Not always. Frequently there's a prolonged, deeply earnest talking in a low voice. A sort of — urgent whispering. But often he talks aloud.

DEFENCE: And continues in this all night?

POLICEMAN: Well, we have to stop him, for the sake of prisoners trying to sleep in neighbouring cells.

DEFENCE: On such occasions did Riel resent being stopped?

POLICEMAN: No. When we spoke to him through the grid he seemed at first not to understand, as if he were still — apart — in some sort of trance or dream. When he did come to, and understood where he was and what we wanted, he would be apologetic and most polite, and would comply.

DEFENCE gives place to the CROWN.

CROWN: In your observation of the prisoner did you at any time form the opinion you were dealing with a lunatic?

POLICEMAN: If by lunatic you mean . . . .

CROWN: A person of unsound mind.

POLICEMAN: I'm not sure what constitutes soundness of mind.

CROWN: So you will not say that you thought the prisoner insane?

POLICEMAN: No. He seems to me one of those . . . singular persons. . . . *(Suddenly.)* After all people have called Hamlet insane.

CROWN: *(Pouncing.)* Ah, but was not Hamlet "putting an antic disposition on"?

POLICEMAN: Yes.

CROWN: Do you think prisoner was "putting an antic disposition on"?

The POLICEMAN pauses, uncertain.

CROWN: *(Sharply.)* Well, do you?

POLICEMAN: *(Slowly, considering it thoughtfully.)* I have never quite been able to make up my mind.

CROWN: Thank you.

The CROWN and the POLICEMAN withdraw. Spots Three and Four are out. Only RIEL and the JUDGE are highlighted, in Spot Two and Spot One.

CLERK: The prisoner Louis Riel.

RIEL: *(Rising and bowing gravely.)* Your Honour. Honourable Court. You will have seen by the papers in the hands of the Crown, I am naturally inclined to think of God at the beginning of my actions. I wish, if I do, you will not take it as a mark of insanity, or as a play of insanity. *(He clasps his hands and closes his eyes, and prays, with deep humility and simplicity.)* Oh my God help me through thy grace and the divine influence of Jesus Christ. Bless me. Bless the honourable Court. Bless all who are around me now through the grace of Jesus Christ our Saviour. Change the curiosity of those who are paying attention to me now. Change that curiosity into sympathy for me. Amen. *(He opens his eyes and looks around. Then, not rhetorical, but intimate, tender.)* The day of my birth I was helpless, and my mother took care of me, and I lived. Today although I am a man, I am as helpless before this Court in the Dominion of Canada, and in this world, as I was helpless on the knees of my mother, the day of my birth.

125

The North-West also is my mother. It is my mother country. And I am sure my mother country will not kill me . . . any more than my mother did, forty years ago when I came into this world. Because, even if I have my faults, she is my mother and will see that I am true, and be full of love for me.

I believe I have a mission. *(The lights begin to dim out, slowly.)* I say humbly that through the grace of God — who is in this box with me — I am the Prophet of the New World.

First I worked to get free institutions for Manitoba. Now — though I was exiled from Manitoba for my pains — they have those institutions, and I am here, hounded, outlawed. . . . *(The stage is now dark.)*

SCENE 8

Vicinity of Courtroom, Regina

Down right, a WOMAN meets the SHERIFF.

WOMAN: Please, Sheriff, please. . . .

SHERIFF: What is it?

WOMAN: I know Louis Riel. I know him since he was a little boy. I want to tell the Judge about Louis.

SHERIFF: No, no, no, no, I'm sorry. . . .

WOMAN: They don't understand Louis in there. It is wrong about him in there. It is not Louis. I know Louis. I know his mother. I knew his father, too, Jean Louis. He was for us too, the half-breed people. . . .

SHERIFF: Yes, yes, I'm sorry, but it's quite impossible for me to . . . . *(She clutches at him imploringly, and he impatiently casts her off.)* Keep your hands off! Let go of me!

WOMAN: Don't put me away, please sir please.

SHERIFF: You can't possibly speak to the Judge.

WOMAN: Then the jury. . . .

SHERIFF: Nor any of the jury. Certainly not!

WOMAN: But they are kind men; they will want to know about Louis; they will see I come to tell the truth for Louis.

SHERIFF: You don't seem to understand. If you try to speak to them . . . .

WOMAN: (Frantic.) I must I must. . . .

SHERIFF: (Sternly.) Do you want to be sent to jail!

The POLICEMAN, walking from the left, has noticed and overheard, the SHERIFF by a nod and glance has him take over. The SHERIFF goes briskly on his way off, left; the POLICEMAN takes the WOMAN's arm kindly and leads her off, right.

POLICEMAN: It'll be all right with him. He'll be all right. Come now, come. The law is very fair. It's better not to interfere. Better for him.

WOMAN: Not to interfere! His friends that knew him, not to interfere!

SCENE 9

Courtroom, Regina

The lights gradually come up on RIEL nearing the conclusion of his speech.

RIEL: Petition after petition was sent from the North-West to the Federal Government, and so irresponsible is that Government that in the course of several years, besides doing nothing to satisfy the just claims of the people, they hardly troubled even to reply. All they have done is to send police and more police. That fact indicates absolute lack of responsibility. Insanity of government! Insanity complicated with paralysis. I was called by the people to lead them in their struggle against this insanity. I came. I came back from exile — to help them. And when I was pounced upon by armed police, I answered with arms. That is what is called my crime of high treason, for which they hold me today and for which they would tear me in pieces. If you take the plea of the defence that I am not responsible for my acts, acquit me completely. If you pronounce in favour of the Crown, which contends I am responsible, acquit me all the same. You are perfectly justified in delaring that, having my reason, I acted with sound mind in quarrelling with an insane and irresponsible Government. If there is high treason, it is not mine but theirs — their high treason against the people of the North-West.

JUDGE: *(Wearied.)* Now are you done?

RIEL: If you have the kindness to permit me. . . .

JUDGE: Well, if you must, you must.

RIEL: I am glad the Crown has proved I am the leader of the half-breeds of the North-West. That is important to remember. It means I stand in this dock not as myself only, but as the chosen representative and leader of a whole people — the half-breed people. Can a whole people be guilty of treason? I beg you to think of that. I am their leader — and one day perhaps I will be acknowledged as more than a leader of the half-breeds — as a leader of good in this great country.

All my life I have worked for practical results. If I have succeeded, after my death my children will shake hands with the Protestants. I do not want those evils which exist in Europe to be repeated here. There will be at last a New World. But not in some days or years. It will take hundreds of years.

Yet, now, we make a beginning. We invite to our new world Italians, Poles, Bavarians, Belgians, the Swedes, the Irish, the Jews — all, all are welcome here, provided only they will help us with their work and with their money, and by acknowledging Jesus Christ as the only hope of mankind and the Saviour of the World.

Now by the soil of this great land they have their start to make a nation. Who starts the nations? God. God is the maker of the universe. Our planet is in His hands. All the nations, the tribes, are members of His family. To each as a good Father He gives their inheritance. God cannot create a tribe, a nation, without locating it. We are not birds. We have to walk on the ground. And this is our ground, our country. And we will enrich it. We will cultivate it. This is the genius of civilization. Honourable Court, that is what as a public man, Riel has said. Of this I am guilty. Of the charge against me I am not guilty. I am confident that for this I will not be destroyed.

JUDGE: Is *that* all?

RIEL: Yes, that is all. Except to put my speech under the protection of my God my Saviour. He is the only one who can make it effective. And He will not fail me. If I have been astray, I have been acting not as an impostor but according to my conscience. Your Honour, that is what I have to say. *(He bows gravely to the Court and then kneels down in the dock in silent prayer.)*

CLERK: The jury will retire to consider their verdict.

JUDGE: Adjourned.

CLERK: Court adjourned.

SCENE 10

Vicinity of Courtroom, Regina

The CROWN and DEFENCE come walking slowly from the right, discussing the case.

CROWN: Must congratulate you. A most skilful defence.

DEFENCE: Thank you. But the jury was with you to the last, I'm afraid.

CROWN: Wish I could think so, but I'm not so sure. They showed lots of sympathy for him at times.

DEFENCE: True, true — if only he hadn't squandered it by tiresome verbosity. French-Canadians will still demand to know why he was tried by an exclusively Anglo-Saxon jury. Not even one Frenchman. And a jury of only six.

CROWN: Our frontier ways are rough sometimes. A bit irregular. But — they get the job done.

DR. JUKES and DR. ROY have come strolling from the left, similarly discussing the case.

JUKES: They'll hang him, doctor.

ROY: Is it so sure? You and I do not agree about him. So — the jury may not either.

JUKES: We shall soon know. Meanwhile, I've found him a most interesting patient. Forces me to re-examine my settled beliefs on many points.

ROY: It is like this, with the deranged. To work with them, it is to see how — what is your word — how — *precarious* is our hold on what we call sanity. What *is* sanity? To think of this — it can be frightening.

JUKES: Speaking of fright, I hate to imagine what *he's* going through now, poor devil. Sitting in there. . . .

ROY: Pardon. Kneeling. He prays. The jury considers, and he prays. He does not stop. He prays in French. In Latin. Mostly French. But sometimes in English! To make quite sure they will understand *(looking upward)* up there! But, I think it is all right, up there. I think *they* know some French!

JUKES: Unless, up there, they've quite lost touch with the French! Quite given them up.

ROY: Ah oui! And heaven now — full only of the English! This would be heaven!

JUKES: This levity, doctor . . . .

ROY: M'm! Not — English.

JUKES: Well, a trifle heartless, perhaps. With prisoner in there, bracing himself for the verdict. Guilty? Not guilty? Must be absolutely agonizing.

They are now joined by the CROWN and the DEFENCE.

ROY: I think he genuinely believes his Saints will save him.

JUKES: Certainly if faith — utter faith could sway a verdict....

CROWN: A court of law's a most unfavourable climate for miracles of faith.

DEFENCE: Even the faith of a prophet.

JUKES: Which reminds me — if it won't strike you as blasphemous, gentlemen — I've been thinking we know a little more now, of the considerations Pilate had to weigh — in a case with, shall we say, certain parallels.

CROWN: *(But lightly, smiling.)* Doctor I consider that remark one of the truest examples of profanity I've heard in a long time.

JUKES: But some truth in it, don't you think? And in that particular connection, gentlemen, isn't it striking how

131

anxious the prisoner is to identify his own predicament with the — Easter tragedy?

DEFENCE: That cross with himself hanging on it.

CROWN: Passion for martyrdom.

DEFENCE: Part of my case for him.

JUKES: Well, he may soon have what his heart desires. Jury may be ready. Shall we go in?

They all go off right. As they are going, two newspapermen come from the left and cross to the right on their way back into the Court.

MARC: I'm *New York Times.* And you?

BILL: Aw, I'm just on the local. Case sure is getting coverage. World-wide!

MARC: Whole thing — Riel himself — newsman's answer to prayer.

BILL: Sure is. Say what do the boys at the hotel think of his chances now?

MARC: Odds this morning were he'd hang.

BILL: That's where I put my money too.

MARC: And me.

BILL: My little all.

MARC: First bet I ever hoped I'd lose.

BILL: Aw, I dunno. But I get you: Guy don't hang, if we lose. Kinda blood-money if we win.

MARC: You got it!

They go off, right.

SCENE 11

Courtroom, Regina

Court assembled as before.

CLERK: Foreman of the jury.

The FOREMAN rises and bows, and remains standing.

CLERK: Are the jury agreed upon their verdict?

FOREMAN: They are.

CLERK: How say you: Is the prisoner guilty or not guilty?

FOREMAN: Guilty.

CLERK: Look to your verdict as the Court records it. You find the prisoner, Louis Riel, guilty — so say you all?

FOREMAN: We do. *(He turns to JUDGE.)* Your Honour, there's something more.

JUDGE: What is it?

FOREMAN: I've been asked by my brother jurors to recommend the prisoner to the mercy of the Crown.

JUDGE: Your recommendation will be conveyed to the proper authorities. Thank you.

The FOREMAN bows and sits down.

JUDGE: Louis Riel, you have been found guilty of a crime the most pernicious that man can commit. You have been found guilty of high treason. For what you did your remarks form no excuse whatsoever, and the law requires you to answer for it. It's true, the jury have asked that Her Majesty give your case merciful consideration, but I can't hold out any hope that Her Majesty will open her hand in clemency to you. As for me, I have only one more duty to perform: that is, to tell you what the sentence of the law is upon you. All I can suggest or advise you is to prepare to meet your end.

RIEL clasps his hands before his breast and bows his head for the blow. The JUDGE puts on the black cap.

JUDGE: It is now my painful duty to pass sentence upon you, and that is, that you be taken now to the police guardroom at Regina, and that you be kept there till the eighteenth September next, and that you then be taken to the place appointed for your execution, and there be hanged by the neck till you are dead. And may God have mercy on your soul.

Spot One, out, on the JUDGE, leaving only RIEL spot-lighted. For an intense, silent moment RIEL stands motionless.

RIEL: *(Then, incredulous.)* St. Joseph! *(Then a cry of anguish.)* "St. Joseph!"

SCENE 12

Corridor to Cells in Police Barracks, Regina

JUKES and the POLICEMAN are conversing anxiously and quietly.

JUKES: How is it with him now?

POLICEMAN: Sometimes he's calm and studiously polite. But sometimes he starts up in a sort of wild delirium, painful to witness. He seems to see people crowding his cell, and to hear voices calling to him, mocking or deriding him.

JUKES: Phantoms. Phantom voices. Hallucinations.

POLICEMAN: But real, terribly real to him. It's as if all he's been through were flooding back, swamping his mind, till

I fear for his reason, or what's left of it. *(A thumping is heard, accompanied by soft cries of lament: "Oh! Oh! Oh!")* There, now! Pounding on the table with his fists and crying to himself — that terrible whimpering cry. . . .

JUKES: Yes, yes it's pitiful, pitiful.

POLICEMAN: Like an animal, trapped.

JUKES: I must observe this. I'll watch through the grid.

JUKES and the POLICEMAN go off, left.

SCENE 13

Cell in Police Barracks, Regina

Phantom tom-toms and mob-singing of "We'll hang him up the river" are heard, at first faintly, but coming up a little as light gradually comes up on RIEL. He is revealed with his arms out and his fists clenched over the small table, almost identical with his position when seen waiting for the volley of the firing-squad at the execution of Thomas Scott. He thumps the table and cries, "Oh! Oh! Oh!" Phantom tom-toms and mob-singing now fade gradually out behind what follows. RIEL clutches the small metal statue of St. Joseph which stands on the table.

RIEL: Oh St. Joseph, St. Joseph you promised me, you can not fail me. Help me. Help me, now. Pray for me. Mercy.

PHANTOM VOICE OF THE JUDGE: And may God have mercy on your soul.

RIEL: Mercy on my soul! Mercy on my soul! *(He looks round apprehensively, and starts up, as if he could see the priest. He picks up and carries, over one arm, the ball of the ball-and-chain shackle fastened to his ankle.)* Père André! Oh Père André, help me.

PHANTOM VOICE OF ANDRE: Our blessed Lady will protect you, pray to her.

RIEL: Oh Mary ever blessed pray for me. Cover me. Hide me. *(Complete change of tone and attitude as he thinks he sees the Judge.)* Honourable Judge why are you wearing the black cap? *(Crescendo to angry outburst.)* Can all the people be guilty? A whole people guilty of treason? Build scaffolds for them all! Make every tree in The Saskatchewan a scaffold and hang us all, all, all by the neck till we are dead, dead, dead and rotten and our rotting corpses make a stench to fill the world. . . . *(Ironic and bitter.)* And fill the noses of fine gentlemen sitting oh so pleased with themselves in Ottawa.

PHANTOM VOICES OF METIS: Louis Riel! Louis Riel!

RIEL: My Métis call me.

PHANTOM VOICE OF MOTHER: Louis my son, Louis!

RIEL: Maman! Maman! They called us savages! A little different tincture in the blood — savages! We own this land! *(A new vision exalts him.)* Look, look, the herds of buffalo, thundering across the plains! The men are riding! *(He moves with their motion as if he saw them.)* Pemmican! There will be lots of pemmican and bonfires on the snow and pipes to smoke and singing by the fires. The spring is on the plains! The sun is strong, strong and rising high. Dance! Dance Métis, dance! *(He claps his hands and sways, and his feet make small motions in time with the dance.)* Eeeeee! Dance, Indians, dance with us! Swing the coloured feathers! Eeeeee! The anklets of angora and the tinkling bells make clouds about your feet! Dance! Dance!

His rhapsody is cut dead by another phantom voice.

PHANTOM VOICE OF SCOTT: Riel!

RIEL: *(Horrified.)* Scott! Thomas Scott!

PHANTOM VOICE OF SCOTT: You'll hang for this!

The volley of the firing-squad is heard far off.

RIEL: Me too! Me too! My life too. . . . Oh there is blood, and blood!

Far off, a solemn bell slowly tolls three strokes.

RIEL: *(After first stroke.)* The bell.

VOICE AS OF ECHO: Riel.

RIEL: *(After the second stroke.)* The passing bell!

VOICE AS OF ECHO: Riel.

RIEL: *(After the third stroke.)* Not for Riel.

VOICE AS OF ECHO: Riel.

RIEL: No! No! Not for Riel! Turn back! Bid them turn back! I have a mission. I say I have a mission. God is with us. The Church is with us! His Grace has brought an amnesty. None will be punished. *(Derisive phantom laughter stops him. He pauses. Then, slow and grave.)* And immediately the cock crew! *(Pause.)* Who has betrayed Riel? They're in our streets! The redcoats riot in our streets, the drunken redcoats, where our young men and girls were dancing. *(The light begins to dim out.)* Dark. Dark. Everywhere. Fall rain! Fall! Black rain and darkness . . . fall on the redcoats . . . on Macdonald's redcoats . . . on the tents of Wolseley. *(Sinking down.)* Oh St. Joseph, hide me, shelter me, pray for me, now and in the hour of death. . . .

SCENE 14

Precincts of Parliament, Ottawa

An excited anti-Riel mob from Ontario demonstrates, down right. A similar pro-Riel demonstration from Quebec is down left. Light comes up first on the Ontario demonstrators. They shout, wave

137

sticks, shake fists, wave flags. Roughly painted on boards that are
hoisted on poles are legends and slogans which are also being
shouted.

>   Death to Riel!
>   Vengeance for Thomas Scott!
>   Hang the traitor!
>   Hang Riel!
>   Hang Riel!
>   Hang Riel!

As light dims out on this Ontario mob it simultaneously comes up
on the mob from Quebec.

>   Sursis Riel!
>   Vive Riel!
>   Reprieve!
>   Sursis!
>   Reprieve!
>   Reprieve!

SCENE 15

Prime Minister's Room, Ottawa

*SIR JOHN A. MACDONALD, now seventy years old, sits at a
table with the Honourable J. A. CHAPLEAU, who is forty-three
years old. Numerous press cuttings and reports are scattered on
the table. There is a tray with whiskey and soda. Both men have*

drinks. Demonstrators in the previous scene are still heard, but now at a distance and dying out behind the discussion. MAC-DONALD rises, with his glass, crosses and stands a moment listening.

MACDONALD: Hang! Reprieve! Hang! Reprieve! *(He returns to his seat.)* Oh hang the whole confounded boiling of them!

CHAPLEAU: It is not a comfortable position: horns of a dilemma!

MACDONALD: It's the very dickens of a position. But as we must somehow resolve the dilemma, let's examine the horns. Suppose the fellow hangs.

CHAPLEAU: If he hangs, Quebec revolts.

MACDONALD: Aye, every flag in Quebec will fly half-mast for him; and we may march behind his hearse into the wilderness perhaps for generations. R.I.P. Riel, R.I.P. Conservative Party. *And*, my dear Chapleau. *(A really important consideration.)* R.I.P. your political career, never to speak of my own.

CHAPLEAU: *(Smiling.)* You *do* regard it seriously, Sir John.

MACDONALD: Aye: what with this bawling for clemency — petitions, petitions, petitions, pleas, demands, threats — your entire French Catholic population, priests, people, press *(He tosses a handful of clippings.)* backed up by all the hysterical and sentimental public blatherers in the press of New York, Boston, Washington, Dublin, London, and even Paris and God alone knows where else besides — all determined, by a sort of inverted lynch law, to see that he doesn't hang.

CHAPLEAU: It demonstrates again the widespread revulsion, especially in America, against capital punishment for what is regarded as a political offence.

MACDONALD: A political *offence*, if we hang Riel, but a political *necessity*, when Riel shot Thomas Scott. An obliging sort of logic. *(Struck by something. Then, slyly.)* By the way, why *must* people associate the trial of Riel with the shooting of Thomas Scott?

CHAPLEAU: A most *dis*obliging sort of logic.

MACDONALD: However, if we take our cue from Quebec and *don't* hang him . . . .

CHAPLEAU: Then, of course, Ontario revolts.

MACDONALD: Ontario votes against us to an Orangeman. And we're back where we started from.

CHAPLEAU: You were so kind as to mention my personal career: I can't hide from myself that if we hang Riel, Quebec will print my signature to the death warrant side-by-side with the speeches I made in defence of his Adjutant, Ambroise Lépine, in the North-West ten years ago. Ah, those magnificent, impassioned speeches! Unfortunately, they would serve equally well in defence of Riel today.

MACDONALD: My dear Chapleau, don't start worrying about your former speeches. Any politician who does that is already among the damned, and he'll be the chief and probably the only mourner at his own funeral before he can say Jack Robinson. *(Struck by something associated with the name.)* Robinson, Henderson. Jack *Hend*erson. *(Having got it.)* Och aye. Chapleau — by another pleasant little masterstroke of irony — the hangman at Regina is to be one, Jack Henderson — a former chum of the late lamented Thomas Scott at Fort Garry. I understand he actually applied — *(Mischievously.)* and to your brother the Sheriff out there — for the privilege, and I'm sure pleasure, of officiating.

CHAPLEAU: How the shade of Thomas Scott will laugh!

MACDONALD: An ugly laugh that will echo around Ontario and go cackling at Quebec till the very mischief is let loose.

CHAPLEAU: Assuming the execution. Are we now, in default of reason, being *(Slyly.)* "led to a decision" following our noses?

MACDONALD: *(His hand to his large nose.)* At least you and I have noses to follow: sound, reliable noses.

CHAPLEAU: Important part of a politician's equipment. Too often his only equipment.

MACDONALD: Unconscionably cynical remark, and I deplore cynicism — at any rate in my younger colleagues. However, while we indulge in these pleasantries, the impasse remains. Hang? Reprieve? One way or the other we must now decide and advise Her Majesty.

CHAPLEAU: If Whitehall would make the decision and save us the embarrassment.

MACDONALD: What else is Whitehall for? However, this time, Her Majesty's Imperial Government flatly refuses to play catspaw for us. Most inconsiderate of them. But this time we must risk burning our own paws — or should I say boats? No, my dear Chapleau, this wretch Riel is actually forcing us to take responsibility and govern Canada. How odd! The outlaw once more shapes the law. Henceforth, Louis Riel's name is scribbled across a chapter of our Constitutional Law! *(Offhand.)* However he's a gone coon.

CHAPLEAU: You are resolved?

MACDONALD: Live or die his miserable existence is nothing compared to what's endangered by it. I will hang or reprieve or do anything else that may be needed to prevent an unfortunate accident — his latest revolt — from fatally marring everything Confederation may mean — for Canada. And that is for the British Empire also, and the U.S.A., in short, for the world. When all has been considered and weighed, I think, perhaps, the public good will best be served if he hangs. There has been postponement already, of the date of execution. If you agree with me . . . .

CHAPLEAU: I do.

MACDONALD: Then we will advise no further interference with the judgment of the Court. I'm sure the Cabinet will concur.

CHAPLEAU: I feel relieved. His death at least removes an endless menace and anxiety.

MACDONALD: And he goes down to history as *(Ironically, slightly burlesque and pompous.)* one of the mortal instruments that shaped our destiny!

CHAPLEAU: As your hymn says, "God moves in a mysterious way. . . ."

MACDONALD: And so, I may add, does Satan. *(He holds up his glass of whiskey. For a moment stares through it meditatively. Then he speaks offhand and rather irritably.)* The execution will take place at Regina on November sixteen at eight o'clock in the morning. *(Swallows his whiskey at a gulp and puts down the glass.)*

SCENE 16

Precincts of Police Barracks, Regina

POLICEMAN, officer of the North-West Mounted Police, already met, gazes across the barrack precincts to the plains.

POLICEMAN: *(To himself.)* At eight he dies. Cold. Very cold. Snow everywhere. *(Pause.)* Now the sun. Gorgeous. Last dawn for Louis Riel. No attempt at rescue — yet. No sign of Gabriel Dumont. Any attempt by him — more than Riel will die. Our scouts — everywhere. The white houses of Regina, bright in the sun. People coming across the plains. So many, coming. On foot. Horseback. *(Sleighbells are heard.)* Buckboards, buggies, democrats, sleighs. All sorts of people. French. Indians. Settlers. Some — here from thousands of miles. Montreal. Toronto. Ottawa. Winnipeg. From across the Rockies. From British Columbia, even. And the U.S.A. (Pause.) Halted now. Our scouts, wheeling their horses across the trails. Thus far, good people! They're kneeling. Kneeling in the snow. Praying. Telling their beads. Some weep. Strange, very strange, this dawn on the prairies. Faces, all staring. Turned to stone. Staring toward this — "place appointed." Riel — quiet now. Waiting. His last hour. Last minutes. Quiet. *(Not reciting it.)*

. . . Seas are quiet when the winds give o'er;
So calm are we when passions are no more.
For then we know how vain it was. . . .

He is abruptly interrupted by a shouted command.

VOICE OF COMMAND: *(From somewhere fairly near by.)*

Leading section, right!
Form — half-sections!
Rear — halt!
Half-section — right!
Halt!
Eyes — right!
Dress!
Eyes — front!

SCENE 17

Cell and Precincts in Police Barracks, Regina

Light first picks up a small group, down left, waiting, as at one entrance to the cell. Nearest this imaginary entrance is the POLICEMAN. Deputy SHERIFF GIBSON, JUKES and pressmen MARC and BILL are there. From the still unlighted area, mid-stage, comes a low murmur of voices — ANDRE and RIEL, reciting the creed. They continue in this throughout what the SHERIFF is saying.

SHERIFF: *(Covering his agitation with an air of a brisk and business-like manner. He looks at his watch.)* What we've arranged: Last thing, when prisoner's on the drop and pinioned, all set, Father André will have him say the Lord's Prayer. At the words "And forgive us our trespasses" — oops! that's it! *(He snaps fingers and gestures.)* Alors, allez au ciel! I've rehearsed it with hangman Henderson. Whole thing should go off without a hitch. Oh! *(Grins.)* Hitch. No pun intended. *(Nervous laugh in which the others do not join.)*

The light remains on the SHERIFF's group; now the mid-stage area, the interior of cell, is also lighted. RIEL is seen facing ANDRE, both kneeling. Another priest, FATHER MCWILLIAMS, stands up-stage from them holding a processional crucifix. RIEL and ANDRE have reached the last phrases of the creed.

RIEL and ANDRE: . . . The communion of Saints; the forgiveness of sins; the resurrection of the body; and life everlasting. Amen.

ANDRE: Rise, my son.

They rise.

RIEL: Resurrection. The resurrection of the body.

ANDRE: The time draws near.

RIEL: I have been given a fine morning — fine frosty morning. I have loved such mornings on the plains.

ANDRE: It is a special favour that you have been given cheerfulness to meet this morning.

RIEL: God is with me.

ANDRE: The time is near. If there is any last thing you wish to tell me.

RIEL: I had a vision, father. Three persons stood before me. My brother, and a priest. And one I did not know, a divine being. He pointed to me and said: "God will be with him. They will destroy his body but God will raise him up on the third day."

ANDRE: *(Embarrassed.)* My son, my son!

RIEL: *(Elated.)* For this my heart leaps up! I laugh! I go with joy! The scaffold waits and I go gladly to it! Happy to die! Oh do not fear. I shall not shame my friends nor please my foes by failing at the end! I shall not die a coward!

ANDRE: Your faith will support you. And now is that all?

RIEL: One last thing. I have one last thing to ask.

ANDRE: *(Being patient.)* What is it?

RIEL: On the scaffold, before I go, may I speak — some last words?

ANDRE: To whom?

RIEL: To my people.

ANDRE: About what?

RIEL: About what I have done. What they should go on to do.

ANDRE: My son I beg you do not ask this.

RIEL: But father . . . .

ANDRE: No. Nothing is proper now but prayer — and silence.

RIEL: I have this right. If I must sacrifice it, too . . . . If it is required of me. . . .

ANDRE: I ask it of you. Your final sacrifice. In spirit you have already passed beyond these earthly things. Do not turn back, my son.

RIEL: *(Submissive.)* Oui, mon père, oui.

ANDRE: And now, are you at peace with all men?

RIEL: I am, father.

ANDRE: Do you forgive your enemies?

RIEL: I do.

ANDRE: Do you give your life a sacrifice to God?

RIEL: To God and my people, my half-breed people.

ANDRE: My son, I give you the kiss of peace.

He embraces RIEL and kisses him, first on one cheek, then on the other. He holds the crucifix he carries before RIEL, who kisses it and gazes at it. Somewhere a clock begins to strike the hour. Down left — the entrance to the cell — the SHERIFF comes to attention.

SHERIFF: Eight o'clock. Now. *(He turns and walks toward his prisoner, the POLICEMAN standing aside to let him pass. JUKES and the PRESSMEN remain behind. The SHERIFF halts beside RIEL and ANDRE.)* It is the time. Are you ready?

ANDRE: We are.

SHERIFF: As Sheriff I'll lead the way.

He moves toward the area down left. In procession behind him follow FATHER MCWILLIAMS with the processional crucifix held aloft, then ANDRE and RIEL. At down left, the procession turns and crosses the stage slowly, down front to down right. At down left, JUKES, the POLICEMAN, and the two PRESSMEN will fall in behind ANDRE and RIEL. From the first steps of this procession ANDRE recites the Confiteor and RIEL repeats it after him as they go forward.

ANDRE: I confess to Almighty God. . . .

RIEL: I confess to Almighty God. . . .

ANDRE: To the blessed Mary ever Virgin. . . .

RIEL: To the blessed Mary ever Virgin. . . .

ANDRE: To blessed Michael the Archangel. . . .

RIEL: To blessed Michael the Archangel. . . .

ANDRE: To blessed John the Baptist. . . .

RIEL: To blessed John the Baptist. . . .

ANDRE: To the Holy Apostles Peter and Paul. . . .

RIEL: To the Holy Apostles Peter and Paul. . . .

ANDRE: And to all the Saints. . . .

RIEL: And to all the Saints. . . .

When ANDRE and RIEL are approaching the corner down right, a bright light from off stage, up left, catches in its beam the HANGMAN, who stands, black-hooded and black-gauntleted, waiting to receive RIEL and lead him off into the light — to the place where the scaffold presumably is.

ANDRE: That I have sinned exceedingly in thought word and deed. . . .

RIEL: That I have sinned exceedingly in thought word and deed. . . .

ANDRE: Through my fault, through my fault, through my most grievous fault. . . .

RIEL: Through my fault, through my fault, through my most grievous fault. . . .

Down right, the procession turns towards the place where the HANGMAN waits, up left. The eyes of ANDRE and RIEL are on the ground, so they do not as yet see the HANGMAN.

ANDRE: Therefore I beseech the blessed Mary ever Virgin. . . .

RIEL: Therefore I beseech the blessed Mary ever Virgin. . . .

ANDRE: Blessed Michael the Archangel. . . .

RIEL: Blessed Michael the Archangel. . . .

ANDRE: Blessed John . . . .

He abruptly breaks off, having lifted his eyes and seen the HANGMAN for the first time. He is so affected that he pauses and utters a small cry of horror. For a moment he seems too distressed to be able to go on. RIEL, by contrast, remains calm and composed, he turns in grave sympathy to encourage ANDRE.

RIEL: Courage, mon père, courage!

ANDRE braces himself and goes on.

ANDRE: Blessed John the Baptist. . . .

RIEL: Blessed John the Baptist. . . .

ANDRE: The Holy Apostles Peter and Paul. . . .

RIEL: The Holy Apostles Peter and Paul. . . .

ANDRE: And all the Saints. . . .

RIEL: And all the Saints. . . .

ANDRE: To pray to the Lord our God for me. . . .

RIEL: To pray to the Lord our God for me. . . .

While the procession is moving off into the light, up left the HANGMAN turns and walks alongside RIEL and upstage of him, with his gauntleted hand on RIEL's shoulder. As they go on, a police TROOPER — *off duty, tunic unbuttoned, smoking a cheroot, abristle with hostility — strolls in from up right and follows, slowly, to mid-stage, where he stands sardonically watching the procession as it passes out of sight repeating the last phrases of the Confiteor.*

ANDRE: And may the Almighty God have mercy upon us.
. . .

RIEL: And may the Almighty God have mercy upon us. . . .

ANDRE: And forgive us our sins. . . .

RIEL: And forgive us our sins. . . .

ANDRE: And bring us to life everlasting. . . .

RIEL: And bring us to life everlasting. . . .

ANDRE: Amen.

RIEL: Amen.

In silence the TROOPER remains a moment gazing toward the light, which has begun to dim. Then:

TROOPER: *(Hoarse with hatred.)* Son of a bitch! *(He spits contemptuously after the procession. Then he throws down his cheroot and savagely grinds it underfoot.)* Goddam son of a bitch!

He lurches off left.

SCENE 18

A Place of Prayer and Mourning

A solemn bell tolls slowly and continues throughout what follows to the end of the play. Simultaneously, in the distance, mob voices may be heard jubilantly singing "We'll hang him up the

river" but with the words changed to "He's hanging up the river."
This distant singing should only be heard during the first eight
strokes of the tolling bell — while MOURNERS are assembling —
and should fade out behind the opening phrases of the requiem,
leaving the remains of the play to the serenity of last things.
Meanwhile, from down right and down left, Riel's MOTHER and
MARGUERITE and PEOPLE come in and, in a sort of ritual
movement, take their places and kneel in a semi-circle with their
backs to the audience. They kneel around ANDRE who is at
centre, with FATHER MCWILLIAMS a pace upstage of him
holding aloft a crucifix. At the seventh stroke of the tolling bell —
there should be an interval of five seconds between successive
strokes — an off-stage male quartet begins to sing a four-part
unaccompanied requiem in Latin.

OFF-STAGE MALE QUARTET:

Requiem aeternam dona eis Domine et
lux perpetua luceat eis. In memoria aeterna erit
justus ab auditione mala non timebit.

At the words "In memoria aeterna erit justus . . .", ANDRE ac-
companies the quartet, speaking the prayer in Latin or in English,
but preferably in Latin.

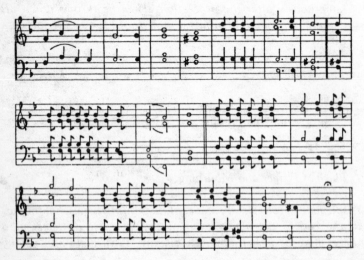

ANDRE:

Fac, quaesumus Domine, hanc cum servo tuo defuncto misericordiam, ut factorum suorum in poenis non recipiat vicem, qui tuam in votis tenuit voluntatem; ut sicut hic cum vera fides junxit fidelium turmis, ita illic cum tua miseratio societ Angelicis choris. Per Christum Dominum nostrum.	*Or*	Grant, O Lord, this mercy to Thy servant departed; that he who in his desires did Thy will may not receive the punishments of his misdeeds: and that as true faith hath joined him to the company of the faithful here below, Thy mercy may make him the companion of the holy Angels in heaven. Through Christ our Lord.

ALL: Amen.

The bell continues to toll.

George Ryga

Indian

EDITOR'S NOTE: George Ryga was born in 1932 in northern
Alberta where his Ukrainian parents were homesteading on
marginal farm land. Largely self-educated — he left school at the
age of 12 — Ryga won a creative writing scholarship at the Banff
School of Fine Arts in summer, 1949. But, in a controversy
characteristic of the outspoken, politically-minded humanist's
career, Ryga found a subsequent IODE scholarship withdrawn
because of one of his poems criticizing the Korean War effort. An
assortment of jobs ranging from farm labourer through radio producer and copy editor to hotel night-clerk supported Ryga until
1961-2 when he sold twelve short stories to the CBC. Since then as
a full-time writer, Ryga has produced well over three dozen stage
plays and radio, television or film scripts, as well as a half-dozen
novels and a small number of essays on Canadian theatre. Among
his stage plays are the highly significant *The Ecstasy of Rita Joe*
(1967) and the controversial *Captives of the Faceless Drummer*
(1971). *Indian* was his first play.

Indian was produced first as a television script on CBC's "Quest"
series in 1962 and published in that version in *Maclean's* that same
year. It was rewritten as a stage play in 1964, published in 1965
(*Tamarack Review*) and staged professionally in 1974 at the
Manitoba Theatre Centre.

Characters:

INDIAN   *Transient Indian labourer. Swarthy, thin, long haired. Wears tight-fitting jeans, dirty dark shirt brightened by outlandish western designs over pockets. Also cowboy boots which are cracked and aged. A wide-brimmed black western hat.*

WATSON   *Farmer and employer of Indian.*

AGENT   *Comfortable civil servant. Works in the Indian Affairs Department as field worker for the service.*

SETTING:

Stage should be flat, grey, stark non-country. Diametric lines (telephone poles and wire on one side, with a suggestion of two or three newly driven fence-posts on the other) could project vast empty expanse.

Set may have a few representative tufts of scraggy growth in distance — also far and faint horizon.

In front and stage left, one fence-post newly and not yet fully driven. Pile of dirt around post. Hammer, wooden box and shovel alongside.

High, fierce white light off stage left to denote sun. Harsh shadows and constant sound of low wind.

Back of stage is a pile of ashes, with a burnt axe handle and some pottery showing.

Curtain up on INDIAN asleep, using slight hump of earth under his neck for pillow. He is facing sun, with hat over his face. WATSON approaches from stage right, dragging his feet and raising dust. Stops over INDIAN's head.

WATSON: *(loud and angry)* Hey! What the hell! Come on . . . you aimin' to die like that?

INDIAN clutches his hat and sits up. Lifts his hat and looks up, then jerks hat down over his face.

INDIAN: Oy! Oooh! The sun she blind me, goddamn! . . . Boss . . . I am sick! Head, she gonna explode, sure as hell!

He tries to lie down again, but WATSON grabs his arm and yanks him to his feet.

WATSON: There's gonna be some bigger explosions if I don't get action out of you guys. What happened now? Where's the fat boy? An' the guy with the wooden leg?

INDIAN: Jus' a minute, boss. Don't shout like that. *(looks carefully around him)* They not here . . . Guess they run away, boss — no? . . . Roy, he's not got wooden leg. He got bone leg same's you an' me. Only it dried up and look like wood. Small, too . . . *(lifts up his own right leg)* That shoe . . . that was fit Roy's bad leg. The other shoe is tight. But this one, boss — she is hunder times tighter!

WATSON: *(squatting)* Is them Limpy's boots?

INDIAN: Sure, boss. I win them at poker las' night. Boss, what a time we have — everybody go haywire!

Watson looks around impatiently.

WATSON: I can see. Where's your tent?

INDIAN: *(pointing to ashes)* There she is. Sonofabitch, but I never see anything burn like that before!

WATSON: The kid wasn't lying — you guys *did* burn the tent.

INDIAN: What kid?

WATSON: Your kid.

INDIAN: *(jumping to his feet)* Alphonse? Where is Alphonse? He run away when Sam and Roy start fight . . .

WATSON: Yeh, he run away . . . run all the way to the house. Told us you guys was drunk an' wild. So the missus fixed him something to eat and put him to bed.

INDIAN: He's all right? Oh, that's good, boss!

WATSON: (smiling grimly) Sure, he's all right. Like I said, the missus fed the kid. Then I took him and put him in the grainery, lockin' the door so he ain't gonna get out. That's for protection.

INDIAN: Protection? You don't need protection, boss. Alphonse not gonna hurt you.

WATSON: Ha! Ha! Ha! Big joke! . . . Where are your pals as was gonna help you with this job? Where are they — huh?

INDIAN: I don't know. They run away when tent catch fire.

WATSON: Great! That's just great! You know what you guys done to me? Yesterday, ya nicked me for ten dollars . . . I'm hungry, the fat boy says to me — my stomach roar like thunder. He's gonna roar out the other end before I'm finished with you an' him! How much you figure the fence you put up is worth?

INDIAN: (rubbing his eyes and trying to see the fence in the distance) I dunno, boss. You say job is worth forty dollars. Five, mebbe ten dollars done . . .

WATSON: Five dollars! Look here, smart guy — ya've got twenty-nine posts in — I counted 'em. At ten cents apiece, you've done two dollars ninety cents worth of work! An' you got ten dollars off me yesterday!

INDIAN: (pondering sadly) Looks like you in the hole, boss.

WATSON: Well maybe I am . . . an' maybe I ain't. I got your kid in the grainery, locked up so he'll keep. You try to run off after your pals, an' I'm gonna take my gun an' shoot a hole that big through the kid's head!

He makes a ring with his fingers to show exact size of injury he intends to make.

INDIAN: No!

WATSON: Oh, sure! So what ya say, Indian? . . . You gonna work real hard and be a good boy?

INDIAN: Boss — you know me. I work! Them other guys is no good —'but not Johnny. I make deal — I keep deal! You see yourself I stay when they run.

WATSON: Sure, ya stayed. You were too goddamned drunk to move, that's why you stayed! What goes on in your heads . . . ah, hell! You ain't worth the bother!

INDIAN: No, no, boss . . . You all wrong.

WATSON: Then get to work! It's half past nine, and you ain't even begun to think about the fence.

INDIAN: Boss . . . a little bit later. I sick man . . . head — she hurt to burst. An' stomach — ugh! Boss, I not eat anything since piece of baloney yesterday . . .

WATSON: (turning angrily) You go to hell — you hear me? Go to hell! I got that story yesterday. Now g'wan — I wanna see some action!

INDIAN: All right, boss. You know me. You trust me.

WATSON: Trust ya? I wouldn't trust you with the time of day, goddamn you! (remembers something) Hey — there's a snoop from the Indian Affairs department toolin' around today — checkin' on all you guys workin' off the reserve. I'm telling you somethin' . . . you're working for me, so if you got any complaints, you better tell me now. I don't want no belly-achin' to no government guys.

INDIAN: Complaints? . . . Me? I happy, boss. What you take me for?

WATSON: Sure, sure . . . Now get back to work. An' remember what I told you . . . you try to beat it, an' I shoot the kid. You understand?

INDIAN removes his hat and wipes his brow.

INDIAN: Sure, bossman — I understand.

INDIAN looks towards the fence in the fields. WATSON stands behind him, scratching his chin and smirking insolently. INDIAN glances back at him, then shrugging with resignation, moves unsteadily to the unfinished fence post. He pulls the box nearer to the post, picks up hammer and is about to step on the box. Changes his mind and sits for a moment on the box, hammer across his knees. Rubs his eyes and forehead.

WATSON: Now what the hell's the matter? Run out of gas?

INDIAN: Oh, boss . . . If I be machine that need only gas, I be all right mebbe . . .

WATSON: So you going to sit an' let the day go by? . . . Indian, I've got lots of time, an' I can grind you to dirt if you're figurin' on bustin' my ass!

INDIAN: Nobody bust you, boss. I be all right right away . . . Sementos! But the head she is big today. An' stomach . . . she is slop-bucket full of turpentine. Boss . . . two dollars a quart, Sam Cardinal says to me . . . with four dollars we get enough bad whiskey to poison every Indian from here to Lac La Biche! Sam Cardinal tell the truth that time for sure . . .

WATSON: What kind of rubbish did you drink?

INDIAN: Indian whiskey, boss. You know what is Indian whiskey?

WATSON: No. You tell me, an' then you get to work!

INDIAN: Sure, boss, sure. As soon as field stop to shake. Indian whiskey . . . you buy two quart. You get one quart wood alcohol . . . maybe half quart formalin, an' the rest is water from sick horse! That's the kind whiskey they make for Indian.

WATSON: An' it makes the field shake for you . . . Christ! *You* make me sick!

INDIAN: Oh, but what party it make!

WATSON: *(irritably)* Come on . . . come on! Get on with it.

INDIAN scrambles on box and starts to drive post into ground. He stops after a few seconds. He is winded.

INDIAN: Sementos! Is hard work, boss! . . . I tell you, Sam Cardinal sing like sick cow . . . an' Roy McIntosh dance on his bad leg. Funny! . . . Alphonse an' I laugh until stomach ache. I win Roy's boots in poker, but he dance anyhow. Then Sam get mad an' he push Roy . . . Roy push him back . . . They fight . . . Boy, I hungry now, boss . . .

WATSON: Tough! I wanna see ten bucks of work done.

INDIAN: Then you feed me? Big plate potatoes an' meat? . . . An' mebbe big hunk of pie?

WATSON: *(laughs sarcastically)* Feed ya? Soon's I get my ten bucks squared away, you can lie down and die! But not on my field . . . go on the road allowance!

INDIAN hits the post a few more times, trying to summon up strength to get on with the work. But it is all in vain. Drops hammer heavily to the box. Rubs his stomach.

INDIAN: You hard man, boss . . . Hard like iron. Sam is bad man . . . bugger up you, bugger up me. Get ten dollars for grub from you . . . almost like steal ten dollars from honest man. Buy whiskey . . . buy baloney an' two watermelon. He already eat most of baloney and I see him give hunk to friendly dog. I kick dog. Sam get mad . . . why you do that? Dog is nothing to you? I say, he eat my grub. He can go catch cat if he hungry. I catch an' eat cat once myself, boss . . . winter 1956. Not much meat an' tough like rope. I never eat cat again, that's for sure. Sementos! But the head hurt!

WATSON: One more word, Indian . . . just one more word an' I'm gonna clean house on you! . . . You wanna try me? Come on!

For a moment the INDIAN teeters between two worlds, then with a violent motion he sweeps up the hammer and begins pounding

the post, mechanically with an incredible rhythm of defeat. WAT-
SON watches for a while, his anger gone now. Scratches himself
nervously, then makes a rapid exit off stage left.
Almost immediately the hammering begins to slow, ending with
one stroke when the hammer head rests on the post, and
INDIAN's head droops on his outstretched arms.

INDIAN: Scared talk . . . world is full of scared talk. I show
scare an' I get a job from mister Watson. Scared Indian is
a live Indian. My head don't get Alphonse free . . . but
hands do.

Sound of motor car approaching. INDIAN lifts his head and peers
to stage right.

INDIAN: Hullo . . . I am big man today! First mister Watson
an' now car come to see me. Boy, he drive! . . . If I not get
out of his way he gonna hit me, sure as hell!

Jumps down from box and watches. Car squeals to stop off-stage.
Puff of dust blows in from wings. Car door slams and AGENT
enters.

AGENT: Hi there, fella, how's it going?

INDIAN: Hello, misha. Everything is going one hunder fifty
percent! Yessiree . . . one hunder fifty percent!

INDIAN rises on box and lifts hammer to drive post.

AGENT: There was talk in town your camp burned out last
night . . . everything okay? Nobody hurt?

INDIAN: Sure, everything okay. You want complaints?

AGENT: Well, I . . . what do you mean, do I want complaints?

INDIAN: I just say if you want complaints, I give you lots.
My tent, she is burn down last night. My partners . . .
they run away. Leave me to do big job myself. I got no

money . . . an' boss, he's got my Alphonse ready to shoot if I try to run. You want more complaints? *(drives down hard on hammer and groans)* Maybe you want know how my head she hurts inside?

AGENT: *(relieved)* Hey — c'mere. I'll give you a smoke to make you feel better. You're in rough shape, boy! Which would you prefer — pipe tobacco, or a cigarette? I've got both . . .

INDIAN drops hammer and comes down from box.

INDIAN: The way I feel, misha, I could smoke old stocking full of straw. Gimme cigarette. *(examines the cigarette AGENT gives him)* Oh, you make lotsa money from government, boss . . . tobacco here . . . and cotton there — some cigarette! Which end you light? *(laughs)*

AGENT: Light whichever end you want. You can eat it for all I care. That's some hat you got there, sport. Where'd you get it?

INDIAN: *(accepting light AGENT offers him)* Win at poker, misha.

AGENT: *(examining him closely)* Aren't those boots tight? I suppose you stole them!

INDIAN: No, boss — poker.

AGENT: And that shirt — will you look at that! Have shirt, will travel.

INDIAN: I steal that from my brother, when he is sick and dying. He never catch me!

AGENT: *(laughing)* That's good . . . I must tell the boys about you — what's your name?

INDIAN: You think is funny me steal shirt from my brother when he die? . . . You think that funny, bossman? I think you lousy bastard! . . . You think that funny, too?

AGENT: *(startled)* Now hold on — did I hear you say . . .

INDIAN: You hear good what I say.

The AGENT takes out his notebook.

AGENT: Just give me your name, and we'll settle with you later.

INDIAN: Turn around an' walk to road. If you want to see stealer in action, I steal wheels off your car. You try catch me . . .

AGENT: *(angrily)* Give me your name!

INDIAN: Mebbe I forget . . . mebbe I got no name at all.

AGENT: Look here, boy . . . don't give me any back-talk, or I might have to turn in a report on you, and next time Indian benefits are given out, yours might be hard to claim!

INDIAN: So — you got no name for me. How you gonna report me when you not know who I am? You want name? All right, I give you name. Write down — Joe Bush!

AGENT: I haven't got all day, fella. Are you, or are you not going to tell me your name?

INDIAN: No! I never tell you, misha! Whole world is scare. It make you scare you should know too much about me!

AGENT: *(slamming notebook shut)* That does it! You asked for it . . . an' by God, if I have to go after you myself, I'm gonna find out who you are!

INDIAN: Don't get mad, misha. I sorry for what I say. I got such hurting head, I don't know what I say . . .

AGENT: Been drinking again, eh? . . . What was it this time — homebrew? Or shaving lotion?

INDIAN: Maybe homebrew, maybe coffee. I don't know. Why you ask?

AGENT: You're no kid. You know as well as I do. Besides, bad liquor's going to kill you sooner than anything else.

INDIAN: *(excitedly)* Misha . . . you believe that? You really mean what you say?

AGENT: What — about bad liquor? Sure I do . . .

INDIAN: Then misha, please get me bottle of good, clean Canadian whiskey! I never drink clean whiskey in my life!

AGENT: Come on, now . . . you're as . . .

INDIAN: I give you twenty dollars for bottle! Is deal?

AGENT: Stop it! . . . Boy, you've got a lot more than a hangover wrong in your head!

INDIAN: *(points off stage)* That car yours?

AGENT: Yes.

INDIAN: How come all that writing on door — that's not your name? Why you not tell truth?

AGENT: Well, I work for the government, and they provide us . . .

INDIAN: Thirty dollars?

AGENT: Look here . . .

INDIAN: How come you not in big city, with office job? How come you drive around an' talk to dirty, stupid Indian? You not have much school, or mebbe something else wrong with you to have such bad job.

AGENT: Shut your lousy mouth, you . . .

INDIAN: Thirty-five dollars? No more! . . . I give you no more!

AGENT: Will you shut up?

INDIAN: *(defiantly)* No! I never shut up! You not man at all — you cheap woman who love for money! Your mother was woman pig, an' your father man dog!

AGENT: *(becoming frightened)* What . . . what are you saying?

INDIAN comes face to face with AGENT.

INDIAN: You wanna hit me? Come on . . . hit me! You kill me easy, an' they arrest you — same people who give you car. Hit me — even little bit — come on! You coward! Just hit me like this! *(slaps his palms together)* . . . Just like that — come on! You know what I do when you hit me?

AGENT: *(looks apprehensively around himself)* What?

INDIAN: I report you for beating Indian an' you lose job. Come on — show me you are man!

He dances provocatively around AGENT. AGENT turns in direction of his car.

AGENT: I'm getting out of here — you're crazy!

INDIAN: *(jumps in front of AGENT)* No . . . you not go anywhere! Maybe nobody here to see what happen, but after accident, lots of people come from everywhere. I'm gonna jump on car bumper, and when you drive, I fall off an' you drive over me. How you gonna explain that, bossman?

AGENT: *(frightened now)* I got nothing against you, boy! What's the matter with you? . . . What do you want with me?

INDIAN: I want nothing from you — jus' to talk to me — to know who I am. Once you go into car, I am outside again. I tell you about my brother, an' how he die . . .

AGENT: Go back to your work and I'll go back to mine. I don't want to hear about your brother or anyone else. *(INDIAN walks offstage to car)* Now you get off my car!

INDIAN: *(offstage)* You gonna listen, misha. You gonna listen like I tell you. *(sounds of car being bounced)* Boy, you ride like in bed! Misha, who am I?

INDIAN returns to stage.

AGENT: How in the devil do I know who you are, or what you want with me. I'm just doing a job — heard your camp got burned out and . . .

INDIAN: How you know who any of us are? How many of us got birth certificates to give us name an' age on reserve? . . . Mebbe you think I get passport an' go to France. Or marry the way bossman get married. You think that, misha?

AGENT: I don't care who you are or what you think. Just get back to your job and leave me alone . . .

INDIAN glances admiringly off stage to car.

INDIAN: Boy, is like pillow on wheels! If I ever have car like that, I never walk again!

AGENT: Get out of my way! I've got to get back into town.

INDIAN: No hurry. Mebbe you never go back at all.

AGENT: What . . . do you mean by that?

INDIAN turns and approaches AGENT until they stand face to face.

INDIAN: You know what is like to kill someone — not with hate — not with any feelings here at all? *(places hand over heart)*

AGENT: *(stepping back)* This is ridiculous! Look, boy . . . I'll give you anything I can — just get out of my hair. That whiskey you want — I'll get it for you . . . won't cost you a cent, I promise!

INDIAN: Someone that mebbe you loved? Misha — I want to tell you somethin' . . .

AGENT: No!

INDIAN catches hold of AGENT's shirt front.

INDIAN: Listen — damn you! I kill like that once! You never know at Indian office — nobody tell you! Nobody ever tell you! . . . I got to tell you about my brother . . . he die three, four, maybe five years ago. My friend been collecting treaty payments on his name. He know how many years ago now . . .

AGENT: You couldn't . . .

INDIAN: I couldn't, misha?

AGENT: There are laws in this country — nobody escapes the law!

INDIAN: What law?

AGENT: The laws of the country!

INDIAN: (threatening) What law?

AGENT: No man . . . shall kill . . . another . . .

INDIAN: I tell you about my brother. I tell you everything. Then you tell me if there is law for all men.

AGENT: Leave me alone! I don't want to hear about your brother!

INDIAN: (fiercely) You gonna listen! Look around — what you see? Field and dust . . . an' some work I do. You an' me . . . you fat, me hungry. I got nothin' . . . and you got money, car. Maybe you are better man than I. But I am not afraid, an' I can move faster. What happen if I get mad, an' take hammer to you?

AGENT: You . . . wouldn't . . .

INDIAN: You wrong, misha. Nobody see us. Mebbe you lucky — get away. But who believe you? You tell one story, I tell another. I lose nothing — but you gonna listen about my brother, that's for sure!

AGENT: (desperately) Look boy — let's be sensible — let's behave like two grown men. I'll drive you into town — buy you a big dinner! Then we'll go and buy that whiskey

I promised. You can go then — find your friends and have another party tonight . . . Nobody will care, and you'll have a good time!

INDIAN: *(spitting)* You lousy dog!

AGENT: Now don't get excited! . . . I'm only saying what I think is best. If you don't want to come, that's fine. Just let me go and we'll forget all about today, and that we ever even seen one another, okay?

INDIAN releases the AGENT.

INDIAN: You think I forget I see you? I got you here like picture in my head. I try to forget you . . . like I try to forget my brother, but you never leave me alone . . . Misha, I never forget you!

AGENT: *(struggling to compose himself)* I'm just a simple joe doing my job, boy — remember that. I know there's a lot bothers you. Same's a lot bothers me. We've all got problems . . . but take them where they belong.

AGENT pulls out cigarettes and nervously lights one for himself.

INDIAN: Gimme that!

AGENT: This is mine — I lit it for myself! Here, I'll give you another one!

INDIAN: I want that one!

AGENT: No, damn it . . . have a new one!

INDIAN jumps behind AGENT and catches him with arm around throat. With other hand he reaches out and takes lit cigarette out of AGENT's mouth. Throws AGENT to the field. The AGENT stumbles to his knees, rubbing his eyes.

AGENT: What's wrong with you? Why did you do that?

INDIAN: Now you know what is like to be me. Get up! Or I kick your brains in!

AGENT rises to his feet and sways uncertainly.

AGENT: Dear God . . .

INDIAN: My brother was hungry . . . an' he get job on farm of white bossman to dig a well. Pay she is one dollar for every five feet down. My brother dig twenty feet — two day hard work. He call up to bossman — give me planks, for the blue clay she is getting wet! To hell with what you see — bossman shout down the hole — just dig! Pretty soon, the clay shift, an' my brother is trapped to the shoulders. He yell — pull me out! I can't move, an' the air, she is squeezed out of me! But bossman on top — he is scared to go down in hole. He leave to go to next farm, an' after that another farm, until he find another Indian to send down hole. An' all the time from down there, my brother yell at the sky. Jesus Christ — help me! White man leave me here to die! But Jesus Christ not hear my brother, an' the water she rise to his lips. Pretty soon, he put his head back until his hair an' ears in slimy blue clay an' water. He no more hear himself shout — but he shout all the same!

AGENT: I wasn't there! I couldn't help him!

INDIAN: . . . He see stars in the sky — lots of stars. A man see stars even in day when he look up from hole in earth . . .

AGENT: I couldn't help him — I don't want to hear about him!

INDIAN: . . . Then Sam Cardinal come. Sam is a coward. But when he see my brother there in well, an' the blue clay movin' around him like livin' thing, he go down. Sam dig with his hands until he get rope around my brother. Then he come up, an' he an' white bossman pull. My brother no longer remember, an' he not hear the angry crack of mud an' water when they pull him free . . .

167

AGENT: *(with relief)* Then . . . he lived? Thank God . . .

INDIAN: Sure . . . sure . . . he live. You hunt?

AGENT: Hunt? . . . You mean — shooting?

INDIAN: Yeh.

AGENT: Sure. I go out every year.

INDIAN: You ever shoot deer — not enough to kill, but enough to break one leg forever? Or maybe hit deer in eye, an' it run away, blind on one side for wolf to kill?

AGENT: I nicked a moose two years back — never did track it down. But I didn't shoot it in the eye.

INDIAN: How you know for sure?

AGENT: Well . . . I just didn't. I never shoot that way!

INDIAN: You only shoot — where bullet hit you not know. Then what you do?

AGENT: I tried to track it, but there had been only a light snow . . . an' I lost the tracks.

INDIAN: So you not follow?

AGENT: No. I walked back to camp . . . My friend an' I had supper and we drove home that night . . .

INDIAN: Forget all about moose you hurt?

AGENT: No. I did worry about what happened to him!

INDIAN: You dream about him that night? . . . Runnin', bawling with pain?

AGENT: What the hell . . . dream about a moose? There's more important things to worry about, I'm telling you.

INDIAN: Then you not worry at all. You forget as soon as you can. Moose not run away from you — you run away from moose!

AGENT: I didn't . . . hey, you're crazy! *(moves towards car off stage, but INDIAN jumps forward and stops him)* Here! You leave me alone, I'm telling you . . . You got a lot of wild talk in your head, but you can't push your weight around with me . . . I'm getting out of here . . . Hey!

INDIAN catches him by arm and rolls him to fall face down in the dust. INDIAN pounces on him.

INDIAN: What you call man who has lost his soul?

AGENT: I don't know. Let go of me!

INDIAN: We have name for man like that! You know the name?

AGENT: No, I don't. *You're breaking my arm!*

INDIAN: We call man like that sementos. Remember that name . . . for *you* are *sementos!*

AGENT: Please, fella — leave me alone! I never hurt you that I know of . . .

INDIAN: Sure.

Releases AGENT, who rises to his feet, dusty and dishevelled.

AGENT: I want to tell you something . . . I want you to get this straight, because every man has to make up his mind about some things, and I've made mine up now! This has gone far enough. If this is a joke, then you've had your laughs. One way or another, I'm going to get away from you. And when I do, I'm turning you in to the police. You belong in jail!

INDIAN: *(laughs)* Mebbe you are man. We been in jail a long time now, sementos . . .

AGENT: And stop calling me that name!

INDIAN: Okay, okay . . . I call you bossman. You know what bossman mean to me?

AGENT: I don't want to know.

INDIAN: *(laughs again)* You wise . . . you get it. I not got much to say, then you go.

AGENT: *(bewildered)* You . . . you're not going to . . . bother me anymore?

INDIAN: I finish my story, an' you go . . . go to town, go to hell . . . go anyplace. My brother — you know what kind of life he had? He was not dead, an' he was not alive.

AGENT: You said he came out of the well safely. What are you talking about?

INDIAN: No . . . He was not alive. He was too near dead to live. White bossman get rid of him quick. Here, says bossman — here is three dollars pay. I dig twenty feet — I make four dollars, my brother says. Bossman laugh. I take dollar for shovel you leave in the hole, he says. My brother come back to reserve, but he not go home. He live in my tent. At night, he wake up shouting, an' in daytime, he is like man who has no mind. He walk 'round, an' many times get lost in the bush, an' other Indian find him an' bring him back. He get very sick. For one month he lie in bed. Then he try to get up. But his legs an' arms are dried to the bone, like branches of dying tree.

AGENT: He must've had polio.

INDIAN: Is not matter . . . One night, he say to me: go to other side of lake tomorrow, an' take my wife an' my son Alphonse. Take good care of them. I won't live the night . . . I reach out and touch him, for he talk like devil fire was on him. But his head and cheek is cold. You will live an' take care of your wife an' Alphonse yourself, I say to him. But my brother shake his head. He look at me and say — help me to die . . .

AGENT: Why . . . didn't you . . . take him to hospital?

INDIAN: *(laughs bitterly)* Hospital! A dollar he took from dying man for the shovel buried in blue clay . . . hospital? Burn in hell!

AGENT: No . . . no! This I don't understand at all . . .

INDIAN: I . . . kill . . . my . . . brother! In my arms I hold him. He was so light, like small boy. I hold him . . . rock 'im back and forward like this . . . like mother rock us when we tiny kids. I rock 'im an' I cry . . . I get my hands tight on his neck, an' I squeeze an' I squeeze. I know he dead, and I still squeeze an' cry, for everything is gone, and I am old man now . . . only hunger an' hurt left now . . .

AGENT: My God!

INDIAN: I take off his shirt an' pants — I steal everything I can wear. Then I dig under tent, where ground is soft, and I bury my brother. After that, I go to other side of lake. When I tell my brother's wife what I done, she not say anything for long time. Then she look at me with eyes that never make tears again. Take Alphonse, she say . . . I go to live with every man who have me, to forget him. Then she leave her shack, an' I alone with Alphonse . . . I take Alphonse an' I come back. All Indians know what happen, but nobody say anything. Not to me . . . not to you. Some half-breed born outside reservation take my brother's name — and you, bossman, not know . . .

AGENT: (quietly, as though he were the authority again) We *have* to know, you understand, don't you? You'll have to tell me your brother's name.

INDIAN: I know . . . I tell you. Was Tommy Stone.

AGENT takes out his notebook again and writes.

AGENT: Stone — Tommy Stone . . . good. You know what I have to do, you understand it's my duty, don't you? It's my job . . . it's the way I feel. We all have to live within the law and uphold it. Ours is a civilized country . . . you understand, don't you? *(turns to car off stage)* I'm going now. Don't try to run before the police come. The circumstances were extenuating, and it may not go hard for you . . .

INDIAN makes no attempt to hinder AGENT who walks off stage.

INDIAN: Sure, misha . . . you're right. *(hears car door open)* Wait! Misha, wait! I tell you wrong. Name is not Tommy Stone — Tommy Stone is me! Name is *Johnny* Stone!

AGENT returns, notebook in hand.

AGENT: Johnny Stone? Let's get this straight now . . . your brother was Johnny Stone . . . and you're *Tommy* Stone? *(INDIAN nods vigorously)* Okay, boy. I've got that. Now remember what I said, and just stay here and wait. *(turns to leave)*

INDIAN: No, misha . . . you got whole business screwed up again! I am Johnny Stone, my brother, he is Tommy Stone.

AGENT pockets his notebook and turns angrily to face INDIAN.

AGENT: Look, Indian — what in hell is your name anyhow? Who are you?

INDIAN: My name? You want my name?

Suddenly catches AGENT by arm and swings him around as in a boyish game. Places AGENT down on the box he used for standing on to drive posts.

AGENT: Hey, you stop that!

INDIAN: An' yet you want my name?

AGENT: Yes, that's right . . . If it's not too much trouble to give me one straight answer, what is your name?

INDIAN: Sam Cardinal is my name!

AGENT rises with disgust and straightens out his clothes.

AGENT: Now it's Sam Cardinal . . . what do you take me for anyway? You waste my time . . . you rough me up like I was one of your drunken Indian friends . . . and now I can't get an answer to a simple question . . . But what the hell — the police can find out who you are and what you've done.

INDIAN: No, sementos! You never find out!

INDIAN throws legs apart and takes the stance of a man balancing on a threshold.

INDIAN: You go to reservation with hunder policemen — you try to find Johnny Stone . . . you try to find Tommy Stone . . . Sam Cardinal, too. Mebbe you find everybody, mebbe you find nobody. All Indians same — nobody. Listen to me, sementos — one brother is dead — who? Tommy Stone? Johnny Stone? Joe Bush! Look — *(turns out both pockets of his pants, holding them out, showing them empty and ragged)* I got nothing . . . nothing . . . no wallet, no money, no name. I got no past . . . no future . . . nothing, sementos! I nobody. I not even live in this world . . . I dead! You get it? . . . I dead! *(shrugs in one great gesture of grief)* I never been anybody. *I not just dead . . . I never live at all.* What is matter? . . . What anything matter, sementos?

AGENT has the look of a medieval peasant meeting a leper — fear, pity, hatred.

INDIAN: What matter if I choke you till you like rag in my hands? . . . Hit you mebbe with twenty pound hammer — break in your head like watermelon . . . Leave you dry in wind an' feed ants . . . What matter if police come an' take me? Misha! Listen, damn you — listen! One brother kill another brother — why? *(shakes AGENT furiously by the lapels)* Why? Why? . . . Why?

AGENT: *(clawing at INDIAN's hands)* Let me go! LET . . . ME . . . GO!

AGENT breaks free and runs off stage for car. Sounds of motor starting and fast departure. Dust. INDIAN stands trembling with fury.

INDIAN: Where you go in such goddamn speed? World too small to run 'way? You hear me, sementos! Hi . . . *sementos*! Ugh!

Spits and picks up hammer. Starts to drive post vigorously.

Curtain.

John Herbert
Fortune and Men's Eyes

EDITOR'S NOTE: The author was born John Herbert Brundage in Toronto in 1926. His life both in and outside of the theatre has been laden wth turmoil and strong emotion. He left school when 17 to take a job as a commercial artist with The T. Eaton Co. Limited. In 1946, in embittering circumstances that have shaped his entire life, he was found guilty of gross indecency and served six months in an Ontario reformatory. After his release, he travelled, worked at an assortment of jobs, studied drawing at the Ontario College of Art, dance at the National Ballet School and theatre at the New Play Society. In the early 1960's he served as Artistic Director of two Toronto theatres, Adventure Theatre and New Venture Players, before founding his own, the Garret Theatre, in 1965. He closed the Garret in 1971 and since has travelled, written and occasionally produced his plays, as well as taught at the Three Schools of Art. Herbert maintains a fiercely critical attitude towards the Canadian artistic environment which he has repeatedly attacked with an acidy tongue. Of his fourteen plays, some of which remain unproduced and/or unpublished, *Fortune and Men's Eyes* has been the most celebrated.

Fortune and Men's Eyes, written in 1963, won the Dominion Drama Festival's Massey Award, which Herbert refused to accept. In 1965, the Stratford Festival workshopped the play, but the first full professional staging was by New York's Actor's Playhouse in 1967. The first Canadian full staging took place in 1968 in French at Montreal's Théâtre de Quatre Sons. This was followed by productions in Ottawa, Winnipeg and Vancouver, among other centres. In 1975 it was presented at the Phoenix Theatre in Toronto and earned the Chalmers Outstanding Play Award for that year. Grove Press published the script in 1967 and a French edition appeared in Quebec in 1971. It was adapted into a graphic film in 1970.

Characters:

SMITTY   *A good-looking, clean-cut youth of clear intelligence
and aged seventeen years. He has the look of a
collegiate athlete. The face is strong and masculine
with enough sensitivity in feature and expression to
soften the sharp outline. He is of a type that
everyone seems to like, almost on sight.*

ROCKY   *A youth of nineteen years who seems older and
harder than his age should allow, though there is an
emotional immaturity that reveals itself constantly.
He has a nature, driven by fear, that uses hatred
aggressively to protect itself, taking pride in
harbouring no soft or gentle feelings. He lives like a
cornered rat, vicious, dangerous and unpredictable.
He is handsome in a lean, cold, dark, razor-featured
way.*

QUEENIE   *A large, heavy-bodied youth of nineteen or twenty
with the strength of a wrestler but the soft white
skin of a very blond person. Physical appearance is
a strange combination of softness and hulking
strength. For a large person he moves with definite
grace and fine precision, almost feminine in
exactness, but in no way frivolous or fluttery.
Movements, when exaggerated purposely, are big,
showy and extravagant. The face is dainty in
features as a "cupie-doll's" . . . plump-cheeked and
small-nosed. The mouth has a pouting, self-indulgent
look, but the eyes are hard, cold, and pale blue like
ice. The hair is fair, fine, and curly, like a baby's.
One looks at him and thinks of a madam in a
brothel . . . coarse, cruel, tough and voluptuously
pretty.*

MONA   *A youth of eighteen or nineteen years, of a physical
appearance that arouses resentment at once in many
people, men and women. He seems to hang
suspended between the sexes, neither boy nor
woman. He is slender, narrow-shouldered, long-
necked, long-legged, but never gauche or ungainly.*

He moves gracefully, but not self-consciously. His nature seems almost more feminine than effeminate because it is not mannerism that calls attention to an absence of masculinity so much as the sum of his appearance, lightness of movement, and gentleness of action. His effeminacy is not aggressive . . . just exists. The face is responsible for his nickname of "Mona Lisa." Features are madonna-like, straight-nosed, patrician-mouthed and sad-eyed. Facial contour is oval and the expression enigmatic. If he had been a woman, some would have described him as having a certain ethereal beauty.

GUARD   *A rugged-faced man of about forty-five to fifty, who looks like an ex-army officer. He has a rigid military bearing, a look of order and long acquaintance with discipline. He presents an impressive exterior of uniformed law enforcement, but one senses behind the unsmiling features some nagging doubt or worry, as if something of his past returned occasionally to haunt him, when he would prefer it forgotten. At these moments, his actions are uneasy and he does not seem so impressive, in spite of the uniform. He has a stomach ulcer that causes him much physical discomfort, that manifests itself in loud belching.*

ACT ONE SCENE ONE

Mid-October, evening.

*Overture: 3 songs — "Alouette" (sung by Group of Boys'
Voices); "Down in the Valley" (One Male Voice); "Jesus Loves
Me" (sung by Group of Boys' Voices).*

*A Canadian reformatory, prep school for the penitentiary. The
inmates are usually young, but there are often older prisoners, as
indicated by the dialogue in places. We are primarily concerned
here with four who are young, though they tell us others exist.
The overwhelming majority of prisoners in a reformatory are in
the late teens and early twenties. Those who are older have been
convicted of offenses that do not carry a sentence large enough to
warrant sending them to a penitentiary. The setting is a dormitory
with four beds and two doorways. One door leads to the corridor, but we do not see it. There is a stone alcove, angled so that
we get the impression of a short hall. We hear the guard's key
open this unseen door whenever he or the four inmates enter or
exit. The whole upstage wall is barred so that we look into the
corridor where the guard and inmates pass in entrance and exit.
Another doorway leads to the toilet and shower room. ROCKY is
stretched on his bed like a prince at rest; QUEENIE sits on his own
bed upstage; MONA leans against the wall of bars, upstage of
QUEENIE. In the distance we hear the clang of metal doors, and a
gruff voice issuing orders. MONA turns at the sounds, and looks
along the hall.*

*Just before lights come up, after curtain has opened, a BOY'S
VOICE is heard singing, at a distance — as farther along a corridor.*

BOY'S VOICE: *(singing):*
  Oh, if I had the wings of an angel
  Over these prison walls would I fly —

*Sound of metal doors clanging open and shut. And sound of
heavy boots marching along corridor.*

VOICE (English accent):   Halt! Attention! Straighten that line! Guard! Take this one down and put him in Observation!

GUARD: Yes sir! Smith! Step out — and smartly!

Lights come up.

BOY'S VOICE *(singing)*:
Oh, if I had the wings of —

QUEENIE *(on stage)*:
Oh, if I had the wings of an angel,
And the ass of a big buffalo,
I would fly to the heavens above me,
And crap on the people below.

VOICE *(English accent; raised now, the voice is not only gruff as before, but high and shrill in overtone, like Hitler's recorded speech)*:   And you, Canary-Bird — shut that bloody row, or I shall cut off your seed supply.

Repeated sound of metal doors, and of boots marching away.

QUEENIE: Oh, oh! That's Bad Bess. The Royal Sergeant don't come this close to the common folk, except when they're bringin' in a batch o' fish.

ROCKY: What's the action out there, Queenie?

MONA *(who stands nearest the bars)*:   It's the new arrivals.

ROCKY: Anybody ask you to open your mouth, fruity?

QUEENIE: Oh, lay off the Mona Lisa, for Christ sake, Rocky.

ROCKY: Always getting her jollies looking out that hole.

QUEENIE: Does Macy's bother Gimbel's?

ROCKY: They got their own corners.

QUEENIE: Well she ain't in yours, so dummy up!

ROCKY: Don't mess with the bull, Queenie!

QUEENIE: Your horn ain't long enough to reach me, Ferdinand.

ROCKY: You might feel it yet.

QUEENIE: Worst offer I've had today, but it's early.

ROCKY: Screw off! (*Turning toward MONA.*) Look at the queer watchin' the fish! See anything you can catch, Rosie?

QUEENIE: How's the new stock, Mona? Anything worth shakin' it for?

MONA: They're all so young.

QUEENIE: That'll suit Rocky. If he could coop a new chicken in his yard, he might not be so salty.

ROCKY: Where'd you get all that mouth . . . from your Mother?

QUEENIE: The better to gobble you up with, Little Red Riding Wolf!

ROCKY: Tell it to your old man.

QUEENIE: Which one? Remember me? I'm my own P. I.

ROCKY: You got a choice?

QUEENIE: I don't mean pimp, like you, I mean political influence, like me!

ROCKY: So you got a coupla wheels in the office! Big deal!

QUEENIE: I like it that way . . . makes it so I don't have to take no crap from a would-be hippy like you.

MONA: They're coming this way.

QUEENIE: Hell! And I didn't set my hair in toilet-paper curls last night. Oh well! I'll try to look seductive.

ROCKY: You better turn around then.

QUEENIE: Well, my backside looks better than your face, if that's what you wanta say.

ROCKY (*with disdain*):   Queers!

Enter GUARD with a youth who is about seventeen.

ROCKY: Hi, screw! What's that . . . your new baby?

GUARD: You planning a return trip to the tower, smart boy?

ROCKY: Just bein' friendly, Captain! I like to make the kids feel at home.

GUARD: So I've noticed. (*To the new boy:*) Okay Smith, this is your dormitory for now. Try to get along with the others and keep your nose clean. Do as you're told, keep your bunk tidy, and no talking after lights out. You'll be assigned your work tomorrow. Meanwhile, follow the others to washup and meals. Pick up the routine and don't spend too much time in the craphouse, or you'll end up in an isolation cell.

ROCKY: He means Gunsel's Alley. Too bad all the queers don't make it there.

QUEENIE (*to the GUARD*):   Now he wants a private room. Take him away, Nurse!

GUARD: Okay you two! Turn off the vaudeville. You'll get your chance to do your number at the Christmas concert. (*He exits.*)

QUEENIE: The Dolly Sisters! After you got your royal uniform, in the delousing room, did Bad Bess challenge you to a duel?

SMITTY: Who?

QUEENIE: Little Sergeant Gritt — that chalk-faced, pea-eyed squirt in the rimless goggles! He's always goin' on about the "Days of Empire" and "God and Country" and all suchlike Bronco Bullcrap.

SMITTY: Oh, yes! He did most of the talking.

QUEENIE: That's our Cockney cunt — never closes her hole.

Didn't he want you to square off for fisticuffs, old chap? Sporting chance an' all that stale roast beef an' Yorkshire pudding?

SMITTY: Well, he did say he'd been boxing champion at some school in England, and that, if any of us thought we were tough, this was our chance to prove it — man to man, with no interference.

QUEENIE: Yeah — that's his usual pitch. Corny, ain't it? It makes him feel harder than those stone lions out front o' Buckingham Palace. Yellow-bellied little rat! When he's outa that uniform, he's scared to death o' any eleven-year-old kid he meets on the street. Did his Lordship get any challengers?

SMITTY: Well, no! I wasn't surprised at that. I felt sure it was just a way of letting the prisoners know who's boss.

QUEENIE: I must say — you ain't exactly a idiot.

ROCKY: One o' these farty Fridays, he's gonna get it good, from some guy faster'n that goddam Indian.

QUEENIE: How stupid kin a Iroquois be? Imagine this jerky Indian from Timmins, takin' that fish-faced little potato chip at his word. The only one ever took the chance — far as I know.

SMITTY: He'd have to have a lot of guts.

QUEENIE: Oh yeah — and they showed them to him fast. He was a brave brave all right — an' stupid as a dead buffalo. The second he an' Bad Bess squared off at each other, two guards jumped Big Chief Running Blood, an' the three British bully boys beat the roaring piss outa him. Heroes all!

ROCKY: What a mess they made o' that squaw-banger!

QUEENIE: You couldn't exactly put that profile on a coin no more — not even a cheap little copper. Oh, well — let's look on the bright side o' the penny; he's in pretty good shape for the shape he's in. After all, he got a free nose-bob an' can pass for a pale nigger now. A darkie can get a better job 'n a redskin any day.

ROCKY: Whoever heard of a Indian what worked? They git government relief.

QUEENIE: Howdya think he got here, Moronia? He was one o' them featherheads from Matachewan Reservation, tryin' t' get a job in the mines. There was this great big ol' riot, an' the cowboys won again. Pocahontas' husband is up here because he tried t' scalp some Timmins cop. An', believe you me, that's the wrong way to get yourself a wig in that tin town.

ROCKY: An' you believe that crap, like he tells you his stories about how some stinkin' bird got its name? Jeez! Maybe you should git yerself a blanket an' become a squaw — you dig those tepee tales so much.

QUEENIE: I dig all kinds o' tail, pale-ass — except yours.

ROCKY: All Indians is screwin' finks an' stoolies, an' I woulden trust 'em with a bottle o' cheap shavin' lotion; and that Blackfeet bum probable slugged some ol' fairy in a public crapper, t' git a bottle o'wine.

QUEENIE: Always judgin' everybody by yourself! Tch! Tch! That's the sign of a slow con man, Sweetie.

MONA *(to new boy):* What's your name? I'm Jan.

SMITTY: Smith.

QUEENIE: But you can call her Mona, and I'm Queenie.

ROCKY: Look at the girls givin' the new boy a fast cruise. Give him time to take his pants off, Queenie.

QUEENIE: So you can get into them, Daddy-O? Don't let him bug you, Smitty. He thinks he's the big rooster here.

ROCKY: You know it too. Welcome home, punk!

SMITTY: This is my first time.

ROCKY: Braggin' or complainin'?

SMITTY: Neither. It's just a fact.

ROCKY: Well, that's nice. You shouldn't be here at all I guess. Got a bum beef?

SMITTY: A . . . a what?

ROCKY: Crap! A beef! A rap! Whose cookies did you boost . . . your mother's?

QUEENIE: What the judge wants to know, honey, is what special talent brought you this vacation . . . are you a store-counter booster or like myself do you make all your house calls when nobody's home?

SMITTY: Neither!

QUEENIE: Rolled a drunk . . . autographed somebody's checks . . . raped the girl next door . . . ?

SMITTY: No, and I . . . I don't want to talk about it.

QUEENIE: You might as well spill it, kid. I can't stand suspense. Ask Mona . . . she screwed all around the mulberry bush until I finally had to go find out in the office.

ROCKY: I coulda saved you the trouble and told you she reached for the wrong joy stick. Did you ever get one you didn't like, Mona?

MONA (to SMITTY): I've learned it doesn't matter what you've done. If you don't say, everyone assumes it's something far worse, so you might as well get it over with.

SMITTY: I just can't.

QUEENIE: OKAY Smitty . . . skip it! I'll find out on the Q.T., but I won't spill it.

ROCKY: Ottawa's First Lady! How did you do it, Ladybird?

QUEENIE: Well . . . I lifted my left leg and then my right, and between the two of them, I rose right to the top.

ROCKY: Of a pile of bull!

MONA: How long is your sentence?

SMITTY: Six months.

MONA: Same as mine. I have a few to go.

SMITTY: Does . . . does it seem as long as . . . as . . .

MONA: Not after a while. You get used to the routine, and there are diversions.

ROCKY: That's an invitation to the crapper.

MONA: Do you like to read?

SMITTY: I never did . . . much.

MONA: Well, this is a good place to acquire the habit.

ROCKY: Yeah! Let Mona the fruit teach you her habits, then you can go and make yourself an extra pack of weed a week.

QUEENIE: She don't go as cheap as you, Rocky. We're tailor-made cigarette girls or nothin'.

ROCKY: I get what I want without bending over.

QUEENIE: Sure! You can always con some stupid chicken into doing it for you. How many left in your harem now, Valentino?

ROCKY: My kids wouldn't spit on the best part of you.

QUEENIE: Who's interested in a lot of little worn-out punks? I've seen them all hustling their skinny asses in the Corner Cafeteria, and if it wasn't for the old aunties who feel them up in the show and take them for a meal, they'd starve to death. Did you tell them before they left that you'd provide them with a whole bus terminal to sleep in when you get out?

ROCKY: After I smarten them up, they don't have to flop in your hunting grounds. They go where the action is and cruise around in Cadillacs.

QUEENIE: Yours, of course?

ROCKY: What I *take*, you can call *mine*.

QUEENIE: What a pity you couldn't get a judge to see it the same way.

ROCKY: You're cruisin' for a bruisin', bitch!

QUEENIE: Thanks awfully, but I'm no maso-sissy, sad-ass. I always kick for the balls when attacked.

(Sings to the tune of "Habanera" from Carmen:)

My name is Carmen,
I am a whore,
And I go knocking
From door to door.

ROCKY: I'll meet you in front of the city hall next Christmas.

QUEENIE: Lovely, but don't ask me for a quarter, like last time.

ROCKY: Since when did you walk on the street with more than a dime?

QUEENIE: After I stopped letting bums like you roost at my place overnight.

ROCKY: Cripes! You'll never forget you played Sally Ann to me once. When you sobered up and felt like a little fun, did you miss me?

QUEENIE: . . . Yeah — also my marble clock, my garnet ring, and eleven dollars.

ROCKY *(laughing)*: Oh jeez, I wish I coulda seen your face. Was your mascara running?

QUEENIE: He's having such a good time, I hate to tell him I like Bob Hope better. So where did you come from Smitty . . . the big corner?

MONA: That means the city . . . it's a slang term. You'll get used to them.

SMITTY: I feel like I'm in another country.

ROCKY: What's your ambition kid? You wanna be a Square John . . . a brown nose?

QUEENIE: Ignore the ignoramus. He loves to play the wise guy.

SMITTY: I'm willing to catch on.

QUEENIE: You will, but you gotta watch yourself . . . play it cool and listen to the politicians.

SMITTY: Politicians?

QUEENIE: The hep guys . . . hippos, who are smart enough to make it into the office. They get the best of it . . . good grub, new shirts, and jeans, lightweight booties and special privileges . . . extra gym, movie shows, and sometimes even tailor-made cigarettes. Like to get in on that?

SMITTY: I don't smoke.

QUEENIE: Well for cripes' sake don't tell them. Take your deck of weed and give it to your mother.

SMITTY: My . . .

QUEENIE: Me, honey! Who else!

SMITTY: Oh! Okay!

MONA: Tailor-made cigarettes are contraband, but your package of tobacco is handed out with a folder of cigarette papers and a razor blade when you go for clothing change once a week . . . it's sort of a payday!

ROCKY: Listen to our little working girl. She works in the gash-house sewing pants together for the guys to wear. Her only complaint is there's nothing in 'em when they're finished.

SMITTY: Is that what I'll be doing . . . ?

QUEENIE: No baby, you won't. The tailor shop and the laundry are especially for us girls. They can make sure that way, we don't stray behind a bush. But I like the laundry since they made me forelady. It's a sweet act of fate because it's the only place in the joint where I can get Javex — to keep myself a natural blonde.

ROCKY: And it's easier to show your ass bending over a tub, than under a sewing machine or a wheelbarrow.

QUEENIE: You've got a one-track mind, and it's all dirt.

ROCKY: My shovel's clean.

QUEENIE: I don't know how. Every time you get in a shower, you've got it in somebody's ditch.

ROCKY: Don't be jealous. I'll get around to shovelling in yours.

QUEENIE: Be sure you can fill it with diamonds when you come callin'.

ROCKY: You'd be happy with a fistful of chocolates.

QUEENIE: Feed the Lauras to your chickens at jug-up, eh Smitty?

SMITTY: Jug-up?

QUEENIE: Meals! Didn't they yell jug-up at you before you ate today?

SMITTY: I wasn't hungry. I thought the food would be the same as at the city jail, and it always made me sick after.

QUEENIE: Don't remind me of that sewage dump on the River. I think they bought that bloody old baloney and those withered wieners once a year . . . and you could put up wallpaper forever with that goddam porridge. Don't worry . . . the pigs they keep here are fed better than that.

MONA: Yes, the meals are good, Smitty. This place has its own farm, so the animals and vegetables are all raised by the prisoners.

SMITTY: I once worked on a farm, between school terms. I wouldn't mind if they put me on that . . . the time would go fast.

QUEENIE: That's the idea, honey! I'll try to wangle you a good go so you don't hafta do hard time. I got some pull in the office.

ROCKY: You'll have to serve a little keester to the politicians who wanna put you in the barn.

SMITTY: What?

ROCKY: But I guess you been in the hay before. Queenie's all for fixin' you up with an old man. You're ripe for tomato season.

QUEENIE: One thing about it, Rockhead. It'll be a hippy who's got it made, and no crap disturber like you that picks him off my vine.

SMITTY: I don't want to hurt anybody's feelings, but I'm not . . . queer. I've got a girl friend: she even came to court.

ROCKY: You shoulda brought her with you. I'da shared my bunk with her.

SMITTY: You don't understand, she's not that kind of . . .

MONA: It's all right, Smitty; he's just teasing you. Life inside is different, but you still don't have to do anything you don't want to, not if you —

QUEENIE: I'm tryin' to smarten him up, Mona, and you try to queer the play. Has sittin' outside the fence got you anything? At jug-up some punk's always grabbin' the meat off your plate and you're scared to say boo.

MONA: I get enough to eat. If anybody's that hungry, I don't begrudge it.

QUEENIE: And look at your goddam rags. They give you that junk on purpose, to make a bloody clown outa you. You ain't had a garment that fits since you come in.

MONA: I can fix them to look better at the shop when the guard's not looking.

QUEENIE: Well I like everything new. I can't feel sexy in rags.

MONA: I don't really care what I look like here.

QUEENIE (*sigh of despair*): See, Smitty! I try to sharpen the girls I like and she don't listen to a screwin' word I say. I coulda got her a real good old man, but she told him she liked her "independence" if you can picture it.

SMITTY: I can understand that.

QUEENIE: Yeah? So what happens? One day in the gym a bunch of hippos con her into the storeroom to get something for the game, and teach her another one instead. They make up the team, but she's the only basket. They all took a whack, now she's public property. You can't say no around here unless you got somebody behind you. Take it from your mother . . . I know the score.

SMITTY: I'll have to think about it.

QUEENIE: Well don't wait until they give you a gang splash in the storeroom. Mona had to hold on to the wall to walk, for a week.

MONA: They won't do it to him. He doesn't look gay, and he's probably not here on a sex charge. They felt I had no rights.

SMITTY: That doesn't seem fair.

MONA: I didn't think so either. It takes a while to get used to the rules of the game, and I've made a few concessions since . . . just to make life bearable. One thing, Smitty; don't depend on protection from the guards, and don't ever go to them. You have to solve your own problems.

ROCKY: And Mona'll show you her scars to prove it . . . fink! Squealed to a goddam screw! Cut you up pretty good after that, didn't we, bitch?

SMITTY: But how could they get away with it?

QUEENIE: The usual way . . . it was an "accident."

SMITTY: Jan?

190

MONA: Everyone agreed it was an accident . . . including me. Be careful, Smitty!

QUEENIE: Now Mona's givin' you some smart news. There's only two kinds of guards: the ones you can use like Holy Face who brought you in — and the fink screws that go straight to the General. When you see one comin' give six so we can play it safe.

SMITTY: Six?

QUEENIE: Say "six" instead of "nix" . . . a warning!

SMITTY: Oh, I get it.

QUEENIE: It's no game, Honey! They got a nice cold tower here with no blankets or mattresses on the iron bunks and a diet of bread and water to tame you. If that don't work, there's a little machine that fastens your hips and ankles, while some sad-ass screw that's got a rod on for you bangs you across the ass with a leather belt fulla holes, and some other son of a bitch holds your arms over your head, twisted in your shirt. They can make you scream for God and your mother before they let you go.

SMITTY *(aghast)*: It sounds like the late late show.

QUEENIE: It's no Hollywood horror-vision. Ask Mona; she was in a fog for a month after.

SMITTY: Mona? . . . Jan?

MONA: I don't want to talk about that, Smitty.

ROCKY: No. She'd rather dream about it.

QUEENIE: She wakes the whole place in the middle of the night with those bloody awful screams — "Mother! Mother!" Crap!

SMITTY *(petrified)*: You're only trying to scare me . . . all of you.

MONA *(gently)*: No, we're not, Smitty . . . someone's always waiting for you to make a misstep. Please be careful.

191

SMITTY: I've heard of lashes, but I thought it was only in very special cases.

MONA (bitterly): They don't keep those little goodies because they have to but because they want to. Learn to look into their eyes before you stick out a hand.

SMITTY: Thanks, Mona, I'll remember.

QUEENIE: Well, now we're gettin' someplace. You see what a wise girl Mona's gettin' to be? She'll know the ropes better than me next time around.

SMITTY: Same thing happen to you?

QUEENIE: Well not exactly, but then I handle myself a little different. Mona's a girl who's gotta learn the hard way. I always see a trap before it springs. But then I have the advantage of early training. I was a Children's Aid ward, and shuffled around from foster homes to farms, to God know what. I been locked in closets so my foster mother could drink and play cards unseen; I had farmers treat me worse'n their dogs, and I learned before I was twelve that nobody gives a crap about you in this cruddy world. So I decided to do something about it. Queenie looks after Queenie, and pretty good too let me tellya.

SMITTY: Sounds like you've had a rough time.

QUEENIE: Skip it! I wouldn't trade places with any soft son of a bitch who needs a goddam mother to tell it what to do and a lousy house in some phony suburb with home-baked pies, and a lot of chitchat around a kitchen table. I've seen what that does to people, and I hate them gutless bastards who go to work eight hours a day, to parties and shows the rest of the time, and walk around with their noses in the air like their own crap don't stink.

MONA: Queenie's never been able to find her mother. The Children's Aid wouldn't give the address because of her criminal record.

QUEENIE: Who wants it anyway? She's probably a pukin'

192

prostitute somewhere, walkin' around the street with a gutful of gin. What dirty bitch would leave a kid before its eyes was open to be pushed around by a buncha bastards who only want some sucker to do the housework for them? I bailed myself outa that crap when I was lucky thirteen and found out somebody liked my body. I been renting it out ever since.

ROCKY: But the offers are gettin' fewer and the rates are gettin' lower. Next year you'll be dishwasher at the corner lunch.

QUEENIE: Listen, asshole, as long as there's houses fulla jewelry an' furs, this girl's hands will help to keep the insurance companies in business, and don't you forget it. It's you stinkin' pimps who better move fast an' get it made before your hair an' teeth rot out on the sidewalk. I'll wave at your bench as I ride past the park in my limousine.

MONA (seeing the GUARD approach): Six!

Enter the GUARD called "Holy Face."

GUARD: Book-up! Okay Curlylocks, it's your turn to wheel the library around, I'm advised from the office, so try not to spend too much time visiting your friends en route . . . everybody's entitled to a book, too. Your pram's in the corridor.

QUEENIE: Thanks Daddy-O, I'll save you a Baby Bunting book.

QUEENIE combs his hair in preparation for the excursion.

GUARD: We have another nice little detail in the V.D. ward. A new patient just puked all over his cell, but he's too weak to mop it up.

MONA: The poor kid!

GUARD: Okay, beautiful. I figure even you might be trusted up there.

QUEENIE: Always the little mother, but don't go giving any kisses till he's had his shots, Nurse. (*QUEENIE exits, passes in corridor wheeling library cart.*) Cigars, cigarettes, vaseline! Everything for the home!

ROCKY: Thanks Captain! I was just about to bash their heads together when you made the scene. You saved me a trip to the tower.

GUARD: It's temporary, believe me. You've been getting closer to it every day. Don't start brooding, Smith . . . that doesn't help in here. Get yourself a book or something before lights out.

SMITTY: Yes sir.

ROCKY: My, my! What a polite little chap. Isn't he sweet, Officer?

GUARD: Lay off him Tibber, or I'll have you moved to a stricter dormitory. Can't you get along anywhere?

ROCKY: Sure, outside!

GUARD: Is that why we're honoured by your presence so often?

ROCKY: Well the law don't like to see a smart guy get ahead. They want suckers who'll take a few cents a week, a row of brass buttons, and call it a living.

GUARD: But we can walk home when the work's done without an armed escort. Think about that, big shot!

ROCKY: I'm thinkin'. (*Gives the GUARD a look that seems to make the GUARD uneasy.*) You wanta stay nice an' honest — and keep it that way. Like, I mean next year ya kin take off wit' yer pension, ain't it? That is — if nothing don't go wrong.

GUARD: Lights out at eight o'clock, Smith! Be ready for bed by then.

SMITTY: Eight?

GUARD: That's right. You're up at six. It won't seem so early when you get used to the idea that, in the evening, there's no place to go.

SMITTY: I guess so.

GUARD: Okay, Florence Nightingale — on the double! *(Exits with MONA.)*

ROCKY: Oh boy! That sucker's ulcer's gonna kill'im afore he gits the chance t' sit at home in a rockin' chair.

SMITTY: He sure did look sick when he went out.

ROCKY: He's sick an' he makes me sick. You ain't smart, ya know, Smitty!

SMITTY: How come?

ROCKY: Fruits always get ya in the deep crap.

SMITTY: I don't know; I never knew any before.

ROCKY: You ain't been around.

SMITTY: No, I guess not.

ROCKY: They'll screw you up every time.

SMITTY: How?

ROCKY: 'Cause they're all phonies . . . gutless; they're all finks.

SMITTY: You sound like you've had experience with them.

ROCKY: An overdose! But no more! I gotta get me one when I get outa the joint. I'm gonna break both her legs . . . then I'm gonna put a coupla sharp chicks out on the hustle for me. That's the real dough.

SMITTY: You mean . . . women?

ROCKY: Let me tell ya! They were fallin' all over Rocky for me to be their boy, but I latched on to this one homo first

195

to make a fast buck. Took him for everything he had . . . almost!

SMITTY: The homo?

ROCKY: Fag!

SMITTY: Oh — queer.

ROCKY: More money than bloody brains! Crazy about me! Old man's a big shot millionaire — stock exchange, race horses — the whole bit, but his one son was real fruit. It took some connin', but I got in solid . . . weekly allowance, swell apartment, lotsa booze and company and a Cadillac convertible.

SMITTY: All yours?

ROCKY: Except the heap! That's how she got me. I was browned off with the freak and split. Sold the works . . . television set, cut-glass decanters and whisky glasses, paintin's and statoos . . . all that crap! I split in the Caddy with a roll would choke a elephant an' had me a ball . . . hotel rooms an' motels from Montreal to Windsor . . . Forty-two street, Frisco . . . dames, cards, booze! Man, was I livin' high!

SMITTY: Money run out?

ROCKY: Hell no! When ya got it, ya can always make it, but that fruit had the brass to call the bulls and get me picked up for takin' the Caddy.

SMITTY: Because it wasn't yours?

ROCKY: What I take is mine — that's my motto. But those queers always like one string to keep ya in line. This bastard kept the car in her name so she could screw me up when the time came.

SMITTY: So he . . . she laid a charge?

ROCKY: Hell, no! She wanted me back, that's all. We agreed on a story to cover all the crap stirred up, but her old man and the bulls stepped in anyways and fixed me good.

They tried to throw the book at me. Now, I'm gonna fix her, an' when I'm finished she won't be able to cruise no more little boys for about a year, except out a window or on a stretcher!

SMITTY: If you do that, maybe they'll send you back again.

ROCKY: You sure are dumb. After you do a job, like I'm gonna, on somebody, they're scared crapless . . . glad to give ya both sides o' the street. Never let a fruit scare ya . . . the cops don't like them either, so underneath they're yellow as a broken egg. Don't ever forget that.

SMITTY: I'll remember.

ROCKY: Ya know, I could make a real sharp guy outa you. Ya got a head an' ya don't shoot your mouth too much.

SMITTY: I don't know too much.

ROCKY: You'll learn, kid! You'll learn. Listen to old Rocky an' you'll get to sit on the sunny side of the yard. See . . . I'm in this dormitory because I raise hell a bit. That's why they put me with these two fruits — to watch me. But there's bigger an' better dorms with more guys, an' that's where I'll be goin' back to . . . an' so could you, if you play along with Rocky.

SMITTY: How do you mean?

ROCKY: Well ya gotta have a buddy, see? Ya can't get chummy with the whole joint, an' specially no fruits. If ya get that name, your ass is cooked when you get to a good dorm. Why d'ya think I give 'em a hard time here? If you're smart, you'll do the same thing. There's real guys in some corridors, so ya wanna keep your nose clean.

SMITTY: I sure don't want anybody to think I'm queer.

ROCKY: Good! That's what I like t' hear.

SMITTY: Why would they put me in this particular dormitory, I wonder? To watch me, too?

ROCKY: Ya musta done somethin' goofy before your bit here

. . . took a poke at a copper or somethin' like that. They won't leave ya in here if Rocky can swing somethin' for us. The other blocks are probably filled up, but we'll be movin' soon. Would you go for that, kid?

SMITTY: Maybe it would be better.

ROCKY: Stick with the Rock an' you'll be looked up at. That ain't easy in the joint. Every jerk's lookin' for your jelly-spot. I didn't get the name I got by takin' it off these goons. Even the screws step easy on me. See how I talk to Holy Face? His blood turns to crap around Rocky.

SMITTY: He doesn't seem to stop you too much.

ROCKY: Nobody stops this boy. Besides I got somethin' on Holy Face. I'll tell you if you make up your mind who your buddy's gonna be. Remember what happened to Mona. You're sittin' duck for a gang splash if y'ain't got a old man. I'm offerin' to be your old man, kid, an' if you're wise you'll think fast. Whadda ya say?

SMITTY: Would it keep me from . . . what happened to Mona . . . in the storeroom?

ROCKY: Ya wouldn't want all those goons to pile on ya, would ya, now?

SMITTY: No . . . for God's sake, no!

ROCKY: Am I your old man then?

SMITTY: Like . . . a buddy, you mean?

ROCKY: Sure, that's the score. I'll kill any son of a bitch lays a hand on ya.

SMITTY: Okay . . . and . . . thanks!

ROCKY (tossing SMITTY his cigarette lighter): Here's a firebox for ya, kid. Keep it! We're gonna get along good, Smitty. Ya wanna know what I got on Holy Face?

SMITTY: Well, sure!

ROCKY: He took a pigeon outa the joint for a pal o' mine, so

I know all about it, an' he knows I got the goods on him. I throw him a hint every once in a while when he thinks he's gonna push me around.

SMITTY: A pigeon?

ROCKY: A letter . . . a message! Jailbird lingo for stuff that ain't allowed — *(with a confiding wink)* like a punk kid is a chicken an' if he gives ya a kiss, that's a bluebird. Everythin' you write's gotta go through a censor in the office, but if ya got somethin' goin' for ya, ya can allays buy some screw. One o' my buddies gave Holy Face fifty bucks t' get a pigeon out for him. That's about as much dough as a lousy screw makes in a week, an' Holy Face ain't so holy as he acts when it comes to makin' hisself a buck.

SMITTY: But there's no money in here. They kept mine at the office.

ROCKY: You're green, kid. There's all kinds of lines goin' around the joint.

SMITTY: But how?

ROCKY: Easy! Some relative calls in for a Sunday visit, slips Holy Face the dough, an' next chance he's got, he divvies up, takes out his half-C note and posts your pigeon.

SMITTY: Why not get the relatives to take a message for nothing?

ROCKY: There's things some relatives won't do. This was a junk deal . . . dope . . . big-time stuff!

SMITTY: What kind of excuse could you give to ask fifty dollars from a relative . . . here?

ROCKY: Plenty! Tell 'em the meals are crap an' cash could get ya candy, magazines, or nice face soap . . . some story like that. Say ya can only get stuff through a good-hearted screw who's takin' a chance for ya. Play it hearts an' flowers . . . works good on most relatives.

SMITTY: I guess so.

ROCKY: So come on, baby, let's me an' you take a shower before bedtime.

SMITTY: A shower?

ROCKY: Sure! I like one every night before lights out!

SMITTY: Go ahead! I had one this afternoon when they brought me in and gave me a uniform.

ROCKY: It ain't gonna kill ya t' take another. I like company.

SMITTY: Tomorrow, Rocky.

ROCKY: Right now!

SMITTY: No . . . thanks!

ROCKY: I like my kids clean.

SMITTY: I'm clean.

ROCKY: Get up!

SMITTY: What . . .

ROCKY: Get movin' . . . into that shower room.

SMITTY: Rocky, you're not . . .

ROCKY: I said *move*, boy!

SMITTY: No! I changed my mind. I don't want an old man.

ROCKY: You got a old man, an' that's better than a store-room, buddy boy!

SMITTY: I'll take a chance.

ROCKY: I'll make sure it's no chance. It's me or a gang splash. Now move your ass fast. I'm not used to punks tellin' me what they want.

He grabs SMITTY's arm, twisting it behind the boy's back. SMITTY gives a small cry of pain, but ROCKY throws a hand over his mouth, pushing him toward the shower room. SMITTY pulls his face free.

SMITTY: Rocky . . . please . . . if you like me . . .

ROCKY: I like you . . . an' you're gonna like me!

Blackout

ACT ONE SCENE TWO

Three weeks later, evening.

As scene opens, SMITTY and MONA are lying or sitting on their own cots, each reading his own book. ROCKY can be heard off-stage, singing in the shower room. QUEENIE and the GUARD are both absent.

ROCKY *(singing)*: Oh, they call me The Jungle King, The Jungle King . . . *(Shouting.)* Hey-y — Smitty!

SMITTY: Yeah? *(Continues reading.)*

ROCKY *(off-stage)*: Hey, Smitty!

SMITTY: Yeah, Rocky?

ROCKY *(off-stage)*: Roll me some smokes!

SMITTY: Okay, okay. *(He moves, still reading, to Rocky's cot, where he finds package of tobacco, but no papers.)*

ROCKY *(still off-stage and singing)*: Oh, the Lion and the Monkey . . .

SMITTY: What you got there, Jan? You must have had thirty takeouts in three weeks.

MONA: It's a book of poems.

SMITTY: Any good?

MONA: Yes, but it's not exactly what I wanted.

SMITTY: I've got something better; well, more useful, anyway. Come here; have a look.

MONA (after crossing to join SMITTY on Rocky's bed): "Advanced Automobile Mechanics." Very practical!

SMITTY: I'm a practical guy. You see, I figure I might not be able to get a job in an office, because — well — bonding, and all that. You know what I mean. Anyway, I worked evenings after school and all day Saturday in my fath — in a garage. I learned a lot about car motors, so I might as well put it to use. Mechanics are paid pretty good, you know.

MONA: That's wonderful, Smitty. This way, your time won't be wasted. You can make your six months really tell, and then after . . .

ROCKY (entering singing and combing his hair): The Jungle King, the Jungle King . . . Say-y! Whadya call this here scene — squatters' rights? Let me tellya somethin' — quick! In good ol' Cabbage-town, there's a li'l joint where me gang hangs out; it's called the Kay Won Cafe. Guess who runs it?

SMITTY: A Chinaman?

ROCKY: Wrong! Charlie owns it, but Rocky runs it. A pretty-boy comes in there 'n' I don't like his face much — me boys wait fer 'im outside, an' grab aholt his arm 'n' legs, an' Rock, who's welterweight champ 'round there, changes the smart guy's kisser a li'l.

SMITTY: You don't like your punching bag to swing too free. Your toughs have to hold him, eh?

ROCKY: I do things my way. There's another spot, on the roughest corner in town, called Eddie's Poolroom. Now — guess who runs it?

SMITTY: Eddie?

202

ROCKY: Oh boy, do you learn slow! Same story. Eddie owns the shack, but ya kin bet yer sweet billiard cue The Rock says who's behin' the eight ball 'round there.

MONA *(rising from Rocky's bed):* All right, Rocky — I get the point.

ROCKY: Ya better see it, Pinhead — or I'll give ya a fat eye t' wear. Now beat it!

SMITTY: Leave him alone.

ROCKY: Oh, you ain't talkin' t' me.

SMITTY: Just don't touch him.

ROCKY: Whadya think he is — precious — or somethin'?

SMITTY: Lay off, that's all.

ROCKY: How come ya talk t' me like that? Ain't I good t'ya, kid? Don't I getya cookies outa the kitchen? An' rubber t' chew, off Holy Face?

SMITTY: You're so good to me — and I'm so sick of it all.

ROCKY: Now, now! That ain't a nice way t' talk, when I just bin fixin' it up wit Baldy t' git us in "D" Dorm. Ain't that whatya wanted all along?

SMITTY: Let's not overdo this "togetherness."

ROCKY: Sad — sad — sad! We-ell — I guess I'll just hafta 'range us a li'l extra gym, so's ya don't feel too neglected. The boys'll wanna meet ya before we move inta their Big Dorm. Tomorrow afternoon, Smitty? Get together wit de gang — just like at Eddie's or the Kay Won?

SMITTY: No, Rocky — no!

ROCKY: No what? No ketchup or no applesauce?

SMITTY: No — no extra gym.

MONA: Please, Rocky — we were only . . .

ROCKY: Shut up, ya wall-eyed whore!

MONA: I only . . .

QUEENIE is heard singing, approaching in corridor.

SMITTY: Six! Six! Forget it!

QUEENIE *(off-stage, singing):*
  I'm a big girl now,
  I wanna be handled like a big girl now;
  I'm tired a stayin' home each evenin' after dark,
  Tired a bein' dynamite without a spark . . .

Let me in. *(Stamping his feet.)* Let me in this cell!

QUEENIE and the GUARD called Holy Face enter, QUEENIE carrying a small, white, cone-shaped Dixie cup. He continues singing.

  I wanna learn what homos do in Old Queen's Park . . .

GUARD: I wanna learn what you do up in that hospital so often.

QUEENIE: I show the surgeon my stretch marks.

GUARD: I know it can't be only for that coneful of cold cream. I'll bet if I gave you a frisk, I'd find scissors or a scalpel tucked in the seam of your shirt. I oughta search you every time out.

QUEENIE *(throwing open his arms):* Oh do, Daddy-O! I just can't wait t' feel your big callous hands on m' satin-smooth bode-ee!

GUARD: I'd as soon have syphilis.

QUEENIE: Who's she? Any relation to Gonorita?

GUARD: Cut it! Let's have a little common decency.

QUEENIE: What's that — somethin' ya eat? Ya know, you're not well at all; the way you been belchin' an' turnin' green around here lately. Maybe that ulcer of yours has soured into cancer, an' you'll never make that first pension check.

GUARD: I'll live to collect it all, and my stomach will sweeten considerably next winter, when I'm down in Florida — away from you bunch of bums. *(GUARD belches loudly.)*

QUEENIE: Pardon *you*! Will the rest be up in a minute? Maybe if the Doc finds out you ain't fit to work, they'll fire ya. Part-pension won't pay the shot for Palm Beach.

GUARD: One thing — I'm going to find out what you do with all those gobs of goo from the dispensary. I suspect it's got somethin' to do with the backside of decency. *(GUARD exits to shower room.)*

QUEENIE: How gross of you, Gertrude. No secret at all! I mix the cold cream with coal dust off the window sills, an' sell it to the screws for mascara. Helen Roobenbitch ain't got nothin' on me. *(Exits to shower room. Sound of a slap. Offstage:)* Brutality! Brutality!

GUARD *(entering):* Next stop for that one is the bug wing. It might as well wear its jacket the same way it does everything else — backwards!

ROCKY: Take it an' tie it up an' don't never ever bring it back no more.

GUARD: Okay. Book-up time. Anybody want a trip to the library?

ROCKY: Yeah! I'll take a book o' matches — t' the works.

GUARD: Pyromania would become you, Tibber; you got all the other bugs.

ROCKY: It bugs me watchin' noses stuck into sheets o' paper day 'n' night. Ain't that right, Smitty?

GUARD: Keep right on reading, Smith! There's no safer pastime around here. Tibber never got past Super-Rat. Well — if that's it, I'll head for a smoke in the lock —

MONA: I'd like to go to the library.

GUARD: Again? You're there every time the doors open.

Can't you wait for the cart to come around?

MONA: It won't have what I'm looking for.

GUARD: Cripes! If there wasn't bars on that book room, you'd be breakin' in.

MONA: Mr. Benson said that I could find something to do for the Christmas concert. *(Shows GUARD library passcard.)*

GUARD: I thought Benson ran the orchestra. Why don't he get you to play the skin flute?

ROCKY: Yah! Yah! The Minnie-Lousy could give him lessons.

MONA: Mr. Benson's in charge of drama for the concert, too. I'm going to do something like that.

GUARD: Why don't you do "I'm A Big Girl Now"? Sassy-face in there could teach you the words.

MONA: I don't sing.

GUARD: Oh, hell! Come on, Hortense; your carriage awaits without.

MONA: Thank you.

SMITTY: See you after, Jan.

MONA: See you, Smitty.

GUARD and MONA exit.

ROCKY *(singing introduction to "I'm A Big Girl Now")*:

Me 'n' my chilehood sweetheart
Ha' come t' de partin' o' de ways . . .

SMITTY: Oh, you're really funny.

QUEENIE *(entering from shower room singing):*
    He still treats me like he did
    In our bab-ee days,
    But I'm a little bit older
    And a little bit bolder
    Since both of us were three . . .

ROCKY: Put down that bloody book, kid!

SMITTY does so, and sits looking at ROCKY.

QUEENIE *(still singing):*
    I'm a little more padded
    Somethin' new has been added . . .

ROCKY: I got best bunk in this joint; can see everything comin' at us down the hall. I wantya t' know I'm real particular who uses it. That thing don't sit on my bunk no more.

SMITTY *(rising):* That'll make two of us . . .

ROCKY *(pushing him back):* What's mine is yours, kid.

QUEENIE: An' what's urine is my-yun.

SMITTY: Keep it! I only want what's mine. *(He gets up again and goes to lie face down on his own cot.)*

ROCKY: Come again on them mashed potatoes.

SMITTY: You heard me.

ROCKY: Watchit! I warned ya 'bout the tomato sauce. Be a good kid now, an' roll me a smoke.

SMITTY casually rolls a cigarette, as though it is second nature to do so for ROCKY.

QUEENIE: And when you've done that, Cinderella — mop the floor, wash the windows, shake the rugs and . . .

SMITTY: Aw, cut it, Queenie!

ROCKY: Smitty likes to keep the old man happy, don't you, kid?

SMITTY: Sure!

QUEENIE (*Singing to tune of "Old Man River"*):
Far far be it from me to free the slaves;
I'm not honest, and my name ain't Abe.
He just keeps rollin'-rollin' those ciggie-boos.

ROCKY: Yer name'll be mud if you keep that up.

QUEENIE: Queen Mud to you, peasant!

ROCKY: I think she's jealous, Smitty.

QUEENIE: Of what, for crap's sake?

ROCKY: 'Cause me an' Smitty is such good buddies. Bugs you, don't it?

QUEENIE: I don't give a damn if you legalize it in church-up next Sunday, and have fourteen babies. It ain't green you see in my eye, it's red, 'cause I hate to see a guy who could be a hippo playin' bumboy to a haywire loony who'll get him an ass-beat or a trip to the tower before his time's up.

ROCKY: You're really askin' for it, ain't ya?

QUEENIE: I'd like nothin' better than for you to take a swing at me, rockhead. Then we'll see who's gonna be called mud!

ROCKY: I'll find a better way, and you can believe it.

QUEENIE: It'll have to be while I'm asleep, 'cause I can see your next move like you drew me a map.

ROCKY: How come you're so smart . . . for a queer?

QUEENIE: 'Cause I get to bed bright an' early, and I'm up with the jailbirds — fresh as a pansy! We can't all be as dumb as you, Dora; it makes for bad publicity.

ROCKY: When you find me underneath, class me with you. For right now you call me Mister!

QUEENIE: How'd you like to say hello to your dear old friend, Baldy, in the office? He tells me he knows you from your first semester here, when you were chicken, like Smitty. I believe he gave your coming-out party, and made you debutante of the year.

ROCKY: I ain't interested in no old fairy's tales.

QUEENIE: May I quote you, or don't you want Baldy to pick you out a nice private room, where you can count your bellybutton and say your prayers, to pass the time?

ROCKY: Shoot off your mouth any way you want. Baldy an' me get along just fine.

QUEENIE: Yeah, he's got a soft spot in his head for you . . . except when he sees Smitty. Your sonny outshines you, it seems.

ROCKY: If he likes me, he's gotta like my buddy too.

QUEENIE: He does. Oh yes indeedy, *how* he does!

SMITTY: Why don't you two turn it off? What am I anyways, a piece of goods on the bargain counter?

QUEENIE: That's up to you, honey. If you smartened up, you could be as high-priced as you want.

SMITTY: I just don't want to be bugged, that's all. Let me do my time the easy way.

QUEENIE: Like the Mona Lisa?

SMITTY: What's Mona got to do with it?

QUEENIE: Well, she don't believe in wheelin' an' dealin' either, and you see what she gets. You gotta hustle inside too, you know, or you end up like a chippy-ass, wipin' up somebody's puke.

SMITTY: I thought you were Mona's friend.

QUEENIE: I am, and I guess I like her 'cause she's different from me. But that don't mean a comer like you has got to settle for the crappy end of the stick. You could have it all your own way . . . by just reachin' for it. You can't park your keester in a corner 'round here.

SMITTY: I'm satisfied to sit it out.

QUEENIE: Okay. Play it safe, but don't be sorry later. Nobody'll bother you while you got a old man, but you'll be anybody's baby when he drops you for a new chicken.

ROCKY sings first two lines of "Jalousie."

QUEENIE: It's Catso-Ratso, your old gearbox buddy who's got the greenies. That Wop's gonna get you good.

ROCKY: No Macaroni scares me, sister!

Sound of metal door opening and closing at a distance.

VOICE *(at distance, along corridor):* Tower up!

SECOND VOICE: Tower screw!

THIRD VOICE *(closer):* Hack from Tower!

FOURTH VOICE: Holy Face with hack!

FIFTH VOICE *(near-by):* Who they after?

SIXTH VOICE *(next cell):* They're still comin'. Must be after Rocky! *(Same.)* Hey Rocky! What'd ya do now?

GUARD *(off-stage):* Shut those goddam traps!

VOICE *(at distance):* Holy Face is a stinkin' lush.

On-stage cell inmates pick it up.

ROCKY: eats his wife an' bangs his daughter.

QUEENIE: Not our Holy Face! He does it on his dear ol' granny.

GUARD *(off-stage):* Who in hell said that?

A short silence.

VOICE *(at distance)*: It was me, Sir — *Gawd*! Ain't you ashamed o' yerself?

General laughter from all voices along corridor and on stage.

GUARD *(to unseen tower guard)*: Jenkins! Go get those bastards!

Sound of a heavy stick banging on metal doors, fading into distance — then silence. GUARD appears.

ROCKY *(singing old hymn)*:
Rock of ages, cleft for me-ee
Let me hide meself in thee-hee —

GUARD *(entering cell)*: That's just lovely — Tibber! I can hardly wait to hear the rest at the Christmas concert.

ROCKY: Thanks, Cap! Bring the wife and kids. They deserve a treat for living with you all year.

GUARD: I'd as soon see them into a monkey cage at the zoo.

ROCKY: Fine sense of loyalty to your students, professor! Tch-tch . . . You hurt my feelin's.

QUEENIE: How do you think the monkeys must feel? Speakin' of monkeys, where in hell's the Mona Lisa?

GUARD: I took it over to the library. It's tryin' to find some book it needs for a number in the Christmas concert.

QUEENIE: I don't need no book for my act! What's she gonna do . . . read "Alice in Wonderland"?

GUARD: I believe it's hunting on the Shakespeare shelf.

QUEENIE: Oh no, who does she think she is . . . Bette Davis?

GUARD: As long as it doesn't ask me to play Romeo, I couldn't care less.

QUEENIE: "But soft, what balcony from yonder Juliet breaks..."

211

SMITTY: Mona shouldn't try to do Shakespeare here. They'd probably laugh, and . . .

QUEENIE: And what? Don't you think we could use a good laugh around this dump? Let her do it if she's fool enough. She'd be worse tryin' to do my act.

SMITTY: But they might hurt her feelings . . .

QUEENIE: Yeah? Maybe *you* should play Romeo. What do you think, Captain?

GUARD: I suppose a little Shakespeare's all right. We've never had the classics before. Maybe it'll start a whole new trend in Christmas concerts.

QUEENIE: Well I'll stick to song and dance and a few bumps and grinds.

SMITTY (*thinking aloud*): But why?

QUEENIE: Why bumps and grinds?

SMITTY: Huh? No . . . no, I was thinking of something else.

GUARD: Come on, Tibber . . . on your feet! They want you in the big office.

ROCKY: What in hell for?

GUARD: Well, I'm reasonably sure it's not to give you the Nobel Peace Prize.

ROCKY: I ain't done nothin'.

GUARD: I wouldn't know. I got a few dozen other characters to watch besides you. Make it fast. I've got to bring the Shakespearean actress back before lights out.

ROCKY: Crap! Roll me some smokes for later, Smitty!

SMITTY: Yeah! I'll try to keep busy so I don't miss you.

ROCKY and GUARD exit.

QUEENIE (*sings first three lines of "I'll See You Again" after them*): You don't smoke, an' you spend half your time rollin' smokes for that haywire goon. What's the matter with you?

SMITTY *(dryly)*: We're "buddies."

QUEENIE: I'd like to know how he got you to make a mistake like that! I had an idea when I first saw you that you're the kind of guy who'd like to be on top.

SMITTY: Of what?

QUEENIE: Of everything. You're no lolliflier — you don't have to play it the way I do. Whatever you're gonna be here . . . you gotta be it in a big way. My way, I'm happy. The hippos know I'm a mean bitch, so I got no questions to answer. But I'm nobody's punk, and you shouldn't be either.

SMITTY: So what am I supposed to do . . . let you pick me an old man? How the hell would that make any difference?

QUEENIE: You don't need a old man, you could be a hippo, if you play your cards right.

SMITTY: So deal me a hand, and see if it comes up a winner.

QUEENIE: Okay. Here's a straight. Rocky's nowhere near top dog in this joint . . . just a hard crap disturber who gets a wide berth from everybody. He ain't in at all, and as long as you're with him, you ain't either. If you get out from under Rocky, and I spread the news you're boss in this block, they'll listen.

SMITTY: So how do I do it? Give him to some sucker for Christmas?

QUEENIE: Who'd take him as a gift? You could wrap him up, just the same.

SMITTY: I'm tempted. What would I use, crap paper?

QUEENIE: You ain't scared of Rocky?

SMITTY: Hell no! I just figured he helped to keep me out of the storeroom. He said if I was asked to that party, I wouldn't be a guest, and I didn't like the idea of providing entertainment for anybody's wolf pack.

QUEENIE: So that's how he caught you . . . the cagey bastard.

SMITTY: You going to sound off about that?

QUEENIE: Not on your life! It wouldn't do me any good to broadcast how Rocky conned you into his nest. When I tipped you off to the storeroom gang splash, it was a cue to get next to the politicians who can do you some good. You shouldn't have give in so soon, or so easy.

SMITTY: Were you here?

QUEENIE: No, damn it!

SMITTY: Well, let me tell you, it wasn't so easy.

QUEENIE: Yeah? Can you go?

SMITTY: You think I didn't fight?

QUEENIE: So how come Rocky won?

SMITTY: With his mouth! Every time he said storeroom, I remembered about Mona, and my fists melted like candy floss.

QUEENIE (excited): You takin' a shower tonight?

SMITTY: I don't know. I try to make them few and far between. If I had a choice, I'd be dirty as a craphouse rat before taking a shower with Rocky.

QUEENIE: Take one tonight, and I'll give six. One thing about Rocky, he don't squeal.

SMITTY: What did you say?

QUEENIE: I'll . . . give . . . six!

SMITTY: Well! How do you think I should play it?

QUEENIE: You wanta be on top, don't ya? I ain't interested in no stars can't live up to their billing. If I put it out that you're tellin' Rocky an' me what to do, I gotta believe half of it.

214

SMITTY: I begin to read you. You want me to punch his head in. Right?

QUEENIE: Have you got what it takes?

SMITTY: All stored up!

QUEENIE: Then let it go.

SMITTY: In the crapper?

QUEENIE: I'll give you six in case Holy Face is hangin' around, but try and make it fast. Turn on a coupla showers to cover the slammin'.

SMITTY: You're on. Oh! Oh! Hold it a minute! What about after?

QUEENIE: What about it?

SMITTY: What will I owe you? You're not doing this out of sweet charity.

QUEENIE: Am I so hard to be nice to?

SMITTY: That depends . . .

QUEENIE: I mean . . . when you want and how you want — I'm nobody's old man, if you know what I mean.

SMITTY: It'd be a change, anyway.

QUEENIE: Whatever you want. You'll be top dog in this corner.

SMITTY: Six!

Sound of key in corridor door . . . enter GUARD and ROCKY.

GUARD: Slipped out of that one like a snake, didn't you, Tibber?

ROCKY: Sure! I don't let no finks hang me on the hook.

GUARD: You'll get caught one day, and when you do, I want to be there.

215

ROCKY: And here I thought you was my true friend.

GUARD: You make no friends, Tibber!

ROCKY: I got Smitty. I tell him everything . . . but everything, screw.

GUARD: That's his business.

ROCKY: Now, don't ya wish ya hadn't slapped me across the mouth three years ago, Mr. Screw?

GUARD: If I had to worry about every mouth I slapped around here, I'd be better off working as a wet nurse.

ROCKY: Well, maybe ya slug so many, ya forgot, but I ain't. It was my first day in the joint, an' I didn't call you "sir."

GUARD: You always were a nervy little brat.

ROCKY: So ya said, an' ya smashed me across the jaw wit' both sides o' yer big mitt, an' when I says, "Ain't y'afraid I'll tell the Warden?" ya says, why should ya be; twenty years ago ya smacked me father in the mouth, an' he was a thief an' a pimp just like me. Ain't that so, Hack?

GUARD: Yeah, that's it all right.

ROCKY: So-o, how's it feel t' have yer own arse roastin' over the pit — an' fer a little fifty-buck boo-boo?

GUARD: You bastard! (Exits.)

ROCKY: Oh, how sweet it is. (Laughing.) See how I shake 'em up, Smitty old kid? (Stretches out on his bed.) Say, where's my weeds, pal?

SMITTY: Roll your own — pal.

ROCKY rolls a cigarette without taking his eyes from Smitty's face.

ROCKY: Gimme a light, kid!

SMITTY (tossing a lighter to ROCKY): Light on your ass!

ROCKY (*carefully*):   You two take a shower while The Rock was out on business?

QUEENIE (*coyly*):   I should be so lucky.

ROCKY: Smitty, come here. I'm gonna tell you what happens to jokers what try to give Rocky the dirty end.

SMITTY: I can hear you.

ROCKY: That phony Wop, Catsolini, finked to a shop screw on me, an' now he's all wrapped up in the General's office . . . wishin' he'd kept his hole closed.

QUEENIE: I thought good old Catso was your machine-shop buddy.

ROCKY: Think again. He mouthed off to the machine-shop screw I lifted his lousy firebox, so they hauled me up to the General, give me a quick frisk, an' when they couldn't find nothin', put the pressure on me. I took it good for you, Smitty.

SMITTY: For me?

ROCKY: Sure! Where d'ya think you got your screwin' firebox — from Ronson's?

SMITTY: But I didn't want the bloody lighter. All I used it for was to light your crappin' smokes when you ask me to come on like your butler.

ROCKY: Alla same, I took it good so's they wouldn't put you on the spot, kid.

QUEENIE: My hero! They make medals for people like you and Saint Joan.

ROCKY: Can it! One thing about it, old Catso's headed for the tower as sure as Christ made little apples an' his mother's ass. His Wop temper got riled up when the screws started shovin' him, and he gave old Sad-Ass Shriker a punch in the mouth. He sure picked the wrong target. Shriker's had a rod-on for that Wop a mile long. Shriker don't like no sissies, micks, Wops, or Kikes, an' when he gets ahold of one, he's just gotta get 'em into the butcher shop so he can have his jollies.

QUEENIE: That's Mona's dearest boy friend . . . the one who slapped her little keester for her. I think she still dreams about him.

SMITTY: That's not funny, Queenie.

QUEENIE: Who says so? It gives me a laugh.

ROCKY: Six!

Sound of key in the door. Enter GUARD and MONA.

GUARD: Make way for the great Sarah Bernhardt . . . or is it Heartburn? *(Exits.)*

QUEENIE: Don't stand up; she's just passing through. No autographs, no interviews, no pictures, and please desist from climbing up on her balcony. Cripes! Look at the expression. She's takin' this tragic stuff serious. Pardon me, madam . . . do we perchance breathe the same air?

SMITTY: Leave her alone, Queenie. You look upset, Mona, what's eating you?

MONA *(trembling):* I . . . I saw something awful as I passed the hospital door.

QUEENIE: Don't tell me one of the boys was havin' a baby?

MONA: Tony . . .

QUEENIE *(quickly interested):* Catsolino?

MONA: Yes, he . . .

ROCKY: Cripes! Those screws musta really marked him up. That circus troupe he calls his family'll be cut off from Sunday visits while old Catso's walkin' around lookin' like a road map.

MONA: It wasn't just that.

SMITTY: What then, for God's sake?

MONA: The doctor was holding a stethoscope to his heart.

ROCKY: Maybe they wanted t' see if Wops has got one.

QUEENIE: I know what she means, an' so do you, rat. Some buddy you are to let him get it. See where Rocky takes his pals, Smitty?

SMITTY: What? Let me in on it.

QUEENIE: You wouldn't know of course. The butcher always tests your heart before he lets 'em cut you up in the kitchen.

SMITTY: What are you blowing about?

QUEENIE: There's a little room off the kitchen where they keep a machine an' a coupla long pieces of cowhide . . . only that torture chamber ain't for the dumb animals.

SMITTY: They're not going to . . .

QUEENIE: You're goddam right they are. You don't slug a screw in the chops an' get off light. Catso's going to get the cat-o'-nine-tails.

SMITTY: God help him.

QUEENIE: Shall we pray?

ROCKY: The only time you get on your knees, bitch, it ain't to pray.

SMITTY: Over a lousy little firebox . . .

QUEENIE: Ease off Smitty. It ain't your beef.

SMITTY: The lighter was lifted for me.

ROCKY: That ain't what he's gettin' a ass-beat for. I got no sympathy for a bloody fink. All squealers oughta be shot.

SMITTY: Because of me . . .

ROCKY: You're buggy . . .

SMITTY (to MONA): What are you doing that for?

MONA *is standing close to the upstage bars at the extreme end of wall, near the exit hall, poised in a position of straining to hear some sound from a great distance away. He seems completely occupied with the effort, unaware of the others in the room.*

QUEENIE: She's listening for the screams. Sometimes the screws leave the kitchen door open, an' you can just hear from that corner. Once I even heard the bloody slaps of the belt. Musta been old Shriker swingin'.

MONA: Oh-h-h . . . *(Does not seem to hear or see SMITTY.)*

QUEENIE: Oh, let her get 'er kicks. I think she's a goddam masochist.

SMITTY *crosses to pull MONA from bars almost brutally, but the boy does not seem to care; he only covers his ears with both hands, as though to shut out some sound.*

SMITTY *(voice shaking):* What do you want to do that for? You trying to bug me? Make me feel guilty?

MONA *(dazed):* I'm sorry . . . I'm sorry. *(Sits in trance on his bed.)*

ROCKY: I'm sick of this crap. Come on, Smitty, let's take a shower. For some reason I feel real good tonight.

SMITTY: Glad to hear it!

ROCKY: Jesus! Don't tell me you're actual gettin' co-operative?

SMITTY: I am . . . tonight.

ROCKY: We-ll, it's about time! Give us six, Mona, if you can come outa that stupor.

QUEENIE: Don't bug her! I'll give ya six tonight.

ROCKY: When did you get so friendly? I had the impression you didn't exactly like us leavin' you alone, Mother dear.

QUEENIE *(sweetly):* Tonight I like it. I'll baby-sit.

220

ROCKY: I smell a sardine, or two.

QUEENIE: What are ya worried about, Rocky? You must have a guilty conscience!

ROCKY: I got no conscience, an' no fat fruit worries me either. Come on, buddy boy.

SMITTY: You can call me Smith.

ROCKY: I don't care what I call ya as long as y' do like you're told. Now move your ass.

SMITTY walks into the shower room. ROCKY turns a questioning look on QUEENIE who smiles in reply like the Cheshire cat. ROCKY goes out to shower room and QUEENIE crosses to stand near door to corridor, without looking toward shower-room door.

MONA *(starting):* Something's wrong in there. What's that?

QUEENIE: Mind your screwin' business.

MONA: But Smitty . . .

QUEENIE: Can take care of himself. He's my boy now, and don't you forget it.

MONA: But Rocky . . .

QUEENIE: Is getting a lesson he's needed for a long time.

MONA: How do you . . . ?

QUEENIE: Because I can pick 'em real good, honey. I know a born hippo when I see one. I ain't spent time around these joints since I was fourteen for nothing. Smitty's got everythin' it takes to run his own show, but he needs me t' help him. I'm big-hearted that way.

MONA: There's no sound now . . .

QUEENIE: I said to make it fast. You give me six. I'm gonna check the damage. *(QUEENIE goes to shower room, returning almost at once.)* You still got that alcohol an' bandages I give you t' hide under your mattress?

MONA: You planned this — to get Smitty.

QUEENIE: Right where I can see him — like I got all the other suckers on this street.

MONA: He could have been caught — or killed. You're not even on his side.

QUEENIE: If he's got a side! Shut your nellie jaw, before I blind you, bitch — an' get me that goddam medicine bag.

MONA: Yes — I'll get it. *(He does so.)*

QUEENIE: An' get ready to bow low, Miss Shakespeare. This block had a good queen; all it needed was a king. *(Exits triumphantly, leaving MONA looking lost and alone.)*

Curtain

ACT TWO

Christmas Eve.

At one end of dormitory, ROCKY lies smoking, on his bed: at the other end, SMITTY is propped up on his, with a book, reading: the GUARD, Holy Face, sits on a high stool, upstage, and a portable record player is going, the music filling the dormitory with something of a night-club atmosphere.

ROCKY: Crap, Captain! The Christmas stunt is lousy enough, without havin' t' watch stinkin' rehearsals.

GUARD: We could always arrange to reserve you a private room, Mr. Tibber. There's a vacancy right now in Gunsel's Alley . . .

ROCKY: Screw off!

GUARD: If you think this is any treat for me, guess again. I got a television when I want to be entertained. The tumblers and acrobats and what-have-you are using up the stage and gym floor, so the leading ladies will just have to practice here at home, with the family. You are what might be described as a captive audience. *(Walking toward shower-room door.)* Move it, girls . . . you're on! These critics of yours will be asleep before you get into those costumes.

QUEENIE *(calling from shower room):* Thank you, Mr. Sullivan. A little cruisin' music, please, while I remove my jock. I'll take it from the top . . . as we used to say at the Casino.

The GUARD crosses to reset the record, and QUEENIE enters, looking like a combination of Gorgeous George, Sophie Tucker and Mae West. He wears a platinum-blond wig, spangled sequin dress, long black gloves, large rhinestone jewelry on ears, neck and wrists, heavy make-up and is carrying a large feather fan. There is no self-consciousness or lack of confidence: movements are large, controlled, voluptuous and sure. He throws open the fan, as ROCKY, SMITTY and the GUARD watch, bending his knees in a slow dip, so the tight gown pulls across his heavy, rounded body, giving the look of an overweight strip teaser beginning the act; slowly he undulates the hips forward and upward in a series of professionally controlled bumps and grinds, the meat and muscle of burlesque dancing. As the record plays the opening to a song, an old night-club favourite, QUEENIE prepares the way with these bold, sex-conscious movements.

SMITTY: Holy mother of . . . you look sexy as hell. Look what we had here, and didn't know it.

QUEENIE: It's all yours, honey — every precious pound. *(Picks up the melody from the recording, to sing a parody of "A Good Man Is Hard to Find.")*

Here is a story, without morals
An' all you fags better pay some mind
'Cause if ya find a man worth keepin'
Be satisfied — an' treat him kind.

A hard man is good to find
I always get the other kind
Just when I think that he's my pal
I turn around an' find him actin' like somebody's gal
And then I rave; I even crave

To see him lyin' dead in his grave.
So if your hippo's nice
Take my advice
Hug him in the shower, kiss him every night
Give him plenty oompah, treat him right
'Cause a hard man nowadays is good to find.

There is spontaneous applause, from even ROCKY and the GUARD, for there is an all-embracing extrovert quality to QUEENIE's performance that is somehow contagious, partly because of a warmth generated by a feeling that QUEENIE seems completely happy with himself and his surroundings.

ROCKY: Come on, Queenie . . . give us another one . . . real lowdown and dirty.

SMITTY: Yeah, Queenie . . . sing it for Daddy, and don't forget I like the wiggle accompaniment.

QUEENIE (*like a famous star*): Sorry, boys . . . that's gotta wait for the show. Get your tickets early, before the front seats are sold out. I wouldn't wantya t' miss anything headed your way.

SMITTY: Throw it here, kid; I don't need a catcher's mitt.

ROCKY: Turn that stuff on again, Queenie; I might get in the mood.

QUEENIE: Put your gloves on, boys. We ain't got that much time before the show starts, an' this is more or less a costume an' make-up rehearsal. We got our numbers down already, but they didn't get these Christmas decorations in till today. Ain't this gown a flip?

SMITTY: Fits like a second skin. What did you do . . . grow into it?

QUEENIE: I hadda get Mona to shove me with a shoehorn.

SMITTY: What you hiding under there?

QUEENIE: Nothing, baby — but your Christmas box.

ROCKY: I'll look after the diamonds for ya.

QUEENIE: They musta took a chandelier apart to get all this glass. Feels good, but you couldn't hock it for a plate o' beans.

ROCKY: Looks like they shot a ostrich for ya, too.

QUEENIE (waving the fan): I hope it ain't moulting season in Africa.

SMITTY: You sprung those curls awful fast.

QUEENIE: My teeth an' my ass are my own, Honey!

GUARD (caught in the mood): If my wife could see me now, she'd start divorce proceedings.

QUEENIE: Never mind, baby; think of the beautiful music you an' me could make while she's in Mexico.

ROCKY: As long as you're spreadin' it around, Queenie . . . my pad's over here. Holy Face ain't got anythin' I can't better.

QUEENIE (enjoying every moment): What am I bid? Line up the Cadillacs on stage left an' the mink coats on the right. What's your offer, Smitty?

SMITTY: All I got is this book on auto mechanics.

QUEENIE (with a wink): Oh, that ain't all you got, Honey.

SMITTY (laughing): You've been peeking again.

ROCKY: Turn on the walkin' music, Queenie, an' give us the strip you did at the last Christmas concert.

QUEENIE: Are you kidding? I did a week in the tower for that surprise performance. I could hear the boys still whistlin', when they turned the key on your mother. Oh well, the bread an' water was good for my figure. I started the New Year lookin' like a cover off Vogue!

GUARD: No more surprises like that one, Queenie, or your concert days will be over. The conveners of this one had a hell of a time getting the General to trust you again.

QUEENIE: Oh, I told them how to fix that up.

GUARD: That's news to me. What did you do?

QUEENIE: I promised the General a little bit.

ROCKY, SMITTY and the GUARD laugh uproariously. At this moment, MONA enters, wearing a makeshift costume for Portia's court scene in The Merchant of Venice. *It is a converted red velvet curtain and becomes him somewhat, but contrast between the graceful, almost classic costume and Queenie's glittering ensemble seems incongruous.*

ROCKY: Flyin' crap! What's that supposed to be? Your bathrobe an' nightcap? What're ya gonna do . . . "The Night Before Christmas"?

QUEENIE *(in impresario fashion):* Ladies and gentlemen, I want you all to meet Tillie — The Birdwoman, God's gift to the Tree People.

ROCKY, SMITTY and GUARD howl at the announcement, but MONA remains as enigmatic in expression as the painting he is named for.

What kinda music do you want, Tillie . . . a slow waltz or a minuet? You'll never get those window drapes off the ground.

MONA: I won't need music.

QUEENIE: Well, you need something. *(Proffering the fan.)* How about these feathers? If you wave 'em hard enough, they might lift you up on your toes; you could call it "The Dying Duck" ballet.

226

ROCKY: Maybe she oughta have a window to hang herself in.

QUEENIE: You better not do a strip, 'cause you'd hafta have red flannel underwear to go with that smock.

MONA: It's from "The Merchant of Venice."

QUEENIE: Well, I'd take it back to him, dearie; you got gypped, whatever you paid.

MONA: This costume is for the courtroom scene . . .

QUEENIE: Oh, I get it. You're gonna play a judge. That should go over big in this joint.

MONA: It's Portia . . .

QUEENIE: It's poor something.

SMITTY (sober and fierce suddenly): Cut it, Queenie!

QUEENIE: What's biting your backside, big boy? She oughta be able to take a little fun.

SMITTY: You go past the point where it's funny.

QUEENIE: When I want you to tell me what to laugh at, I'll write you a certificate of authority.

GUARD (standing): Okay, children . . . cool it! Or we cut the run-through right here.

QUEENIE: Let's have Miss Shakespeare's number. I'm sure Rocky and the other boys will just love it, especially the ones who write poems on the wall of the crapper.

SMITTY: I know the scene, Mona; we took it in high-school English. It's where Portia goes to court for her boyfriend. Isn't that the part?

MONA (attention on SMITTY only): Yes . . . it is the plea she makes in the name of human charity and . . .

SMITTY (gently): Mercy?

MONA: Yes.

227

SMITTY: I'd like to hear it again. Will you say it for me?

QUEENIE: Oh mercy my me!

The others move into the background, sitting on beds, the GUARD returns to his stool. They watch, as though at some amusing spectacle, where one should not laugh, but cannot resist. QUEENIE pokes ROCKY in the ribs with his elbow. Then opens the fan over his face, holding it as a shield. ROCKY casually lights a cigarette and the GUARD yawns with indifference. Only SMITTY moves to hear MONA, looking into the serious, sad face.

MONA begins very hesitantly, stuttering (with comic pathos and badly spoken) — as others giggle and roll eyes, etc.

QUEENIE and ROCKY interrupt Mona's speech throughout.

MONA:
  The quality of mercy is not strained,
  It droppeth, as the gentle rain from heaven
  Upon the place beneath: it is twice blessed;
  It blesseth him that gives, and him that takes:
  'Tis mightiest in the mightiest; it becomes
  The throned monarch better than his crown;
  His sceptre shows the force of temporal power
  The attribute to awe and majesty,
  Wherein doth sit the dread and fear of kings;
  But mercy is above this sceptred sway,
  It is enthroned in the hearts of kings,
  It is an attribute of God himself;
  And earthly power doth then show likest God's,
  When mercy seasons justice.

QUEENIE *(to SMITTY, standing):* Down in front.

SMITTY sits and MONA strives to continue.

(With finality)

  Thank you!

MONA continues.

ROCKY: Take it off.

QUEENIE: Put it on.

ROCKY: Ya dropped yer lunch.

QUEENIE: Encore!

ROCKY: Turn off the lights.

QUEENIE: Gee, you're pretty, lady!

ROCKY: Pretty ugly.

QUEENIE: Would you mind terribly — coming out of a cake?

MONA falters and seems unable to continue.

Oh, she doesn't know it by heart.

SMITTY *(turning to the GUARD):* Will you make them shut up?

GUARD: Okay. Good enough! The guys are waitin' and they won't know them words any better 'n you do. Let's go, Christmas dolls! Come on, Shirley Dimples — and you too, Raggedy Ann!

QUEENIE *(grabbing MONA away from SMITTY):* Laws has muhcy, Miss Melanie — de Yankees is hyeah. Ain' you skeered dey gonna find yoah sissy brudder in dat closet?*(Propelling MONA toward corridor and concert.)* Run foh yoah life; all Atlanta am on fiyah!

They exit.

GUARD *(to ROCKY and SMITTY):* You bums get busy with a boot brush, and button up those shirt fronts. The General's wife and the Salvation Army are out there tonight. *(He exits.)*

ROCKY *(shouting after him):* Yeah! I'll wear my best tie — de one wit' de stripes. Queenie's browned off with you, Smitty.

SMITTY: Who gives a screw?

ROCKY: Mona . . . maybe?

SMITTY: How come Mona bothers you so much? You got a rod-on for her?

ROCKY: I got something I'd like t' give all fruits, but it ain't what they're lookin' for.

SMITTY: Seems to me that Mona doesn't know you're alive.

ROCKY: Oh, the Mona knows I'm here all right, only it's too lily-livered to look.

SMITTY: For a joker who claims he doesn't go in that direction, it looks to me like you ride the train awful hard.

ROCKY: You tryin' t' prove somethin', wise guy?

SMITTY: I don't have to. You prove the point every time you open your trap . . . it snaps shut on what you are.

ROCKY: Don't ever get the idea I'm a pansy, punker!

SMITTY: Watch your words there, Rocky. I'm nobody's punker these days, or have you forgotten what the floor of the crapper smells like . . . up close?

ROCKY: I ain't forgot.

SMITTY: Don't make me remind you too often.

ROCKY: Y' use your meat hooks pretty good, but that don't make you big time, Mister. Queenie tells me you're doin' a lousy little joy-ride rap. That's kid stuff.

SMITTY: It's big enough for me.

ROCKY: Ya didn't know yer ass from a hole in the ground before ya hit this joint here. It took me and Queenie t' smarten y' up.

SMITTY: I'm not interested in getting smart like you or Queenie. Did you get a chance to keep any of the stuff you got knocked off for? I guess not. And it must have taken a lot of Queenie's guts to smash a little old lady over the head for a closetful of diamonds and furs.

ROCKY: I'da got away clean if the lousy heap didn't run outa stinkin' gas, but Queenie screwed herself . . . she hadda play the actress before sluggin' some old bitch, by standin' in the hall singin' Happy Birthday to cover up the screams. Too bad the next-door neighbour knew it wasn't the old dame's birthday, and called the cops. Crap! I'da gave my right eye to 'a seen Queenie's face when they put the arm on her with that load of mink coats and diamonds. I'll bet she was plannin' to wear 'em, like Queen Elizabeth, on Halloween.

SMITTY: So today she's wearing a neckload of cheap glass and singing her songs to a gymnasium full of pickpockets and petty boosters.

ROCKY: Well, I ain't in that class. When my bit's up here, my real old man'll be outa Kingston, and me and him's gonna hit the big time together. I guess a pun . . . (he thinks better of using the term) . . . a joy-rider like you don't know who Tiger Tibber is.

SMITTY: Sure . . . I've read about your father . . . the high priest of pipe dreams.

ROCKY: But you wouldn't know what kinda cash a guy gets, dealin' out the junk.

SMITTY: Look Rocky, I don't give a crap what you and your old man do to get back here or someplace else. Queenie's always telling me what a big thing it is to pry open somebody's door or window, and you want to impress me by telling me your father peddles dope and your mother sells bingo to wine-hounds. Well, it cuts no ice with me. If I was to choose a racket it wouldn't be lousy drugs and cheap booze.

ROCKY: Well, ya better find somethin', buddy boy, 'cause y'ain't gonna be able t' git a decent job no more — maybe not even a half-assed one. Lookit Queenie! She wuz

231

workin' the counter o' a Chinatown restaurant, after her first bit here. She wuzn't there two weeks when Seven-Foot Tiny o' the Morality Squad steps inta the kitchen t' scoff a free cuppa coffee. He catches sight o' sweet Queenie playin' tea maid t' all them tourists 'n' square Chinks, so sends down t' the cash register fer the manager. He asks him does he know he's got a queer an' a thief workin' fer 'im. Dear Queenie, who planned on gittin' fat that winter, wuz out in the alley wit' the rest o' the cats — before Big Tiny finishes his bummy cuppa coffee.

SMITTY: So? Queenie made a try, anyway. It was probably better than selling bingo to wine-hounds. You pick your form of animal life; I'll find mine.

ROCKY: You keep my old lady outa it. When she was a big-time bootlegger she use'ta eat little boys like you for breakfast.

SMITTY: I can believe it!

ROCKY: And she still rakes in more dough in a day than you seen in a year.

SMITTY: I hope she saves it to pay her fines. They must love her at City Hall.

ROCKY: Can it.

SMITTY: You started this bomb rolling, big mouth.

ROCKY: That's what I get for tryin' to level withya about Queenie! She's bugged by you playin' nursemaid to Mona.

SMITTY: I don't like to see somebody shoved around by a couple of yellow-bellied crapheads.

ROCKY: You tangled with Queenie yet?

SMITTY: I'm ready when it comes!

ROCKY: I got news for you. Queenie's in solid with the politicians. She keeps old Baldy fixed up with punkers, and he pays by takin' the jokers she fingers, and lockin' em up in Gunsel's Alley.

SMITTY: I'm worried sick; notice how my nails are chewed to the elbow.

ROCKY: You ain't done hard time till they make you sit it out in Gunsel's Alley. Y'eat, crap, wash, jerk an' flop . . . all in a lonely little six-by-six. It's real cozy if ya don't go haywire the first month. A couple goons smashed their own heads on the brick wall . . . wide open like eggs. They figgered they was better off in the hospital than locked alone in a cage, like a screwin' canary.

SMITTY: I'd sing all day long, if I thought I wouldn't have to look at your ugly map for the rest of my time.

ROCKY: Yeah? Well they don't let little Mona drop in for visits, y' know.

SMITTY: Let's take a shower, Rocky!

ROCKY: I'm nice and clean right now, thanks.

SMITTY: Well don't rub any more of your dirt on me, 'cause I'll get the urge to clean it off . . . on you. Dig me, punk?

GUARD (entering with MONA): Okay Hans and Fritz! Patch it up and come on to the Christmas concert. They've got a bag of candies and an orange waiting for you at the door.

SMITTY: Why aren't you backstage, Mona? It's about time to start.

MONA: They decided I shouldn't do any Shakespeare.

SMITTY: Who decided?

MONA: Mr. Benson said they would only laugh at me and make life more unpleasant afterwards.

SMITTY: Well come on and watch with me, then.

GUARD: No, leave it here! Whenever that one gets into an assembly, there's trouble. Last time it was at church-up

. . . somebody split its pants down the back with a razor blade.

SMITTY: You wouldn't call that his fault.

GUARD: Look, Junior! If you had a bunch of hunters waving rifles around, you wouldn't throw a bird in the air, and expect nobody to shoot, would ya? It stays here.

SMITTY: This is Christmas!

GUARD: I don't care if it's the day of the Second Coming, the target stays here. Anyhow, it's got the whole corridor to roam around in tonight. The cell doors are all open, an' silly-bitch can go sniffin' around the empty beds for entertainment.

SMITTY: Isn't there a rule that says everybody attends the Christmas concert?

GUARD: You ask too many questions, Smith.

SMITTY: I thought you went by *all* the rules.

GUARD (*uneasy, as sometimes with Rocky's words*): Yeah! Come on, let's go.

SMITTY: I'll celebrate right here.

GUARD: Pick the kind of company you want, Smith, but take my advice . . . don't get caught. Come on, Tibber.

ROCKY: Let's move! The concert can't be as corny as this act. So long, sweethearts.

GUARD and ROCKY exit.

In the distance, Boys' voices can be heard singing a round of:

Row, row, row your boat,
Gently down the stream
Merrily, merrily, merrily, merrily,
Life is but a dream . . .

Sounds are from gathering in auditorium.

234

SMITTY: I hate that son of a bitch, and I'm soon going to show him how much. Then, he'll know the shower of knuckles I gave him was only a baptism.

MONA: Rocky can destroy himself soon enough.

SMITTY: He ought to be squashed — like a bedbug.

MONA: What would you expect of him? Do you know that his father . . .

SMITTY: Hell, yes! He takes great pride in his parents — the famous dope-peddler and the fabulous bootlegger. He sure rounds out that family circle.

MONA: Before he came here, this time, his mother was sent to jail. She's been convicted so many times, the court wouldn't accept another fine.

SMITTY: My heart bleeds for the dear, lost lady and her deprived offspring. Who'll make the pancakes now and run the still?

MONA: Rocky's sixteen-year-old brother took over the boot-legging and began, besides, to sell his teen-age girl friends to anybody who has five dollars.

SMITTY: Say! Outside, did you live near that slum?

MONA: No, I probably wouldn't have lived this long, or, at least, my nose would be a different shape.

SMITTY: How come you know so much about the rockhead?

MONA: I listen to him and read between the lines.

SMITTY: What a waste of time! That's their mess — not ours. I'm interested in you and me. You make excuses for them, but you keep your secrets, like Greta Garbo — under a hat.

MONA: You haven't said much about your life outside.

SMITTY: I'm forgetting, that's why — I'm going to spend the rest of my life forgetting my father. He put me here. To hell with him! Who put you in?

MONA: No one — really! It just — happened.

SMITTY: Happened? How can a thing like getting here just happen?

MONA: My life — like that from the start; I expect what comes.

SMITTY: That tells me a lot.

MONA: It's just that I can't . . .

SMITTY: So shove it, then!

MONA: A gang — of guys — in the neighbourhood — that night — pushed me around. My payday — had it on me — they knew. Next thing — I'm on the ground — kicking me — kicking. I look up — all those legs, but there's a big cop. Thank God! Thank God! Bleeding — numb — on my feet at last! Then — he looked at me, and I saw his sympathy shift — to the gang. Forgot my money — excited; asked were they mixed up with me — sexually. Smitty?

SMITTY: Don't get off the damn pot! Crap it out!

MONA: A — a huddle — like a football game — formation; all came out, laid charges — said I made passes. Four gave witness in court. Only voice for me — my poor, shocked mother, and sitting out there, trying to smile at me — eyes dark, afraid — God help her — my young sister!

SMITTY: But you should have had a lawyer.

MONA: Oh, I had one — or did I? Yeah — too late, after he got his money — we saw he didn't care — to tarnish his reputation. No real defense. A deal. Magistrate's court is like trial in a police station — all pals, lawyers and cops together! Threw me on the mercy of the court. Oh, Christ — that judge, with his hurry-up face, heard the neat police evidence and my lawyer's silly, sugar-sweet plea. So halfhearted — I wanted to shout, "Let me speak; leave me some damn dignity!" The fat, white-haired frown looked down at me — "Go to jail for six months!" — like I'd dirtied his hands, and that would wipe them clean.

Six months! Six thousand would have sounded the same.

SMITTY: Well, things are going to be a lot different by next month. There's a brand new year on the way.

MONA: How — "different"?

SMITTY: I mean, you're not going to be pushed around by anybody — goons, like Rocky and Queenie. They taught me more than was good for them. I'm on my way to being a politician, and I don't plan to do anymore hard time because of anybody. We've had it rough lately, but I'm about to even the score.

MONA: I don't know how that can be done.

SMITTY: Hell, kid! What I'm saying is we're going to wear the best of everything — new shirts, fresh from the tailor shop, and lightweight boots. We'll get extra grub — candy and fresh fruit — everything good that's going around. What do you say to that?

MONA: What do you expect me to say — about those things?

SMITTY: Well, for cripe's sake you might say "thanks." I'll have to. Or, "I like you, Smitty," or even — you might —

MONA: What's happened to you, Smitty?

SMITTY: I discovered I'm human. You're not blind. Who's been acting like your old man lately?

MONA: I don't have any old man. I thought you understood that.

SMITTY: You only think you don't. Look, Jan, when I came to this joint, I didn't know up from down. I've made a few mistakes since the one that got me here, and that's the only one I'm not sorry for. I stole a car — to get my mother out of town, away from my drunken slob of a father. I had to — he had the keys. I was helping her to run away with Ben — Ben's a nice guy. They tried to get me out of this jackpot, together, but I slugged a cop when they were arresting me. My dear father got back at us all. He didn't have a good word for me in court. After all, he was the respectable married man, a substantial citizen with his own business — the hardhearted bastard! Hard is a good word for him. He likes hard women, hard liquor, and hard words. For all he wanted from my mother, he might as well have hired a housekeeper and visited a prostitute regularly. Screw him! What I'm saying is you've got to work at it to make things go your way.

MONA: I can see you're not going to park your keester in a corner. Your father and Queenie have taught you well.

SMITTY: And I'm sick of that fat whore treating me like a piece of her property. I'll pick my own bedmate from here in. I shouldn't have to give you all this jazz, you know what I need. Haven't you any feelings after all?

MONA: Yes — some, but not the kind you're getting at — at least, not with you.

SMITTY: What did you say?

MONA: I said — not with you, Smitty.

SMITTY: Saving yourself for those dirty bastards in the gym? Is that what you enjoy — being forced into a corner?

MONA: It's better that way.

SMITTY: Better? Are you playing hard to get or something? Because, I know different; anybody who grabs you, gets you.

MONA: Slicings — patterns — blind and empty release; sure, I'll go on being a party to it.

SMITTY: Do you like that? I thought you liked me.

MONA: I do, Smitty — a great deal.

SMITTY: I knew you put up with what you got because you had no choice; that you really went for me. You showed it in a hundred ways, so now, while we're alone — a chance —

MONA: Just a minute! How do you feel with Queenie — afterward?

SMITTY: I could spit on her.

MONA: It would be the same with me; it's not in your nature.

SMITTY: I came to you.

MONA: No! Just circumstance! You're looking for a girl — not for me.

SMITTY: Do I smell or something? What's wrong with *my* body?

MONA: Nothing — it's very — Smitty, don't ask me to.

SMITTY: Should I ask you to do it with somebody else? Keep on being public property? I guess you like change — a different one every day, for variety. What do you do? Make comparison?

MONA: I — separate! Yes, that's right. I separate things in order to live with others and myself. What my body does and feels is one thing, and what I think and feel apart from that is something else.

SMITTY: You're crazy.

MONA: It's to the world I dream in you belong. It endures better. I won't let you move over, into the other, where I would become worthless to you — and myself. I have a right to save something.

SMITTY: I was afraid of everyone — everything — except you — until now. You're trying to shake me.

MONA: You're trying to kill me. You think I can be used just any old way — even by you.

SMITTY: To hell with me then!

MONA: No — listen! It's the sight of myself I can't stand — the way you throw it back.

SMITTY: Where do you get the goddam gall to tell me how I see you?

MONA: The right to say or be anything or everything or nothing to myself — and not a tame little fruit. Wasn't that it — soft, worshipping, harmless? Now you've flexed your muscles and found power, I'm an easy convenience. Not a Queenie! Oh no; I'd never turn on you. If I mattered, you'd be afraid of my feelings — not sure of them. You're offering me — indifference. Well, I don't want it.

SMITTY: Did you think I wanted your body? You make me sick. I wanted some kind of reaction to me, and only because I'm caught in this hellhole, you filthy fairy! You cocksucker!

MONA: You see? You see?

SMITTY (runs to the bars): Let me out of here! I'll go to the bloody concert — anywhere — where there's life —

He bangs wildly on bars with his fists. MONA follows to stand behind SMITTY, puts out a hand gently, but not touching him, then with difficulty, punches him on the shoulder. SMITTY reacts violently, turning on MONA.

MONA: No! Wait a minute! (Goes to Smitty's bunk, picks up a book and holds it out.) Look — listen — you read it.

SMITTY goes slowly to sit beside MONA and begins to read, clumsily, haltingly. They laugh, embarrassed, and continue to read until they are in a slight hysteria of laughter that causes them to break up and fall against each other.

When in disgrace with fortune and men's eyes
I, all alone, beweep my outcast state,
And trouble deaf heaven with my bootless cries,
And look upon myself, and curse my fate,
Wishing me like to one more rich in hope,
Featur'd like him, like him with friends possess'd,
Desiring this man's art, and that man's scope,

With what I most enjoy, contented least;
Yet in these thoughts myself almost despising,
Haply I think on thee, and then my soul
(Like to the lark at break of day arising,
From sullen earth) sings hymns at heaven's gate;
For thy sweet love remembered such wealth brings,
That then I scorn to share my state with kings.

SMITTY and MONA are laughing, heads close together, when QUEENIE and ROCKY enter.

QUEENIE: I'll give the bitch a bluebird! *(Smashes his fist into Mona's cheek.)*

ROCKY: Give it to the dirty little fruit.

SMITTY *(who has leaped up, fists ready to swing. He punches QUEENIE on the jaw):* Screw off, bastard!

QUEENIE *(backing away, but preparing to fight):* I'll take the punk, Rocky. Put your boots to the bitch.

SMITTY turns to take ROCKY, and QUEENIE uses the advantage to put a wrestling hold on SMITTY, pinning his arms behind his back.

I got him. Go, Rocky! Go!

ROCKY *(shaking MONA as though he were a rag doll):* I'm gonna smash your face, fairy.

He throws MONA to the floor, raising his foot to kick, but SMITTY breaks from QUEENIE, hurling the heavy blond to the floor, and kicks ROCKY in the groin. ROCKY screams, doubling over with pain. SMITTY then goes after QUEENIE just as the GUARD comes in, gun drawn.

GUARD: To the wall fast, or I cut your feet off.

All except MONA, who lies on the floor, move toward the wall.

Raise those mitts, children!

The three raise hands.

Okay, crap-disturbers, what's the score here?

QUEENIE / ROCKY / SMITTY *(together):* That dirty little bitch
. . . The goddam fruit . . . These filthy bastards . . .

GUARD: Cut it! One at a time! *(To QUEENIE:)* You, Goldi-
locks, what's your story?

QUEENIE: When me an' Rocky come in from the concert,
that looliflier on the floor was tryin' to make the kid here.
(Wide-eyed.) We done it for his own good, Cap!

GUARD: Yeah! I can just imagine your motives. *(To ROCKY:)*
Okay, you now, Terrible Tibber! Let's hear your phony.
Who were you saving?

ROCKY: Queenie give it to you straight, Cap; an' I'm stickin'
with that story. The fruit was gropin' pretty good when
we made the scene. We don't want that kinda stuff in
here. You know how it is. Just turn your back an' that
little queer's reachin' . . .

GUARD: Okay, turn it off, Tibber! Next thing you'll be telling me you want to go to church next Sunday to pray. *(To
SMITTY:)* All right, Romeo! Let's have your version of the
balcony scene.

SMITTY: My name is Smith.

GUARD: Well, well! May I call you Mister Smith? Names
don't mean a damned thing in here, sonny. Actions mean
everything. Did that thing on the floor make a pass at
you?

SMITTY: Nobody made a pass.

GUARD: Oh, now, this isn't your mother or a judge you're
talking to, Smarty Smith. We know by now a pass was
made. I'm not asking you if you liked it. I want to know
who made the pass.

SMITTY: Nobody made any pass at anybody.

GUARD: Real stubborn, aren't you?

SMITTY: You asked me. I can't help it that you don't believe me. We were talking when these haywire goons hit the block. They started the hey rube and I took over, since they seemed to want to play.

GUARD: You're not only getting too smart, Smith, you're becoming arrogant as well. Where do you think this attitude's going to lead you?

SMITTY: Into the office, where I can put an end to this crap.

GUARD: You're right . . . the General's office, where you'll need some much smarter answers.

SMITTY: I've got them.

GUARD: Your answers aren't worth much when you get hauled up on the big guy's carpet, kid.

SMITTY: Says you! Don't you think they might be worth about . . . fifty bucks?

The GUARD is stunned into silence. He steals a quick accusing look at ROCKY, who averts his eyes carefully.

GUARD *(shakily):* I don't think you know what you're talking about. What is this . . . some kind of bluff?

SMITTY: I don't say anything I can't back up with facts . . . like names, dates and letters. Dig me, screw?

GUARD *(enraged but cornered):* You crapping fink! Learned it all, haven't you? Found a way to save your precious little hide? *(To ROCKY:)* I ought to shoot you a second mouth, Tibber.

ROCKY just grins in reply, now enjoying the Guard's discomfiture.

There's one hide's not going to get off so easy. *(GUARD pushes MONA with his foot.)* Up off your ass, you little pansy! You know what you got the last time this happened, don't you? *(He pushes MONA ahead of him, toward the corridor door.)* You can bend over all you want, in the kitchen.

MONA (*realizing*): No! Oh, no, no, no, no . . . (*Protest mounts to screams off-stage.*)

SMITTY (*running to the bars*): Stop it! Stop it! I did it! I made the pass. (*Shouting after them.*) Do you hear? I made the pass . . . I made the . . .

QUEENIE *and* ROCKY *begin to laugh in derision.*

(*Turning vicious.*) Shut up you yellow bastards! I'll wipe the floor with your rotten guts. One more laugh out of your ugly kissers and I'll spray teeth from here to hell.

QUEENIE: We didn't mean anything, Smitty. What are you so hot about? That little . . .

SMITTY: Shut your filthy hole, you fat whore!

ROCKY: Jeez, Smitty; that thing ain't worth . . .

SMITTY: Listen to me, Rock-ass! Before I leave this stinking joint I'm going to demolish your mug so bad that no fruit will ever look at you again . . . let alone a woman. When will depend on you. Ask for it once and you've got it. This is my show from now on. I got that lousy screw over a barrel, and I'm going to keep him there. Also, Baldy's making me a politician . . . a wheel in the office. You see, Queenie, I wasn't hustling my little ass in the park at thirteen for peanuts. I went to school; I got typing and bookkeeping, so Baldy's put me where I can make things move my way. If you'd learned to write, maybe you'd be better off . . . but you'll swallow chicken crap when I make up the menu. And you, monkey; would you like to be my punchin' bag around here or should I ship you into Gunsel's Alley for safekeeping? Choose fast!

ROCKY: I . . . I'll take it off you.

SMITTY: Okay. You'll volunteer to be my sparring partner in the gym every time I want to box somebody, and, sweetie, I'm gonna knock you senseless. Now get into that goddam crapper and stick your heads into a coupla bowls, till I yell for you to come out. That'll be after lights out, 'cause I don't want to see your ugly maps again today.

ROCKY and QUEENIE *look at each other, dazed.*

You know who Baldy is? You know what he can do?
Well, I'm his boy now.

QUEENIE: Ain't it the bitter truth? *(Pulls ROCKY away.)* Come
on, Snake-Eyes; we rolled too low in the game — this
time around.

SMITTY: So move, goddam it! *(A step toward them.)*

*In their haste to get out, the two bump into each other, ridiculous
and clumsy in their new roles. SMITTY laughs loudly, revealing a
cruelty that fills the room with its sound. Suddenly his head turns
in another direction as though just recalling something. He steals
a quick look toward the shower room, then stealthily and lithely
as a cat, he moves to the corner of the dorm where MONA had
listened to the sound of Catsolino's beating. From an attitude of
strained listening, SMITTY suddenly contorts in pain as MONA
had done before, but there is no sound from his distorted mouth.
He seems to be whipped by unseen strokes of a lash, until he is
spread-eagled across the upstage bars. When it seems he can bear
no more he covers his ears with both hands, stumbling blindly
downstage. Standing thus, head and shoulders down, he rises
slowly out of the hunched position to full height, hands lowering.
His face now seems to be carved of stone, the mouth narrow,
cruel and grim, the eyes corresponding slits of hatred. He speaks
in a hoarse, ugly whisper.*

I'm going to pay them back.

*He then walks, almost casually, down to Rocky's bunk where
cigarettes, which we have not seen him use before, and a lighter,
lie on the side table. He picks up a cigarette, lights it, then stretches
out on Rocky's bed, torso upright against the back of it. Looking
coolly out to the audience with a slight, twisted smile that is
somehow cold, sadistic and menacing, he speaks his last line.*

I'll pay you all back.

Light fades to black, and there is heard a final slam of jail door.

Curtain

245

William Fruet
Wedding In White

EDITOR'S NOTE: William Fruet was born in Lethbridge, Alberta in 1933. He turned down scholarships at R.A.D.A. and the University of Alberta to study at the Canadian Theatre School in Toronto under Ernest Sterndale Bennett. However, his early professional work was chiefly as a photographer and writer, rather than as an actor. He wrote the script for "Goin' Down the Road", winner of the Canadian Film Award for Best Screenplay in 1969, and for "Rip-Off" in 1971, as well as "Slipstream." In recent years he has remained in Canada and continued his film work concentrating on directing.

Wedding in White was conceived as a television script but received its first production as a stage play opening at Toronto's Poor Alex Theatre in 1970. In 1972, William Fruet directed *Wedding in White* as a film starring Donald Pleasence and Carol Kane.

Characters:

JIM	*A middle-aged army veteran*
MARY	*His wife*
JEANIE	*Their daughter*
JIMMIE	*Their son*
BILLY	*Jimmie's friend*
DOLLIE	*Jeanie's friend*
SANDY	*Old army friend of Jim's*
SARAH	*Old friend of Mary's*
BARNIE	*An old wino*
HATTIE	*His wife*
JOCK	*A soldier*
	Assorted soldiers in club;
	Sundry wedding guests

SCENE ONE

The play takes place somewhere in Western Canada, in a small town, near the end of the Second World War.

The master set consists of a large living room, stage left and a small dining room, stage right. The front door to the house and a stairway indicating an upper floor, are on the extreme left of the living room. Beneath the stairway another door opens to the cellar. This same corner of the room has become Jim's personal little sanctuary consisting of a large black leather chair, an old gramophone, a small whisky cabinet, a display of shell casings and other war souvenirs. Several army group photos hang beside pictures of King George V and Queen Mary. A Union Jack is draped as a background. The remainder of the living room is a clutter of odd pieces of old worn out furniture: a faded and sagging chesterfield, covered in doilies and needlework, scatter rugs and cheap bric-a-brac everywhere. An old dresser sits strangely alone and out of place in this setting.

The dining room is separated by a small archway. In the centre of the room sits a large circular table with an old tarnished brass chandelier hanging directly above. One naked bulb lights the room in a dim yellow pallor. A china cabinet sits along one wall and French doors open to a partial kitchen set seen in the back.

Throughout the house, gaping cracks in the plaster and a lack of general upkeep over the years will indicate the kind of people and conditions lived under here. An atmosphere of mustiness and slow decay.

The house lights slowly dim. Fade in the distant sound of drums and bagpipes, playing a stirring march tune of war.

The music builds as the theatre grows darker, giving the illusions of coming closer. When the theatre has reached complete darkness, the music will be a deafening pitch with the clapping bam of the bass drum and the wheezing whine of the pipes everywhere.

The music suddenly stops abruptly and we hear only the crisp noise of hobnailed boots marching in unison . . .

The curtain rises on the stage in darkness.

Cut sound.

Silence . . . four beats.

The setting is plunged into light.

The front door opens and three men in army uniforms enter with a lot of noise and laughter. The two younger men are of the regular army and carry duffel bags, while old JIM wears the uniform of the Veteran's Guard, and carries a large case of beer under his arm. He is a puffy cheeked Scot in his early sixties, whose dialect is a combination of British and Scots slang, carried over from the days of the First World War. When he speaks, it is in a wheezing raspy voice, from years of tobacco smoking. Usually a sober and self-centered man, he is presently experiencing a rare moment of joy, having just met his son JIMMIE and friend BILLY, who have come for a weekend leave. JIMMIE is about thirty-five but looks much older because of his missing top teeth and sunken cheeks. He is a loud-mouthed, illiterate and obnoxious extrovert, with an answer for everything delivered at the top of his voice. To old JIM however he is a model son, who can do no wrong; a hard-drinking, whoring soldier. BILLY, his friend, is a contrast to JIMMIE: a shy quiet introvert, until he has drunk his fill . . . then the shyness leaves him and an ugly meanness takes over. . He speaks in a broken harsh Newfoundland accent.

JIM: *(Calling)* Hi there we're home! Tip, he's home!

JIMMIE: *(With a loud "whoop")* YAAAAA-AAAA-HOOOOOOOOO! Where the hell are ya Mom?

MARY: *(Off)* Is it youse, Jim?

JIMMIE: There's my girl!

MARY: *(Crying out.)* Och Jimmie, my boyyyy!

JIMMIE gives her a swat on the behind and picking her up, swings her off her feet.

JIMMIE: WHEEEEEEE!

MARY: Oh Jimmie, be careful!

JIMMIE: Ha Ha just look at her willya! Stil got an eye for the good lookers eh?

JIM: *(Slapping him on the back.)* Well dammit man, look who you take after, heyyy!

Loud guffaws of laughter.

JIMMIE: Yes sir! Ya know, you're still the only woman I'm gonna marry Mom! That's what I used to tell her, Billy!

MARY: *(Holding him at arm's length.)* Let me look at you, let me look at you. Oh, tch, I think you've lost weight!

JIMMIE: You're gettin' skinny as hell yourself!

Laughter

MARY: Oh, you!

JIMMIE: *(Pulling BILLY over.)* Billy boy I want you to meet the finest little woman in this damn town — my Mom! Mom, this here's my mate Billy. He didn't have nowheres to go to on his leave, so I brought him home with me!

BILLY: *(Nods with a forced smile.)*

249

MARY: Pleased to meet you, I'm sure.

JIMMIE: Bloke didn't want to come! So I says look here boy, any pal of mine is always welcome in my folk's home!

JIM: (Patting JIMMIE on the back again.) The lad's right! I've always told him that.

MARY: Oh yes, any friend of Jimmie's is always welcome here. Come in, Billy.

JIM: (Closing the front door.) Why don't we all come in? What the devil are we standing here for?

JIMMIE: (Spotting JEANIE.) Well I'll be gone to hell!

Entering, they are now able to see JEANIE standing at the top of the stairs watching. She is a sloppy unkempt girl of sixteen; a late child left with the mark of feeble-mindedness. She is indifferent towards her mother, but regards her father with respect heavily blended with fear.

JIM: (Gruffly) Hey you, don't you see who's here?

JIMMIE: She's all growed up! That's the kid sister, Billy. I told you about her sure! Well you come on down here and let us have a look at you Jeanie!

JIM: Come on, come on, your brother wants to see you!

MARY: (To BILLY) Cat's got her tongue. She's shy that one.

JEANIE: (Slowly coming down.) . . . Hi Jimmie.

JIMMIE goes to meet her at the foot of the stairs, lifting her off.

JIMMIE: Hi yourself! Come on, give your brother a big hug! (He gives her a quick embrace, taking her over to the group.) Say hello to Billy, my buddy!

JEANIE: Hello. . . .

BILLY: How are ya kid.

JIMMIE: Ho ho, she's no kid anymore! Even got a couple of plums growing under that sweater!

MARY: Jimmie!

Old JIM breaks into loud guffaws of laughter, hanging on every word his son says, ready to laugh, to please, to impress.

JIM: *(To BILLY.)* Ain't he a devil, this one!

JIMMIE: *(Giving JEANIE a squeeze.)* Ah hell Ma, she knows I'm only kidding her! *(He goes to his duffel bag.)* Hey, I think there's something in here for you!

JEANIE: *(Her eyes lighting up)* . . . me?

JIMMIE: Yep. Don't know any other Jeanies, and that's what this says on it — "To Jeanie".

JEANIE: Gee, what is it?

JIMMIE: Open it up and see! Heyyy, I smell something cooking! *(They all follow JIMMIE into the living room leaving JEANIE forgotten.)* Billy you just sit yourself down! This here's home for a couple of days, and you act like it was, see!

JIM: *(Echoing JIMMIE.)* Aye you do like the lad says Bill, make yourself at home.

MARY: I been holding supper for youse. Was the bus late or something?

JIM: Good God, woman, can't I buy my boy a beer, after not seeing him for a year?

JIMMIE: Me and Billy worked us up one hell of a thirst on that bus, eh boy?

BILLY: You said it!

JIMMIE: Actually we did get hung up. Where was it, Calgary? Yeah, that's right. This driver guy says fifteen minutes stop, see? So me and Billy beats it over to the beer parlour and this SOB took off without us. I was sayin to Billy here, what if we'd been shippin overseas or something? Where the hell would we have been then? Now that ain't no way to run no bus company!

JIM: You're absolutely right son. They got no right doing that. You paid for your ticket and it's their job to see that you get there!

JIMMIE: Oh those buggers ain't heard the last of me yet, I'll tell you Dad, no sir! We had to wait a whole stinkin hour for the next one! Christ, I mean they don't even stop that thing long enough to let you have a leak!

BILLY: I'm still splitting. Where's the head?

JIMMIE: (Making a complete production of it.) Well ya see those stairs? Straight up and the door on the right, and she's starin you in the face. (BILLY stares up.) An don't fall in mate!

JIM: (Chuckles) I'll take the bags up to the room.

JIMMIE: Here let me give you a hand.

JIM: No, no, just sit yourself down and take the weight off your feet.

MARY: Aye, you must be weary after that long ride, and hungry too I'll bet.

JIMMIE: Starving, Mom, starving!

MARY: Well it's only going to take me a minute to put it on the table.

She scurries off to the kitchen. JIMMIE goes over to where old JIM struggles with the bags and the case of beer.

JIMMIE: Here mate.

JIM: I can manage.

JIMMIE: Come on now don't argue with me or I'll take you over my knee! (Sweeps up one of the bags and the case of beer.)

JIM: *(Chuckling)* Alright alright. By God, I bet you could too! You're gettin bigger every time I see you!

JIMMIE: 'Sides you didn't think I was going to trust you all alone with this do you? *(Holds up case of beer.)*

JIM: *(Eyes lighting.)* Hah! Aye, we'll have us a fast one before supper, eh?

They have now reached the top of the landing and JIMMIE gives the bathroom door a kick as he passes.

JIMMIE: That's a hell of a waste of good beer! *(JIM bursts into laughter.)* . . . and don't shake it more than twice or you're playing with it!

We hear an inaudible comment from BILLY. The old man pats his son affectionately on the back as they enter one of the bedroom doors.

JIM: Still the same kidder, aren't ya! You an Bill can have your old room an Mother an me will take Jeanie's. She can sleep on the chesterfield downstairs.

The stage is empty except for JEANIE, who still clutching her gift goes quickly into the living room and begins to unwrap it, being careful not to wrinkle the tissue paper in order to save it. She takes out a small brooch of the Maple Leaf, framed in rhinestones. It is a cheap and gaudy piece of jewellery but she is pleased with it. BILLY comes out of the bathroom still zipping his fly. He sees her and stops, just standing and watching her for a brief time; he surveys the setting, noticing the absence of the others, then starts slowly down the stairs.

BILLY: Like it? Pretty nice, huh?

JEANIE: Yeah. Wait'll I show Dollie this!

BILLY: Who?

JEANIE: Dollie, she's my best friend. She's got lots of nice things like this.

BILLY: Your friend, huh? Same age as you?

JEANIE: Two years older, but that don't matter. Do you think it does?

BILLY: I dunno . . .

JEANIE gets up and going to the dresser to see, pins it close to one shoulder. BILLY watches her every move.

BILLY: If you want, I can send you a couple more things like that . . . ?

JEANIE: *(Taken)* . . . for me?

BILLY: Sure . . . guy I know, s'got lots of 'em . . .

JEANIE: Gee, yeah! *(Swinging back to the mirror.)* Boy will that brown her off!

BILLY: Whozat?

JEANIE: Dollie. She's just like that, that's all. She's my friend, but boy does she think she's smart. Doesn't like anybody having things she hasn't got. I only got one other brooch that Mom gave me, but you should see all the things she's got. Earrings and even a pearl necklace. It ain't real but it looks pretty nice.

BILLY: Why don't you bring her around? I wouldn't mind meeting her . . .

He gives a silly laugh, but JEANIE misses the implication.

JEANIE: You will. She's going to call on me later . . . *(Forced sigh.)* She'll probably start putting on the dog for Jimmie. She saw an old picture of him and she thinks he's real cute. I got it in my wallet. Want to see it?

BILLY: *(Shrugs)* Yeah, sure.

JEANIE: I don't have very many . . . you should see all she's got. All the kids at school have.

BILLY: You an her still go to school?

JEANIE: Naw, she works. I'm gonna quit after this summer. I hate it.

BILLY: Never did me no good. *(Hands her back the wallet.)*

JEANIE: I could get a job as a waitress tomorrow, and you make pretty good money too. I mean, what good's going to school if you don't want to be something special?

BILLY: Where ya's goin later?

JEANIE: *(Shrugs)* Just fool around, I guess . . .

BILLY: Maybe we can all get together an do something.

JEANIE: What . . . ?

BILLY: I don't know. Ain't you got any shows around here? Or scoff a few beers maybe.

JEANIE: *(Wide eyed)* In a beer parlour?

BILLY: Don't matter to me. Beer's — beer . . .

JEANIE: My dad would crown me.

BILLY: Well good beer never hurt anybody.

JEANIE: Yeah but he treats me like I'm still a child. He don't like me going out nowhere.

BILLY: You look pretty grown up to me . . .

JEANIE blushes. BILLY comes closer, keeping an eye out for the others.

BILLY: You know, you shouldn't wear that thing there . . . here let me show you.

He removes it and leaning closer to her, pins it over one of her breasts. JEANIE is taken by this small show of attention, unaware of any ulterior motive on his part.

BILLY: There . . . that's how you should wear it.

We hear a burst of laughter from upstairs, causing BILLY to step back quickly. JEANIE crosses to the mirror to admire herself.

JEANIE: Let me see . . .

As she admires herself, BILLY smirks to himself behind her back, confident and sure of himself with this girl. MARY appears in the dining room carrying a dish of steaming potatoes.

MARY: You'll wear that mirror out, the way you're always in front of it. I could use a little help, ya know . . . *(Seeing BILLY she changes to complete sweetness.)* Oh . . . I didn't mean to interrupt, Mr. Billy.

BILLY: We was just talking.

MARY: *(Sweetly)* Come on then Jeanie and give me a hand dear. *(To BILLY)* Would you mind calling Jimmie and Dad then? I don't want it to get cold. I spect they're in one of the bedrooms upstairs.

JEANIE gives a weary sigh and goes into the dining room while BILLY goes upstairs.

JEANIE: *(Anxious)* Do you like Jimmie's friend?

MARY: *(Absently)* Aye, he seems nice. Very quiet.

JEANIE: He promised to send me some things.

MARY: What sort of things?

JEANIE: Some more nice things like this that Jimmie brought.

MARY: You no asked him I hope?

JEANIE: No! *(Catching her mother's intent stare.)* What's wrong?

MARY: *(Scornfully)* Have you no decency? What do you mean by putting that brooch there? If your father sees that . . .

Loud burst of laughter from upstairs.

. . . now put it on properly, or don't wear it at all! *(Shaking her head.)* I don't know what's to become of you . . .

MARY angrily exits to the kitchen. JEANIE sighs and goes to the mirror.

BILLY: *(Off)* Aye, well drink up then, drink up!

The bedroom door opens and the three come out of the room.

JIMMIE: *(Suddenly)* Hey hey, show the old man some of those pictures ya got Billy! Wait'll you see these Dad!

They stop on the stairway landing as BILLY reaches into his tunic and produces some postcard photos. BILLY and JIMMY watch the old man's reactions with sheepish grins. None of them notice JEANIE below in the living room.

JIM: *(His eyes lighting up.)* Ho ho, the old sixty-niner eh! *(Goes to the next.)* My God, where did you get these?!

JIMMIE and BILLY burst into snorts of laughter.

BILLY: Guy I know s'got lots of 'em . . .

They start down the stairs chuckling.

Curtain

SCENE TWO

One hour later.

Dinner finished and the three men sit about the dining room table engaged in conversation. Old JIM rambles on about conditions at the POW camp, but it is DOLLIE sitting in the living room who holds the attention of JIMMIE and BILLY. She is well developed physically and covered in an array of cheap jewellery. Excessive makeup covers her pouty face, and while she is attractive, she has an unwashed grimy look about her. Throughout the scene she is aware of the admiring eyes upon her, and goes through a series of exaggerated sighs and gestures as she waits for JEANIE. (Throughout the play she chews gum feverishly.)

JIM: . . . that's what's wrong. They're too easy on 'em. Spect we should treat 'em like bloody royalty, they do!

DOLLIE: *(Calling)* Hurry up Duke!

JEANIE: *(Off)* Relax, eh?

DOLLIE: *(For the benefit of JIMMIE and BILLY.)* Some people!...

JIMMIE and BILLY give her acknowledging smiles, and each other knowing looks.

JIM: . . . no, as far as I'm concerned prisoners of war got no privileges. They're nothing but bastards what gave up!

JIMMIE: *(Making conversation, his eyes still on DOLLIE.)* Dad's one of the guards at this POW camp they got outside town.

JIM: *(Eager to impress.)* Four thousand men in that camp! Mind you it's not like being in the regular service. Don't I wish I was young enough, but someone's got to watch 'em. And I do my job well if I do say so myself.

BILLY: Don't make no sense to me. Looking after a bunch of bastards you're supposed to kill.

JIM: My very sentiments. But they're clever beggars though. Here, I'll show you something, I'll wager you never seen before . . .

He gets up, and passes through archway past DOLLIE, to his private corner, where he keeps a shrine of souvenirs. Once more there is an interplay of looks between DOLLIE and the other two.

BILLY: *(Hushed whisper.)* What do you say mate?

JIMMIE: . . . a week's pay says she's handled more meat than a barracks butcher!

DOLLIE flips through a magazine aware they are discussing her, but unable to hear their comments.

JIM: Here it is, I knew it was somewhere . . . *(He returns carrying a whiskey bottle with a model ship built inside)* . . . ever see anything like that?

JIMMIE: *(Taking it.)* Well I'll be gone to hell! How about that Billy? !

BILLY: Jeeeze, how'd that ship get in there?

They are putting the old man on, while he oblivious to this, babbles on, colouring his story.

JIM: Ho ho, there's a story behind that, let me tell you. Went into the compound one day an there's this kraut hiding something behind his back. "Hand it over", I says. He shakes his head. So I says to the S.O.B., I says, "You step out of line with me you bastard, and I'll crack your bloody skull open with the butt of this gun . . ." *(He takes a dramatic pause, the other two nodding mockingly.)* . . . well he backs off see.

JIMMIE: *(Helping him along.)* Shit pouring out of his pants I'll bet.

JIM: *(Laughing)* Aye aye! "Give it over", I says. He drops it right there and is gone like a shot out of hell!

He slaps himself on the knee, breaking into loud laughter. The other two laugh at him.

JIMMIE: Should have put the boots to him dad!

JIM: (Quickly) I woulda I woulda, if I could have caught him! Aye, I'd of taught him a lesson for once an all, I'll tell ya!

BILLY: *(Handing it back,)* Pretty sharp Pop . . .

JIM: It's a very complicated business. Ya see they build it a little bit at a time. Got all kinds of strings and things they do it with. Clever buggers alright . . .

He is interrupted as MARY bustles through from the kitchen wearing a faded old hat and putting on a shabby coat.

MARY: Well I'm on my way. I hope the supper was good Billy?

BILLY: Just fine just fine . . .

JIMMIE gives a belch of approval.

MARY: It wasn't much I'm afraid, but it's so hard to get things these days with a war on an all.

JIMMIE: *(Suddenly aware of her.)* Where you going Ma? Ain't you comin' over to the Legion with us?

MARY: No no I've got to go out for a few hours . . . I'll see you when you get home, son.

She glides through the living room, stopping at the foot of the stairs.

MARY: Jeanie you clear up for me now hear? . . . Well, bye bye again — I'll have some nice hot rolls and tea waiting for you when you get home.

JIMMIE: So long kid . . .

JIM gives an acknowledging grunt and BILLY a slight wave as the old woman disappears out the front door.

JIMMIE: *(No real concern)* Where's she goin anyways?

JIM: *(Brushing it off.)* Oh she's got to help out for a few hours . . . anyway, like I was sayin' . . .

We hear the barking and whimpering of a dog coming from the cellar.

. . . Oh God, didn't anybody feed me dog yet? !

JIMMIE: You got a dog now?

JIM: *(Rising and scraping some scraps together.)* Aye. Figured it might be safer for mother, with me away so much. We've had a couple of escapes from that camp. Trouble is no one feeds the poor bugger. Ain't going to have a dog long that way I always say.

JIMMIE winks to BILLY and follows the old man through the living-room to the cellar stairs.

JIMMIE: *(To DOLLIE as he passes.)* How you doing kid . . . ?

She shrugs giving him a smile. When he is behind her back, JIMMIE makes a goose gesture with his finger to BILLY, and they exchange broad grins.

JIM: *(Entering the cellar.)* Hi Rex, come on boy! Ain't had him long . . . still got to be trained a bit . . .

JIMMIE: *(Entering cellar.)* S'long as he knows who's master!

BILLY rises and casually saunters into the livingroom. DOLLIE pretends to be engrossed in her magazine. BILLY slowly eyes her up and down before he speaks.

BILLY: How's she goin . . . ?

DOLLIE: *(Shrugs)* Okay I guess . . .

BILLY: Yeah, Jeanie was sayin ya might come over tonight . . . I'm Billy.

DOLLIE: Hi . . . *(Yelling out.)* Jeeze Dougal how much longer ya going to be? ?

JEANIE: *(Off)* A minute . . .

JIM'S VOICE: *(Off)* No ya don't . . . get down damn it! . . . Alright now — heel! Come on come on, ya don't get a bloody thing til ya do like I said — HEEL!

We hear loud laughter from JIMMIE, then a burst of barking.

JIM'S VOICE: *(Off)* Son-of-a-bitch! !

Loud yelping from the dog.

Aye you know that don't you! That's my foot! Let's try it again . . . up now . . .

JEANIE bounds down the stairs and noticing the absence of her father, makes a "s-h-h-h" gesture with her finger and motions for DOLLIE to follow her sneak out.

BILLY: Hey where ya's goin?

DOLLIE: *(Teasing)* Could be anywhere . . .

JEANIE: *(Urging)* Come on quick.

BILLY: *(Quickly)* I mean, maybe we could meetcha's later huh?

DOLLIE: *(As they disappear out the door.)* Maybe . . . So long.

BILLY: *(Following to the open door.)* Okay then don't forget . . . later huh!

JIMMIE comes stumbling through the cellar door, snorting with laughter. BILLY curses himself at having let the thing slip out of his hands.

JIMMIE: *(Still laughing.)* Keeey-Rist, you should see him down there, beating the shit out of that poor thing!

JIM'S VOICE: *(Off)* . . . now play dead . . . *(Whine from the dog.)*

JIMMIE: *(A new burst of laughter.)* Hear him hear him! !

BILLY: *(Angry)* Hey look how long we gonna hang around? I don't want to go no friggin Legion tonight!

JIMMIE: Awww, now I can't just walk out on the old man yet . . . It'll be okay . . . We'll find some poon tang boy . . . *(He playfully puts his arm around BILLY in a hug.)*

BILLY: *(Trying to shove him off.)* Fuck off Jimmie!

JIMMIE: *(Still hanging on to him.)* That little piece really got your stones hard eh! *(Grabbing at him.)* Hey let's have a feel!

BILLY: Bastard! *(He manages to free himself and he and JIMMIE giggling like kids jockey for position each trying to grab the other's crotch.)*

JIM'S VOICE: *(Off)* . . . Now sic em! Sic emmm! ! ! !

Loud frustrated barks from dog.

SCENE THREE

Legion Club.

Two flats mask off the master set. The setting now is a service-men's Legion club, where dart boards, beer tables, flags and shields are situated about the room. In the background we hear the clink of glasses and the steady drone of conversation and laughter. Old time music is provided by an off stage accordion and saxophone.

At a table centre stage, completely filled with glasses of draught beer, sit JIMMIE and BILLY with SANDY and his lady friend SARAH, two old friends of Jim's. SANDY is also a wheezing old Scots in his early sixties, who loves drink, song and army life. Froth coats his mouth, and his face wears a permanent flush, from the many years of such a life. SARAH is round, middle aged and also Scots. She has been widowed from the First World War and is still bitter for her fate; that of having had to be a cleaning woman, to scrape together a living and raise her children. SANDY has escorted her for years, and the relationship has grown to be the same as that of an old married couple. While she tends to nag him, she knows her place; submissive respect, predominant among these women toward their men. An ugly hump protrudes from her back.
Seated at a table next to them is HATTIE, a vinegar faced and dirty old hag and her husband BARNIE, a seedy looking heap, in paint splattered overalls. They have one glass of beer before them and hungrily eye Jimmie's table. They are the kind who frequent a place like this, conning all the free beer they can get. Throughout

the scene they hang on every word at Jimmie's table, throwing in comments, laughing at all times with the group . . . and always working closer in an attempt to integrate.

JIMMIE, BILLY and SANDY have had a good deal to drink, so voices are loud, and spirits brave.

SANDY: *(Wagging a finger in BILLY's face.)* Yes sir, I've known Jimmie . . . well me and his father's been friends since . . . since I can remember! So . . . I've known Jimmie since he was a wee boy . . . A baby! Isn't that right Jimmie?

JIMMIE: *(Giving him a teasing punch.)* Ah hell Sandy, it must of been before that!

(A cackle from HATTIE and BARNIE.)

SANDY: *(Puff of laughter.)* Ah he's a kidder this boy . . . always been a kidder, yes sir. *(Laughs)*

JIMMIE: *(Amused)* Drink up Sandy drink up, we're gettin way ahead of you!

SANDY: Hell I been here all day! You . . . you could never catch up to me! *(Burst of silly giggling.)* Nobody can drink Sandy under the table!

SARAH: Aye, an ain't you the proud one.

SANDY: *(Moaning)* Awww, God almighty . . .

SARAH: Well where's the fun in just sittin drinking all the time?

JIMMIE: The little woman wants to dance Sandy!

BILLY: *(Mischievously)* How bout me Mam, how bout me? !

SARAH: *(Standing)* Aye, why not. Come on then son.

BILLY grabs her and clumsily begins to whirl her about, causing her to cry out good naturedly.

SANDY: Aww, he's a good bloke!

JIMMIE: But no friggin dancer I'll tell ya!

HATTIE: You should see my old man here, dance. Eh Honey?! *(BARNIE's head bobs in agreement.)*

As JIMMIE and SANDY laugh at the antics of BILLY, JIM appears leading another old VET by the arm.

JIM: *(Bursting with pride.)* Here he is! Aye Scotty, this here's wee Jimmie! Home on leave he is. You remember Scotty don't you Jim?!

HATTIE: *(Trying to get JIM's attention.)* Hey Mister . . . ? *(But no one pays her any attention.)*

JIMMIE: *(Standing and offering an unsteady but vigorous hand-shake.)* How are ya mate. Sure sure, you . . . now don't tell me. It was at the post office with dad here!

SCOTTY: *(Pleased)* Aye, that's right. Worked together with your dad for years.

JIMMIE: Sure, I never forget a face! Names . . . now that's a different matter. But I never forget a face!

JIM: That's one thing I'll say for the boy; never forgets a face.

HATTIE: An that's a fine looking boy you got there too!

JIMMIE: Never forget a good screw either.

Round of smutty laughter. HATTIE and BARNIE scream at this.

On the far end of the room BILLY begins to get playful, patting SARAH on the buttocks. She ignores it, but when he persists, she makes him release her and waddles indignantly back to the table.

SCOTTY: Have you been over yet Jimmie?

JIMMIE interprets this as a pointed question, and his gay clownish mood switches to sober hostility.

JIMMIE: That's a very interesting story . . .

JIM: *(Cutting in.)* He's asked for active duty a hundred times now. Haven't you son? They won't let him off.

JIMMIE: You know what that prick of a sarge tells me? "Dougal, you're the only guy who knows where the hell anything is in this place . . . " Sure!

JIM: *(Adding)* See, he's head of the stores, there at the base where he is.

BILLY and SARAH have taken their seats . . . She looks appealing to SANDY who hasn't noticed any of the carrying on. BILLY just sits with a pious smirk on his face.

JIMMIE: *(His anger growing, he bangs the table.)* That's what he said! Remember Billy, me telling you? !

BILLY: Jim's the boy. Don't matter what you want! Want a new duffel bag or a stinkin pair of shoe laces . . . Jimmie's the only guy who can get it for you!

HATTIE: You tell em soldier! *(BILLY grins back.)*

JIMMIE: *(The martyr.)* That's what I get for doing my job so well . . .

SCOTTY: *(Offering consolation.)* Every job counts. They'll give you your chance in time . . .

JIMMIE: *(Waving him off.)* Ohhhh no, that's not what you were gettin at . . . *(A hush falls over the group.)* Listen commere . . . *(His hostility growing.)* Commere commere! *(Pointing him out.)* You don't think it's important what I do, the crap I got to put up with huh? !

JIM: Scotty didn't mean anything like that Jimmie . . .

JIMMIE: *(Waving him off.)* No no let him speak for himself dad! . . .

HATTIE has now gotten up and stands right at their table, eager for the action.

You're so smart you tell me something then, you tell me; somebody needs a rifle and I don't give him one, what happens then, huh? What happens eh? !

SCOTTY: *(Lost)* I don't know . . . ?

JIMMIE: He's S.O.L. — that's what! !

BILLY bursts into snorts of laughter.

JIMMIE: Am I right Billy, am I right? ! You damn right I am! !

HATTIE: *(Cackling)* Jeeze that's a good one! This boy's got a head on his shoulders. *(To BILLY)* What's your name Honey?

BARNIE quickly moves over.

JIMMIE: *(Eager to pick a fight with anyone.)* Field-Marshal Montgomery . . .

HATTIE: *(Realizing she isn't going to make it with JIMMIE.)* Hah, you ain't no Field-Marshal Montgomery . . . anyway I was talkin to him.

JIM: *(To HATTIE and BARNIE.)* Come on come on you two...

BILLY: *(Grinning)* He was just pulling your leg. I'm Billy.

HATTIE: 'At's a nice name. Very nice. Mine's Mrs. Smith, but my friends call me Hattie. That's Barnie, my old man . . . *(BARNIE reaches across to shake hands and reaches for a glass of beer with the other)* . . . Betcha can't guess what he does for a living?

JIMMIE: *(Scoffing)* Nothing!

HATTIE: Who asked you?

JIMMIE: Piss off!

JIM: *(Intervening)* Listen, you two, what is it you want here?

BARNIE: Jiss trynna be friendly that's all.

JIMMIE: *(Losing his temper.)* Horse shit! You get your arse and your old lady's out of here!

BARNIE: It's a free country!

JIMMIE: *(Giving BARNIE a shove.)* We ain't feedin no pikers beer. Get the hell out of here!

JIM: You heard the boy, shove off!

HATTIE and BARNIE off stage cussing between themselves.

SANDY: Ah those two are always sponging. I don't know why the hell they let them in here. This is supposed to be a club for servicemen only!

JIM: Aye.

BILLY: *(Amused by the episode.)* I think they're goofy as hell. *(Giggles)*

BARNIE'S VOICE: *(Off)* That's the one there!

BARNIE and HATTIE return with a very husky young soldier. A small group follows behind and forms about the table.

BARNIE: *(To soldier.)* You know what he said? He called me a piker!

SOLDIER: *(To Jim.)* You say that?

BILLY: He didn't say nothing.

SOLDIER: You shut up, I ain't talking to you!

JIM: *(Not backing off.)* Go on get out of here, we don't want no trouble!

HATTIE: He said it Jock! I was right here!

BARNIE: Called me a piker! *(Thrusting his hand into his pocket and producing a few bills.)* I got money . . . see see! Yes sir, ain't nobody can call Barnie a piker!

SOLDIER: *(Thumping JIM on the chest.)* You better watch who you're calling names old man!

JIM: *(Pointing to JIMMIE.)* Listen, you want me to put the boy on you? !

JIMMIE goes white. The crowd begins to intervene.

VOICE ONE: Here Here!

VOICE TWO: Take your fight outside!

ANOTHER VOICE: We don't want it in here!

A chorus joins in.

SOLDIER: *(Challenging JIMMIE.)* Come on outside then! I'll
   take you anytime!

*A hush falls and all eyes are on JIMMIE, waiting to see if he will
meet the challenge . . . he sits frozen in fear.*

SOLDIER: Ahhh, you chicken livered . . . *(He takes a wild
   swipe at JIMMIE from across the table, sending several glasses
   crashing to the floor.)*

*The crowd quickly steps in, repeating "No fighting in here":
"Break it up", etc. JOCK is led off as some sort of hero with a
chorus of comments such as "That a boy Jock" "Guy must be
yellow" "Good boy Jock", etc.*

*JIM is unable to hide his shame and disappointment as he just
looks to JIMMIE. JIMMIE trying to cover, attempts to pick up a
glass of beer but is trembling so much he can't.*

JIMMIE: *(His lips quivering.)* The bastard . . . let's get the hell
   out of here!

Curtain

269

SCENE FOUR

The house, later that night.

The living and dining room are dark. A beam of light spills across the set, from the kitchen where we hear the muffled conversation of the men. MARY comes from the kitchen, in her robe and slippers.

MARY: *(Weary)* Good night then . . .

JIMMIE appears from the kitchen carrying a bottle of beer. He is very drunk now, and can hardly steady himself. He feigns a false cheerfulness.

JIMMIE: Going to bed Ma?

MARY: Aye, I'm a bit weary . . .

He puts his arm around her, walking her to the stairway.

JIMMIE: How hell are ya Ma? How's going kid?

MARY: Seem to be having a lot of back aches lately Jimmie...

JIMMIE: Ahh, you're the hardest little worker in the world, ya know that.

MARY: I guess me age is catching up with me though.

JIMMIE: *(Patting her on the back.)* You never looked better . . . take it from me.

MARY: Ohh, you always was a flatterer.

JIMMIE: You got good ole Jimmie's word. An if I say it, then it's God's truth . . . *(His head bobbing in agreement with himself.)* . . . yes sir.

MARY: Don't be drinkin too much tonight eh son . . . ?

JIMMIE: *(Tilting up the bottle.)* Last one — right here.

MARY: Alright then. I'll see you in the morning. I won't wake you early; let you sleep in good and late. *(Kisses him on the cheek.)*

JIMMIE: *(With a wave.)* Keep smiling . . . keep smiling kid.

MARY disappears into the darkness of the stairs and into one of the rooms. JIMMIE, unable to stand anymore, flops down on the chesterfield, and sits alone in the darkness, feeling sorry for himself. He mutters inaudibly. JIM and SANDY wander in from the kitchen.

JIM: What you sitting in here all alone for lad?

SANDY switches on a light, and BILLY staggers in plopping a case of beer in the centre of the floor.

BILLY: Ahhh, forget it Jim! *(He plops down in a chair. JIMMIE glares at him.)*

SANDY: *(Trying to cheer JIMMIE.)* Suuuuure. I've always said it, and I'll say it again, "Ain't nothing worth gettin in a fight over."

JIMMIE: *(Growling)* Then shut your God damn mouth.

SANDY: Now hold on Jimmie, hold on. It's old Sandy your friend. I didn't mean nothing by it.

JIM: Aye son, that's no way to talk.

JIMMIE: Awww, the stupid ole bugger's been going on about it all night!

JIMMIE struggles to stand up. It is not a vicious or loud threat, but merely a drunken threat.

JIMMIE: *(To SANDY.)* You wanna fight me? You wanna fight me huh? ! Come on then, come on . . . *(Puts his fists up.)*

SANDY: *(Wounded)* Jimmie boy . . .

JIMMIE: Put up or shut up! Just shut up hear? ! *(Kicking the case of beer.)* Go-waan, take your bloody beer with you!

JIM takes hold of JIMMIE before he falls down.

JIM: Now come on son, come on, sit down!

JIMMIE attempting to wave his father off, keels over onto the chesterfield.

JIMMIE: I'm alright, I'm alright . . . Listen listen . . . you wanna know something? You wanna know why I didn't kick the crap out of that guy dad? Ca . . . cause that's all it would mean . . . that's all! Woulda been the end of it! I come home on leave . . . to see you an mom . . . an they throw me in the jug. That what you want? Huh? !

JIM: I know I know son. *(Taking him by the arm.)* Come on, you better go up to bed. You've had too much to drink. Give me a hand Billy.

JIMMIE: *(Whimpering with self pity.)* I'm okay . . . I'm okay . . . *(He struggles to his feet.)* I'm sorry . . . *(Backing off and up the stairs.)* . . . soooorry . . .

JIMMIE stumbles off up the stairs. SANDY slowly rises, a hurt man.

JIM: *(Following SANDY to the door.)* Sandy you're no leavin... Listen I know that boy. He's just had too much to drink. He'd never say those kind of things if he was sober . . .
But SANDY is the wounded man and drunkenly fumbles for the door-knob.

SANDY: *(Wagging his head.)* I know I know . . . Jim you and me's always been friends — right?

JIM: . . . Right.

SANDY: Friends?

JIM: Friends . . .

They shake hands vigorously.

SANDY: Best friend I ever had!

He weaves out the door and into the darkness. JIM closes the door, and drifts back into the room — a sorry man.

JIM: *(Half to himself.)* Never seen the boy act like that before. He's a good boy. You're his friend Billy . . . you never seen him act like that before did you?

BILLY: Good head Jimmie . . . good head.

JIM: *(Reassured)* Sure. God I ought to know, he's my own son! . . . Ah, I think I've had enough myself. I'd better go up and make sure he's okay . . .

JIM heads for the stairs slowly. BILLY stays in his chair facing the front doorway. He gives the old man a wave.

BILLY: Okay, night Pop. Don't worry bout him . . . Jimmie's a hundred per cent . . . hundred per cent.

JIM nods with gratitude, starts up the stairs. BILLY gives a big yawn, looks at his watch, and settles himself more comfortably in the chair. His eyes fix on the front door . . . waiting.

BLACKOUT:

Lights come up on BILLY still in the chair, his shoes and jacket now off and tie loosened. He is on the verge of dozing, when the laughter of JEANIE and DOLLIE can be heard outside. He comes to, quickly.

The door opens and they enter, flopping about in fits of laughter. JEANIE suddenly realizes where they are, waves DOLLIE to kill it. They continue in muffled giggles . . .

A silly smile comes over BILLY's face, as he watches their antics. They come in and flop down beside his chair, and between fits of hysterical laughter, relate their story of the evening, as though they were sharing it with an old friend.

DOLLIE: Ohhhh, you should have seen these two goons that followed us home! Eh Duke? !

JEANIE: Yeah!

DOLLIE: Boy did they like you!

JEANIE: *(Shrieking)* Me? ? ! You ya mean! !

They nearly collapse laughing. BILLY half joins them, but doesn't follow the conversation at all.

DOLLIE: If you could have seen their faces!

JEANIE: Real jerks!

DOLLIE: Ever see Mutt and Jeff in person? !

More laughter.

BILLY: This a couple of guys you met?

DOLLIE: Met! We did everything we could not to meet them! They wouldn't leave us alone. Everywhere we went . . . they were sure to go . . . wagging their tails behind them!

JEANIE: *(Snorts of laughter.)*

DOLLIE: An herrrrr, "please ta meetcha!". Honestly Duke!

JEANIE: Well they paid for our coffee and stuff didn't they! Sides I can't be like you. You should see her Billy. She tells the guy to . . . well I can't say, but boyyyyy!

BILLY: *(Eager)* What'd she say?

DOLLIE: *(Daring her)* Go ahead . . . tell him.

JEANIE: Oh no, not me!

DOLLIE: What'd I tell you about starting things you can't finish? *(Teasing BILLY.)* Anyway I told him . . .

She stops, she and JEANIE bursting into another fit of giggling, BILLY scowls, becoming impatient with them.

BILLY: Well common. What'd ya say?

274

DOLLIE: *(Playing with him.)* You shouldn't be so curious . . . it killed the cat . . .

BILLY *waits with a blank look on his face.*

DOLLIE: . . . You know what I mean?

BILLY: *(Annoyed)* Well what's so funny about that?

DOLLIE: Ooooooo-kay then . . . *(She takes a long teasing pause and speaks in suggestive tones.)* . . . What's something . . . you got . . . that I haven't?

BILLY: *(A silly grin lighting his face.)* Well let's see . . . that's an open question . . .

DOLLIE: *(Before he can give an answer.)* Bad breath!

BILLY: *(Feeling foolish.)* Hah! Real funny.

The girls go through another session of giggling.

DOLLIE: Awww, it's just a joke you play on fellows. Don't be a sore head.

BILLY: *(No humour.)* Ummm. You want a beer?

DOLLIE: *(Making a face.)* Beer — yuk!

BILLY: *(To JEANIE.)* How about you?

JEANIE: *(Wishing she could please him.)* Gee I . . . I can't.

It is DOLLIE who interests BILLY, by being coy and putting him down. JEANIE is unable to compete, not having Dollie's looks or drive. She is soon a forgotten party as BILLY and DOLLIE engage in their childish game.

DOLLIE: *(Challenging)* I used to know a guy who could take a bottle down without stopping . . .

BILLY: Hell that's easy! Watch this.

He tilts the bottle and drains it. While it has not gone down too easy, he manages to conceal his discomfort and smirks back at her defiantly.

DOLLIE: *(Poking him playfully in the stomach.)* He was an idiot too! *(Laughter)* Boy if I hit you in the gut now — bam, beer all over the place! . . . *(She gives a teasing laugh.)*

BILLY: . . . go ahead.

DOLLIE: Are you kidding?

BILLY: Gwan, hit it . . .

DOLLIE: *(Drawing back her fist, teasing.)* . . . Ooo-kay . . . *(She holds.)*

BILLY: *(Tensing)* Come on . . .

She suddenly unleashes, hitting him hard in the stomach. He flushes having obviously felt pain, but forces a leering grin back.

BILLY: See, you can't hurt me.

DOLLIE: *(Wringing her hand.)* Jeeze, I hurt my knuckle on one of those buttons!

BILLY: Hurt yourself instead huh? ! Hell you'll be okay. *(Fumbles with her hand awkwardly, then lets go.)*

DOLLIE: I've got to put some cold water on it . . .

She moves off into the dark kitchen, dragging JEANIE with her. BILLY quickly rises, checking for any sounds from upstairs. We hear the running of the tap and a muffled argument between the girls.

DOLLIE: *(Off)* Go-wan, I said.

JEANIE: Boyyyy . . .

JEANIE comes out, stands looking at him embarrassed.

JEANIE: *(Shrugs)* . . . She wants you to go in there.

276

BILLY *gets up and quickly goes in. There is a long silence, then giggling and muffled sounds from the kitchen. JEANIE lost for something to do, sighs to herself and begins to make up the chesterfield into a bed.*

JEANIE: *(Giving a feeble warning.)* I'm still here you know Dollie . . . *(No answer.)* An I'm sleeping down here tonight . . . soooo.

Silence is her only answer. She shrugs, plops the pillow down on the sloppily made bed, and goes up the stairs and into the bathroom. There is a long silence with occasional sounds of heavy breathing . . . then . . .

DOLLIE'S VOICE: *(Off)* Okay okay sonny.

BILLY'S VOICE: *(Off)* What's wrong . . . ?

DOLLIE'S VOICE: *(Off)* I-said-quit-it!

Sounds of a struggle.

BILLY'S VOICE: *(Off)* Shit! !

DOLLIE *suddenly plunges out of the darkness of the kitchen, her hair all tossed.*

DOLLIE: *(Grabbing her coat.)* I'm getting out of here, you're nuts!

BILLY: *(Following)* God damn cock teaser!

DOLLIE: Get you!

BILLY *starts to cross, now enraged.*

DOLLIE: *(Stopping him cold.)* I'll yell so loud, this whole house'll be awake in one second! *(She scurries out the front door.)*

BILLY *stands there cursing under his breath, wanting to go after* her, afraid the commotion may have already awakened those upstairs.

JEANIE comes out of the bathroom, in a nightie and an old robe thrown about her. She stops surprised when she sees him standing there alone, then continues down the stairs. She tosses her bundle of clothes on one of the chairs saying nothing as BILLY watches her every move.

BILLY: (Feeling he must say something.) . . . Your friend went home.

JEANIE: (Shrugs) I didn't know whether you wanted to go in there or not. She made me ask you. She has to always get her way . . .

BILLY: (Lamely) Nothing happened you know . . . hell just kidding around a bit. (Notices the chesterfield made into a bed.) You sleeping down here?

JEANIE: Mom and dad got my room. You an Jimmie are sleeping in theirs.

BILLY's eyes go to the quietness upstairs, then back to her. Awkwardly he begins to fumble with little pieces of business, stalling for time.

BILLY: Yeah . . . it's gettin late. Guess everybody's asleep up there . . . huh?

JEANIE: (Not sensing anything.) Guess so . . . Hey don't tell em what time I came home eh?

BILLY: Naw . . .

As BILLY moves about, he comes to her heap of clothing on the chair. His eyes fall upon her exposed undergarments; the brassiere, panties. He studies her.

BILLY: That . . . that Dollie, ah, she ain't much you know. Hell you're prettier than . . . she is even.

JEANIE: Are you kidding? All the fellows go after her.

BILLY: You . . . you got great long red hair . . . *(Awkwardly moves closer to her.)* . . . all ya gotta do, is fix it different. I mean more grown up.

His eyes keep darting to the rooms upstairs, then back to her. She just stands listening.

BILLY: You know? Curl it up like women do.

He gives a final heavy sigh, then awkwardly gives her a quick rough kiss. It has caught her completely by surprise, and she doesn't respond in any way.

BILLY: *(Releasing her.)* Well, you . . . go to bed then an' I'll turn off the lights on my way up . . .

He stands there watching as she obeys, taking off her robe and slipping into bed. He tip-toes across to the light switch and the lights go out. There is a short silence and we hear only his heavy breathing.

BILLY'S VOICE: Well . . . goodnight then.

JEANIE'S VOICE: Night Billy . . .

We see his silhouette cross back to the foot of the chesterfield.

BILLY: *(Clearing his throat.)* You don't really want me to go up, do you?

JEANIE'S VOICE: What do you mean . . . ?

BILLY'S VOICE: . . . You know.

No answer. We see his form go to the chesterfield and sit on the edge.

BILLY'S VOICE: . . . Huh?

We see his form disappear into the darkness of the chesterfield and hear a startled noise from Jeanie.

JEANIE'S VOICE: What . . . what are you doing?

BILLY'S VOICE: *(Angry)* Don't play dumb now you!

We hear the sounds of someone getting up from one of the beds upstairs. Quietness.

JEANIE'S VOICE: Please don't Billy . . .

From the darkness upstairs, we hear JIMMIE puking in his room.

JEANIE'S VOICE: *(Whimpering)* No please don't do that . . .

BILLY'S VOICE: *(Snarling)* You make one more god damn sound, and I'll smash your head to a pulp! !

End of Act One Curtain

ACT TWO

Three months later . . .

It is the evening of a cold November day. When the curtain rises JIM wanders about the living room in a state of confusion.

JIM: Tip? . . . Tip what time is it?

MARY: *(Off)* You've plenty of time. It's only six thirty Jim.

JIM: Fussin' with a lot of fancy duds that's all. Well it's not for me I'll tell ya!

MARY enters from the kitchen carrying a freshly pressed pair of men's trousers. She hurries along to the stairs.

MARY: I know, I know. There's your pants. Mind not to get 'em creased now.

JIM: Alright, woman, alright!

JIM goes upstairs as JEANIE enters, shivering and bundled in a heavy winter coat.

MARY: *(Coming down the stairs.)* Do you have any idea of the time, girl?

JEANIE: *(Shrugs)* Around six ain't it?

MARY: I mean your supper. I bin keepin it warm three quarters of an hour now!

JEANIE: I can't help it, there were no buses. I ain't hungry anyway.

MARY: Nonsense, a body can't live without food. Everything's on the stove. I haven't much time.

JIM: *(Off)* Tip! Where the devil are my medals? ?

MARY: *(Sighing)* Your father's fit to be tied tonight.

JIM: You didn't leave 'em on the blazer when you sent it for cleaning, did you?

MARY: They're in where they should be! With your cuff links in the top drawer!

Pause

JIM: So they are, so they are . . . confound it, they could get marked up just lying about like this you know!

MARY: *(Exasperated)* Listen to him. Did you ever hear so much complaining from one man? Been a bundle of nerves all afternoon. Pretends not to be the least bit interested in the presentation. To hear him tell it, he's doing them a big favour just by showing up tonight.

JEANIE: *(Distant)* What presentation?

MARY: Now I told you about it. Sometimes I don't think you hear a word I say! The Legion get-together tonight. Your Dad's going to be honoured by his squad.

JEANIE: . . . Oh that . . .

MARY: What do you mean, "oh that"? It's a real fine thing that they're doin! *(To herself.)* I hope it cheers him some. He's been so with the moods since Jimmie was here in the summer . . . *(Afterthought)* . . . so strange, them just up and leavin like that the next mornin . . . not even a good-bye . . . it's all the drinking they do . . . *(Seeing JEANIE staring off.)* . . . what's wrong with you?

JEANIE: *(Over-reaction.)* Nothing . . .

JIM has started down the stairs. He moves with a certain care, as though he may soil the fresh blazer he wears.

JIM: Well . . . how do I look?

MARY: Very becoming Jim.

JIM: Aye they must have shrunk me blazer a bit at the cleaners . . . tight fit. Darn thing's always catching lint too.

MARY: Did you prepare a thank you speech Jim?

JIM: I said it before, I'll not be making any fancy speeches. I'll say thank you an that's all.

MARY: Jim you must say something.

JIM: Aw now look here, did I ask 'em to give me any blinkin award? Did I now?

MARY: I hope not.

JIM: It wouldn't be me if I said anything else! My boys know me as a man of simple tastes and one who expresses himself the same way.

MARY: It seems a shame.

JIM: Aye, well that's the way it's gonna be. Did you get the job girl?

JEANIE: *(Quietly)* . . . No.

MARY: You didn't? But I'm sure Grace said they needed help bad. You didn't tell them about your last job, did you?

JEANIE: They talked with me, then said there were no positions open.

MARY: What a pity. You might've been able to get a little extra sugar too. Grace always does . . . Maybe you could get on doing the offices with me.

JEANIE: I'm not doing cleaning!

MARY: I'd rather you had a nice job in a shop too, but . . .

JEANIE: I won't do it!

JIM: You'll bloody well do what your mother tells you! Going to that blinking high school for two years taking up typing and everything an what the hell good did it do you? Got the sack first week you had a job. And that was a good job in an office an everything!

JEANIE: Yes sir.

MARY: I'll talk to Mr. Rogers an see if I can get you on a couple nights a week with me, till you can find a good job, eh! *(Knock on door.)* . . . That must be Sarah. Come in.

SARAH enters laden down with pastry tins and packaged food.

SARAH: Just me it is!

MARY: Here, let me give you a hand dear. Oh my goodness, what have you got in all these things?

SARAH: I made up three dozen cookies this aft and the rest is mostly sandwiches for the darts tournament. Hullo Jim, Jeanie!

JEANIE: Mrs. McIver.

JIM: Well I dare say it looks like we'll have us quite a feed tonight. I'm just going up to get my coat, Sandy should be here any minute.

He exits upstairs.

MARY: Isn't that a new coat you're wearing Sarah? I don't think I've seen it before.

SARAH: Aye, got it the Eagle's rummage sale last week, so it isn't really new.

MARY: Near new though. Oh that was lucky, finding something that nice.

SARAH: Found me three nice dresses too.

MARY: Tch! Oh I do wish I'd been able to peek in. Isn't it lovely Jeanie?

JEANIE: Uh huh.

MARY: I'd love to see the dresses! I'll just fetch me salad and cake and we'll be off then.

Exits to kitchen.

SARAH: How have you been Jeanie?

JEANIE: Okay I guess.

SARAH: And how's school?

JEANIE: *(Making a noise with pursed lips.)* Quit!

SARAH: Oh I didn't know that.

JEANIE: Dad says "what do I need an education for anyways . . . girls only end up getting married and then it's all a waste". I didn't like it anyway . . .

SARAH: Oh learnin's a good thing. Though I think it's most important a girl should learn the makin of a good home . . . *(Sound of car horn off. SARAH goes to the front door window.)* . . . that must be Sandy now! Aye it's him. He's here — Jim, Mary!

She quickly gathers her belongings as JIM comes down the stairs with his heavy army winter coat and hat.

JIM: Here, is he? Tip . . . !

SARAH: *(Starting out the front door.)* Well, bye bye Jeanie.

JIM: And no running around now, hear? I don't want you hanging around that dance hall on 13th street! Come on, Tip!

MARY: *(Rushing through)* I'll be but a second! *(She fumbles about putting on her heavy coat, powdering her nose and a last look in the dresser mirror.)*

JIM: *(Off)* She can't go nowhere without a tea and a pee . . . Tip! ! !

MARY: Alright alright. Bye bye Jeanie. Mind what your father said and clean up for me now. An see if you can find some scraps for the dog.

She exits on the run. JEANIE pushes her food aside and begins wandering aimlessly about the house, lost in thought. She cranks the gramophone and puts on a record, The White Cliffs of Dover by Gracie Fields. Going past the mirror, she hesitates to study herself. Slowly she runs her hand across her abdomen. The front door flies open, causing her to jump with a start. DOLLIE enters.

DOLLIE: God what a time I had getting out tonight! You'd think I was some little kid! Nobody home is there?

JEANIE: *(Still nervous)* Th . . . they just left.

DOLLIE: *(Flopping down on the sofa.)* "Stay away from the goddam soldiers" he says. The only guy I know who isn't a soldier is him! Oh, I just love that song . . . My mother nearly cries every time she hears it. *(Suddenly up and wandering into the dining room.)* Hey, got anything to eat? I'm starving! *(Picks at Jeanie's plate.)* If my mother serves potatoes again tomorrow, I'll vomit! Get the job?

JEANIE: Naww, they wanted someone older.

DOLLIE: No loss. I wouldn't want a job like that. "Yes Mam", "No Mam", "What's it gonna be today Mam?", "Oh thank you Mam" *(Making a face.)* Ouuuuck! And you'd have to dress up all the time.

JEANIE: I know. I didn't want the darn thing anyway. I don't like addin' up money and everything . . . just don't like doin' it, that's all.

DOLLIE produces a package of cigarettes and offers one to JEANIE. Throughout the rest of the scene they go through a series of smoking gymnastics.

DOLLIE: My father says if I don't get a job soon, he's kicking me out — yuk yuk! 'Sides he hasn't got any room to talk. Every time I see the old fart, he's just sitting there with a gut full of beer! Aw, I'll go back to the cannery in the spring. Have to get some money somewhere if I want to go to the coast to see my sister.

She wanders about.

JEANIE: *(Enviously)* You really going to Vancouver Dollie?

DOLLIE: *(From kitchen)* Maybe. I don't know. If I can get some money somewhere. Bus is about eighty bucks return. Won't cost me nothing to stay there though. My brother-in-law told me to come and see them anytime. Jeeze you ought to see him too Jeanie! Is he ever cute! And he got a real terrific job in one of the defence plants. He treats me real swell, which bugs my sister.

JEANIE: Is he the one who . . . ?

DOLLIE: . . . Yeah.

JEANIE: You shouldn't go there then Dollie.

DOLLIE: *(Mocking)* Oh jeeze Dougal, when you gonna learn that all guys want that! You just gotta make up your mind who you're givin and who you're not. *(Snickers)* Anyway he gave me ten dollars not to tell my sister. *(Challenging)* Why don't you try it some time? It won't kill ya.

JEANIE: No thanks.

DOLLIE: *(Exasperated)* Ohhh! That's your trouble, ya never

try nothin! After the first time — pffffttt! . . . But you'll never know 'cause you're gutless!

JEANIE: I am not!

DOLLIE: Oh yes you are! You got a yellow streak right up the middle of your back!

JEANIE: Well if you're so smart, I could tell you something too!

DOLLIE: *(Sarcastic)* What? !

JEANIE is sorry she said anything . . . remains silent.

DOLLIE: *(Badgering her.)* What — come on — what? I'm waiting!

Jeanie's lip begins to quiver.

DOLLIE: What, I said? What? What? What? See, you're yellow!

JEANIE bursts into tears and runs up the stairs into her room. DOLLIE gives an exasperated sigh, calling up after her.

DOLLIE: Oh come on Dougal I was only kidding! *(Waits)* What a creep! *(Realizes JEANIE is not coming back.)* Aww come on Dougal, I got a whole pack of cigarettes tonight an everything . . . *(Angry)* Well I'm going then! *(She starts from the door.)* You coming? ? *(Waits)* I'm leaving! *(Exiting)* Creep!

Curtain

SCENE TWO

The Dougal home later that night. JEANIE sits in a faded housecoat, curling her hair at the dining-room table. The sounds of approaching voices and laughter grow louder with the singing of "I've Got Sixpence". The front door opens and MARY and

*SARAH enter, followed by JIM and SANDY, who, very intox-
icated, struggle to support one another. SANDY is in the same age
group as JIM with the same red face from too much drinking during his life and a heavy wheeze at all times. The two of them take
a stance in the doorway and put the finishing touches to the last
chorus.*

JIM and SANDY:
    I've got no pence . . .
    Jolly Jolly no pence . . .
    I've got no pence . . . to send home to my wife!
    I've got no pence to spendddd . . .
    And no pence to lendddddd . . .
    And no pence to send home to my wife!
    Pooooor wife!

*SANDY and JIM applaud themselves with laughter, while MARY
and SARAH pretend to be annoyed but are delighted by every
second of it.*

MARY: Come in now and close the door, before we all freeze
    to death! *(To JEANIE)* Did you ever hear the likes of it? All
    the way home they've been carrying on like that!

SARAH: *(To JIM and SANDY)* A pair of fools; that's all ya are.

MARY: I thought for sure we'd be arrested.

JIM: *(Very drunk)* Hah! Ne . . . Need more an the bloomin
    police force to take a couple of infantry men . . . Eh
    Sandy? !

SANDY: At's for sure — I'll tell you!

SARAH: Sandy ya no have to shout like that!

SANDY: *(Wagging his finger.)* I mean if a man can't sing a bit
    . . . when he's happy, what is there? Nothing — that's
    what! Nothing! !

SARAH: You're disgustin.

JIM: *(His head bobbing in agreement.)* Ayeeeee. An if it weren't fer a few chaps like us . . . there wouldn't be no Canada! Right? ?

SANDY: Right! You said it Jim boy. You said it.

MARY: *(To JEANIE.)* Tonight they won the whole war an are gonna make short work of this one.

JIM: *(Drunken anger.)* Listen here, lookin after them bloody Jerries in a camp, is just as important as any other job in this war — Hear!

MARY: *(Trying to calm him.)* I no meant anything by it Jim . . .

JIM: *(Raving on)* An you show me anyone what says different an I'll show you a son-of-a-bitchin liar! Aye an just show me one of em blinkin police what could do the job we do! It's something for them to keep an eye on just a couple of prisoners! Sandy and me is been trained to guard a whole camp with thousands in it. Every one of em a hundred times dangerouser an somebody who broke into a shop or somethin!

SANDY: Aye, an people ought to be more aware of it!

JIM: It's us what looks out fer the bloody police an every one else in this country, when it comes down to it!

SANDY: *(Clapping)* I could no said it better myself! *(Sees JEANIE for the first time.)* Ahhhhh, there she is. By golly if she doesn't get prettier everytime I see her! Have ya got a kiss for ole Sandy lass?

SARAH: Sandy you behave yourself.

(JIM joins SANDY's loud laughter at JEANIE's embarrassment.)

SANDY: Ahh, I guess I'm not the handsome beggar I use to be! If I was a few years younger I could give some lad a run for his money, eh Jim!

JIM: *(Knowing laugh.)* Aye . . . that you could, that you could! Mother you got a few ales in the fridge for me an Sandy?

JIM starts off in the direction of the kitchen. MARY on his heels.

MARY: Oh Jim, now I don't think you should be having any more . . . Have some tea instead, why not . . . ?

SANDY holds his gaze on JEANIE, a silly smile on his face. While she is frightened a little, she is enjoying his attention.

SANDY: You know it's true Jeanie. I was a real terror in France . . . *(Laughing)* Aye, old Sandy here, if you'll believe it!

JEANIE: Were you?

SANDY: Them French women just wouldn't leave me alone! An them women are really something let me tell you!

SARAH: Tch, Sandy . . .

SANDY: You just ask your Dad, he'll tell you! *(Begins to move closer to JEANIE.)* Yes Sir . . . ole sad eyes Sandy they use to call me . . . cause that's what the women use to like — my sad eyes!

SANDY begins to sing in a very shaky voice.

SANDY: I — I — I dream of Jeanie with the light brown hairrrr . . . La da da da — daaaa Da da da daaaa . . .

He gives her a little pat on the shoulder, then lets his arm rest there. SARAH comes over.

SANDY: You don't mind ole Sandy singing a wee bit do you?

JEANIE: *(Awkwardly)* No . . .

SARAH: You'll not be winning any awards for singing Sandy. Now sit down.

SARAH gently takes SANDY's arm trying to guide him away, but he does not budge.

SANDY: It's not awards I'd be wanting if I had a daughter lovely as Jeanie here . . .

SARAH: Don't be making a fool of yourself.

SANDY: *(Maudlin)* Aye, that's what I am an I know it. A fool I never married and had a family of my own. A little girl . . .

SARAH: . . . good grief.

SANDY: *(To JEANIE)* You don't know how lonely it can be by yourself all the time. When you're young you manage, but who cares about me now eh? No one . . . Aye when you're old . . . *(His arm falls about her waist now.)* Ahhh, do you no remember when you were a little one lass, and you use to sit on my lap and cuddle up to ole Sandy? Eh? You were always giving me kisses then . . . *(Whispering)* Just a wee one eh . . . ?

SARAH: *(Embarrassed)* Sandy, leave Jeanie be!

SARAH pulls at him. SANDY suddenly reels about on her snarling.

SANDY: Who the hell you think you're pushin? ! Keep your bloody hands to yourself!

JIM enters from kitchen, his arms filled with bottles of open beer.

JIM: Hi Sandy, the ship'll not run dry tonight!

SANDY: Glory be! Here let me give you a hand, man!

He goes quickly to JIM and they divide the load, laughing and nearly falling over one another.

SARAH: You're not going to be drinking more are you?

MARY: Jim please . . . I wish you wouldn't.

JIM: Listen, since when the hell can't I have a few quiet drinks with a friend in my own home? !

SANDY: Sh-h-h-h Jim. Don't be yelling in front of wee Jeanie. She's just a young lass.

MARY: You'll have regrets tomorrow.

JIM: Come on boy, we'll go down the cellar, so's we don't disturb certain folks.

They exit through the doorway beneath the stairs, going to the cellar.

SANDY: Ahhh, you're a lucky man Jimmie Dougal; your own house, fine wife and a lovely beautiful daughter . . .

SARAH: *(With a sigh)* Ah, it always ends up with too much drinking. I like a pint or two myself, now or then but . . .

MARY: It's men's ways Sarah. I just made us a pot of tea and we can sit down and have a nice chat of our own without them. It'll just take me a minute to get it. Jeanie, will you put some cups love. I've scads of things to tell *(Going into kitchen)* you Sarah! You'll not guess who's getting married? Joe and Mollie's girl, and that little bit of nothing no more than nineteen!

SARAH: Aye they seem to grow up a lot faster these days. I guess the war's got to do with it . . .

SARAH's eyes follow JEANIE as she sets some places at the table. The old woman feels a certain resentment because of SANDY's flirtation with the girl. We hear a burst of laughter from SANDY and JIM in the cellar as they break into song in the background.

JEANIE: *(Giggles)* Gee they're funny when they drink. Specially Sandy and everything he said. Listen to them!

SARAH: Aye they can never seem to hold their tongues when they've got the drink in 'em. You mustn't pay him too much attention when he gets like that. Old men like flattering young girls with a lot of sweet talk, but it don't mean anything with 'em.

JEANIE: Mom always tells Dad the same thing — and she's never wrong. Tomorrow he'll wish he hadn't.

MARY: Here we are. Oh you should have seen it all Jeanie, it was so nice. I dare say I was so touched by it, I nearly came to tears two or three times. All the clapping and cheers — well I knew your Dad was liked, but I nay knew that much. Did you see the lovely plaque they gave him?

JEANIE: Oouu, that's nice! Is it gold?

MARY: Well the plate part with the writing on is, I guess. Wouldn't it Sarah?

SARAH: Oh yes they always make them out of gold.

MARY: An when he got up and made his thank you speech, he made 'em laugh, didn't he Sarah?

SARAH: Aye.

MARY: I don't mind saying Isabel Mckay looked a bit green with it all.

SARAH: Oh she was that all right. Seen her and the Sergeant Major going home early, saying she had her bad headache.

MARY: Aye, well she'd best not try her bossiness with me anymore. And your Dad and Sandy won the doubles too! Although the Calgary group tallied more points for the evening. Your Dad says it was luck, that's all.

JEANIE: Did they give anything away?

MARY: Aye, Elsie won the door prize. It was a nice lamp too. *(Sitting heavily)* Ohhh that feels good. Nothing like a wee cup of tea when you want relaxation. I thought sure my poor legs were going to give out on me tonight.

SARAH: I'm a bit weary myself, Mary.

MARY: It's the veins. I should go to the doctor, but I know he'll want me to go into the hospital . . . and it would cost so much money.

A loud burst of laughter from the cellar.

SARAH: It's not right you know . . .

MARY: Oh Sarah, let them be. I suppose they've got good reasons for celebrating tonight.

SARAH: If Harry were alive he'd not be down there. He was a gentleman, Mary, that he was . . . a gentleman. God bless him.

MARY: He was a fine man. It's been hard for you living alone these years, eh Sarah?

SARAH is almost on the verge of tears as she goes on in choking tones.

SARAH: It was no' as bad when my daughter Betty was with me. But she has her own family now. Aye there've been times when it's been so lonely . . . *(Blows her nose)* . . . A body has to manage the best it can though.

MARY: Have you no ever thought . . . Jeanie not so much cake, you'll be a mess of pimples in the morning. You know that! *(Back to SARAH)* Have you no ever thought of wedding again Sarah?

SARAH: *(Laughing)* Ach, and who'd want the likes of me? A few years ago when I was younger, I thought about it, but I couldn't find eyes for any other man. And I was busier then, doing more things . . . If you were meaning him downstairs there — not on your life. The only thing that man wants, is someone looking and cleaning up after him. Aye a housekeeper!

MARY: I spect he is a bit difficult.

SARAH: Oh he can be sweet enough when he wants inviting to dinner or something. Aye it will have to be a patient woman who'll put up with Sandy Travers.

MARY: Let me fill you again . . .

SARAH: No thank ye Mary. I best get on my way if I'm going to catch the last bus.

MARY: You're not going home on the bus are you? Get Sandy to drive you.

SARAH: He'll not be in any condition for driving a car. Besides, once he's started drinking and singing, he's settled in for the night. I don't feel like waiting about for hours. *(Rising)* I'll just get my purse an coat.

MARY: Sarah, it's a bitter night. If you won't call him, I will. *(Going to doorway to basement.)* Sandy! Sarah's leaving now!

Continued laughter and song is their answer.

SANDY and JIM:
I don't care — what the hell ya say!
I don't give a damn — any any — way!

She closes the door, muffling their song to the background again.

MARY: Take yourself another sweater then. Jeanie fetch it.

SARAH: No no Mary I'm fine. Don't go fussin.

MARY: You'll catch your death of cold standing there on the corner waiting for that bus. You bundle up!

SARAH: My coat's fine . . .

MARY: *(Helping her on with clothes.)* It's damp out tonight. Just slip it on now. Don't be telling me. I ride them buses enough to know the heating's no good in em!

SARAH: It's not too bad if you get a seat away from the doors. Bye bye Jeanie, take care of yourself.

MARY: I'll be calling you Sarah . . .

SARAH: Aye. Will you be going to the church for Bingo on Wednesday?

MARY: Aye.

SARAH: Bye bye then.

MARY goes out on the veranda with SARAH. We hear them call their "goodbyes". The laughter and singing of JIM and SANDY rises, then fades off again. MARY comes back shivering, and closing the door peers out into the darkness, through the window.

MARY: It's turned even colder. I do hope she'll not have a long wait . . .

JEANIE: Why does Mrs. McIver walk all bent over like that?

MARY: *(Distant)* Ah, she had a bad fall when she was young . . . Her husband was very drunk . . . and beat her up. She no remembers it though . . . *(Aware)*

And those aren't things for your ears young lady. Ahh me, I'll just clear the dishes and turn in. You sure aren't much help to your old mother. Didn't I ask you to clear up for me when I was leaving . . . ? Turn out the parlour lights and get yourself to bed now.

MARY moves tiredly through her task of clearing the table and taking the dishes into the kitchen. Always in the background the sudden bursts of laughter and song; then quiet again. JEANIE starts to turn out the lamps, when she catches her form in the dresser mirror. She studies herself for a long time, then gently brings her hand to her abdomen and touches it. The kitchen light goes out and MARY comes through the darkness of the dining-room and upon JEANIE. She watches the girl's ritual.

MARY: What are you doing? . . .

JEANIE startled, swings about. There is a long pause; the girl's eyes cast to the floor.

MARY: Jeanie . . . ?

JEANIE: *(Mumbling)* . . . nothing.

MARY: Why were you looking at yourself like that?

JEANIE does not look at her, just shakes her head.

MARY: Is something . . . wrong?

JEANIE: *(Afraid)* You won't tell Dad?

MARY: *(Frightened)* Tell him what?

JEANIE: I think I'm in trouble . . .

MARY: *(Afraid to ask)* How?

JEANIE: *(A whisper)* . . . a . . . a baby.

MARY gives a reflex gasp, bringing her hand to her mouth to muffle it. There is a long stunned silence as she stares horrified at JEANIE.

MARY: . . . you've been with a man.

JEANIE nods

MARY: *(Broken)* . . . God in heaven.

JEANIE: . . . Just once.

MARY: *(In agony)* Shhhhhh! *(Sotto voce)* Go upstairs.

JEANIE begins to whimper, quickly vanishes up the stairs. The old woman moves with a numbness about the room, turning off the lights. Slowly she walks through the semi-darkness to the stairs. Unable to bear the strain any longer, she sinks to a sitting position on the stairs, and dropping her head on her knees, begins to quietly weep.

MARY: . . . oh God . . . God no . . .

A bright edge of light spills through from the partly open cellar door. There is a round of laughter from JIM and SANDY as they break into an old army song.

JIM and SANDY:
　Roll me oooooover . . .
　In the clooooover
　Roooll me over — lay me down — an do it againnnnn . . .

Blackout

SCENE THREE

It is early next morning in the Dougal home. The stage is empty except for SANDY asleep on the chesterfield. He cuddles a small scatter rug, thrown over him and snores gently. MARY, in robe and slippers, enters dining room from the kitchen. She sits at the table, sipping on a cup of tea, lost and heavy in thought. Her thoughts are suddenly interrupted by the retching of JIM clearing his throat upstairs. She moves quickly across to the stairs, watching for any sign of him.

JIM: *(Off)* Oh my God . . . my God . . . *(Moans)*

His bedroom door is heard opening, and he stumbles across and into the bathroom, flushing the toilet and running the taps as he clears his throat. Another groan.

MARY: *(Calling)* Is it you Jim?

JIM: *(Off)* Ayee . . .

MARY: *(Hopefully)* It's early. You've only been to bed a few hours. Why don't you try an get more sleep.

JIM: *(Off)* Ayee.

JIM comes out of the bathroom, crosses to his bedroom. MARY goes quickly up the stairs and enters JEANIE's bedroom.

MARY: *(Off)* Jeanie . . . get up now.

JEANIE: *(Sleepy sounds)* What for? It's so early.

MARY: Do as I say. Get up.

MARY comes silently down the stairs. She feels the chill in the air and goes to one of the heating vents in the living room, feeling for heat. She goes down the cellar. The dog starts barking. JEANIE crosses into the bathroom.

MARY: *(Off)* Shhhh Rex! It's only mother . . .

From the cellar come the sounds of coal being shovelled. Upstairs JIM begins to retch again. His door is heard opening and he crosses, trying the bathroom door.

JIM: Are ya in there Jeanie?

JEANIE: I'll be out in a second.

JIM: Well hurry it up. Your old dad's in a bad way.

SANDY stirs, shivers, bringing the rug closer about himself.

JIM: *(Insistent)* Jeanie? !

Toilet flushes. Door opens and JEANIE comes out.

JEANIE: I just only went in there . . .

JIM enters, slamming the door behind him. Inside more coughing and retching. JEANIE comes down the stairs, shivering from the cold. She enters the living room, stops and stares briefly at the form of SANDY, then crosses to the heating vent and tries warming herself. SANDY's head slowly comes up and he watches her. Not noticing him she turns her backside toward the vent and lifts her nighty and robe higher about her so the heat will go up and inside her clothing. SANDY's head slowly looks about to see if they are alone.

He sinks back into sleep again. MARY comes up from the cellar.

MARY: What are you doing, standing there displaying your-self like that? Get in there and have your breakfast.

JEANIE: It's too cold.

MARY: I've put coal in the furnace. The house'll be warm soon.

JEANIE crosses and sits shivering at the dining room table.

MARY: I've not slept a wink all night. (*A hushed last hope.*) Are you sure Jeanie?

JEANIE: (*Lazily*) Well nothing's happened for three months.

MARY: Don't be smug! Do you realize the trouble you're in?

JEANIE: Yes.

MARY: (*Wrathfully*) Who was he?

JEANIE: . . . just a soldier.

MARY: Why do you want to protect this man?

JEANIE: I don't want to protect nobody.

MARY: Then tell me who he is!

JEANIE: (*After a long pause.*) . . . it was that Billy.

MARY: (*Stung*) . . . Jimmie's friend?

JEANIE nods

MARY: But how? Where?

JEANIE: He did it to me while you were all sleeping.

MARY: . . . You let him?

JEANIE: He made me! I didn't want to, but he made me.

MARY: (*Enraged*) What's wrong with your tongue? Why didn't you yell so someone would hear you? ? ?

JEANIE: (*Whimpering*) He has his hand over my face . . . I could hardly breathe . . . an I was scared. It was so fast . . . he was on top of me . . . I started crying. Then it was over an he said everything would be okay if I didn't tell nobody . . .

MARY: (*To herself*) . . . and your brother brought him here . . .

JEANIE: The next morning he came down by himself, just before they left. An he told me I'd better not tell anybody ever, or he'd come back . . . and get me for it . . .

MARY: It's filth! Do you understand that — filth!

JEANIE nods. JIM is heard coughing and moving about upstairs.

JIM: *(Off)* Tip, I can't sleep no more. You can start my breakfast.

MARY: I knew he'd not last long.

JIM's bedroom door is heard opening upstairs. MARY quickly goes about setting the breakfast table. JIM starts down the stairs. He stops when he gets to SANDY in the living room.

JIM: Has Sandy no moved about yet Tip?

MARY: Shhh, you'd best not wake him Jim.

JIM: *(Loud laugh)* That ole bugger'll have one big head this morning I'll wager. *(Enters dining room)* I'll say one thing for that man. He can be flat on the floor from drink, but he'll no pass out. Never in all the time I've known him! No sir! *(To JEANIE)* Well don't you say good morning anymore?

JEANIE: Morning sir.

MARY: I'll have it for you in a second Jim. *(Scurries off into the kitchen.)*

JIM: *(Holding his head)* Ohhh, God almighty, you'd think a man could have a wee bit of pleasure without paying such a price.

MARY: *(Off)* Bit under are ya?

JIM: Aye.

MARY: *(Entering with cereal.)* You should know when to stop.

JIM: *(Growling)* I know. I know.

MARY: Here's your porridge. Eat it while it's hot. I'll start your eggs. *(Goes off)*

JIM: Turn em over. I don't want em looking at me this morning.

MARY: *(Off)* What time are you on duty?.

JIM: Not till noon. *(Groans)* It was a good night wasn't it Tip? I mean I think it went over don't you? Everyone seemed to be having a good time.

MARY: Aye it was lovely.

JIM: Aye it was a good evening if I do say so myself. Did my thank you speech go off all right?

MARY: You were fine Jim.

JIM: *(A grunt of agreement)* Aye, well that's the part I don't care for. Don't mind when it's just my boys. But when there's strangers about, and ladies . . . Never was much for that stuff you know.

MARY: Here's your toast dear.

JIM: So if they ask me again, I'll make that part clear right at the beginning. No speech makin! . . . what's this? No butter?

MARY: Jeanie wasn't able to get any yesterday.

JIM: Well hell's bells I can't eat my toast without butter woman!

MARY: I can't help it Jim.

JIM: *(Standing and banging fist.)* It don't matter a damn anyway! Just try and get a little butter in this town, just try! I'd like to know where in hell it's going, that's what I'd like to know! I know there's plenty of butter in that camp there, for them Gerries! It's a fine mess when you're feedin it for them and not ourselves isn't it! *(He sits again, now calmer.)* I'll see if I can wangle some from Nelson in stores.

MARY: Aye why don't you.

JIM: Hate toast without butter. *(To JEANIE)* Pour your dad some coffee. I hope the hell there's sugar in the house.

MARY: Aye, there is, there is. *(Exits to the kitchen.)*

JEANIE pours the coffee. She begins to exit.

JIM: Where you going?

JEANIE: Get dressed . . .

He gives a grunt signifying permission to leave. JEANIE goes upstairs. MARY returns from the kitchen with the eggs.

MARY: *(Calling)* You can lay out your dad's uniform Jeanie.

JIM: You not eatin Tip?

MARY: Aye. Been up for some time. *(Waiting)* I could no sleep last night.

JIM: Oh, the leg actin up on ya again is it?

MARY: A bit . . . along with other things . . .

There is a long pause as MARY searches for words. JIM dunks his toast and noisily slurps at the hot coffee, not concerned.

MARY: *(Hushed)* I'm afraid something's happened, and I can no find the words to tell you Jim.

JIM: *(Grunts)* . . .

MARY: It's to do with Jeanie.

JIM: What about her? *(Long empty pause. JIM continues to eat.)* Come on, come on, what is it Tip?

MARY: *(Whispers)* She's in trouble . . .

JIM: Aye, you already said that.

MARY: Woman trouble.

JIM stops eating, now aware of the subject matter and tries to comprehend it. There is a pause.

MARY: . . . she's pregnant . . .

He sits staring at her, his mouth tight, his eyes cold.

JIM: My Jeanie?

MARY: Now Jim please before . . .

He leaps to attention almost upsetting the table.

JIM: Where is she? !

MARY: Jim listen first.

JIM: *(Starting towards the stairs.)* Jeanie? ! *(He reaches the stairs and stands at the foot of them waiting.)* . . . Jeanie! ! !

MARY: Please Jim what are you going to do?

JIM: I want to hear it from her.

MARY: *(Hovering about him.)* It wasn't her fault. You didn't let me finish.

JIM: *(Sharp)* Let her tell it!

They both stand waiting. JEANIE's head slowly peeks from the doorway of her bedroom.

MARY: *(Meekly)* Come down dear.

Slowly JEANIE makes her way down until she is standing in front of her father. There is a long silence.

JIM: . . . what is it your mother says?

JEANIE: I'm sorry.

JIM stands there trembling. Suddenly he lashes out, sending JEANIE sprawling to the middle of the living room floor.

JIM: You little bitch! !

MARY: *(Grabbing onto him.)* Jim Jim stop it! !

JIM: *(Standing over her and striking her several times as he screams.)* You're disgusting do you hear! ! A slut! ! ! A good for nothing — bloody slut! ! !

MARY stands screaming trying to pull him off while JEANIE has crouched into a ball to protect herself from the rain of blows.

MARY: Jim in the name of God!

JIM: I'll show you what I think of you slut! Where's my belt? ! !

He lunges off toward the kitchen, MARY following, pleading for him to stop. She rushes back and sees SANDY half sitting, awake and bewildered from all the noise and commotion. JEANIE lies crumpled on the floor sobbing.

MARY: Sandy! Oh God Sandy come quick! !

SANDY: *(Getting to his feet.)* What is it? ? What's wrong? ? !

MARY: *(Pointing to the kitchen.)* He'll kill her he'll kill her! Stop him, you've got to stop him — please! ! !

SANDY: *(Moving quickly to the kitchen.)* Jim come to your senses man!.

MARY: *(Gathering JEANIE up by the arms and helping her toward the stairs.)* Oh Jeanie Jeanie Jeanie. My Jeanie.

MARY guides the sobbing girl quickly up the stairs and into Jeanie's bedroom. The door is locked after them. Over this action we hear the arguing of JIM and SANDY from the kitchen.

SANDY: Hey Jim, are you daft man?!

JIM: Get out of my way damn it! !

SANDY: Take it easy man. Give me the belt! . . . Jim! !

JIM comes through from the kitchen wielding a large strap. SANDY, having a hard time, clings to him.

JIM: Leave go, I'll teach her! ! !

SANDY: Jim! Come on now Jim!

JIM: *(Screaming)* Dammit do you understand what I said! ! !

SANDY: You'll no hit her or I'll call the police, so help me!

JIM stands there trembling.

JIM: You don't understand do you? ! I've got a whore for a daughter! I'm a disgraced man Sandy!

Quick blackout Curtain

ACT THREE   SCENE ONE

A week later . . .

Evening, one week later. JEANIE sits at the dining room table cutting pictures from a magazine. There are sounds of footsteps on the veranda outside and she hurries upstairs. The front door opens and MARY enters. The old woman moves with weariness as she removes her coat, etc. She shuffles towards the kitchen as JEANIE slips halfway down the stairs, calling to her.

JEANIE: *(Loud whisper)* Is Dad with you?

MARY: *(With a start)* Oh Jeanie you startled me.

JEANIE: Is he?

MARY: No it's alright, come down. He'll not be off till eight. Did you prepare the vegetables like I asked?

JEANIE: *(Eager)* Uhhuh! And I cleaned the bathroom and made the beds.

MARY: *(Sitting with a sigh.)* Oh, I'm a bit weary. Got to catch my breath. I just dread these Wednesdays and doing that big office.

JEANIE: I'll put the kettle on for some tea for you Mom.

MARY: Thank ye Jeanie. It's just too big an office for one person. I was chatting with the manager tonight. He even knows me by name. Always telling me how nice and clean I get the place for them. He was saying tonight that they can't remember ever having anyone who did as good a job as I do . . . What's this you been doing? Cutting out? Oh, this here's a nice one Jeanie. What are you going to do with them?

JEANIE: Hang them up in my room with the others I guess.

MARY: How about this one with all the food in it?

JEANIE: (Shrugs) I don't know. I just like it so I cut it out too. (Pause) Has Dad said anything about me . . . ?

MARY: (Quietly) Aye. He says you're to go away.

JEANIE: (Shocked) Go away? Where?

MARY: I don't know Jeanie. It's only what he said.

JEANIE: (Frightened) But I don't want to go away. I want to stay with you.

MARY: We'll just have to wait and see . . .

JEANIE: (Starting to whimper) I'd . . . I'd be afraid all alone . . .

She bursts into sobs and falls at her mother's knee, clinging to her.

MARY: I know I know . . . don't cry now. (She rocks JEANIE gently in her arms as she would a child.)

JEANIE: I don't ever want to go away . . .

MARY: Some day you'll have to. You'll be getting married and having a family of your . . . (She stops suddenly aware of what she is saying.) . . . aye. I've planned so long how some day, you'd have a fine wedding . . . all lovely at the church and everything . . . and I could start saving a little now and then . . . so we could maybe have the reception at the King George Hotel . . .

JEANIE: *(Faintly)* It's so fancy there . . .

MARY: Aye. I've worked some of the big banquets that have been there. Not out front, but I could see all the fine trays and things going in and out. When I'd tell dad about it he'd say "don't make the food taste any better" . . . *(Pause)* . . . Imagine, inviting all our friends there. And my Jeanie in a long white dress . . . *(Heavy sigh)* . . . it'll no be now I guess.

JEANIE: Last year at school a girl got rid of one with a knitting needle . . .

MARY: God forgive you!

JEANIE: I didn't mean anything.

MARY: Don't even think such thoughts, or He'll strike you down where you stand! To give birth is a sacred thing.

JEANIE: But I don't want no baby.

MARY: *(Fatalistic)* It's His will, and punishment for tempting the lust of a man.

JEANIE: I didn't mean to tempt nobody.

MARY: No woman does. It's something . . . a cross our good Lord gave us to bear.

Sounds of someone tramping snow from their feet are heard outside on the veranda. JEANIE becomes alert and scrambles upstairs. JIM enters the front door.

JIM: Damn cold wind out there tonight, I'll tell ya . . .

MARY: *(Quickly on her feet getting dinner.)* Soon's you get your things off, come sit down and get some warm supper in ya.

JIM: . . . Aye.

MARY: *(From the kitchen.)* Bit early aren't ya?

JIM: Gerries inside tonight. Don't need all of us freezing our asses off in them towers in this kind of weather. Smitty can handle things.

JIM sits, trying to rub the circulation back into his hands. MARY casually goes through the motion of making up a tray, watching him closely to determine his mood.

MARY: I'd better take Jeanie up something. You know, she prepared most of the dinner for me tonight . . . *(No answer)* . . . Cleaned the house up real nice too, don't you think? *(Still no answer)* She's a big help to me when she wants to be . . . Could I call her down to eat with us Jim?

JIM: I no want to see the likes of her . . .

MARY: You must . . . still love her some Jim? No matter what happened . . .

JIM: She can come down when I've finished.

MARY: Have you nothing in your heart? *(No answer)* You no really want her to go away I hope?

JIM: I'm a man of my word.

MARY: But where?

JIM: At's her bloody worry not mine!

MARY: Ah but she's only sixteen. She's never been away from us. Where could she possibly go?

JIM: Aye she's been about more than we imagined. A regular little woman of the world.

MARY: That's not so. She never had so much as a boyfriend all through school.

JIM: Mary I've travelled half the world and I know the kind of women that take up with men the way she did. It's in em and there's nothing you can do about it! Loose women eager for the pleasures of the flesh. In the army we call them sluts.

309

MARY: Jeanie's not that kind of girl! I brought her up best I know how — to believe in God and what's good.

JIM: It's in em! Oh I've had my eye on that one for a while now. I could see the makins of a tramp. Struttin about in them high heel shoes, her tits stickin out. Plastering all that red shit on her face!

MARY: What about the man? Does he get no blame?

JIM: Bah! What woman don't know! When they're off in the dark with a man and he's feeling them all over! I knew she weren't the brightest, but I no thought her to be a bloody fool!

MARY: (Sadly) Aye, but she's good and could love and make a fine house for some man.

JIM: (Sarcastic) Oh God, love is it now! Ayee like in the movie pictures ehhh? With all the fine music and all. No man would want her now.

A long pause.

MARY: (Quietly) Wasn't much different with you and me Jim . . .

JIM: . . . what do you mean?

MARY: You took me before we were wed.

JIM: It was a hell of a lot different, I'll tell ya.

MARY: I was but sixteen . . . just taken my first job then with the Kerr family, remember? They'd all gone out that night . . . and you came over. They were shipping you overseas and you'd come to tell me. Just the two of us in that big house. I knew you wanted me that way . . . but I was so afraid and I knew it wasn't right. We were in my room, on the bed . . . I tried, but I couldn't stop you.

JIM: (Defensive) I don't remember that.

MARY: I understood and I wanted to be good to you . . . I just didn't want it to be there like that. Women dream there really will be fine music like in the pictures. And everything will be wonderful. How I cried afterwards, remember? And I prayed to God a thousand times to forgive me . . .

JIM: That was all a long time ago Tip. Anyway you know I wanted to marry you.

MARY: It was a long wait those years, wondering if you'd come back. If you'd still want me. I asked you to marry me before you went, but you wouldn't.

JIM: There was a war on. I might have been killed.

MARY: Aye . . .

JIM: (Flustered) Why do you twist things like this, trying to make me look no better than he is?

MARY: Jim, if you'd no come back, I'd been no better off than Jeanie. I would have been a terrible disappointment to some other man on his wedding night.

JIM: (Growing angry) Listen, there's plenty of difference! We don't even know who the son of a bitch is! He could be a bloody chink or a wog for all I know! And I no left you pregnant, woman . . .

MARY: You took me though didn't you?

JIM: (Losing his temper.) Yes dammit I took you! What of it?

MARY: I'll not let you send Jeanie away Jim.

JIM: (Astounded) **You'll** not let me . . . ? and what is it **you** will do?

MARY: I want her to stay here with us . . . and have her baby.

JIM: (Not believing his ears.) What? !

MARY: (Urgent plea.) Oh look Jim, I've thought about it. After she's had the baby, she could find herself a job, and

311

I could watch it through the day, while she was away working.

JIM: Are you daft?

MARY: It would be something for me. You've got the service and Jeanie's young with her whole life yet. I'd look after and care for the baby real well.

JIM: Aye . . . you could wheel it down the street and say, "Good morning, Mrs. Brown. How do you like our wee bastard today?"

MARY: It will still be Jeanie's . . . a warm little baby. I want it.

JIM: To hell with it! Have I no been shamed enough already? God knows how many times and **who** she spread her legs for! And now you ask me to keep the offspring of this filth! She's to leave and not set foot back here again, do you hear? I never want to be reminded of the shame she brought in this house!

MARY: It was that Billy who brought it!

JIM: *(Crashing his fist to the table.)* That's a bloody lie and you know it! He's Jimmie's friend! He's a soldier! A man of honour!

MARY rises, drained of any further fight. It is probably the first time the old woman has stood up to JIM in all the years of their marriage, and she has lost. Slowly she climbs the stairs . . .

MARY: I no understand, I guess. A wee baby . . . honour . . .

JIM waits until she has disappeared, then moves to the living room. He goes to his corner and cranks the phonograph. From the cabinet he takes a full whisky bottle. He places the needle on the record, and sitting in his large leather chair, pours a drink. The whine of the bagpipes playing a stirring march tune fills the room . . .

Blackout

SCENE TWO

The scene is several hours later as the lights come up on JIM sprawled asleep in the large armchair. The clock chimes four . . . then silence. JIM snores quietly. There is a knock on the front door and then scratching on the window pane. The door opens and SANDY totters in, very drunk. His hat sits crooked and a silly smile is glued to his face.

SANDY: *(Singing)* Just a wee doch an doris . . . just a wee doch eh loveeee . . . Hey Jimmie — ho ho! Come on, wake up Jim boy. *(Sees bottle)* Well now what ya got here? How now brown cow!

JIM: *(Slowly waking)* Aye . . . ? Sandy is it?

SANDY: Aye it's your ole buddy Sandy at's who!

JIM: Huh! Must have dozed off, that's what I did.

SANDY: That's what you did alright. I bet that's what ya did. I seen the light still on. I says, "Is that my friend Jim's house?" "Yep" I says. "Well what's he doin up at this hour?" I asked. "Well I don't know" I says. "Might be something wrong so I better go in an see" says I. An there you were — just like that when I came in. *(He eyes the bottle.)*

JIM: No no, just dozed off that's all. Well go on man, have some. *(Holds out his glass.)* Pour me a wee drop too.

SANDY: Well I don't mind if I do — aye!

JIM: At the club were you?

SANDY: *(Wagging his head.)* Noooooo . . .

JIM: Not on duty?

SANDY: Nope.

JIM: Well come on!

SANDY: *(Giggling)* Was looking after Sarah tonight, I was.

JIM: Ah, Sarah!

313

SANDY: Felt it was my duty after the dreadful way I behaved last Saturday night. Staying here and drinking an all!

Bursts out giggling

JIM: She's a good woman.

SANDY: *(Sober)* My very words Jimmie, my very words. Made up a real fine dinner too she did. A meal fit for a king!

JIM: Tell me . . . is she any good in bed?

SANDY: *(Feigning innocence)* Ehhh?

JIM: Come on you ole bugger.

SANDY: How could you think it of me Jimmie? ?

JIM: She's been without a husband a good many years. I fancy she'd be alright?

SANDY: Like it was her last! *(Gleeful laughter)* Aye Jimmie, we'll say she's appreciative as hell! Let's put it that way eh!

JIM: Ach, you could fall in a shit house an come up covered in diamonds! I'll be damned if I know where you get your strength!

SANDY: I'm just a young boy at heart, that's what! It's what's in the heart.

JIM: *(Scoffing)* It's what's in the balls ya mean! Travers you're luckier than a dog with two cocks! Still screwin at your age.

SANDY: *(Swaggering pride)* Right! An listen Jimmie, I can give em women anythin those green laddies can — an a hell of a lot longer too! Nawww, they're not the men we was in our day. You show me one who could stand up to me even now! Go on show me one!

JIM: Aye, I believe ya.

SANDY: Can't be done I'll tell ya! An they're not men of principle anymore, like we was Jimmie. Now you take the rat's ass who did wee Jeanie in. An then up an deserts her! A fine soft young girl like her . . . You can no call that a man! *(Seeing JIM)* Ahhh, I should have no mentioned it. I'm sorry.

JIM: My shame is that you were here to see such happenings that morning. *(Woeful shake of his head.)* I don't know where I might a gone wrong. Always I did my best to be a good husband and father.

SANDY: *(Patting JIM's shoulder.)* You've done well.

JIM: No I've not. I've failed.

SANDY: Listen there ain't a better man anywhere what I know. An anybody what says different, will have to account to me!

JIM: *(Depths of self pity)* Aye, thank ye Sandy.

SANDY: And you must never think any of it your fault. The shame's that it could ever happen in the house of such a fine honourable man.

JIM: Here let me fill ya . . . *(Pours SANDY a drink)*

SANDY: Aye, just a wee one. Thank ye. Yes, there should be some kind of laws or something. 'S'not right . . . *(Wags his head.)*

JIM: The law's for the rich, not the likes of you and I. Not the men who have known hard work all their lives.

SANDY: Aye, but we're the ones they call Johnnie on the spot when they go an get a war on their hands! Chaps like you an me. Yet anyone who pleases can come and cast shame on your home and name, and they don't give a damn 'bout that!

JIM: Aye.

The two sit quietly considering these thoughts and sipping their drinks.

SANDY: Maybe you can find her a husband somewhere . . .

aye that's what you gotta do Jimmie.

JIM: Bahhh! Who the hell would want her now?

SANDY: If I was younger I sure as hell would! She's a fine looking girl. *(Snaps his finger)* I'd marry her like that!

Loud raptures of laughter from JIM.

SANDY: I would, I would! A wee wife and little ones, something I've always wanted. But it's never been found to happen that way for me.

JIM: *(Being serious)* Aye man but you'd no take one who'd fallen?

SANDY: Ahh, that's where you're wrong Jim. There's no finer girl. Cause she was taken advantage of, don't change the fact that she's bred from good stock. Don't I know it! An that's what counts. She strayed, ayeee. But I could straighten her out fast!

JIM: *(Studying him.)* Oh it's with kindness you speak now . . .

SANDY: Jeanie's a lovely . . . any man would be honoured — I've said. But the lass has a mind of her own. She'd never want the likes of an old man like me. She's young . . . aye young and soft . . . *(His voice trails away as he dwells on this image.)* . . .

JIM stands and paces in thought for a while. He keeps stopping as though studying SANDY, who continues contentedly on his drink. A smile comes to JIM's face and he chuckles to himself, having reached a decision. He fills the glasses once more.

JIM: *(Toasting)* . . . to our friendship.

SANDY: Aye. Thank ye Jimmie.

JIM walks over to the stairs.

JIM: Jeanie!

SANDY: *(Quickly)* Oh Jim Jim, shhh. Don't be waking the Mrs. an all.

JIM: Drink up my friend! Put on the victrola and give us some music.

MARY appears from her bedroom pulling her robe about her. She comes quickly down the stairs. SANDY struggles over to the phonograph humming and ready for the start of a good party.

MARY: *(Frightened)* What is it Jim?

JIM: Wake the girl and bring her down.

MARY: But why Jim?

JIM: Do as I say Tip. An tell her to brush her hair a bit.

MARY, frightened, obeys and goes up to JEANIE's bedroom. JIM goes back to where SANDY stands, teetering, attempting to read the label of the record. JIM begins to chuckle loudly.

SANDY: What's so funny Jimmie?

JIM: *(Putting on the record.)* I was only thinking. If you were to marry Jeanie, you'd be my son-in-law! *(Loud laughter.)*

SANDY: *(A big grin.)* Aye, that's right! *(Pause)* An, an you'd be my father-in-law! ! !

They lapse into raptures of laughter, each considering the other in their respective roles. The record begins to play but the machine has run down and we get the whining wheeze of the bagpipes in slow time, setting a mocking background to their laughter.

Blackout

SCENE THREE

Week later. Lights come up on JEANIE alone in the living room, slumped across a sofa chair. She chomps on an apple and leafs through a comic book. Her whole attitude is once again relaxed and lazy.

MARY: *(Off from kitchen)* Jeanie? Are you comin in here to help me or not?

JEANIE: *(Not moving)* . . . uh huh . . .

Brief silence.

MARY: *(Off)* You know it's for you that all this is being done?

JEANIE: I know . . .

MARY: *(Off)* Well, then, you might lend a hand!

JEANIE: *(Impatient sigh)* What do you want me to do?

MARY: *(Off)* Oh honestly! You know right well there's a million things you could be helpin me with. There's sandwiches to be made. The whole house'll have to be gone over. Or did you think these things just get done by themselves before a wedding? *(Peeking in)* Look at you just lolling about! Pity we don't all have us such leisure time. It'll be different after ya married ya know. *(Pointed)* I'll not be picking up around here after the two of you.

JEANIE: I'm not feeling so good . . .

MARY: The baby?

JEANIE rises, goes over to the full length mirror.

JEANIE: I guess so . . . *(She studies her now slightly protruding tummy showing beneath the tight jeans. She gently rubs herself in a circular motion.)* . . . there it goes again!

MARY: *(Coming over)* What is it?

JEANIE: Something inside.

MARY: *(Brightly)* Aye. It's the baby kicking.

JEANIE: *(With distaste)* Is it alive already?

MARY: It's early for movement but that's a good sign.

JEANIE: *(Viewing her stomach)* Goooood!

MARY: Let me. *(Places her hand on JEANIE's abdomen.)*

JEANIE: Feel anything?

MARY: No . . .

JEANIE: How can it move when it hardly even shows?

MARY: Ahh, it's wee but it's alive.

JEANIE: I'm not going to like this.

MARY: *(Bringing her hand away.)* It's been a long time, but once you've had the feeling you never forget it. You were a restless one. Started kicking right at three months and didn't let up till you were born.

JEANIE: What are they kicking for?

MARY: They're just movin about.

JEANIE: *(Hopefully)* Maybe I shouldn't do anything. Can't tell, I could strain something.

MARY: Aye, you best sit for a spell. Keep comfy. *(Weary)* The good Lord should have given me another pair of hands. I don't know how I can get it all done in time.

JEANIE: Why aren't we having the reception at the Legion instead of here?

MARY: Cause it cost too much and there won't be very many. Just a few friends of Dad's and Sandy's.

JEANIE: Huh. That isn't going to be much of a wedding.

MARY: Dad says it's best that way. I wanted so much just to have your Aunt Lil, but he says no. I spect it would take a lot of explaining.

JEANIE: There won't be anyone here that I know. I want Dollie to come.

MARY: That rascal. I don't know that I want her about here.

JEANIE: *(Pouting)* She's my best friend. I want somebody.

MARY: If your Dad says . . . *(There is a knock at the door.)* Oh tch . . . who can that be? I've so much to do . . .

She bustles to the door and opens it.

MARY: *(Surprised)* Sarah . . . Well fancy, come in, come in . . .

SARAH: *(Entering)* Hello, Mary . . .

MARY, not prepared for this visit, behaves in a strained and nervous manner. SARAH's eyes keep constantly going to JEANIE, who has edged off to a distant corner.

MARY: *(Exaggerated)* I was just sayin to myself in the kitchen "I must call Sarah soon one of these days. It's been nearly two weeks now." Give me your coat . . .

SARAH: Thank ye Mary . . . *(Removing it.)* I've only stopped by for but a minute . . . *(Nods)* . . . Hello Jeanie . . .

JEANIE: *(Quietly)* Mrs. McIver . . .

MARY: I do think it's turned colder again don't you? Either that or my blood's gettin thinner. You're just in time for a cup of tea Sarah.

SARAH: Like I say I can't stay long. I only dropped in to see if you'd heard the news of poor Mrs. Black?

MARY: No, I didn't. What happened to the dear thing?

SARAH: Had another attack, she did.

MARY: Ohhhh tch! How bad is it?

SARAH: She's no strength at all. The doctor said she's not to leave her bed.

MARY: The doctor was there an all was he? My goodness, who's looking after her?

SARAH: I was with her through the night, and Elsie said she'd do her best to spend most of today with her.

MARY: I'll take her some broth, and look in on her over the weekend and see if there's anything needs doing. Will they be notifying the boy I wonder?

SARAH: I don't think she knows where he is. He no writes her any more.

MARY: Someone's going to have to watch her. She's too old to be on her own anyway.

SARAH: Aye. Age is an unkind thing.

MARY: Well I'm glad you told me. The poor thing. Jeanie, fix the kettle, love.

SARAH: I really mustn't stay Mary.

MARY: Nonsense, you can't be leavin without at least havin a cup of tea to warm your innards. Sit down, sit down, Sarah.

SARAH: *(Awkwardly, not knowing how to start.)* I had wanted to ask you something as well . . .

MARY: *(Suddenly nervous)* Oh? What is it Sarah?

SARAH: *(Embarrassed)* To tell the truth I feel very silly even askin, mind you. Knowing my Sandy and the way he's always carrying on havin his jokes on people.

MARY: Aye. He's always been that way.

SARAH: He was to dinner last night, as he is most Thursday nights . . . Course he always comes on Sundays. First time he ever missed was last Sunday. *(Her gaze falling on JEANIE.)* He told me something very funny on Thursday. Said he wouldn't be coming no more. *(Nervous laugh)* Said he and Jeanie there . . . were going to be married?

There is no answer. JEANIE looks away and SARAH's eyes come then to MARY questioning.

SARAH: Surely it's not true . . . ?

MARY: I'm . . . sorry Sarah.

SARAH: *(Hushed)* Jeanie and Sandy . . . ? I thought it was just a joke he was havin on me. *(Faltering)* Who would have ever imagined. *(Staring at JEANIE.)* God in heaven! *(She stands just shaking her head.)* Well I hope you're both very happy. May I please have my coat Mary.

MARY: *(Weakly)* No one meant to hurt you Sarah.

SARAH: *(Getting her coat herself.)* No, no, please, don't start offering me sympathy. It only just came as such a shock, that's all. Finding out people that you think are your friends . . . *(Choking on the words.)* have been carrying on behind your back.

MARY: It's not true Sarah.

SARAH: But it is the truth! *(To JEANIE, losing all her composure.)* You, you little scamp! What do you want with someone like Sandy? ? Why don't you get somebody younger like yourself? ! Disgustin cheap people, that's what ya are! ! *(She bursts into tears.)*

MARY: Sarah! !

SARAH: An you Mary . . . all these years, all these years . . .

SARAH exits sobbing. MARY follows, standing in the doorway and calling after her.

MARY: Don't ever come back here again, ya hear? ! You don't call us things like that!

MARY's voice trails off, and covering her face she crosses quickly to the sofa where she sobs quietly. JEANIE crosses and closes the front door.

JEANIE: Whew, she really flipped.

MARY: *(Angered)* Do you no see the trouble you've made for everyone Jeanie! She's been my best friend all my life.

JEANIE: It wasn't my idea to marry him!

MARY: I pray God it's a wise decision your father has made.

JEANIE: She can have him for all I care . . .

MARY: Hold your tongue! It's all been done for you!

JEANIE: I'll make you some tea.

MARY gives a weary nod. JEANIE exits to the kitchen. The old woman blows her nose a few times and collects her composure. The front door opens and JIM enters carrying a large parcel.

JIM: Hi Tip, was that Sarah I just passed goin down the street? *(MARY nods.)* Thought it was. Didn't say a bloody word she didn't. Fact she never even looked up at me.

MARY: She was here asking about the wedding.

JIM: Ummmmmm. Well . . . can't be helped. She's a good woman. Always liked Sarah. Where's Jeanie?

MARY: Making the tea . . .

JIM: Don't be letting it bother you Tip, somes always got to be hurt by these things. Jeanie!

JEANIE cautiously enters from the kitchen.

JIM: Come in here. Picked up a little something for you on the way home I did. *(Indicates the parcel.)*

JEANIE: For me?

JIM: Darn it, that's what I said didn't I! Well go on, open it!

JEANIE goes to the parcel and slowly unwraps it. JIM stands with a pleased smile waiting. She removes a white wedding gown, not boxed, but merely folded and wrapped in the brown paper.

JIM: Well . . . ?

JEANIE: Oh, it's beautiful. See mom?

MARY rises, her attention completely captivated by the gown now.

MARY: Aye . . . Where'd ya get it Jim?

JIM: Got it at the seconds on Fourth street. It ain't brand new, but I'll be damned if I'll be payin out a whole lot of money for a dress you wear one day. The fellow there told me it cost fifty dollars when it was new.

MARY: *(Taking it.)* Here let me see Jeanie . . . *(She examines it closely.)* . . . bit soiled near the bottom, but spect we can clean that up easy enough.

JIM: Sure ya can! Go over it a bit with an iron an it'll look good as new. Only been worn once.

MARY goes to the full length mirror, and instinctively holds it up to herself. She is enchanted with the dress.

MARY: Aye . . . it is beautiful isn't it. *(Second thought)* Do you think it will be proper, her wearin this? I mean seein we're not having it in the church an all?

JIM: Hell a wedding's — a wedding and that there's a wedding dress ain't it!

MARY: I know, but . . . *(Dismisses it.)* Come here Jeanie and see how it fits on you.

JEANIE comes over and MARY holds it up to the girl.

MARY: Ahh . . . you'll look lovely.

JEANIE: Wait'll Dollie sees this! Dad can I have Dollie come?

JIM: I guess so.

JEANIE: *(Overjoyed)* Weeeeee! ! Thanks dad! ! *(She bounds off toward the phone.)*

324

MARY: O dear we're going to have to make a few adjustments. Upstairs now young lady and put it on.

JEANIE: I'm just going to call Dollie first!

MARY: Now don't be fooling about Jeanie! I've so much to do as it is.

JEANIE grudgingly consents and is followed up the stairs by MARY nattering behind her.

JIM: *(Calling after them.)* You help your mother now Jeanie! I want everything ship-shape. You'll be married at four pm tomorrow.

Quick curtain

SCENE FOUR

Late afternoon the next day — the Dougal home. The stage is empty and in semi-darkness. We hear the laughter of voices and singing, approaching, growing louder as they reach the veranda outside. The door flies open and JIM, quite high, enters, his arm around SANDY's neck. SANDY is very drunk. Three or four guards enter, all laughing and talking at one. Then JEANIE in her gown and carrying a small bunch of flowers. DOLLIE wearing some of her mother's clothes enters. She carries a small Brownie box camera with a flash on it. MARY is the last to enter. The entire scene hums with noise as everyone talks at once, removing their coats, etc. DOLLIE approaches one of the VETS and discusses something.

TOMMIE: *(Above all the noise.)* Well come on man, break out the drinks damn it!

Loud approval from all the men.

ART: Wait a minute everybody! Over here first! *(Starts herding them towards one end of the room.)* Come on, the little girl wants to take a nice photo of the whole bunch of ya!

Loud "ohs" and "ahs" from everyone, reluctant to oblige.

JIM: Oh to hell with it! I don't want my picture taken!

ANOTHER: Aye, me neither!

MARY: Please Jim, it's Jeanie's weddin photos!

BOB: Yeah come on Jim you have to be in em! You're the bride's father!

Agreement from all. JIM grumbles and joins the rest, shuffling about awkwardly, forming a group. DOLLIE stands off to the side looking down into her camera, waiting.

ART: That's right everybody. Wait a minute, I'll get in there myself!

TOMMIE: Fer Christ sakes, Sandy, you're spose to stand next to your new wife! *(Gives him a shove.)*

Everyone breaks into laughter and SANDY is handled along by each person. ART places him beside JEANIE then puts his own arm around SANDY and takes a pose.

DOLLIE: Get ready now . . .

They all freeze except SANDY who can't stop weaving. The flash goes off and the group instantly breaks, groaning about how they can't see, all talking and laughing again.

TOMMIE: Well, where the hell are those drinks? !

JIM: Aye aye! Tip, come on give me a hand! *(He guides her off into the kitchen with him.)*

Everyone starts talking and laughing again. DOLLIE and JEANIE pose with their arms round each other for ART to take a picture.

BOB: *(To all)* Now listen everybody; we don't want to be staying too long! Sandy and his bride got things of their own they want to do!

Loud round of laughter from everyone except JEANIE. DOLLIE whispers the meaning into her ear.

TOMMIE: Ahh, you don't want to be saying them kinds of things! Look at the lass, she's embarrassed!

ANOTHER: She don't look bare-assed to me!

Another round of laughter. JIM and MARY enter carrying several beers which are quickly handed about. A cheer comes from all.

BOB: Give the girls one too Jim!

JIM: What? I'll be damned! They're too young!

This is met with jeers from all. Reluctantly he hands JEANIE and DOLLIE each a bottle of beer. The group approves of him once more.

JIM: Now I want you all to drink your share! There's a whole ice box full out there!

BOB: God bless you for your generosity Dougal!

JIM: Aye it's not every day a man gives away his daughter!

TOMMIE: Hear hear! and a finer man you couldn't have found! *(Agreement from all)*

JIM: Ahhh, love works in strange ways I'll tell ya. There he is . . . my best friend . . . my daughter. And I have nary an idea how they feel over each other. Then one day my Jeanie comes to me and she says, "Dad, I love Sandy." . . . *(Appreciative ohs and ahs from the group.)* . . . An there he is . . . not sayin a word! For obvious reasons of course. Because he's a deceitful old man! *(Round of laughter and clapping.)* . . . Well I got them together. And I said, "I'm a man of a few years myself ya know. And I hope I've

327

gathered a bit of wisdom with it . . . Now Sandy," I says, "it's true you're a few years older than my lass, but! I know the man that you are too. I know you'll treat my Jeanie right . . . an them's the things that's important to me!" So I said to them, "You have my blessing". And a finer man it couldn't be, as you already said gentlemen . . .

With this JIM gives a nod of the head and tilts back his bottle of beer. There is a loud round of "hear hear" and clapping.

TOMMIE: Well I was the best man and I'm suppose to make a speech. But I'll be damned if I'm gonna!

BOB: That's a blessing!

TOMMIE: Enough from you Bob. Really I don't have much to say. Sandy's been a friend of mine for a good many years an . . . it's nice to see him settling down at last. I hope the both of you are very happy. I think I'm suppose to propose a toast to . . . ah to the bride. So gentlemen if you'll rise an join me in this toast. "To a very lovely bride."

ALL: Hear hear! *(They all drink up.)*

BOB: In case you don't know it, you're suppose to respond to that toast Sandy! *(Group laughter.)*

SANDY: I never been married before — how was I to know? But it's the truth anyway. It comes a wee bit late for me in life . . . But I — I'll be a good husband you know. I want to thank you Tommie for what you said about my wee wife . . . *(Looks at Jeanie.)* . . . she's — she's a lovely thing alright . . . an I'm a lucky man. *(Awkwardly wipes the froth from his mouth with his cuff.)* An I think the drink's catching up on me too! *(Snorts with laughter.)*

BOB: There ain't enough drink in the world for Sandy Travers!

All agree!

SANDY: To hell with you too Bob!

TOMMIE has wound the gramophone and put on a record of The Anniversary Waltz. He begins humming with it.

TOMMIE: Dahhh — dadada . . . dadadahhhhh . . . dadada . . . You're supposed to dance with your bride, Sandy!

Everyone agrees and they drag SANDY over to JEANIE and DOLLIE seated on the sofa. JEANIE is embarrassed and, giggling, hides her face and turns away. DOLLIE tugs at her.

DOLLIE: Come on, Dougal, you're suppose to dance with him!

JEANIE: I don't want to. *(Gives Dollie a playful shove back.)* You dance with him!

Loud round of laughter and they pull her up and hand her to SANDY. The two of them stumble about awkwardly, JEANIE not knowing how to dance and SANDY too drunk. Everyone breaks into song, singing with the music. A VET dances with MARY and ART takes DOLLIE for a few whirls.

ALL:
So tell me I may always dance
The anniversary waltz with you
Tell me this is real romance
An anniversary dream come true
Let this be the answer to all future years . . .
Millions of smiles and a few little tears . . .

SANDY suddenly loses his balance, falling flat on his face. Everyone begins laughing and teasing him.

BOB: Come on Sandyyy!

TOMMIE: Will you look at the fine groom now! ! That's the way you're suppose to be the morning after! ! !

All jeer with delight at this and coax JEANIE to make him get up and dance some more.

SANDY: *(On all fours.)* What I need is another bloody beer, that's all!

ALL: Give him a beer, Jim!

JIM: I'll give him a beer alright! Here ya're, my fine laddie!

He stands pouring it on SANDY's head. Everyone approves with laughter.

SANDY: That's a hell of a thing to do to a good beer!

JIM: An that's no way to be talking to your father-in-law!

SANDY: *(Falling back on the floor with laughter.)* I nay heard anything so funny! Help me up, for God's sake, Jimmie!

There is a good deal of grunting and wheezing and JIM helps him to his feet. Slowly the laughter subsides.

TOMMIE: I think it was time we was on our way. Leave the loved ones alone.

JIM: What the hell ya sayin man? We're just startin to have us a party here!

TOMMIE: Oh, I think Sandy's got other things on his mind Jim!

Snickers from everyone.

JIM: No, you can't go. Good Lord, I got all the drink in the cooler and Mary here prepared a lot of food an all!

BOB: It wouldn't be fair to Sandy, Jim. They want to be alone.

JIM: To hell with em!

TOMMIE: I tell ya what. We'll take it over to my place — how's that Jim?

BOB: It's okay by me! *(Others all join in agreement.)*

JIM: Well alright then. *(Starting for the kitchen.)* Come on, give me a hand. Good God, I thought you were all losing your heads for a minute!

Some follow him into the kitchen to help; others begin to put their coats on. SANDY has been placed in a chair and sits in a stupor with glazed eyes.

DOLLIE: Well I'll see you, kiddo. Everybody's going.

JEANIE: *(Suddenly frightened.)* Gee you don't have to go already. Mom, you're not going too are you?

MARY stands helpless wanting to say something consoling to the girl at this time, but she cannot find any words.

MARY: We must, Jeanie . . . *(Lost for words.)* . . . it'll be alright . . .

The group suddenly sweeps back through carrying sandwiches, beer, etc.

JIM: Come on Tip, we're going over to Tommie's!

JIM is the first one out the door. The others follow, all bidding their goodbyes. DOLLIE whispers something to JEANIE and then disappears with the rest. MARY takes a quick look back and exits. Bob peeks back in before closing the door.

BOB: Sandy, I don't want you misbehavin now! *(Loud snort of laughter.)*

The door slams shut and the noise from the group quickly fades. There is a long silence. Then a few sniffles from JEANIE. It is so quiet you can hear SANDY wheezing as he breathes. He groans, belches loud and suddenly realizes everyone has left.

SANDY: Where the hell . . . they all gone . . . ?

His head bobs and he notices JEANIE on the far side of the room, sobbing quietly. He struggles to his feet, stands trying to get his co-ordination in check. He watches her.

SANDY: Ahhh, you're not cryin are you? . . . *(He shuffles over toward her.)* . . . Ohhh Jeanie come on, come on . . . *(He reaches down and gently touches her arm. She pulls away. He speaks to her with kindness.)* Ohh now don't be frightened of old Sandy . . . come on . . . my head's splittin. I need ya to help me up the stairs, lass . . .

She looks up at him now as she begins to regain her courage. She wipes away the tears.

SANDY: *(Big smile.)* See. It's only me . . . *(She slowly stands)* That a girl . . . there's nothin to be scared of . . .

He turns and shuffles towards the stairs. She walks hesitantly a few steps behind him. He stops when he reaches the stairs, and looks back to her for help.

SANDY: Oh I don't trust meself on these stairs . . . will ye give me a hand?

She stands beside him and he gently leans on her, his arm about her shoulder. He keeps purring in soft tones as they start slowly up the steps, their backs to the audience.

SANDY: Easy now . . . that a girl . . . *(Pause)* . . . that a girl . . .

Reaching the top of the stairs, his hand slowly slides down her back, and he gently caresses her buttocks . . . suddenly clutching them firmly.

SANDY: *(Breaking into a loud hoarse laugh.)* That a girl!

Quickly he pushes her into the bedroom and the door slams shut.

Four beats of silence.

Slowly fade the setting to darkness.

End Curtain

David E. Freeman
Creeps

EDITOR'S NOTE: David E. Freeman was born in 1945 in Toronto. Handicapped by cerebral palsy, he attended Sunnyview School where he was encouraged in creative writing. On leaving Sunnyview at age 17, he entered a sheltered workshop which created the kind of frustration mirrored in *Creeps*. Freeman's reaction was to begin writing for a number of Canadian magazines, and at the urging of CBC producer William Davidson, to draft a play. In 1966, Freeman left the workshop — and creative writing — to attend McMaster University, graduating with a degree in political science in 1971. With no apparent job prospects, he called his friend Bill Glassco who was looking for plays to do at Toronto's Factory Theatre Lab. Their association resulted not only in Freeman's rewriting his early play as *Creeps* and its being staged at the Factory, but in its being the first play in Bill Glassco's founding season at the Tarragon Theatre in 1971-2. Since then, David E. Freeman has written three more plays which have received professional productions, but none has equalled the success of *Creeps*.

Creeps opened on 3 February 1971 at the Factory Theatre Lab in Toronto and then with essentially the same cast, but in a revised script, opened the Tarragon Theatre on 5 October 1971. It won the Chalmers Outstanding Play Award for that year, the New York Drama Desk Award for Outstanding New Playwright in 1973, and one of six Edinburgh "Fringe" Festival awards in 1979. The play was published in 1972 by the University of Toronto Press.

Characters:

PETE
JIM
SAM
TOM
MICHAEL
SAUNDERS
CARSON
GIRL
SHRINERS

The actor playing the role of Michael also plays the Chef, Puffo The Clown, and the Carnival Barker in the three Shriner sequences.

The play is set in the washroom of a sheltered workshop for cerebral palsy victims. A "sheltered workshop" is a place where disabled people can go and work at their own pace without the pressure of the competitive outside world. Its aim is not to provide a living wage for the C.P., but rather to occupy his idle hours.

SOME NOTES ON THE CHARACTERS' MOVEMENTS

Each actor taking a role of one of the characters with cerebral palsy is faced, as the character, with major physical problems, the practical solution of which is paramount to a successful rendering of the play. It is to be noted that there are many kinds of spasticity, and each actor should base his movements on one of these. There can be no substitute for the first-hand observation of these physical problems, and one might even suggest that the play not be attempted if opportunities for such first-hand observation are not available. These notes indicate the approach taken by the actors in the original production.

PETE
   The actor in the original production developed a way of speaking that is common to many spastics. The effort required to speak causes a distortion of the facial muscles. The actor was able to achieve this by thrusting the jaw

forward, and letting the lower jaw hang. Whatever speech problem is adopted for this role, no actor should attempt it unless he has an opportunity for first-hand observation.

    The deformed hand was not held rigid in one position. The actor used the hand for many things, keeping the fist clenched and employing the fingers in a clawlike manner.

JIM

The actor walked with his knees almost touching, feet apart, back bent much of the time, using his arms more than any other part of his body for balance.

SAM

Sam is a diaplegic, his body dead from the waist down (except for his genitals). He is in a wheelchair. The problem for this actor was to find how to make the wheelchair an extension of his body.

TOM

The actor walked with one hip thrust out to the side. Forward motion always began with the foot of the other leg, rising up on the toe, and then thrusting downward on the heel. His arms were held in front of him, his fingers splayed, upper arms and shoulders constantly being employed for balance.

MICHAEL

The actor always staggered, his head lolling, his body very loose, constantly on the edge of falling. He fell, or collapsed, rather than sat, and grinned most of the time. He too had a speech problem, very slurred, not employing the facial muscles like Pete.

A men's washroom in a sheltered workshop. The hall leading to the washroom is visible. In the washroom are two urinals and two stalls. A chair is set against one of the stalls and there is a bench.

When the lights go up one of the stalls is occupied. MICHAEL, a mentally retarded C.P. of about eighteen, comes along the hall, enters the door of the washroom, and starts flushing the toilets, beginning with the urinals. He comes to the occupied stall and knocks on the door.

PETE: Who is it?

THELMA: *(An offstage voice. It is important that this voice be spastic, but that what she is saying always be clear)* I need a priest!

MICHAEL *chuckles to himself, does not answer. Meanwhile TOM has entered, walking in a sway and stagger motion. Having observed the game MICHAEL is playing on PETE, he ushers MICHAEL out, then sits in the chair up against the stall occupied by PETE. PETE drops his pack of cigarettes.*

TOM: *(Disguising his voice)* Hey, Pete, you dropped your cigarettes. *(Pause. A comic book falls)* Hey, Pete, you dropped your comic book.

Pete's pants drop to the floor.

TOM: *(His own voice)* Hey, Pete, you dropped your pants.

PETE: That you, Tom?

TOM: Course it's me. Who were you expecting, Woody the Pecker?

PETE: Why didn't you answer?

TOM: When?

PETE: Didn't you knock on the door just now?

TOM: No.

PETE: Must have been Michael flushing toilets.

TOM: Doing his thing.

PETE: He wants to be toilet flushing champion of the world.

TOM: Well at least he's not like some lazy bastards who sit on their ass all day reading comic books.

PETE: I'm on strike. They only pay me seventy-five cents a week. I'm worth eighty.

TOM: You're always on strike.

PETE: How many boxes did you fold today, smart ass?

TOM: Oh, about two hundred. How's the rug?

PETE: Fucking rug. I wish to hell she'd put me on something else. At least for a day or two. It's getting to be a real drag.

TOM: Yeah, that's the way I feel about those boxes.

THELMA: I need a priest! Get me a priest!

TOM: *(Wearily)* Oh, God.

PETE: Old Thelma kind of gets on your nerves, doesn't she?

TOM: Yeah.

THELMA: Someone get me a priest!

TOM: Pete, I gotta talk to you about something.

PETE: Okay, shoot.

TOM: No, I'll wait till you're out of the can.

Knock at the door.

SAM: Open up! *(Pause)* Who's in there?

TOM moves to open the door

SAM: Come on, for Chrissake.

TOM: All right, hang on.

With difficulty TOM gets the door open. SAM wheels by him into the washroom.

TOM: Wanna take a leak, Sam?

SAM: No, I wanna join the circle jerk. Where's Pete?

PETE: In here.

SAM: Well, well, Pete is actually using the shithouse to take a shit.

337

PETE: Okay, Sam, knock it off.

Pause.

TOM: *(To SAM)* How are you making out with the blocks?

SAM: Screw the blocks. You know how many of those fuckin' things I done today? Two. Do you know why? Because that half-ass physical therapist . . .

TOM: Physio.

SAM: Physio, physical, what the fuck's the difference? They're all after my body. She keeps making me do the same damn blocks over again. "That's not good enough," she says. "Get the edges smoother," she says. *(Pointing to his crotch)* Take a bite of this.

PETE: *(Flushing the toilet)* She can be a pretty miserable old cunt at times.

SAM: All the time. How's the rug, Pete?

PETE: That thing.

TOM: I told him, he's never gonna finish it sitting in the john all day.

PETE: *(Emerging from the stall)* I've been weaving that stupid rug beside that hot radiator every day now for three months. And what has it got me? A big fat zero.

SAM: That's because you're a lazy bugger. You know what that stupid idiot who runs this dump says about you.

PETE: Yeah, I know. "Pete, if you worked in my factory, you wouldn't last a day . . ."

TOM: "But since you're a helpless cripple, I'll let you work in my workshop . . ."

SAM: "For free!"

PETE: And the government will give me a pension, just for breathing.

TOM: And the Rotary and the Shriners will provide hot dogs and ice cream.

SAM: And remember, boys, "If they won't do it . . . "

ALL: "Nobody else will!"

Blackout. Circus music and bright lights. Enter two SHRINERS, a girl (MISS CEREBRAL PALSY) in a white bathing suit, and a chef. They dance around the boys, posing for pictures, blowing noise-makers, and generally molesting them in the name of charity. The chef stuffs hot dogs into their hands. They exit, the music fades, the light returns to normal. The boys throw their hot dogs over the back of the set.

PETE: Sometimes I wonder how I ever got myself into this.

TOM: Good question, Pete. How did you?

PETE: Another time, Tom, another time.

THELMA: I need a priest!

PETE: What's this big piece of news you have to tell me?

TOM: It doesn't matter.

PETE: Come on, Tom, crap it out.

TOM: It's okay, forget it.

PETE: I postponed my shit for this.

TOM: That's your problem.

SAM: Hey, I bet he's gonna get laid and he doesn't know what to do.

PETE: Well the first thing he better learn is how to get undressed faster.

TOM: Very funny.

PETE: What's the matter? This place still getting you down?

TOM: Yeah, I can't hack it much longer.

SAM: Can't hack what?

TOM: Everything. Folding boxes, the Spastic Club, Thelma, the whole bit.

PETE: How's the art coming?

TOM: Didn't you hear me?

PETE: Sure I heard you. You said you couldn't hack folding boxes. Well I can't hack weaving that goddamn rug. So how's the art?

TOM: Screw the art. I don't want to talk about art.

PETE: Okay.

SAM: Chickentracks.

TOM: What's that?

SAM: Chickentracks. That's what you paint, Tom. Chickentracks.

TOM: I paint abstract. I know to some ignorant assholes it looks like chickentracks. . .

SAM: Listen, Rembrandt, anything you ever tried to paint always looked like shit warmed over, so you try to cover it up by calling it an abstract. But it's chickenshit and you know it.

TOM: You wouldn't know the difference between a tree and a telephone pole, Sam.

SAM: There isn't any difference. A dog'll piss on both of them.

TOM: And you'll piss on anything, won't you?

PETE: Okay, Tom, cool it.

TOM: Why the fuck should I cool it? This prick's attacking my art.

PETE: You shouldn't take yourself so seriously.

TOM: Oh, do forgive me, gentlemen. I took myself seriously. *(Getting up)* I shall go to Miss Saunders and insist she castrate me.

He starts for the door.

SAM: Castrate what?

PETE: Where are you going?

TOM: Where does it look like?

PETE: Dammit, Tom, come on back and stop acting like an idiot.

TOM: Why should I? Whenever anyone tries to talk serious around here, you guys turn it into a joke.

PETE: Nobody's making a joke.

SAM: Look, Tom, even if you do have talent, which I seriously doubt, what good is it to you? You know bloody well they're not going to let you use it.

TOM: Who's they, Sam?

SAM: The Rotary, the Shriners, the Kiwanis, the creeps who run this dump. In fact, the whole goddamn world. Look, if we start making it, they won't have anyone to be embarrassed about.

PETE: Come on, Sam, there's always the blacks.

TOM: And the Indians.

SAM: Yeah, but we're more of a challenge. You can always throw real shit at a black man or an Indian, but at us you're only allowed to throw pityshit. And pityshit ain't visible.

TOM: I think you're stretching it just a bit.

SAM: The only way you're going to get to use that talent of yours, Tom, is to give someone's ass an extra big juicy kiss. And you ought to know by now how brilliantly that works for some people round here.

TOM: You mean Harris?

SAM: If the shoe fits.

TOM: You lay off Jim, 'cause if you'd had the same opportunity you'd have done the same thing.

SAM: So now he licks stamps in the office on a weekly salary, and he's president of the Spastic Club. Whoopee!

TOM: *(To PETE)* Are you going to talk to me or not?

JIM enters and goes to the urinal. He is surprised to see TOM. His walk is slow and shaky, almost a drunken stagger.

SAM: Here's Mommy's boy now.

Pause.

PETE: Things slack in the office, Jim?

JIM: Naw, I just thought I might be missing something.

SAM: Oh you're sweet. Isn't he sweet? I love him.

PETE: Cigarette?

JIM: No thanks, I'm trying to give them up.

He flushes the urinal.

SAM: Shouldn't be difficult. Giving up is what you do best.

JIM: Aren't you guys worried about getting caught? *(To PETE)* You know you've been in here for over an hour.

SAM: Shit time. Push me into the crapper, will ya, Pete.

PETE: Saunders won't come in here.

JIM: She might, Pete. Remember Rick and Stanley.

PETE: I do, but I'm not Rick and Stanley.

342

TOM: Jim, that story's horseshit. Those guys weren't queer.

SAM: *(From the stall)* Sure they were queer. Why do you think they always sat together at lunch, for Chrissake?

PETE: I'll never forget the day she caught them in here necking. Screamed her bloody head off. *(To TOM)* Of course the reason she gave for separating them was that they were talking too much and not getting their work done. Right, Jim? *(JIM says nothing)* No, Saunders won't come in here now. Not after a shock like that.

SAM: Maybe not, but she might send Cinderella to check up on us. How 'bout it, Princess?

JIM: Why would I do a thing like that?

PETE: Then why did you come in?

JIM: Is this washroom exclusive or something?

TOM: It's not that, Jim. It's just that you haven't been to one of our bull sessions for a long time. Not since your promotion.

JIM: I already told you. I just wanted to see if I was missing something.

SAM: You are. Your balls.

Knock at the door.

SAUNDERS: Jim! What's happening in there? I haven't got all day.

Silence. PETE and TOM look at JIM.

JIM: Okay, so she asked me. But I didn't come in here to spy.

SAM: Well move your ass, Romeo. You heard what the lady said, she can't wait all day.

SAUNDERS: Jim?

SAM: Bye-bye.

SAUNDERS: Jim, are you there?

JIM moves towards the door.

TOM: Wait, Jim, you don't have to go.

SAM: Dammit, let the fucker go. His mommy wants him.

PETE: Shut up, Sam.

SAM: I wasn't talking to you.

TOM: Why don't you stay for a while?

PETE: Yeah, tell old tight-cunt you're on the can or something.

He grabs JIM and pulls him away from the door.

SAUNDERS: Jim Harris! Do you hear me!?

PETE signals to JIM to answer.

JIM: Yes, Miss Saunders, I hear you. But I'm on the toilet at the moment.

SAUNDERS: What are you doing on the toilet?

PETE: *(At the door)* He's taking a shit. What do you do on the toilet?

SAUNDERS: If you boys aren't back to work in five minutes I'm reporting you to Mr. Carson.

She walks back down the hall.

SAM: Once upon a time, boys, there was a boudingy bird, and the cry of the boudingy went like this . . .

TOM and PETE: *(In falsetto, forestalling SAM)* Suck my boudingy!

Silence while PETE listens at the door.

344

JIM: I could use that cigarette now.

PETE: *(Bringing him one)* Thought you were trying to quit.

JIM: I am.

Pause.

TOM: Jim, why did you lie?

JIM: I did not lie. Saunders saw me coming in, and she thought I might remind you that you'd been in here a long time. That's all.

TOM: Then why didn't you say so when Sam asked you?

SAM: Because he's so used to telling lies, if anyone said he was spastic, he'd deny it.

TOM: Will ya shut up, Sam.

JIM: That's okay. Sam didn't care for me when I was sanding blocks with him.

SAM: Pete, push that chair in here, will you?

JIM: Now that he thinks I've gone over to the other side, he's got even less reason to like me.

SAM: Listen, Princess, nobody likes a white nigger.

TOM: What's that mean, Sam?

PETE: *(As he holds the chair for SAM)* Why don't you use a bedpan?

SAM: Why do you think, dummy? Because my ass begins to look like the other side of the moon. *(By now he is off the toilet and back in the chair.)* All right, all right.

He wheels backwards out of the stall.

JIM: Well, Sam?

SAM: Well what, stooge?

JIM: What do you mean, white nigger?

345

SAM: Well since you're all so fired fuckin' dyin' to know, I'll tell you. You finished high school, didn't you?

JIM: Yes.

SAM: And you went to university?

JIM: Yes.

SAM: And you got a degree?

JIM: So?

SAM: Well, you went to university. You wrote all that crap for the paper about how shitty it was to be handicapped in this country. Then what do you do? You come running down here and kiss the first ass you see. That's what I mean by being a white nigger, and that's what fuckin' well pisses me off.

JIM: All right, Sam, now you listen to me. I still believe everything I wrote, and I intend to act on it. But you can't change things until you're in a position to call the shots. And you don't get there without being nice to people. By the way, what are you doing about it? All I ever get from you is bitch, bitch, bitch.

SAM: I got every fuckin' right to bitch. You expect me to sand blocks and put up with the pityshit routine for ninety-nine years waiting for you to get your ass into a position of power? Fuck you, buddy! You give me a choice and I'll stop bitching.

TOM: Now look who's taking himself seriously.

SAM: (To TOM and PETE) What do you guys know about the bullshit I put up with? My old lady, now get this, my old lady has devoted her entire goddamn life to martyrdom. And my old man, you ever met my old man? Ever seen him give me one of his "Where have I failed?" looks? Wait'll ya hear what happened last night. He invited his boss over for dinner, and you know where the old bugger wanted me to eat? In the kitchen. First I told him to go screw the dog — that's about his style — and then, at the

346

height of the festivities, just when everything was going real nice for daddy, I puked all over the table.

TOM: Charming.

SAM: It was beautiful. Stuck my finger down my throat and out it all came: roast beef, mashed potatoes, peas, olives. There was a *real* abstract painting, Tom. You should have seen the look on his boss's face. Be a long time before he gives at the office again.

MICHAEL enters. During the ensuing dialogue he attempts to flush the urinals, but is stopped by signals from PETE.

JIM: You know, Sam, you amaze me. You say you don't want to wait ninety-nine years, but you're happy if you can set us back a few. A stunt like that doesn't make Carson's job any easier.

PETE: Okay, Timmy, you're not addressing the Spastic Club.

SAM: Piss on Carson! He doesn't give a shit about us and you know it.

JIM: I don't know it. I don't know what his motives are. But I do know he's trying to help us.

PETE: His motives are to keep the niggers in their place.

SAM: Yeah, by getting Uncle Timmy here to watch over them.

TOM: *(To SAM and PETE)* What are you guys, the resident hypocrites? Look, no one twists your arm to go to those Spastic Club meetings. No one forces those hot dogs down your throat.

PETE: Sure, we take them. Why not? They're free. Why look a gift horse in the mouth? But at least we don't kiss ass.

JIM: No, you let me do it for you. *(Slight pause)* But that's beside the point. The point is that Carson does care about what happens to us.

SAM: He does?

JIM: You're darn right he does.

SAM: You ever been over to his house for dinner?

JIM: Yes.

SAM: Ever been back?

JIM: No.

SAM: In other words, you got your token dinner, and now you only see him at Spastic Club meetings and here at the workshop?

JIM: That's not true. He comes to my place sometimes, doesn't he, Tom?

TOM: Yeah, but what about all those times your mother invited him for dinner and he cancelled out at the last minute?

JIM: So? That doesn't prove anything.

SAM: It proves a helluva lot to me.

MICHAEL pokes PETE on the shoulder.

PETE: What is it, Michael?

MICHAEL: Cigarette, please.

PETE: Okay, Michael, but smoke it this time, don't eat it. Last time everyone accused me of trying to poison you.

Banging at the door.

SAUNDERS: Boys! What's going on in there? If you don't come out this minute I'm coming in.

SAM: We dare you!

TOM: Shut up, Sam.

SAUNDERS: What was that?

PETE: Nothing, Miss Saunders. Sam just said, "We hear you."

SAUNDERS: Oh no he didn't. I know what he said. He said, "We dare you."

PETE: Well Christ, if you already knew, what the fuck did you ask for? *(To himself)* Stupid bitch!

SAUNDERS: Jim. What's happening in there? Are they doing something they shouldn't?

SAM: Yeah, we're pissing through our noses!

JIM: Cut it out, Sam. No, Tom and Pete are on the toilets, and I'm holding the bottle for Sam.

SAM: Hey, that hurts! Don't pull so hard, you idiot!

SAUNDERS: *(Nonplussed)* Well hurry up, and stop fooling around. I can't wait on you all day.

She starts down the hallway, stops when she hears

SAM: *(To the door)* That's it, Pete, no more blowjobs for cigarettes! Jim, take your hands off me, I've only got one! Michael, don't use your teeth! Christ, I've never seen so many queers in one place. I could open a fruit stand!

SAUNDERS listens, horrified, then runs off down the hall. MICHAEL sits on the floor and begins to eat the cigarette. The laughter subsides.

PETE: I think she left.

Pause.

TOM: Do I finally get to say something?

PETE: Oh yeah, where were we? You couldn't hack folding boxes.

TOM: Or the Spastic Club.

349

PETE: Or the Spastic Club.

TOM: Or Thelma.

PETE: Or Thelma.

TOM: Pete.

PETE: What's the matter now?

TOM: Cochran, for once in your life, will you be serious?

PETE: I'm fucking serious.

SAM: It's the only way to fuck.

PETE: If I was any more serious, I'd be dead. I wish to hell you'd get on with it, Tom.

Pause.

TOM: You guys ever read a story called "Premature Burial"?

SAM and JIM shake their heads.

PETE: What comic was it in?

TOM: Edgar Allen Poe.

PETE: Oh.

TOM: Anyway, it's about this guy who has this sickness that puts him into a coma every so often. And he's scared as hell someone's going to mistake him and bury him alive. Well, that's the way I feel about this workshop. It's like I'm at the bottom of a grave yelling "I'm alive! I am alive!" But they don't hear me. They just keep shovelling in the dirt.

THELMA: I need a priest!

JIM: Tom, if you really feel that way, you ought to talk to Carson.

TOM: Oh, fuck off.

JIM: He's not an idiot, you know.

350

PETE: Tom, you want to know what I think? I think you should stop reading junk like Edgar Allen Poe. You take that stuff too seriously.

SAM: Pete's right. You should stick to your regular diet.

TOM: What's that crack supposed to mean?

SAM: It's sticking out of your back pocket, sexy.

TOM reaches round and removes a book from his pocket.

TOM: *(Tossing it to SAM)* Here, Sam, why don't you take it for a while? Maybe it'll shut you up.

SAM: *(As he flicks through the book)* Hey, he's got the dirty parts underlined in red.

PETE: Read some.

SAM: *(Reading)* "Nothing like a nice yellow banana," she said aloud. It touched every sensitive area of her pussy. Tears came to her eyes in shots of violent lust. Then her movements began to increase and she spliced herself repeatedly . . .

TOM: That's enough, Sam.

SAM: The thick banana swirled in her cunt like a battering ram. She grasped it hard and shoved it faster and faster. Then she sat up, still gorged with the banana . . .

TOM: I said, that's enough!

He gets up and moves to take the book away from SAM.

SAM: *(Who has not stopped reading)* It hit high up against the walls of her wet cunt. She could move whichever way she liked. "Oh, shit, this is juicy," she said aloud. The reflection she saw in the mirror was ludicrous and made her even more hot. "Oh you big banana, fuck me! . . . "

TOM grabs the book.

PETE: Wait. I want to find out about the banana split.

TOM: If you're so hot about the banana, you can have the goddamn book.

He gives it to him.

SAM: It'll only cost you a nickel, Pete, it's underlined.

TOM: Okay. So I get a charge out of dirty books. What does that make me, a creep?

SAM: Well at least I don't pretend to be something I'm not. I don't work myself up during office hours.

TOM: No, you just do it at picnics.

SAM: What about a goddamn picnic?

JIM: Come on, Sam, you remember the Rotarian's daughter.

SAM: So I remember a Rotarian's daughter. What now?

PETE: She was sitting beside you and you were feeling her up like crazy, that's what now.

SAM: If the silly little fart is stupid enough to let me, why not?

JIM: You were making a bloody spectacle of yourself.

SAM: Love is where you find it.

PETE: Yeah, but with you working her over like that, I could hardly keep my mind on the three-legged race. Didn't she even say anything?

SAM: Nope, she just sat there. Smiled a lot.

THELMA: I need a priest! *(Pause)*

JIM: There's a girl who isn't smiling, is she, Sam?

SAM: Shut up, Harris.

THELMA: Get me a priest!

TOM: Ever since I've been here, Thelma's always calling for a priest. How come?

PETE: Sam knows.

SAM: Yeah, well mind your own business.

THELMA: Someone get me a priest!

SAM: *(Screams, overlapping THELMA)* Dry up, you stupid fuckin' broad!

PETE: Why don't you go comfort her, Sam? You used to be pretty good at comforting old Thelma.

JIM: Yeah, you couldn't keep your hands off her.

SAM: What's the matter, were ya jealous, princess?

TOM: Hey, I'd like to know what the hell's going on.

PETE: This was before your time, Tom. Thelma was all right then. Cute kid, as a matter of fact. Until old horney here got his hands on her and drove her off her rocker.

SAM: That's a fuckin' lie. The doctors said it wasn't my fault.

JIM: They only told you that to make it easy for you.

SAM: Look, it wasn't my fault.

JIM: What you did sure didn't help any.

SAM: Well why bring it up now?

PETE: Because we're sick and tired of having you put everybody down. It's time someone put you down for a change.

TOM: Well, what did he do? Will you please tell me?

PETE: From the day Thelma got here, Sam was after her like a hot stud. Being so nice to her, and then coming in here and bragging how she was letting him feel her up, and bragging how he was gonna fuck the ass off her soon.

THELMA: I want a priest!

PETE: Maybe you've heard, Tom, that Thelma's parents are religious. I don't just mean they're devout, they're real dingalings about it. Like they believe Thelma's the way she is because of some great sin they've committed. Like that. Anyway, she was home in bed one weekend with a cold, and Sam went over to visit her, and her parents weren't out of the room two seconds when Sam was into her pants.

SAM: That's another goddamn lie. It didn't happen that way.

PETE: Okay, so it took a full minute. Don't quibble over details.

SAM: Look I didn't mean for anything to happen that day. What do you think I am, stupid? In the first place, she had a cold, and in the second place, her parents were out on the goddamn porch. I just wanted to talk. She started fooling around, trying to grab my cannon and everything. Naturally I get a hard-on. What am I supposed to do? Silly little bitch! We were just going real good when she changed her mind. That's one helluva time to exercise her woman's prerogative, isn't it? Anyway, we . . . she fell out of bed. In a few seconds in come Mommy and Daddy. They thought I'd fallen out of my chair or something. Well, there I am in bed with my joint waving merrily in the breeze, and Thelma's on the floor minus her P.J.'s, and all hell broke loose. You'd have thought they'd never seen a cock before. The old man, he bounced me out of bed along the floor and into the hallway. The old lady, she dragged Thelma up behind. Then they held us up in front of a little Jesus statue and asked it to forgive us 'cause we didn't know what we were doing. (*Pause*) The doctors said it wasn't my fault.

JIM: They were only feeling sorry for a horny cripple in a wheelchair.

PETE: Yeah, but we all know the truth, don't we Sam?

SAM: (*Overlapping*) Why don't you shut the fuck up, Cochran!

JIM: Hey Pete, remember how Thelma used to dress before Sam put his rod to her? So pretty.

TOM: Okay, guys, knock it off.

PETE: Yeah, but that's all over now. Now she only wears black and brown, and everything's covered, right up to the neck.

JIM: She used to laugh a lot too.

TOM: That's enough!

THELMA: I need a priest!

MICHAEL: *(Sing-song)* Thelma needs a priest. Thelma needs a priest.

SAM: Fuck off! Piece of shit!

SAM goes for MICHAEL, who is sitting on the floor, and hits out at him. MICHAEL is surprised, but hits back. To stop the fight, PETE grabs Sam's chair from behind. SAM then lashes out at PETE. At the same time, JIM and TOM go to rescue MICHAEL. JIM falls while TOM tries to get MICHAEL's attention away from SAM. Throughout the commotion MICHAEL continues to yell, "Thelma needs a priest." Finally, SAM wheels angrily away and PETE helps JIM up.

TOM: *(At one of the urinals)* Hey, Michael, look, a cockroach. Big fat one.

MICHAEL sees the cockroach and gets very excited. PETE, TOM, and JIM gather round him at the urinal.

PETE: Hey, Sam, there's livestock in the pisser.

TOM: *(To MICHAEL)* Why don't you use your ray gun and disintegrate it?

MICHAEL: What ray gun? I got no ray gun.

SAM: Yes, you have. That thing between your legs. It's a ray gun.

MICHAEL looks down and makes the connection.

MICHAEL: *(Delighted)* I disintegrate it. I disintegrate it all up.

He turns into the urinal.

SAM: You do that.

SAUNDERS returns and knocks at the door.

SAUNDERS: For the last time, are you boys coming out or not?

SAM: Go away, we're busy.

SAUNDERS: Very well, then, I'm coming in.

She enters the washroom.

PETE: Have you no sense of decency?

SAUNDERS: All right, I don't know what you boys have been doing in here, but I want you back to work immediately. Pete, you've still that rug. Tom, there's boxes to be folded. Sam, you'd better get busy and sand down the edges of those blocks if you expect to earn anything this week. As for you, Jim, well, I'm beginning to have second thoughts.

JIM: Yes, ma'am.

Pause. No one makes a move to go.

SAUNDERS: Well, get moving!

PETE: I have to take a crap.

He heads into one of the stalls.

TOM: Me too.

He goes into the other one.

SAM: I have to use the bottle.

SAUNDERS: And how about you, Jim? Don't you have something to do?

SAM: He has to hold the bottle for me.

SAUNDERS: He has to what, Sam?

SAM: Well, it's like this. I don't have a very good aim, so Princess here is gonna get down on her hands and knees . . .

SAUNDERS: (Cutting him off) All right, that's quite enough. When you're through here, I want you back to work. And fast. Michael, you come with me.

MICHAEL turns around from the urinal. His pants are open, his penis exposed.

MICHAEL: (To SAUNDERS) I'm gonna disintegrate you.

SAUNDERS: (Screams) Michael! Oh, you boys, you put him up to this! Didn't you?

PETE: We did not.

SAUNDERS: Right! Mr. Carson will be here any minute. We'll see what he has to say.

She opens the door to leave.

SAM: (Calling after her) Hey, be careful. He's got one too.

More screams. She exits, and is seen running down the hall. PETE and TOM emerge from the stalls laughing. JIM tidies MICHAEL and sends him out the door.

PETE: Sam, you have a warped sense of humour.

SAM: Yeah, just like the rest of me.

JIM: Proud of that, aren't you Sam? Professional cripple.

SAM: Eat shit, princess.

JIM: And such a sterling vocabulary.

Pause. JIM begins to pick up cigarette butts and matches, which by now litter the floor.

TOM: Hadn't you better go before Carson gets back?

JIM: The office can wait.

TOM: What'll you do when he gets here?

JIM: I'll cross that bridge when I come to it.

TOM: Well, we'll all have to cross that bridge soon. We've been in here for over half an hour.

SAM: Yeah, we do tend to take long craps.

PETE: I don't care how long it takes me to crap.

Pause.

TOM: Did you get your typewriter fixed yet, Jim?

JIM: No, I haven't had time.

TOM: Well, my dad's offer still stands . . . If you'd like him to take a look at it.

JIM: Thanks, I would. How is your father?

TOM: He's okay. Why don't you bring it over Sunday?

JIM: I'll have to see. I'm kind of busy at the club. Christmas is coming.

TOM: It will only take an hour.

JIM: You wouldn't like to give us a hand this year, would you?

TOM: What did you have in mind?

JIM: I thought you might like to do our Christmas mural.

TOM: No, I don't think so.

JIM: Spastic Club's not good enough for chickentracks, eh? Seriously, Tom, I could use some help. Not just for the mural, but to paint posters, stuff like that.

TOM: How much is the Spastic Club willing to pay for all this?

JIM: Come on, you know there's no payment. All the work for the club is done on a voluntary basis. Carson's never paid anyone before.

SAM: So why should the old fart break his record of stinginess just for you?

JIM: It may interest you to know, Sam, that Carson doesn't get paid for his services either.

SAM: Bwess his wittle heart.

TOM: In that case, the answer's no. If I get paid for folding boxes, why the hell should I paint a lousy mural for free?

JIM: I just thought it might keep you busy.

TOM: I'm busy enough.

JIM gets up, staggers over to the waste basket and deposits his litter. SAM applauds.

PETE: Jim, what's the Spastic Club planning for us boys and girls this year?

JIM: Oh, we've got a few things up our sleeve. Actually, we'd appreciate it if some of the members were a bit more co-operative. So far the response has been practically nil.

TOM: That's horseshit.

PETE: What about my idea of having that psychologist down from the university?

JIM: Well, since you're so interested, Pete, I'll tell you. Carson didn't think too much of it. He was afraid the members would be bored. I don't happen to agree with him, but that's the way he feels.

SAM: What about my idea for installing ramps in the subway?

JIM: It's a good idea, Sam, but that sort of thing doesn't come under our jurisdiction.

SAM: Who says so?

JIM: It's up to the city. We're not in a position . . .

TOM: Okay, Jim, what does the Spastic Club have up its sleeve for this year?

JIM: There's a trip to the Science Centre. One to the African Lion Safari. We're organizing a finger painting contest, that Sorority is throwing a Valentine's day party for us . . .

PETE: Wheee! A party!

Circus music is heard low in the distance.

TOM: What's the entertainment, Jim?

JIM: Puffo the Clown, Merlin the Magician . . .

PETE: And Cinderella, and Snow White and the Seven Fucking Dwarfs. Jesus Christ, Jim, Puffo the Clown! What do you and Carson think you're dealing with, a bunch of fucking babies?

Blackout, circus music at full and bright lights. PUFFO, in clown suit, has arrived, carrying balloons. Enter also the GIRL and two SHRINERS, the GIRL dressed in circus attire. She is marching and twirling a baton. One of the SHRINERS is wearing a Mickey Mouse mask and white gloves. He follows the GIRL, weaving in and around the boys, dancing in time to the music. The other SHRINER appears on a tricycle (or on roller skates, if preferred) waving to the audience. PUFFO presents SAM, TOM and PETE each with a balloon, and exits following the GIRL and SHRINERS. The music fades.

PETE: Who was that masked man, anyway?

On a signal from PETE, the boys burst their balloons with their lighted cigarettes.

JIM: Wait a minute, Pete, let me finish. We've got other things planned.

PETE: Like what?

JIM: Well, for one, we're planning a trip to a glue factory.

TOM: You're kidding.

JIM: No, I'm not. Carson thinks it might be very educational.

TOM: What do you think, Jim? Do you think it will be very educational?

JIM: I don't know. I've never seen them make glue before.

PETE: Well, you take one old horse, and you stir well . . .

JIM: We're planning other things too, you know.

TOM: What other things?

JIM: Well you know, theatre trips, museum trips. These things take time, Tom. We've written letters and . . .

TOM: What letters? To whom?

JIM: Letters. Lots of letters. They're at home in my briefcase. I'll show them to you tomorrow.

TOM: Any replies?

JIM: What?

TOM: How many replies did you get to the letters?

JIM: Look, am I on trial or something?

TOM: I don't know, Jim. Are you?

JIM: Okay, maybe some of the things we do aren't as exciting as you and I'd like them to be, but I'm doing the job as well as I can, and I can't do it all on my own. You guys

361

bitch about the programme, but you won't get off your asses and fight for something better. That idea of Pete's about the psychologist, I really pushed that idea. Pushed it to the hilt . . .

PETE: But Carson didn't like it.

JIM: Carson didn't like it, and the more I pushed the firmer he got.

SAM: Why didn't you push it right up his ass?

JIM: *(Ignoring this)* So I told Pete he should go down and talk to Carson himself. I even made him an appointment. But he never showed up, did you, Pete?

PETE: I was busy.

TOM: Why the hell should you or Pete or anyone else have to beg that prick for anything?

JIM: Tom, that's not fair. So he's a little stuffy, at least he's interested. He does give us more than the passing time of day.

PETE: Sure, he was in for a whole hour this morning.

JIM: Pete, you may not like Carson, but just remember. If he, or the Kiwanis, or any of the other service clubs decide to throw in the towel, we're in big trouble.

SAM: "If they won't do it . . . ."

JIM: If they won't do it, who will? You?

A long pause.

PETE: I've got nothing against the Rotary or the Kiwanis. if they want to give me a free meal just to look good, that's okay with me.

TOM: You're sure of that?

PETE: Tom, the Bible says the Lord provides. Right now He's providing pretty good. Should I get upset if He sends the Kiwanis instead of coming Himself?

JIM: If you feel like getting something, why don't you give something?

PETE: No, sir. I don't jump through hoops for nobody, and certainly not for a bastard like Carson. I might have nothing to say against the groups, but I don't have anything to say for them either.

TOM: You can't stay neutral all the time.

PETE: Tell that to Switzerland. Tom, you're young. You don't realize how tough it is for people like us. Baby, it's cold outside.

SAM: *(Under his breath)* Christ!

PETE: When I came to this dump eleven years ago, I wanted to be a carpenter. That's all I could think about ever since I can remember. But face it, whoever heard of a carpenter with a flipper like that? *(Holds up his deformed hand)* But I had a nice chat with this doc, and he told me I'd find what I'm looking for down here. So I came down here, and one of Saunders' flunkies shoves a bag of blocks in my hand. "What gives?" I said. And then it slowly dawned on me that as far as the doc is concerned, that's the closest I'll ever get to carpentry.

And I was pissed off, sure. But then I think, good old doc, he just doesn't understand me. 'Cause I still have my ideals. So in a few days I bust out of this place and go looking for a job — preferably carpentry. What happens? I get nothing but aching feet and a flat nose from having fucking doors slammed in my face all the fucking time.

And I'm at my wits end when I got a letter from the Spastic Club. And I said fuck that. I'm about to throw it in the furnace, but I get curious. I've heard of the Spastic Club and I always figured it was a load of shit. But I think one meeting isn't going to kill me.

So I go, and I find out I'm right. It's a load of shit. It's a bunch of fuckheads sitting around saying, "Aren't we just too ducky for these poor unfortunate cripples?" But I got a free turkey dinner.

When I got home I took a good look at myself. I ask myself what am I supposed to be fighting? What do these jokers want me to do? The answer is they want to make life easier for me. Is that so bad? I mean, they don't expect me to keep you guys in your place or nothing. They just want me to enjoy life. And the government even pays me just for doing that. If I got a job, I'd lose the pension. So why have I been breaking my ass all this time looking for a job? And I got no answers to that. So I take the pension, and come back to the workshop. The only price I gotta pay is listening to old lady Saunders giving me hell for not weaving her goddamn rug.

Blackout. Fanfare. Light up on far side of the stage. The actor playing MICHAEL enters dressed as a freak show barker. With him is the girl, his assistant, dressed in similar carnival attire. The following sequence takes place in a stage area independent of the washroom.

BARKER: *(To the audience)* Are you bored with your job? Would you like to break out of the ratrace? Does early retirement appeal to you? Well, my friends, you're in luck. The Shriners, the Rotary, and the Kiwanis are just begging to wait on you hand and foot.

Charleston music. The BARKER and the GIRL dance. The music continues through the next several speeches until he is handed the brain.

To throw you parties, picnics. To take you on field trips. To the flower show, the dog show, and to the Santa Claus Parade.

More dancing.

Would you like to learn new skills? Like sanding blocks, folding boxes, separating nuts and bolts? My friends, physiotherapists are standing by eager to teach you.

The GIRL hands him a wooden block and another block covered with sandpaper. More dancing as he sands the block.

Whoopee, is this ever fun.

He hands the block back to the GIRL.

Now, I suppose you good people would like to know, how do I get this one-way ticket to paradise? My props, please.

The GIRL hands him a life-size model of a human brain which has the various sections marked off, and a hammer. The music stops. He walks downstage into a pool of light directly in front of the audience.

Now all you do is take a hammer and adjust the motor area of the brain. Like this. Not too hard, now, we wouldn't want to lose you.

He taps the brain gently.

Having done that, you will have impaired your muscle co-ordination, and will suddenly find that you now *(Speaking with the speech defect of the character Michael)* "talk with an accent". You will then be brought to our attention either by relatives who have no room for you in the attic, or by neighbours who are distressed to see you out in the street, clashing with the landscape.

Now, assuming you are successful in locating the proper point of demolition, we guarantee that this very special euphoria will be yours not for a day, not for a week, but for a lifetime. There's no chance of relapse, regression, or rehabilitation because, my friends, it's as permanent as a hair transplant. It's for keeps. Should you, however, become disenchanted with this state, there is one recourse available to you, which while we ourselves do not recommend it, is popular with many, and does provide a final solution to a very complex problem. All you do is take the hammer and simply tap a little harder.

He smashes the brain. At the moment of impact, he becomes spastic, and slowly crumbles to the floor. Blackout.

The lights come up on the four boys.

SAM: Guys like you really bug me. You got two good legs and one good hand. So the other's deformed. Big Fuckin' Deal. By the way, who the hell said you couldn't be a carpenter? You had your loom fixed up in five minutes last week while that old fart of a handyman was running around town looking for something to fix it with.

PETE: That was just lucky.

TOM: You know what I think, Cochran? I think you're lazy. I think eleven years ago you were looking for a grave to fall into, and you found it in the Spastic Club.

PETE: Don't be self-righteous about things you don't understand.

TOM: I understand laziness.

PETE: You don't understand. I tried.

TOM: Aw, c'mon, Pete, you didn't try very hard.

PETE: There's no place in the outside world for a guy who talks funny.

SAM: Aw, you poor wittle boy. Did the big bad mans hurt your wittle feelings?

PETE goes for SAM, is about to hit him, but is restrained by TOM.

TOM: That's not funny, Sam. *(To PETE)* But it is a bit ridiculous. Here you are, you're thirty-seven years old, and you're still worried about something as small as that.

PETE: It may be a small thing to you, Tom. It's not to me.

JIM: Howdya like to have kids following you down the street calling you drunk? I get that all the time, but you learn to live with it.

SAM: Sure you learn to live with it. You learn to rub their noses in it too. Last week I was at this show and I had to be bounced about twenty steps in the chair just to get to the lobby. Well, you know what that does to my bladder, eh? So naturally I make for the washroom. The stalls are two inches too narrow, of course. As for the urinals, I never claimed to be Annie Oakley. They don't have urinal bottles 'cause they'd fuck up the interior decoration. But then I did spy this Dixie cup dispenser . . .

JIM: Sam, you didn't!

SAM: Yeah, sweetie, I did. I was just doing up my fly when the usher walked in, saw the cup sitting on the edge of the sink. He thought it was lemonade. Told me patrons weren't allowed to bring refreshments into the washroom. Then he moved closer and got a whiff.

PETE: What happened?

SAM: Another United Appeal supporter had his dreams all crushed to ratshit.

JIM: And Sam set us back another twenty years.

SAM: What do you expect me to do, Harris? Piss my pants waiting for everything to come under your jurisdiction?

PETE: Sam's right. It's like you said, Jim. You do the best with what you got.

TOM: Come on, Pete, that's a cop-out and you know it. Sam should have got rid of that cup as soon as he took his leak. Putting it on the sink in plain view of everyone, for Chrissake!

PETE: Don't be so smug. A guy survives the best way he knows how. You wait, you'll find out. They don't want us creeps messing up their world. They just don't want us.

TOM: Tough! They're going to get me whether they want me or not. I'm a man, and I've got a right to live like other men.

PETE: You're the only man I know who can make a sermon out of saying hello.

He goes into one of the stalls, slamming the door behind him.

TOM: Yeah and pretty soon I'm gonna say goodbye. You expect me to spend the rest of my life folding boxes?

PETE: *(Over the top of the stall)* Look, Rembrandt, we know you're a great artist and all that shit. But if you paint like you fold, forget it.

JIM: Wait a minute, Pete. I've seen some of Tom's paintings. I'm no expert on abstract, but I think they're pretty good. They're colourful and . . .

SAM: Colourful chickentracks?

TOM: Fuck off!

JIM: Still, I'm not other people. I might like them, but folks on the outside might not. People get pretty funny when they find out something's been done by a handicapped person. Besides, we both know you can't draw.

TOM: That doesn't make any difference. I paint abstract.

SAM: So you'll win the finger painting contest.

JIM: Tom, we've been over this I don't know how many times. Name me one good abstract painter who isn't a good draftsman.

SAM: Name me one good writer who'd be caught dead in a glue factory.

JIM: Seriously, can you think of one famous artist who was spastic?

TOM: Jim, if you're sure I can't make it, what about the letter?

PETE: What letter?

JIM: *(Shrugs)* Oh, a letter he got from an art critic.

PETE: *(Emerging from the stall)* What did it say?

TOM: Here, you can read it yourself.

He hands the letter to PETE who begins to read it to himself.

SAM: Out loud.

PETE starts to read it, gives up, hands the letter to JIM.

JIM: *(Reading)* Dear Mr. March, I was fascinated by the portfolio you submitted. I cannot recall an artist in whose work such a strong sense of struggle was manifest. You positively stab the canvas with bold colour, and your sure grasp of the palette lends a native primitivism to your work. I am at once drawn to the crude simplicity of your figures and repulsed by the naive grotesqueries which grope for recognition in your tortured world. While I cannot hail you as a mature artist, I would be interested in seeing your work in progress this time next year.

SAM: Which one of your father's friends wrote it?

TOM: None of them.

SAM: One of your mother's friends?

TOM: The letter's authentic. I'll bring the guy's magazine column if you don't believe me.

PETE: Oh, we believe you, Tom. Critics are so compassionate.

TOM: You shit all over everything, don't you?

PETE: *(Handing TOM the letter)* It's a good letter, I guess.

TOM: You guess?

PETE: Well, what the hell am I supposed to say? You're the artist. I don't even like the Mona Lisa. To me she's just a fat ugly broad. But I can't help wondering, Tom . . .

TOM: What?

PETE: If he wouldn't have said the same thing if you'd sent him one of your boxes. (TOM starts to protest but PETE goes on) Like when I'm weaving that goddamn rug and we have visitors. Now I'm no master weaver. Matter of fact, I've woven some pretty shitty rugs in my time. But whenever we have visitors, there are always one of two clowns who come over and practically have an orgasm over my rug, no matter how shitty we both know it is.

SAM: It's the same with the blocks. They pick one up, tell me how great it is, and then walk away with a handful of splinters.

TOM: It's not the same. This guy happens to be one of the toughest art critics around.

JIM: Even tough art critics give to the United Appeal.

TOM: Yes, and sometimes writers write for it.

JIM: Well, it keeps me off the streets.

SAM: Yeah, Jim peddles his ass indoors where it's warm.

PETE: And Carson has an exclusive contract on it. Right Jim?

JIM: I work because I want to work. It's a challenge, I enjoy it, and I can see the results.

PETE: Sure. So can we. Hot dogs, ice cream, balloons, confetti . . .

JIM: Well at least I don't have illusions of grandeur.

TOM: What illusions have you got, Jim?

JIM: Tom, you've got to come down to earth sooner or later. For someone in my situation the workshop makes sense. I can be more useful in a place like this.

TOM: Useful to Carson?

JIM: No, to people like Michael and Thelma.

TOM: What about Carson? Are you going to go on kissing his ass?

JIM: Call it what you like. In dealing with people, I have to be diplomatic.

TOM: Fine, Jim. You be diplomatic for both of us.

He gets up.

PETE: Where are you going?

TOM: I'm bored. I'm leaving.

PETE: What's the matter?

TOM: Nothing, Cochran, go back and finish your shit.

JIM: Tom, what is it?

TOM: I'm quitting.

JIM: You're not serious?

TOM: Getting more serious by the minute.

JIM: You're building a lot on a few kind words, aren't you?

TOM: The man doesn't know I'm spastic.

JIM: He's going to find out. And you know what'll happen when he does. You'll be his golden boy for a few weeks, but as soon as the novelty wears off, he'll go out of his way to avoid you.

TOM: What if the novelty doesn't wear off?

JIM: Tom, I don't think you should rush into this.

TOM: How long do I have to stay, Jim?

JIM: Stay until Christmas. Stay and do the mural.

TOM: No.

JIM: But you like painting. It won't hurt you.

TOM: I said no!

JIM: Why not?

TOM moves towards the door.

JIM: Won't you at least talk about it?

TOM: *(He turns and looks at JIM.)* That's all you know how to do now, isn't it? No writing, no thinking, just talking. Well get this straight. I don't want any part of the Spastic Club or the Workshop. It's finished, okay?

JIM: Look, I know this place isn't perfect. I agree. It's even pretty rotten at times. But, Tom, out there, you'll be lost. You're not wanted out there, you're not welcome. None of us are. If you stay here we can work together. We can build something.

SAM: Yeah, a monument to Carson. For the pigeons to shit on.

TOM: How long are *you* going to stay here?

JIM: How long?

TOM: Are you going to spend the rest of your life being Carson's private secretary?

JIM: Well, nothing's permanent. Even I know that.

TOM: Stop bullshitting and give me a straight answer.

JIM: Okay, I'll move on. Sure.

TOM: And do what?

JIM: Maybe I'll go back to my writing.

TOM: When? *(No reply)* When was the last time you wrote anything?

JIM: Last month I wrote an article for "The Sunshine Friend."

PETE: *(Joined by SAM)* "You are my sunshine, my only sunshine . . . "

TOM: Shut up! I mean when was the last time you wrote something you wanted to write?

JIM: Well, you know, my typewriter's bust . . .

TOM: Don't give me that crap about your typewriter. You don't want to get it fixed.

JIM: That's not true . . .

TOM: Do you know what you're doing here? You're throwing away your talent for a lousy bit of security.

JIM: Tom, you don't understand . . .

TOM: You're wasting your time doing a patch up job at something you don't really believe in. (*JIM does not reply. TOM moves towards him.*) Jim, there are stacks of guys in this world who haven't the intelligence to know where they're at. But you have. You *know*. And if you don't *do* something with that knowledge, you'll end up hating yourself.

JIM: What the hell could I do?

TOM: You could go into journalism, write a book. Listen, in this job, who can you tell it to? Spastics. Now think. Think of all the millions of jerks on the outside who have no idea of what it's really like in here. Hell, you could write a best-seller.

JIM: I've thought about it.

TOM: Well *do* something about it.

JIM: Don't you think I want to?

TOM: Jim, I know you're scared. I'm scared. But if I don't take this chance, I won't have a hope in hell of making it. And if you keep on doing something you don't want to do, soon you won't even have a mind. Do you think if Michael had a mind like yours he'd be content to hang around here all day flushing toilets?

PETE: He's right, Jim. You don't belong here. Why don't you and Tom go together?

TOM: Look, I'll help you. We can go, we can get a place, we can do it together. Come on, what do you say?

SAUNDERS and CARSON enter the hallway.

SAUNDERS: They've been in here all afternoon. I tried to reason with them, but they refused to come out. I know you're busy, and I hate to bring you down here, but I'm really afraid this Rick and Stanley business is repeating itself . . .

CARSON: Miss Saunders.

SAUNDERS: Yes?

CARSON: Thanks, I can take it from here.

SAUNDERS exits. CARSON opens the door and stands in the doorway.

CARSON: Okay, guys, out.

Brief pause, then JIM moves to go.

TOM: Jim, how about it?

JIM: Later, Tom.

CARSON: Much later. It's time to get back to work.

TOM: I'm quitting, Carson.

CARSON: First things first. We can discuss that in the morning. *(He waits)* Let's go.

JIM: I'm quitting, too, sir.

CARSON: Right now I've got a good mind to fire you. Go to my office and wait for me.

SAM: He's making it real easy for you Jim. He just fired you.

CARSON: You, too, Sam. Out.

SAM: I need the bottle. Hand me the bottle, Carson.

CARSON: You've had all afternoon to use the bottle. Now, out!

SAM: I need the fucking bottle!

TOM goes to get the bottle, is stopped by CARSON.

CARSON: You leave that bottle alone. I want you all out of here.

PETE gets the bottle, gives it to SAM.

CARSON: Pete! Goddamn it, what's wrong with you guys?

SAM now has the bottle in his lap.

CARSON: Give me that bottle! *(He takes it away from SAM.)* Now get out of here, all of you. *(Nothing happens, so he starts to wheel SAM's chair.)*

SAM: Take your fuckin' hands off my chair!

JIM: Listen! You never listen to me!

CARSON: For God's sake, Jim, I'll listen, but in my office.

JIM: No, here. Now!

CARSON: What's eating you?

SAM: Give me the goddamn bottle.

He tries to get it, but CARSON holds it out of his reach.

CARSON: Get out of here, Sam!

He pushes the chair away.

SAM: Fucking prick!

CARSON: *(Shaken)* All right, what is it?

TOM: Jim, he's listening.

JIM: I don't want to spend the rest of my life here.

CARSON: Fine. You probably won't. Now can we all get back to work?

SAM: I need the fucking bottle!

TOM: Didn't you hear what he said? He said he doesn't want to spend his whole life in this dump.

CARSON: Look, March, you've been in here all afternoon. You've got Miss Saunders all upset because of Michael, and . . .

SAM: *I need the bottle!*

CARSON: Shut up, Sam!

TOM: Do you know why we've been here all the afternoon? Did you ever think of that?

SAM: Son of a bitch! Do you want me to piss my pants?

CARSON shoves the bottle at him, SAM wheels into the doorway of one of the stalls.

TOM: Did it ever enter your head that we might think of something besides the workshop, the club, and making you look good?

CARSON: Look, I don't know what you think, and right now I really don't care. All I'm concerned with is that you get out of this washroom. If you've got a complaint, you can come and talk to me.

TOM: I won't be there. Neither will Jim.

CARSON: I said, we can discuss that in the morning. *(He turns to SAM and PETE.)* Come on Sam, Pete, let's go.

PETE: He can't find it, Carson.

JIM: I want to be a writer.

CARSON: *(To SAM and PETE.)* Quit fooling around, and hurry up.

JIM: I want to be a writer!

CARSON: You are a writer.

JIM: You don't understand. I want to make my living from it.

CARSON: Maybe you will, some day. But it's not going to happen overnight, is it?

TOM: If you stay here, Jim, it won't happen at all.

CARSON: It sure as hell won't if he runs off on some half-assed adventure with you.

TOM: Come on, Jim, the man's deaf.

CARSON: And what is it this time, Rembrandt? Poverty in a garret somewhere?

TOM: Better than poverty at the workshop.

CARSON: What are you going to paint, nude women?

TOM: You son of a bitch!

CARSON: Okay, Tom. Let's go.

He moves to usher TOM out.

TOM: You fucking son of a bitch! (*In pushing him off, TOM loses his balance and falls. CARSON tries to help him up.*) Get the fuck off me, Carson! (*Slowly JIM and PETE help him to his feet.*) Jim, you can stay and fart around as much as you like, but I'm going. Now are you with me or not?

CARSON: No, he's not. Now beat it.

TOM: Is that your answer, Jim?

JIM: Tom, wait . . .

TOM: I'm tired of waiting.

JIM: Maybe if I had just a little more time.

TOM: There's no time left.

JIM: Couldn't we wait till the end of the week?

CARSON: No, Jim. If you're serious about going, go now.

JIM: What about the Christmas programme?

CARSON: I can find someone else.

JIM: But Christmas is the busiest time.

PETE: Go, Jim! Go with Tom!

SAM: *(Overlapping)* Don't let him do it to you, baby. Go!

JIM: But Tom, it's Christmas!

TOM: Jim, please!

JIM: I can't let him down now. Maybe after Christmas . . .

SAM: Fuck Christmas! What about Tom?

JIM: I've written all these letters, made all the arrangements...

TOM turns and moves towards the door.

SAM: Piss on the arrangements! Are you going to let him walk out that door alone?

PETE: If you don't go now, Tom will be alone, but you'll be more alone. Believe me, I know.

JIM: I can't go! I can't go, Tom, because, if you fall, I'll be the only one there to pick you up. And I can hardly stand up myself.

TOM has gone.

SAM: How did you get around on campus, princess? Crawl on your belly? *(He wheels angrily to the door.)* Fuckin' door! Hey, Carson, how about one cripple helping another?

CARSON: Get him out, Pete.

SAM and PETE exit. They wait outside the door, listening. JIM staggers over to the bench and sits.

378

CARSON: Why don't we talk about this over dinner? At my place, if you like.

THELMA: I need a priest! Get me a priest! Someone get me a priest!

Slow fade to the sound of Thelma's sobbing. PETE wheels SAM down the hallway. SAM is laughing.

David French

Of the Fields, Lately

EDITOR'S NOTE: David French was born in Coley's Point, New-foundland in 1939, but moved with his family to Toronto in 1945. After graduating from high school, he took a variety of jobs while studying acting in Toronto and the Pasadena Playhouse in California. Professional acting afforded him a livelihood until 1965 when he had become established as a writer of television and radio scripts. In 1972 *Leaving Home*, about a Newfoundland family transplanted to Toronto, was staged by Tarragon Theatre and became a finalist for the annual Chalmers Outstanding Canadian Play Award. *Leaving Home*, which has had at least 80 different productions, was followed by five more stage plays, all done at the Tarragon, including *Of the Fields, Lately* and *Jitters* (1979), a witty comedy about Canadian theatre and social manners which has had over 100 productions to date.

Of the Fields, Lately opened its first run on 29 September 1973 at Toronto's Tarragon Theatre, and won the Chalmers Outstanding Canadian Play Award for that year. It was first published in 1973 by Playwrights Canada and in 1975 by New Press. The play has had over forty productions to date.

Characters:

BEN
JACOB
MARY
WIFF

The scene: A house in Toronto, January, 1961.

ACT I
Scene 1 *early Sunday evening:*
Scene 2 *two hours later.*

ACT II
Scene 1 *Monday morning:*
Scene 2 *early Monday evening.*

NOTE: *Music for the scene changes and the epilogue:*
Bach's Variation No. 25 played on piano, from Bach's Goldberg Variations.

ACT ONE SCENE ONE

Limbo. Light up on BEN.

BEN: *(to the audience)* It takes many incidents to build a wall between two men, brick by brick. Sometimes you're not aware of the building of the wall, and sometimes you are, though not always strong enough or willing enough to kick it down. It starts very early, as it did with my father and me, very early. And it becomes a pattern that is hard to break until the wall is made of sound brick and mortar, as strong as any my father ever built. Time would not level it. Only death.

I don't know if my father ever remembered one such incident. He never spoke of it to me, but I often thought it was the emotional corner-stone of the wall between us.

Light up on JACOB.

JACOB: It was summer, 1952, and I had just come home from work, later than usual. It was going on nine in the evening, and as I stepped in the door, Mary said to me, "Ain't tonight the night Ben's team plays for the championship?"

BEN: He rushed out the door and down to the school-yard, the first game he had ever come to, and my mother put his supper in the oven, for later . . . I hadn't reminded my father of the game. I was afraid he'd show up and embarrass me. Twelve years old, and ashamed of my old man. Ashamed of his dialect, his dirty overalls, his bruised fingers with the fingernails lined with dirt, his teeth yellow as old ivory. Most of all, his lunchpail, that symbol of the working man. No, I wanted a doctor for a father. A lawyer. At least a fireman. Not a carpenter. That wasn't good enough . . . And at home my mother sat down to darn his socks and watch the oven . . . I remember stepping up to bat. The game was tied; it was the last of the ninth, with no one on base. Then I saw him sitting on the bench along third base. He grinned and waved, and gestured to the man beside him.

JACOB: *(at game)* That's my son.

BEN: But I pretended not to see him. I turned to face the pitcher. And angry at myself, I swung hard on the first pitch, there was a hollow crack, and the ball shot low over the short-stop's head for a double. Our next batter bunted and I made third. He was only a few feet away now, my father.

JACOB: Ben! Ben! Over here! Ben!

BEN: But I still refused to acknowledge him. Instead, I stared hard at the catcher, pretending concentration. And when the next pitch bounced between the catcher's legs and into home screen, I slid home to win the game.

JACOB: His team-mates pounced on him and hefted him up on their shoulders and lugged him around the infield. A hero.

BEN: And there he was, jumping up and down, showing his teeth, excited as hell.

JACOB: 'Ben!' I shouted my level best. 'Ben!' And I seen him look my way . . . and then look off . . . *(Light fades slowly on JACOB.)*

BEN: And as the crowd broke up and our team stampeded out of the school-yard, cleats clicking and scraping blue sparks on the sidewalk, I looked back once through the wire fence and saw my father still sitting on the now-empty bench, alone, slumped over a little, staring at the cinders between his feet, just staring . . . I don't know how long he stayed there, maybe till dark, but I do know he never again came down to see me play. At home that night he never mentioned the game or being there. He just went to bed unusually early . . .

A hymn begins: "Abide with Me", softly at first as BEN turns and walks into the kitchen, removes his shirt and drops it into the bushel basket beside the ironing board. The light has been slowly fading, and the hymn rising in volume as the light fades to black, then comes up onstage.

The stage is divided into two rooms: living-room and kitchen. In addition there is a hallway with the front door offstage. A staircase leads up from the hallway to the second floor, to the bedrooms and bathroom, all unseen.

The kitchen contains an ironing board, a small arborite table and four chairs, a stove, fridge, cupboards over the sink containing dishes, a wall telephone, a calendar and kitchen prayer. There is also a back door leading off the kitchen and a window.

The living-room contains a bay window, a knick-knack cabinet, chesterfield and arm-chair, T.V. and radio. There are various family photographs around the room.

It is a few minutes past seven, Sunday evening, January, 1961.

JACOB sits on the chesterfield in the living-room, listening with a preoccupied look to the hymn which comes from a nearby radio. He wears casual clothes.

MARY is in the kitchen, ironing. She sings along with the hymn. There is a bushel basket of clothing on the floor beside the ironing board, and now and then she helps herself to a shirt or blouse, irons and folds it. She wears black.

MARY: Remember that time Dot and me was crossing Water Street with Ben in the carriage? You and Wiff was behind.

JACOB looks up and turns down the radio.

The streetcar had stopped to let us cross, and that old car shot out from behind it and took the carriage right out of our hands.

JACOB: Can still hear the t'ump. And you screaming like a tea-kettle.

MARY: Poor Dot. She fainted dead away. T'ought he was killed for sure. Remember that?

JACOB: A wonder he wasn't, the way the carriage was all squashed up.

MARY: A miracle she called it. Suppose it was . . . *(pause)*

JACOB: He hardly said hello, Mary . . .

MARY: What?

JACOB: Two years away, and he hardly gives me a glance.

MARY: Well, give him time, he just got in. Besides, you wasn't much better, the way you kept your distance.

JACOB: Not so much as a handshake . . .

MARY: Perhaps if you'd put your hand out first . . .

JACOB: Yes, and have him chop it off. *(He rises, crosses to archway.)* What's he home for? Did he say?

MARY: Dot's funeral, I imagine.

384

JACOB: What? All the ways from Saskatchewan? He wasn't that close to Dot.

MARY: Look, Jake, I don't know any more than you do. I was just as surprised as you when he walked in tonight. He never mentioned he was coming home.

JACOB: You sure, Mary?

MARY: Well, you was listening into my ear when I called him yesterday. Did I once ask him to? Did I?

At that moment BEN comes down the stairs, and JACOB returns to the chesterfield. BEN's hair is slightly long, and he wears blue jeans and a white T-shirt. He looks at JACOB, who looks away and turns up the radio. BEN enters the kitchen.

BEN: My shirt ready yet, Mom?

MARY: Not yet, my son. Did you find everyt'ing okay?

BEN: Yeah. Hey, I like the new house.

MARY: Do you?

BEN goes to the fridge and pours himself a glass of milk and takes a biscuit from the bread-box.

BEN: You surprised to see me, Mom?

MARY: I still ain't recovered.

BEN: You don't seem too excited.

MARY: Don't I?

BEN: No. I thought you would be.

MARY: Well, you never said you was coming home when I talked to you on the phone. You never gave any hint.

BEN: So what? I'm impulsive, okay?

MARY: I only called to let you know about Aunt Dot. I never expected you to come all this ways. Why did you?

BEN: How's Uncle Wiff taking it?

MARY: Wiff? Don't mention Wiff to me.

BEN: You two still not getting along?

MARY: I never expected him to sink as low as he done this time.

BEN: Why? What'd he do now?

MARY: Never had the decency to go down to the hospital when Dot died. His own wife.

BEN: Really?

MARY: Not a word of a lie. The hospital phoned to tell him Dot never had long, so he called us. Then he never showed up. Later, we drove up to the Oakwood and found him drunk at one of the tables. Couldn't stand on his own. *(slight pause)* Ben?

BEN: What?

MARY: You never answered my question. Why did you come home?

BEN: Why? I wanted to. What do you mean why? I liked Aunt Dot. Do I have to have any other reason? *(MARY just looks at him.)* All right. I wanted to see you, too. Is that good enough? Missed your cooking. *(He hugs her.)* Hey, you lost weight.

MARY: What about your father?

BEN: What about him?

MARY: Don't he enter into it? He lives here, too. He ain't just a stick of furniture, you know.

BEN: Look, if you don't want me here, Mom, just say so . . .

MARY: At least you could speak to him. Is that too much to ask? A few words, at least.

BEN: I already said hello. What more do you want? He doesn't want to talk to me.

386

MARY: Don't he? *(slight pause)* You might've shook his hand, Ben. He stood there, waiting . . . Both of you too proud to make the first move. What a pair.

BEN: How come he's listening to the church service? He never used to.

MARY: That's not'ing. He even lets me drag him there on occasion — Christmas and Easter.

BEN: What's happened to him?

MARY: Who knows, my son? Never t'ought I'd see that day, though, did you? *(slight pause)* Ben?

BEN: Yeah?

MARY: I'm telling you right now, there's to be no fighting. Is that understood? I won't have it.

BEN: Don't worry. I won't start anything.

MARY: No, and don't finish it, either, or else. *(BEN looks at her.)* Or *else.*

BEN: What if he picks on me? What then? What am I supposed to do, let him?

MARY: Ignore him.

BEN: Just like that?

MARY: Yes, just like that. He ain't a well man, Ben, and I don't want him upset.

BEN: Why? What's wrong with him? His back still bothering him?

MARY: What? . . .

BEN: His back.

MARY: Oh, yes . . .

BEN: What does the doctor say? Is he okay now?

MARY: Look, why don't you go in and speak to him. Break the ice. Go on now. And don't forget what I said. No fighting.

BEN enters the living-room, takes a few hesitant steps towards his father, stops, his hands jammed into his pockets. He is about to return to the kitchen when JACOB turns his head.

JACOB: *(quickly)* How was your flight?

This stops BEN.

BEN: *(turns)* What? . . .

JACOB: The plane ride . . . You never said . . . How was it?

He switches off the radio. During this scene they look awkwardly at one another, separated by a continent of a few feet. Each waits for the other to speak first and each suffers the discomfort of selfconsciousness.

BEN: Oh? . . . Bumpy . . . You know.

MARY: You used to like those old planes, Jake. He was up a lot during the War. Wasn't you, boy?

BEN: *(to JACOB)* Yeah?

JACOB: *(to BEN)* When I worked at the Gander . . . I was there when Dr. Banting crashed. We heard his plane take off that morning in the fog, and not long afterwards we heard he went down . . .

Pause.

BEN: *(finally, for something to say)* Didn't Uncle Fred work for the Air Force or something? Around the same time?.

JACOB: No, the Army.

BEN: Was it the Army? *(He nods.)*

MARY: Tell him about Fred, Jake. How he couldn't read or write, and he was putting up towers.

JACOB: No, he don't want to hear about that. A telegram would arrive from Ottawa, and Fred'd say to the nearest man, "Read it, I left my glasses home." What a man. Couldn't read or write his own name, and he was building towers for the Army. *(pause)* Don't let on I said it, but your mother was worried half to death, these past two years.

MARY: *Who* was? I heard that.

BEN: What for? I can take care of myself.

JACOB: Well, you might've wrote more often. Four or five letters ain't much. There was months there we never knowed whether you'd been kidnapped or killed.

BEN: It's not the Wild West any more, you know.

JACOB: That ain't the p'int, now, and you knows it. Don't argue.

MARY: Jake!

BEN: Dad, look . . .

JACOB: What's you doing out there? Is you still working?

BEN: Yeah. Didn't Mom tell you?

JACOB: Don't tell me you'm still sorting letters at the Post Office?

BEN: So? What's wrong with that?

JACOB: Ah, my Jesus . . .

BEN: It's a job, okay? I don't know what I want to do yet.

JACOB: That's for men without schooling. You went to university.

BEN: Yeah, for two whole months. Big deal.

JACOB: Whose fault is that? Mine, I suppose?

BEN: Did I say it was anybody's fault? Did I?

JACOB: No, and that you didn't. Well, don't blame me. You didn't have to run off like a common hobo and quit school, just because I struck you once.

BEN: Once?

JACOB: How many times did my own father take the skin off me, and I never held a grudge. I never let it ruin my life, a few strokes of the belt.

MARY: All right, that's enough! Ben, get in here quick and get your shirt.

BEN: *(to JACOB)* I didn't come home to fight, okay? I came for the funeral. So lay off. *(He enters the kitchen.)*

JACOB: Would you've come home so quick if *I'd* died?

MARY: What a t'ing to say, Jake. Shame on you.

JACOB: *(to himself, as he switches on the radio)* Be lucky if he sent flowers . . .

Another hymn plays.

MARY: *(angrily)* I t'ought I asked you not to fight with him? Not home ten minutes and already it's started. If there's any more of that, you can go straight back where you came from, and I means it. I won't warn you again.

BEN: Look, you asked me to talk to him, Mom. It was your idea.

MARY: Talk, yes.

BEN: So I tried.

MARY: Did you?

BEN: Yeah, I did.

JACOB: What's you two doing in there, Mary — scheming?

MARY: No, we're not scheming. *(to BEN)* He don't hear too well these days, except when he ain't supposed to.

JACOB: Instead of plotting behind my back, you'd best get ready. Wiff'll soon be here and he's still half-naked.

MARY: Well, *I'm* ready. Is you? I don't see you getting dressed in a hurry.

JACOB: No, I'll wrinkle my good suit if I sits around. *(then)* T'row me out yesterday's paper. I ain't finished it yet.

MARY: *(winking at BEN)* What's wrong with your two feet, boy?

JACOB: Not'ing. I just don't wish to *intrude*, Mary. *(He turns up the radio.)*

BEN: See? That's what I mean, Mom. That.

MARY: Never mind. Get dressed and forget it. Pretend you don't hear. That's what I does.

BEN crosses to the foot of the stairs, buttoning his shirt.

JACOB: And change your pants. You'm not wearing old blue jeans down to the funeral parlour.

BEN: Did I say I was?

MARY: Leave him alone, Jake!

JACOB: Uncle Wiff'll want you for a pallbearer on Tuesday, now you'm home.

MARY: Your dark suit's still in our closet, my son. I kept it. Didn't need to be cleaned or pressed, even.

JACOB: Well, shine your shoes. Have some respect for your Aunt Dot, if you got none for yourself. *(BEN goes up the stairs.)* And cut your hair!

With that JACOB switches off the radio and rises with sudden weariness. He wanders into the kitchen, looks for the newspaper on top of the fridge.

MARY: A fine welcome home this is. And you wonders why he stays away?

JACOB: Oh, he'll be back, Mary, as long as you'm alive. No fear of that, my lady. He ain't home to see me. That much is certain.

MARY: Can't you just be civil, Jake?

JACOB: Civil?

MARY: Yes, you've heard of the word. He's only home for two days.

JACOB: T'ank God.

MARY: Yes, you'll be some glad to see him go, won't you? Then you can go back to reading his letters on the sly.

JACOB: Never even asked how I was . . . T'inks more of his Aunt Dot than he do of me.

MARY: That ain't true.

JACOB: Even when I was in the hospital, did I get so much as a Get Well card? Poor Billy was there every weekend. If it'd been you, Mary, had a heart attack . . .

MARY: Keep your voice down . . .

JACOB: And you expects me to be civil? Well, he can kiss my ass, and you can tell him so for me. Is that civil enough?

MARY: Look, Jake, don't let's quarrel on account of Ben, okay? We've been fine, ain't we, just the two of us, until now? Ain't we?

JACOB: Not a harsh word between us. (*He sits at the table with his newspaper.*)

MARY: So let's keep it that way. We was never so close as when the boys left, never. (*slight pause*) Why, I even went to wrestling.

JACOB: And who went to bingo with you and Dot once a week, rain or shine?

MARY: Well, don't spoil it then. Don't let him be a wedge between us. Not again. (*then*) Go on, boy. Read your newspaper. Find somet'ing in there to complain about. (*pause*) I don't t'ink I'll go to bingo anymore, Jake.

JACOB: Oh? Just when I was getting the hang of it.

MARY: No. My heart ain't in it anymore, boy. Won't seem the same without Dot. What luck she had, poor soul. Won more door prizes . . . Chandeliers, toasters . . . (*Her attention is suddenly focussed on JACOB, who holds the newspaper close, then studies it at arm's length.*) "The wise man's eyes are in his head; but the fool walketh in darkness."

JACOB: What?

MARY: *Ecclesiastes.*

JACOB: And what's that supposed to mean, may I ask? "The fool walketh in darkness."

MARY: That's where you'll be, my son, in darkness, if you don't soon get glasses.

JACOB: Ah . . . (*He rises and gets MARY's glasses from a cupboard shelf. A pair with rhinestones and winged sides.*)

MARY: All kidding aside, Jake, you really ought to. You needs them now you're starting back to work. A wrong step and . . .

JACOB: (*slipping on the glasses*) I don't require glasses.

MARY: Don't you?

JACOB: (*crosses back to his chair, sits, read*) No. How often must I tell you? I got along without 'em this long.

MARY: What's you wearing mine for then?

JACOB: Making out the fine print.

MARY: Yes, like the headlines. And you calls *me* vain.

JACOB: Besides, I owns my own pair, if you ain't t'rowed 'em out already like you t'reatened to.

MARY: What? Those old t'ings you bought off the counter at Woolworth's? I wouldn't trust you to cross the street with those on.

JACOB continues to read. Pause.

JACOB: *(musing aloud)* Is that the same Sam Morgan, I wonders?

MARY: Who'd you say?

JACOB: Sam Morgan. "Suddenly, at St. Joseph's Hospital, on Wednesday, January 10, beloved husband of . . . "

MARY: *(snatches the newspaper from his hands)* That's enough of that! What's wrong with you, lately?.

JACOB: Give that back. I wasn't reading the obituaries.

MARY: No? What was it — the comic strip? You promised you wouldn't.

JACOB: I just happened to glance t'rough it. Give it here. I t'ought Dot might've been mentioned.

MARY: How? She only passed away yesterday. It was too late for Saturday's paper. She'll be in tomorrow's, if Wiff ain't forgot to phone it in. *(She hands back the newspaper and crosses back behind the ironing board.)*

JACOB: Don't be foolish, Mary, the funeral parlour does that. And listen here, you let up on Wiff, you hear? "Blessed are the merciful", or is that one not in the same Bible you reads?

MARY: If I had my way, he wouldn't put his foot in the door.

JACOB: Well, Wiff's me oldest friend, and he's welcome in this house anytime, day or night.

MARY: This is my house, too.

JACOB: All right, but if he goes, I goes.

MARY: He don't deserve your sympathy, and he won't get mine. As if his philandering wasn't bad enough . . .

JACOB: By the Jesus, Mary, I wouldn't wish you for an enemy. You'm some hard case at times. Wouldn't move you with a winch, once your mind's set. *(He returns to his newspaper. Pause.)*

394

MARY: Still can't believe she's gone . . .

JACOB: Sam Morgan. Ain't that a kick in the ass. We worked together a few years back, Mary. You minds him.

MARY: Don't recall.

JACOB: Yes, you do so, now. Second cousin to Skipper Dick Chard from Buttercove. Married a Drudge from Tickle Harbour.

MARY: Sam Morgan?

JACOB: Had a glass eye.

MARY: Oh?

JACOB: A blue one. We was mates together over at Canada Packers, hanging doors. What a great one for fun, Sam. He'd sit on the crowded streetcar mornings, up to his old devilment, his eye in backwards . . .

MARY: And he passed away?

JACOB: Wednesday. They buried him yesterday, it says. Mount Pleasant Cemetery. And I never knowed he was sick, even. Never got a chance to pay my respects. *(slight pause as he scans the obituary)* Don't say what he died of. But knowing Sam, I dare say he choked to death on his own eye. He'd pop it in his mouth for fun.

MARY: Yes, and two guesses who egged him on.

JACOB: Just fifty, Mary. Fifty.

MARY: Is that all he was? That's young, fifty.

JACOB: Two years younger than us.

MARY: Look, boy, put down that old newspaper and get dressed. You're getting on my nerves. Go on.

JACOB: *(stands, crosses into living-room, looks for photo album)* Strong as a sled-horse, Sam. He'd pick up a keg of nails and lug it under his arm.

MARY: Is it worth it to iron your old workshirt for tomorrow?

395

JACOB: We was in the Church Lads' Brigade together, years and years ago . . . *(finds the photo album in a drawer)* Don't we have a snapshot here somewhere? I'm sure of it . . . The two of us in our little blue pillbox hats, khaki puttees, and blue breeches . . . "Fight the good fight." That was our motto.

MARY: Jake?

JACOB: Friends dropping like flies . . . First your sister, and now . . .

MARY: *(sharply)* Jake!

JACOB: What? *(He crosses to the arm-chair and sits looking through album.)*

MARY: You don't listen. You want your workshirt ironed or not?

JACOB: Well, speak up if you wants an answer. Yes, and I needs a clean pair of woollen socks as well. Is my long underwear clean?

MARY: I bought you a new pair at Eaton's.

JACOB: Did you take the pins out?

MARY: I did. *(chuckling)* That won't happen again. *(slight pause)* Jake?

JACOB: What?

MARY: *(crosses to JACOB)* About tomorrow . . .

JACOB: What about it?

MARY: If you're doing this on my account . . .

JACOB: Oh, for Christ's sake, don't start in on that again. I'm tired of it.

MARY: I'm only t'inking of you, boy.

JACOB: Well, you just tell the Honeydew you'm quitting on Friday. There's no need of both of us working.

MARY: But the doctor said . . .

JACOB: I don't care what he said. I've been off seven weeks, and that's long enough.

MARY: Another month or two won't make no difference . . .

JACOB: Look, I can't sit around on my ass like some men can. I don't know what to do with myself. If I don't get to work I'm as dead as Dot.

MARY: Will you take it easy then? Will you do that for me? Don't take on more than you can handle.

JACOB: Never had much use for doctors the best of times. Still don't.

MARY: *(crosses back to the ironing board)* No, except when it's me that's sick.

JACOB: He don't understand what it's like, not working. How could he? Never done a honest day's work in his life. So don't mention him again.

MARY: All right, I won't.

JACOB: Takes out a tonsil or two and calls it work. He don't know what work is. Can't remove a wart, for Christ's sake, without he burns it off with acid. Even Dot could do better than that. Why, you'd rub your hand across her fur coat and the wart'd drop off within a week or two — without Blue Cross.

MARY: Yes, well, some good it done her, poor soul . . .

JACOB: As much good as those goddamn butchers with their knives.

MARY: Well, if Dot had only listened to the doctor and had her check-ups, she might be alive today. *(pause)* Don't seem fair, do it? How someone that gentle could die in such pain.

JACOB: *(slight pause)* Mary?

MARY: What, boy?

JACOB: I ain't had a single pain in weeks, Mary. Not a single pain.

MARY: No? I heard you the other night . . . groaning. What was that?

JACOB: Heartburn.

MARY: Was it?

JACOB: Heartburn, I tells you.

MARY: If you says so . . .

JACOB: That damn margarine again. And don't put any on my sandwiches. If you does, I'll toss my lunchpail and all to the sparrows.

MARY: Don't you dare.

JACOB: And they'll suffer. *(pause)*

MARY: *(placing iron on counter)* What's the forecast say? Did you look?

JACOB: *(into his newspaper)* Ten above.

MARY: How cold's that if you're high up?

JACOB: Ten below, perhaps.

MARY: That cold? Perhaps you'll work inside.

JACOB: Perhaps.

MARY: Might they let you off early?

JACOB: *(teasing her)* The wind's the worst, Mary. Seen a young lad one time, lugging a pane of glass; the wind took it like a sail and off he went . . .

MARY: *(dismantles the ironing board, crosses to the cupboard, puts it away)* T'anks for telling me, boy. I needed to hear that. Got any more good news you're keeping back?

JACOB: Fifteen stories below . . .

MARY: Enough. I'll have bad dreams tonight.

JACOB: Don't be foolish. I ain't some young Eye-talian the first day on the job, tripping over his own toes. Will you stop worrying?

MARY puts the bushel basket on the counter, puts the ironing inside it.

MARY: You could've been a carpenter foreman today, if you'd a mind to . . .

JACOB: Well, I ain't, so forget it . . .

MARY: You was asked often enough.

JACOB: I couldn't do figures.

MARY: Nonsense. Could Fred? He couldn't read or write, even, and look what he done.

JACOB: That was twenty years ago. Times've changed.

MARY: You can read a blueprint, can't you? And you measures better with your eye than most can with a slide rule. You just don't t'ink enough of yourself, Jake. You never did.

JACOB: Look, the truth is I'm fortunate to be working. How many companies you suppose wants to hire you, once word gets around you got a bad heart? Don't want to risk it. If it wasn't for Wiff . . .

MARY: You could've been more, Jake.

JACOB: What odds? I'm a damn good carpenter. Ain't that enough? I never wished to be more.

MARY: No?

JACOB: I ain't cut out to be a slave driver, Mary.

Enter BEN, dressed in his dark suit. JACOB quickly removes MARY's glasses, reads his newspaper.

399

BEN: Uncle Wiff not here yet?

MARY: Not yet, my son. (*She crosses to BEN.*) Well, look at you. Look, Jake. All growed up. Don't you look smart. I see you borrowed one of your father's ties. (*JACOB reacts.*) Looks nice. You looks good in a shirt and tie. Don't he, Jake?

JACOB: Just make sure you leaves the knot in, that's all.

MARY: (*trying to laugh it off*) He still ain't learned to tie a knot yet. Can you beat that? Still relies on your brother to do it for him, whenever he's in town.

JACOB: At least Billy takes an interest in the family. That much you can say for him. Don't find him gallivanting all over the country.

MARY: (*changing the subject quickly*) Suit still fits, I see . . .

BEN: Yeah, but the ass is shiny. Will there be many people there?

MARY: Oh, I wouldn't worry. No one will see that, I'm sure.

JACOB: (*rises, puts away album*) No, his father's the only one he shows his ass to. Well, you may not have me around much longer to run down. (*He starts up the stairs.*) Once the heart goes . . . (*He exits.*)

BEN: (*to MARY*) The what? . . . (*calling up the stairs*) Wait a minute. What are you talking about? Dad!

But JACOB has gone. A beat or two. BEN turns and looks at MARY, who enters the kitchen. He follows her.

What'd he mean — the heart? What's he talking about? Is there something wrong with his heart? Mom?

MARY: Sit down, Ben. And don't be angry with me.

BEN: No, I'll stand . . .

MARY: Suit yourself. (*She sits, looks at her hands.*) I've wanted to tell you ever since you walked in tonight, but I was afraid you'd come down on me for not telling you before. *(She turns and looks at BEN.)*

BEN: I'm listening . . .

MARY: I lied to you, Ben. Your father never strained his back. That wasn't why he was in the hospital.

BEN: What was it then?

MARY: A heart attack.

BEN: A heart at — ?

MARY: A coronary. Back in November. And he wasn't in the hospital for just a week. It was more like a month.

BEN: Why didn't you tell me?

MARY: I had my reasons.

BEN: What reasons? What possible reason could there be? Didn't you think I cared?

MARY: Wasn't that at all. I just didn't want you here.

BEN: What do you mean, you didn't want me here? Why not? He's my father, isn't he?

MARY: Yes, and he's my husband, and he comes first, now. I do what's best for him, not you. For *him*, do you understand?

BEN: So? What's that got to do with it?

MARY: What would you've done, Ben, had I told you the truth? You'd've been the first on the plane.

BEN: So?

MARY: Well, I wasn't about to risk losing him on account of you. How was I to know what might happen if you showed up at the hospital?

BEN: I wouldn't have fought with him, for Christ's sake. Don't you know me better than that?

MARY: It wasn't you I was worried about, it was him. He wasn't supposed to move, even. What if he saw you and went into one of his rages? What then? As it was, he had two more attacks in the hospital that almost finished him.

BEN: *(angrily)* Wait a minute. You mean he almost died and you didn't tell me?

He turns away to the sink, stands for a moment with his back to MARY. Then suddenly, violently, he smashes his fist into the cupboard door. He leans over the sink, motionless.

MARY: You got his temper, all right. I hoped you'd be different . . . *(pause)*

BEN: *(turning)* How'd it happen?

MARY: Oh, it was stupid, stupid. We was lugging that fridge down off the back of the truck, just the two of us. I wish to goodness I'd never heard tell of it. Stupid old fridge.

BEN: Why didn't you have it delivered?

MARY: We could've, if he'd just waited another day. But no, no, he's got no patience. Had to have it right away, that very afternoon. It was too much for just the two of us. I ain't that strong, and he knowed it. He had most of the weight on his end . . .

BEN: *(crosses to MARY)* All right, Mom, it's not your fault.

MARY: The fridge was my idea . . .

BEN: You couldn't know . . .

MARY: . . . He just let it drop, suddenly, and went inside. Stretched out on the chesterfield. Not a word out of him. I had no idea what was wrong, no idea. Started to frighten me, just lying there with his eyes closed, the beads of sweat on his forehead.

BEN: Didn't you call the doctor?

MARY: He wouldn't hear tell of it, at first. I had to practically t'reaten him, and when the doctor showed up, there was no way he was going to the hospital.

BEN: That figures.

MARY: "I ain't going!" he said. "You'll have to drag me! I wants to die in me own bed!" All because he had no clean underwear . . .

BEN: Jesus.

MARY: Oh, I'm glad you wasn't here, my son. He'd never've wanted you to see him carried out, shivering, on a stretcher, all wrapped in blankets. It was all I could do not to turn away my head. He looked so *puzzled* . . .

BEN: How could it happen, Mom? I mean he's not like other men. He's so strong.

MARY: Was, Ben.

BEN: Christ, when we were growing up, he'd make fun of us, Billy and me, if we got a blister. Like it was a sign of weakness or something.

MARY: Imagine then what this's done to him, a man that proud of his health and strength. Always wore it like some men wear a medal. T'ought he'd have it always like the colour of his eyes. *(slight pause)* I t'ink he's frightened, now. Frightened and ashamed.

BEN: Ashamed? Of what?

MARY: He can't keep up with others, even men his own age, and he knows it. I t'ink it preys on his mind like an insult. *(slight pause)* I never wanted you here, my son, but since you is, perhaps you can talk some sense into him, without getting into a row. Before it's too late.

BEN: What do you mean "too late"?

MARY: I'm frightened to death, Ben. He starts back to work tomorrow. Wiff got him a job. He ain't ready.

BEN: Is that what the doctor says?

MARY: He warned him against it.

BEN: Can't you talk to him?

MARY: I've tried my best, but he t'inks I'm in league with the doctor. Perhaps you'll have better luck.

BEN: He'd never listen to me, Mom. We'd just get in another argument.

MARY: It's worth a try, ain't it? Do it for me. I'm at my wit's end, my son.

BEN: What the hell's he trying to do, Mom — kill himself?

MARY: Don't say that.

BEN: Well, Christ, that's what it looks like.

MARY: No, Ben, it's my fault. I made the mistake of mentioning my legs was hurting. All that standing at work. That's all the excuse he needed. The very same night he was on the phone to Wiff. *(Doorbell rings.)* Speak of the devil, that's him now. *(She crosses to the foot of the stairs.)* Jacob!

JACOB: *(off)* What?

MARY: Wiff's here! Hurry up! Answer the door!

JACOB: *(off)* What's wrong with *your* two feet? I'm dressing.

MARY: *(as she crosses back to the counter and gets the bushel basket, to BEN)* I t'ought he only took a minute? You answer it. *(She crosses back to the archway.)* I'm going upstairs. I don't want to see his ugly face.

BEN: *(crossing to archway)* Mom, did you tell Billy about the heart attack?

MARY: Yes . . . He came to the hospital.

BEN: Great. No wonder Dad's so pissed off. He thinks I knew, too, right?

MARY: What could I do, Ben? He'd have t'ought it strange if I hadn't let both you know.

She exits upstairs. Doorbell rings again. BEN crosses out into the hallway and answers the door.

BEN: *(off)* Hello, Uncle Wiff.

WIFF: *(off)* Who's that? Is that you, Billy?

BEN: *(off)* Ben.

WIFF: *(off)* Ben? No. Is that you, Ben?

He follows BEN into the hall. WIFF is dressed in an overcoat and dark suit. He wears a black fedora with a red feather in the brim, and has the red nose of a drinker.

Well, for crying out loud I never recognized you, duckie, it's been so long. Your old Uncle Wiff never recognized you. When'd you get in?

BEN: Just a while ago. I flew home.

WIFF: Jacob must be some t'rilled, I dare say. *(He takes off his rubbers.)* You all alone?

BEN: No. Mom and Dad're upstairs. They'll be right down. *(WIFF removes his hat, places it on the banister.)* I was sorry to hear about Aunt Dot, Uncle Wiff.

WIFF: Terrible, my son, terrible. And just when we was planning a trip home this summer. *(He crosses to the chesterfield.)* Our first since we left. Even got the old car fixed . . . Oh, well, Dot's better off now. This life was too much for her. Perhaps the next'll be a little kinder . . . *(He sits on the chesterfield.)*

BEN: Would you like a drink, Uncle Wiff?

WIFF: No, I don't dare touch it. Your mother'd crown me, duckie, if she caught me . . . You say she's upstairs? Your Uncle Wiff'll have a whiskey then, as long as you makes it quick. And straight.

BEN enters the kitchen, gets the whiskey and a glass from the cupboard, pours a drink. WIFF takes a mickey from the inside pocket of his overcoat and takes a quick drink, slips it back.

How long you home for, Ben? For good?

BEN: No. Just till the funeral.

WIFF: Oh? A good excuse to come home, eh, my son? *(BEN doesn't answer. WIFF rises, removes his coat and scarf, hangs them over the banister.)* Too bad you couldn't stay a spell longer. Your father could do with some help now. He ain't at all well. Scares me sometimes to look at him.

BEN: Yeah, I've noticed.

WIFF: *(crosses to archway)* A lot of changes in two years, boy . . . Even the cold bothers him, now. *(BEN returns from the kitchen and hands WIFF his drink.)* And I can recall times he'd find fun with it all, even the cold . . . Did he ever tell you the time back home me and him was in Holyrood?

BEN: *(sitting in the arm-chair)* No, I don't think so.

WIFF: What a bugger of a cold night that was. Freeze your poor pecker off. We drove into this little town one night in the winter, Jake and me. Just boys, the two of us. I had my father's old coal truck. Checked into the first hotel we saw — what we called back home a "baseball hotel".

BEN: What's that?

WIFF: A baseball hotel? That's a pitcher on top of the dresser and a catcher underneath. *(BEN laughs.)* Holyrood's a Catholic town, and the room we had was all decked out in religious pictures of bleeding hearts. Never seen so many in me life. Just a little room with a bare bulb hanging down over the bed. And the last t'ing we seen before I reached up and switched off the light was this big picture of Jesus on the far wall. There he was, poor old Jesus, with his halo and crown of t'orns and this big red heart dripping down on his white gown, with a flame shooting out the top of the heart, and him standing there with his arms stretched wide open — *(he gestures)* — and it was that cold in our room, duckie — and Jacob'll back me up — it was that cold that in the morning when we looked up, Jesus had his hands over his ears like this. *(He demonstrates.)*

BEN: *(laughing)* Christ!

WIFF: Yes, that's right, my son — poor old Jesus Christ! *(then — seriously)* Oh, he ain't the same man, Ben, since the night you run off. I can testify to that. And what a state he was in at the time. Worse than your mother. Never ate for days. I doubt he slept a wink till he knowed where you was.

BEN: He shouldn't have beat me, Uncle Wiff. I warned him.

WIFF: Forget it. You're a bigger man than that, duckie. Make up. Take your Uncle Wiff's advice. Stay home and give him a hand. He's worked hard for you all his life. You might do the same in return. *(BEN says nothing.)* Some sons would, gladly.

BEN: I don't want to live at home any more. I like being on my own. He'll be all right.

WIFF: Will he? Have you taken a good look at him, lately? Have you, my dear? A close look? That's a man walking in the valley of the shadow. Mark my words.

BEN: Then why'd you get him the job? Did you have to?

WIFF: Wait a minute, now, duckie, wait a minute. *(He sits on the chesterfield.)* I ain't denying he wants to work. Your Uncle Wiff never said that, did he? All I'm saying is he oughtn't to. He ain't in no shape.

BEN: Did you tell him that?

WIFF: Bless your heart, I did so. I advised him to wait a few months, after he's more rested up . . .

BEN: So what do you think I should do?

WIFF: He might listen to reason, if he t'ought you was staying home. That might do the trick, if all else fails.

Enter JACOB. WIFF quickly passes his glass to BEN.

JACOB: Wiff, my son, how is you? Still holding up?

WIFF: Oh, as good as can be expected, duckie. As good as can be expected.

JACOB: *(to BEN)* Where's your manners? Get your uncle a drink.

MARY: *(entering, sitting on the far end of chesterfield, away from WIFF)* He don't want a drink, and neither does you. Have a grain of sense. Look what happened yesterday.

JACOB: *(ignoring MARY)* Wiff?

WIFF: No, my son, I'm off it for Lent, as the old man used to say. Off it for Lent.

JACOB: Suit yourself. I t'ink I'll have a quick one. *(He enters the kitchen, pours himself a drink.)* Been down to Jerrett's yet, Wiff?

WIFF: Just come from there, duckie. Saw Dot for a few minutes.

MARY: Oh? How do she look?

WIFF: Lovely, maid, lovely. Never know it was the same person. Just like she's sleeping.

JACOB: Did you see our flowers?

WIFF: I did, bless your heart. T'anks ever so much. They's lovely. Even the Oakwood Hotel sent a big wreath signed by all the waiters.

MARY: Not surprising. You're the best customer they ever had. Even Dot's dying couldn't keep you out on a Saturday afternoon.

BEN: Mom, for Christ's sake . . .

WIFF: Must be our time of life, Mary. Flowers don't smell of the fields, lately . . . only of the funeral parlour . . . of death. *(pause)*

408

MARY: What dress did you settle on?

WIFF: What dress . . . ?

MARY: Wasn't a black one, was it? You know how she felt about black.

WIFF: No, maid, wasn't black . . .

MARY: Did any of her dresses fit her? I wouldn't t'ink they would, all the weight she lost.

WIFF: Well, one did, Mary. Just the one, my dear . . .

MARY: Which one?

WIFF: Well . . . *(He rises, moves nervously behind the chester-field.)*

MARY: No, don't tell me, Wiff. *(She stands.)* If you done what I t'ink you done I'll wring your neck for sure. That's a promise.

JACOB enters with his drink and glances from WIFF to MARY.

JACOB: What in Christ's name's going on now? Can't I step out of the room for two minutes, Mary?

MARY: Oh, I could murder him, I could. Do you know what this . . . this . . . ? Guess what he's went and done, Jake? You won't believe this. Not in a million years.

JACOB: What?

MARY: Stuck Dot in her wedding dress. After what I told him Dot said.

JACOB: Did you, Wiff?

WIFF: That was the custom, Mary. You knows yourself. Why, the day we was married your poor mother said to Dot, "Now, me baby *(rhymes with abbey)* pack your dress away, that's for your funeral."

MARY: And what was it I told you Dot said just before she died? Her very last words: "Don't let Wiff bury me in my wedding dress."

BEN sits on sofa, lights a cigarette.

WIFF: She never knowed what she was saying, Mary. She never meant that, for crying out loud. That wasn't Dot speaking. Not my Dot.

MARY: No? How would you know? Was you there? Here I is, trying to keep my husband alive at all costs, and you ain't got two minutes to give to a dying woman! *(She enters the kitchen, sits at the table.)*

JACOB: Leave my name out of it. *(then)* She's just upset, Wiff. Pay her no mind.

WIFF follows MARY into the kitchen.

WIFF: Look, Mary . . .

MARY: You just never loved her, Wiff, or you'd've made it to the hospital.

WIFF: That's a lie, Mary. I loved Dot, and don't you say I didn't. And once she loved me, too.

JACOB sits in the arm-chair.

By Jesus, there was a time I couldn't pass her chair without she'd reach out and touch me. And I was the same. I couldn't get close enough. I would've crawled down and lived inside her bowels. We was the perfect pair . . .

MARY: You took up with the boarder. That's what ruined it. And after Dot treated that girl like a daughter . . .

WIFF: I never looked at another woman, including Marie, till Dot went t'rough the change of life. Wouldn't have a t'ing to do with me, after that. Too tired, she'd say. Always tired . . .

MARY: All right, but was it too much trouble to sit with her till she went? You could've done that much.

WIFF: For crying out loud, Mary, I was on my way to the hospital, no odds what you believes. I wanted to say good-bye.

MARY: You wanted a whiskey more.

WIFF: I just stopped off at the Oakwood for a minute. For a quick one, I told myself.

MARY: You might've waited.

WIFF: No, duckie, I needed a good stiff drink right then, that's all there was to it. I'd been down to that hospital night after night for six weeks, watching her waste away to not'ing . . . hoping every day would be her last. I could hardly bear to look at her . . . One quick glass of Scotch. Should've only took two minutes, if that.

MARY: Why didn't it, then?

WIFF: Why? If you're ready to listen, I'll tell you why . . . I had my first whiskey, and no sooner had I drunk it than somet'ing came back to me so clear . . . *(He sits.)* The first time Dot and me ever met. T'irty-five years ago. Me on my way down to the coal shed to unload the steamer, her on her way to the church to light the fire. How it all came back, suddenly, sitting at that table. That dark road, the stars still out, and me with my flashlight and lunchpail, no older than Ben. And who comes tripping along the road towards me, but Dot, the beam of her flashlight bouncing and swinging. I puts the light in her young face, and for a moment I don't recognize her, she's blossomed out that much in the time I was away in Boston . . . "Is that you, Dot Snow?" And she laughs. I'd forgot how gentle laughter could be. "Is that you, Wiff Roach?" Well, duckie, I never made it to the coal shed that morning. No, by God, I never. And my father couldn't have dragged me, had he kicked me ass all the way with his biggest boots. I walked her up the road, instead, and we sat in her family pew till the sun come up. Two months later we was married. You remembers, Mary. You was the bridesmaid. *(slight pause — WIFF stands)* So that's how come I

411

never made it to the hospital yesterday. I had another whiskey to ease the pain I was feeling, and a t'ird because the second never helped . . . So if you wants to hurt me, Mary, you go right ahead, my dear, but you're too late . . . and not'ing you can ever say or do will make me feel any worse than knowing what Dot and me once had and what it come to in the end, without either one of us ever knowing why . . . *(He sits again.)* And that's why I wants her buried in her wedding dress, if you must know, in spite of what she said at the last. What she wanted in those days past is just as real to me as what she wanted yesterday. Nor do it have the same sadness, Mary, not the same sadness at all . . .

MARY turns to WIFF. Slow fade to black. Music.

SCENE TWO

Lights up. Two hours later. MARY rushes in, followed by BEN. She removes her coat and thrusts it at BEN, who hangs it up. She crosses into the kitchen, fills the electric kettle, plugs it in.

BEN: *(removing his coat, hanging it up)* Quit it, Mom. *(He enters the living-room.)* How long you going to keep this up? You didn't speak once all the way home.

MARY: No, and you don't deserve to be spoken to. And the same goes for your father.

BEN crosses to the chesterfield, sits reading a magazine.

What'd you let him get in a row for?

BEN: What do you mean let him? I didn't let him.

MARY: Didn't you see it coming? Couldn't you stop it?

BEN: How? I was ten feet away talking to somebody. I still don't know what happened. He was talking to Uncle Wiff and some other guy . . .

MARY: Ike Squires.

BEN: Who?

MARY: Your father never had much use for him, even back home.

BEN: Anyway, the next thing I knew this guy was running out the front door with Dad after him.

MARY: Well, he's just lucky Ike can run faster than him. Wouldn't that be a nice sight — two growed men going to it on the street? What'll people say, for goodness sake?

BEN reaches over and flicks on the radio. A late-night jazz piece plays.

BEN: Actually, it was pretty funny . . . *(He laughs.)*

MARY: *(crosses to archway)* Funny? There was not'ing funny about it. He ought to be ashamed. And you're just as bad as him, if you laugh. That only encourages him. *(She returns to the kitchen.)*

BEN: Come on, Mom, where's your sense of humour? Look at it this way . . . Who else do you know would pick a fight inside a funeral parlour?

MARY: Yes, and my poor sister lying dead a few yards away. What a sin. *(slight pause)* I stood there tonight looking down at Dot — and God forgive me — all I could t'ink about was perhaps your father was next. *(She crosses to the archway.)* Did you speak to him yet, like I asked you to?

BEN: No. Not yet.

MARY: Why not? He'll soon be off to bed.

BEN: I just haven't had a chance. I will, when he comes in from the garage.

MARY: See that you do. *(crossing to BEN)* Oh, Ben, I've been some uneasy, lately, I don't mind telling you. At night I've been coming awake and listening for your father's

413

breathing in the dark. If I don't hear it, I gets frightened and jabs him in the ribs with my elbow. If that don't wake him, I gets more frightened and snaps on the light. And on top of that, last night I had a bad dream. Can't get it out of my mind.

BEN: Really? What was it like?

MARY: Not now. Your father might come in any second. Later. *(She starts for the kitchen.)*

BEN: No. Come on, Mom. I'd like to hear it, okay? I've had a strange one myself, lately.

MARY: *(turns back to BEN)* I took it for a warning, Ben. Like a bird in the house . . . Death ain't always a pale rider on a pale horse, my son. Sometimes . . . like last night . . . he's just a man dressed all in black. Wearing a peaked cap and holding a black lunchpail. Standing high on a rooftop . . . *(She pauses.)*

BEN: Yeah? Is that all?

MARY: It was windy, and the wind took his cap off, and he just stood there staring out over the city . . . as though he was beside the shore, looking out to sea for something lost . . .

Stamping of feet is heard outside the kitchen door, and MARY returns to the kitchen counter, just as JACOB enters, carrying his rubbers. As he closes the door behind him, she picks up a cup and saucer and turns. The cup falls to the floor and shatters.

JACOB: That's one you won't t'row at me. *(He crosses to the hallway closet.)*

MARY: The night ain't over yet, boy.

JACOB: *(hanging up his coat, to MARY)* At least she's speaking to me.

MARY: *(as she sweeps up the broken cup)* I oughtn't to, after the fool you made of yourself tonight. Where did you t'ink you was — the beer parlour?

414

JACOB: Go on with you. We had a few words, that's all.

He enters the kitchen, crosses to the fridge. He removes a wedge of cheese and cuts off a slice with his penknife.

MARY: Words? Is that what you calls it? Well, I'd hate to be the one has a conversation with you. *(She deposits the broken cup in the garbage receptacle.)* What brought that on?

JACOB: Not'ing. I don't wish to talk about it.

MARY: Well, get out of the kitchen, then. Go in the other room. Ben wishes to speak to you.

JACOB: He do? What do he want?

MARY: How should I know? Go and find out.

JACOB: You come in with me, Mary.

MARY: Don't be silly. Go on. He won't bite. *(as JACOB picks up a newspaper off the top of the fridge)* And leave the paper right where it is. You won't need to hide behind that. *(pushing him towards the door)* Go on, I said.

As JACOB enters the living-room, BEN switches off the radio. JACOB removes his tie and hangs it over the banister. He looks at BEN's back a moment. Then he crosses behind the chesterfield to the window.

JACOB: Wonder how much Wiff paid for that casket? Bronze is the most expensive there is. Must've set him back two t'ousand, at least, wouldn't you say?

BEN: Probably more than that. *(slight pause)* Dad . . .

JACOB: *(not hearing BEN)* Back home we never had funeral parlours in my day.

BEN: No?

JACOB: No. When Father died, he was kept home in bed, and somebody — mostly Mother and me — sat with him for the t'ree days, every hour. *(Out of his embarrassment he takes a pack of cigarettes from his shirt pocket, discovers it empty, then crosses to the arm-chair and sits.)* Some would keep their blinds drawn for months on end. Once the preacher preached a sermon saying what a sin it was to keep out the Light of God that way. *(BEN quickly offers his father a cigarette. JACOB takes one.)* T'anks. *(He breaks off the filter, and BEN lights the cigarette for him.)* They never embalmed in those days, either. And lots couldn't wait the t'ree days, let me tell you. Had to be buried sooner.

(Pause.)

BEN: How did your father die?

JACOB: Cancer, my son. Like Dot. He was only forty-six.

BEN: What was he like?

JACOB: Father? Oh, that depended on who crossed his path and what mood he was in. On good days he'd give you the bread out of his mouth. He was a hard man to know. Don't suppose many knowed him well, except Mother. She was the only one wasn't frightened of him. *(slight pause)* The first time they operated on him, four men had to hold him down on the kitchen floor. No morphine, no kind of pain-killer, just the knife and four men kneeling on his arms and legs. A ball of flesh as big as a marble popped out of his mouth and rolled across the floor. Never let out a whimper, just kicked and t'rashed. The cancer was in his mouth, you see, and Mother said she'd pick up teeth in the bedclothes weeks later. *(slight pause)* The night he died he was in such torment he reached up and took hold of the frame of the bed and bent the brass out of shape. Still never made a sound . . . The doctor later said he never knowed how any normal man could've stood it without screeching out . . .

BEN: Were you there?

JACOB: No. Mother told me later. She wouldn't let me near the room. Never wished me to see him, the shape he was

416

in. At t'ree or four that morning she came out, rolling down her sleeves, and closed the door, and I knowed before she spoke he was gone, just the way she came out that way and closed the door . . . When I did see him, at last, after they'd made him up, he looked so small lying there in bed that I wondered to myself how I ever could've been so frightened of him, such a small man. In life, I'd never noticed that, how small he was . . . *(slight pause)* By the way, your Mother said you wished to speak to me.

BEN: Yeah, I do . . . *(He stands.)*

JACOB: What about?

BEN: Well, Mom told me you're going back to work tomorrow . . . and I was thinking . . .

JACOB: Don't waste your breath, my son. I've heard it all before. Did she put you up to this?

BEN: Put me up to what? You haven't let me finish. I'd like to stay home for a while if that's okay with you, and work.

JACOB: What'd you say? . . .

BEN: I said I'd like to stay home for a while and work. I mean, if you don't mind.

JACOB: Mind?

BEN: Maybe you don't want me here. It's your house.

JACOB: That ain't true, now. Your mother owns half. She's got as much say in the matter as I does. *(He stands.)* Did you mention this to her yet?

BEN: No.

JACOB: Good. Watch me surprise her. Mary, come in here quick. Hear the good news. *(to BEN)* She'll be some overjoyed, Ben. *(then)* Mary! *(He crosses to the archway.)* Drop what you'm doing and get in here before he changes his mind.

MARY: *(crosses to the sink, deposits her cup)* What is it?

417

JACOB: Hang onto your bonnet, Mary. You'll never believe what I just heard with my own two ears, bad as they is. You ready for this?

MARY: *(crosses to JACOB)* You won the Sweepstakes.

JACOB: Better. Your son wishes to stay home.

MARY: *(to BEN)* Oh?

JACOB: "Oh?" Is that all you can say is "oh?" Make a liar out of me, why don't you?

MARY: What was you expecting?

BEN: Well, why not, Mom?

JACOB: I t'ought the least you'd do is jump and smack your hands. You does that much at the bingo. Didn't you hear me? He wishes to stay home for good.

BEN: For a while.

JACOB: For a while? What's the good of that? *(then)* All right. For a while.

MARY: *(to BEN)* What for?

JACOB: There she goes again. What does you mean "what for?" By the Christ, if you ain't contrary. For two years she's been praying for not'ing else . . .

MARY: Who has?

JACOB: . . . and now she asks "what for?"

MARY: Perhaps we'd be better off if he never, Jake.

JACOB: In the name of Christ, Mary, what's got into you?

MARY: Remember what we talked about earlier? Just the two of us?

JACOB: All right, my son, pack your bag, your mother don't want you here.

MARY: It ain't that.

418

JACOB: Well, what kind of a way is that to speak? *(crosses to BEN)* Look, this is *my* house, and you're bloody well welcome if you likes, no questions asked. There's a spare bedroom. You can come and go to please yourself. And neither your mother nor me will interfere. Will we, Mary? *(then)* Will we?

MARY says nothing.

Well, this calls for a drink. I'll break out the whiskey. Billy gave me a bottle for Christmas. *(He rushes off into the kitchen and pours two drinks, singing.)*

"Up and down the southern shore
Go to bed after supper
See the great big ugly t'ing
Go after Charlie Tucker"

(then) Don't go back on your word, now.

MARY: What's the idea, Ben? You was supposed to convince him not to work. What's staying home got to do with it?

BEN: Look, Mom, I'm going to get a job, and he won't have to work. I just haven't told him yet.

MARY: So that's it. Well, my son, you'd better let him know what you intends. He might not go for it. I don't t'ink he will.

JACOB rushes back with the two drinks, hands one to BEN.

JACOB: Here you is, my son. Here's to us, to the t'ree of us. Down the hatch. *(He drinks. BEN doesn't.)* This is some night, ain't it? Just like old times. My only regret is poor Billy ain't here. *(slight pause)* Why the long faces? Look at the two of you. What gives? *(then)* Mary? . . .

MARY: You never let him finish, Jake. There's more. I t'ink you ought to hear the rest of it.

JACOB: The rest of what?

419

Doorbell rings, then pounding on the door.

What's that? . . .

MARY: Someone's at the door.

BEN: I'll get it. *(He exits.)*

JACOB: *(to MARY)* At this hour? *(He crosses to the window, looks out.)* Why, it's Wiff . . .

MARY: Wiff? What's he want?

JACOB: Now how should I know? *(He crosses into the hall.)*

MARY: Don't you dare give him anyt'ing to drink. We'll never get rid of him.

WIFF rushes in, holding his heart. BEN follows. WIFF is dressed only in his suit. He is agitated, breathless, dishevelled, and shivering from the cold.

JACOB: Wiff, my son, what's wrong? What's you doing out like that?

WIFF: Let me catch my breath. I'm half froze . . .

JACOB: Who's after you, boy — the devil?

WIFF: No, duckie, Dot. *(He warms his hands on the radiator.)*

JACOB: *(to MARY)* What'd he say?

MARY: *(her eyes on WIFF)* Dot . . .

JACOB: Dot . . .?

MARY: Has you been drinking, Wiff?

WIFF: No, bless your heart, I ain't been drinking. Nor will I touch another drop as long as I lives, if I lives to be two hundred, so help me Jesus. Not after tonight . . . *(He collapses on the chesterfield.)*

MARY: He must've been dreaming.

JACOB: How could he? We just dropped him off. He hardly had time to take off his coat.

WIFF: Close to t'ree t'ousand dollars, almost a year's salary, I paid for her funeral. What more do she want? And she calls me heartless. *(to BEN)* Your Uncle Wiff's heartless. *(then grabbing BEN's drink)* Is you drinking that, duckie? I needs to calm my nerves, love.

MARY: *(to herself)* The shortest two hundred years I ever seen.

WIFF: What's she want to come after me for, for crying out loud. We had plenty of good times in the past . . . One time I come home drunk from the Union meeting and she'd locked me out. So I sat down on the steps and took a spell. All of sudden up went the window overhead and down came a pan of cold water. I jumped halfway out in the road, with the fright. Then she come downstairs and let me in, laughing to beat the band . . .

JACOB: All right, boy. Tell us what happened.

WIFF: . . . Well, when I got home, duckie, I hung up my overcoat, switched on the basement light and went down to the furnace. Dam t'ing's been acting up, lately, clicking off when it shouldn't . . . and there she was, Dot, standing in the shadows beside the washing machine, as real as you or me.

MARY: Blessed God.

WIFF: Walked right up to me, love, wearing that old rag-gedy dressing-gown of hers.

JACOB: Mother saw Father about the house, weeks after he died.

WIFF: Oh, she laid right into me, Ben. The names she called your old Uncle Wiff. And I t'ought Dot never knowed a single one of them words, Jake. Said I ought to have tried to reach her when she was alive. Said I never cared enough. "Why'd you let it happen?" she said. "Why didn't you reach out?" Said she'd follow me the rest of my days for what I done . . . Well, duckie, I got out of there some quick, let me tell you. And when I looked back, she was starting up the stairs after me, crying to beat hell . . . That's when I took off out the door. I run all the way here.

JACOB: Don't you worry none, Wiff. We'll put you up. Plenty of room here.

MARY: Where will he sleep? Is you forgetting who's home?

BEN: I'll sleep on the chesterfield. He can have the bedroom.

MARY: Suit yourself. I'll get the blankets. *(She exits upstairs.)*

WIFF: I couldn't go back there, Jake. I just couldn't, love. I'd die of fright, if I was to wake up in the middle of the night with Dot leaning over me, as much as I adored her . . .

JACOB: Say no more, Wiff. I understands. *(to BEN)* Bring in the bottle, will you, my son? *(BEN exits into the kitchen.)* What do you say to another drink, Wiff, old boy? Take the chill out of your bones.

WIFF: No, bless your heart, I had one already tonight. One's my limit, after this. *(then)* She always wanted a blue silk dress, and I was always too stingy. Oh, my son, I wish I had it all to do over . . .

BEN enters with the whiskey bottle and a glass for himself.

BEN: Uncle Wiff?

WIFF: Well, perhaps I'll have a drop after all. A little one, my dear. *(as BEN pours)* Not too little . . .

MARY comes downstairs, carrying a pillow, sheets and blankets.

MARY *(as she deposits the bedclothes on the chesterfield)* Before I forgets it, Wiff, what was that row about tonight down at Jerrett's? Jacob's too modest to tell.

JACOB: Won't sleep till you knows, will you, Mary? No mistake.

WIFF: Oh, 'twas not'ing, Mary. Ike was boasting how they made him foreman.

JACOB: Foreman! Don't know his ass from a blueprint. He married the superintendent's daughter. That's how he got the job.

WIFF: Jake took him down a peg or two, didn't you, duckie? T'ought he'd come to his own funeral by mistake.

MARY: Not carpenter foreman, Wiff?

WIFF: Yes. T'inks he's King Shit, now.

MARY: On what job?

WIFF: Ours, my dear.

JACOB: What've I told you all these years, Ben? It's who you knows, not what you knows.

MARY: Oh, you fool! He'll work you ragged, just to get back. You've done it this time, boy.

JACOB: Go on with you. I'll crown him with a two-by-four if he so much as looks at me sideways.

MARY: Yes, you will so.

JACOB: Oh, won't I?

MARY: No, and I'll tell you exactly what you'll do, knowing you. You'll do whatever he tells you to do and do it twice as quick as you ought to and then ask for more. That's what you'll do. As if it wasn't bad enough before! . . . (She sits on the chesterfield.)

WIFF: Come to t'ink of it, Jake, Ike's a mean bastard when he's sore. He don't forget an insult, that one. Watch out for him, boy. He might try to get back at you.

MARY: How?

WIFF: Oh, I've seen it before, Mary, more than once. A foreman's got it in for you, he gives you the worst job there is.

MARY: Which is?

WIFF: Rigging beam bottoms and beam sides. You got to climb out along the steel with your toolbox. That's what makes it so dangerous.

BEN: How high are they up?

WIFF: Twenty floors.

JACOB: For Christ's sake, Wiff, what's you trying to do — frighten her? Now lay off.

WIFF: All right, my son, I won't say another word. But if I was you . . .

JACOB: Well, you ain't me, and that's that.

WIFF: No, but if I was, I knows what I'd do, duckie. I'd tell him where to shove it or I'd quit first. It ain't worth it.

JACOB: I won't do no such t'ing. Do you t'ink I'd let that little bastard get the best of me? That'd be the day.

MARY: (desperately) All right, but what does you want more? To get the better of Ike Squires or for Ben to stay home? You'd better make up your mind right now, Jake, 'cause you can't have it both ways, not this time. Can he, Ben?

JACOB: What's you talking about? (to BEN) You'm staying home, ain't you?

MARY: Tell him, Ben. Go on.

JACOB: You made a promise, now. Don't go back on your word.

BEN: Yeah, but you never let me finish, Dad. I wanted to stay home so you wouldn't have to work. That's what I was getting at before. Even Uncle Wiff thinks it's a good idea.

JACOB: *(to WIFF)* Oh, he do, do he? What is this, Wiff — a goddamn conspiracy? All of you ganging up on me.

WIFF: Now don't take it the wrong way, my son, I wouldn't go behind your back. You've been looking kind of pekid, lately, that's all I meant.

MARY: Yes. You've earned a good rest, Jake. Ben's young and strong. Let him pitch in for a spell.

WIFF: Jesus, if I had a son . . .

MARY: Just till you gets a clean bill of health, Jake. Not a second longer.

WIFF: For crying out loud, you're too good a man to be taking orders from that arsehole.

BEN: And what do you care what he thinks of you?

WIFF: I'd give a week's pay to watch King Shit crawling out on that cold steel with a heavy toolbox.

JACOB: *(chuckling)* Did you see him tonight? Couldn't move his ass quick enough, could he, Wiff? Lickety-split like a jack-rabbit.

MARY: Jake, please . . . Reconsider, won't you? Do it for me, if not for yourself.

BEN: I want to, Dad.

Pause.

JACOB: Oh, for Christ's sake, Mary, if it's that important to you . . . *(He crosses into the kitchen with his glass and gets the whiskey bottle.)*

MARY: You won't go in then?

JACOB: No, I won't go in. Satisfied? You got your own way, as usual.

MARY: T'anks, Jake. *(to BEN and WIFF)* Now you both heard that. *(to JACOB)* And I'm holding you to it.

BEN: I'll look for a job tomorrow.

MARY: Do that. *(to JACOB as she crosses into the kitchen and pours herself a tea)* And you and me can take it easy for a spell.

JACOB: You'm to quit the Honeydew next Friday, don't forget.

MARY: I will, I will.

JACOB: And see the doctor about those legs. *(He sits at the table.)*

MARY: I'll make an appointment. Oh, you was right, Jake, you was right, boy. This is a night to celebrate and give t'anks. Wouldn't you say, Wiff? In spite of Dot?

WIFF: I would, my dear, yes . . . *(He sits.)*

JACOB: But it's only for a short spell, Mary. Get that t'rough your head. A few weeks.

MARY: Until the doctor says . . .

JACOB: No. Until Ben goes. *(BEN nods to MARY.)* Believe it or not, Mary, I was looking forward to going back to work. That's somet'ing you just don't seem to understand, even after all these years . . .

MARY: I do, Jake.

JACOB: No, you don't. What am I supposed to do — slouch about the house growing fat and lazy? I'm only fifty-two. What have I got to live for without my work? You tell me that, Mary, if you can. What have I got to live for?

He pours WIFF another drink as the lights fade slowly to black.

ACT TWO SCENE ONE

Early next morning. On the kitchen table are two empty whiskey bottles and three glasses. One of the glasses still contains a little whiskey. There is also an ashtray overflowed onto the table.

In the living-room a song plays softly on the radio. The chester-field has not yet been made up, and the sheets and blankets are tangled. BEN's pyjama bottoms are tossed carelessly over the armchair.

At rise, BEN is beside the fridge, drinking thirstily from a bottle of orange juice. He wears pyjama tops and blue jeans. He is barefoot. When he has drunk enough, he replaces the bottle and closes the fridge.

MARY: *(off)* Jake, is that you down there?

BEN: No, he went out, Mom. It's me.

MARY: *(off)* Take the butter out of the fridge, will you, my son? And plug in the kettle.

BEN does, as WIFF, freshly scrubbed, comes down the stairs and enters the kitchen.

WIFF: Hello, my precious. How's your head this morning? Care for some breakfast? *(He begins to prepare himself scrambled eggs and toast.)*

BEN: No, thanks. I couldn't look at food. *(slight pause)* Uncle Wiff?

WIFF: What can I do for you, love?

BEN: You ever have the same dream over and over?

WIFF: Yes, but I wouldn't dare tell you, you'd t'ink for certain your Uncle Wiff belonged in a cage. For years it was always me and Veronica Lake . . . Ah, my son, we're odd creatures. For months after Dot lost interest in me, I never looked at another woman, and yet when me and her was most happy, I wanted to drive the boots home to every beautiful woman in the street . . .

Just then MARY comes down the stairs dressed in her 'Honeydew' uniform. She is spraying with a can of lilac air freshener. BEN enters the living-room.

MARY: Morning, my son.

BEN: Morning, Mom. *(He sits on the chesterfield and slips on his socks and boots.)*

MARY: Morning, Wiff.

WIFF: Mary.

MARY circles the living-room spraying, then enters the kitchen and sprays.

MARY: You don't have to do that, Wiff. I'll make your breakfast. Sit down, boy.

WIFF: No, bless your heart, I can do it myself. I ain't helpless.

MARY: Wiff?

WIFF: Yes, my dear?

MARY: T'anks for last night. Jake'll listen to you before he will to me.

WIFF: Oh, don't t'ank me, love. It was all Ben's doing. Jake'd agree to leprosy to keep him around. You and me had little to do with it.

MARY, smiling, deposits the can on top of the fridge and returns to the living-room.

MARY: How'd you sleep?

BEN: Not too good.

MARY: Well, your first night back, that's to be expected. You're used to your own bed, now.

BEN: It wasn't the bed, Mom.

MARY: Hardly slept myself.

BEN *(as he helps MARY fold the sheets and blankets)* How come? I thought you'd sleep okay last night.

MARY: No. Your father kicked and twisted all night. Wonder I ain't black and blue, or scratched to pieces. Never cuts his toe-nails.

BEN: Where'd he go?

MARY: Out back. He's warming up the truck.

BEN: What for?

MARY: He drives me to work.

BEN: Oh.

MARY: Not that he needs to . . . I suppose he feels funny, still in bed with me off to work. *(The sheets and blankets are now folded.)* I'd better see what he's up to. He ought to've been in by now. *(then)* Wiff? Is Jake out back?

WIFF: One second, maid, I'll look.

As WIFF looks out the kitchen window, MARY folds BEN's pyjama bottoms neatly over the back of the arm-chair.

No, no sign of him, Mary. *(He returns to making his breakfast.)*

MARY: Where could he be at? *(She crosses to the living-room window, looks out.)* No, there he is, shovelling the sidewalk. Without gloves, as usual. *(She watches.)*

BEN: *(crosses to the window)* I'd've done that. Next time get me up, okay?

MARY: No, leave it be. He's got to have somet'ing to do. *(quickly)* Don't let him see you . . .

BEN: Why not?

MARY: Look how he leans on his shovel . . .

BEN: He looks old, Mom. I noticed that last night. Smaller . . .

MARY: Come away, now, before he catches you. *(as she moves away from the window)* You want some breakfast?

429

BEN: No. Just a coffee. I'll get it. (He follows MARY into the kitchen. As she cleans the table of the whiskey bottles, glasses and ashtray, he unplugs the kettle and makes himself a mug of instant black coffee.) . . . Mom, remember that dream I mentioned? I had it again this morning, the same one.

MARY: Oh?

BEN: Yeah. I think it woke me. I haven't been able to shake it off.

MARY: Is it that bad, my son?

BEN: It never made any sense before I came home. I think it does now.

MARY: You any good at dreams, Wiff?

WIFF: Not me, maid. Dot was the one. (He crosses to the table with his plate, sits.)

BEN: It's always the same, Mom . . . I'm on a brass bed, a big brass bed like the one we had back home when I was a kid. Remember?

MARY: (to WIFF) He always t'ought it was gold. The way it shone.

BEN: Whatever happened to it?

MARY: Oh, we left it back in Bay Roberts, my son, along with all that other old junk we never knowed was antiques.

BEN: (as he sits at the table) . . . Anyway, the bed's sitting at a crossroads, two dirt roads, and I can see a cliff behind me, and the sea beyond that.

MARY: Might be Conception Bay.

BEN: Except I'm the same age I am now. It's a beautiful day, summer, and I'm just lying there on the bed at this crossroads, wide awake, looking up at the blue sky, the sun sparkling on the bedposts . . . Suddenly the sky's full of butterflies, all different colours, millions of beautifully coloured wings . . . and then . . .

MARY: Yes? *(She crosses to BEN.)*

BEN: Then two people without faces, a man and a woman . . .

MARY: A man and a woman?

BEN: Yeah, they come up one road and look at me and go down the other . . . and suddenly the sky's black, it's night, and the butterflies become snowflakes, and I'm running, really scared for some reason, stumbling along this snowy road, running home, running like crazy, and all I know is that I have to get home fast because . . . *(He pauses.)*

MARY: *(sitting)* Because what, my son?

BEN: Because something . . . terrible is happening there, and I don't know what . . . something terrible . . .

BEN and MARY stare at one another. A beat. Then JACOB enters offstage and slams the door. He stamps his feet and begins to cough a hacking cough.

MARY: I wish he wouldn't smoke. Sometimes he can't catch his breath when he goes outside.

WIFF: Another reason he shouldn't be working up high.

JACOB: *(appearing in the hallway, wearing his coat and cap; he sniffs)* Goddam place smells of lilacs! *(He hangs up his coat and cap in the closet.)*

MARY: Now if I hadn't sprayed, he would've complained it smelled of cigarettes. Contrary as the day is long. *(to BEN)* Was he cross before he went to bed last night?

BEN: No.

WIFF: He was telling jokes, love.

MARY: First t'ing he noticed when he opened his eyes this morning, was the venetian blinds in the bedroom was dusty. Done not'ing but complain ever since.

431

JACOB: *(entering the kitchen)* Ain't my breakfast ready yet? You've had all morning for Christ's sake.

MARY: *(to BEN)* What'd I say? *(to JACOB, as she rises)* No, and Wiff made his own. I just got downstairs.

JACOB: Wiff.

WIFF: Duckie.

MARY: Sit down, boy. I'm just making the tea.

She puts three tea bags into the teapot and pours in hot water. BEN takes the newspaper off the counter and spreads out the want ads on a corner of the table. JACOB watches him a moment.

JACOB: *(to BEN)* Well, you'm up bright and early this morning. Can't wait step into my shoes. *(to WIFF)* Look at him. *(He remains standing.)*

BEN: *(running his fingers down the want ad columns)* I couldn't sleep, that's all.

JACOB: Makes no bloody wonder, after last night. You keeps drinking like that, you'll have the d.t.'s. I t'ought you could put it away fast, Wiff.

BEN: Get serious. I only had a few.

JACOB: A few?

BEN: He drank two to my one, didn't he, Uncle Wiff?

WIFF: Leave me out of it, duckie.

JACOB: He calls that a few, Wiff. Picked up some fine habits out west, I see. Nineteen years old . . .

BEN: Twenty.

JACOB: Twenty, is it?

BEN: I'll be twenty-one soon.

MARY: All right, just stop it, the both of you. Stop it. What's you want for breakfast, Jake? Bacon and eggs?

JACOB: Home one night, and staggering off to bed . . .

MARY: Is you hungry or not?

JACOB: Hungry? How the hell would I be hungry? I lost my appetite the day I stopped working. A bird could live on less.

MARY: Well, sit down and have a cup of tea, at least. You're making me nervous.

JACOB: *(sitting)* I suppose you'm working Wednesday, Wiff?

WIFF: Oh, yes, boy. Sooner the better. Best t'ing for me right now. Too much time on my hands is no good. Allows you to t'ink too much . . .

JACOB: You can say that again, Wiff. I never could sit on my ass for very long, even when I was laid off. Feel every minute, if I ain't active. Every goddamn minute. *(He looks at BEN.)* Ain't that Saturday's paper?

BEN: Yeah.

JACOB: This is Monday. What's the good of Saturday's paper to you? Why don't you look at last summer's? *(BEN says nothing.)* What a way he goes about t'ings, Wiff. My Christ. And he went to university, too.

BEN: Lay off, will you? I'll get the other papers, later. It's not going to hurt if I look, is it?

JACOB: No, don't give me no heed, I'm uneducated.

MARY: *(changing the subject, as she crosses to the table, puts down a cup of tea for JACOB and WIFF)* I'm surprised the t'ree of you never slept in. It must've been late when you come to bed.

JACOB: Who said it was late?

MARY: I t'ought it was. I never heard you come to bed.

WIFF: It was only one, Mary.

MARY: That's late for Jake.

433

JACOB: It might've been, when I was working. Not now. I can stay up to all hours, now.

MARY: *(changing the subject again)* More coffee, Ben?

BEN: *(looking curiously at JACOB)* No, thanks, Mom.

JACOB: *(to BEN)* What's you staring at? Never seen me face before?

BEN: What's wrong with you this morning? All you've done is bitch.

MARY: *(to herself, as she crosses back to the counter and pours her own tea):* Worse than an old woman.

JACOB: *(to BEN)* I don't like to be spied on, for starters. Is that good enough?

MARY: That ain't what's bothering you. Own up to it.

BEN: Who was spying on you?

JACOB: The two of you.

MARY: Oh, we was not.

JACOB: Liar. I seen you at the window. Next you'll be telling me I'm blind. I ain't some specimen under glass, Mary.

MARY: Did I say you was?

JACOB: Then don't watch me like a goddamn hawk. *(then)* Tea's like bark.

MARY: Why don't you just come out with what's eating at you and get it over with?

JACOB: Eating at me? What in Christ's name could be eating at me, Mary? I've got it all to my liking, now.

MARY: Well, there's no need to put us all t'rough this. Next t'ing you'll take after Wiff.

WIFF: *(quickly)* I'm just going, my dear. Just on my way out the door. *(He half-rises but JACOB stops him with a gesture.)*

JACOB: How many men you suppose would leap at the

chance not to work? Most would give their eye-teeth. Bet Wiff would, if Dot was still alive.

MARY: All right, I've took all I can. If you wants to go to work so bad, go . . . Go! . . . Did you hear what I said?

JACOB: *(glancing at BEN)* Ah . . .

MARY: I won't stop you this time, if this is how you intends to carry on. I can't take much more. I'll pack your lunchpail, if you likes. *(She steps to the fridge and takes down his lunchpail.)*

JACOB: You will, like hell! *(He jumps up, follows her, snatches the lunchpail from her hands, and smashes it on the floor.)* There! *(Silence. MARY bends down and picks up his lunchpail and opens it. She removes the thermos and shakes it. It rattles.)* Now see what you made me do! *(He rushes out to the hall closet.)* Can't leave well enough alone for a second, can you, Mary? My good t'ermos. *(He returns to the kitchen, struggling to put on his coat and cap.)*

MARY: Don't be foolish, boy. Where do you t'ink you're off to?

JACOB: Out. And I don't know when I'll be back — if ever. Find your own way to work.

He exits the kitchen door, slamming it behind him. MARY rushes after him.

MARY: *(off)* Jake! Wait! Your rubbers! . . . *(Slowly, MARY returns, closing the door. She walks to the counter. We hear the truck drive off. As she picks up her teacup. . .)* Well, I got my wish, didn't I . . . And now it's started . . .

BEN: What has?

MARY: What I was afraid of . . .

Slow fade to black. Music.

Lights up. Early the same evening. The kitchen table has been set for four. MARY is alone onstage, standing at the living-room window. The curtains are pulled aside slightly, and she stares out at the street. Finally, she draws the curtains, crosses and enters the kitchen, checks the oven.

MARY: *(to herself)* Where could he be to? *(Offstage, the front door opens and closes. MARY darts to the table, quickly scoops up the plates, and begins slowly and casually to reset the table, humming a little tune. BEN enters the hallway, carrying a book. He removes his things and crosses to the archway, thumbing his book. MARY, turning.)* Oh, it's you . . . I t'ought it might be your father.

BEN: Why? Isn't he home yet?

MARY: No.

BEN: What time is it?

MARY: Just after six. I'm worried sick. It ain't like him to miss his supper. He's always home at five sharp, no odds what.

BEN: I wouldn't worry, Mom. He'll be back. You know how he talks.

MARY: What if he had an accident with the truck? I'm afraid to turn on the radio, in case . . .

BEN: Look, you're getting all worked up for nothing. If anything did happen, they wouldn't put it on the radio before notifying us.

MARY: *(returns and sits at the table)* I've always knowed where he was, at all times. This is the first time I wouldn't know where to reach him in case of an emergency. The first time since we was married . . .

BEN: *(crosses into kitchen)* Is Uncle Wiff here?

MARY: No.

BEN: So maybe he's with him.

MARY: I t'ought of that. Did Wiff say where he was going to this morning?

BEN: No. (then) Yeah, wait a minute, he did. He said he was going to the cemetery to pick out a plot.

MARY: They might be at the Oakwood together. He may've dropped in for a beer and seen Wiff. He'd soon forget the time.

BEN: Why don't you phone?

MARY: No. He don't like that. Makes him feel foolish, he says, in front of the other men. Would you?

BEN: All right. In a few minutes, okay? Give him a while longer. (He crosses to the fridge and gets a Coke.)

MARY: I'll get changed then. Keep an eye on the oven, will you? I won't be long. And yell up if he comes in. (She crosses to the archway, then remembers, crosses back.) Oh, by the way, how'd it go today? Any luck? You get a job?

BEN: No, I didn't, Mom.

MARY: Oh.

BEN: I didn't look.

MARY: You didn't look? Why not? What was you doing all day?

BEN: I was at the library.

MARY: The library?

BEN: I needed some time to think, I just lost track of time. When I looked out the window, finally, it was dark. So I came home.

MARY: What was you t'inking about?

BEN: Mostly Dad, I guess.

MARY: (as BEN enters the living-room, sits in the arm-chair with his Coke) Well, the best way you can help your father is get a job. You can't look tomorrow, but you can start again Wednesday. *(She turns to exit, then turns back to BEN.)* Since when did you start going to the library? You was never that fond of books, even in school.

BEN: Yeah, I know. It happened in Regina last winter. I ran into the library one day to get out of the cold, on my way home from the Post Office. I saw a girl there behind the desk.

MARY: A girl?

BEN: The most beautiful girl I've ever seen. So I picked up a book, any book, just as an excuse to hang around, you know. I did that for weeks, every day except Sunday. I'd go to the library after work and read and look at this girl. Even gave her a name: Sarah.

MARY: Did you talk to her?

BEN: No. I was too shy . . . And one day she wasn't there. I still don't know what happened to her: whether she quit or got fired, moved away or got married or what. I kept going back for weeks, hoping to see her again . . . and then one day I realized I was going there just for the books . . . *(He laughs.)*

MARY: *(laughing too)* Well, just don't tell your father where you was at the whole day. He'd have a fit if he knowed.

She exits upstairs. BEN rises, takes a few paces.

BEN: *(exasperated)* Shit! *(He paces a moment, then crosses to the window, looks out. Suddenly, he knocks on the window and waves, enters the hall, out of sight. The front door opens.)*

BEN: *(off)* You want a hand with that, Uncle Wiff?

WIFF: *(off)* I wouldn't mind, love. Just put it down anywhere.

BEN enters carrying two fair-sized cardboard boxes. WIFF follows behind, removes his rubbers. BEN sets the boxes down on a chair in the hall.

MARY: *(off)* Is that you, Jake?

WIFF: No, it's Wiff, Mary. *(to BEN)* Ain't he home yet?

BEN: No. Mom's worried.

WIFF: Yes, well, he's usually home by this time . . .

BEN: She thinks he might've had an accident or something.

WIFF: Well, I wouldn't go that far, duckie. Jake's not the kind to do somet'ing rash, for all that. He's a good driver.

BEN: Yeah, but he needs glasses. And you saw the mood he was in this morning.

WIFF: Still and all — Jesus! — it don't help to jump to conclusions. Did you phone the hospitals?

BEN: No. I didn't want to frighten Mom. I thought I'd phone the Oakwood first.

WIFF: Now that's an idea. He just might've tied one on.

BEN: *(as he enters the kitchen)* You know the number?

WIFF: *(absently)* No, my son . . .

BEN walks to the counter, picks up the telephone book, opens it.

BEN: Uncle Wiff?

WIFF: Yes, my son?

BEN: About this morning . . . Have they been fighting a lot like that, lately?

WIFF: No. No, come to t'ink of it, they've been getting along famously. Like two kids.

BEN: So it's only since I've been home . . .

Sound of truck.

WIFF: Sounds like him, now.

439

They both look out the kitchen window.

BEN: *(crossing to the stairs)* Mom, he's home!

MARY: *(off)* Yes, I heard his truck!

BEN picks up his book and sits on the chesterfield.

WIFF: *(as he crosses to the stairs and hangs his coat, hat and scarf on the banister)* T'ank Christ. That's a load off my mind. I t'ought he'd gone off the road and was freezing to death in some ditch. *(He crosses to the chesterfield, sits beside BEN.)* Ben, my son, I just hope we done the right t'ing, persuading him to stay home. I don't mind telling you I've had my doubts, after today.

BEN: So have I, Uncle Wiff.

WIFF: I wish I'd never interfered.

BEN: What if he went in? What do you think would happen?

WIFF: Ben, I wish I had the answer to that one.

BEN: He might be better off, Uncle Wiff.

WIFF: Yes, and who knows? It might be the last t'ing he ever does.

BEN: Well, he'll die if he stays home. At least if he went to work he could keep a little self-respect.

MARY comes quickly down the stairs. She is dressed in slacks, blouse and cardigan. WIFF gets himself a magazine.

MARY: Hello, Wiff. *(to herself, as she rushes into the kitchen)* Better get the supper on the table or he'll have another excuse to be cranky.

She takes the casserole from the oven and is crossing to put it on the table, just as the kitchen door opens and JACOB enters. He shields his left cheek with a rolled-up newspaper.

440

MARY: *(casually)* You're just in time, boy. Just this second took the supper out of the oven. You must be famished.

JACOB: *(as he crosses to the hall closet and hangs up his coat and cap)* No, I ain't a bit hungry. I ate downtown.

BEN and WIFF pretend to be engrossed in their reading.

MARY: I made macaroni and cheese, special.

JACOB: Goddamn it, Mary, why won't you listen to me? I said I wasn't hungry. Don't you understand English? And then you wonders why I loses my temper so much of the time. *(As he crosses and sits in the arm-chair with his newspaper we can see the bruise and cut on his left cheek.)*

WIFF: *(casually, from behind his magazine)* How'd it go today, Jake? What was you up to?

JACOB: *(sitting)* Not a goddamn t'ing, Wiff, and I'm the tiredest I've ever been. Doing not'ing takes the good right out of me.

WIFF throws down his magazine and looks at JACOB for the first time.

WIFF: What the hell . . .!

BEN: *(looking over)* What happened, Dad?

JACOB puts his finger to his lips, indicating MARY.

WIFF: Where'd you get the souvenir, Jake?

JACOB: *(smiling)* Where else? — the Oakwood.

WIFF: Who'd you run into? Anybody we knows?

JACOB: Only Ike Squires.

WIFF: How is Ike, Jake?

JACOB: Well, a funny t'ing happened, Wiff. Somebody bloodied his nose while I was there.

441

WIFF: Is that a fact? Sorry I missed it. What hospital's Ike in, Jake?

As MARY enters the living-room and stands behind his arm-chair, JACOB covers his cheek with his hand.

MARY: Is that where you was all day, at the hotel?

JACOB: No, I wasn't. I drove around most of the day and for a short spell I parked in front of the job.

BEN: What for?

JACOB: Don't know. Just to have a look, I suppose.

MARY: What's wrong? You got a toothache?

JACOB: No. What put that in your head?

MARY: What's you trying to hide then?

JACOB: I ain't hiding a blessed t'ing.

MARY: No? Then let me look. *(She pulls away his hand.)* What in the world! . . . Have you been in a fight?

JACOB: *(laughing)* What makes you t'ink that?

MARY: Stand up and let me look. Stand up. *(He does.)* Stand still. *(He lets her inspect the bruise.)* Better put some Mercurochrome on it. Who hit you? *(She touches his cheekbone.)*

JACOB: *(dancing away)* Goddamn it, Mary, that stings. Keep your fingers to yourself.

MARY: Who hit you?

JACOB: None of your business.

MARY: Well, I hope it hurts. Who was it, Ike Squires? I heard you say somebody bloodied his nose. You set some example, you do.

JACOB: That's right, Mary, pour on the sympathy. All I did was what you suggested last night.

MARY: What was that, pray tell?

JACOB: *(to WIFF)* I went after Ike in the beer parlour, instead of the funeral parlour.

Laughing, he exits. BEN and WIFF laugh, too, and so does MARY, in spite of herself.

MARY: Well, come on, you two, supper's ready. *(She crosses toward the archway.)* Jake ain't eating. We might as well start.

WIFF: *(rising)* No, t'ank you kindly, Mary, I ate before. I just come by to drop some of Dot's t'ings off. *(He crosses to the chair and picks up one of the boxes.)*

MARY: Oh? *(She takes the box.)*

WIFF: *(putting on his overcoat)* T'ought you might like to look t'rough it and pick what you likes. The rest you can give to the Salvation Army.

MARY: *(crosses to the chesterfield, puts down the box)* So you went home after all? I t'ought you'd never set foot in there? *(She sits.)*

WIFF: *(crosses to MARY, who slowly removes a beautiful shawl and stares at it)* Well, Mary, I left here this morning and went to the cemetery and picked out a plot, two plots, one for each of us, and I stood there with me breath blowing, looking at the white ground and all the headstones round about, and suddenly it went t'rough me like a cold wind: Dot's *dead.* I don't t'ink it had really sunk in before, that fact, even when I bent over her casket last night and kissed her cold lips. Not even then for some reason. Perhaps because she was there in body if not in spirit. Not until that moment in the cemetery did it strike me: Dot's *dead.* Dead. The word itself was like a nail in me own coffin. Tomorrow, I said to myself, she'll be under the snow forever in a bronze box and I'll never see her face again, even in death. In time I'd forget what she even looked like . . . So I had a good cry right there in the cemetery, as much for myself as for her, I suppose, the

443

first tears I shed since she died . . . And then I got in the car and drove home. Went t'rough the house, top to bottom.

MARY: What for, Wiff?

WIFF: Looking for Dot, maid. Only this time she never appeared. Even sang out her name.

MARY: Wasn't you frightened to, after last night?

WIFF: (sitting) Mary, I suddenly felt that anyt'ing was better than not'ing, maid . . . anyt'ing. I t'ink I understands for the first time a little what Jacob feels . . .

MARY: It ain't the same, Wiff.

WIFF: Ain't it, Mary?

Enter JACOB, carrying a bottle of Mercurochrome and a box of Band-Aids. He crosses to the arm-chair.

JACOB: Here, Mary, put this on for me.

MARY: (rises, crosses to JACOB) Did you wash it with hot water?

JACOB: I did. Just stick on the Band-Aid and don't say another word. And don't be rough, it smarts.

MARY: (as she administers to his cheek) What'd you do — follow Ike from the job?

JACOB: No, I never. He just happened to be there. Him and a few of the other boys. I sat by myself.

MARY: Yes, for how long?

JACOB: Until I heard them laughing and looking my way. Then I pushed back my chair and went over to his table and asked him to repeat what was so goddamn funny.

WIFF: Wish I'd been there. I'd like to've seen that. That must've shut him up in a hurry.

JACOB: No, Wiff. He t'ought he was safe among his friends. Only a good swift kick in the arse would shut that one up.

MARY: Yes, and you have just the boots to do it. Hold still. *(She pushes him down on the arm of the arm-chair.)*

JACOB: Hold your tongue, Mary. You don't even know what he said to me.

MARY: What?

JACOB: "Sit down, Mercer," he says. "The drinks's on me."

MARY: And for that you bloodied his nose?

JACOB: "You won me five dollars today," he says. "How's that?" says I. "I bet one of the boys five dollars you wouldn't show up." And he gave a great loud horse-laugh. Could've heard him a block away with a band playing.

WIFF: Is that when you struck him, duckie?

JACOB: No, first off I t'rowed his beer in his face, and he lunged up knocking over the table, walloped me one right in the cheek.

WIFF: Sneaky little bugger, ain't he?

JACOB: By Jesus, Wiff, I'll hand him that much, he's fast. Never saw it coming. I only got one good one in before the waiters rushed over and broke it up.

WIFF: Well, next time, duckie, he'll save his bets for the race-track.

MARY: *(sticking on the Band-Aid)* There. Serve you right if you gets a black eye. That'd teach you.

JACOB: *(walking away)* Dared me to come into work. Right there in front of the other men. Said I wasn't man enough . . . never had the guts is how he put it. Holy Christ, Wiff, I'd like to make him eat those words.

WIFF: Dare say you would.

JACOB: I'd like to cram every goddamn word down his gullet.

BEN: Why don't you, Dad?

JACOB: What?

BEN: Make him eat his words.

JACOB: How?

BEN: How else? Go in to work.

JACOB: What? . . .

MARY: Ben . . .

BEN: Don't let me stop you. I might as well tell you now as later. I'm going back out west.

JACOB: You is not, now. You just got here.

BEN: I am. I've thought it over.

MARY: Ben, what's come over you?

BEN: Christ, he wants to work, Mom. Let him.

JACOB: Who says I wants to work? I never said a word, did I, Mary? *(slight pause)* Did I, Wiff?

BEN: Come on, Dad, you know you would've gone to work today if we hadn't blackmailed you. You only agreed to keep me home.

JACOB: Listen here, I couldn't care less if I never lifts a bloody hammer again. What's it ever done for me? I'm just a workhorse.

BEN: That's bullshit, and you know it. It's your whole life. *(slight pause)* Anyway, I'm going home . . .

JACOB: Home? . . .

BEN: . . . right after the funeral tomorrow, so you can do what you want. I'm sorry, Mom. *(He enters the kitchen.)*

MARY: *(going after BEN)* Sorry? You'll be sorry all right.

JACOB: *(to himself)* I t'ought it was too good to be true . . . *(He sits in the arm-chair.)*

MARY: *(to BEN)* Have you lost your mind? What do you suppose'll happen now, if he goes in? Have you forgot Ike

446

Squires? He has double the excuse to go after your father now.

BEN: What if he doesn't go in, Mom? Did you ever consider that? Or doesn't it matter?

MARY: He'll never let up on him, Ben. He's that type. You heard Wiff.

JACOB: *(explosively)* Will you shut up about Ike Squires, Mary? I can snap him in two like a stick of pencil.

BEN: *(crosses to JACOB)* You'd never let up on yourself, Dad. Or Mom. *(to MARY)* You're the one has to live with him.

WIFF: Ben's right, Jake, as much as I hates to admit it. The boy's right.

JACOB: What? Whose side is you on, Wiff? Mine or his?

WIFF: There's no sides this time, duckie. Don't you know that?

BEN: Look what happened this morning, Mom. That was just the beginning.

JACOB: This morning? What happened this morning? Oh, I see. I ain't allowed to get up on the wrong side, is that it? It's a crime not to have a smile on my face every blessed morning.

BEN: *(crosses into the kitchen to MARY)* Let him go, Mom. It'll only get worse if you don't.

JACOB: *(jumps up, crosses to the hall closet, and gets his coat and cap)* All right, Mary. See that, now? He don't give a shit if I lives or dies. He never has. Perhaps you'll believe me now.

BEN: Oh, don't be ridiculous. *(He crosses to the table, sits.)*

JACOB: Well, don't you come to my funeral, you hear? *(to MARY)* And don't you let him within a hundred yards or else. *(to WIFF)* Some friend you turned out to be, taking his part. I never would've believed it, Wiff.

WIFF: Now, duckie . . .

JACOB: Don't duckie me, goddamn it!

He heads for the kitchen door and manages to get just outside, but MARY's next line brings him back.

MARY: *(to BEN)* Even if what you says is true, Ben, he still ain't fit to work!

BEN: I know that . . .

JACOB: *(to MARY)* Who ain't fit?

MARY: You ain't, boy. And I'm in no hurry to be a widow, even if Ben's intent on killing you.

JACOB: Goddamn it, Mary, I'll put my fist t'rough that wall if you says I ain't fit one more time. I can still work as good as Wiff here, no odds what you says to the contrary.

MARY: All right, but admit it or not, you're in no condition to be up twenty stories in ten-below cold!

JACOB: Is that a fact? *(He crosses into the living-room, tossing his cap at the foot of the stairs.)*

MARY: *(following him)* What if you're hanging on with your toolbox and you take a fit of coughing? Sometimes you can't catch your breath. I've seen it on cold mornings. Even the wind can take your breath away when you goes outside. Or what's worse — what if you has a sudden pain in your chest? What then, boy? Do you t'ink I wants to be sick with worry every day you sets off for the job, not knowing whether you'll be back or not? *(She crosses into the kitchen.)* Ben don't care. He don't have to live with it. *(She crosses to BEN.)* But you'll have to live with it, my son, if anyt'ing should happen to him. It'll be on your conscience for the rest of your life. Is that what you wants? Is it? *(BEN says nothing.)* Well, I just hopes you don't live to regret it, my son. For your sake, I wouldn't want it on my mind, I can tell you. *(She turns and starts wearily for the stairs.)* If anyone wants supper it's on the table. I'm going to lie down. *(She starts up the stairs, then stops.)* He can battle all he wants to, Ben, we're all up against the same enemy: time . . .

She exits. Pause.

WIFF: *(rises)* Well, I . . . I must be off. *(He crosses into the hall.)* I'd like to be alone with Dot for a spell. May be my last real chance. I won't be back tonight, love. I already told Mary. I'm going home.

JACOB: Oh?

WIFF: Will I see you all later?

JACOB: We'll be there, Wiff, we'll be there. *(then)* Wiff?

WIFF: What, my son?

JACOB: I never meant what I said before. You're the best friend I ever had, outside Mary.

WIFF: Don't you t'ink I knows that, boy. *(slight pause)* And Wednesday morning we'll go to work together. Just like old times. Is that a deal, duckie?

JACOB: That's a deal. I'll pick you up, same time as always.

WIFF: See you later, love. You too, Ben. *(He exits.)*

JACOB removes his coat, hangs it over the banister. Then slowly crosses into the kitchen and gets down a bottle of whiskey from the cupboard. He turns and looks at BEN.

JACOB: You want a drink?

BEN: No, thanks. *(A beat. Then he enters the living-room, sits on the chesterfield.)*

JACOB: *(as he pours himself a drink)* I never knowed how growed up you was till tonight. *(He crosses to the archway.)* What made you do it?

BEN: Do what?

JACOB: *(moves close to BEN)* One minute you was willing to stay, the next you wasn't. It wasn't all for me, now, was it? Tell the truth. *(slight pause)* You wouldn't have a girl out west, would you? Is that it? Did I guess right? I did, didn't I?

BEN: . . . Yeah, that's it. How'd you know?

JACOB: *(sits in the arm-chair, picks up his newspaper)* Well, that puts a different light on t'ings. You ought to've mentioned it before. Now, that I can understand. I missed your mother when I come up here alone to look for work and left her back home. Well, perhaps you'll settle down, at last. What's she like?

BEN: *(with difficulty)* She's beautiful, Dad. She works in a library. That's how we met.

JACOB: What's her name?

BEN: Sarah . . .

JACOB: Well, you bring her home next time you comes, you hear? I'd like to meet her. Will you do that for me?

BEN: Sure, Dad. . . *(He rises.)*

JACOB: *(as BEN crosses behind the arm-chair)* And don't stay away so long next time, Ben. *(a beat)* Your mother worries . . .

He buries himself in his newspaper. Cross fade of lights so that BEN and JACOB end up in spots, BEN facing the audience. JACOB remains sitting in the arm-chair, his face hidden by the newspaper.

BEN: Seven weeks later I took another jet home and stood in a winter cemetery, stamping my feet against the cold, feeling somehow he'd set me free with his death. Keeled over on the job, was how Uncle Wiff put it. Hammering a nail in a joist . . .

I never did get any closer to my father, thoug. learned to take him seriously as a man, not an obst. But the wall was still there, a little cracked maybe, b still dividing us, still waiting to be toppled.

And I never did get to ask him that one simple question that has haunted me all my life, ever since that summer evening when I was twelve and he came down to the school-yard to watch me play . . . "How did you like the game?"

Slowly JACOB lowers and folds his newspaper as though he has heard the question. The lights fade slowly to black.

James Reaney
Handcuffs

EDITOR'S NOTE: James Reaney was born in 1926 in a rural community near Stratford, Ontario. He attended high school in Stratford, received his doctorate from the University of Toronto where he studied under Northrop Frye, and has taught in the Department of English at the University of Western Ontario since 1960. His distinguished career includes over thirty stage plays, a half-dozen radio scripts, the libretti for three operas, and two Governor-General's Award-winning volumes of poetry. In 1960, his second play, *The Killdeer*, also won a Governor-General's Award. In 1967 *Colours in the Dark* was the first major Canadian play to be done at Stratford; *Sticks and Stones*, the first of the Donnelly trilogy, was staged in 1973 at the Tarragon Theatre and was a Chalmers Award finalist; *St. Nicholas Hotel*, the second part of the Donnellys, appeared at Tarragon in 1974 and won a Chalmers Outstanding Canadian Play Award; *Handcuffs* completed the trilogy. Since then Reaney has continued his active playwriting with over a half-dozen new plays.

Handcuffs: The Donnellys, Part Three, which opened on 29 March 1975 at Toronto's Tarragon Theatre, was a Chalmers Outstanding Canadian Play finalist. It was first published by Press Porcépic in 1977.

AUTHOR'S NOTE: Like slowly closing handcuffs people (priests, bishops, constables, farmers, tavern keepers, traitors, threshers, among others) openly and secretly, legally and illegally fasten the disturbing Donnelly family still so that it can murder them . . . Tuesday, 3 February, 1880.

But although no one was ever *legally* punished for this crime, there are stories still told of how almost a year later the ghosts of Mr & Mrs Donnelly managed to execute four or five of their enemies. Where the Donnelly house once stood the remaining family place four stones; it's hard to handcuff wheat.

ACT I

From somewhere behind a bare stage dominated by a large sideboard or buffet comes the sound of a family group singing to themselves Victorian parlour songs, some of them in four part harmony. Then they enter & cued by a visible pianist whose piano stands directly behind the cupboard they direct at us "When You & I Were Young, Maggie" (with tenor soloist) and then "Grandfather's Clock". JENNIE CURRIE, née Donnelly, comes forward and arranges four chairs or partners in a reel; she then winds up a gramophone on Stage Right & places on it a record playing an Irish reel. She proceeds to dance all by herself. Having finished the Clock Song the rest of the cast form a "house" about this dancing figure and soon THERESA O'CONNOR comes visiting with her children; they open the door and surprise JENNIE who says:

JENNIE: Oh, Theresa O'Connor, I never expected you'd catch me doing this. Dancing by myself. *(The shebeen lady enters with PEGGY and grandchildren, bonneted for a summer afternoon.)*

THERESA: Jennie Currie. We thought you were having a party in the middle of the afternoon. When I pushed open that door you children fully expected to see a fiddler and

PEGGY: But there was only you, Jenny

JENNY: And these chairs

THERESA: And that gramophone

CHILD: Jennie Currie, what's in this box you've got on top of the buffet here?

JENNY: Theresa, do they know of my mother?

THERESA: Children, Jenny's mother was Mrs James Donnelly

JENNY: It's a piece of bone from my mother's arm.

Out of the corner of our eye we see a tall woman fling her arms up, turn and fade away

THERESA: Your mother had arms like wings, Jenny, I remember you saying that at the wake.

JENNY: I remember. Children, my mother what was left of her, was brought into your house, Theresa, your house and waked there

THERESA: It was a rough wooden box the bones were in. I can

JENNY: My mother, Theresa, had arms like wings. We'd be all alone in the house and she'd teach me how to dance

THERESA: And the handwriting there'd be in that arm. Peggy, she sent a note in with Johnny once

JENNY: You gave it to me at the wake and I've wrapped the piece of bone up in it

CHORUS: November 23rd, 1879 (*They sit on church pews on either side; enter as needed*)

MRS DONNELLY: Theresa O'Connor. I want Peggy over there to sew me — us nine — nine handkerchiefs edged with black in time for my son Michael's funeral

On Stage Left there is a sewing machine PEGGY will soon be sewing at.

CHILD: Mother, when did they kill her?

PEGGY & CHORUS: Midnight, Tuesday, February the 3rd.

JENNY: Oh Peggy, I asked your mother here at the wake as we stood looking at my mother's handwriting

THERESA: We stood there, Jenny, and you asked me to tell you every last single time I saw your mother between the time she wrote that note

CHORUS: November 23rd, 1879

JENNY: And the time she died

PEGGY: Tuesday, February the 3rd

THERESA: Jenny, those last two months they were alive your brother Tom came twice, and I saw your brother John thrice and your father once and your mother four times and her niece

THERESA begins to take bottles out of the cupboard and puts them on top — changing Jenny's house into hers.

JENNY: Oh Theresa, show me. Show me the twice and the thrice and the once and the four

PEGGY goes to sewing machine. Its whirring sound rises and falls as part of the play's spirit.

THERESA: At the wake you asked me, you ask me now and I tell you it was time flowing by in our little house we had no idea at first where time was flowing your mother on her visits to our house, you would be sewing over at the sewing machine more than likely, Peggy and —

JENNY: It isn't summer any more outside my windows, it's snowing

THERESA: The last two months went by like this: remember Peggy? I said one day to put up a curtain, now why did I tell you that —

PEGGY: Well. Weren't they always saying that

455

THERESA: Hush! Peggy, yes that I was running an illegal tavern, a shebeen

CARROLL: *(entering abruptly)* There was a cupboard in her house made into a bar with bottles, glasses, whiskey, wine and pop in those bottles and she justified their presence by saying:

THERESA: Aw for the love of Heaven, it's for the convenience of our boarders and roomers and I dare you to call me a liar.

CARROLL: Theresa O'Connor, you've only got four rooms in this house. What boarders, what roomers?

THERESA: Come this evening and you'll see them, Mr Inspector. We've small quarters but large hearts and — is he gone, children? Peggy, while you're sewing there could you just run me up a curtain there to hide our cupboard that they're *(kissing the sideboard)* darling cupboard — making such a fuss about?

PEGGY: I will ma, but I wish you'd watch your tongue.

THERESA: Heavens preserve us it's Mrs Donnelly coming to our door and she's got a strange young girl with her, who in the name of Heaven can that girl be? Peggy, darling, put on the kettle and we'll boil you's all a cup of tea.

PEGGY: She wants to give Mrs Donnelly a cup of tea. Kitty, will you put the kettle on for ma?

KITTY: Pat will you please put the kettle on for ma?

PAT: Johnny, will you put the kettle on.

MRS DONNELLY: Good day to you Theresa O'Connor, I would like you to meet my husband's niece Bridget who's just come over on the boat from Ireland. And we're back from town meeting her.

BRIDGET: I'm very pleased to meet you, Mrs O'Connor.

MRS DONNELLY: Theresa, Mr Donnelly was wondering if we could take Johnny back with us to the farm. We need a good boy like Johnny here to do the chores while we're away.

THERESA: Johnny shall go with you as he has before and he likes going out to hear your boys talk and sing — Bridget, my darling, what's scaring you?

MRS DONNELLY: It's the sewing machine, Theresa.

THERESA: Bridget have you never heard one go that fast before?

BRIDGET: I've never set eyes on a sewing machine before, Mrs O'Connor. Such a great fearsome roaring sound, what ever are you sewing on it girl?

PEGGY: A curtain.

BRIDGET: That's a very big curtain, is it Peggy O'Connor's your name?

Children are involved in shadowmaking.

PEGGY: It has to be, Bridget Donnelly is that your name, it has to be a big curtain to hide the very big shame that my mother must keep a shebeen when you'd think it was only where you come from, girl, that they'd have that kind of drinking place.

THERESA: Peggy O'Connor, more sewing, less jawing. Bridget Donnelly, your aunt and uncle can explain better than I ever can why we must keep a supply of whiskey for certain of our friends. How would they get home on a cold wet night when by the time they leave one of the taverns on the Main Street and travel a bit they're half frozen through and that's where we come in — helping everybody we can the rest of the way home with the — you're scared again, girl. Sure have you never heard a piano before, it's hidden there where we store it for a friend behind the bar — whoops, cupboard, it's the piano belonged to old Mrs Flaherty who's in jail for poisoning Mr O'Flaherty, whoops — Pat stop strumming the piano and let Peggy here play a bit or perhaps you'd favour us with a song, Bridget, and Peggy would pick up behind you.

BRIDGET: I do have a song. It's a song about coming here and how grateful I am to my uncle and my aunt for taking the weight of me off my father's family with times so hungry in Ireland. Aunt Julia, may I sing it?

MRS DONNELLY: Yes, Bridget. You may sing here whenever you please.

BRIDGET:
My heart's like a bird that has flown from her nest
For the harsh winter winds would give her no rest
Cross the seas and the wilderness she's rowed with her
   wings
Till at last in Ontario her freedom she sings.

I felt free, I guessed I would go on missing my mother and father back in Ireland, but I knew as soon as the horses' heads that afternoon pointed towards my uncle's gate that I was going to — it would be the happiest time of all my days.

PEGGY has finished sewing the curtain and it is put up. It can be drawn completely across the stage, not only hiding the cupboard, but becoming an important, constantly moving character in the play as well.

THERESA: The days of December, for that girl went out there to live with the Donnellys just before December began in 1879 and the first day of December was a

CHORUS: Monday, Tuesday, Wednesday, Thursday, Friday, Saturday, Sunday, Monday, Tuesday, December the 9th, one of Mr and Mrs Donnelly's sons, Michael, was murdered in a bar room at Waterford, Wednesday —

PEGGY: I sewed them all handkerchiefs bordered with black and took them out to them on

& CHORUS: Thursday

THERESA: The wake, and the funeral was on

& CHORUS: Friday

THERESA: Was it a large funeral, Peggy.

PEGGY: Yes, but there were mainly Protestants at the funeral as many of their Catholic friends are afraid to go near them.

PAT & CHORUS: Sunday,

PAT: We had sore throats and stayed home from church,

PAT & JOHNNY are always playing with the shadows they can produce with a candle & cut out cardboard figures.

PAT & CHORUS: Monday

Enter a young doctor; we may remember him as the tenor soloist in the family entertainment.

THERESA: Jerome O'Halloran, Dr Jerome O'Halloran, you're the new young doctor we've all been praying for as giving us some sort of choice away from that skull and cross bones that's been purging and amputating us all these years

JEROME: Open your mouth, boy, till I get a look at this throat

O'HALLORANS: Jerome, what are you doing in this woman's shebeen? We happened to see you entering as we cuttered by.

JEROME: Mother and father, what do you suppose I would be doing at Theresa O'Connor's. Her children are ill

O'HALLORANS: *(suddenly appearing)* A likely story. Theresa is more then likely leading you astray as she has many other sons, brothers and fathers by serving you whiskey and

Divide into Mr and Mrs after initial "solid" feeling is attained.

JEROME: I apologize for the lunacy of my parents, Theresa O'Connor

O'HALLORANS: And we apologize, my son Jerome, we have to apologize daily to the good people of the settlement for your shameless behaviour.

JEROME: Father, what shameless behaviour?

O'HALLORAN: William Donnelly was in your office yesterday.

JEROME: William Donnelly hurt his shoulder lately. Am I not to heal

O'HALLORAN: / / Never a sick Donnelly. May they die in a ditch for his brothers Tom and John would let nobody thrash for me all fall and the grain rotted in the field

/ / equals two stamps ((will equal clappings. Generally speaking friends of the Donnellys clap their hands a lot, while their enemies stamp their feet.

JEROME: (Oh you're mad with hatred of them.) I love the Donnellys.

O'HALLORANS: Get out of here you miserable ingrate, get out

JEROME leaves

THERESA: (Wait a minute, Mr and Mrs O'Halloran, whose house is this anyhow I love the Donnellys too.

O'HALLORANS: No one lives in a proper house that loves the Donnellys.

THERESA gives a derisive "Hah!"

O'HALLORANS: As the godparents of Peggy and Johnny, Theresa, we cannot help but notice how evilly you are bringing them up. You still keep the shebeen here, clandestinely, don't you, and if you do not mend your evil ways we will as the children's godparents see if we cannot get these children away from your influence.

THERESA: Mr and Mrs O'Halloran, what is it you really mean? That I'm friendly to the Donnellys whom all you church proud people have taken to hating so much, go away with you O'Halloran, you're a total abstainer now, but if you don't go away and mind your own business I'll tell the children's godmother here about the time you puked all over my front steps and all the way home as far as the church

PEGGY: Mother!

CHORUS: Tuesday. Wednesday.

THERESA: Johnny, you're back.

PEGGY: It's a letter from Mrs Donnelly, mother.

She & PEGGY are revealed in the Donnelly kitchen by the Stage Left curtain being drawn back

MRS DONNELLY: Theresa, Bridget and myself would appreciate your sending out Peggy to sew for us — 2 dresses & a quilted petticoat.

PEGGY: Johnny, what else did you bring from their place?

JOHNNY: Some apples, some loneliness.

THERESA: Why loneliness? They've heaps of friends out that way.

JOHNNY: Oh, no one comes to neighbour with the Donnellys any more.

THERESA: What about the Keefes and the Feenys and the Macdonalds.

JOHNNY: Only those three families.

THERESA: I do not understand it, only

461

JOHNNY: They are being hounded out of the township, mother, and no one will come near them after what the priest said about them after mass last Sunday.

THERESA: Speak of the devil, here comes the priest to our door — children! *(they quickly close the curtain)* Your reverence, Father Connolly.

PRIEST: Good morning, Theresa O'Connor. Theresa O'Connor, I have heard bad things spoken about the use you make of your house and I have descended like fire from Heaven to see if it is so what I've heard. Draw back that curtain, please. *(A statuette of Mary is revealed.)*

THERESA: We like to keep her on top of the cupboard, sure it makes the whole room like a chapel and with a curtain in front of her there's a greater power to her mystery and greater mystery to her power. Would your reverence not take a cup of tea with us? Kitty . . .

PRIEST: I have no time for tea, Theresa O'Connor, and I want you to know that I am by no means satisfied in this matter of the curtain that hides what's on the cupboard and I also want you and your children to be at mass next Sunday and every mass from now on.

THERESA: Sir, they had the quinzy till their throats were puffed up like bladders, his throat's still . . .

PRIEST: You're good at sewing up curtains, Peggy O'Connor, what else do I see you sewing?

PEGGY: A dress for Bridget Donnelly, your reverence.

PRIEST: Oh, their niece from Ireland, yes, her you may sew for, for she is innocent, but I would not waste my time if I were you sewing shirts for the sons or shifts for that mother of theirs. Good day to you Theresa O'Connor, no do not ask for my blessing.

CHORUS: Tuesday, Wednesday early evening . . .

A young woman comes for a dress fitting.

THERESA: Children, you'll set fire to the house playing with the candles that way. Peggy, perhaps you'd be wisest to give Miss Johnson her fitting up in my bedroom, I see someone coming to our door and it's a man.

JOHNNY: They say there's a secret society formed against the Donnellys.

PAT: What's a secret society, Johnny?

DR JEROME O'HALLORAN enters. The boys retreat behind the ½ drawn Stage Right curtain.

JOHNNY: Well, Pat — it's swear   drink   midnight   attack

& CHORUS: swear   drink   midnight   attack

THERESA: Dr O'Halloran, you've come back to look at the children's throats.

JEROME: Yes, Mrs O'Connor. Even Father Connolly said I should look in.

THERESA: Oh well then, your mother and father cannot take offence.

JEROME: I know for a fact they're not in the village. Open up Patrick. Johnny. Now that's an awful shadow you're casting, my boy. Go to the druggist, Theresa, take this and he'll give you a bottle of the sweetest tasting nasty looking stuff you ever swallowed, children.

A curious pause.

THERESA: Jerome O'Halloran, what is it you really want?

JEROME: Theresa O'Connor. I saw Miss Johnson come in here and I did not see her leave. I can't help it, I've got something very important I'd like to say to her.

THERESA: She's upstairs with my daughter, but you should knock on the door first for they're trying on a new dress.

JEROME hurries off behind the curtain.

JOHNNY: There was once a man dug a tunnel out to his haystack so that when the secret society attacked, why he was able to get away and they . . .

THERESA: Hush, children, you make my blood run cold, Peggy, what's the matter?

PEGGY bursts out from behind the curtain.

PEGGY: Mother, this is the worst yet you've done to us.

THERESA: What on earth do you mean?

PEGGY: Dr O'Halloran came in to the bedroom upstairs and just looked at Miss Johnson, and she just looked at him.

THERESA: And what did you look at?

PEGGY: I looked at them.

THERESA: They're a handsome young couple. You should have stayed by as chaperone. They shouldn't be left alone in a bedroom together, they've been hopelessly in love for years.

PEGGY: I can well believe it, mother, chaperone. Chaperone! I always feel that when people start unbuttoning their clothes and falling into each other's arms it's a bit late to play chaperone, so I ran out. Mother, what are you going to do?

THERESA: Nothing.

PEGGY: Your house is well known for its cupboard, now it's getting a reputation for its bed.

THERESA: Oh Peggy, run off with this up to the drugstore, it's some medicine for the children and think as you're going up that sure Jerome O'Halloran and Katie Johnson have been in love since they were sixteen and she the daughter of the Grand Master of the Orange Lodge and he the beloved son of the most pious Catholic family in the settlement and they've waited long enough for their hardhearted parents to melt so I said yes, I said to him yes . . . go up and see if she's in the room, but if you'd had the courage to stay this'd never happened.

PEGGY: They'll come and burn down our house for a bawdy house, mother, and don't you dare ask me to sew you up another curtain!

THERESA: She's right, and yet I don't know how I let this happen. Uh, the poor young lovers there's little chance they'll ever get together again — go easy on the bed O'Halloran, men are always like that, shaking and shaking you till the bed starts squeaking and the bottom right leg is half broke as it is, I always felt like asking Mike when he was alive and he'd be on top of me, or under me sometimes what it was he was trying to shake out of me, the truth? Rattling you away like a box with a piece of bone in it when if the truth were known they would have just as much pleasure if they just held you in their arms and were still for a while. Jerome O'Halloran and Katie Johnson I hope you've come to the little garden you're knocking at the door of before Peggy gets home from the drugstore . . .

CHORUS: Monday, Tuesday, Wednesday, Thursday. . . .

JOHNNY: Mother, I just seen a man tramping round the house.

THERESA: It's the new constable, Jim Carroll, children! Good evening, Constable Carroll, and what can I do for you?

CARROLL: You can serve me some of your old Hennessy, Theresa O'Connor and see if I know it.

THERESA: And you can wipe your face on my arse, Jim Carroll if you think I'll fall for that trick of yours. There's not a drop in the house.

CARROLL: Draw that curtain aside if you please. I want to know what is behind it.

A crucified Jesus is revealed.

THERESA: There does that satisfy you?

CARROLL: *(afraid)* Draw it again, Theresa. Theresa, if you'd only shun the Donnellys I might be able to do something for you.

THERESA: Well we will not shun the Donnellys and there is nothing you might ever be able to help us with. Shut the door behind you, please.

CARROLL: Didn't realize you had a door, Theresa. Most places like yours don't, they just have an old piece of sacking stretched across — a hole — in the wall.

CHORUS: Thursday, December the 25th.

THERESA & CHORUS: 26th, 27th, 28th, 29th, 30th.

THERESA: Thirty days hath December.

PEGGY: Mother, 31 days hath December.

THERESA, PEGGY & CHORUS: Friday, New Year's Day, 1880.

THERESA: Oh excuse me for yawning so much.

PEGGY: It's been extremely quiet lately, mother.

THERESA: It's a humdrum day, all hum and no drum.

PEGGY: No visitors is the best sort of day. There goes John Donnelly.

Window filled with kids' faces looking at John.

JOHN: Yes, I was murdered on the 4th of February, early in the morning. On New Year's day 1880 that was still a month away. I forget why I rode into Lucan, the snow so deep. Some errand for my parents and as I passed Connor's — how was I to know they would hold an inquest on my body there with you, coroner, cutting open my body and saying:

his shadow on curtain

CORONER: What a large and well formed heart John Donnelly had. Look!

JOHN: And my brother Will saying:

shadow on opposite curtain

WILL: This is more than flesh and blood can endure. *(Pause)* I will live through this circus.

THERESA: Here comes the eleven o'clock freight. You can hear it blowing for all the crossings — that'll be the Cedar Swamp Line, now the Chapel crossing line, now . . .

CHORUS: Monday Tuesday Wednesday the 7th of January, 1880 Thursday Friday Saturday Sunday Monday Tuesday Wednesday Thursday the 15th Friday . . .

PEGGY: Oh Mother, such a strange thing happened out at the Donnellys' there was a barn across the road from them burnt down in the middle of the night. Patrick Marksey's barn, and in the morning he came over and accused the Donnelly boys of burning it down, but they'd been at the Keefe's at the wedding dance all night. So he couldn't say very well they done it, so he turned on old Mr Donnelly and said,

MARKSEY: You burnt my barns.

PEGGY: How could he have burnt the barns — there was fresh snow fell in the night and I looked out into the yard and not one track went from the Donnellys' house anywhere. Hark, mother, here's Tom driving Mrs Donnelly to our door.

MRS DONNELLY: Yes, Theresa, is this not a pretty way we are used. But I have no time to sit down and tell you the full lunacy of it all. Peggy, I'll take the pillow slips with me now, for I'm catching the train this morning and going to visit my daughter Jennie in St Thomas. I'm promised to see her and my grandchildren since the wake for Michael. What is it, Tom?

TOM: Mother, we're cutting it awful close.

MRS DONNELLY: Goodbye Theresa. Thank you Peggy.

THERESA: She's not herself. She doesn't want to stay out there where you are being accused all the time of doing things it would take an athletic hoyden of sixteen all her time doing let alone an old woman in her sixties.

CARROLL: I've a subpoena here for Peggy O'Connor. You by the sewing machine over there, come here and sign this piece of paper for me.

THERESA: What's this about, Constable Carroll?

CARROLL: Well, your daughter consorts with the Donnellys doesn't she? So she was out there the night of the fire and when she appears at the hearing tomorrow perhaps she can tell us what went on that night when

MARKSEY: They burnt my barns.

PEGGY: Yes, perhaps I can.

CARROLL: Remember Peggy O'Connor. Two o'clock sharp at the Council Chambers.

CHORUS: Saturday Sunday Amen Monday

THERESA: I'm waving goodbye to Johnny he's going out with the boys to the farm again. The Donnellys'll need him to feed the pigs and cattle while they go to the hearing at Granton they're now draggin them to

PEGGY: Now they're saying Mrs Donnelly set the fire and she's arrested too.

THERESA: What did you forget, child?

JOHNNY: My cap, goodbye mother. Goodbye Peggy. Wait for me John!

CHORUS: Tuesday Wednesday Thursday Friday the 30th, Saturday the last day of January.

THERESA: They're still having the hearings drag on about the fire and it is Candlemas and now it's Tuesday.

THERESA & CHORUS: February the third

THERESA: and it's St Blaise's Day — keep that blessed candle near your throat, Pat, it's blessed by the priest today and is bound to drive the quinzy away Mr Donnelly is there no stopping them from dragging you all over the country examining about this fire business?

MR DONNELLY: No stopping them. They've adjourned the hearings three times now. Why, Theresa, they're advertising my wife and myself as if we were mad dogs. Johnny, button up that coat for it's a cold day out on the line and the wind'll whistle right through you. Good day to you, Theresa O'Connor.

THERESA: And good day to you, Mr Donnelly. Now the next day was

THERESA & CHORUS: Wednesday the 4th

THERESA: Johnny, you've come back from the Donnellys all by yourself whatever happened to your cap where'd you get that big lady's hat and — Johnny, where's your coat?

JOHNNY has a blanket around his shoulders.

JOHNNY: It's burned up in the fire. Mother, my hat and my coat got burnt up last night. Old Mrs Whalen gave me her hat to wear.

THERESA: Burnt up — where?

JOHNNY: With the Donnellys.

THERESA: What?

JOHNNY: It's burned in the fire, the house was burned. Bridget's dead, they're all dead and burned.

THERESA: *(scream)*

JOHNNY: Mother, there was a whole bunch of men came into their house. I hid under the bed while they killed them and then they set the house afire.

THERESA: I don't want to hear anymore who did this! Did you recognize the men?

JOHNNY: Yes! The Donnellys are all dead.

THERESA: *(scream)* All dead?

JOHNNY: Mother — what I want to know is should I tell the names of the men, I know three of them, should I. . . .

THERESA: If you tell the names they'll kill you. *(He whispers to her)* This is too wicked to go unpunished. Tell yes. It is too bad to let them go, Peggy, Mrs Donnelly is dead and Bridget — stop sewing the dress for you're sewing the dress of a dead woman. *(the sewing machine rattles furiously)*

PAT: Mother, Will Donnelly wants to know if they can bring the bodies here for the wake.

THERESA: *(scream — loudest)* Oh my God, whoever burnt down the Donnellys will be after us next. Peggy, I beg you to stop sewing that dress. She's dead. We'll have to get the house ready for the wake, children get those chairs out of the attic. *(The sewing machine stops!)*

PEGGY: I've finished the dress. Now they're bringing in John's body and there is an opening of that body by the coroner and then an inquest and he is taken away to the undertaker's. Then he comes back in his coffin. Oh Jennie Donnelly, when you ask us to teach you what it was like to live in my mother's shebeen the last month your mother was alive, it was like — it was *(holding out the dress as the wake abruptly starts with coffins entering. JOHN's coffin has a candle in it; the other coffin — a rough wooden box — contains four stones.)*

PEGGY: Those that love them clap (those that hate them stamp /

CHORUS:

De profundis clamavi ad te, Domine
                    Domine, exaudi vocem meam
Si iniguitates observaveris, Domine, Domine, quis
    Sustinebit
Five dead people lying in a house[3]*
These four stones once were people and this candle
Once was he who held it — John Donnelly
Five dead people lying in a house
Five dead people are coming to this house
Five dead people have come into this house
On Alice Street near the tracks in Lucan
The last tollgate before harvest in God's eye
The bridegroom's thigh, the Holy Spirit's sigh
//((//((//((//((//((//((//((//((//((//((//

*Vary with toe taps and fingersnaps. The five dead people, their
eyes bandaged with gauze, enter from behind the curtains, present
themselves and fade away.*

Who has entered this room whom I cannot see
Five dead people have come to this house
Mourn their collections, their sheaves of time
A stone for Bridget, a stone for Tom
A stone for James, a stone for Judith
                            we mourn them till dawn
And a candle for John
It's twelve o'clock, Jennie Donnelly, you're late, you're
    late

JENNIE: My mother. Was it because she was tall that you
    hated her so much? And burnt her first with your words,
    then with your kerosene? Explain then why   she had
    to die

CHORUS: It's half past twelve, Will Donnelly, you're late,
    you're late Cripple. Here comes Cripple! Cripple Cripple
    hey Cripple!

---

*To be repeated three times (likewise throughout).

471

WILL: (and who the hell are you over there ((((

STAMPERS: //// We're we were we are their enemies /

WILL: And who the hell are you over there?

CLAPPERS: (We are we were we will be — their friends?

In and out of the clapping & stamping, WILLIAM DONNELLY takes up the stone that represents TOM and presses it against O'HALLORAN (WILL is backed by clappers) and asks:

WILL: These are the bones of my brothers, O'Halloran. Tell us why you killed them or I'll beat you to death with them

CLAPPERS:
Bones of my brothers, O'Halloran
Or I'll beat you to death with them

O'HALLORAN: // You'll remember that last summer — this is Malachi O'Halloran speaking — my big field of wheat ripened and was cut and bound and we stooked it and it stood there and it stood there yes because of the quarrel between us and two of your brothers, yes two of your brothers dead there — yes, John said Tom said — *(The brothers with eyes bandaged enter abruptly. People at the wake are smoking and drinking from bottles.)*

TOM & JOHN: O'Halloran, you will, we swear by the Holy Name, you will never thresh that grain.

TOM: You've had me up in court just five times too often. You and your neighbours on their horses after me one whole night too many.

O'HALLORAN: Curtin's threshing machine came up the front road and you stopped him off

CURTIN: I came down the back road and you

TOM & JOHN: No one threshes for O'Halloran do you hear, Marty Curtin? No one do you hear? After what he has done to us may your grain rot in your fields.

472

O'HALLORAN: And I watched it do so. If I killed the mother and father, helped kill them, I killed the source of the men who meant that my seed was spilled on the ground.

TOM: O'Halloran, what's this my ghost found in your granary today then? *(throws the grain at him)* Grain? We let you thresh after we'd shown you we could stop you forever if we wanted to. *(The brothers throw the grain hither & thither.)*

O'HALLORAN: Yes, in the end my big field was threshed, but we'll see just how. But I still had to kill them for there was never any peace with them around like I'll show you, I'll show you what Tom was like — there's a tavern at Elginfield called Glass's Hotel and he rode by it once with his pal who's more here than I am tonight — Jim Feeny. Mrs Glass came out for some water and she saw Donnelly about to

MRS GLASS: *(We see her shadow — her mobcap silhouette)* Don't water your horses there, Tom Donnelly. There's no water for Donnelly horses at this tavern, your friend there can have a drink if he must. *(She comes out from behind the curtain.)*

O'HALLORAN: She went inside again. Micky Glass her husband said to her:

MR GLASS: Who was that in the yard, missus?

TOM: *(from behind curtain with hobbyhorses)* It was me Tom Donnelly and my horse Ploughboy and Jim Feeny and his horse — Whirlwind, *(they enter on their horses)* and we'll teach you to say no Donnellys get a drink at your horse trough, my horse is very upset, we'll drink your cellar dry, Mrs Glass and Mr Glass. Jim, start drinking. *(Slurp)*

MR & MRS GLASS: Not if this poker — and this axhandle — can persuade you to do otherwise. Out of here out of that out here out of that. Don't you touch that cask tap. Get your damn thumb off that bung. *(Their pursuit of TOM & JIM turns into the boys' pursuit of them!)*

CHORUS: *(with bottles)*
The table and punch was upsot
And the row it commenced in a
minit, shure.
Niver a tast of a shtick had he   *the Glasses are stuffed*
got   *into a cubbyhole*
So he picked up a piece of the
furniture
Gurgle gurgle gurgle gurgle
gurgle gurgle gurgle[32]

A concrete sound chorus ending with an exhausted slurp

JIM: This is Jim Feeny's arm. When we were boys he made me cut my name — no, his name, he made me cut his name into the flesh of my arm and he cut my name Jim Feeny into the flesh of his arm:

JIM & TOM: My blood, your blood / Sealed in brotherhood[2]

JIM: I've always liked being with him, except he sometimes goes a bit farther than my nerves can stand. Like now. And he knows that when I'm drunk I cannot stand the mention of Hell or devils, so why does he — Through clouds of tobacco smoke at the wake his sister Jennie comes towards me and she says:

JENNIE: Jim Feeny. Jim, my brother tells me you almost stayed the night at our place.

JIM: Yes, Jennie. Tom wanted me to stay, but I'd been told not to sleep at the Donnellys' any more.

JENNIE: And, Jim, what's this I hear about Tom drinking again. I took him to the priest and he took the pledge, for oh that was much of his trouble.

JIM: It was when his horse was denied drink, Jennie, that he started up again. I told her what happened at Glass's Tavern, but oh not all of it. She has the look they all have, commanding you to tell it all, he had it, well I won't, they're all too bossy, Tom was too bossy, especially right after breakfast the Donnellys are too bossy, and yet I'd have given anything to've been raised by his parents. You should see my father and mother — always fighting, always drinking with the farm dribbling through their fingers. We're poor. We need money.

TOM: What's the matter, Jim. You're — stop drinking, you're getting into one of those sulky fits again where — you want to kill Tom Donnelly your only friend.

JIM: Stay away from me, Tom Donnelly, or I'll shoot your friggin knees off.

TOM: Come on, Jim. Try to kill me. That's great fun

JIM: Try to kill you, why you nearly killed me.

TOM: Jim, the silly girl never thought what she was doing and I can't share everything with you and besides your leg is mended.

JIM: Yes, my leg's mended. Give me an ax and I'll chop off your feet — Oh I hear the dead men tramping by.

Bearing the coffins, the people at the wake march away with the coffins.

TOM: That's right, Jim, the graveyards are on the march.

JIM: Oh Tom, I'll — I know I'll die a hard death.

TOM: Home. Let's go home so Mr and Mrs Glass can go to bed. *(groans from the cubbyhole)*

JIM: Well, I'm not going home, you bugger, because you pushed me off the ladder.

The curtains swag back to reveal a girl lolling on top of the cupboard like a barroom picture.

GIRL: What they're got onto is me. I was in love with Tom Donnelly once. When I was fourteen on the Main Street of Lucan I saw him go by and I took a *(about to jump*

475

down) scissors — Tom Donnelly, kin I have a lock of your hair!

TOM: Kin you, you just have.

GIRL: I was crazy about the Donnelly boys. I'd have danced naked for Tom and told my parents of this desire which prompted them to move from Lucan as fast as they could to Brooke Township. But there was a man owned the swamp there decided to cut her all down, so that who should show up at my window last winter out of the lumber camp but Tom Donnelly with Jim Feeny holding the ladder. *(This scene is played on top of the cupboard.)*

TOM: Look, my pal out there, Jim Feeny wonders if he can come up too.

GIRL: Jim Feeny your pal, eh. Well, I told you I'd do anything for you, Tom, call him up he looks cold.

TOM: Wait a minute I might just marry you. If it's a boy. But if my friend lies with you how will we know if it's his or mine?

GIRL: That's very true, Tom Donnelly, said I and I tipped the ladder over with Jim Feeny halfway up it. *(He crashes over.)*

TOM: Jim how was I to know you'd break your leg, and you start pounding me and I'll start hammering you. Let's get out of here, the constables are coming. Now come home.

A demon holds two moons in front of JIM.

JIM: Do you see the moons, Tom?

TOM: Yes, Jim, I'll bet there are two of them tonight.

JIM: Do you see the devil peeking out at us from behind that bush?

TOM: No. Yes. Oh, Jim Feeny, let's get it over with. I always say if you're going to vomit, vomit and if you're going to have the D.T.'s damn your heart, the sooner you have them the better and you're over with them.

Nightmare devils attack JIM FEENY.

JIM: Don't you tell me when to have the D.T.'s! I'll kill you.

TOM: Jim, old pal, when I go to Hell, will you come along with me?

JIM: I told you not mention Hell or devils.

TOM: I see the one that's about to pull your guts out. I'll fight him for you.

JIM: I told you, Tom Donnelly, not to mention Hell. Hell. Oh God, there's a tree after me *(One of the demons does pull JIM's guts out — a long magenta ribbon & dances away with it. Up in the air & over the demons lift him!)*

CHORUS: Hell hell hell hell hell hell hell hell hell hell[42]

fade to the Feeny house

JIM: *(screaming)* Tom will you forgive me what I done to you if I can make you see what my soul was like?

CARROLL is behind the bed listening. Use curtain as head of bed.

MATER: Bless you, my son, *(the demons whisk away!)* it's not Tom Donnelly, it's your very own mother, *(hiccough.)*

PATER: And your very own father — *(hiccough.)* Tom Donnelly brought you home to us two days ago and you've been raving in your sick bed now for

JIM: Tom Donnelly sneaked away did he when the devils came to get me did he, well I'll get him. I'll kill him.

MATER: Son, son I always thought that you liked Tom Donnelly quite a lot.

JIM: I hate him, he makes me see devils.

CARROLL: Now Michael and Bridget Feeny, this is a very interesting thing you're telling me about your son when he was ill in bed with the D.T.'s. You see something awful is going to happen to the Donnellys, so tell your son not to sleep there anymore, Bridget Feeny, not to sleep there anymore when Tom invites him to stay the night — why are you crying, Mrs Feeny, Jim Feeny's mother? You see the whole plan for ridding us once and for all of this disturbing family depends a great deal on getting inside their house without their knowing it so that, we need someone to — someone that used to be, well used to be Tom Donnelly's friend.

PATER: Jim Carroll, how much would you be willing to pay for this getting inside the Donnelly house?

CARROLL: For the key to the Donnelly house, the skeleton key? Well, it's a pretty sick and feeble and used up looking and undependable key lying there, isn't it.

MATER: For $500 his mother and his father might clean some of the rust and the cobwebs off it, Jim Carroll. They might.

Fades away. A prim, strict knocking comes from behind the curtains which part to reveal:

MR O'HALLORAN: Mickey Glass, open up your tavern, it's Malachi O'Halloran and his wife and we want a dish of hot tea on this cold night at the bottom of the hill coming in out of town.

MR GLASS: We can't serve you, for Donnelly's locked us up in the cubbyhole over here.

MRS O'HALLORAN: My soul, Malachi O'Halloran, the place looks as if a hundred devils had run through it.

MR O'HALLORAN: Mickey Glass. Mrs Glass. What on earth's footstool has happened here?

MRS GLASS: Donnelly. Donnelly came along and he brought his horses in to drink at our bar and

MR GLASS: *(crawling about)* Oh if this is what Hell is like, what can Paradise be up to?

MRS GLASS: You must excuse my husband, Mr and Mrs O'Halloran as I know you're the most upstanding people we've ever had in the settlement, but as the whiskey kept pouring in on us in there in the cubbyhole there he couldn't help but lick a few drops of his own whiskey off his very own floor.

MRS O'HALLORAN: *(loud)* Can no justice, can no constable do nothing, anything, about this?

MR GLASS: Malachi O'Halloran, I am a justice and I know for a fact that no constable of mine would dare arrest Tom Donnelly for this. He's got them all scared — if this is one corner of Hell called Mickey Glass's Tavern, what must the other corners be like?

MRS O'HALLORAN: Well this carnival has gone on too long, husband. Sober up Mr Mickey Glass. *(stamping her foot)* Is there no end in view? That family has bought law and used it like gipsies. And like gipsies that family must leave this parish, what hope of that, eh?

MR O'HALLORAN: Honoria O'Halloran, the only hope is that — the bishop is moving his palace and see back — back from the border, back to London which is but 18 miles away and now — he's close enough to see what's the matter and to sort the wheat from the chaff. *(Bells, big & little. THE O'HALLORANS ring handbells)*

CHORUS: Ash Wednesday. The Bishop that was always far away is now close by. Amen *(sung)*

Organ peals as curtains part to reveal BISHOP preceded by proud hobbyhorsemen drawing him in his carriage.

BISHOP: And I consulted with and visited every priest in my diocese until I felt as if I had become a shepherd striding across the field where my sheep grazed and my sheepdog priests kept them from straying. Father Girard, what is going on in your parish? I see from my tower the twinkling lights of burning barns. I see crops rotting in the field, I hear a constant gnashing of teeth, and of one family I hear — I see in the daily press constant reference.

FATHER GIRARD: Your excellency, in my parish there is a feud between certain families. I am not Irish as they are and you are, your excellency I do not understand the feud, but my impression is that this family of the Donnellys is slowly losing ground.

BISHOP: Losing ground.

FATHER GIRARD: For example, your excellency their reputation is far worse than they actually are. Even I who do not listen to stories, I am aware that outrages are purposely committed which will be blamed on them.

BISHOP: And what do you yourself think of them, Father Girard?

FATHER GIRARD: The Donnellys are like lions attacked in the desolate wilderness by a pack of wild dogs.

BISHOP: Father Girard, there are changes, certain changes I wish to initiate in your particular parish. Two changes. The first is the pattern your parish has of voting for a Liberal candidate. I hope to change that.

FATHER GIRARD: Your excellency the second change must be involved with the first, for it is my removal from the parish is it not?

BISHOP: Down in Belle River where you will have a French speaking parish you will still be able to drive your flock into the Liberal fold, but up here — you see we are hoping for a Catholic Conservative member of Parliament. So the Donnellys must change their voting pattern.

FATHER GIRARD: They will not change, your excellency.

BISHOP: Will they not? Well, it is unfortunate for them that this riding cannot be won unless a party takes a majority of the votes, the Catholic votes in their ward, and the Conservative party shall take a majority of those votes. They must kneel with the rest of the parish.

FATHER GIRARD: Your excellency, what Conservative priest will next be the shepherd of my erstwhile flock?

BISHOP: A very strong man. Even now I see his loving parishioners in Quebec bidding him farewell.

FATHER CONNOLLY faces us with his flock kneeling in front of him. Organ.

CHORUS:
Advent shadows in December
Violet branches on the snow
Help the Christian to remember
This babe returns to judge us now.

PRIEST: My dear people of Kelly's Corners, tears fill my eyes as I hear for the last time your sweet voices. Oh no, this is too much, you are all kneeling with a parcel, no, no, what can be in this parcel?

CHORUS & SOLO: We, the parishioners of Saint Malachy's Parish take this opportunity, Father Connolly, to make you a farewell gift as well as the purse we have made up for you. The winters of Biddulph we hear are even longer and colder than those here at Kelly's Corners, Quebec. It is a coat, Father Connolly.

PRIEST: What warm thoughts you have had towards me, my dear parishioners. Of what animal is this extremely thick and handsome fur?

CHORUS & SOLO: The wolf, Father Connolly. It is a wolfskin coat.

PRIEST: *(dressed in the coat which radiates a strange elegant power.)* I think I was sent to this neighbourhood of Biddulph up in Ontario partly for the purpose of putting all lawless conduct down. There was no time to know the people at all; there I was, here I am, having said my first mass in St Patrick's and I barely know the altarboys' names. *(The kneelers imperceptibly change to the Biddulph congregation with the DONNELLY family on Stage Right.)*

SOLO: In their hands they shall bear Thee up, lest Thou dash Thy foot against a stone.

CHORUS: Thou shalt walk upon the asp and the basilisk,

PRIEST: and Thou shalt trample under foot the lion and the dragon.

CHORUS: Amen.

PRIEST: Now, what was I going to say to you, people of St Patrick's, Biddulph? Why it is simply this — before the week is out I hope to have visited each and every one of my parishioners.

JENNIE: Father Connolly was as good as his word and soon one heard that Father Connolly had

CHORUS:
visited Barry   visited Trehy
visited Feeny   visited O'Halloran

O'HALLORAN under or over this gestures and tells the priest of his troubles with the DONNELLYS.

O'HALLORAN:

At night — someone takes out my horses — after we've gone to bed, father, and after we are sound asleep, and they ride those horses from one toll gate to another all night. But in the morning I find my horses back in my stables again — out of breath and nigh death.

CHORUS:

Domine, non sum dignus/ ut intres sub tectume meum:/ sed tantum dic verbum/ et sanabitur anima mea[3]

CHORUS:
visited Cahill   visited Cassleigh
visited McCann   visited O'Halloran again

O'HALLORAN is seen telling the priest an earful.

O'HALLORAN:

Father Connolly, this summer my big field of wheat ripened and was cut and bound and we stooked it and it stands there and it stands there yes because of the quarrel between us and two of the Donnelly family, the brothers John and Tom. Father Connolly, they have sworn that I will not thresh that grain. Must my grain rot in the field and must my granaries cobweb because so says Donnelly?

CHORUS:

In thine infinite goodness, we beseech Thee, O Lord, to watch over Thy household, that even as it relies solely upon the hope of Thy heavenly grace, so it may ever be defended by Thy protection. Through our Lord. In nomine Patris et Filii, et Spiritus Sancti. Amen. Visited Donnelly

PRIEST: Mrs Donnelly, I have been hearing about your boys' bad doings.

MRS DONNELLY: Let us their mother and father hear of them too, Father Connolly.

PRIEST: They will let no one thrash the grain belonging to Malachi O'Halloran and it lies rotting in his field. Your son Will, I want particularly to visit him. Where does he live?

MRS DONNELLY: Father Connolly, he lives in a house by the blacksmith's at Whalen's Corners.

PRIEST: I understand he is harbouring a youth who has been taking out Mr O'Halloran's horses and

O'HALLORAN:

At night — someone takes out my horses — after we've gone to bed, father, and after we are sound asleep, and they ride

CHORUS:

Domine, non sum dignus/ ut intres sub tectume meum:/ sed tantum dic verbum/ et sanabitur anima mea[3]

those horses from one toll
gate to another all night.
But in the morning I find
my horses back in my
stables again — out of
breath and nigh death.

PRIEST: Mrs Donnelly, your boys shall change their ways,
or I'll straighten them.

MRS DONNELLY: Father Connolly, there are worse than my
sons in the neighbourhood, but the biggest crowd is
against them. Father, we are being persecuted.

PRIEST: I have also heard that your niece, Mr Donnelly, has
come out from Ireland to live with you. Bridget Donnelly
how long is it since you were in Ireland?

BRIDGET: I was still there last harvest, Father, and I have not
seen spring here in Canada.

PRIEST: After I see your son William, Mrs Donnelly, I will
make up my mind about what you have said, I wish you
good day.

WILL: But when Father Connolly in his visiting tour came to
my house only my wife was there to receive him. We had
a sick boy in the house; I was away in the village waiting
at young Dr O'Halloran's office.

DR O'HALLORAN: Will Donnelly, you appear to be the last
customer this afternoon. How's the healing process going
on with your shoulder?

WILL: My wife was dressing it last night. Norah thinks it
needs some more probing. You see, Jerome, when my
stallion tried to pin me against the walls of his box stall he
picked a rather slivery four by four to grind me against.

O'HALLORAN: What makes this horse do things like this,
Will. You usually get along well with all your beasts,
don't you?

WILL: There's been someone throwing stones at our house late at night. I've taken to locking his stable, but he gets nervous at the stones and the shouting.

DR O'HALLORAN: What are they trying to do to you, Will?

WILL: Jerome O'Halloran, I'm not going to tell you, you were whistling when I came in here, why should our miseries interrupt your happiness?

JEROME: Yes, Will, I am very happy.

WILL: And I bet I know why you're happy.

JEROME: *(Laughing)* I suppose the whole village knows that I spent the night at Theresa O'Connor's with

WILL: with Katie Johnson

JEROME: It happened so suddenly, Will. Our respective parents will have to let us get married now.

WILL: Jerome, I also need some medicine for the sick lad we have staying with us. He is hot with fever, but feels so cold he clings to our stove.

JEROME: *(Opening drawer of cupboard. Then writing prescription.)* Half of the people in the township have the symptoms you describe, Will. *(a curious pause)* What are you thinking, Will.

WILL: That you and Katie Johnson will never be happy inside the tollgates of this township, Jerome.

JEROME: *(Emotion)* Oh Will, we're sick of being afraid of them. No, no. We're staying where we were born & where I practise. Tomorrow I'm to see Father Connolly about our marrying

PRIEST: *(in wolfskin coat)* Yes, it was after my attempt to visit Will Donnelly at Whalen's Corners that his friend the young doctor came to me with his miserable adventure at that woman's house with the curtain over the cupboard.

Stephen, that is William Donnelly's house, why is their dog barking so ferociously at me?

BOY: Your reverence, I don't feel that it's barking at you.

PRIEST: You'll have to tie the horse to that tree or it will bolt. What a bitterly cold day and this is the last visit I have to make. They do so sic their dog on me, listen to it. Why do they not open the door. Open the door at once. Call off that beast of a dog!

GIRL: Good day to you, sir.

PRIEST: Is your husband at home? I pray do not bar me from entering your house, your dog is snapping at our heels.

GIRL: Joe, off with you. I am their hired girl, sir. Joe! My mistress is lying down just at present and my master is away. Yes, Mr Donnelly is away from home and he warned me not to let any stranger into the house while he was gone. Gipsies and other such mountebanks are rife in all sorts of disguises.

PRIEST: Get down on your knees, girl, when you address your priest with such nonsense.

GIRL: Norah Donnelly, do I have to get down on my knees if this fellow in the great big fur coat says?

PRIEST: I am not a gipsy, I am not a mountebank. You could not have been at mass last Sunday, I am the new priest of the parish.

NORAH: Father Connolly. Pardon us, Father. We did not know who you were if you are what kind of fur is that?

PRIEST: What business is it of yours what kind of fur —

NORAH: It's wolfskin, isn't it?

PRIEST: Yes, Mrs Donnelly, it is wolfskin, what of that? My parishioners presented it to me as a parting gift and I wish I were back with them now.

NORAH: Your reverence, forgive me. I honestly did not recognize you as a priest dressed — it's very dangerous to wear that fur when there are so many fierce dogs about, they smell the wolf, Father Connolly, welcome to our house.

PRIEST: Thank you. And you are Norah Donnelly, then, William Donnelly's wife?

NORAH: Yes, your reverence. The reason I was not at mass last Sunday is that I was ill. And my husband is not at home. He is out looking for some medicine for the sick boy we have here behind the stove.

PRIEST: Who is this lad? What name is upon you, boy?

NORAH: I doubt if he hears you, father. He has been so feverish.

PRIEST: Surely he is no boy of yours, what is his name then?

NORAH: Tom Ryan.

PRIEST: I was told by the O'Hallorans that you harboured a lad here who is accused of stealing a horse of theirs.

NORAH: Your reverence, he is an outcast boy thrown out of his home by his father. Sometimes he makes his home with us and I have heard another side to the story about O'Halloran's horse.

PRIEST: Young woman, are you calling the most respectable family in my parish liars?

NORAH: No, father, I am simply saying there are always two sides to a story.

PRIEST: Well, Mrs William Donnelly, in that supposition you are wrong. There are not always two sides to a story. There is one side, mark this, and one side only *(he climbs into the pulpit / step ladder & the scene dissolves into a church scene)* Last Sunday I spoke of making things better in this parish. Have they been getting better? No. No, they have been getting worse, for last week someone whose name I think I know although no one will tell me his name because they are terrified of a certain gang of roughs and toughs in the neighbourhood, that someone took out one of Mr O'Halloran's horses in the dead of night and rode him from tollgate to tollgate until the poor beast was nigh dead. I told the culprit to come and see me. He came to see me and brought with him his lame friend who on finding me out left me a threatening letter.

The congregation are kneeling in front of him & cower in terror, beating their breasts when he starts "cursing".

WILL: It is not fair, Father Connolly, that you should ask this lad's master to discharge him.

PRIEST: He is a drifter, one of the young ne'er do wells who hang out at a certain house not three miles from where you are kneeling and I am standing.

WILL: First prove that he took the horse, we can give you proof of the lad's innocence.

TOM RYAN: *(lounging on the cupboard which has lately been used for an altar)* By the way, in this particular instance, I, Tom Ryan, did not take out O'Halloran's horse, although at three other times I had — just for the hell of it. But whoever this time did take out O'Halloran's horse picked just the right moment to do it.

PRIEST: I curse the man or boy who took out the horse and nearly killed it.

WILL: *(at first as a silhouette, then slowly out with the congregation on this side of the curtain)* You have paid his master twenty dollars to let him go; you had him put in a buggy and driven to the borders of Biddulph where I met him, drove him back to Lucan and got him a job with a threshing gang.

PRIEST: Who is the priest in this parish? I tell you I curse the man or boy who did this deed. I ask the congregation to mark this prophecy of mine — the guilty party shall be a corpse inside a month. Whoever took out O'Halloran's horse — shall be a corpse inside a month.

WILL: Everybody stand up. Father Connolly . . . what are you saying — that the person in this community, the person who dies within the next month is the person who stole O'Halloran's horse?

PRIEST: I have received a threatening letter from a cripple and a devil notorious in this parish.

WILL: Are you all alive now? You alive, Tom Ryan?

TOM RYAN: Yes, Mr Donnelly.

WILL: At the end of thirty days let us see, Father Connolly, who has keeled over. The month of June has thirty days;

CHORUS: Four Thursdays four Fridays four . . . One day, two days, 3/4/5/6/7/8/9/10 days 11/12///////////// 14/15/16/17/18/19/20/21/22/23/24/25/26/27/28/29/ thirty days . . . Saturdays, Five Sundays, Five Mondays, Four Tuesdays, Five Wednesdays

PRIEST: I ask this congregation to mark this prophecy of mine — the guilty party will be a corpse inside a month so now that thirty days have passed — who is dead? And who is dead is he or she who took out O'Halloran's horse?

SOLO MAN: Phil Flannery, aged pauper. Too weak at the time to steal a horse.

SOLO WOMAN: Old Mrs O'Flaherty. After a year in the county jail on suspicion of poisoning my late dear husband, and I'm seventy seven years old.

WILL: Tom Ryan, are you still alive?

TOM RYAN: Still alive, Mr Donnelly.

O'HALLORAN: And so you are mocked, Father, in their rat-hole tavern by that William Donnelly and that ne'er do well Tom Ryan whom we cannot seem to get expelled from the township and who has not even the grace to die when he has been cursed from the altar.

PRIEST: Mr O'Halloran is it true that no thresher is brave enough to thresh your grain for you because of the Donnelly boys' threats

O'HALLORAN: All too true, Father.

PRIEST: Who has the nearest threshing machine in these parts?

O'HALLORAN: Oh Marty Curtin has one, but he won't use it. He doesn't want it destroyed.

The congregation form a threshing machine & are led offstage by the thresher, CURTIN, and followed by FR CONNOLLY.

PRIEST: I personally, Mr Curtin, with cash of my own will guarantee any damage to your machine even to complete destruction. We shall just see who is the priest of this parish, a lame man who trades horses and leads around a stallion in the spring for she mares, or he who has been vouchsafed the sacrament of ordination.

MRS DONNELLY: *(revealed in her kitchen by the drawing of Stage Left curtain)* How quiet it is on the line tonight, Mr Donnelly. I can hear Bridget ironing handkerchiefs and you mending harness and Tom polishing it, but there's nothing else to hear.

TOM: The leaves are all off the trees, that's why. And there's no wind, mother.

MRS DONNELLY: When's John coming home?

TOM: When the threshing's through at Trehy's unless they have a dance. If they have a dance then — daybreak.

MRS DONNELLY: Oh well, then I'll lock him out and he can knock on the windows if he wants in.

TOM: Mother, you've taken such a fancy lately to locking up the house. What's got into you?

MRS DONNELLY: Fewer and fewer people are neighbouring with us. Back in the old country that sometimes meant they visited you at other times. What's that sound?

490

MR DONNELLY: Mrs Donnelly, read that paper out you found hidden under Tom's mattress this morning. I want to hear that again.

MRS DONNELLY: Northern Sparks. A hotel wrecked by roughs in London Township. A few of the natives deliberately took possession of Glass's Hotel, Elginfield, London Township and commenced a fearful scrimmage. Poor Glass had no chance whatever. The table and punch was upsot / An' the row it commenced in a minit, shure. Niver a taste of shtick had he got, / So he picked up a piece of the furniture. Probably it was a bad job for him he did so, as they soon made splinters of all the sundry of the bar furniture, and Glass fled in all directions . . .

TOM: Aw they left out the best part. We shoved them in the little cubby hole they have under the stairs and we let the whiskey barrel bung out right beside so you could hear old Glass getting drunk, sad, wet, mad and glad all at once.

MRS DONNELLY: How would you like it Tom if someone put you under a stair and drowned you in whiskey?

TOM: Mother, how would you like it if you were riding along with your friend and old Mrs Glass comes out into her yard and says: Donnellys must not drink from our trough. Her trough's too good for Donnelly horses is it, well I'll show her, her decanters aren't good enough for our horses.

MR DONNELLY: It's true. At your age I'd have done something. I don't think I'd have taken my horse into the bar though. Your horse might have hurt his feet in the barroom, Tom. What are you rummaging about in the cupboard for, Tom, don't you see they partly know they'll get a rise out of you.

TOM: I think I hear a constable coming to arrest me. Oh it's John. That's none of our horses though, I knew it was a strange horse.

JOHN: Tom! I caught them trying to sneak the threshing machine into O'Halloran's through the back of Trehy's farm. Listen you can hear it. Tom, they've got the priest with them.

Threshing machine slowly approaches with PRIEST intoning the following litany as the machine is elaborately cranked & set going by CURTIN. This human threshing machine should behave with busybody solemnity led in by the cleric chanting from a small black book:

Holy Mary, *pray for us.*
Holy Mother of God,*
Holy Virgin of virgins,*
St Michael*

fades into O'HALLORAN's speech & under the noise of the machine

St Gabriel,*	**O'HALLORAN:**
St Raphael,*	We got it nearly all
All ye holy Angels	threshed. Well more than
& Archangels,*	half way. And they stood
All ye holy order	on the road looking over
of blessed Spirit,*	at us with broad grins. I
St John Baptist,*	guess they knew what was
St Joseph,*	going to happen. One of
All ye holy Patriarchs	the sheaves I was pitching
& Prophets &c.*	in felt a bit heavy.† By the
	name of God they had
	hidden horseshoes and
	iron pins in the sheaves by
	the road and small stones
	that —

JOHN: There's a saying O'Halloran, heavy in the sheaf, full in the granary.

*pray for us

†TOM: Lift it Malachi, heavy though it be.

492

As the machine breaks down, FR CONNOLLY's face is blackened by an inner explosion.

PRIEST: *(pulpit)* Things will be better in Biddulph. *(Congregation kneels in front of him.)* I do not care if I get a bullet through my head, but they will be better. I propose to form a Peace Society. I have stated the purpose here at the head of this paper. *(The paper is the same prop scroll used to represent the petition for Donnelly's life in Part One.)* I want all the men who are interested in preserving peace and order in the parish of St Patrick's, Biddulph, to sign their names. All those who do not sign I shall consider backsliders, blacklegs and sympathizers with this gang of evildoers and ruffians in our midst. Any of you who do not sign if they take sick they may send for William Donnelly. Do not send for Father John Connolly. As an indication of who is with me and who is against me will those that intend signing — kneel

This leaves the DONNELLYS standing. They leave the church and the paper is signed as in Part I with congregation intoning the Roman Line names.

CARROLL: For those of us who had some time ago decided that handcuffs must be forged and plans must be made this was the moment we had waited for over a year. *(cartwheels & yells!)* Now we had a screen to work behind and a petition was soon forwarded to the Court House too — we had the Priest and the Conservative Party behind us. Now we needed the law. For years the Donnellys had been using the law, protected by the Grit Sheriff, pampered by Grit magistrates — so we said:

CHORUS: *(they face us in a compact line)* To the Judge of the County of Middlesex. We the undersigned inhabitants of Biddulph humbly pray, humbly petition. Whereas for some time past evil-minded persons have robbed us, slashed our animals, burnt our barns, broke my threshing machine, deluded our females, bullied us, tormented us, stole my cow, laughed at us, looked right through us, mocked us . . . we want James Carroll to be of said Township Constable therein and the following respectable farmers and landowners to be magistrates: Messrs Cassleigh and O'Halloran.

CASSLEIGH & O'HALLORAN: Mr Carroll, you're in a position to catch them now.

CARROLL: Yes, yes. I'll be the cause of the Donnellys being banished out of Biddulph or lose my life in the process.

CHORUS: *(joining hands, dancing & singing about him)* There came one day to Lucan town / A man of mighty frame / His beard was black, his shoulders broad / James Carroll was his name. *(fiddle)*

CARROLL: Then we went after them . . .

BISHOP: Father Mahoney, let us go up in the tower of my cathedral — higher, higher, higher yet till we see?

At the huge step ladder behind everything, the BISHOP & his secretary climb up to survey what is happening.

MAHONEY: I see a mob invade the Donnelly farm in search of a lost cow. I see them drag the Ryan boy off to jail at last . . . I see the Donnelly family cleaning wheat at their kitchen door.

BISHOP: Are they looking dejected?

MAHONEY: Not very. Some, your excellency.

BISHOP: Now that we have punished them, we will show them some kindness in some unexpected way. You will see, we will bring them round. First severity, then love. And then — they will kneel.

MRS DONNELLY: John! John and Tom Donnelly, don't sow this wheat! Have you been sowing any of it?

JOHN: Yes, mother. We have.

MRS. DONNELLY: What's the use of sowing wheat in a township that hates us?

TOM: Shall we go about the front field picking up all the grain we've sown then, mother?

MR DONNELLY: Your mother's tired of Biddulph, John.

MRS DONNELLY: I'm sick of Biddulph. Why don't we take our wheat with us somewhere and sow it there. Not here.

MR DONNELLY: When there's children to this, we will.

MRS DONNELLY: I'll never see this harvested. James, you'll never see it harvested. John I thought you were to sow the wheat tomorrow. I never dreamed you were . . .

JOHN: Mother, we were, but then the boy came to tell us not to bother going to his father's threshing today,

TOM: and not to neighbour with his father anymore because of what the men said to his father last night —

JOHN: so Tom started sowing and I did too,

TOM: tramping up and down the field right out there, I thought you looked dreaming about something.

JOHN: was it Bridget talking about the old country, or — time passing by without your noticing until the wheat is nearly all sown except for this.

We are back at the wake again. The coffins return; all lie asleep by them.

MRS DONNELLY: Into the ground with them, then, John. *(she throws a handful of wheat at us)* And burn these bad seeds, Mr Donnelly, burn them over here. *(A brazier of bad seeds is burnt.)* November! November I shall say to you, John, your wheat's up. *(Her form towers & fades in & out behind the smoke & fire of the brazier)* Next month I'll go to see Jennie in St Thomas. She used to ask me to lift my arms like this and then bring them down like wings and lift her up in them, until she got bigger and instead I taught her to dance when we'd be all alone here, my daughter and myself. Even if she's dancing all alone she's really dancing with me.

495

JENNIE: That clock strikes the hour nearest dawn. Am I only left awake to watch? No. William's gone to look after the horses.

CHORUS:
Five dead people lying in a house
The last tollgate before harvest and heaven

JENNIE:
But at dawn comes a sleigh to bear you away

CHORUS:
Five dead people are leaving this house

The blindfolded dead come out from behind the curtain & follow their coffins but —

JENNY:
But at dawn comes a sleigh to bear you away

CHORUS:
Five dead people are leaving this house

The blindfolded dead come out from behind the curtain & follow their coffins but —

JENNY: No, not yet

MRS DONNELLY, her eyes bandaged, dances with JENNIE to the gramophone & then leaves.

CHORUS: *(record)*
Five dead people are leaving this house[3]

JENNY:
At dawn comes a sleigh to bear you away
The snow has come down
To cover the ground
Where you will lie buried today

Two times cross each other — the morning of Friday, 6 February, 1880 and the summer afternoon in 1900. We hear sleighbells, then the chuff-chuff of the gramophone.

CHORUS: End of Act One

ACT II

Organ. The coffins arrive at the church. FR CONNOLLY comes to meet the DONNELLYS. The scene shifts to the Bishop's Palace.

CHORUS: *sung*

  Exsultabunt Domine ossa humiliata
  They shall rejoice in the Lord, the bones that have been
    humbled
  Requiem aeternam dona eis, Domine. Et lux perpetua
  luceat eis.

CORCORAN: Two years before the Donnelly Tragedy if tragedy it can be called, I, Timothy Corcoran, was almost their member of Parliament, and after the results came out I paid a visit to His Excellency the Bishop, Francis McSweeney

BISHOP: Appointments, Father Mahoney?

MAHONEY: Mr Corcoran is soon here to see you, Your Excellency. And the chimney sweeps are coming at half past. In these few spare moments might we, Your Excellency, just go through your speech at four o'clock at the Academy of the Sacred Heart.

BISHOP: My dear children I have assisted at this annual distribution of prizes with much gratification. Father Mahoney, weren't our chimneys just swept?

MAHONEY: Your Excellency, the bird, the wild bird that has been trapped in the fire place chimney here for three or four days now.

BISHOP: Ah yes, Father Mahoney. It's not making much of a sound this morning, is it? The child when brought to school is not only an ignorant being but it is also a being inclined to evil. How important, therefore . . .

MAHONEY: Your Excellency, I beg your pardon. I forgot that Mr Corcoran is already here.

BISHOP: Timothy Corcoran. May I congratulate you, Mr Timothy Corcoran, on your victory at the polls yesterday. We Conservatives who are Catholics are marching forward to greater and greater strengths.

CORCORAN: *(who has kneeled & kissed the Bishop's ring)* Your Excellency, there's

BISHOP: Who says this is not an age for miracles, Mr Corcoran? Sir John A Macdonald waves his magic wand — good Catholics everywhere vote for

CORCORAN: Your Excellency, there has been a final tally of the votes. I lost by seven votes.

BISHOP: By how many votes? Mr Corcoran, are you telling me that you lost the riding by just seven votes? Then the Protestants did not vote for you as they promised. Some Orangemen. Although you were the Conservative candidate you were also a Catholic and they

CORCORAN: Your Excellency, it was some Irish Catholics who did not

BISHOP: Where?

CORCORAN: By a large margin I lost in Ward Three, Biddulph.

BISHOP: That should have been the safest spot in the world for an Irish Catholic candidate. Whatever has gone wrong?

CORCORAN: There is a family there that is Catholic and Irish, but we cannot persuade them to vote Conservative. They influence the whole neighbourhood to vote the Protestant ticket. Grit.

498

BISHOP: What name is upon them?

CORCORAN: Donnelly.

BISHOP: Father Mahoney?

MAHONEY: Your Excellency may remember that a letter came to you from a member of that family — William Donnelly. *(draws the curtain aside to reveal this person)*

WILL & BISHOP: Your reverence. Our new parish priest, Father Connolly, has formed a Peace Society in direct opposition to our family. I wonder if Father Connolly knows that the members

BISHOP: What beautiful handwriting.

WILL & BISHOP: of this society are sworn to each other? I wish that you would bring Father Connolly and I face to face before you and decide who is in the wrong.

BISHOP: The man should have been a priest.

WILL & BISHOP: Our name is continually referred to in church in connection with crime, but the names of others known to have committed crimes are never even hinted at. For God's sake, do something before it is too late.

BISHOP: But he doesn't know how to address his bishop. No, I am not your reverence, William Donnelly, I am your Excellency. And. He doesn't know that before you can stand you must learn to kneel. Seven votes. *(Rescues the bird at the fireplace / sewing machine)* So, Mr Corcoran, this William Donnelly did not vote for you then, and he is just one of a whole family of such people?

CORCORAN: Your Excellency, yes. He is the very worst one of all the Donnellys.

BISHOP: You said just now that they influence the whole neighbourhood, why would you say that now?

CORCORAN: The kind of influence they use is to ride the horses of my supporters all night until they are nigh dead and leave tied to their tails if they have not cut them off — Vote Tory, Be Sorry.

BISHOP: Father Mahoney. You may tell the chimney sweeps to go away. We have no need of their service now the trapped bird has fallen down into the grate. . . . *(Bird shadow on the curtain now.)* Black with soot, ashes. Dead? No. With the warmth of my hands, the pressure of the ring on my finger, the bird revives. Its heart is beating; its wings flutter: — open that window if you please — *(both MAHONEY & CORCORAN rush to obey)* and after four days and nights in our dark chimney off the wretched bird flies, free out of my palace, away from my cathedral, trapped in our flues no longer. *(Gesture of arms up)* Free, yes free. But black marked, dirty with soot and ashes. He flies to his familiar or her familiar branch in the grove — oh Father Mahoney, this is the turn I shall give the speech this afternoon, *(Wing Shadows on Curtain.)*

MAHONEY: Your Excellency, this is the trope we have been searching for.

BISHOP: Does this sooty bird resemble its fellow birds now? Is it as it looked before? No. The other birds turn away. What bird is this so different.

MRS DONNELLY: Shure, don't you see how my family is being treated. We are being shunned. No one neighbours with us any more.

BISHOP: All the birds of the grove give it a roost by itself, a wide roost

MR & MRS DONNELLY are about to be surrounded by a mob and killed.

MRS DONNELLY: at first.   *Vicious chirping*

MR DONNELLY:
They are using us worse than   *(Bird starling sounds)* mad dogs.

BISHOP: At first, then the other birds can bear the stranger no longer. Cruel are the laws of nature. At first a peck. And then a buffet.

MR DONNELLY: I was not in the least afraid of them.

BISHOP: Peck peck peck Buffet buffet buffet

CHORUS: A gang of masked men murder an entire family. Intense excitement.

Birds attack the "different" bird & kill her & him with chirping sounds.

BISHOP: My dear children, would you have joined with those cruel birds driving away the stranger who was after all their brother but only changed by the soot of our chimneys? Tree cross roost Arimathea work that around some more, Father Mahoney and let me see it at eleven.

A servant pours water into a basin and brings it to his master. The BISHOP washes his hands.

Mr Corcoran, we have been chastizing this family, we have been trying to teach them not to be so different — or else. Now when they have had time to think it all over, we will show them the other side of our power, the power to overlook, to forgive. Be patient likewise, Mr Corcoran. We are working with the government to free the son who is in prison — Robert. I want you to take him home to his father and you will see and we shall see — if that does not change matters with this family cleanse the soot off their feathers as it were. Ah, your wrath against this family can only with difficulty be assuaged. Timothy Corcoran, try to forgive them, have you forgiven them? Can you forgive them, ever?

He nods his head after a long pause

And when the next election, the provincial one is held in your riding and you run again, this time you will win, by a large margin. You will win because you have swallowed your pride and helped us give this family one more chance. (*Crossing and climbing as in the diocesan walk scene to FR*

GIRARD.) Father Mahoney, did I write to Crinnon, Bishop of Hamilton, a short while ago?

JIM FEENY takes a rope & starts to hang himself from another stepladder.

MAHONEY: Yes, your Excellency, and you asked him this question: Why did you not invite Father Connolly to your thirty-fifth anniversary celebrations?

The two prelates climb the two sides of the great stepladder at the back of the stage.

BISHOP: You invited all the other priests from all the other missions to which you had once ministered, except Father Connolly, and he is the priest of St Patrick's, Biddulph, your very first pastorate. It was noticed by many too and even hinted at as a scandal that you did not send an invitation to the incumbent at your very first mission, St Patrick's

CRINNON: McSweeny, he will never get one. I consider it one of the duties of a pastor to keep his parishioners alive.

BISHOP: Spiritually alive.

CRINNON: Alive. Why there is the son of one of my old parishioners throwing a rope over a tree branch in the forest.

BISHOP: The Feeny boy. A difficult case. How can Connolly help him when he is too weak and drunken and generally besotted even to come near the church.

CRINNON: McSweeny, it is not only Feeny who is sick of life. Go down the steps of your steeple with its bells and see what you find stretched out at the foot of your altar.

BISHOP: Crinnon, I know, I know. Father Connolly came into town this morning from Biddulph and he has been mysteriously praying at my altar ever since.

CONNOLLY at foot of altar. Young lovers in doctor's office

CRINNON: Do you want me to show you why he is doing this?

BISHOP: No. I know. It concerns that wretched young doctor, Jerome O'Halloran. How on earth, Crinnon, could Connolly have foreseen that turn to events. Yes, a few days ago, I know, you do not have to tell me, this young man met his — concubine in his office and

KATE: Jerry, I slipped out through the back door of the milliner's. They will all think I have gone home, but of course there I cannot go.

JEROME: Why what have they said?

KATE: Not to come home again.

JEROME: Home here then. Kate, my hands. These hands have just examined a dead man at the inquest.

KATE: I don't care. I'll kiss away the death.

JEROME: So there's that and there's also the fact that I kept my appointment with Father Connolly. I went to see him at his office.

KATE: What did he say, Jerome.

JEROME: He says that if I marry you he will excommunicate me and that I will be damned. He says that . . . I told him of what we had done at Mrs Connors', that in effect we are married already, and he called me a fornicator and you were called such a name that I struck him. I struck him. He then told me that I was a disgrace to my pious old mother and father, and that I was even worse than the very very worst of the Donnellys — that cripple and devil, Will Donnelly. Later at the inquest as I was cutting open that man's body in order to get at the heart it suddenly came to me that tonight when you came — why *(Gets both poison and wine from altar)* we would drink this in some wine — from this glass and we would at last be free. What are you thinking?

KATE: Yes. Jerome, you know I will go with you wherever you go.

They drink, he first

JEROME: Do you want to know where we are going now, Kate?

KATE: If you know, tell me.

JEROME: We'll put on our coats because the thing works through various stages of increasing drowsiness and we'll walk down the road to the tollgate. *(They walk towards us)*

KATE: Once past the tollgate we're out of Biddulph, Jerome. Jerome, may I turn back just once?

JEROME: When we get to the tollgate. *(They have disappeared.)*

BISHOP: *(down from ladder now & bending over the abject priest)* Connolly, I want you to come with me to my study. What happened then?

CONNOLLY: They were found dead just this side of Kelly's toll house. Kelly brought them back into the village in a cart. Tell me, your Excellency, where I am to bury him?

BISHOP: What does the church say with regard to the burial of those who take their own lives?

CONNOLLY: The gravedigger without waiting for my authority went ahead and dug the young man's grave in their family plot by the chancel.

BISHOP: Tell him to dig another one outside the fence. He must not be buried in consecrated ground.

CONNOLLY: You tell him, because I'm not going back there ever again. Here's the key to the church.

BISHOP: Connolly, I am going to get Father Mahoney to walk over to the Huron Hotel and get you a hack. He will tell the driver to take you back to your presbytery and the first thing you must do is tell the sexton to fill in the grave by the chancel and dig the new one outside the church yard. Don't you realize the good that will come of this severity? Now if you go back you will be respected as you have never been respected before. Connolly, who has the key to that church and the key to their souls, you or William Donnelly? It is a battle, lives are lost in battles, but to save men's souls we must fight on. The unfaithful shepherd

CONNOLLY: Wolf. Yes. Your Excellency, you are sending a wolf back to them. I am one, I cannot sleep, I hear both sides of the feud confess opposite things until I, I feel graceless.

BISHOP: Get up Connolly

CONNOLLY: How much longer do I have to stay there then if I do go back.

BISHOP: If! Until you die, Connolly. Get up and out of here. Father Mahoney!

He beats FATHER CONNOLLY with his crozier out of the church — towards us as TOM races across to the tree where FEENY is hanging himself.

TOM: Jim Feeny, you young bugger, what are you trying to get away with this time? I'll hang you. Just because Jerry O'Halloran did himself in you feel it's the fashionable thing to do, do you, hang yourself? Jimmy. God you've been drinking.

JIM: A man can't even die around here anymore. Let me have my rope back.

TOM: Nothing doing. I'm hiding this rope on you. *(Exit behind curtain to hide same)*

JIM: Why was I hanging myself anyhow? The time I was so sick after Tom and me smashed up Glass's Tavern there was somebody at my bedside, no not my mother

505

CARROLL: It was I, Jim Carroll, when your mind was open like a cracked egg, I suggested

JIM: That I should change sides! Well. And yet to all the world and the Donnellys I'd still appear a Donnelly man

CARROLL: Oh, you want to join us, do you? Well.

JIM: Yes, Jim Carroll, if I am to change sides just where is the other side and how do I join?

CARROLL: Let's put you through your paces. I sent him one of my anonymous notes. Towards the end I got rather famous for these, my stepmother's hair fell out after one I sent her.

JIM & CARROLL: Shun the Donnellys, or you will be used in the manner they will be used. Signed — Vigilant.

Suggest the Donnelly house with small windows held up by actors.

JIM: I spent the next few weeks hanging around the Donnellys as I never hung around them before. And

CARROLL: I've a warrant here for your arrest, Jim Feeny, but if you leave the township nothing more will be heard of it.

JIM:
My feelings were hurt, they didn't want me to join their society after all. He wanted me not. He wanted me to leave the township. Well, I like Tom again. To hell with you Carroll, I'm never leaving this township. Now's your time to arrest me:
Here's my hands and here's my fists
Put them round my dimpled wrists

CARROLL: I have an object of my own in view just now, Jim Feeny, but I will arrest you the first time I find you in Lucan.

JIM: Then Jim, I'll walk into Lucan with you and here, everybody, (*much pursuing of CARROLL in & out of the curtains which part, sway, close)* in front of the Post Office, Constable Carroll, arrest me. *(and move as of themselves to suggest a whole day's chasing of CARROLL by FEENY)* Am I not even worth arresting? *(The citizens of Lucan freeze in surprise.)*

POSTMASTER: Letter for you, Jim. That's a good pair of lungs you have there, almost blew all the stamps and telegraph forms we got in here out of their respective drawers. Woke the baby.

JIM & CARROLL: So you're tired of the crowd you're with, come to the dance tonight.

JIM: Dance tonight. There were dances all over the township. *(Three Dances. These dances whirl about JIM FEENY without letting him join.)* I must have visited three of them before I finally stumbled *(The last dancers disappear behind the curtain.)* into the deserted house on a side road not far from the Donnellys. The house was under a big elm and you'd see a flock of crows fly in one window of the house and out another.

The curtains draw back; organ chord out of horror movies; a row of heads rise slowly up from behind the altar — the Secret Society in council.

CHORUS: Here, you can't come in here. You're not a member.

JIM: If this is the Peace Society I'd like to join. My father signed the book in the church, why can't I join?

O'HALLORAN: Prove you're an enemy of the Donnellys.

JIM: How can I prove that now, tell me how.

CARROLL: Bring us a pair of Tom Donnelly's old shoes, an old shirt of his and some pants and a coat, a coat he used to wear a lot.

TOM & JIM: *(TOM quietly crossing to him)* But — Your blood, my blood / Sealed in brotherhood

TOM: When he remembers me signing his name on my arm, he loves me. But when he remembers the sting of my knife signing my name on his arm he hates me

JIM: I was like a girl who couldn't make up her mind. And I said no.

CARROLL: Yes

JIM: No!

CARROLL: Yes, the trouble with Jim Feeny is he never has and never will be able to make up his mind, so we'll make it up for you. Handcuff him. Because a girl that can't make up her mind, but has gone this far with her petticoat up and the man has it out

He handcuffs FEENY who is hanged behind & over the altar this time by his wrists.

JIM: I'm not that much of a whore yet that you'll get me to get you Tom Donnelly's clothes.

CARROLL: Well, we'll see about that, and here's a bell you can ring when your wrists feel ready to steal Tom's clothes. Don't let it drop now, we'll tie it to your hand.

JIM: Carroll, I'll never ring it. You haven't broken my backbone yet, I won't give in even if it's to old Christ himself.

The curtains fold over to conceal FEENY.

CARROLL: That's the spirit, Jim. Me, I had got what I wanted behind me. All the things I mentioned before, priest, law and this group of men sworn to each other, but there were still one or two gaps to be filled — our strongwilled friend back there and the fact that there was one strong man in the land just around the Donnellys' place whose help we needed. Patrick Marksey. *(We hear the cane of an old, yet tough, strong farmer tapping on the frozen ground.)*

508

TOM: Patrick Marksey. Yes, behind my back they strung up my friend in a deserted house they had no permission to occupy.

MARKSEY: Who the hell do you men think you are trespassing on my property?

CARROLL: Good night, Pat.

MARKSEY: Get out of here, Jim Carroll and take your friends with you. Get out!

CARROLL: Pat, it's a great deal of trouble you'd be saving us if you let us use this old place. Sure there's nobody living here before we came except Mrs Wind and Mr Rain, are they such better tenants of yours?

MARKSEY: I don't want any of your secret people money, and don't ask me to join you or to swear your oath or help you in any way. O'Halloran, I'm surprised to see you in this gang, has God not punished you enough?

O'HALLORAN: Marksey, the Donnellys have insulted us for years till it's now we have marked them down and God punishes them through us. I swear it was them misled my boy who killed himself and is now lying in a ditch, yes God will punish those whose strength and place was needed in the holy work and they hid their talent, Patrick Marksey.

CARROLL: We can't move without a man of standing like you, Pat, in on it.

MARKSEY: I know you can't, Jim Carroll, and I'll say this: I have not got a thing against the Donnellys. I'm tired of your always being after them. Leave them alone or I'll advertise you and this old house even if the crows nest in it it is my house, not your house, Jim Carroll. Good night to you, boys. (*They leave. Crow sounds.*) Ah, I'll clear the rest of you vermin out tomorrow and break up your nests — Jim Feeny. What have they got you strung up there for, tinkling a bell like a blind beggar. *(He lowers JIM & CARROLL enters to seize him.)*

CARROLL: Pat! Jim. I can leave the handcuffs on you and it's the lock-up or — you can come with us forever and I'll take them off.

JIM: Take them off.

MRS DONNELLY: *(from her kitchen)* It was late in the fall now, the roads iron with frost, and the men were sitting in the kitchen mending harness. Bridget was baking. I was knitting and listening to the quiet outside as I had begun to more and more. I thought *(we hear a tiny bell tinkling; so does she)* that at a great distance I could hear — there it is again, a tinker's bell, no not a tinker's bell, but a leper's bell. Some story my mother read me by the fire a very long time ago — about a saint who was a leper and had to wear a bell to warn people that he was coming. . . . *(Sudden noise at the door. Horsemen have thrown a briefly dressed FEENY on to their doorstep.)*

TOM: In the name of Heaven, what happened to you, Jim Feeny. Stand back, mother and Bridget. He's not decent. Jim, here's a pair of my old shoes. An old shirt of mine and some pants.

JIM: They strung me up, Tom, and left me hanging. Then they stripped me and burnt my clothes and when I said I wouldn't join them they brought me here and threw me at your mother's door.

MRS DONNELLY: And a coat. A coat Tom used to wear a lot, Jim. Put it on.

JIM: and I put them on. Then it was like clapping drowned out by stamping for I went back to them with Tom's clothes and they took them off me — made me watch while they gambled for them.

Card game with vigilantes smacking cards on floor and reciting Roman Line litany sotto voce. Leave clothes on FEENY, have identical Tom's clothes on dummy. This takes place in silhouette behind the curtain.

TOM: When Jim would stay at our place some nights I'd wake up and look at your face beside me because something had changed about you

JIM: Couldn't you see what was happening?

TOM: Stuck eyelid! *(He draws back the curtain to reveal the card game.)*

VIGILANTE: You're it, Barry! You've won the clothes of Tom Donnelly

CARROLL: Wait a minute, according to the rules — it's O'Halloran who's won!

ALL: O'Halloran!

O'HALLORAN: Jim Carroll, what am I to do with Tom Donnelly's clothes.

CARROLL: Dress up in them.

O'HALLORAN: I'm too stout

CARROLL: But your servant Jim Purtell is Tom's size, is he not?

O'HALLORAN: Yes, and dressed as Tom Donnelly what does he do?

CARROLL: Don't you see? He burns down Patrick Marksey's barns.

The curtains close cutting us off from the vigilantes.

TOM: And so the clothes my mother and myself gave you when you were naked, Jim were used to bring in Marksey on their side. In fire or flood or field or air where we wander now I ask you, Jim Feeny.

JIM: Yes, Tom, I helped close the ring around you. Then it was the day before Christmas and seemed as good a day as any, so I found a rope in my father's driving shed and walked into the Donnellys' woods to hang myself. And all is done as you have seen, Tom's now coming back from hiding the rope, I the whore told you they were always like that, bossy, try to hang yourself and they won't let you, what'd you do with the rope?

TOM: Hid it on you, Jim. Look, Jim, I want you to come home with me, it's Christmas Eve.

JIM: If you hadn't interrupted me I'd have been all right by now.

TOM: Not by a long shot, you'd have been choking for hours, I never seen a hangman's knot tied more ill, you just don't know how to do it, Jim.

JIM: I could see the door of the Donnelly kitchen getting closer and closer. Mr and Mrs Donnelly and John were all dressed up for church.

JIM: That's a new suit, John.

JOHN: Yes, it's the first time I've worn it.

TOM: Whatever happened to your old suit, why everything you're wearing is new?

JOHN: Burnt them

MRS DONNELLY: Now why would you do that now?

JOHN: I read something in the newspaper made me do it, mother, if you must know. If you remember that woman I was married to for a week and twice she said bad things about us, and I said once more hurt us like that and I'll go back, and so she did it the third time?

MR DONNELLY: John, your mother and myself are sorry we asked.

JOHN: Well, she got married again, father, and I burnt the suit I married her in.

MR DONNELLY: Tonight, John, confession and mass. And the old year is ended.

512

JOHN: Father. Mother. *(Kneels and receives their blessing)*

MR & MRS DONNELLY: Bless you my son. In nomine patris et filii et spiritus sancti. Amen.

JIM: They left the house when Mr Keefe's sleigh called for them. Tom and Bridget went out to the barn to do the chores. *(Pause, kissing the cupboard)* I love the house of the Donnellys. *(Caressing other pieces of furniture, curtains, invisible tables)* I love their chairs and their John's mother and father still kiss him *(Some emotional cry or scream or choked anguish as the love turns to hatred at his arm being cut, probably by the cupboard again, kicking cupboard)* Burn to the ground, burn to the ground. *(Pause before leaving)* I leave. Only saw Tom Donnelly once ever again, saw him the night they got him.

Curtains

CHORUS:
(sing "The snow lay on the ground" under)

PRIEST: Who is next? *(He draws the Stage Left curtain in front of himself, then ducks down behind altar and stands behind Stage Right curtain. MRS DONNELLY knocks at the Stage Left curtain: FR CONNOLLY opens his curtain.)* Come in, Mrs Donnelly. *(She opens the Stage Left curtain)*

MRS DONNELLY: Father Connolly. *(She shuts the curtain front of her)*

PRIEST: Father Connolly *(He shuts curtain in front of himself.)* She says it as if she were my equal. Father Connolly. Mrs Donnelly.

MRS DONNELLY: Mrs Donnelly. He is afraid of me, I can tell by the way his lips purse my name. *(She opens Stage Right curtain and appears at it: he opens Stage Left curtain and appears.)*

PRIEST: To see me about? Yourself, your husband, and your son John were just at confession, were you not?

MRS DONNELLY: Are you sure John came to you? *(The PRIEST draws his curtain shut)*

PRIEST: Yes

MRS DONNELLY: What I should have said was — yes, John came to you, but did you receive him.

PRIEST: Ah, but you didn't ask that you see.

MRS DONNELLY: So that I went on for an hour with you *(she comes out and goes over to confront his curtain after closing her curtain:)* telling you the story of my life ever since *(she draws aside the curtain: he has vanished)* yes, the story of my life has been this *(she draws the Stage Left curtain too and he is not behind it.)* If you could see my face and I could see yours, but no

PRIEST: *(appearing at Stage Right opening his curtain)* Mrs Donnelly, when people have a hard name, as a priest, having the charge of souls, I must set my face against their deeds.

MRS DONNELLY: Why is it that you have a face for our deeds but no face at all for the lives that are explainers of these deeds. *(He draws the other curtain sharply in front of him. The curtains both wave out at her; she touches them to see who, if anybody, is behind.)* Is it that when you first came to our neighbourhood — her farm on the road is before our farm and with her sable coat and her sable muff and her fur hat driving down to the church to suck the toes of Jesus in her jet black cutter, the soul of respectability . . . Mrs O'Halloran. *(MRS DONNELLY reveals her by sharply drawing aside the Stage Right curtain.)*

MRS O'HALLORAN: *(in her usual regalia)* Father Connolly, my mother was sitting in her parlour when my infant brother came running in from the road.

BOY: Mammy! There's a strange woman coming down the street out of Connors' shebeen and she's drunk!

MRS DONNELLY: And so, Father Connolly — when you see me you don't see me you always see — this! (*Drawing the Stage Left curtain aside to reveal the AXWOMAN — JAMES CARROLL dressed up as the MRS DONNELLY of the vigilante version: coarse, pipe-smoking, rough, jug-toting and a giantess to boot!*)

MRS O'HALLORAN: It was Mrs Donnelly, Father Connolly, walking! down! the middle! of the

AXWOMAN: My husband's got seven years in Kingston, and my seven sons'll each kill their man for each year their darling father's in the cage.

MRS O'HALLORAN: Shut up the shutters, my mother then said. Shut them up till Mrs Donnelly goes past and away. (*AXWOMAN draws Stage Left curtain across her face and MRS O'HALLORAN draws her shutters.*)

MRS DONNELLY: I am not like that. Keep that curtain away from your face, Father, when you talk to me — stop that! (*Every time she gets one curtain open, it is shut. The space before the altar fills with worshippers. She has a piece of cloth in her hands.*)

PRIEST: (*rapidly drawing aside, then shutting the Stage Right curtain*) Good evening, Mrs Donnelly.

CHORUS: Sanctus!

MRS DONNELLY: Yes, good evening Father Connolly. Perhaps at mass, Mr Donnelly, John (*She and the DONNELLY men are now at the back of the church. FATHER CONNOLLY is celebrating mass and we cut to his administering the sacrament. The DONNELLYS with others proceed to the communion rail, but JOHN hangs back.*)

MR DONNELLY: John. Why are you not coming forward with us?

JOHN: Mother and father, Father Connolly refused me confession — I cannot go up.

MRS DONNELLY: WHY?

JOHN: Because, because he said I probably intended to confess to a lie in order to shield Tom at the trial when the case comes up about Glass's tavern.

MRS DONNELLY: *(Tears her veil apart. She turns sharply away. The DONNELLYS leave the church)* This is the last time we come to your altar, Father Connolly. Oh no — we will come once more. Once more!

MUSIC: *("I Dreamt of Marble Halls" & Wedding Dance at Donnelly School. The mandolin plays the tune very coldly & the dance is sluggish.)*

BISHOP: Father Mahoney, my hand is stained with ink. Ask the servant to bring me a basin of water. I look down from my tower and over my diocese. There is Corcoran driving down from Biddulph. Are all those people at the wedding party friends of the Donnellys, Mr Corcoran?

CORCORAN: And vote as they vote. If they vote for me tomorrow I win the riding.

BISHOP: And will they vote for you? *(From the stepladder he views the dance & washes his hands.)*

MARIA: It's not like my wedding dance at all at all if the Donnelly boys don't show up at it, father. Does anyone know if they're coming?

MR KEEFE: Maria, darling, the Donnelly boys may not be anxious to come to the dance with a brother dead just a month ago.

GIRL: There's some say their good shirts were out on the line drying all afternoon, and they've disappeared.

WOMAN: They've trouble finding handkerchiefs, they had no handkerchiefs but ones edged in black

GIRL: They're still in town getting proper handkerchiefs, they couldn't dance with those in their pockets.

MARIA: Can they hear the music from the dance up at their house there? Sure, they can, I used to hear Will playing at the Donnellys' when I was a girl at school here, but you aren't playing loud enough, all of you put your heart into it, open the windows and the doors so the sound of it makes their feet tap and their father and mother say, go — mourning or no, get out of the house and off to Maria and Nick's wedding party.

This sequence is a reprise that brings together the musical & dance themes of the whole trilogy. What the dancers are trying to do is make enough noise to attract the DONNELLY boys to the dance. What they don't realize, of course, is that if the boys do come to the dance CARROLL cannot accuse them of burning down MARKSEY's barn which is about to go up in flames; he will then in desperation turn upon their mother and father.

We hear Will's fiddle and soon the four DONNELLY boys appear and each perform a solo dance "The Haymakers' Reel"

The feeling of this sequence should be of a last desperate fling on the part of the DONNELLYS and their friends. As CORCORAN speaks the dances become shadows and the fiddle music weakens.

DANCES

1. Schottische

2. Buffalo Gals

3. Elgin Girls

4. John Barley Corn

5. Sticks & Stones

6. Schottische

7. Stamping & Clapping

8. Jig with Solos

9. Curtain Dance

"The Haymakers' Reel"

CORCORAN: Oh your Excellency, I went to the prison. I showed them your letter, I received Bob Donnelly, I drove with him towards his father's farm and could see in the distance Old Donnelly waiting at his gate

MR DONNELLY: I saw Mr Corcoran driving towards me, my son Bob beside him.

The BISHOP washes his hands, scrub, brush his nails

CORCORAN: Jim. I know you and your sons worked against me last election. No hard feelings, Jim, we've got Bob out of prison six months before his sentence

MR DONNELLY: He should never have gone to prison in the first place.

CORCORAN: Jim, you're glad to see him back, aren't you?

MR DONNELLY: Bob

BOB: Father, forgive me. They pried me loose. *(He kneels to his father)*

MR DONNELLY: Mr Corcoran, on Sunday last after mass Father Connolly told the parish we should all vote for you. He said you were a good man.

CORCORAN: Mr Donnelly, Father Connolly is a good and wise man. As much as the bishop he worked for Bob's release.

MR DONNELLY: We didn't go to mass, Mr Corcoran. On Christmas Eve Father Connolly refused to confess another son of mine, John.

CORCORAN: Mr Donnelly

MR DONNELLY: Mr Corcoran, all my life men have come to my door both here and in Ireland and asked me to do something I do not want to do — you and your pals have taken away from us half my farm most of our reputation. But he has a few friends left.

CHORUS: Seven votes!

MR DONNELLY: Yes, we lost you the riding, so what you're really saying, Mr Corcoran, is — Donnelly, you've still got something left, some votes and we want them too and if you don't give me them votes, out of the township, I won't vote for you, I'm not in the least

BISHOP: Corcoran, are you quite sure of that

CORCORAN: Yes, your Excellency, his answer was

MR DONNELLY: *(Directly up to BISHOP)* No!

MR DONNELLY & CHORUS: *(Directly up to BISHOP)* No!

BISHOP: You know I must have signed a hundred letters to get that man's son out of prison. Here, take this water and throw it away.

Continue with dance scene which comes out from behind the shadow curtain once more threading through it will be MAHONEY descending with basin to servant who passes basin to another servant until the basin cuts across the dance and its water is thrown out in the centre of the dancing floor.

DANCERS: *(whispering)* We've danced till dawn. That's not the dawn that's the moon. That's not the moon, that's a barn burning, it's Pat Marksey's barn! *(A blazing model of a barn is brought in.)*

MARKSEY: I got my horses and cows out, I had enough time to do that, but there's all my grain and tons of hay and implements and the new buggy my son Morris bought last summer and waggons, the new buggy. . . . There they are going by on the road, I saw them, Tom and Bob and John and Will. I said — they burnt my barns!

BRIAN: Father, they couldn't have. I'm just home from the dance at the school and the Donnelly boys were there the whole night. Tom and Bob and John and Will.

MARKSEY: Was Tom Donnelly at the dance, Brian?

BRIAN: Father, ask others than your own son if you must, but I swear you are wrong — why would they want to burn down your barns.

MARKSEY: I swear I saw Tom Donnelly come out of our granary with a lighted torch, it's the old man then, for who else but the Donnellys

BRIAN: Why would old Donnelly burn you out, give me one reason.

MARKSEY: If he didn't, who did? Where's Jim Carroll, well where is the man, he's generally skulking at their gate. Carroll!

"Sweet & Low" hummed under — first line under of BRIDGET's speech only

Use the human house convention

BRIDGET: I waved goodbye to Mrs Donnelly who that morning was off on a long promised visit to her daughter in St Thomas. Tom was driving her to catch the train at Lucan Crossing. I was sweeping the snow from the doorstep. . . .

CARROLL: Out of my way, girl, I've business inside this shanty. Mr James Donnelly, the Elder, I've a warrant here for your arrest.

MR DONNELLY: *(smiling)* Jim, you haven't visited us for over two months now. Where have you been?

JOHN: Get those handcuffs away from my father. Read the warrant first, Carroll.

CARROLL: You, James Donnelly, are charged with — the burning down last night of Patrick Marksey's barns. Where's the old woman, where's your wife, Donnelly?

JOHN: It's not our job to hunt down our mother for you, Carroll. *("Sweet & Low" BRIDGET's speech under again.)*

BRIDGET: By that time my aunt would have been at the O'Connor house in the village where she *(we suddenly shift to the O'Connor shebeen and for the first time repeat verbatim one of the scenes from Act One.)*

MRS DONNELLY: Yes, Theresa, is this not a pretty way we are used. *(The audience should now begin to grasp the structure of the play and experience a "double" feeling about the next events. The sewing machine sound here should help us transfer our mind back to the earlier shebeen scenes.)* But I have no time to sit down and tell you the full lunacy of it all. Peggy, I'll take the pillow slips with me now, for I'm catching the train this morning and going to visit my daughter Jennie in St Thomas. I'm promised to see her and my grandchildren since the wake for Michael. What is it, Tom?

TOM: Mother, we're cutting it awful close.

MRS DONNELLY: Goodby Theresa. Thank you Peggy.

THERESA: She's not herself. She doesn't want to stay out there where you're being accused all the time of doing things it would take an athletic hoyden of sixteen all her time doing let alone an old woman in her sixties.

CARROLL: I've a subpoena here for Peggy O'Connor. You by the sewing machine over there, come here and sign this piece of paper for me.

THERESA: What's this about, Constable Carroll?

CARROLL: Well, your daughter consorts *(Humming of "Sweet & Low" under & on. This Victorian tune is MRS DONNELLY's mind thinking of her grandchildren as she takes the long complex rail journey to St Thomas; a lullaby, a world so different from the Biddulph world she is escaping from.)* with the Donnellys doesn't she? So she was out there the night of the fire and when she appears at the hearing tomorrow perhaps she can tell us what went on that night when

MARKSEY: They burnt my barns

PEG: Yes, perhaps I can.

CARROLL: Remember Peggy O'Connor. Two o'clock sharp at the Council Chambers.

The actors sit as if on a gaslit train (the L.H.&B.) going down to London

TRAVELLER: Gaslight. I was asleep, but at Lucan Crossing an old woman in black got on and sat beside me. Snowflakes on her bonnet. Gaslight.

MRS DONNELLY: All the fields covered in snow up over the fences. Snow. *(Train whistle as train enters London station & screech of brakes.)* At the station in London I suddenly realized how sick I was of Biddulph and when no one was looking I put up both my arms just to see I still could. *(The actors get off the train & become the Market Square at London; silhouettes of the hotels and halls there.)*

STATION AGENT: I saw her when I was putting more coke in the waiting room stove. I could see her reflection in the mica windows. All dressed in black and — *(Imitates her but he can't get his arms up as high as she can.)*

MAN: Who is that old woman? Crossing the Market Square where only snow is being sold this day at one gust of wind a peck.

CHORUS: I saw her . . . Sam Kelly, Thomas Varley, Thomas Hodgins —

MAN: See the old woman go into the dining room at the City Hotel.

WOMAN: She's somebody from Biddulph isn't she, Tom?

Use a "held" window to establish the dining room.

HOSTESS: Good day to you, Mrs Donnelly. Are you all alone in town or are you expecting some other members of your family

MRS DONNELLY: I'm all alone, Mrs McMartin, for I'm going down to St Thomas to see my daughter, Jennie. I'll have a glass of port, and a piece of seed cake, if you please.

CHORUS & PAPERBOY: Through the thick glass of the dining room window and the snow comes

PAPERBOY: My voice selling papers. Great victory in Zululand, Burmese Rebels Routed and . . . . Incendiarism in Biddulph, the barns of . . .

MRS DONNELLY: There was time before the other train to St Thomas to buy the children a toy, and then my tracks in the deep snow behind me

Now the London & Port Stanley train is mimed; MRS DONNELLY walks toward us down a line of kneeling passengers.

CHORUS

John Wood William Ramsay Hugh McDonald Andrew McCauslin	
Pond Mills	3.30
North Westminster	3.40
Westminster	3.57
Glamworth	4.05
Yarmouth	4.09
St Thomas	4.15

train whistle & brake screech

GRANDCHILD: I can remember her visiting us. I said to my mother — *(at JENNIE's house)* was looking out the window in the front room down the street and there was this old woman coming up the street with her footsteps behind her.

JENNIE: That old woman is your grandmother, children. What do you mean at all, old woman. Mother. At last you've come down from Biddulph to see us. At last at last.

GIRL: Then she picked us up and whirled us around — it was then that she seemed to change —

BOY: She wasn't a grandmother any more, boy she was strong and if she'd ever let you go *(stop humming "Sweet & Low")* it'd been like a cannon or an eagle.

GIRL: I remember she asked us a riddle.

MRS DONNELLY: I have seven sons and each of them a sister. How many children have I?

BOY: Grandmother, two of your sons are dead.

MRS DONNELLY: Oh yes, but they're still my sons. Seven sons have I, and each of them has a sister. How many in my family? I'll fly through the air with the right answer.

CHILD 1: Fourteen

CHILD 2: Fifteen, grandmother.

BOY: Eight! *(She picks him up & whirls him about.)*

MRS DONNELLY: Right. Eight is right, your mother is sister to seven brothers. Now fly over my head, for eight children, seven boys and a girl have I. *(Clock strikes seven.)*

JENNIE: Mother, sit down and rest yourself now. They won't go to bed until they see the toy you brought them, and it's dark enough now — it's a magic lantern. Hush, your grandmother's gone to sleep. Nellie, could you see who that is at the door. I'm terrified to leave this thing shining by itself, flaming away in there, well I guess it's . . . Who are you and what do you want? *(The shadow of the hand and the handcuffs comes on the screen.)*

The magic lantern should show a brightly colored garden scene, the garden, or a matter of fact, mentioned earlier by THERESA O'CONNOR in connection with JEROME & KATIE

CONSTABLE: I have a warrant for a Mrs James Donnelly. Where is she?

JENNIE: My mother. Asleep in that chair over there.

CONSTABLE: Constable Carroll, is this the woman you mean.

CARROLL: Yes, and I told you what a hard lot she is. Wake her up.

MRS DONNELLY: There's no need to wake me up. I'm just keeping my eyes closed so as not to see your face, Jim Carroll.

CONSTABLE: Mrs Donnelly. You are to come along with me to the police station, and from there Constable Carroll will take you back to Biddulph.

MRS DONNELLY: Read the warrant first, if you please.

CONSTABLE: Constable Carroll will do that. Mrs Currie, tell your mother she must get up out of that chair.

JENNIE: I will tell her no such thing.

MRS DONNELLY: I know my law. If he has the warrant then let him come in here and read it.

CARROLL:

Mrs Donnelly, you are charged with incendiarism. Patrick Marksey alleges that on January the 15th you aided your husband in burning down his barns.	*Handcuffs her. There is a struggle. She tries to embrace her grandchildren, but her wings have now been clipped.*

JENNIE: No! you're not taking her back there alone with you. Nellie, you'll have to take care of the children for a few days. Slow down your sleigh. Wait up, Mother. I'm coming with you. I'm coming with you. (*Use Roman Line Convention with its litany of names which imprisons MRS DONNELLY once more*) When we reached home, my father and brothers had the bail papers ready and he took off the handcuffs. (*MRS DONNELLY falls to the ground on her face.*) Mother, I've talked to William and he says there is nothing to worry about. It is only their law and they are making fools of themselves, but I won't leave you unless you raise up your head. (*MRS DONNELLY doesn't*)

525

MRS DONNELLY: Oh God, I thought to myself, If I said so despite her children she'd stay with me and they'd get her too, so raise your head Judith Donnelly although when you raise it and my head is so heavy, it is to *(Slowly she gets up: she & JENNIE come towards each other — but the LAWYER's voice interrupts.)*

LAWYER: *(at the Lucan Council Chambers)* Mrs Donnelly, at the preliminary hearing today as your lawyer I want you to promise me one thing

MRS DONNELLY: Very well, Mr McDiarmid. What one thing?

LAWYER: Even if what you and your husband say is true about these magistrates and your accuser, do not even dream of telling them so to their faces.

MRS DONNELLY: Mr McDiarmid, do you mean to tell me that Squire Cassleigh is to sit in judgement on us when it is he murdered a man on the road, oh years ago now, and they could never pin it on him, and do you tell me that this knife which I myself took away from him, oh years ago now at the bee, this knife — do you not want to know what he was doing with this knife? yes, torturing a man, clipping off his ears, am I not then to give him back his knife — and shame him? Or is it that I tell you what is not true about him.

LAWYER: Mrs Donnelly, I do believe you, but with persons of power it is wise to be discreet

CONSTABLE: Oyez, oyez, the court is in session.

CHORUS: Will all those present rise.

MAGISTRATE CASSLEIGH: Patrick Marksey versus James Donnelly and Julia Donnelly who are charged with incendiarism. The Prisoners are called and answer to their respective names.

He enjoys this hugely; perhaps we do remember his activities in Part One where his gavel did more than just tap a magisterial table.

MR DONNELLY: I am James Donnelly

MRS DONNELLY: I am Julia Donnelly

JUDGE: How plead you, James Donnelly.

MR DONNELLY: Not guilty.

JUDGE: How plead you, Julia Donnelly with regard to the charge that you helped your husband burn down Patrick Marksey's barns on the night of January the 15th.

MRS DONNELLY: Not guilty

MARKSEY: My name is Patrick Marksey. My reasons for suspecting the Donnellys of burning my barns was — That I heard a neighbour, Mrs John Carroll told my daughter Mary that my son would not be long riding in his new buggy — and this buggy was burned in the barn, the driving shed. Further she said that Mrs Donnelly made this threat. Yes, this threat alarmed me.

LAWYER: Have you any other reason, Mr Marksey?

MARKSEY: No.

MRS DONNELLY: *(Advancing down stage)* Oh of course, Mr Marksey, no other reason and who dared to speak in my defence, who dared to say that I, who dared to say that we had not scampered through the snow drifts to light this man's barns, why who but three women — Peggy O'Connor who had been dressmaking at our house that evening

PEGGY: Donnelly boys went to the wedding just before dark. *(At the sewing machine)* Prisoners and Miss Donnelly and myself remained afterwards in the house, went to bed about 11 o'clock *(Clock strikes)* all of us did

MRS DONNELLY: And my niece Bridget said:

BRIDGET: Mrs Donnelly slept in the middle of the bed between me and Miss Connors and was not out of the bed all night.

MRS DONNELLY: And the neighbour, Mr Marksey, Mrs John Carroll she was brave enough to stand up in court and say that

MRS JOHN CARROLL: Mrs Donnelly visits with me sometimes. Mr Marksey, Mrs Donnelly did not say that your son would not have his buggy long I am positive of this. What she did say was that

MRS DONNELLY: I'll put a blush in his face and make him lie back in his grand buggy because that particular Marksey boy had been part of a mob trampling through our yard in search of the famous cow that was lost

MRS JOHN CARROLL: No, I have not heard Mrs Donnelly say anything against the Markseys since.

JOHN & TOM: The magistrates adjourned, this time to Granton for February the 4th

MR DONNELLY: They are treating us like mad dogs. We have been dragged all across the township to make us laughing stocks, an old man and an old woman over sixty years old. We are being advertised as barn burners.

MRS DONNELLY: Good evening, Mr & Mrs O'Halloran

MR DONNELLY: My wife said good evening, Mr & Mrs O'Halloran.

MRS O'HALLORAN: Malachi, let us leave this room where we won't be bothered by barn burners. Father Connolly should tell this family to leave the parish. *(This snub is the breaking point and)*

MRS DONNELLY: *(turning back)* Mr Cassleigh. Magistrate Cassleigh, your honour.

CASSLEIGH: Why, Mrs Donnelly, are you showing me this knife?

MRS DONNELLY: Because I once was the woman who stopped you from tormenting a man with this knife and I am now the woman who tells you that with the exception of Mr

Lindsay over there my husband and myself are being tried, accused and judged by thieves and murderers. *(She throws the knife at his feet; he picks it up.)*

CASSLEIGH: *(Starts to whet the knife on a stone)* I'm not facing that woman again, Carroll in daylight. I'll show her who's master of this neighbourhood get me a calendar. Marksey, we've been through this before. Can we use your old house to meet in?

CARROLL: We'll need some whiskey. Better make up a list of our men.

CASSLEIGH: Everybody got a pen and some ink, O'Halloran. Here's some paper.

CARROLL: Sunday's out. There are only two possible days — this and this.

MARKSEY: Why?

CARROLL: Unless you want to wait until after the hearing which is going to fall through and then they're at our throats for malicious arrest.

MARKSEY: Tell us what to write. No, Ash Wednesday would be bad luck, you're

CARROLL: *(directly at us)* "Tie up your dogs tonight. Keep them inside. If you hear any noise outside, pay no heed." We'll need fifty copies of that

MARKSEY: When do we hand them out? *(They tear paper.)*

CARROLL: Not until after we hear what this priest has to say at mass on Sunday.

CHORUS: Amen!

PRIEST: Then at the harvest-time, I will order the harvesters: "Collect the weeds first, and bundle them up to burn. But gather the wheat into my barn." . . . Bundle them up to burn. And I say to you that whoever has burnt down the barns of Patrick Marksey, their house — a ball of fire from Heaven shall fall on that house before this month is out.

CHORUS: February the third dawn *(clock strikes five)* And there was a house built by James Donnelly on the Sixth Concession it was filled with living people and on the last day on which this house stood the following events happened. Nine o'clock *(clock)*

JOHN: After breakfast my father asked me to get ink and pen and we wrote a letter to a lawyer in town

MR DONNELLY: I want you to attack them at once, as they will never let us alone until some of them are — made an example of.

JOHN: James Donnelly, X his mark

CHORUS: Ten o'clock *(clock)*

JOHN: My brother Will came riding up to borrow the cutter. As he left I called after him: Will, expect me this evening, I'll ride over and get the cutter back to drive them to Granton tomorrow.

CHORUS: One o'clock *(clock)*

TOM: After dinner I took my father into Lucan on our sleigh. We posted a letter to the lawyer, bought some tobacco, and then went to Connors' place to pick up Johnny.

THERESA: Mr Donnelly, is there no stopping them from dragging you all over the countryside examining you about this fire business.

MR DONNELLY: Apparently not, Theresa O'Connor. They're advertising my wife and myself as if we were mad dogs. Johnny, button up your coat, for it's a cold day out on the line and the wind'll whistle right through you. Theresa, we'll bring Johnny back tomorrow if we have no more hearings ahead of us. If he's not back they've put us in jail, you'll know . . . .

THERESA: Oh Mr Donnelly, sufficient unto the day is the evil thereof. Be a good and helpful boy out at Donnellys', Johnny. Goodbye now.

CHORUS: Six o'clock *(clock)*

CASSLEIGH, MARKSEY & CHORUS: There they go. Tom and his father. Going a bit fast, Tom's drunk. Bags of grain under the buffalo robe? Tie up your dogs tonight. Keep him inside. If you hear . . . .

CHORUS: A quarter past six

JOHNNY: Good evening, Mrs Donnelly. May I take my outer pants off and dry them by the stove?

MRS DONNELLY: Shure, Johnny. Bridget, watch the stove for me. Boys your mitts'll burn there. Up here with them. Did you post the letter, Mr Donnelly?

JOHNNY: It got dark, and just after dark, after we had tea, John Donnelly put the harness loose on his pony, and he rode off to Will's place at Whalen's Corners to get the cutter.

CHORUS: Seven o'clock (clock)

JOHN: (on hobbyhorse) As I went up to the Town Line and then down to Whalen's Corners the moon went behind a cloud. I tied up my horse in Will's stable, the one next to the locked one where he kept his stallion.

WILLIAM's house at Whalen's Corners should be established in front of the closed curtain.

CHORUS: *Humming until WILLIAM's speech*

NORAH: Through this doorway my brother-in-law John came into our house. Just after dark. I went to bed about nine. Will and John stayed up talking with their friend, Martin Hogan. John was to sleep closest of all to this door.

CHORUS: Midnight, midnight (clock)

WILLIAM: Gentlemen, I'm winding the clock, (he winds up the gramophone whose chuff-chuff sound continues until the end of this act) and then I'm retiring. Talking about the Vigilantes or the Secret People or the Happy Gang as I

531

prefer to call them is never as much fun as slumber. Norah's been in bed these last three hours.

NORAH: Give the men the buffalo robe. It's cold in that room, Will

JOHN: Good night, Will. Hey, Martin, what're you putting your mitts on for?

MARTIN: I'm staying the night at Morkin's, Jack. We're threshing there tomorrow.

JOHN: Martin, it's all hours and Mrs Morkin's got all those children, wake one up and the whole house wakes up, poor woman, stay with us, Martin. Will, tell him to stay the night.

WILLIAM: I did, in there Martin. Goodnight.

MARTIN: Lots of fresh air in here. John Donnelly, there's someone cut off a swatch of your hair lately.

JOHN: Good night Martin. (*Looks at him. As in the case of TOM's girl, people are getting relics of the DONNELLY boys while there is still time.*) I went right to sleep. But when you sleep there's a part of yourself that wakes up, the cat's whisker two miles long inside your brains comes twitching out fishing and although you are asleep it roams the yard and road outside Will's house, then the fields so that deep as the dreamsea was that waved over me I knew that something was wrong. There were no dogs barking in Biddulph, but the dogs in Blanshard were, why? Someone is coming up the road to spy on us. At one o'clock part of me knew already that a tall narrow light had sprung up over my father's house and that mother and father were walking in a fiery furnace. A greasy, sweaty blood ball of (*We see rifle-bearing silhouettes waiting at the door.*) humanity was rolling towards us now and at a quarter to two early ones were whispering to each other

CARROLL: Get the stallion. When he hears it kicking he'll come running out. (*Use hobbyhorse head for stallion*)

JOHN: But Will's sleep was too deep for their line, my sleep began to flow back and more and more of me knew that they wanted my brother Will to come to this door. It mustn't be Norah because her brother, John, and three other men were pointing at the door with guns, no — it's the Cripple they want, my lame brother I love with all my heart, and I swam up on top of the dreamriver and made my eyes open

MARKSEY: Give over that. You'll never wake him up that way. Call him by name.

CARROLL: Kick at the door. Fire, fire. Open the door Will. Fire, fire. Open the door, Will

JOHN: I got up out of bed, I began to open the inner door, they had opened the outer one, and I said: I wonder who's hollering fire and rapping at the door? ///// Will. Will. I'm shot and may the Lord have mercy on my soul.

MACDONALD: Brother-in-law is easy at last.

CARROLL: What next?

MARTIN: Don't move Will, it's you they want and they think they got you.

MARTIN and NORAH drag in JOHN and place candle in his hand. WILL walks down stage towards us and draws aside an invisible curtain which is repeated by a curtain motion upstage revealing just disappearing vigilantes.

WILL: When I woke up to John's voice, then the shots ///// I reached up to the window and pulled the curtain aside. I saw Carroll's hand and heard my brother-in-law's voice.

MACDONALD: Brother-in-law is easy at last.

CARROLL: What next?

NORAH: *(Rises from JOHN's side and screams at the door)* Murderers!

533

WILL: When I raised the curtain again they were gone. *(Clock strikes two.)* It was all over in five minutes.

NORAH: As I walk back and forth the window gets bigger. Then smaller.

Clock strikes the hours.

WILL: Just before daybreak it began to snow.

NORAH: At eight o'clock Will asked a neighbour to drive over to his father's place and see if anything was the matter. If not — to tell them that John was dead.

WILL: I stayed at home till my neighbour came back.

NEIGHBOUR: Will Donnelly, your mother and father are dead. Last night. They were all murdered last night and their house set fire upon them. *(We look directly at WILLIAM's face.)*

Train whistle. WILL DONNELLY is remembering a train whistle a very long time ago when his father came home to them one summer evening after being seven years away.

ALL: End of Act Two

ACT III

We open in the graveyard of St Patrick's, Biddulph in the early 1970's. On the anniversary of the murder it is the custom for crowds of people in cars to come up, park and wait for a possible ghostly appearance at the Donnelly grave. In the centre of the stage stand the ghosts of MR & MRS DONNELLY behind two cloths representing their first and second gravestone.

CHORUS: February the third, 1974. St Blaise's Day falls on Shrove Tuesday this year.

A car radio blares out "At the Hop"

CHORUS: This is the night the Donnellys got killed.

GIRL: Oh Verne, let's drive up to Lucan and go out to the graveyard and see if we can see their ghosts.

OLD MAN: I am the sexton of St Patrick's Church and I draw my churchyard with a stick on this floor. Yes, the Donnellys are buried here.

GIRL: Tonight's the night they killed the Donnellys.

CHORUS: There are seventy five cars parked by the churchyard with two hundred people in them waiting for midnight when Mrs Donnelly's ghost will appear.

BOYS: Waiting for what?

CHORUS: For the Donnellys to appear. Smoking dope, drinking beer. Listening to our car radios. Blowing our horns. Hey. Look at him jump over the fence.

OLD MAN: Get out of the churchyard. Stay clear off that gate. Get down off of that fence.

BOY: Hey. Look at the old guy after him with the rake.

CHORUS: Thaw. Violent thunder. *(Use camera flash cubes)* Ice on the roads. Rain.

BOY: He's got to the grave.

GIRL: The old fellow's slipped.

BOY: He's standing on top of it.

YOUTH (TOM): *(in hockey windbreaker)* Johannah and James Donnelly. Rise up. Rise up and show yourselves. *(He falls down drunk close by the gravestone.)*

CHORUS: February the third, 1974. St Blaise's Day falls on Shrove Tuesday this year.

CHORUS (PART): This is the night the Donnellys got killed.

GIRL: Oh Verne, let's drive up to Lucan and go out to the graveyard and see if we can see their ghosts.

OLD MAN: I am the caretaker of St Patrick's churchyard and with this stick I draw my churchyard on this floor. Get out of the churchyard. Stay clear of that gate. Stop taking pictures of me. Get out of the churchyard.

Use flashlights for headlights, kids' wagons. Underneath banners that have the 2 inscriptions on them lie the DONNELLYS.

MRS DONNELLY: Who's that walking over our grave? Who's that screeching for us to rise from our tombs.

MR & MRS DONNELLY: Well, young fellow, you may get the worst thing in the world and that is to get what you want.

MRS DONNELLY: Get that false gravestone off us. — We weren't died, we were killed, we were murdered. That's better now heave that one up too till we get at this young bastard. Grab him Jim. For I am buried here, oh yes, with my husband and my sons, they buried what's left of me. Here's the coffin four of us lie in. Hear our bones rattling? *(They have grabbed the drunken youth and are turning him into their son, TOM.)*

OLD MAN: Get out of the churchyard! Get down off that fence. Stay clear of that gate.

MR DONNELLY: But they never finished the older gravestone that says we were murdered. My remaining sons wanted to put on top of it a statue of my son Tom whom they handcuffed before they butchered him. My youngest son in only his shirt sleeves, blood spurting from his wounds and on his strong arms they, all twenty of them were that afraid of — HANDCUFFS!

YOUTH: Let me go you old bugger. Keep your hands off me. I dreamt then that they handcuffed me, you old harridan, don't look at me with your hell eyes.

MRS DONNELLY: Yes, we've handcuffed you and we've handcuffed their church, they dare not leave it open because James Donnelly what happened the last time they did so.

MR DONNELLY: Toughs from Grand Bend came in with their trulls in search of us into the house of God and desecrated the altar.

MRS DONNELLY: And we've handcuffed their priest. Are you there, priest — no, the presbytery's not a good place to sleep at nights for there's a certain unused rocking chair that all by itself . . .

YOUTH: Let me go, please let me go. Take the handcuffs off me.

MR DONNELLY: Make up your mind what you want then, soft tough, is it too much when the curtain between you and us, between your life and our life, between life and death starts wavering and swaying and

MRS DONNELLY: drawing back like a foreskin from the thigh of demon lover Christ himself.

MR DONNELLY: like the mighty eyelid of God the Father's eye.

MRS DONNELLY: like the wind from the mouth of the Holy Ghost that flutters her veil as she speaks:

BOTH: UNDO THE HANDCUFFS, Indeed! First unlock the handcuffs in your mind that make you see us as

MR DONNELLY: that fierce harridan

MRS DONNELLY: that old barnburner!

BOTH: We weren't like that/this! I take you by the hair down into our grave and beyond where

MRS DONNELLY: you'll be our son Tom

MR DONNELLY: you'll see that

BOTH: I was a child once, a spring.
(These speeches involve fluttering, waving curtains and the movement of the ghosts behind the gravestone curtains.)
I became a river when my body united with his/hers
From that river came seven sons and one daughter
We were all right, they said, if you left us alone

But there was something about us that made people
Never able to leave us alone and we fought them
Until the river fell into the sea of Death and the Sun of Hell
Changed us into the fog outside this winter night
With our handcuffed boy —

& TOM:

look we are everywhere
In the clouds, in the treebranch, in the puddle,
There. Here. In your fork. In your minds.
Your lungs are filled with us, we are the air you breathe
And you say —

MARY DONOVAN & CHORUS: *(in nightgown. A window is held in front of her. She is watching the DONNELLY house go up in flames. A fierce red glow lights up her face.)*
Mary Donovan
                        Watches   the Fiery Furnace

MARY, MR & MRS DONNELLY & TOM:
There burn four of her neighbours
James and Judith Donnelly, Tom and Bridget

MARY:
Kerosene angel do not forget
To grind my enemies all to dust
In your fiery furnace, fiery furnace, fiery furnace &c.

MARY: *(knocking)* Go see who's knocking at our door, Bill.

BILL: *(her husband who seems slow to understand the delights of revenge)* Can't you tear yourself away from that window?

MARY: I won't stop watching, Bill Donovan, till there's nothing more to watch.

BILL: What are you looking at anyhow — just a house burning.

MARY: Oh no, Bill. It's not just a house burning. Inside that house is the woman who once said that my mother was so fat she had to be pulled in and out of a bed with a pulley. There goes the chimney, Bill! And did you get him, Jim?

he enters still excited from what he has lately accomplished

CARROLL: Yes, we got him.

MARY: So Cripple's dead. How'd you get him?

CARROLL: *(laughing hysterically)* We called Fire at his door. Will, Will, Fire. fire. And he came and we shot him.

BILL: How'd you get them over here, Jim?

CARROLL: Handcuffs. We handcuffed them.

BILL: Jim, you're weeping.

CARROLL: It's the first time I've wept since my mother died. I swore then — a lad of ten that I was — that I'd not weep again till the night I got them for her

BILL: The flames from their house are reflected in your tears, James Carroll.

even in death the DONNELLYS still offend

CARROLL: Will their house never stop burning? How can I get any sleep with it so bright all over your house, Mary and Bill?

MARY: You'd better get some sleep, Jim. You have to be at the hearing over at Granton by ten, don't you?

BILL: *(stupidly)* What's the use of your going to that. They won't be there.

CARROLL: Bill Donovan, it'd be just like the Donnellys not to show up, wouldn't it. Just like them

MARY: Jim has to go to the hearing, Bill. Otherwise people would say he knew they were dead. Bill, tie this around Jim's face. *(She gives BILL a long white bandage)* Lead him off to his bed. Lead him off to his bed. *(He is led off with his eyes bandaged.)*

CHORUS:
   Pillar of fire turns to pillar of smoke
   Pillar of fire, pillar of smoke

LINDSAY: I am one of the magistrates in the Marksey fire hearing. Squire Lindsay. Just before ten I showed up at Middleton's Hotel. The Donnellys had not arrived as yet. Way off to the west of the village there was a pillar of smoke. Good morning, Cassleigh, Carroll. Mr Pat Whalen, what are you doing here?

WHALEN: Ask Jim Carroll, Squire Lindsay.

CARROLL: Pat's wife, Mr Lindsay, I've heard heard old Mrs Donnelly making some more threats about Marksey's barns and I came to Pat's house with a subpoena but Pat here saw fit to wave an axe at me when all the world knows his old woman is dying to testify. So — Pat is up for assaulting me.

LINDSAY: Mr Whalen

WHALEN: Squire Lindsay

LINDSAY: You live across from the Donnellys, don't you?

WHALEN: I do that

LINDSAY: Any signs of them turning out. They're late and that's not their custom

WHALEN: Oh, sir, it will be their custom this morning.

CARROLL: I wonder what can be keeping them?

CASSLEIGH: What do you mean, Pat, it will be their custom this morning.

WHALEN: I mean that smoke over there. Their place got burnt down last night.

CARROLL: Cold day to be without a house

CASSLEIGH: Seen Tom and the old man go by in the sleigh yesterday. Going fast. Drunk. They'd quarrel among themselves a lot.

WHALEN: Yes, they'll quarrel no more then. Yes, they're dead. I saw their bodies burning. But not all of them that were in the house last night lie there with it snowing on them. Yes, there was a boy with them last night and he got out of the house and came over to our place sometime after one o'clock. In his bare feet.

CARROLL: A boy. What was this boy doing there, Pat?

WHALEN: Cassleigh, you didn't see him in the sleigh, did you, because he was there, still going to haul me up for waving the axe, Jim, because that boy was sleeping with Old Donnelly and he says there was a man came into the house to arrest the Donnellys and then there were thirty men came in and beat them to death, but he was hiding under the bed.

CARROLL: Pat, what will you be telling us next. Did he recognize the man?

CASSLEIGH: Where is this little firebug at this very moment, Pat?

They elbow WHALEN out of the room.

CARROLL: Join us at the bar, Squire Lindsay.

LINDSAY: I couldn't take my eyes off their sleeves. They hadn't had time to change their shirts yet. *(CARROLL and CASSLEIGH re-emerge from behind the curtain with terror on their faces; something has scared them & they are getting away from it!)*

LINDSAY: What's the matter, gentlemen?

Enter WILLIAM DONNELLY who should play the Prosecuting Attorney's role in the coming trial scenes since in real life it was his intelligence that directed the prosecution

WILLIAM: The matter, Squire Lindsay, is that when they came into the bar here they learned from the boy they sent over to spy on my house this morning that they didn't succeed in shooting me last night. My brother, not his brother. I'm very much alive still, and very much in their minds.

something darkens the stage

LINDSAY: A wind from the west came up and drove the pillar of smoke over the village darkening the sun. The bodies of Mr and Mrs Donnelly lay open to the sky until someone came to rake them up.

We now move to the ruins of the DONNELLY homestead repre-sented by four stones. A long line of people representing the endless line of sightseers' cutters and sleighs that went by in the days after the murder circle the four stones. Sometimes when KEEFE's back is turned they snatch at a souvenir, i.e. — a skull, a teapot lid or a piece of Mrs DONNELLY's stove. MR KEEFE is collecting the bones of the DONNELLYS with the same sort of rake that the sexton held at the opening of this act.

KEEFE: When I, Jim Keefe, told Father Connolly at Christ-mas that I would give Jim Donnelly rides in my cart as long as I had a horse to drive him I never thought I would be doing this.

Some choral funeral service round here: Amen or Ora pro nobis

PRIEST: Dear Friends, you are in the presence of one of the most solemn scenes which I have ever witnessed, but I have witnessed many a solemn scene, but never like this. I am heart broken . . . I never suspected. *(He is agitated, yet strangely calm.)* The guilty men who imbued their hand in innocent blood will have to answer for this awful crime before the living God.

In other words on one level we are proceeding through the funeral service and its images sift in with images from the trials &c.

542

KEEFE: Yes, before the living God, I seen Marksey ride by Donnelly's gate last night with a sword wrapped up in a blanket

NEIGHBOUR: Oh Mr Keefe, you should never tell that to anyone.

KEEFE: I should tell if it were my own son and he were to hang for it. Hhrrout of that, stranger, don't touch the bones of the dead. Before the living God, I am their only friend it seems left to guard their bones and there's not enough of me.

PRIEST: I believed that there were men who would give a man a clout when half drunk in Biddulph but I never thought that they could commit such a Oh! God in Heaven, who would have thought it would I can't say anymore *(He falls face down on the altar)*

PATRICK: *(standing up in the congregation)* Father Connolly, I wish you to give a more detailed account.

PRIEST: What do you ask me, Patrick Donnelly?

PATRICK: I would like you to tell the whole matter, giving particulars more fully.

PRIEST: Well, perhaps it would be better for me to tell. I remember saying that and then — I told this and I told that it was reported in the newspapers, but to tell *(exaggerated gesture using the curtain)* the whole matter, Oh God in Heaven, no, Patrick Donnelly, you don't know what you are asking — no, no — to circumcize this veil that hides each and every one of us from each other and from God?

He slides away from view behind the curtain. Suddenly we are in court & listening to MARY DONOVAN's testimony; she wears loud clothes, an awful bonnet and is supremely smiling & confident.

MARY: Yes, I am Mary Donovan, wife of Bill Donovan. Yes, my house is near the Donnellys

LAWYER: Mrs. Donovan, is there anything to intercept the view between your house and the Donnellys?

MARY: Not a thing. We were next neighbours on the same side of the road. On the night of the murder James Carroll stayed at our house. He went to bed before we did and did not get up till after we did

CHIEF: I am the Chief of Police for London. On the day following the murder I asked you if your bedroom door was shut.

MARY: Yes, but I could hear if they went out.

LAWYER: Did you sleep sound last night, Mrs Donovan?

MARY: I slept very sound, always do nights. That's what I go to bed for.

LAWYER: Did you hear any noise in the night?

MARY: No, nor anything about the fire until we looked over in the morning.

LAWYER: Surely Mrs Thompson, if James Carroll's brother says that he woke up at one o'clock having heard the clock strike would he not have seen the fire at Donnellys' through that window. Your honour, the window in question looked directly over to the Donnelly homestead. It would seem to me that when you see a house burning *(A model of the DONNELLYS' curtilage — house, outbuildings and barn — is brought in and set down.)*

MARY: Ah, his brother didn't want to bother him about a little thing like that.

JUDGE: May I ask this witness a question? Mrs Donovan, I suppose when you heard the next day that not three hundred feet away four people had been murdered the night before — I suppose you were greatly alarmed?

MARY: Well, no — nothing extra.

CHIEF: The first time I questioned her there was nothing down in front of this window which overlooks the Donnellys place. (*The window in question is held up.*)

MARY: What was that question again, Chief?

CHIEF: Anyone lying on this bed could have seen the fire at one o'clock.

MARY: — Not if they put up a blanket. Maybe they put up a blanket. (*She places a towel across the window.*)

CHORUS: The Queen against James Carroll. For the murder of Julia Donnelly . . .

FRAMER: I am a house framer by occupation. This is the Donnelly house ten years ago I built — one and a half storey log house.

JUDGE: Who were the neighbours to this house?

4 NEIGHBOURS: We are

Have the model set fire to and burning now by two Vigilante "ladies" with torches.

JUDGE: And what did you do the night Neighbour Donnelly was murdered and his house burned over his head.

4 NEIGHBOURS: Our houses were, our houses still are only a few rods, a few yards away

CAIN: John Cain. I live on the south half of lot 18. I heard no noise all that night. There's been a good many fires in that neighbourhood and sometimes people get into trouble by being too quick to turn out to a fire.

JUDGE: After you heard of their murder did you go over to the Donnellys?

RYDER: No. I had some potatoes to take in and I went to take them in.

JUDGE: Even though you knew that four of your neighbours had been killed and their house burned, you never went to see anything about it?

Four neighbours turn their back on a blazing house

RYDER: No, we had our work to do.

WHALENS: Patrick Whalen, Ann Whalen

ANN: We live just across the road from the Donnellys.

& PAT: Concession 7, lot 18.

ANN: I was waked up by someone
rapping on the kitchen door.
Who is it?

JOHNNY: Johnny Connors.

PAT: Who?

JOHNNY: Call up the old man and the boys and quench the fire at Donnellys'. A lot of men — dressed in women's clothes and set fire to the two beds.

PAT: It's not a fire . . . seems more like a lamp burning.

JOHNNY: A lot of men came over

PAT: Do you be dreaming boy? Why you're walking in your sleep.

JOHNNY: Mr Whalen, I'm not. Mr & Mrs Donnelly. Tom murdered. Might still be alive.

ANN: Pat, don't listen to him. You're a smart little fire bug. Don't call up the boys. They might get killed.

PAT: Annie, his little feet are frozen. Now I'll get the fire going here and just get these poor little bare feet warm. Put them up on the oven door. That's the way. Why you're right. It is a fire. Annie. I'll go over and tell Jack.

LAWYER: Did you know anybody there, Johnny Connors?

JOHNNY: Yes. Jim Carroll.

ANN: *(slaps him)* Be careful of what you're saying, boy. You mightn't be telling the truth. We might all be brought to court and I wouldn't want that.

CHORUS: It's a dangerous thing to find a dead man.

LAWYER: Mrs Donovan again, please.

MARY: William Donnelly? I can't think of anyone I hate more in the township. *(She leans down over the model house & sings:)*
Cain killed Abel, Donnelly killed Farrell
Your old man killed Farrell, Will
Where's your father they asked young Cripple
He's down at Kingston on the old treadmill

LAWYER: Mrs Donovan, at the preliminary hearings the Chief of Police said that the window overlooking the Donnelly house had no curtain.

MARY: No, he could not have said that. Because over that window there was always a curtain of double thickness. I put it up there when they were sowing their fall wheat to keep out the rain and the snow. So neither we nor James Carroll could have possibly seen their

LAWYER: Then if the Police Chief says that the curtain was not there at his first visit, but only appeared some time afterwards, he says what is not true?

MARY: No man can say I was mistaken in that. No one lying on that bed could see the Donnelly house burning down because it was a double thickness double thickness double thickness double thickness

CLERK: The next witness, Johnny Connors.

LAWYER: Coming to the boy Connors I would ask you to weigh very carefully his evidence because it is the main upon this child's

MARKSEY: That son of a bitch, he'd swear to anything.

All the actors available get on their hands & knees and crawl downstage to represent the pigs in the DONNELLYS' barn waiting for their nightly feed.

JOHNNY: After tea, after John went over to Will's, Tom and I did the chores.

TOM: Here Johnny. Take my whip. I'll show you how to keep the pigs back with one hand while your other gets the feed in the trough. Otherwise they'll get the pail away on you. Hrrout of that! Get back there you fat devil. Now Johnny, climb up in the loft and throw down straw till I tell you enough . . . enough. That's for the cattle. Always check the blanket on my horse, Indian. Because he's always getting it off. There. Johnny will take good care of yous all.

JOHNNY: Then we went back into the house. Then we sat for a while. Mrs Donnelly was reading the paper. Bridget was knitting. Tom said

TOM: Bridget, get some more apples for Johnny. I can tell he's thinking of them down there in the cellar. Aren't you, Johnny?

MR DONNELLY is kneeling at a chair saying his evening prayers.

JOHNNY: Then when we got the apples eat, the old man said his prayers.

MR DONNELLY: World without end. Amen.

JOHNNY: Then he said

MR DONNELLY: Take off your boots, Johnny. You'll sleep alongside of me tonight.

TOM: Johnny's staying out here with me, Father.

MR DONNELLY: More room in my four poster, Johnny.

JOHNNY: So I did. Mr Donnelly got into the bed first. I climbed over him. As I was falling asleep I thought I heard someone in the kitchen with the old woman, Tom and Bridget . . . I think it was Jim Feeny. Then I went to sleep.

MRS DONNELLY: Are you off to the dance tonight, Jim Feeny?

JIM: *(wearing a peculiar coat)* Mrs Donnelly. Only I can't make up my mind which one to go to.

MRS DONNELLY: Tomorrow's Ash Wednesday. Don't the dances and weddings come thick and fast just before it comes. Well, there was a carnival you might have frolicked at up at Parkhill last Saturday.

TOM: Jim, you should wear that coat to the carnival. I didn't recognize you in it I swear to God you've never worn that before. At least I've never seen it on your back before.

JIM: Oh — I've just got this coat, Tom. Got it over in Michigan. Johnny not in tonight?

BRIDGET: He's gone to bed with Uncle Jim.

JIM: You're right Bridget, it is all hours. I'll be saying goodnight to yous all.

MRS DONNELLY: Come here, Jim Feeny. Come and let me look at your wrists. Where did you get that nasty red welt around your neck? Bridget, bring this man a cup of tea, he's cold and trembly.

JIM: Oh no thank you, Mrs Donnelly. I was only trying to get my cap out of the threshing machine a couple of days ago at Morkin's the silly old cap had blown off my head into all those moving up and down parts, for shure I didn't want to see my cap turned into a bushel of wheat, eh Bridget, and goodnight, Mrs Donnelly.

TOM: Drink the tea! My mother says you're to have a cup of tea before you leave the premises.

MRS DONNELLY: Tom, don't be so harsh with your friend. You might roll up your sleeve and show Bridget how you've got Jim's name carved on your arm, and he's got

549

your name on his arm. It's years ago I caught them doing that out on the door step. Jim Feeny these red marks about your wrists I understand, but

TOM: Mother, why don't we undress him, take off his shirt and we'll give him a scratch and bruise catechism.

MRS DONNELLY: Jim Feeny, look me in the eye.

JIM: You know I can't do that, Tom's mother. If only I could.

MRS DONNELLY: You wore handcuffs for our sake, who made you wear rope for us too?

JIM: Mrs Donnelly.

MRS DONNELLY: She didn't hand you lately and give you a red necklace. No. Who? I know who — them. But why? Jim Feeny. All your life Jim Feeny you've been handcuffed and tethered by one fear or another. Tell me. Speak out! James Feeny, is it true what your mother once told me that you're still a child, that you can't raise your arms over your head. Try. Try. (*she raises her arms but he cannot quite raise his*)

JIM: My nerves. My nerves.

MRS DONNELLY: Tom, take care of your friend.

TOM: What's the matter, Jim. Get hold of yourself. Stay the night and talk it over with me.

They are now in front of the model. We should glimpse MRS DONNELLY checking doors and saying her prayers before retiring. The curtains close.

JIM: I'm promised I'd drop over at the Whalens' and walk Temperance Trehy home, Tom.

TOM: Oh, it's Temperance Trehy is it. I wish you luck there Jim, shure she was born with her legs crossed.

JIM: Tom she'll laugh at me in this coat. Could I leave it here and pick it up later on?

TOM: Shure. Pick it up tomorrow.

JIM: Tom, it's the sort of night when it's cold enough to wear the damn thing all the way home, but not to visit across the road.

TOM: Come back this night, Jim, and get it then. I'll be in bed though. We're up early tomorrow to go to the trial.

JIM: No Tom, I wouldn't want to wake yous. Give it here.

TOM: Jim, I'll leave the kitchen door on the latch. Mother always bolts it, but after she's gone to bed, I'll fix it so you can let yourself in when we're all asleep. Don't make any noise though.

JIM: Fine, Tom. Fine. I'll tiptoe so you'll never hear me. Goodnight, Tom.

TOM: Goodnight Jim.

JIM: Goodbye Tom.

JOHNNY: Then I went to sleep and between twelve and two o'clock a man came into the house to arrest the old man and Jack.

LAWYER: Today in court do you see this man?

JOHNNY: Yes, there he is. James Carroll.

MR DONNELLY: What have you got against me now, Jim?

CARROLL: I've got another charge against you and Jack. Where is he?

MR DONNELLY: He's not in.

CARROLL: Where'd you say he was?

MR DONNELLY: Didn't I tell you, he's not in. Hold the light now till I dress myself. Judy, where's my coat?

MRS DONNELLY: Bridget, up and light the fire.

CARROLL is whistling the "St Patrick was a gentleman" song.

JOHNNY: I said, "Here's your coat, Mr Donnelly. I'm using it for a pillow."

BRIDGET: Uncle Jim, could I have your knife to make shavings with to light the fire?

MR DONNELLY: Tom, are you handcuffed?

"Ladies" are already prowling about.

TOM: Yes, he thinks he's smart. Read me your warrant Carroll.

CARROLL: There's lots of time for that

In shadow we see the confused forms of a massacre, what a child might see from under a bed. In front of the curtain four "ladies" beat the stones with pickaxes.

JOHNNY: Then a whole crowd jumped in and commenced hammering them with sticks and spades. Tom ran out into the front room and got outside. Bridget ran upstairs and I ran after her. She shut the door and I ran back again in the room and got under the bed behind a clothes (*TOM should pick up his stone & run away with it. We see BRIDGET on top of one of the stepladders.*) basket. I could only see their feet, but I got a look at some faces by
They carried Tom inside the house again. They said (*TOM is dragged behind the curtain again.*)

MARKSEY: Hit that fellow with a spade and break his skull open.

CARROLL: Here — hold the candle here. Get those handcuffs off of him

MACDONALD: Where's the girl.

JOHNNY: Then one of them said, Where's the girl?

Quite quickly we are at the trial again. CARROLL collapses in front of the curtain.

552

DEFENCE LAWYER: My Lord, we crave the court's permission to allow the prisoner to retire. He has taken ill.

JUDGE: What does the Gaol Surgeon say?

DOCTOR: The prisoner is suffering from heart disease, my Lord, and is too ill to attend today.

JUDGE: *(pause)* Very well. The court stands adjourned until 9:30 a.m. tomorrow. *(CARROLL proceeds over to BRIDGET and takes the stone away from her.)*

BRIDGET: When I got upstairs I went to the window and knelt by it hoping to see a star if the one cloud that covered the whole sky now would lift. I knew they would come to get me and they did. They dragged me down the stairs. The star came closer as they beat me with the flail that unhusks your soul. At last I could see the star close by; it was my aunt and uncle's burning house in Ontario where — and in that star James and Judith and Tom and Bridget Donnelly may be seen walking as in a fiery furnace calmly and happily forever. Free at last.

The O'HALLORANS dart out from behind the curtains.

MRS O'HALLORAN: The boy is lying, lying, lying when he says our hired man was present at the house.

JUDGE: Mrs O'Halloran, if you do not keep quiet how would you like it if I put you in jail for twenty-four hours.

MRS O'HALLORAN: Put me in jail for twenty-four years I will have my say. Jim Purtell our hired man could not have left our house without upsetting a chair which my father-in-law always puts against the front door.

DEFENCE LAWYER: *(blocking out the JUDGE with a skilful tug at the curtain.)* Try that Mr O'Halloran, if you please.

MR O'HALLORAN: The boy is lying, lying, lying when he says our hired man was present at the house.

DEFENCE LAWYER: No. Mrs O'Halloran says it with more conviction. You see we've got to break the jury's trust in the boy's testimony. As one of your defence lawyers let me tell you that unless, O'Halloran, you put more conviction into your statements Carroll's bound to hang, so it's Mrs O'Halloran.

MR O'HALLORAN: *(he's getting mad!)* Why don't you get up and testify yourself, McWhin, sure you're the lawyer that helped us plan so many of the things, but your foresight didn't deal with a boy under a bed.

DEFENCE LAWYER: Well, patience. You see our difficulty is, O'Halloran, that the boy is telling the truth. And the jury knows that. But we have to . . .

MR O'HALLORAN: *(angrily shouting)* Johnny Connors is not telling the truth. He's lying, he's been posted by Bill Donnelly, he's

DEFENCE LAWYER: Bravo! That's it. Now don't be afraid to make a scene in court. Before they can stop you, Mr & Mrs O'Halloran — you should plant a few ideas in everybody's heads. Let's have it all again. *(Draws curtains aside so as to reveal the Judge.)*

MR O'HALLORAN: My wife's statement I beg leave to corroborate and if this boy's testimony is wrong with regard to one person he says he saw at the Donnelly house

MRS O'HALLORAN: They were not people, everyone knows they were fond of animal fighting among themselves, some of them got drunk, a lamp upset — if a mob came to the house as the child says then why weren't the barns burnt down too? Why just the house?

MR O'HALLORAN: Many agree with the very believable theory that William Donnelly killed them. Half of the farmers in Oxford County believe this.

MRS O'HALLORAN: What about the pair of pants in the basin of blood found in my back yard on a post. Well, with this a very laughable story is connected; we took the basin to a doctor in Granton to have it analyzed and it was, he said, red dye. Red dye not blood.

JOHNNY: I am not lying. I saw him there. *(JOHNNY yanks the curtains apart revealing people who seem involved in odd activities. They start when the curtain reveals their tricks.)* I saw him, and him and Mr & Mrs O'Halloran — my own godfather and godmother as a matter of fact — I saw your hired man there and — but what is one clap of two hands against the thunder of hundreds of stamping feet?

A stamping & clapping contest between the O'HALLORANS & the CONNORS. The others stamp too & march out with the model.

JUDGE: There had to be a second trial because the jury disagreed. Four for hanging Carroll. One undecided, and seven for acquittal.

It is years afterward. Son and mother by the fireplace.

THERESA: Johnny Connors, what are you thinking of, my God what are you doing with that toy train over and over again playing in front of the fire, you're a bit full grown to be still playing with such a toy.

JOHNNY: Do you remember the O'Hallorans, mother, and how they fought so against my testimony that Jim Purtell had been at the Donnelly's killing them?

THERESA: They were such a proud pair of them with their rich farm and their children all lawyers and doctors, oh dear, so respectable looking.

JOHNNY: They were lying. I used to watch them in court and think — you're not really respectable at all, Mr & Mrs O'Halloran.

THERESA: What does that matter — they looked so. Well. *(The O'HALLORANS with hobbyhorsemen prance through.)* Look at them the proud ones that Christmas their sleigh prancing down the snowy roads.

JOHNNY: The last time I saw the Donnellys — they were lying bleeding on the floor, smashed and battered. As I fled their burning house my bare foot stepped on Mrs Donnelly's face. Oh and the O'Hallorans had led the pack of the highflyers against the Donnellys. But I see them triumphant over their enemies. I see the ghosts of Mr & Mrs Donnelly, not their ghosts — them *(JOHNNY should begin to walk about here — glorying in his Donnellys. MR & MRS DONNELLY come out from behind the curtains; well, their ghosts do and they are waiting for somebody.)* See them come from wherever the dead wait in fire or flood or cloud or field — see them waiting in the ditch by the road where the O'Hallorans will come by. *(The O'HALLORANS drive up & the DONNELLYS hold their horses' reins so that the sleigh is pinned to the railway tracks. A train runs over them, but a baby is thrown free.)*

FARM WIFE: Mr & Mrs O'Halloran were coming to have dinner with us. *(The farm wife puts 4 plates on the altar.)* I had finished setting the table, it was Christmas 1880, dark and snowing heavily outside and I thought the train whistled oddly. There was a strange sound, the brakeman of the 6 o'clock freight train came to our door

BRAKEMAN: Missus, I'm the brakeman of the freight train's just had an accident at the crossing over there.

FARM WIFE: My God, what's that baby you hold in your arms!

BRAKEMAN: Missus, I guess whoever was driving that sleigh we hit got trapped on the tracks and when we hit them the baby was thrown clear into the snow.

FARM WIFE: This baby is my brother's youngest, Denis O'Halloran. I sewed this baby's petticoat, my God man are all the people on the sleigh dead then. All the O'Hallorans save this baby?

THERESA: You make my blood run cold, Johnny, do you suppose it could be true?

JOHNNY: Country people say the old man and woman then disappeared and that it was revenge on O'Halloran who was the secret leader of the gang that killed them.

THERESA: They say they still walk it's true. Oh that was a good many years ago, Johnny.

JOHNNY: *(coming downstage & facing us with his arms held up)* They held the horses, two strong horses just by with the reins of their eyes, my Mr Donnelly and my Mrs Donnelly. So that at the second trial there was not one O'Halloran left to call me a liar.

FARM WIFE: Take these four plates away, Kitty, and break them. The O'Hallorans and their son and wife will never eat with us again. *(We hear the first plate cracking and so to the others; the fourth is broken at the very end of the play. Organ chord. The coffins are brought in & the funeral service sweeps on to its conclusion.)*

WOMEN: *(sung)* Deliver me, O Lord, from everlasting death on that day of terror.

MEN: Quando caeli movendi sunt et terra

WOMEN: When Thou shalt come to judge the world by fire.

MEN: Dread and trembling have laid hold on me

WOMEN: et timeo, dum discussio venerit at que ventura ira.

MEN: When Thou shalt come to judge the world by fire.

ALL: Kyrie eleison. Christe eleison. Kyrie eleison

PRIEST: Dominus vobiscum *(sprinkling holy water on the coffins. The altar boy lights the candle which will also be used in censing the two closed boxes.)*

ALL: Et cum spiritu tuo.

PRIEST: Oremus.

PRIEST: O lord, do not bring your servants to trial, for no man becomes holy in your sight unless you grant him forgiveness of all his sins . . . By the help of your grace, may they escape the sentence which they deserve, for during their earthly lives, they were signed with the seal of the Holy Trinity: you who live and reign forever and ever.

ALL: Amen.

PRIEST: Pater noster . . . (While he silently prays and moves sprinkling about in the background we are also in the jury-room.)

JUROR #1: How many, Mr Foreman, here believe, just let me poll my fellow jurors, just how many of you believe the boy's testimony?

JUROR #2: And how many of you would hang Carroll even if you saw him doing it?

JUDGE: Gentlemen of the jury

VOICES: Vote for Corcoran or your barns burn.

JURY:

Horace Hyatt	Joe Lamont
B. Francis	Dugal Graham
Jas F. Elliott	Jas A. Waterworth
James Dores	Hopper Ward
Asa Luce	Benjamin Kilburn
John Carrothers	William Hooper

Eleven yeomen and one baker, good men and true of Middlesex County.

JUDGE: Is the prisoner James Carroll guilty or not guilty of having murdered Julia Donnelly? Have you agreed upon your verdict?

JURY: We have.

JUDGE: What say you then, guilty or not guilty?

CARROLL appears behind the jurors.

VOICES: We will visit you at all hours of the night when you least expect it. The only difference between them and mad dogs was in the face. (It is obviously CARROLL who says this.)

JURY: Not guilty.

CARROLL: Before I got out of jail I wrote a song, when we were acquitted we hired an Italian band to go back with us to Lucan on the train. So ladies and gentlemen, when you hear me sing this — there's a harp! *(Mandolin & Piano as in a John McCormack recording.)*

The Vigilant boys, like heroes, from the prison dock will go
When the jury gives their verdict and the world their truth shall know
It is then they'll join their many friends whose hearts will jump with glee
We'll soon be all safe home again, for the Vigilant boys are free.
I now must take my leave of you
Tis all I have to tell
All those who chance to hear my song
I bid you all farewell.
One last thing! I remember the look on Jim Feeny's face when we told him that — Jim we can't pay you the $500. *(This scene is a farewell close up of JAMES CARROLL.)*

PRIEST: . . . And lead us not into temptation

CHORUS: But deliver us from evil.

PRIEST: Requiescant in Pace

CHORUS: Amen

The coffins are taken out of the church into the graveyard.

Sung to*

May the angels take you into paradise
in tuo adventu suscipiant te Martyres
And lead you into the holy city of Jerusalem
Chorus angelorum te suscipiat

Three crouching forms are left on stage — MR & MRS DONNELLY, JAMES CARROLL

And with Lazarus who was poor
Aeternam habeas requiem
May you have everlasting rest.*

The pall bearers, all actors — return to the stage miming the growth of a wheatfield.

March! the snow has gone
The green field John & Tom sowed
Still there green
April! growing again growing again
May! taller and longer with longer
Days until
June and July
July! until ready for harvest
August
Shivering and rippling
cloud shadows summer wind
cloud shadows

A golden light sweeps the stage. We should feel that around the Donnelly farmyard lies a big field of wheat ready for harvest.

CHORUS: To the yard of the house which once had stood by this wheat field came the Donnellys who were left. Patrick Donnelly! tell us now something that you once did or wrote or said. Pat Donnelly. *(pp)* Four stones where there once was a house/home

PAT: *(placing stone)* I, Pat Donnelly, blacksmith from St Catharines, once heard James Feeny say that there was only one thing he ever done that he was sorry for. I asked him what that was. He said he sold Tom Donnelly the best friend he ever he had. *(He begins to beat the handcuffs apart with his hammer.)*

CHORUS: Robert Donnelly

BOB: *(placing stone)* Bob Donnelly, drayman from Glencoe. They told me it was the remains of my father. I knelt down and picked up his heart *(Kisses it then slowly puts it down.)*

CHORUS: William Donnelly

WILLIAM: Weep for one, not for four.

CHORUS: Jennie Currie that once was Jennie Donnelly from St Thomas.

JENNIE: My husband tells me that you, William, have preserved one of the bones of my mother's arms. If so, when you come to St Thomas let him bring it with him, so that I may kiss the loving arm that never failed to throw protection around and provide for all of us in the darkest day of our need.

CHORUS:
Where there once was a house/home, four stones.
Handcuffs, The Donnellys, Part Three

THE END

Middlesex Town,
University College, University of Western Ontario,
London,
Ontario.
January 15, 1976

Sharon Pollock

Blood Relations

EDITOR'S NOTE: Sharon Pollock was born in 1936 in Fredericton, New Brunswick but went to school in the Eastern Townships region of Quebec. Her early work in the theatre as an actress and director was interrupted when she won the Alberta Playwriting Competition with *A Compulsory Option* which was staged by Vancouver's New Play Centre in 1973. That, combined with the sale of radio and television scripts to CBC, launched her vigorous writing career. *Walsh*, her first major drama, was produced by Theatre Calgary in 1973 and in 1974 by the Stratford Festival's Third Stage. Over the next six years, she taught at the University of Alberta and the Banff School of Fine Arts, served as writer-in-residence for Alberta Theatre Projects and wrote four major plays: *The Komagata Maru Incident, One Tiger to a Hill, Generations* and *Blood Relations.* She is currently Artistic Director at Theatre Calgary where her two newest plays, *Whisky Six* and *Doc*, have been staged in the past two years.

An early version of *Blood Relations* was presented in 1976 as "My Name Is Lisbeth" by Douglas College in British Columbia with Sharon Pollock in the role of Lizzie Borden. Rewritten under its present title, it was performed by Edmonton's Theatre Three in 1980 before being staged by Ottawa's National Arts Centre in 1981. Its first publication was by NeWest Press in 1981.

Characters:

MISS LIZZIE	*Who will play BRIDGET, the Irish maid.*
THE ACTRESS	*Who will play LIZZIE BORDEN.*
HARRY	*Mrs. Borden's brother.*
EMMA	*Lizzie's older sister.*
ANDREW	*Lizzie's father.*
ABIGAIL	*Lizzie's step-mother*
DR PATRICK	*The Irish doctor; sometimes THE DEFENSE.*

SETTING

The time proper is late Sunday afternoon and evening, late fall, in Fall River, 1902; the year of the "dream thesis", if one might call it that, is 1892.

The playing areas include (a) within the Borden house: the dining room from which there is an exit to the kitchen; the parlour; a flight of stairs leading to the second floor; and (b) in the Borden yard: the walk outside the house; the area in which the birds are kept.

PRODUCTION NOTE: *Action must be free-flowing. There can be no division of the script into scenes by blackout, movement of furniture, or sets. There may be freezes of some characters while other scenes are being played. There is no necessity to "get people off" and "on" again for, with the exception of The Actress and Miss Lizzie (and Emma in the final scene), all characters are imaginary, and all action in reality would be taking place between Miss Lizzie and The Actress in the dining room and parlour of her home.*

The Defense may actually be seen, may be a shadow, or a figure behind a scrim.

While Miss Lizzie exits and enters with her Bridget business, she is always a presence, observing unobtrusively when as Bridget she takes no part in the action.

ACT ONE

Lights up on the figure of a woman standing centre stage. It is a somewhat formal pose. A pause. She speaks:

> "Since what I am about to say must be but that
> Which contradicts my accusation, and
> The testimony on my part no other
> But what comes from myself, it shall scarce boot me
> To say "Not Guilty".
> But, if Powers Divine
> Behold our human action as they do,
> I doubt not than but innocence shall make
> False accusation blush and tyranny
> Tremble at . . . at . . ."

She wriggles the fingers of an outstretched hand searching for the word.

> "Aaaat" . . . Bollocks!!

She raises her script, takes a bite of chocolate.

> "Tremble at Patience", patience patience! . . .

MISS LIZZIE enters from the kitchen with tea service. THE ACTRESS' attention drifts to MISS LIZZIE. THE ACTRESS watches MISS LIZZIE sit in the parlour and proceed to pour two cups of tea. THE ACTRESS sucks her teeth a bit to clear the chocolate as she speaks:

THE ACTRESS: Which . . . is proper, Lizzie?

MISS LIZZIE: Proper?

THE ACTRESS: To pour first the cream, and add the tea — or first tea and add cream. One is proper. Is the way you do the proper way, the way it's done in circles where it counts?

MISS LIZZIE: Sugar?

THE ACTRESS: Well, is it?

MISS LIZZIE: I don't know, sugar?

THE ACTRESS: Mmmn. *(MISS LIZZIE adds sugar.)* I suppose if we had Mrs. Beeton's *Book of Etiquette*, we could look it up.

MISS LIZZIE: I do have it, shall I get it?

THE ACTRESS: No. . . . You could ask your sister, she might know.

MISS LIZZIE: Do you want this tea or not?

THE ACTRESS: I hate tea.

MISS LIZZIE: You drink it every Sunday.

THE ACTRESS: I drink it because you like to serve it.

MISS LIZZIE: Pppu.

THE ACTRESS: It's true. You've no idea how I suffer from this toast and tea ritual. I really do. The tea upsets my stomach and the toast makes me fat because I eat so much of it.

MISS LIZZIE: Practice some restraint then.

THE ACTRESS: Mmmmm. . . . Why don't we ask your sister which is proper?

MISS LIZZIE: You ask her.

THE ACTRESS: How can I? She doesn't speak to me. I don't think she even sees me. She gives no indication of it. *(She looks up the stairs.)* What do you suppose she does up there every Sunday afternoon?

MISS LIZZIE: She sulks.

THE ACTRESS: And reads the Bible I suppose, and Mrs. Beeton's *Book of Etiquette*. Oh Lizzie. . . . What a long day. The absolutely longest day. . . . When does that come anyway, the longest day?

565

MISS LIZZIE: June.

THE ACTRESS: Ah yes, June. *(She looks at MISS LIZZIE.)* June?

MISS LIZZIE: June.

THE ACTRESS: Mmmmmm. . . .

MISS LIZZIE: I know what you're thinking.

THE ACTRESS: Of course you do. . . . I'm thinking . . . shall I pour the sherry — or will you.

MISS LIZZIE: No.

THE ACTRESS: I'm thinking . . . June . . . in Fall River.

MISS LIZZIE: No.

THE ACTRESS: August in Fall River? *(She smiles. Pause.)*

MISS LIZZIE: We could have met in Boston.

THE ACTRESS: I prefer it here.

MISS LIZZIE: You don't find it . . . a trifle boring?

THE ACTRESS: Au contraire.

MISS LIZZIE gives a small laugh at the affectation.

THE ACTRESS: What?

MISS LIZZIE: I find it a trifle boring . . . I know what you're doing. You're soaking up the ambience.

THE ACTRESS: Nonsense, Lizzie. I come to see you.

MISS LIZZIE: Why?

THE ACTRESS: Because . . . of us. *(Pause.)*

MISS LIZZIE: You were a late arrival last night. Later than usual.

THE ACTRESS: Don't be silly.

MISS LIZZIE: I wonder why.

THE ACTRESS: The show was late, late starting, late coming down.

MISS LIZZIE: And?

THE ACTRESS: And — then we all went out for drinks.

MISS LIZZIE: We?

THE ACTRESS: The other members of the cast.

MISS LIZZIE: Oh yes.

THE ACTRESS: And then I caught a cab . . . all the way from Boston. . . . Do you know what it cost?

MISS LIZZIE: I should. I pay the bill, remember?

THE ACTRESS: *(Laughs.)* Of course. What a jumble all my thoughts are. There're too many words running round inside my head today. It's terrible.

MISS LIZZIE: It sounds it.

Pause.

THE ACTRESS: . . . You know . . . you do this thing . . . you stare at me . . . You look directly at my eyes. I think . . . you think . . . that if I'm lying . . . it will come up, like lemons on a slot machine. *(She makes a gesture at her eyes.)*Tick. Tick . . . *(Pause.)* In the alley, behind the theatre the other day, there were some kids. You know what they were doing?

MISS LIZZIE: How could I?

THE ACTRESS: They were playing skip rope, and you know what they were singing? *(She sings, and claps her hands arhythmically to:)*

"Lizzie Borden took an axe
Gave her mother forty whacks,
When the job was nicely done,
She gave her father forty-one."

MISS LIZZIE: Did you stop them?

THE ACTRESS: No.

MISS LIZZIE: Did you tell them I was acquitted?

THE ACTRESS: No.

MISS LIZZIE: What did you do?

THE ACTRESS: I shut the window.

MISS LIZZIE: A noble gesture on my behalf.

THE ACTRESS: We were doing lines — the noise they make is dreadful. Sometimes they play ball, ka-thunk, ka-thunk, ka-thunk against the wall. Once I saw them with a cat and —

MISS LIZZIE: And you didn't stop them?

THE ACTRESS: That time I stopped them.

THE ACTRESS crosses to table where there is a gramophone. She prepares to play a record. She stops.

THE ACTRESS: Should I?

MISS LIZZIE: Why not?

THE ACTRESS: Your sister, the noise upsets her.

MISS LIZZIE: And she upsets me. On numerous occasions.

THE ACTRESS: You're incorrigible, Lizzie.

THE ACTRESS holds out her arms to MISS LIZZIE. They dance the latest "in" dance, a Scott Joplin composition. They chat while dancing.

THE ACTRESS: . . . Do you think your jawline's heavy?

MISS LIZZIE: Why do you ask?

THE ACTRESS: They said you had jowls.

MISS LIZZIE: Did they.

568

THE ACTRESS: The reports of the day said you were definitely jowly.

MISS LIZZIE: That was ten years ago.

THE ACTRESS: Imagine. You were only thirty-four.

MISS LIZZIE: Yes.

THE ACTRESS: It happened here, this house.

MISS LIZZIE: You're leading.

THE ACTRESS: I know.

MISS LIZZIE: . . . I don't think I'm jowly. Then or now. Do you?

THE ACTRESS: Lizzie? Lizzie.

MISS LIZZIE: What?

THE ACTRESS: . . . did you?

MISS LIZZIE: Did I what?

Pause.

THE ACTRESS: You never tell *me* anything. (*She turns off the music.*)

MISS LIZZIE: I tell you everything.

THE ACTRESS: No you don't!

MISS LIZZIE: Oh yes, I tell you the most personal things about myself, my thoughts, my dreams, my —

THE ACTRESS: But never that one thing. . . . (*She lights a cigarette.*)

MISS LIZZIE: And don't smoke those — they stink.

THE ACTRESS ignores her, inhales, exhales a volume of smoke in MISS LIZZIE's direction.

MISS LIZZIE: Do you suppose . . . people buy you drinks . . . or cast you even . . . because you have a "liaison" with Lizzie Borden? Do you suppose they do that?

THE ACTRESS: They cast me because I'm good at what I do.

MISS LIZZIE: They never pry? They never ask? What's she really like? Is she really jowly? Did she? Didn't she?

THE ACTRESS: What could I tell them? You never tell me anything.

MISS LIZZIE: I tell you everything.

THE ACTRESS: But that! (Pause.) You think everybody talks about you — they don't.

MISS LIZZIE: Here they do.

THE ACTRESS: You think they talk about you.

MISS LIZZIE: But never to me.

THE ACTRESS: Well . . . you give them lots to talk about.

MISS LIZZIE: You know you're right, your mind is a jumble.

THE ACTRESS: I told you so.

Pause.

MISS LIZZIE: You remind me of my sister.

THE ACTRESS: Oh God, in what way?

MISS LIZZIE: Day in, day out, ten years now, sometimes at breakfast as she rolls little crumbs of bread in little balls, sometimes at noon, or late at night . . . "Did you, Lizzie?" "Lizzie, did you?"

THE ACTRESS: Ten years, day in, day out?

MISS LIZZIE: Oh yes. She sits there where Papa used to sit and I sit there, where I have always sat. She looks at me and at her plate, then at me, and at her plate, then at me and then she says "Did you Lizzie?" "Lizzie, did you?"

THE ACTRESS: *(A nasal imitation of EMMA's voice.)* "Did-you-Lizzie — Lizzie-did-you." *(Laughs.)*

MISS LIZZIE: Did I what?

THE ACTRESS: *(Continues her imitation of Emma.)* "You know."

MISS LIZZIE: Well, what do you think?

THE ACTRESS: "Oh, I believe you didn't, in fact I know you didn't, what a thought! After all, you were acquitted."

MISS LIZZIE: Yes, I was.

THE ACTRESS: "But sometimes when I'm on the street . . . or shopping . . . or at the church even, I catch somebody's eye, they look away . . . and I think to myself "Did-you-Lizzie — Lizzie-did-you."

MISS LIZZIE: *(Laughs.)* Ah, poor Emma.

THE ACTRESS: *(Dropping her EMMA imitation.)* Well, did you?

MISS LIZZIE: Is it important?

THE ACTRESS: Yes.

MISS LIZZIE: Why?

THE ACTRESS: I have . . . a compulsion to know the truth.

MISS LIZZIE: The truth?

THE ACTRESS: Yes.

MISS LIZZIE: . . . Sometimes I think you look like me, and you're not jowly.

THE ACTRESS: No.

MISS LIZZIE: You look like me, or how I think I look, or how I ought to look . . . sometimes you think like me . . . do you feel that?

THE ACTRESS: Sometimes.

MISS LIZZIE: *(Triumphant.)* You shouldn't have to ask then. You should know. "Did I, didn't I." You tell me.

THE ACTRESS: I'll tell you what I think. . . . I think . . . that you're aware there is a certain fascination in the ambiguity. . . . You always paint the background but leave the rest to my imagination. Did Lizzie Borden take an axe? . . . If you didn't I should be disappointed . . . and if you did I should be horrified.

MISS LIZZIE: And which is worse?

THE ACTRESS: To have murdered one's parents, or to be a pretentious small-town spinster? I don't know.

MISS LIZZIE: Why're you so cruel to me?

THE ACTRESS: I'm teasing, Lizzie, I'm only teasing. Come on, paint the background again.

MISS LIZZIE: Why?

THE ACTRESS: Perhaps you'll give something away.

MISS LIZZIE: Which you'll dine out on.

THE ACTRESS: Of course. (Laughs.) Come on, Lizzie. Come on.

MISS LIZZIE: A game.

THE ACTRESS: What?

MISS LIZZIE: A game? . . . And you'll play me.

THE ACTRESS: Oh —

MISS LIZZIE: It's your stock in trade, my love.

THE ACTRESS: Alright. . . . A game!

MISS LIZZIE: Let me think . . . Bridget . . . Brrridget. We had a maid then. And her name was Bridget. Oh, she was a great one for stories, stood like this, very straight back, and her hair . . . and there she was in the courtroom in her new dress on the stand. "Do you swear to tell the truth, the whole truth, and nothing but the truth, so help you God?" (Imitates Irish accent.)

"I do sir," she said.

"Would you give the court your name."

"Bridget O'Sullivan, sir."

Very faint echo of the voice of THE DEFENSE under MISS LIZZIE's next line.

"And occupation."

"I'm like what you'd call a maid, sir. I do a bit of everything, cleanin' and cookin'."

The actual voice of THE DEFENSE is heard alone; he may also be seen.

THE DEFENSE: You've been in Fall River how long?

MISS LIZZIE: *(Who continues as BRIDGET, while THE ACTRESS — who will play LIZZIE — observes.)* Well now, about five years sir, ever since I came over. I worked up on the hill for a while but it didn't — well, you could say, suit me, too lah-de-dah — so I —

THE DEFENSE: Your employer in June of 1892 was?

BRIDGET: Yes sir. Mr Borden, sir. Well, more rightly, Mrs Borden for she was the one who —

THE DEFENSE: Your impression of the household?

BRIDGET: Well . . . the man of the house, Mr Borden, was a bit of a . . . tightwad, and Mrs B. could nag you into the grave, still she helped with the dishes and things which not everyone does when they hire a maid. *(HARRY appears on the stairs; approaches BRIDGET stealthily. She is unaware of him.)* Then there was the daughters, Miss Emma and Lizzie, and that day, Mr Wingate, Mrs B.'s brother who'd stayed for the night and was — *(He grabs her ass with both hands. She screams.)*

BRIDGET: Get off with you!

HARRY: Come on, Bridget, give me a kiss!

BRIDGET: I'll give you a good poke in the nose if you don't keep your hands to yourself.

HARRY: Ohhh-hh-hh Bridget!

BRIDGET: Get away you old sod!

HARRY: Haven't you missed me?

BRIDGET: I have not! I was pinched black and blue last time — and I'll be sufferin' the same before I see the end of you this time.

HARRY: (Tilts his ass at her.) You want to see my end?

BRIDGET: You're a dirty old man.

HARRY: If Mr Borden hears that, you'll be out on the street. *Grabs her.* Where's my kiss!

BRIDGET: (Dumps glass of water on his head.) There! (HARRY splutters.) Would you like another? You silly thing you — and leave me towels alone!

HARRY: You've soaked my shirt.

BRIDGET: Shut up and pour yourself a cup of coffee.

HARRY: You got no sense of fun, Bridget.

BRIDGET: Well now, if you tried actin' like the gentleman farmer you're supposed to be, Mr Wingate —

HARRY: I'm tellin' you you can't take a joke.

BRIDGET: If Mr Borden sees you jokin', it's not his maid he'll be throwin' out on the street, but his brother-in-law, and that's the truth.

HARRY: What's between you and me's between you and me, eh?

BRIDGET: There ain't nothin' between you and me.

HARRY: . . . Finest cup of coffee in Fall River.

BRIDGET: There's no gettin' on the good side of me now, it's too late for that.

HARRY: . . . Bridget? . . . You know what tickles my fancy?

BRIDGET: No and I don't want to hear.

HARRY: It's your Irish temper.

BRIDGET: It is, is it? . . . Can I ask you something?

HARRY: Ooohhh — anything.

BRIDGET: *(Innocently.)* Does Miss Lizzie know you're here?. . . I say does Miss Lizzie —

HARRY: Why do you bring her up.

BRIDGET: She don't then, eh? *Teasing.* It's a surprise visit?

HARRY: No surprise to her father.

BRIDGET: Oh?

HARRY: We got business.

BRIDGET: I'd of thought the last bit of business was enough.

HARRY: It's not for — [you to say]

BRIDGET: You don't learn a thing, from me or Lizzie, do you?

HARRY: Listen here —

BRIDGET: You mean you've forgotten how mad she was when you got her father to sign the rent from the mill house over to your sister? Oh my.

HARRY: She's his wife, isn't she?

BRIDGET: *(Lightly.)* Second wife.

HARRY: She's still got her rights.

BRIDGET: Who am I to say who's got a right? But I can tell you this — Miss Lizzie don't see it that way.

HARRY: It don't matter how Miss Lizzie sees it.

575

BRIDGET: Oh it matters enough — she had you thrown out last time, didn't she? By jasus that was a laugh!

HARRY: You mind your tongue.

BRIDGET: And after you left, you know what happened?

HARRY: Get away.

BRIDGET: She and sister Emma got her father's rent money from the other mill house to make it all even-steven — and now, here you are back again? What kind of business you up to this time? (Whispers in his ear.) Mind Lizzie doesn't catch you.

HARRY: Get away!

BRIDGET: (Laughs.) Ohhhh — would you like some more coffee, sir? It's the finest coffee in all Fall River! (She pours it.) Thank you sir. You're welcome, sir. (She exits to the kitchen.)

HARRY: There'll be no trouble this time!! Do you hear me!

BRIDGET: (Off.) Yes sir.

HARRY: There'll be no trouble. (Sees a basket of crusts.) What the hell is this? I said is this for breakfast!

BRIDGET: (Entering.) Is what for — oh no — Mr Borden's not economizin' to that degree yet, it's the crusts for Miss Lizzie's birds.

HARRY: What birds?

BRIDGET: Some kind of pet pigeons she's raisin' out in the shed. Miss Lizzie loves her pigeons.

HARRY: Miss Lizzie loves kittens and cats and horses and dogs. What Miss Lizzie doesn't love is people.

BRIDGET: Some people. (She looks past Harry to ACTRESS/ LIZZIE. HARRY turns to follow BRIDGET's gaze. BRIDGET speaks, encouraging an invitation for THE ACTRESS to join her.) Good mornin' Lizzie.

THE ACTRESS: *(She is a trifle tentative in the role of LIZZIE.)* Is the coffee on?

BRIDGET: Yes ma'am.

LIZZIE: I'll have some then.

BRIDGET: Yes ma'am. *(She makes no move to get it, but watches as LIZZIE stares at HARRY.)*

HARRY: Well . . . I think . . . maybe I'll . . . just split a bit of that kindling out back. *(He exits. LIZZIE turns to BRIDGET.)*

LIZZIE: Silly ass.

BRIDGET: Oh Lizzie. *(She laughs. She enjoys ACTRESS/LIZZIE's comments as she guides her into her role by "painting the background.")*

LIZZIE: Well, he is. He's a silly ass.

BRIDGET: Can you remember him last time with your Papa? Oh, I can still hear him: "Now Andrew, I've spent my life raisin' horses and I'm gonna tell you somethin' — a *woman* is just like a *horse!* You keep her on a tight rein, or she'll take the bit in her teeth and next thing you know, road, destination, and purpose is all behind you, and you'll be damn lucky if she don't pitch you right in a sewer ditch!"

LIZZIE: Stupid bugger.

BRIDGET: Oh Lizzie, what language! What would your father say if he heard you?

LIZZIE: Well . . . I've never used a word I didn't hear from him first.

BRIDGET: Do you think he'd be congratulatin' you?

LIZZIE: Possibly. *(BRIDGET gives a subtle shake of her head.)* Not.

BRIDGET: Possibly not is right . . . And what if *Mrs* B. should hear you?

LIZZIE: I hope and pray that she does. . . . Do you know what I think, Bridget? I think there's nothing wrong with

Mrs B. . . . that losing 80 pounds and tripling her intellect wouldn't cure.

BRIDGET: *(Loving it.)* You ought to be ashamed.

LIZZIE: It's the truth, isn't it?

BRIDGET: Still, what a way to talk of your mother.

LIZZIE: Step-mother.

BRIDGET: Still you don't mean it, do you?

LIZZIE: Don't I? *(Louder.)* She's a *silly ass* too!

BRIDGET: Shhhh.

LIZZIE: It's alright, she's deaf as a picket fence when she wants to be. . . . What's he here for?

BRIDGET: Never said.

LIZZIE: He's come to worm more money out of Papa I bet.

BRIDGET: Lizzie.

LIZZIE: What.

BRIDGET: Your sister, Lizzie. *(BRIDGET indicates EMMA, LIZZIE turns to see her on the stairs.)*

EMMA: You want to be quiet, Lizzie, a body can't sleep for the racket upstairs.

LIZZIE: Oh?

EMMA: You've been makin' too much noise.

LIZZIE: It must have been Bridget, she dropped a pot, didn't you, Bridget.

EMMA: A number of pots from the sound of it.

BRIDGET: I'm all thumbs this mornin', ma'am.

EMMA: You know it didn't sound like pots.

LIZZIE: Oh.

EMMA: Sounded more like voices.

LIZZIE: Oh?

EMMA: Sounded like your voice, Lizzie.

LIZZIE: Maybe you dreamt it.

EMMA: I wish I had, for someone was using words no lady would use.

LIZZIE: When Bridget dropped the pot, she did say "pshaw!" didn't you, Bridget.

BRIDGET: Pshaw! That's what I said.

EMMA: That's not what I heard.

BRIDGET will withdraw.

LIZZIE: Pshaw?

EMMA: If mother heard you, you know what she'd say.

LIZZIE: She's not my mother or yours.

EMMA: Well she married our father twenty-seven years ago, if that doesn't make her our mother —

LIZZIE: It doesn't.

EMMA: Don't talk like that.

LIZZIE: I'll talk as I like.

EMMA: We're not going to fight, Lizzie. We're going to be quiet and have our breakfast!

LIZZIE: Is that what we're going to do?

EMMA: Yes.

LIZZIE: Oh.

EMMA: At least — that's what I'm going to do.

LIZZIE: Bridget, Emma wants her breakfast!

EMMA: I could have yelled myself.

LIZZIE: You could, but you never do.

579

BRIDGET serves EMMA, EMMA is reluctant to argue in front of BRIDGET.

EMMA: Thank you, Bridget.

LIZZIE: Did you know Harry Wingate's back for a visit? . . . . He must have snuck in late last night so I wouldn't hear him. Did you?

EMMA shakes her head. LIZZIE studies her.

LIZZIE: Did you know he was coming?

EMMA: No.

LIZZIE: No?

EMMA: But I do know he wouldn't be here unless Papa asked him.

LIZZIE: That's not the point. You know what happened last time he was here. Papa was signing property over to her.

EMMA: Oh Lizzie.

LIZZIE: Oh Lizzie nothing. It's bad enough Papa's worth thousands of dollars, and here we are, stuck in this tiny bit of a house on Second Street, when we should be up on the hill — and that's her doing. Or hers and Harry's.

EMMA: Shush.

LIZZIE: I won't shush. They cater to Papa's worst instincts.

EMMA: They'll hear you.

LIZZIE: I don't care if they do. It's true, isn't it? Papa tends to be miserly, he probably has the first penny he ever earned — or more likely *she* has it.

EMMA: You talk rubbish.

LIZZIE: Papa *can* be very warm-hearted and generous *but he needs encouragement.*

EMMA: If Papa didn't save his money, Papa wouldn't have any money.

580

LIZZIE: And neither will we if he keeps signing things over to her.

EMMA: I'm not going to listen.

LIZZIE: Well try thinking.

EMMA: Stop it.

LIZZIE: *(Not a threat, a simple statement of fact.)* Someday Papa will die —

EMMA: Don't say that.

LIZZIE: Some day Papa will die. And I don't intend to spend the rest of my life licking Harry Wingate's boots, or toadying to his sister.

MRS BORDEN: *(From the stairs.)* What's that?

LIZZIE: Nothing.

MRS BORDEN: *(Making her way downstairs.)* Eh?

LIZZIE: I said, nothing!

BRIDGET: *(Holds out basket of crusts. LIZZIE looks at it.)* For your birds, Miss Lizzie.

LIZZIE: *(She takes the basket.)* You want to know what I think? I think she's a fat cow and I hate her. *(She exits, but will return to observe scene.)*

EMMA: . . . Morning, Mother.

MRS. BORDEN: Morning Emma.

EMMA: . . . Did you have a good sleep?

BRIDGET will serve breakfast, then join "LIZZIE" to observe scene.

MRS BORDEN: So so. . . . It's the heat you know. It never cools off proper at night. It's too hot for a good sleep.

EMMA: . . . Is Papa up?

MRS BORDEN: He'll be down in a minute . . . sooo . . . What's wrong with Lizzie this morning?

EMMA: Nothing.

MRS BORDEN: . . . Has Harry come down?

EMMA: I'm not sure.

MRS BORDEN: Bridget. Has Harry come down?

BRIDGET: Yes ma'am.

MRS BORDEN: And?

BRIDGET: And he's gone out back for a bit.

MRS BORDEN: Lizzie see him?

BRIDGET: Yes ma'am.

EMMA concentrates on her plate.

MRS BORDEN: . . . You should have said so. . . . She have words with him?

EMMA: Lizzie has more manners than that.

MRS BORDEN: She's incapable of disciplining herself like a lady and we all know it.

EMMA: Well she doesn't make a habit of picking fights with people.

MRS BORDEN: That's just it. She does.

EMMA: Well — she may —

MRS BORDEN: And you can't deny that.

EMMA: *(Louder.)* Well this morning she may have been a bit upset because no one told her he was coming and when she came down he was here. But that's all there was to it.

MRS BORDEN: If your father wants my brother in for a stay, he's to ask Lizzie's permission I suppose.

EMMA: No.

MRS BORDEN: You know, Emma —

EMMA: She didn't argue with him or anything like that.

MRS BORDEN: You spoiled her. You may have had the best of intentions, but you spoiled her.

MISS LIZZIE/BRIDGET is speaking to ACTRESS/LIZZIE.

MISS LIZZIE/BRIDGET: I was thirty-four years old, and I still daydreamed. . . . I did . . . I daydreamed . . . I dreamt that my name was Lisbeth . . . and I lived up on the hill in a corner house . . . and my hair wasn't red. I hate red hair. When I was little, everyone teased me. . . . When I was little, we never stayed in this house for the summer, we'd go to the farm. . . . I remember . . . my knees were always covered with scabs, god knows how I got them, but you know what I'd do? I'd sit in the field, and haul up my skirts, and my petticoat and my bloomers and roll down my stockings and I'd *pick* the scabs on my knees! And Emma would catch me! You know what she'd say? "Nice little girls don't have scabs on their knees!"

They laugh.

LIZZIE: Poor Emma.

MISS LIZZIE/BRIDGET: I dreamt . . . someday I'm going to live . . . in a corner house on the hill. . . . I'll have parties, grand parties. I'll be . . . witty, not biting, but witty. Everyone will be witty. Everyone who is *any*one will want to come to my parties . . . and if . . . I can't . . . live in a corner house on the hill . . . I'll live on the farm, all by myself on the farm! There was a barn there, with barn cats and barn kittens and two horses and barn swallows that lived in the eaves. . . . The birds I kept here were pigeons, not swallows. . . . They were grey, a dull grey . . . but . . . when the sun struck their feathers, I'd see blue, a steel blue with a sheen, and when they'd move in the sun they were bright blue and maroon and over it all, an odd sparkle as if you'd . . . grated a new silver dollar and the gratings caught in their feathers. . . . Most of the time they were dull . . . and stupid perhaps . . . but they weren't really. They were . . . hiding I think. . . . They knew me. . . . They liked me. . . . The truth . . . is . . .

ACTRESS/LIZZIE: The truth is . . . thirty-four is too old to daydream. . . . *(They observe scene.)*

MRS BORDEN: The truth is she's spoilt rotten. *(MR BORDEN will come down stairs and take his place at the table. MRS BORDEN continues for his benefit. MR BORDEN ignores her. He has learned the fine art of tuning her out. He is not intimidated or hen-pecked.)* And we're paying the piper for that. In most of the places I've been the people who pay the piper call the tune. Of course I haven't had the advantage of a trip to Europe with a bunch of lady friends like our Lizzie had three years ago, all expenses paid by her father.

EMMA: Morning Papa.

MR BORDEN: Mornin'.

MRS BORDEN: I haven't had the benefit of that experience. . . . Did you know Lizzie's seen Harry?

MR BORDEN: Has she.

MRS BORDEN: You should have met him downtown. You should never have asked him to stay over.

MR BORDEN: Why not?

MRS BORDEN: You know as well as I do why not. I don't want a repeat of last time. She didn't speak civil for months.

MR BORDEN: There's no reason for Harry to pay for a room when we've got a spare one. . . . Where's Lizzie?

EMMA: Out back feeding the birds.

MR BORDEN: She's always out at those birds.

EMMA: Yes Papa.

MR BORDEN: And tell her to get a new lock for the shed. There's been someone in it again.

EMMA: Alright.

MR BORDEN: It's those little hellions from next door. We had no trouble with them playin' in that shed before, they always played in their own yard before.

EMMA: . . . Papa?

MR BORDEN: It's those damn birds, that's what brings them into the yard.

EMMA: . . . About Harry . . .

MR BORDEN: What about Harry?

EMMA: Well . . . I was just wondering why . . . *[he's here]*

MR BORDEN: You never mind Harry — did you speak to Lizzie about Johnny MacLeod?

EMMA: I ah —

MR BORDEN: Eh?

EMMA: I said I tried to —

MR BORDEN: What do you mean, you tried to.

EMMA: Well, I was working my way round to it but —

MR BORDEN: What's so difficult about telling Lizzie Johnny MacLeod wants to call?

EMMA: Then why don't you tell her? I'm always the one that has to go running to Lizzie telling her this and telling her that, and taking the abuse for it!

MRS BORDEN: We all know why that is, she can wrap her father round her little finger, always has, always could. If everything else fails, she throws a tantrum and her father buys her off, trip to Europe, rent to the mill house, it's all the same.

EMMA: Papa, what's Harry here for?

MR BORDEN: None of your business.

MRS BORDEN: And don't you go runnin' to Lizzie stirring things up.

EMMA: You know I've never done that!

MR BORDEN: What she means —

EMMA: *(With anger but little fatigue.)* I'm tired, do you hear? Tired! *(She gets up from the table and leaves for upstairs.)*

MR BORDEN: Emma!

EMMA: You ask Harry here, you know there'll be trouble, and when I try to find out what's going on, so once again good old Emma can stand between you and Lizzie, all you've got to say is "none of your business!" Well then, it's *your* business, you look after it, because I'm not! *(She exits.)*

MRS BORDEN: . . . She's right.

MR BORDEN: That's enough. I've had enough. I don't want to hear from you too.

MRS BORDEN: I'm only saying she's right. You have to talk straight and plain to Lizzie and tell her things she don't want to hear.

MR BORDEN: About the farm?

MRS BORDEN: About Johnny MacLeod! Keep your mouth shut about the farm and she won't know the difference.

MR BORDEN: Alright.

MRS BORDEN: Speak to her about Johnny MacLeod.

MR BORDEN: Alright!

MRS BORDEN: You know what they're sayin' in town. About her and that doctor.

MISS LIZZIE/BRIDGET speaks to ACTRESS/LIZZIE.

MISS LIZZIE/BRIDGET: They're saying if you live on Second Street and you need a housecall, and you don't mind the Irish, call Dr Patrick. Dr Patrick is very prompt with his Second Street house calls.

ACTRESS/LIZZIE: Do they really say that?

MISS LIZZIE/BRIDGET: No they don't. I'm telling a lie. But he is very prompt with a Second Street call, do you know why that is?

ACTRESS/LIZZIE: Why?

MISS LIZZIE/BRIDGET: Well — he's hoping to see someone who lives on Second Street — someone who's yanking up her skirt and showing her ankle — so she can take a decent-sized step — and forgetting everything she was ever taught in Miss Cornelia's School for Girls, and talking to the Irish as if she never heard of the Pope! Oh yes, he's very prompt getting to Second Street . . . getting away is something else. . . .

DR PATRICK: Good morning, Miss Borden!

LIZZIE: I haven't decided . . . if it is . . . or isn't . . .

DR PATRICK: No, you've got it all wrong. The proper phrase is "good morning, Dr Patrick", and then you smile, discreetly of course, and lower the eyes just a titch, twirl the parasol —

LIZZIE: The parasol?

DR PATRICK: The parasol, but not too fast; and then you murmur in a voice that was ever sweet and low, "And how are you doin' this morning, Dr Patrick?" Your education's been sadly neglected, Miss Borden.

LIZZIE: You're forgetting something. You're married — and Irish besides — I'm supposed to ignore you.

DR PATRICK: No.

LIZZIE: Yes. Don't you realize Papa and Emma have fits everytime we engage in "illicit conversation". They're having fits right now.

587

DR PATRICK: Well, does Mrs Borden approve?

LIZZIE: Ahhh. She's the real reason I keep stopping and talking. Mrs Borden is easily shocked. I'm hoping she dies from the shock.

DR PATRICK: (Laughs.) Why don't you . . . run away from home, Lizzie?

LIZZIE: Why don't you "run away" with me?

DR PATRICK: Where'll we go?

LIZZIE: Boston.

DR PATRICK: Boston?

LIZZIE: For a start.

DR PATRICK: And when will we go?

LIZZIE: Tonight.

DR PATRICK: But you don't really mean it, you're havin' me on.

LIZZIE: I do mean it.

DR PATRICK: How can you joke — and look so serious?

LIZZIE: It's a gift.

DR PATRICK: (Laughs.) Oh Lizzie —

LIZZIE: Look!

DR PATRICK: What is it?

LIZZIE: It's those little beggars next door. Hey! Hey get away! Get away there! . . . They break into the shed to get at my birds and Papa gets angry.

DR PATRICK: It's a natural thing.

LIZZIE: Well Papa doesn't like it.

DR PATRICK: They just want to look at them.

LIZZIE: Papa says what's his is his own — you need a formal

invitation to get into our yard. . . . *Pause.* How's your wife?

DR PATRICK: My wife.

LIZZIE: Shouldn't I ask that? I thought nice polite ladies always inquired after the wives of their friends or acquaintances or . . . whatever.

HARRY observes them.

DR PATRICK: You've met my wife, my wife is always the same.

LIZZIE: How boring for you.

DR PATRICK: Uh-huh.

LIZZIE: And for her —

DR PATRICK: Yes indeed.

LIZZIE: And for me.

DR PATRICK: Do you know what they say, Lizzie? They say if you live on Second Street, and you need a house call, and you don't mind the Irish, call Dr Patrick. Dr Patrick is very prompt with his Second Street house calls.

LIZZIE: I'll tell you what I've heard them say — Second Street is a nice place to visit, but you wouldn't want to live there. I certainly don't.

HARRY: Lizzie.

LIZZIE: Well, look who's here. Have you had the pleasure of meeting my uncle, Mr Wingate.

DR PATRICK: No Miss Borden, that pleasure has never been mine.

LIZZIE: That's exactly how I feel.

DR PATRICK: Mr Wingate, sir.

HARRY: Dr . . . Patrick is it?

DR PATRICK: Yes it is, sir.

HARRY: Who's sick? [In other words, "What the hell are you doing here?"]

LIZZIE: No one. He just dropped by for a visit; you see Dr Patrick and I are very old, very dear friends, isn't that so?

HARRY stares at DR PATRICK.

DR PATRICK: Well . . . (*LIZZIE jabs him in the ribs.*) Ouch! . . . It's her sense of humour, sir . . . a rare trait in a woman. . . .

HARRY: You best get in, Lizzie, it's gettin' on for lunch.

LIZZIE: Don't be silly, we just had breakfast.

HARRY: You best get in!

LIZZIE: . . . Would you give me your arm, Dr Patrick? (*She moves away with DR PATRICK, ignoring HARRY.*)

DR PATRICK: Now see what you've done?

LIZZIE: What?

DR PATRICK: You've broken two of my ribs and ruined my reputation all in one blow.

LIZZIE: It's impossible to ruin an Irishman's reputation.

DR PATRICK: (*Smiles.*) . . . I'll be seeing you, Lizzie . . .

BRIDGET: They're sayin' it's time you were married.

LIZZIE: What time is that?

BRIDGET: You need a place of your own.

LIZZIE: How would getting married get me that?

BRIDGET: Though I don't know what man would put up with your moods!

LIZZIE: What about me putting up with his!

BRIDGET: Oh Lizzie!

LIZZIE: What's the matter, don't men have moods?

HARRY: I'm tellin' you, as God is my witness, she's out in the walk talkin' to that Irish doctor, and he's fallin' all over her.

MRS BORDEN: What's the matter with you. For her own sake you should speak to her.

MR BORDEN: I will.

HARRY: The talk around town can't be doin' you any good.

MRS BORDEN: Harry's right.

HARRY: Yes sir.

MRS BORDEN: He's tellin' you what you should know.

HARRY: If a man can't manage his own daughter, how the hell can he manage a business — that's what people say, and it don't matter a damn whether there's any sense in it or not.

MR BORDEN: I know that.

MRS BORDEN: Knowin' is one thing, doin' something about it is another. What're you goin' to do about it?

MR BORDEN: God damn it! I said I was goin' to speak to her and I am!

MRS BORDEN: Well speak good and plain this time!

MR BORDEN: Jesus christ woman!

MRS BORDEN: Your "speakin' to Lizzie" is a ritual around here.

MR BORDEN: Abby —

MRS BORDEN: She talks, you listen, and nothin' changes!

MR BORDEN: That's enough!

MRS BORDEN: Emma isn't the only one that's fed to the teeth!

MR BORDEN: Shut up!

MRS BORDEN: You're gettin' old, Andrew! You're gettin' old!
(She exits.)

An air of embarrassment from MR BORDEN at having words in front of HARRY. MR BORDEN fumbles with his pipe.

HARRY: *(Offers his pouch of tobacco.)* Here . . . have some of mine.

MR BORDEN: Don't mind if I do. . . . Nice mix.

HARRY: It is.

MR BORDEN: . . . I used to think . . . by my seventies . . . I'd be bouncin' a grandson on my knee. . . .

HARRY: Not too late for that.

MR BORDEN: Nope . . . never had any boys . . . and girls . . . don't seem to have the same sense of family. . . . You know it's all well and good to talk about speakin' plain to Lizzie, but the truth of the matter is, if Lizzie puts her mind to a thing, she does it, and if she don't, she don't.

HARRY: It's up to you to see she does.

MR BORDEN: It's like Abigail says, knowin' is one thing, doin' is another. . . . You're lucky you never brought any children into the world, Harry, you don't have to deal with them.

HARRY: Now that's no way to be talkin'.

MR BORDEN: There's Emma . . . Emma's a good girl . . . when Abbie and I get on, there'll always be Emma. . . . Well! You're not sittin' here to listen to me and my girls, are you, you didn't come here for that. Business, eh Harry?

HARRY whips out a sheet of figures.

MISS LIZZIE/BRIDGET: I can remember distinctly . . . that moment I was undressing for bed, and I looked at my knees — and there were no scabs! At last! I thought I'm the nice little girl Emma wants me to be! . . . But it wasn't that at all. I was just growing up. I didn't fall down so often. . . . *She smiles.* Do you suppose . . . do you suppose there's a formula, a magic formula for being "a woman"?

Do you suppose every girl baby receives it at birth, it's the last thing that happens just before birth, the magic formula is stamped indelibly on the brain — Ka Thud!! *(Her mood of amusement changes.)* . . . and . . . through some terrible oversight . . . perhaps the death of my mother . . . I didn't get that Ka Thud!! I was born . . . defective. . . . *(She looks at THE ACTRESS.)*

LIZZIE: *(Low.)* No.

MISS LIZZIE/BRIDGET: Not defective?

LIZZIE: Just . . . born.

THE DEFENSE: Gentlemen of the Jury!! I ask you to look at the defendant, Miss Lizzie Borden. I ask you to recall the nature of the crime of which she is accused. I ask you — do you believe Miss Lizzie Borden, the youngest daughter of a scion of our community, a recipient of the fullest amenities our society can bestow upon its most fortunate members, do you believe Miss Lizzie Borden capable of wielding the murder weapon — thirty-two blows, gentlemen, thirty-two blows — fracturing Abigail Borden's skull, leaving her bloody and broken body in an upstairs bedroom, then, Miss Borden, with no hint of frenzy, hysteria, or trace of blood upon her person, engages in casual conversation with the maid, Bridget O'Sullivan, while awaiting her father's return home, upon which, after sending Bridget to her attic room, Miss Borden deals thirteen blows to the head of her father, and minutes later — in a state utterly compatible with that of a loving daughter upon discovery of murder most foul — Miss Borden calls for aid! Is this the aid we give her? Accusation of the most heinous and infamous of crimes? Do you believe Miss Lizzie Borden capable of these acts? I can tell you I do not!! I can tell you these acts of violence are acts of madness!! Gentlemen! If this gentlewoman is capable of such an act — I say to you — look to your daughters — if this gentlewoman is capable of such an act, which of us can lie abed at night, hear a step upon the stairs, a rustle in the hall, a creak outside the door. . . . Which of you can plump your pillow, nudge your wife, close your eyes, and sleep? Gentlemen, Lizzie Borden is not mad. Gentlemen, Lizzie Borden is not guilty.

MR BORDEN: Lizzie?

LIZZIE: Papa . . . have you and Harry got business?

HARRY: 'lo Lizzie. I'll ah . . . finish up later. *(He exits with the figures. LIZZIE watches him go. MISS LIZZIE/BRIDGET watches.)*

MR BORDEN: Lizzie?

LIZZIE: What?

MR BORDEN: Could you sit down a minute?

LIZZIE: If it's about Dr Patrick again, I —

MR BORDEN: It isn't.

LIZZIE: Good.

MR BORDEN: But we could start there.

LIZZIE: Oh Papa.

MR BORDEN: Sit down Lizzie.

LIZZIE: But I've heard it all before, another chat for a wayward girl.

MR BORDEN: *(Gently.)* Bite your tongue, Lizzie.

She smiles at him, there is affection between them. She has the qualities he would like in a son but deplores in a daughter.

MR BORDEN: Now . . . first off . . . I want you to know that I . . . understand about you and the doctor.

LIZZIE: What do you understand?

MR BORDEN: I understand . . . that it's a natural thing.

LIZZIE: What is?

594

MR BORDEN: I'm saying there's nothing unnatural about an attraction between a man and a woman. That's a natural thing.

LIZZIE: I find Dr Patrick . . . amusing and entertaining . . . if that's what you mean . . . is that what you mean?

MR BORDEN: This attraction . . . points something up — you're a woman of thirty-four years —

LIZZIE: I know that.

MR BORDEN: Just listen to me, Lizzie . . . I'm choosing my words, and I want you to listen. Now . . . in most circumstances . . . a woman of your age would be married, eh? have children, be running her own house, that's the natural thing, eh? (Pause.) Eh, Lizzie?

LIZZIE: I don't know.

MR BORDEN: Of course you know.

LIZZIE: You're saying I'm unnatural . . . am I supposed to agree, is that what you want?

MR BORDEN: No, I'm not saying that! I'm saying the opposite to that! . . . I'm saying the feelings you have towards Dr Patrick —

LIZZIE: What feelings?

MR BORDEN: What's . . . what's happening there, I can understand, but what you have to understand is that he's a married man, and there's nothing for you there.

LIZZIE: If he weren't married, Papa, I wouldn't be bothered talking to him! . . . It's just a game, Papa, it's a game.

MR BORDEN: A game.

LIZZIE: You have no idea how boring it is looking eligible, interested, and alluring, when I feel none of the three. So I play games. And it's a blessed relief to talk to a married man.

MR BORDEN: What're his feelings for you?

LIZZIE: I don't know, I don't care. Can I go now?

MR BORDEN: I'm not finished yet! . . . You know Mr MacLeod, Johnny MacLeod?

LIZZIE: I know his three little monsters.

MR BORDEN: He's trying to raise three boys with no mother!

LIZZIE: That's not my problem! I'm going.

MR BORDEN: Lizzie!

LIZZIE: What!

MR BORDEN: Mr MacLeod's asked to come over next Tuesday.

LIZZIE: I'll be out that night.

MR BORDEN: No you won't!

LIZZIE: Yes I will! . . . Whose idea was this?

MR BORDEN: No one's.

LIZZIE: That's a lie. She wants to get rid of me.

MR BORDEN: I want what's best for you!

LIZZIE: No you don't! 'Cause you don't care what I want!

MR BORDEN: You don't know what you want!

LIZZIE: But I know what you want! You want me living my life by the Farmers' Almanac; having everyone over for Christmas dinner; waiting up for my husband; and *serving at socials!*

MR BORDEN: It's good enough for your mother!

LIZZIE: She is *not* my *mother!*

MR BORDEN: . . . John MacLeod is looking for a wife.

LIZZIE: No, god damn it, he isn't!

MR BORDEN: Lizzie!

LIZZIE: He's looking for a housekeeper and it isn't going to be me!

MR BORDEN: You've a filthy mouth!

LIZZIE: Is that why you hate me?

MR BORDEN: You don't make sense.

LIZZIE: Why is it when I pretend things I don't feel, that's when you like me?

MR BORDEN: You talk foolish.

LIZZIE: I'm supposed to be a mirror. I'm supposed to reflect what you want to see, but everyone wants something different. If no one looks in the mirror, I'm not even there, I don't exist!

MR BORDEN: Lizzie, you talk foolish!

LIZZIE: No, I don't, that isn't true.

MR BORDEN: About Mr MacLeod —

LIZZIE: You can't make me get married!

MR BORDEN: Lizzie, do you want to spend the rest of your life in this house?

LIZZIE: No . . . No . . . I want out of it, but I won't get married to do it.

MRS BORDEN: *(On her way through to the kitchen.)* You've never been asked.

LIZZIE: Oh listen to her! I must be some sort of failure, then, eh? You had no son and a daughter that failed! What does that make you, Papa!

MR BORDEN: I want you to think about Johnny MacLeod!

LIZZIE: To hell with him!!!

MR BORDEN appears defeated. After a moment, LIZZIE goes to him, she holds his hand, strokes his hair.

LIZZIE: Papa? . . . Papa, I love you, I try to be what you want, really I do try, I try . . . but . . . I don't want to get married. I wouldn't be a good mother, I —

MR BORDEN: How do you know —

LIZZIE: I know it! . . . I want out of all this . . . I hate this house, I hate . . . I want out. Try to understand how I feel. . . . Why can't I do something? . . . Eh? I mean . . . I could . . . I could go into your office. . . . I could . . . learn how to keep books?

MR BORDEN: Lizzie.

LIZZIE: Why can't I do something like that?

MR BORDEN: For god's sake, talk sensible.

LIZZIE: Alright then! Why can't we move up on the hill to a house where we aren't in each other's laps!

MRS BORDEN: *(Returning from kitchen.)* Why don't you move out!

LIZZIE: Give me the money and I'll go!

MRS BORDEN: Money.

LIZZIE: And give me enough that I won't ever have to come back!

MRS BORDEN: She always gets round to money!

LIZZIE: You drive me to it!

MRS BORDEN: She's crazy!

LIZZIE: You drive me to it!

MRS BORDEN: She should be locked up!

LIZZIE: *(Begins to smash the plates in the dining room.)* There!! There!!

MR BORDEN: Lizzie!

MRS BORDEN: Stop her!

LIZZIE: There!

MR BORDEN attempts to restrain her.

MRS BORDEN: For god's sake, Andrew!

LIZZIE: Lock me up! Lock me up!

MR BORDEN: Stop it! Lizzie!

She collapses against him, crying.

LIZZIE: Oh, Papa, I can't stand it.

MR BORDEN: There, there, come on now, it's alright, listen to me, Lizzie, it's alright.

MRS BORDEN: You may as well get down on your knees.

LIZZIE: Look at her. She's jealous of me. She can't stand it whenever you're nice to me.

MR BORDEN: There now.

MRS BORDEN: Ask her about Dr Patrick.

MR BORDEN: I'll handle this my way.

LIZZIE: He's an entertaining person, there're very few around!

MRS BORDEN: Fall River ain't Paris and ain't that a shame for our Lizzie!

LIZZIE: One trip three years ago and you're still harping on it; it's true, Papa, an elephant never forgets!

MR BORDEN: Show some respect!

LIZZIE: She's a fat cow and I hate her!

MR BORDEN slaps LIZZIE. There is a pause as he regains control of himself.

MR BORDEN: Now . . . now . . . you'll see Mr MacLeod Tuesday night.

LIZZIE: No.

MR BORDEN: God damn it!! I said you'll see Johnny MacLeod Tuesday night!!

LIZZIE: No.

MR BORDEN: Get the hell upstairs to your room!

LIZZIE: No.

MR BORDEN: I'm telling you to go upstairs to your room!!

LIZZIE: I'll go when I'm ready.

MR BORDEN: I said, Go!

He grabs her arm to move her forcibly, she hits his arm away.

LIZZIE: No! . . . There's something you don't understand, Papa. You can't make me do one thing that I don't want to do. I'm going to keep on doing just what I want when I want — like always!

MR BORDEN: *(Shoves her to the floor to gain a clear exit from the room. He stops on the stairs, looks back to her on the floor.)* . . . I'm . . . *(He continues off.)*

MRS BORDEN: *(Without animosity.)* You know, Lizzie, your father keeps you. You know you got nothing but what he gives you. And that's a fact of life. You got to come to deal with facts. I did.

LIZZIE: And married Papa.

MRS BORDEN: And married your father. You never made it easy for me. I took on a man with two little ones, and Emma was your mother.

LIZZIE: You got stuck so I should too, is that it?

MRS BORDEN: What?

LIZZIE: The reason I should marry Johnny MacLeod.

MRS BORDEN: I just know, this time, in the end, you'll do what your Papa says, you'll see.

LIZZIE: No, I won't. I have a right. A right that frees me from all that.

MRS BORDEN: No, Lizzie, you got no rights.

LIZZIE: I've a legal right to one-third because I am his flesh and blood.

MRS BORDEN: What you don't understand is your father's not dead yet, your father's got many good years ahead of him, and when his time comes, well, we'll see what his will says then. . . . Your father's no fool, Lizzie. . . . Only a fool would leave money to you. *(She exits.)*

BRIDGET approaches "LIZZIE."

BRIDGET: Ah Lizzie . . . you outdid yourself that time. *(She is comforting LIZZIE.)* . . . Yes you did . . . an elephant never forgets!

LIZZIE: Oh Bridget.

BRIDGET: Come on now.

LIZZIE: I can't help it.

BRIDGET: Sure you can . . . sure you can . . . stop your cryin' and come and sit down . . . you want me to tell you a story?

LIZZIE: No.

BRIDGET: Sure, a story. I'll tell you a story. Come on now . . . now . . . before I worked here I worked up on the hill and the lady of the house . . . are you listenin'? Well, she swore by her cook, finest cook in creation, yes, always bowin' and scrapin' and smilin' and givin' up her day off if company arrived. Oh the lady of the house she loved that cook — and I'll tell you her name! It was Mary! Now listen! Do you know what Mary was doin'? *(LIZZIE shakes her head.)* Before eatin' the master'd serve drinks in the parlour — and out in the kitchen, Mary'd be spittin' in the soup!

LIZZIE: What?

BRIDGET: She'd spit in the soup! And she'd smile when they served it!

LIZZIE: No.

BRIDGET: Yes. I've seen her cut up hair for an omelette.

LIZZIE: You're lying.

BRIDGET: Cross me heart. . . . They thought it was pepper!

LIZZIE: Oh, Bridget!

BRIDGET: These two eyes have seen her season up mutton stew when it's off and gone bad.

LIZZIE: Gone bad?

BRIDGET: Oh and they et it, every bit, and the next day they was hit with . . . *stomach flu!* so cook called it. By jasus Lizzie, I daren't tell you what she served up in their food, for fear you'd be sick!

LIZZIE: That's funny. . . . *(A fact — LIZZIE does not appear amused.)*

BRIDGET: *(Starts to clear up the dishes.)* Yes, well, I'm tellin' you I kept on the good side of cook.

LIZZIE watches her for a moment.

LIZZIE: . . . Do you . . . like me?

BRIDGET: Sure I do. . . . You should try bein' more like cook, Lizzie. Smile and get round them. You can do it.

LIZZIE: It's not . . . *fair* that I have to.

BRIDGET: There ain't nothin' fair in this world.

LIZZIE: Well then . . . well then, I don't want to!

BRIDGET: You dream, Lizzie . . . you dream dreams . . . Work. Be sensible. What could you do?

LIZZIE: I could

MISS LIZZIE/BRIDGET: No.

LIZZIE: I could

MISS LIZZIE/BRIDGET: No.

LIZZIE: I could

MISS LIZZIE/BRIDGET: No!

LIZZIE: I . . . dream.

MISS LIZZIE/BRIDGET: You dream . . . of a carousel . . . you see a carousel . . . you see lights that go on and go off . . . you see yourself on a carousel horse, a red-painted horse with its head in the air, and green staring eyes, and a white flowing mane, it looks wild! . . . It goes up and comes down, and the carousel whirls round with the music and lights, on and off . . . and you watch . . . watch yourself on the horse. You're wearing a mask, a white mask like the mane of the horse, it looks like your face except that it's rigid and white...and it changes! With each flick of the lights, the expression, it changes, but always so rigid and hard, like the flesh of the horse that is red that you ride. You ride with no hands! No hands on this petrified horse, its head flung in the air, its wide staring eyes like those of a doe run down by the dogs! . . . And each time you go round, your hands rise a fraction nearer the mask . . . and the music and the carousel and the horse . . . they all three slow down, and they stop. . . . You can reach out and touch . . . you . . . you on the horse . . . with your hands so at the eyes. . . . You look into the eyes! *(A sound from Lizzie, she is horrified and frightened. She covers her eyes.)* There are none! None! Just black holes in a white mask. . . . *(Pause.)* . . . The eyes of your birds . . . are round . . . and bright . . . a light shines from inside . . . they . . . can see into your heart . . . they're pretty . . . they love you. . . .

MR BORDEN: I want this settled, Harry, I want it settled while Lizzie's out back.

MISS LIZZIE/BRIDGET draws LIZZIE's attention to the MR BORDEN/HARRY scene. LIZZIE listens, will move closer.

HARRY: You know I'm for that.

MR BORDEN: I want it all done but the signin' of the papers tomorrow, that's if I decide to —

HARRY: You can't lose, Andrew. That farm's just lyin' fallow.

MR BORDEN: Well, let's see what you got.

HARRY: *(Gets out his papers.)* Look at this . . . I'll run horse auctions and a buggy rental — now I'll pay no rent for the house or pasturage but you get twenty percent, eh? That figure there —

MR BORDEN: Mmmn.

HARRY: From my horse auctions last year, it'll go up on the farm and you'll get twenty percent off the top. . . . My buggy rental won't do so well . . . that's that figure there, approximate . . . but it all adds up, eh? Adds up for you.

MR BORDEN: It's a good deal, Harry, but . . .

HARRY: Now I know why you're worried — but the farm will still be in the family, 'cause aren't I family? and whenever you or the girls want to come over for a visit, why I'll send a buggy from the rental, no need for you to have the expense of a horse, eh?

MR BORDEN: It looks good on paper.

HARRY: There's . . . ah . . . something else, it's a bit awkward but I got to mention it; I'll be severin' a lot of my present connections, and what I figure I've a right to, is some kind of guarantee. . . .

MR BORDEN: You mean a renewable lease for the farm?

HARRY: Well — what I'm wondering is . . . No offense, but you're an older man, Andrew . . . now if something should happen to you, where would the farm stand in regards to your will? That's what I'm wondering.

MR BORDEN: I've not made a will.

HARRY: You know best — but I wouldn't want to be in a position where Lizzie would be havin' anything to do with that farm. The less she knows now the better, but she's bound to find out — I don't feel I'm steppin' out of line by bringin' this up.

LIZZIE is within earshot. She is staring at HARRY and MR BORDEN. They do not see her.

MR BORDEN: No.

HARRY: If you mind you come right out and say so.

MR BORDEN: That's alright.

HARRY: Now . . . if you . . . put the farm — in Abbie's name, what do you think?

MR BORDEN: I don't know, Harry.

HARRY: I don't want to push.

MR BORDEN: . . . I should make a will . . . I want the girls looked after, it don't seem like they'll marry . . . and Abbie, she's younger than me, I know Emma will see to her, still . . . money-wise I got to consider these things . . . it makes a difference no men in the family.

HARRY: You know you can count on me for whatever.

MR BORDEN: If . . . *If* I changed title to the farm, Abbie'd have to come down to the bank, I wouldn't want Lizzie to know.

HARRY: You can send a note for her when you get to the bank; she can say it's a note from a friend, and come down and meet you. Simple as that.

MR BORDEN: I'll give it some thought.

HARRY: You see, Abbie owns the farm, it's no difference to you, but it gives me protection.

MR BORDEN: Who's there?

HARRY: It's Lizzie.

MR BORDEN: What do you want? . . . Did you lock the shed? . . . Is the shed locked! *(LIZZIE makes a slow motion which MR BORDEN takes for assent.)* Well you make sure it stays locked! I don't want any more of those god damned . . . . I . . . ah . . . I think we about covered everything, Harry, we'll . . . ah . . . we'll let it go till tomorrow.

HARRY: Good enough . . . well . . . I'll just finish choppin' that kindlin', give a shout when it's lunchtime. *He exits.*

LIZZIE and MR BORDEN stare at each other for a moment.

LIZZIE: *(Very low.)* What are you doing with the farm?

MR BORDEN slowly picks up the papers, places them in his pocket.

LIZZIE: Papa! . . . Papa. I want you to show me what you put in your pocket.

MR BORDEN: It's none of your business.

LIZZIE: The farm is my business.

MR BORDEN: It's nothing.

LIZZIE: Show me!

MR BORDEN: I said it's nothing!

LIZZIE makes a quick move towards her father to seize the paper from his pocket. Even more quickly and smartly he slaps her face. It is all very quick and clean. A pause as they stand frozen.

HARRY: *(Off.)* Andrew, there's a bunch of kids broken into the shed!

MR BORDEN: Jesus christ.

LIZZIE: *(Whispers.)* What about the farm.

MR BORDEN: You! You and those god damn birds! I've told you! I've told you time and again!

LIZZIE: What about the farm!

MR BORDEN: Jesus christ . . . You never listen! Never!

HARRY: *(Enters carrying the hand hatchet.)* Andrew!!

MR BORDEN: *(Grabs the hand hatchet from HARRY, turns to LIZZIE.)* There'll be no more of your god damn birds in this yard!!

LIZZIE: No!

MR BORDEN raises the hatchet and smashes it into the table as LIZZIE screams.

LIZZIE: No Papa!! Nooo!!

The hatchet is embedded in the table. MR BORDEN and HARRY assume a soft freeze as ACTRESS/LIZZIE whirls to see MISS LIZZIE/BRIDGET observing the scene.

LIZZIE: Nooo!

MISS LIZZIE: I loved them.

Blackout

ACT TWO

Lights come up on ACTRESS/LIZZIE sitting at the dining room table. She is very still, her hands clasped in her lap. MISS LIZZIE/BRIDGET is near her. She too is very still. A pause.

ACTRESS/LIZZIE: *(Very low.)* Talk to me.

607

MISS LIZZIE/BRIDGET: I remember . . .

ACTRESS/LIZZIE: *(Very low.)* Don't.

MISS LIZZIE/BRIDGET: On the farm, Papa's farm, Harry's farm, when I was little and thought it was my farm and I loved it, we had some puppies, the farm dog had puppies, brown soft little puppies with brown ey . . . *(She does not complete the word "eyes")* And one of the puppies got sick. I didn't know it was sick, it seemed like the others, but the mother, she knew. It would lie at the back of the box, she would lie in front of it while she nursed all the others. They ignored it, that puppy didn't exist for the others. . . . I think inside it was different, and the mother thought the difference she sensed was a sickness . . . and after a while . . . anyone could tell it was sick. It had nothing to eat! . . . And papa took it and drowned it. That's what you do on a farm with things that are different.

ACTRESS/LIZZIE: Am I different?

MISS LIZZIE/BRIDGET: You kill them.

ACTRESS/LIZZIE looks at MISS LIZZIE/BRIDGET. MISS LIZZIE/BRIDGET looks towards the top of the stairs. BRIDGET gets up and exits to the kitchen. EMMA appears at the top of the stairs. She is dressed for travel and carries a small suitcase and her gloves. She stares down at LIZZIE still sitting at the table. After several moments LIZZIE becomes aware of that gaze and turns to look at EMMA. EMMA then descends the stairs. She puts down her suitcase. She is not overjoyed at seeing LIZZIE, having hoped to get away before LIZZIE arose, nevertheless she begins with an excess of enthusiasm to cover the implications of her departure.

EMMA: Well! You're up early . . . Bridget down? . . . did you put the coffee on? *(She puts her gloves on the table.)* My goodness, Lizzie, cat got your tongue? *(She exits to the kitchen. LIZZIE picks up the gloves. EMMA returns.)* Bridget's down, she's in the kitchen. . . . Well . . . looks like a real scorcher today, doesn't it? . . .

LIZZIE: What's the bag for?

EMMA: I . . . decided I might go for a little trip, a day or two, get away from the heat. . . . The girls've rented a place out beach way and I thought . . . with the weather and all . . .

LIZZIE: How can you do that?

EMMA: Do what? . . . Anyway I thought I might stay with them a few days. . . . Why don't you come with me?

LIZZIE: No.

EMMA: Just for a few days, come with me.

LIZZIE: No.

EMMA: You know you like the water.

LIZZIE: I said no!

EMMA: Oh, Lizzie.

Pause.

LIZZIE: I don't see how you can leave me like this.

EMMA: I asked you to come with me.

LIZZIE: You know I can't do that.

EMMA: Why not?

LIZZIE: Someone has to *do* something, you just run away from things.

Pause.

EMMA: . . . Lizzie . . . I'm sorry about the − *[birds]*

LIZZIE: No!

EMMA: Papa was angry.

LIZZIE: I don't want to talk about it.

EMMA: He's sorry now.

LIZZIE: Nobody *listens* to me, can't you hear me? I said *don't* talk about it. I don't want to talk about it. Stop talking about it!!

BRIDGET enters with the coffee.

EMMA: Thank you, Bridget.

BRIDGET withdraws.

EMMA: Well! . . . I certainly can use this this morning. . . . Your coffee's there.

LIZZIE: I don't want it.

EMMA: You're going to ruin those gloves.

LIZZIE: I don't care.

EMMA: Since they're not yours.

LIZZIE bangs the gloves down on the table. A pause. Then EMMA picks them up and smooths them out.

LIZZIE: Why are you leaving me?

EMMA: I feel like a visit with the girls. Is there something wrong with that?

LIZZIE: How can you go now?

EMMA: I don't know what you're getting at.

LIZZIE: I heard them. I heard them talking yesterday. Do you know what they're saying?

EMMA: How could I?

LIZZIE: "How could I?" What do you mean "How could I?" Did you know?

EMMA: No, Lizzie, I did not.

LIZZIE: *Did-not-what.*

EMMA: Know.

610

LIZZIE: But you know now. How do you know now?

EMMA: I've put two and two together and I'm going over to the girls for a visit!

LIZZIE: Please Emma!

EMMA: It's too hot.

LIZZIE: I need you, don't go.

EMMA: I've been talking about this trip.

LIZZIE: That's a lie.

EMMA: They're expecting me.

LIZZIE: You're lying to me!

EMMA: I'm going to the girls' place. You can come if you want, you can stay if you want. I planned this trip and I'm taking it!

LIZZIE: Stop lying!

EMMA: If I want to tell a little white lie to avoid an altercation in this house, I'll do so. Other people have been doing it for years!

LIZZIE: You don't understand, you don't understand anything.

EMMA: Oh, I understand enough.

LIZZIE: You don't! Let me explain it to you. You listen carefully, you listen. . . . Harry's getting the farm, can you understand that? Harry is here and he's moving on the farm and he's going to be there, on the farm, living on the farm. *Our farm*. Do you understand that? . . . Do you understand that!

EMMA: Yes.

LIZZIE: Harry's going to be on the farm. That's the first thing. . . . No . . . no it isn't. . . . The first thing . . . was the mill house, that was the first thing! And *now* the farm. You see there's a pattern, Emma, you can see that, can't you?

EMMA: I don't —

LIZZIE: You can see it! The mill house, then the farm, and the next thing is the papers for the farm — do you know what he's doing, Papa's doing? He's signing the farm over to her. It will never be ours, we will never have it, not ever. It's ours by rights, don't you feel that?

EMMA: The farm — has always meant a great deal to me, yes.

LIZZIE: Then what are you doing about it! You can't leave me now . . . but that's not all. Papa's going to make a will, and you can see the pattern, can't you, and if the pattern keeps on, what do you suppose his will will say. What do you suppose, answer me!

EMMA: I don't know.

LIZZIE: Say it!

EMMA: He'll see we're looked after.

LIZZIE: I don't want to be looked after! What's the matter with you? Do you really want to spend the rest of your life with that cow, listening to her drone on and on for years! That's just what they think you'll do. Papa'll leave you a monthly allowance, just like he'll leave me, just enough to keep us all living together. We'll be worth millions on paper, and be stuck in this house and by and by Papa will die and Harry will move in and you will wait on that cow while she gets fatter and fatter and I — will — sit in my room.

EMMA: Lizzie.

LIZZIE: We have to do something, you can see that. We have to do something!

EMMA: There's nothing we can do.

LIZZIE: Don't say that!

EMMA: Alright, then, what can we do?

LIZZIE: I . . . I . . . don't know. But we have to do something, you have to help me, you can't go away and leave me alone, you can't do that.

EMMA: Then —

LIZZIE: You know what I thought? I thought you could talk to him, really talk to him, make him understand that we're people. *Individual people*, and we have to live separate lives, and his will should make it possible for us to do that. And the farm can't go to Harry.

EMMA: You know it's no use.

LIZZIE: I can't talk to him anymore. Everytime I talk to him I make everything worse. I hate him, no. No I don't. I hate her.

EMMA looks at her broach watch.

LIZZIE: Don't look at the time.

EMMA: I'll miss my connections.

LIZZIE: No!

EMMA: *(Puts on her gloves.)* Lizzie. There's certain things we have to face. One of them is, we can't change a thing.

LIZZIE: I won't let you go!

EMMA: I'll be back on the week-end.

LIZZIE: He killed my birds! He took the axe and he killed them! Emma, I ran out and held them in my hands, I felt their hearts throbbing and pumping and the blood gushed out of their necks, it was all over my hands, don't you care about that?

EMMA: I . . . I . . . have a train to catch.

LIZZIE: He didn't care how much he hurt me and you don't care either. Nobody cares.

EMMA: I . . . have to go now.

LIZZIE: That's right. Go away. I don't even like you, Emma. Go away! *(EMMA leaves, LIZZIE runs after her calling.)* I'm sorry for all the things I told you! Things I really felt! You pretended to me, and I don't like you!! Go away!! *(LIZZIE runs to the window and looks out after EMMA's departing figure. After a moment she slowly turns back into the room. MISS LIZZIE/BRIDGET is there.)*

LIZZIE: I want to die . . . I want to die, but something inside won't let me . . . inside something says *no. (She shuts her eyes.)* I can do anything.

THE DEFENSE: Miss Borden.

Both LIZZIES turn.

THE DEFENSE: Could you describe the sequence of events upon your father's arrival home?

LIZZIE: *(With no animation.)* Papa came in . . . we exchanged a few words . . . Bridget and I spoke of the yard goods sale downtown, whether she would buy some. She went up to her room . . . .

THE DEFENSE: And then?

LIZZIE: I went out back . . . through the yard . . . I picked up several pears from the ground beneath the trees . . . I went into the shed . . . I stood looking out the window and ate the pears . . .

THE DEFENSE: How many?

LIZZIE: Four.

THE DEFENSE: It wasn't warm, stifling in the shed?

LIZZIE: No, it was cool.

THE DEFENSE: What were you doing, apart from eating the pears?

LIZZIE: I suppose I was thinking. I just stood there, looking out the window, thinking, and eating the pears I'd picked up.

THE DEFENSE: You're fond of pears?

LIZZIE: Otherwise, I wouldn't eat them.

THE DEFENSE: Go on.

LIZZIE: I returned to the house. I found — Papa. I called for Bridget.

MRS BORDEN descends the stairs. LIZZIE and BRIDGET turn to look at her. MRS BORDEN is only aware of LIZZIE's stare. Pause.

MRS BORDEN: . . . What're you staring at? . . . I said what're you staring at?

LIZZIE: *(Continuing to stare at MRS BORDEN.)* Bridget.

BRIDGET: Yes ma'am.

Pause.

MRS BORDEN: Just coffee and a biscuit this morning, Bridget, it's too hot for a decent breakfast.

BRIDGET: Yes ma'am.

She exits for the biscuit and coffee. LIZZIE continues to stare at MRS BORDEN.

MRS BORDEN: . . . Tell Bridget I'll have it in the parlour.

LIZZIE: *Is making an effort to be pleasant, to be "good". MRS BORDEN is more aware of this as unusual behaviour from LIZZIE than were she to be rude, biting, or threatening. LIZZIE, at the same time, feels caught in a dimension other than the one in which the people around her are operating. For LIZZIE, a bell-jar effect. Simple acts seem filled with significance. LIZZIE is trying to fulfill other people's expectations of "normal".*

LIZZIE: It's not me, is it?

MRS BORDEN: What?

LIZZIE: You're not moving into the parlour because of me, are you?

MRS BORDEN: What?

LIZZIE: I'd hate to think I'd driven you out of your own dining room.

MRS BORDEN: No.

LIZZIE: Oh good, because I'd hate to think that was so.

MRS BORDEN: It's cooler in the parlour.

LIZZIE: You know, you're right.

MRS BORDEN: Eh?

LIZZIE: It is cooler. . . .

BRIDGET enters with the coffee and biscuit.

LIZZIE: I will, Bridget.

She takes the coffee and biscuit, gives it to MRS BORDEN. LIZZIE watches her eat and drink. MRS BORDEN eats the biscuit delicately. LIZZIE's attention is caught by it. BRIDGET exits.

LIZZIE: Do you like that biscuit?

MRS BORDEN: It could be lighter.

LIZZIE: You're right.

MR BORDEN enters, makes his way into the kitchen, LIZZIE watches him pass.

LIZZIE: You know, Papa doesn't look well, Papa doesn't look well at all. Papa looks sick.

MRS BORDEN: He had a bad night.

LIZZIE: Oh?

MRS BORDEN: Too hot.

LIZZIE: But it's cooler in here, isn't it . . . *(Not trusting her own evaluation of the degree of heat.)* Isn't it?

MRS BORDEN: Yes, yes, it's cooler in here.

MR BORDEN enters with his coffee. LIZZIE goes to him.

LIZZIE: Papa? You should go in the parlour. It's much cooler in there, really it is.

He goes into the parlour. LIZZIE remains in the dining room. She sits at the table, folds her hands in her lap. MR BORDEN begins to read the paper.

MRS BORDEN: . . . I think I'll have Bridget do the windows today . . . they need doing . . . get them out of the way first thing. . . . Anything in the paper, Andrew?

MR BORDEN: *(As he continues to read.)* Nope.

MRS BORDEN: There never is . . . I don't know why we buy it.

MR BORDEN: *(Reading.)* Yup.

MRS BORDEN: You going out this morning?

MR BORDEN: Business.

MRS BORDEN: . . . Harry must be having a bit of a sleep-in.

MR BORDEN: Yup.

MRS BORDEN: He's always up by — *(Harry starts down the stairs.)* Well, speak of the devil — coffee and biscuits?

HARRY: Sounds good to me.

MRS BORDEN starts off to get it. LIZZIE looks at her, catching her eye. MRS BORDEN stops abruptly.

LIZZIE: *(Her voice seems too loud.)* Emma's gone over to visit at the girls' place. (*MR BORDEN lowers his paper to look at her. HARRY looks at her. Suddenly aware of the loudness of*

617

her voice, she continues softly, too softly.) . . . Till the week-end.

MR BORDEN: She didn't say she was going, when'd she decide that?

LIZZIE looks down at her hands, doesn't answer. A pause. Then MRS BORDEN continues out to the kitchen.

HARRY: Will you be ah . . . going downtown today?

MR BORDEN: This mornin'. I got . . . business at the bank.

A look between them. They are very aware of LIZZIE's presence in the dining room.

HARRY: This mornin' eh? Well now . . . that works out just fine for me. I can . . . I got a bill to settle in town myself.

LIZZIE turns her head to look at them.

HARRY: I'll be on my way after that.

MR BORDEN: Abbie'll be disappointed you're not stayin' for lunch.

HARRY: Nother time.

MR BORDEN: *(Aware of LIZZIE's gaze.)* I . . . I don't know where she is with that coffee. I'll —

HARRY: Never you mind, you sit right there, I'll get it. *He exits.*

LIZZIE and MR BORDEN look at each other. The bell-jar effect is lessened.

LIZZIE: *(Softly.)* Good mornin' Papa.

MR BORDEN: Mornin' Lizzie.

LIZZIE: Did you have a good sleep?

618

MR BORDEN: Not bad.

LIZZIE: Papa?

MR BORDEN: Yes Lizzie.

LIZZIE: You're a very strong-minded person, Papa, do you think I'm like you?

MR BORDEN: In some ways . . . perhaps.

LIZZIE: I must be like someone.

MR BORDEN: You resemble your mother.

LIZZIE: I look like my mother?

MR BORDEN: A bit like your mother.

LIZZIE: But my mother's dead.

MR BORDEN: Lizzie —

LIZZIE: I remember you told me she died because she was sick . . . I was born and she died . . . Did you love her?

MR BORDEN: I married her.

LIZZIE: Can't you say if you loved her.

MR BORDEN: Of course I did, Lizzie.

LIZZIE: Did you hate me for killing her?

MR BORDEN: You don't think of it that way, it was just something that happened.

LIZZIE: Perhaps she just got tired and died. She didn't want to go on, and the chance came up and she took it. I could understand that. . . . Perhaps she was like a bird, she could see all the blue sky and she wanted to fly away but she couldn't. She was caught, Papa, she was caught in a horrible snare, and she saw a way out and she took it. . . . Perhaps it was a very brave thing to do, Papa, perhaps it was the only way, and she hated to leave us because she loved us so much, but she couldn't breathe all caught in the snare. . . . *(Long pause.)* Some people have very small wrists, have you noticed. Mine aren't. . . .

There is a murmur from the kitchen, then muted laughter. MR BORDEN looks towards it.

LIZZIE: Papa! . . . I'm a very strong person.

MRS BORDEN: *(Off, laughing.)* You're tellin' tales out of school, Harry!

HARRY: *(Off.)* God's truth. You should have seen the buggy when they brought it back.

MRS BORDEN: *(Off.)* You've got to tell Andrew. *(Pokes her head in.)* Andrew, come on out here, Harry's got a story. *(Off.)* Now you'll have to start at the beginning again, oh my goodness.

MR BORDEN starts for the kitchen. He stops, and looks back at LIZZIE.

LIZZIE: Is there anything you want to tell me, Papa?

MRS BORDEN: *(Off.)* Andrew!

LIZZIE: *(Softly, an echo.)* Andrew.

MR BORDEN: What is it, Lizzie?

LIZZIE: If I promised to be a good girl forever and ever, would anything change?

MR BORDEN: I don't know what you're talkin' about.

LIZZIE: I would be lying . . . Papa! . . . Don't do any business today. Don't go out. Stay home.

MR BORDEN: What for?

LIZZIE: Everyone's leaving. Going away. Everyone's left.

MRS BORDEN: *(Off.)* Andrew!

LIZZIE: *(Softly, an echo.)* Andrew.

MR BORDEN: What is it?

LIZZIE: I'm calling you.

MR BORDEN looks at her for a moment, then leaves for the kitchen.

DR PATRICK is heard whistling very softly. LIZZIE listens.

LIZZIE: Listen . . . It's stopped.

DR PATRICK can't be seen. Only his voice is heard.

DR PATRICK: *(Very low.)* Lizzie?

LIZZIE: It sounded so sad I wanted to cry. I mustn't cry.

DR PATRICK: I bet you know this one. *(He whistles an Irish jig.)*

LIZZIE: I know that! *(She begins to dance. DR PATRICK enters. He claps in time to the dance. LIZZIE finishes the jig.)*

DR PATRICK applauds.

DR PATRICK: Bravo! Bravo!!

LIZZIE: You didn't know I could do that, did you?

DR PATRICK: You're a woman of many talents, Miss Borden.

LIZZIE: You're not making fun of me?

DR PATRICK: I would never do that.

LIZZIE: I can do anything I want.

DR PATRICK: I'm sure you can.

LIZZIE: If I wanted to die — I could even do that, couldn't I.

DR PATRICK: Well now, I don't think so.

LIZZIE: Yes, I could!

DR PATRICK: Lizzie —

LIZZIE: You wouldn't know — you can't see into my heart.

DR PATRICK: I think I can.

LIZZIE: Well you can't!

621

DR PATRICK: . . . It's only a game.

LIZZIE: I never play games.

DR PATRICK: Sure you do.

LIZZIE: I hate games.

DR PATRICK: You're playin' one now.

LIZZIE: You don't even know me!

DR PATRICK: Come on Lizzie, we don't want to fight. I know what we'll do . . . we'll start all over. . . . Shut your eyes, Lizzie. *(She does so.)* Good mornin' Miss Borden. . . . Good mornin' Miss Borden. . . .

LIZZIE: . . . I haven't decided. . . . *(She slowly opens her eyes.)* . . . if it is or it isn't.

DR PATRICK: Much better . . . and now . . . would you take my arm, Miss Borden? How about a wee promenade?

LIZZIE: There's nowhere to go.

DR PATRICK: That isn't so. . . . What about Boston? . . . Do you think it's too far for a stroll? . . . I know what we'll do, we'll walk 'round to the side and you'll show me your birds. *(They walk.)* . . . I waited last night but you never showed up . . . there I was, travellin' bag and all, and you never appeared . . . I know what went wrong! We forgot to agree on an hour! Next time, Lizzie, you must set the hour. . . . Is this where they're kept?

LIZZIE nods, she opens the cage and looks in it.

DR PATRICK: It's empty. *(He laughs.)* And you say you never play games?

LIZZIE: They're gone.

DR PATRICK: You've been havin' me on again, yes you have.

LIZZIE: They've run away.

DR PATRICK: Did they really exist?

LIZZIE: I had blood on my hands.

DR PATRICK: What do you say?

LIZZIE: You can't see it now, I washed it off, see?

DR PATRICK: *(Takes her hands.)* Ah Lizzie . . . .

LIZZIE: Would you . . . help someone die?

DR PATRICK: Why do you ask that?

LIZZIE: Some people are better off dead. I might be better off dead.

DR PATRICK: You're a precious and unique person, Lizzie, and you shouldn't think things like that.

LIZZIE: Precious and unique?

DR PATRICK: All life is precious and unique.

LIZZIE: I am precious and unique? . . . I *am* precious and unique. You said that.

DR PATRICK: Oh, I believe it.

LIZZIE: And I am. I know it. People mix things up on you, you have to be careful. I am a person of worth.

DR PATRICK: Sure you are.

LIZZIE: Not like that fat cow in there.

DR PATRICK: Her life too is —

LIZZIE: No!

DR PATRICK: Liz —

LIZZIE: Do you know her!

DR PATRICK: That doesn't matter.

LIZZIE: Yes it does, it does matter.

DR PATRICK: You can't be —

LIZZIE: You're a doctor, isn't that right?

623

DR PATRICK: Right enough there.

LIZZIE: So, tell me, tell me, if a dreadful accident occurred . . . and two people were dying . . . but you could only save one. . . . Which would you save?

DR PATRICK: You can't ask questions like that.

LIZZIE: Yes, I can, come on, it's a game. How does a doctor determine? If one were old and the other were young — would you save the younger one first?

DR PATRICK: Lizzie.

LIZZIE: You said you liked games! If one were a bad person and the other was good, was trying to be good, would you save the one who was good and let the bad person die?

DR PATRICK: I don't know.

LIZZIE: Listen! If you could go back in time . . . what would you do if you met a person who was evil and wicked?

DR PATRICK: Who?

LIZZIE: I don't know, Attila the Hun!

DR PATRICK: (Laughs.) Oh my.

LIZZIE: Listen, if you met Attila the Hun, and you were in a position to kill him, would you do it?

DR PATRICK: I don't know.

LIZZIE: Think of the suffering he caused, the unhappiness.

DR PATRICK: Yes, but I'm a doctor, not an assassin.

LIZZIE: I think you're a coward.

Pause.

DR PATRICK: What I do is try to save lives . . .

LIZZIE: But you put poison out for the slugs in your garden.

DR PATRICK: You got something mixed up.

624

LIZZIE: I've never been clearer. Everything's clear. I've lived all of my life for this one moment of absolute clarity! If war were declared, would you serve?

DR PATRICK: I would fight in a war.

LIZZIE: You wouldn't fight, you would kill — you'd take a gun and shoot people, people who'd done nothing to you, people who were trying to be good, you'd kill them! And you say you wouldn't kill Attila the Hun, or that that stupid cow's life is precious — *My life is precious!!*

DR PATRICK: To you.

LIZZIE: Yes to me, are you stupid!?

DR PATRICK: And hers is to her.

LIZZIE: I don't care about her! *(Pause.)* I'm glad you're not my doctor, you can't make decisions, can you? You are a coward.

DR PATRICK starts off.

LIZZIE: You're afraid of your wife . . . you can *only* play games. . . . If I really wanted to go to Boston, you wouldn't come with me because you're a coward! *I'm not a coward!!*

LIZZIE turns to watch MRS BORDEN sit with needle work. After a moment MRS BORDEN looks at LIZZIE, aware of her scrutiny.

LIZZIE: . . . Where's Papa?

MRS BORDEN: Out.

LIZZIE: And Mr Wingate?

MRS BORDEN: He's out too.

LIZZIE: So what are you going to do . . . Mrs Borden?

MRS BORDEN: I'm going to finish this up.

LIZZIE: You do that. . . . *(Pause.)* Where's Bridget?

MRS BORDEN: Out back washing windows. . . . You got clean clothes to go upstairs, they're in the kitchen.

Pause.

LIZZIE: Did you know Papa killed my birds with the axe? He chopped off their heads. *(MRS BORDEN is uneasy.)* . . . It's alright. At first I felt bad, but I feel better now. I feel much better now. . . . I am a woman of decision, Mrs Borden. When I decide to do things, I do them, yes, I do. *(Smiles.)* How many times has Papa said — when Lizzie puts her mind to a thing, she does it — and I do. . . . It's always me who puts the slug poison out because they eat all the flowers and you don't like that, do you? They're bad things, they must die. You see, not all life is precious, is it?

MRS BORDEN: *(After a moment makes an attempt casually to gather together her things, to go upstairs. She does not want to be in the room with LIZZIE.)*

LIZZIE: Where're you going?

MRS BORDEN: Upstairs. . . . *(An excuse.)* The spare room needs changing.

A knock at the back door . . . A second knock.

LIZZIE: Someone's at the door. . . . *(A third knock.)* I'll get it.

She exits to the kitchen. MRS BORDEN waits. LIZZIE returns. She's a bit out of breath. She carries a pile of clean clothes which she puts on the table. She looks at MRS BORDEN.

LIZZIE: Did you want something?

MRS BORDEN: Who was it? — the door?

LIZZIE: Oh yes. I forgot. I had to step out back for a moment and — it's a note. A message for you.

MRS BORDEN: Oh.

LIZZIE: Shall I open it?

MRS BORDEN: That's alright. *(She holds out her hand.)*

LIZZIE: Looks like Papa's handwriting. . . . *She passes over the note.* Aren't you going to open it?

MRS BORDEN: I'll read it upstairs.

LIZZIE: Mrs Borden! . . . Would you mind . . . putting my clothes in my room? *(She gets some clothes from the table, MRS BORDEN takes them, something she would never normally do. Before she can move away, LIZZIE grabs her arm.)* Just a minute . . . I would like you to look into my eyes. What's the matter? Nothing's wrong. It's an experiment. . . . Look right into them. Tell me . . . what do you see . . . can you see anything?

MRS BORDEN: Myself.

LIZZIE: Yes. When a person dies, retained on her eye is the image of the last thing she saw. Isn't that interesting? *(Pause.)*

MRS BORDEN slowly starts upstairs. LIZZIE picks up remaining clothes on table. The hand hatchet is concealed beneath them. She follows MRS BORDEN up the stairs.

LIZZIE: Do you know something? If I were to kill someone, I would come up behind them very slowly and quietly. They would never even hear me, they would never turn around. *(MRS BORDEN stops on the stairs. She turns around to look at LIZZIE who is behind her.)* They would be too frightened to turn around even if they heard me. They would be so afraid they'd see what they feared. *(MRS BORDEN makes a move which might be an effort to go past LIZZIE back down the stairs. LIZZIE stops her.)* Careful. Don't fall. *(MRS BORDEN turns and slowly continues up the stairs with LIZZIE behind her.)* And then, I would strike them down. With them not turning around, they would retain no image of me on their eye. It would be better that way.

LIZZIE and MRS BORDEN disappear at the top of the stairs. The stage is empty for a moment. BRIDGET enters. She carries the pail for washing the windows. She sets the pail down, wipes her forehead. She stands for a moment looking towards the stairs as if she might have heard a sound. She picks up the pail and exits to the kitchen. LIZZIE appears on the stairs. She is carrying the pile of clothes she carried upstairs. The hand hatchet is concealed under the clothes. LIZZIE descends the stairs, she seems calm, self-possessed. She places the clothes on the table. She pauses, then she slowly turns to look at MRS BORDEN's chair at the table. After a moment she moves to it, pauses a moment, then sits down in it. She sits there at ease, relaxed, thinking. BRIDGET enters from the kitchen, she sees LIZZIE, she stops, she takes in LIZZIE sitting in MRS BORDEN's chair. BRIDGET glances towards the stairs, back to LIZZIE. LIZZIE looks, for the first time, at BRIDGET. BRIDGET starts up stairs.

LIZZIE: Don't go up there. *(Pause.)* We must hurry before Papa gets home.

BRIDGET: Lizzie?

LIZZIE: I have it all figured out, but you have to help me, Bridget, you have to help me.

BRIDGET: What have you done?

LIZZIE: He would never leave me the farm, not with her on his back, but now *(She gets up from the chair)* I will have the farm, and I will have the money, yes, to do what I please! And you too Bridget, I'll give you some of my money but you've got to help me. *(She moves towards BRIDGET who backs away a step.)* Don't be afraid, it's me, it's Lizzie, you like me!

BRIDGET: What have you done! *(Pause.)* You've killed her!

LIZZIE: Someone broke in and they killed her.

BRIDGET: They'll know!

LIZZIE: Not if you help me.

BRIDGET: I can't, Miss Lizzie, I can't!

628

LIZZIE: *(Grabs BRIDGET's arm.)* Do you want them to hang me! Is that what you want! Oh Bridget, look! Look! *(She falls to her knees.)* I'm begging for my life, I'm begging. Deny me, and they will kill me. Help me, Bridget, please help me.

BRIDGET: But . . . what . . . could we do? A denial.

LIZZIE: *(Up off her knees.)* I have it all figured out. I'll go downtown as quick as I can, you go back outside and work on the windows.

BRIDGET: I've finished them, Lizzie.

LIZZIE: Then do them again! Remember last year when the burglar broke in? Today someone broke in and she caught them.

BRIDGET: They'll never believe us.

LIZZIE: Have coffee with Lucy next door, stay with her till Papa gets home and he'll find her, each of us swears she was fine when we left, she was alright when we left! — it's going to work, Bridget, I know it!

BRIDGET: Your papa will guess.

LIZZIE: *(Getting ready to leave for downtown.)* If he found me here he might guess, but he won't.

BRIDGET: Your papa will know!

LIZZIE: Papa loves me, if he has another story to believe, he'll believe it. He'd want to believe it, he'd have to believe it.

BRIDGET: Your papa will know.

LIZZIE: Why aren't you happy? I'm happy. We both should be happy! *(LIZZIE embraces BRIDGET. LIZZIE steps back a pace.)* Now — how do I look?

MR BORDEN enters. BRIDGET sees him. LIZZIE slowly turns to see what BRIDGET is looking at.

LIZZIE: Papa?

MR BORDEN: What is it? Where's Mrs Borden?

BRIDGET: I . . . don't know . . . sir . . . I . . . just came in, sir.

MR BORDEN: Did she leave the house?

BRIDGET: Well, sir . . .

LIZZIE: She went out. Someone delivered a message and she left. (*LIZZIE takes off her hat and looks at her father.*)

LIZZIE: . . . You're home early, Papa.

MR BORDEN: I wanted to see Abbie. She's gone out, has she? Which way did she go? (*LIZZIE shrugs, he continues, more thinking aloud.*) Well . . . I . . . I . . . best wait for her here. I don't want to miss her again.

LIZZIE: Help Papa off with his coat, Bridget. . . . I hear there's a sale of dress goods on downtown. Why don't you go buy yourself a yard?

BRIDGET: Oh . . . I don't know, ma'am.

LIZZIE: You don't want any?

BRIDGET: I don't know.

LIZZIE: Then . . . why don't you go upstairs and lie down. Have a rest before lunch.

BRIDGET: I don't think I should.

LIZZIE: Nonsense.

BRIDGET: Lizzie, I —

LIZZIE: You go up and lie down. I'll look after things here.

LIZZIE smiles at BRIDGET. BRIDGET starts up the stairs, suddenly stops. She looks back at LIZZIE.

LIZZIE: It's alright . . . go on . . . it's alright. (*BRIDGET continues part way up the stairs. She stops, turns to watch the scene.*) Hello Papa. You look so tired. . . . I make you

unhappy. . . . I don't like to make you unhappy. I love
you.

MR BORDEN: *(Smiles and takes her hand.)* I'm just getting old,
Lizzie.

LIZZIE: You've got on my ring. . . . Do you remember when
I gave you that? . . . When I left Miss Cornelia's — it was
in a little blue velvet box, you hid it behind your back,
and you said, "guess which hand, Lizzie!" And I guessed.
And you gave it to me and you said, "it's real gold, Lizzie,
it's for you because you are very precious to me." Do you
remember, Papa? *(MR BORDEN nods.)* And I took it out
of the little blue velvet box, and I took your hand, and I
put my ring on your finger and I said "thank you, Papa, I
love you." . . . You've never taken it off . . . see how it
bites into the flesh of your finger. *(She presses his hand to
her face.)* I forgive you, Papa, I forgive you for killing my
birds. . . . You look so tired, why don't you lie down and
rest, put your feet up, I'll undo your shoes for you. *(She
kneels and undoes his shoes.)*

MR BORDEN: You're a good girl.

LIZZIE: I could never stand to have you hate me, Papa.
Never. I would do anything rather than have you hate
me.

MR BORDEN: I don't hate you, Lizzie.

LIZZIE: I would not want you to find out anything that
would make you hate me. Because I love you.

MR BORDEN: And I love you, Lizzie, you'll always be precious to me.

LIZZIE: *(Looks at him, and then smiles.)* Was I — when I had
scabs on my knees?

MR BORDEN: *(Laughs.)* Oh yes. Even then.

LIZZIE: *(Laughs.)* Oh Papa! . . . Kiss me! *(He kisses her on the
forehead.)* Thank you, Papa.

MR BORDEN: Why're you crying?

LIZZIE: Because I'm so happy. Now . . . put your feet up and get to sleep . . . that's right . . . shut your eyes . . . go to sleep . . . go to sleep . . .

She starts to hum, continues humming as MR BORDEN falls asleep. MISS LIZZIE/BRIDGET is still on the stairs. LIZZIE still humming, moves to the table, slips her hand under the clothes, withdraws the hatchet. She approaches her father with the hatchet behind her back. She stops humming. A pause, then she slowly raises the hatchet very high to strike him. Just as the hatchet is about to start its descent, there is a blackout. Children's voices are heard singing:

"Lizzie Borden took an axe,
Gave her mother forty whacks,
When the job was nicely done,
She gave her father forty-one!
Forty-one!
Forty-one!"

The singing increases in volume and in distortion as it nears the end of the verse till the last words are very loud but discernible, just. Silence. Then the sound of slow measured heavy breathing which is growing into a wordless sound of hysteria. Light returns to the stage, dim light from late in the day. THE ACTRESS stands with the hatchet raised in the same position in which we saw her before the blackout, but the couch is empty. Her eyes are shut. The sound comes from her. MISS LIZZIE is on the stairs. She moves to THE ACTRESS, reaches up to take the hatchet from her. When MISS LIZZIE's hand touches THE ACTRESS', THE ACTRESS whirls around to face MISS LIZZIE who holds the hatchet. THE ACTRESS backs away from MISS LIZZIE. There is a flickering of light at the top of the stairs.

EMMA: *(From upstairs.)* Lizzie! Lizzie! You're making too much noise!

EMMA descends the stairs carrying an oil lamp. THE ACTRESS backs away from LIZZIE. EMMA does not see her. MISS LIZZIE turns to see EMMA. The hand hatchet is behind MISS LIZZIE's back concealed from EMMA. EMMA pauses for a moment.

EMMA: Where is she?

MISS LIZZIE: Who?

EMMA: *(A pause then EMMA moves to the window and glances out.)* It's raining.

MISS LIZZIE: I know.

EMMA: *(Puts the lamp down, sits, lowers her voice.)* Lizzie.

MISS LIZZIE: Yes?

EMMA: I want to speak to you, Lizzie.

MISS LIZZIE: Yes Emma.

EMMA: That . . . actress who's come up from Boston.

MISS LIZZIE: What about her?

EMMA: People talk.

MISS LIZZIE: You needn't listen.

EMMA: In your position you should do nothing to *inspire talk.*

MISS LIZZIE: People need so little in the way of inspiration. And Miss Cornelia's classes didn't cover "Etiquette for Acquitted Persons".

EMMA: Common sense should tell you what you ought or ought not do.

MISS LIZZIE: Common sense is repugnant to me. I prefer uncommon sense.

EMMA: I forbid her in this house, Lizzie!

Pause.

MISS LIZZIE: Do you?

EMMA: *(Backing down, softly.)* It's . . . disgraceful.

633

MISS LIZZIE: I see.

MISS LIZZIE turns away from EMMA a few steps.

EMMA: I simply cannot —

MISS LIZZIE: You could always leave.

EMMA: Leave?

MISS LIZZIE: Move. Away. Why don't you?

EMMA: I —

MISS LIZZIE: You could never, could you?

EMMA: If I only —

MISS LIZZIE: Knew.

EMMA: Lizzie, did you?

MISS LIZZIE: Oh Emma, do you intend asking me that question from now till death us do part?

EMMA: It's just —

MISS LIZZIE: For if you do, I may well take something sharp to you.

EMMA: Why do you joke like that!

MISS LIZZIE: *(Turning back to EMMA who sees the hatchet for the first time. EMMA's reaction is not any verbal or untoward movement. She freezes as MISS LIZZIE advances on her.)* Did you never stop and think that if I did, then you were guilty too?

EMMA: What?

THE ACTRESS watches.

MISS LIZZIE: It was you who brought me up, like a mother to me. Almost like a mother. Did you ever stop and think that I was like a puppet, your puppet. My head your hand, yes, your hand working my mouth, me saying all the things you felt like saying, me doing all the things you felt like doing, me spewing forth, me hitting out, and you, you — !

THE ACTRESS: (Quietly.) Lizzie.

MISS LIZZIE is immediately in control of herself.

EMMA: (Whispers.) I wasn't even here that day.

MISS LIZZIE: I can swear to that.

EMMA: Do you want to drive me mad?

MISS LIZZIE: Oh yes.

EMMA: You didn't . . . did you?

MISS LIZZIE: Poor . . . Emma.

THE ACTRESS: Lizzie. (She takes the hatchet from MISS LIZZIE.) Lizzie, you did.

MISS LIZZIE: I didn't. (She puts the hatchet on the table.) You did.

Blackout

Margaret Hollingsworth

Ever Loving

A PLAY IN TWO ACTS

EDITOR'S NOTE: Margaret Hollingsworth was born during the war in England and moved to Canada in 1968. She graduated with a degree in psychology from Lakehead University in Thunder Bay, then moved to Vancouver where she received her M.F.A. in theatre and creative writing at the University of British Columbia. She went on to teach for the University of Victoria at David Thompson University Centre in Nelson, B.C. Her first professionally-produced play was *Bushed* done by the New Play Centre in Vancouver in 1973, who also staged *Operators*, the following year. *Apple in the Eye*, a radio play little known in Canada, has had numerous broadcasts outside the country and was re-written and staged in Vancouver in 1983. *Alli Alli Oh* and *Mother Country* have had professional productions in Toronto; *Islands* and *War Babies*, her most recent works, have been produced by the New Play Centre. *War Babies* was also staged by the Belfry Theatre in Victoria, B.C.

Ever Loving was first produced at the Belfry Theatre, Victoria, B.C. in November 1980 and has had subsequent performances in Halifax, Montreal, Toronto and Vancouver.

AUTHOR'S NOTE: *The action of the play takes place between 1938 and 1970. The set should be flexible, at one time or another it represents a bar, a café, three railway stations, a train, a farm, various domestic interiors, La Gondola (an Italian supper club), etc. Costume changes are quick indicators of changes of period and leaps in time and it is recommended that costumes be as realistic as possible.*

Characters:

RUTH WATSON (RUTHIE)
JAMES MICHAEL O'SULLIVAN (DAVE)
PAUL TOMACHUK
DIANA MANNING
CHUCK MALECARNE   *A musician, preferably a*
                     singer/pianist
LUCE MARIA MARINI

ACT ONE SCENE ONE

In "La Gondola", a supper club in Niagara Falls, 1970. Italian decor. DIANA, PAUL, RUTH, and DAVE are eating in silence at a table illuminated by a single candle. DIANA's accent is less pronounced than in the following scenes, and PAUL has picked up a slightly British intonation. LUCE sits nearby smartly dressed and coiffed, alone at a table. CHUCK is playing and singing, his style exaggeratedly Mediterranean, smooth. He sings "I Never Promised You a Rose Garden" in Italian.

DIANA: Well, this is really nice. *(smiles)*

Silence. DIANA pats PAUL's hand

RUTH: I still have your fur. It's a bit yellow, but it's all right. I've kept it in tissue. Do you want it back?

DIANA: I'd forgotten about it.

DAVE: *(prodding his meat)* What is this anyway?

637

RUTH: It's veal. You've had it before.

DAVE: Yeah . . . I mean the sticky stuff.

DIANA: Marsala — it's a sauce.

DAVE: Mmmm.

DIANA: This is all such a revelation to me.

DIANA smiles. She is far more socially at ease than RUTH and DAVE.

PAUL: D'you know Dave, this is the first trip we've ever taken out east. . .

DIANA: *(to RUTH)* Apart from that dreadful train ride — you remember? *(pauses)* Niagara Falls. We planned it as a silver wedding gift to each other. *(pauses)* In another five years we'll be retiring to the west coast — *(to PAUL)* somewhere around '75, isn't that right? Paul's been having a bit of trouble with the old war wound, so there's no sense pressing our luck.

PAUL: Yes. Going to try some city living for a change — Victoria. *(to RUTH)* Ever been there?

RUTH: No.

DAVE: *(suddenly, to PAUL)* Seems to me you were a bit of a womanizer, isn't that right? I was looking for you in the old regimental photograph — you weren't there.

PAUL: We weren't in the same regiment.

RUTH: I told you that.

DIANA: Well it's so nice to know that we've all done so well.

PAUL: *(pouring wine)* Come on — try some of this. My wife claims it's a good vintage, don't you Di? *(holds the bottle up to LUCE, mistaking her for the hostess)* Waiter . . . another bottle. *(to DAVE)* It's all right, it's on us. We're celebrating.

DAVE: *(preventing PAUL from pouring into RUTH's glass)* It doesn't agree with her.

CHUCK: *(to LUCE)* Friends of yours?

LUCE: I never set eyes on them.

CHUCK: Just as well. I wouldn't wanna know you if they were.

LUCE: Snob!

CHUCK: Just choosy, that's all. Always was. *(touches LUCE's hand)*

DIANA: It was an inspiration thinking of you, wasn't it, Paul?

PAUL: Sure was.

DIANA: And then finding you at the same address. As soon as we got here I called directory assistance for Hamilton. I couldn't think of your married name. All I could think of was Watson. Ruthie Watson.

RUTH: O'Sullivan. *(prods her food)* It's Irish.

DIANA: Yes. *(nods at RUTH's food)* Aren't you enjoying it?

RUTH: We don't come out to restaurants very often.

PAUL: Neither do we. *(to DIANA)* When did we last eat out?

DIANA: We only have one good restaurant within a hundred miles. My brother came over a few years ago . . . I think that's what bugged him most. It's funny what you can get used to. Paul went through hell with me the first year or two, didn't you?

PAUL: Well . . . I guess all the girls put up a bit of a fight didn't they? *(pauses)* So . . . did you make it to Expo?

DAVE: No . . . no, we didn't bother.

PAUL: We're planning to look in — better late than never, eh?

DAVE: They coulda spent that money on something better. Stamp out crime across the country eh Ruthie?

RUTH: Aye.

PAUL: You a cop?

DIANA: I was a policewoman during the war.

DAVE: You?

RUTH: He's a security guard.

PAUL: Good job?

DAVE: Security officer. Lousy pay but I'm not complaining. You don't see us going on strike. We do that and the whole goddamn country falls apart. *(blows out the candle on the table)* Biggest fire hazard there is. Yeah . . . *(to DIANA)* Look where strikes got your country . . . down the drain.

(RUTH is searching in her purse)

(to RUTH) What are you looking for?

RUTH: Matches. *(to DIANA)* I didn't bring any.

DAVE gives RUTH a thunderous look

DIANA: I'll do it. *(lights the candle)*

Pause

DIANA: Well . . . it's been a long time eh? A heck of a time. Too long of course . . . Yes . . . well, nothing comes easily does it? I can't say I'd've changed anything though — looking back. It's extraordinary really. I don't know where the years've gone.

They all stare into the flame. The lights dim. Searchlights sweep across the stage accompanied by an air raid siren and blackout. The three couples dive offstage. The scene is struck in a frenzy of activity. The siren dies and an ominous silence prevails. "All clear" is heard. The sound of the sea as the lights come up a little. Music — "Will Ye Ne'er Come Back Again." The voice of COLONEL W.E. SUTHERLAND, O.B.E., Commander of the Queen Mary, is heard. He has an English accent

COLONEL SUTHERLAND: Ladies and gentlemen, this is your captain speaking. In less than an hour we will be docking in Halifax. Canada is just ahead and I want particularly to address this message to all of you who are representative of the true flower of English womanhood. Canada's fighting men have placed their trust in you, and I am confident that you and your lovely children, the like of whom I have rarely seen, will not betray this trust. The dark years are over. Your courage, sacrifice and bravery have helped to make victory possible. You have won the admiration of decent peoples throughout the world. . .

(COLONEL SUTHERLAND's voice begins to fade)

Canada welcomes you as citizens of whom she may be justly proud. . .

Lights up on CHUCK, at home, practising "Don't Sit Under the Apple Tree." Lights fade

ACT ONE   SCENE TWO

Fall, 1945. Onstage we see a Union Jack and three railway stations: Halifax, Hamilton, and Regina. In Halifax, a banner reads "Welcome to Canada British War Brides." LUCE sits brooding under the banner. There is also a wartime poster which should show the Canadian, American, and British heads of state. DIANA and RUTH enter. They have luggage. RUTH has a baby in a carry-cot. They walk past LUCE, looking for the train.

DIANA: It's over there — that must be it.

RUTH: Are you sure? If we get on the wrong one we might end up with the Eskimos. *(pauses)* Shall I ask? *(glances at LUCE)*

DIANA: I doubt if she'd know. Don't stare.

RUTH: Why wouldn't she know?

DIANA: She doesn't look English.

RUTH: Well, none of them are.

They stop and examine the poster

RUTH: Look, there's Mr Churchill and President thingama-
bob in his wheelchair — who's that one?

DIANA: That's their prime minister I think. King —

RUTH: King what?

DIANA: Ruthie!

RUTH: He doesn't look like a prime minister. *(glances back at
LUCE)* It's awful . . . *foreign* isn't it, I mean . . .

*They get in the train and settle themselves. The lights dim. The
train is in motion. LUCE is still wrapped in her cape, at the station. CHUCK, at home, plays a snatch of "Sentimental Journey".*

DIANA: *(indicating a paper bag which RUTH is holding)* What's
that?

RUTH: Oh . . . nothing.

DIANA: It's dripping.

RUTH: Yes. *(sniffs it)* It's maybe a bit mouldy. Well, I
couldn't eat it on the boat. I couldn't let it go to waste . . .
all that real white bread, and cornflakes . . . and did you
see the tinned peaches? It's not fair I had to go and get
seasick.

DIANA: But you can't keep the stuff. The train meals are
enough for an army.

RUTH: Aye . . . I suppose.

DIANA: Here . . . let me throw it out of the window.

RUTH: No . . . no . . . maybe someone'll want it.

Pause. DIANA stares out the window

What's he going to think of me — I haven't slept for three nights. I look like a witch.

DIANA: You look all right to me.

RUTH: Aye, but you don't know me. You don't know how nice I can look.

DIANA: We've been in pretty close proximity for the last three weeks.

Pause.

RUTH: I shouldn't've put my frock on in Halifax. *(looks out the window)* It's not very green is it . . . Not *green* green — more black.

DIANA: Fir trees.

RUTH: Aye. And do you know they're full of bears. Dave told me. I wonder what the cows eat? It's all trees.

DIANA: Lovely colours. They must be maples . . . See . . . those red ones. That's their national tree.

RUTH: National *tree*? *(thinks)* We've got the thistle.

DIANA: They call autumn fall.

RUTH: It feels . . . different. Creepy. Foreign. *(pauses, has no word to express her feelings)* Big.

DIANA: Don't look at it.

RUTH: I can't help it.

DIANA: *(irritated)* Well don't.

RUTH: Don't shout at me.

Pause. RUTH is near to tears.

DIANA: *(sighs)* It's going to take time isn't it? Getting the hang of . . . *(makes an expansive gesture)*

RUTH: Oh, it'll be all right — as soon as I see Dave — as soon as I see my house. He's going to love Rita. *(pauses)* How many are you going to have?

DIANA: We've decided on two. I'd like a boy and a girl.

RUTH: You can't stop them coming just like that.

DIANA: Oh we're not catholics.

RUTH grimaces. They stare out the window. The sound of a train whistle. In the distance, strains of "The Wedding March" are heard

RUTH: They're playing it again. Someone's getting out.

DIANA: *(getting up to look)* It's not even a station! There's not a house in sight. There's someone with a violin. How jolly. *(hums along)*

RUTH: We're not brides. Half the women are pregnant.

DIANA: Poor soul. She's crying.

RUTH: *(not looking)* Yes.

DIANA: There's four or five fellows out there to meet her. They're all kissing her on both cheeks. That's the way the French do it. Whoops — we're off. *(lurches back into seat)* I'm glad it wasn't me.

They sit in silence

ACT ONE   SCENE THREE

Halifax Station, fall, 1945.

CHUCK: Come on, Loose. I don't get it. Why do you have to spend all your time on the railway station?

LUCE: People.

CHUCK: Well, there's people at home. All you gotta do is walk to the corner store to see people. Go downstairs and talk to Mama once in a while. She's people. She'll be glad to show you what's what.

LUCE: People, la gente. Vengano, vanno. Dove vanno?

CHUCK: What?

LUCE: Where they go? La gente?

CHUCK: How should I know? On journeys — they're travelling.

LUCE: Stranieri. Da dove? Where from they come? Are my brothers. Fratelli. Tutti fratelli.

CHUCK: Where?

LUCE: *(vaguely)* Là.

CHUCK: I'm your brother!

(LUCE stares at him)

Godammit, Loose. I'm not coming down to the railway station every day to bring you home for supper.

LUCE: Non è necessario. I come back. Sola. *(makes no move)*

CHUCK: So what do you think Mama and Papa are thinking? They're thinking you're not happy with me. With us. Well, if you'd rather spend your days here. . .

(LUCE shrugs)

This is the last time I'm coming looking for you. Okay? You just come home.

LUCE: Home?

CHUCK: Casa. Casa mia. Okay? Now! *(leaves)*

ACT ONE SCENE FOUR

Fall, 1945. RUTH and DIANA are still on the train.

DIANA: It's all . . . untouched. London's horrible now . . . ugly. Here everything's so splendidly . . . untouched. No bombing. . . nothing destroyed . . . mile upon mile . . . well, there's nothing to bomb is there? There's no one to kill.

RUTH: Bears.

DIANA: It's quite beautiful really.

RUTH: Yes. But it's not like Scotland.

DIANA: Space. That's what Paul said. A blank page just waiting for us to write on. *(shakes her head)* I thought I understood him. Did you notice that Canadian in the restaurant car this morning? He was reading a comic. A grown man!

RUTH: Yes . . . Dave likes comics. I hope he'll be there to meet me. I hope his family likes me. What if they don't? What'll you do if Paul's don't like you?

DIANA: Oh, they will. There might be a slight problem with the father not speaking fluently — he's Ukrainian.

RUTH: What's that?

DIANA: Oh . . . a part of Russia. Luckily I speak German. We won't be seeing much of Paul's family, anyway. They're country people. Farmers. Paul's not like that. *(pauses)* I hope he's not crippled. He says he's all right but . . .

RUTH: I'd'a died if Dave'd got hurt.

DIANA: He writes these incredible letters. I shall miss them.

RUTH: They'll think I look all right, won't they? *(looks at her dress)* My mother helped me alter it. She got it off a friend who died.

646

DIANA: Was she a big woman? The friend?

RUTH: Big? Aye, she was bonny, why?

DIANA: Nothing.

RUTH: It's the shoulders, isn't it?

DIANA: I'll tell you what. I'll give you something to go with it. *(gets her case from under the seat)* There . . . *(brings out a white fox wrap)*

RUTH: *(overwhelmed)* Oh! . . .

DIANA: Go on. Try it on.

RUTH: No. No, I couldn't.

DIANA: I don't need it. It's hot on the prairies.

RUTH: Aye. It's hot in Hamilton too — when it's not snow-ing. *(tries on the wrap)*

(RUTH fantasizes. Music — a Viennese waltz. RUTH wears a tiara and waltzes wearing the wrap, tosses a single rose to an admirer. Fantasy ends)

If I could borrow it. . . I could maybe post it back to you. . .

DIANA: It's yours.

Pause. RUTH gets the feel of the wrap. She takes it off with a quick gesture.

RUTH: I can't take it. *(bursts into tears)*

DIANA: *(hugs RUTH)* Oh Ruthie.

RUTH: You don't have to be nice to me . . . It's all so . . . so . . .

DIANA: It's going to be all right. Don't worry. We've got to make it all right. They'll be waiting for us — as long as we love them nothing else matters.

RUTH: I don't know. I don't know . . .

ACT ONE SCENE FIVE

PAUL and DAVE are waiting for the train on Regina and Hamilton stations. PAUL has flowers. Their monologues should run over each other, though some phrases should stand alone.

DAVE: What's taking her so long? Shouldn't have to wait like this. . . You watching over me Rita? *(pats his pocket)* You better be . . . Why the hell didn't I get a photograph? How come she sent me a picture of the kid when I asked for one of her? Does that mean she's fat? Jesus! What if I don't recognize her? What if she's fat? What if she doesn't love me . . . loves the kid and . . . Well if she doesn't love me I won't love her . . . eh Rita? That's only right isn't it? Verna. Why does she keep hanging around? Should'a told her about . . . about the kid. What's she gonna say? She'll make a big scene. Jesus! Well, I wasn't engaged to her or nothing. She can't fool me she was waiting around for me . . . I don't care what she said in her letters I know what she was doing . . . Well Jackie Cranmer as good as he said it didn't he? Even with my own brother . . . no . . . *(pauses)* Hope she doesn't want me to finish high school. No, she won't want that. If only Dad coulda held out another couple of months. Wish she'd get here. Hold my hand Rita. . . hold my hand . . .

PAUL: God she can't hate it . . . she'll love it . . . she'll go along with . . . we can build it up together. . . So why doesn't she wanna talk about it in her letters? God! She can't hate it. What if she's changed? People don't change . . . yes they do . . . No — that's crazy. Look on the bright side. Well, we're still the same people — underneath — she's the same person. I'm . . . oh, God! For ever and ever . . . I'll never get to sleep on my own again. It's gonna be okay. Isn't it? Hell, we'll get old together. . . we'll read books in the winter, yeah, that's it, read out loud, I'll read to her when she gets near-sighted, she can nurse me when I'm sick . . . What if I do get sick? Yeah, we'll read Shakespeare. Why doesn't she get here? *(suddenly)* She's not coming. Well, I can get by without a woman — sure, I mean, I never laid a hand on one of those nurses did I? Never. How come? Don't remember. Maybe I'm undersexed. Jees! It'll be okay when she gets here. She's that kind of person, makes things happen. None of the great philosophers were married were they? Didn't have wives . . . Kant, Heidegger, did Buddha get married? Wish there'd never been a war . . . wish I'd never been over there. Wish I'd stayed.

ACT ONE SCENE SIX

Fall, 1945, on the train. DIANA is looking at the baby.

DIANA: I think she's hungry.

RUTH: Aye . . . it's time . . . I'll go and warm the bottle.

DIANA: Should we wake her?

RUTH: Of course. It's time.

DIANA: Let me do it.

RUTH: No . . . thanks all the same.

DIANA: Just once more.

RUTH: Everyone's wondering whose baby she is —

DIANA: I know but . . .

RUTH: So I'll do it.

DIANA: I have been rather hogging her —

RUTH: It's all right. You can practise on your own one. *(tries to pass DIANA)*

DIANA: Ruthie . . . do you mind if I ask you something — it's a bit silly — I mean, I was always giving advice to people before . . . but it was all so, sort of abstract. *(suddenly)* Did it hurt?

RUTH: What?

649

DIANA: Having her? She's got such a big head.

RUTH: She has not!

DIANA: You don't have to talk about it.

RUTH: Ach, we all talk about it when we get together up the train. Haven't you listened?

DIANA shakes her head

RUTH: It wasn't as bad as some of them make out. I'd've liked it better if Dave'd been there with me though.

DIANA: Don't be silly — men are far too squeamish.

RUTH: Not Dave. He says that after what he's seen nothing'll set him back.

DIANA: *(doubtful)* I don't think I'd like Paul to be in on it.

RUTH: Yes you will.

DIANA: My father never came within two hundred miles of my mother when she had us.

RUTH: Aye, but they're old-fashioned.

DIANA: We were twins.

RUTH: You and your brother? You never said —

DIANA: We weren't that close.

RUTH: Won't you miss him?

DIANA: Hugh? No, of course not.

RUTH: No?

DIANA: To hell with all of them anyway! *(bites her lip)*

RUTH: Here . . . you can take her.

(RUTH pushes the baby into DIANA's arms. DIANA clings to the baby, rocking it closely)

Just this one last time, mind . . .

DIANA leaves, carrying the baby. RUTH is left alone in the carriage

ACT ONE SCENE SEVEN

As the scene begins, RUTH and DIANA are on the train and LUCE is still at Halifax station, 1945. After the first three lines, the scene changes to 1938. RUTH is in a fish shop, DIANA on a tennis court, and LUCE at home.

RUTH: *(staring out the window of the train)* I wonder how many of my friends've got babies? They'll all have gone back to the fish market now that the war's over. *(defiantly)* Well, I'm glad I'm not in their boat.

DIANA: *(elsewhere on the train, imitating the train, rocking the baby)* Da da da dum, da da da dum, da da da dum. One da da equals about two feet, say, da dum equals two more feet, how many feet in a mile, five thousand two hundred and eighty? Multiplied by how many miles? . . .

LUCE: *(on the platform, mesmerised)* Treni, guardando . . . i treni . . . guardando, treni passando — passare la vita guardando treni — sognando, sognando, tanti sogni . . . sogni . . . sogni — dreams. *(hisses very softly, as if letting out stream)*

Scene changes to 1938. Music — "Bonny Dundee"

RUTH: *(scaling fish)* It's not fair. Maggie's been on the counter for over a month and you promised me you'd get me off scaling. I'm going as fast as I can, Mr. MacKie — well, you promised. *(to girl beside her)* He'd have us here all night if he could.

Music — "Il Lombardino", an Italian folk song

LUCE: *(with an English textbook)* Il mio nome . . . my name is Luce Maria Marini . . . How do you do? *(closes the book and closes her eyes, trying to memorize)* I am Luce Maria Marini *(extends her hand)* How do you do . . . Yank? I am mighty fine. *(closes the book)*

Music — "Hearts of Oak"

DIANA: *(on the tennis court, playing, shout)* Love-fifteen. I'm sure Anthony. Really. *(to herself)* Why aren't you more mysterious? What if you spoke with an accent? Come into ze Casbah. *(giggles)* Well at least you could learn to roll your "r"s Maybe they'll make you in the navy. The war might be good for something! Come on!

LUCE: I have twenty — one, two — twenty-two years. *(calls out, answering her mother's shout)* Si, vengo Mama, vengo.

RUTH: *(looks at clock)* Ten past two. Will Andy take me to the pictures tomorrow night? There's Jeanette MacDonald and Nelson Eddy on . . . "Your eyes are like two spoonfuls of the blue Pacific."

DIANA: It might even liven things up a bit 'round here. Daddy doesn't think so. He has too much business with Germany. Well, they're not really *enemy*. How can they be? They can capture me any day! Must try not to think about it. It's such an awful word . . . war. *(to Anthony)* Out!

LUCE: Dicono che si sarà una guerra. *(looks up the word)* Warrr. Will to be warrra. They say . . . no? Is true, Yank? E vero? You want me come to bed? *(giggles at her audacity, opens book)*

RUTH: Five more minutes and I'll shut one eye, then if I sit on the stool for ten minutes . . . He's given me these spots on my chin. Clark Gable wouldn't rub my chin. He'd go straight for my lips. I hope I wouldn't get lipstick on him. *(dreams)*

LUCE: I like New York.

DIANA: Now Hugh's been called up. . . . I wouldn't mind being a pilot, if he can do it why can't I?

(The three women begin to speak in concert. These speeches should be orchestrated so that the occasional phrase stands alone)

RUTH: Oh, Humphrey! He comes straight for me and touches my face. "You're exquisite", and everyone hears and he doesn't care. "You're coming away with me, doll." "Oh Humphrey, how can I? . . . What about Andy?" His eyes burn and I think he's going to kiss me, but instead I feel him slipping a ring on my finger and I almost faint. And he carries me to his Rolls Royce and drives me to Hollywood and we sit in his mansion and sip green goddesses and talk about our love.

LUCE: Here women is making only bambini, more bambini! Is nothing other to make. In America . . . *(dreams herself into perfect English)* For Christ's sake tell those people to stop following me . . . and there is no one can tell me I can't smoke. It is my voice. Mine. My apartment. My manager. I'm just too busy.

And I don't give autographs!

DIANA: Last summer in Heidelberg . . . the boys were fabulous . . . Are you sure you wouldn't like to take a breather Anthony? Fabulous — just the way I always imagined. Fantabulous dancers . . . frightfully . . . masculine . . . in that sort of . . . German way. Not a bit like English men. Why do you let your mouth hang open when you serve?

LUCE: I want to go to America!

RUTH: *(looks at the clock)* An hour and three quarters. *(changes feet)*

DIANA: Out!

653

RUTH: When I get married, I'll have a bedroom with a dressing table with three mirrors and a frill on the bottom, and I'll have four bridesmaids in pink dresses. *(looks at the clock)* An hour and a half.

LUCE: I will to be cantatrice. *(sings)* You like? I like you, Yank. I like to go to New York. Non è possible. E cattiva — ogni giorno . . . take lesson make practise, hello Mama, hello Papa, eat food, stay house, learn English, for what? Ogni giorno lo stesso. Same. No thing to make. Che noioso. In America non è così. My mother wishes I sposare . . . marry with Angelo . . . my cugino — cowsin. Non voglio, non voglio sposarmi. I will not marry with Italian boy. I marry with American man. You come to bed, Yank?

DIANA: I always did like foreign men, I don't know why.

That's game and set Anthony, I hated to do it to you. *(smiles broadly)*

RUTH: *(looks at clock)* An hour and fifteen minutes!

LUCE: Dicono che ci sarà una guerra . . . warrrr!

DIANA: *(laughs)* War? Oh how silly. It can't possibly last!

Scene shifts between CHUCK in Halifax, 1941, and DAVE in Hamilton Station, 1939. Both are in new uniforms. At first, CHUCK at home, practising "There'll Always Be an England" throughout the scene.

CHUCK: *(sings the first line in a bland, neutral voice)* No . . . no . . . boring! This could be my big break. Well, there's never been a war where they didn't need music. *(croons the first couple of lines of the song)* Close, but no cigar!

CHUCK fantasizes. He is in a spotlight. Caruso-like he soars above a huge choir or orchestra version of "There'll Always Be an England". Fantasy lights dim on CHUCK, lights up on DAVE, in uniform, on Hamilton Station, 1939

DAVE: Jeez — won't they ever run to time again? *(looks at his watch. Paces. Pacing becomes marching. Comes to attention, salutes)* I got shoes that fit and they're not my Dad's hand-me-downs. I got a uniform . . . I got a job . . . *(throws his hat in the air)*

Fantasy lights up on CHUCK, who bows to the sound of waves of applause. Fantasy lights down, normal lighting up

CHUCK: Paris . . . Rome . . . Berlin, here I come!

DAVE fantasizes

DAVE: How we gonna get there? Troop ship from Halifax. *(salutes)* For king and country. *(dives onto his stomach and defends his position with a gun. Crawls on his stomach)* For the British Empire! Okay, Johnny . . . hold on there while I defuse this mine . . .

The mine explodes. DAVE looks up and sees Mackenzie King

DAVE: Mr Prime Minister, sir! *(assumes the voice of Mackenzie King)* "Welcome back to Canada, son. It's been a long year." *(DAVE's voice)* Thank you Mr King, sir. *(Mackenzie King's voice)* "What can we do for you?" *(DAVE's voice)* I just wanna carry on, sir — some kinda work like I been doing, to suit my talents. *(Mackenzie King's voice, in a confidential whisper)* "Well, it just so happens we need someone to test this new fighter plane and I think you're our man . . ."

CHUCK plays "There'll Always Be an England"

CHUCK: Canadian guy wrote it, so a Canadian guy can sing it, right? *(tries a new style, sings)* "The empire too, we can depend on you . . ." *(glances across at DAVE, ends with a crashing chord)*

ACT ONE SCENE NINE

A dingy English café, 1941. PAUL and DIANA face each other, drinking tea. PAUL, nervous, sticks his finger out as he drinks.

DIANA: Why are you doing that?

PAUL: What?

DIANA sticks her finger out. PAUL spills his tea. He is tongue-tied, embarrassed

DIANA: Oh, it's all right. It'll wash. You don't have to drink it you know. I won't be offended.

(PAUL puts his cup aside gratefully)

It's not a very good brand — dusty. Shall I be mother? *(refills his cup)* You should have seen this place two years ago. They had lovely china and lace cloths and real cream.

PAUL: Really?

DIANA: Yes. You really should've seen it before the war.

(Silence)

Have you been to Europe before?

(PAUL shakes his head)

What were you doing before you joined up?

PAUL: I used to read a lot.

DIANA: No . . . I mean work? What did you work at?

PAUL shrugs. Silence

PAUL: Look . . . I . . . I don't know why you invited me.

DIANA: You said you were lonely.

PAUL: Yes . . . but . . .

DIANA: Well it's not such a big event. We're only having tea . . .

PAUL: I'm sorry.

DIANA: That's all right.

PAUL: Why did you join the police?

DIANA: My mother thought it was safer — if she only knew! *(laughs)* I was going to join the WAFs actually — that's what I've always wanted to do — fly, or explore the Amazon in a boat — well, I suppose everybody does.

PAUL: The Amazon?

DIANA: I mean who wants to stick around here all their life? If the war hadn't happened I was enrolled in a secretarial college. I was going to be a bilingual secretary — you know, French and German. Maybe work in France . . . Do you?

PAUL: What?

DIANA: Know French and German?

657

PAUL: Only Ukrainian.

DIANA: What?

PAUL shrugs

DIANA: But why? I mean . . . Ukrainian?

PAUL: My old man came over from the Ukraine in twenty-three. He brought my mother. They didn't speak English. My dad doesn't speak too much of it even now.

DIANA: Well why doesn't he learn?

PAUL: Never had to I guess. He had to break land, no one to talk to. Mom died when I was a little kid . . . No medical facilities or anything. We were out in the sticks, see — still are come to that.

DIANA: What sticks?

PAUL: What?

DIANA: Sticks?

PAUL: Oh . . . it means nowhere. You know?

DIANA: Say something. Go on.

PAUL: I have.

DIANA: In Ukrainian.

PAUL: No, I can't. I don't want to have anything to do with that. *(pauses, then suddenly)* Tea dusza krasna. *(shrugs, confused)*

DIANA: Then you must be a farmer too.

PAUL: Me? *(suddenly animated)* Not me. You wouldn't get me near a farm.

DIANA: What then? Let me look at your hands. Come on . . . I'll guess.

PAUL puts a hand on the table, then pulls it away suddenly

PAUL: I was gonna be a printer. I had an opportunity. It wasn't exactly what I wanted but it was a job . . . We were printing a translation of Goethe. Poetry . . . and then . . .

DIANA: Well you can always go back to it. Goethe'll always be there.

PAUL: No he won't. I won't go back there.

DIANA: Why is everyone so negative? Of course you'll go back.

PAUL: They stopped the printing. He was a German. Anyway, I got fired.

DIANA: Oh? Why?

PAUL: For printing . . . something I shouldn't'a been.

DIANA: What?

PAUL: Illegal material.

DIANA: What kind?

(Pause)

Paul?

(Pause)

Paul?

PAUL: *(looking away)* Pamphlets — stuff like that. They got this War Measures Act, see. So they can stomp on everyone — Close the meeting halls, shut down the presses — they have informers.

DIANA: Who's they?

PAUL: The government, who else? The goddamned Liberals — oh, I'm sorry.

DIANA: That's all right. I'm not made of gossamer you know.

PAUL: It's never gonna happen again — I'll tell you — if this war changes anything it'll change that . . . bourgeois tyranny.

659

DIANA: I don't understand.

PAUL: Communism — what would you know about that? Communism — I had a job — when you were sixteen you wanted to fly. I had a job and when they found out I got turned in, some s.o.b. turned me in, kaput, finished, they sent me back to the farm, there was nowhere else to send me, was there? So there. There you are — I told you didn't I. I was a communist.

DIANA: I think that's fantastic.

PAUL: (taken aback) You do?

DIANA: My father'd have a fit! He's terrified of commies . . .

PAUL: Sssssh!

DIANA: Be like dad, keep mum. (puts her finger over her lips, imitating a wartime poster, then tries to stop giggling)

PAUL: My old man, he used to be pretty active in the old country, left wing stuff of course, still talks a lot but he licks the Anglicki's boots, yes. Sold out for the land, sold himself, and licks their boots even though he hates their guts. You can't talk to him, he never listens, goes ahead and does what he thinks, talk, talk, talk, talk and he never even listens.

DIANA: What's an Anglicki?

PAUL: (not listening) But I'm not gonna do that. Shall I tell you something? I'm going to be a writer, I'm going to write it all down, tell about Estevan and the strikes, they shot them all on the street you know, I'm gonna write — I don't tell that to everyone. In fact, you're the first person I've told.

DIANA: Paul? What's an Anglicki?

PAUL: Anglicki? English of course.

DIANA: (stiffly) You don't like the English?

PAUL: I didn't say that did I? I got nothing against England as long as it stays right here — I volunteered didn't I? When this war's over there's a few things gonna change. . . it's the end of imperialism, all that stuff's dead. Canadians aren't licking any more boots . . . if I'm still alive I'll . . .

DIANA: *(standing)* Well, I've really enjoyed this. I have to go now.

PAUL: *(confused)* You do?

DIANA: I'm on duty at four . . .

PAUL: Yes but you said . . .

DIANA: *(puts her gloves on)* Bye-bye Paul. *(holds out her hand briefly, then starts to leave)*

PAUL: Here . . . here, I brought you something. I didn't like to give it to . . . here . . . *(takes out a chocolate bar and thrusts it at her)*

DIANA: *(unenthusiastic)* Chocolate. How nice . . .

PAUL: I can get more . . . They told me that all the English girls . . .

DIANA: Yes.

Awkward pause

PAUL: What I said in Ukrainian . . .

DIANA: I must go. *(leaves)*

PAUL: I said you were beautiful. *(puts his head in his arms)*

This scene melds into next, at least as far as PAUL's line in Scene Ten

CHUCK and LUCE's room, Halifax, 1946. LUCE stares out the window. She is deeply depressed.

CHUCK: Loose. Hey, Loose. Loose. *(waves, tries to attract her attention)*

PAUL: Anglicki.

CHUCK: Here. Here . . . I got you something. Dictionary. Help you to know the words. Come on, Loose . . . ah, c'mon. I know you don't have to be like this. It doesn't fool me. Come on, Loose. *(embraces her)* Ti amo. Ti . . . well, we gotta talk. We got a lifetime ahead of us, Loose. We gotta find something to say.

LUCE: *(mutters)* Non mi capisci. Senti . . . senti . . . perchè non puoi sentire?

CHUCK: Come down off your high-class pedestal. You're in Canada now. Halifax. You don't have a big house in Milan and another goddamn mansion on lake whatever and a grandmother with a villa in Florence and . . . well —

LUCE: *(mutters)* Ma, non dev'essere così . . . need not to be so . . .

LUCE fantasizes. She sits comfortably curled up, reading a magazine. CHUCK enters, gives her a cigarette, perches on the arm of the chair

CHUCK: D'you want me to stay around, darling?

LUCE: *(no accent)* Not today, it's been a long day — I just wanna settle down and relax for a while, sleep a bit maybe.

CHUCK: *(ruffling her hair)* Okay, I won't pressure you.

LUCE: Come back when I'm feeling like it and make me laugh.

CHUCK: Sure — I got things of my own to do anyway.

LUCE: You don't mind if I go down to New York in the morning? I have an audition.

CHUCK: Great, need some spondoolix? *(takes out a fistful of dollars)*

LUCE: No — I have my own money.

CHUCK: Well, if I don't see you before you go . . . good luck —

LUCE: That's what I like most about you, Chuck, you give me room . . . you let me breathe and be free . . . and whenever I need you . . .

LUCE's fantasy ends

CHUCK: Listen to me, Loose! I take you to live in the Italian part of town, don't I? I find us a room in . . . At least you could talk to my papa when he calls, it's not like he doesn't speak Italian.

LUCE: He is not Italian.

CHUCK: Look . . . what d'you want? You want roses? I'll bring you roses . . . you want me to carry you away on a white horse? I'll carry you . . . I can't even ride a goddamn horse. Want me to stand on my head?

LUCE: *(not watching)* Is Napolitano. Your papa. Napolitano is not Italian.

CHUCK falls in a heap, defeated

CHUCK: You're home now, Loose.

(LUCE shrugs, goes back to her magazine)

You're home. You're just gonna have to get used to it. *(pauses)* And nobody here has time to spend a whole week reading one magazine. And sitting in one place. Okay? You just gotta get used to it, that's all.

ACT ONE SCENE ELEVEN

The train, fall, 1945.

DIANA: Yes . . . this is it. The guard says another couple of minutes. *(gathers RUTH's things together, straightens her fur)* This is where you have to change trains, Ruthie.

RUTH: Maybe I should stay on.

DIANA: What?

RUTH: Just for another day or two . . . as far as Lethbridge. So I can see you off — I could always catch a train back — if I wanted to.

DIANA: What a way to talk! Besides, I'm not going to Lethbridge. We're staying with Paul's father first, near Regina. I told you, I'm going to see where he grew up.

RUTH: You'll come and see me?

DIANA: Yes . . . and you must come out to us. You and David . . . come for Christmas.

RUTH: I'm nearly there and you'll still be on the train. Even tomorrow when I'm in my house. . .

DIANA half pushes RUTH out of the train

ACT ONE SCENE TWELVE

Fall, 1945. CHUCK and LUCE are in their room in Halifax. DAVE is at Hamilton Station, and PAUL at Regina Station. CHUCK is playing "Der Fuhrer's Face" in a Spike Jones imitation. Suddenly he stops, realizing he is not too brilliant.

CHUCK: Well, I'm just a boy from Halifax — what d'you expect, Glen Miller? *(plays another snatch, stops)* Jesus, the war's over — that doesn't mean anything any more . . . Loose . . .

664

(LUCE is too far away to hear)

Loose . . . I gotta find some other songs . . . *(shakes his head, mystified, picks out the melody of "Sentimental Journey")* Loose . . .

DAVE: Ruthie . . .

PAUL: Diana . . . can you cook?

CHUCK: *(stops playing)* You're home, Loose . . .

PAUL: Canadian style, I mean — Canadian style — can you make pyrogies?

DAVE: Will I recognize you?

PAUL: What if it isn't . . .

DAVE: What if? . . .

PAUL: . . . like in the letters. . . What if . . .

DAVE: What? . . .

CHUCK: Loose you're in Canada now!

CHUCK begins the melody of "Sentimental Journey" again

ACT ONE SCENE THIRTEEN

A seaside promenade, 1941. RUTH sits on a bench. DAVE, wearing his uniform, enters.

DAVE: Anyone sitting here?

RUTH: I was waiting on a friend.

DAVE: Male or female?

RUTH: A girl.

DAVE: *(imitates RUTH)* A girl? Oh, she can sit on my lap. *(sits down)*

RUTH: *(flirtatious)* Who do you think you are?

665

DAVE: James Michael O'Sullivan. You can call me Dave. *(holds out his hand)*

RUTH: *(not taking it)* Dave . . . oh. Not James?

DAVE: That's my dad. I chose Dave —

RUTH: You christened yourself?

DAVE: Yeah . . . sure. It's a better name. Tougher. Well, don't you have a name?

RUTH: Oh . . . Ruthie. Ruth Watson.

DAVE kisses her hand. RUTH withdraws her hand, giggles

RUTH: What'd you do that for?

DAVE: Haven't you ever met a Canadian? We all kiss hands . . . or rub noses.

RUTH: You talk funny.

DAVE: You don't wanna say that. Last person said that to me I said, "You wanna talk funny too?" So I broke a few of his teeth. I was real polite about it. Offered to pick them up after. *(laughs)*

RUTH: Poor man.

DAVE: Yeah. Poor knuckles.

RUTH: D'you fight a lot?

DAVE: Sure. That's what we're here for.

(RUTH grimaces)

Oh . . . I'm putting you on. I never done nothing like that. I been sitting on my knuckles for two years just about. You know, we're the only outfit in military history with a birthrate higher than the deathrate! Wait 'til they let me at them, though. *(aims his fist)* Where are you from anyways? You talk funny too.

RUTH: Dundee. Scotland . . . I joined the land army and came down south.

DAVE: You mean you milk cows?

RUTH: No. I get put on the hedging mostly . . . Sometimes they let me prune.

(DAVE pulls a face)

What?

DAVE: My mom used to feed me those when I couldn't go.

RUTH: Not that kind. (giggles) Pruning. (shows him)

DAVE: Can I buy you a drink?

RUTH: What?

DAVE: In the pub. (nods in direction of pub)

RUTH: Thanks all the same — I'm listening to the band.

DAVE: Oh . . . well, in that case . . . (gets up as if to leave)

RUTH fantasizes. She is tied to a tree by her hands

RUTH: Help me . . . help me . . . the Indians are going to burn my bones!

DAVE becomes part of her fantasy without turning around. He sings the "Indian Love Call" elongating the words ". . . calling you-ooo-oo-ooo."

DAVE: (singing) "When I'm calling you-ooo-oo-ooo, will you answer true-ooo-oo-oooo?"

RUTH: Help, help, help.

DAVE: (He turns, becomes a Mountie and goes into the "Mountie's Song" riding like a "pack of angry wolves" chasing some unknown assailant, ready to get his quarry dead or alive. He fires a volley of shots and unties RUTH)

RUTH: Oh, thank you, thank you.

DAVE: Think nothing of it, Ma'am. Just a day in the life of a Mountie. (salutes, goes away whistling "Indian Love Call")

667

RUTH: I think I'm in love.

RUTH's fantasy ends

DAVE: I should be . . . *(meaning "pushing on")*

RUTH: *(quickly)* Are you in the army?

DAVE: Yeah. I'm a general.

RUTH: Well, if you're a general, you can afford to buy me a green goddess — after my friend comes.

DAVE: *(sits down)* So. Where are you from in Scotland?

RUTH: I told you. Dundee.

DAVE: That's a cake.

RUTH: It's a place.

DAVE: Yeah, you're right. It's in Canada.

RUTH: You . . . *(hits him in mock frustration)*

DAVE: *(protecting himself)* Wrong again — I meant Dundas — now you're not gonna tell me that's in Scotland too. Last time I saw it, it was ten miles up the road from where I live, but they could'a moved it, it's been two years. You know something? You can drive 'round the world in Canada — no need to go outside of Ontario — we got a Paris and a Melbourne and a Delhi . . . and a Hamilton, that's where I'm from.

RUTH: Ontario?

DAVE: Yeah. That's the best part of Canada.

RUTH: Isn't it awful cold there?

DAVE: Cold? In summer it gets up over a hundred. We drive out to the cottage in summer. We got this cottage, see, on the lake there, and we get the boat out and . . . it's up over a hundred degrees every day.

RUTH: A cottage? And a boat?

DAVE: Yeah, sure. We drive out there on weekends.

RUTH: You got a car?

DAVE: Sure. Everyone has a car.

RUTH fantasizes. Music: wedding bells, wedding march

RUTH: Ruth O'Sullivan. The supper's ready, Davie darling. I'm just picking some roses to put on the snowy white table cloth. If they grow any thicker we'll never get through the door into our cottage.

DAVE: Good. I'm starving. I've been hewing wood and drawing water all day.

RUTH: Have you parked the car?

DAVE: I left it in the paddock. It's too big for the garage.

RUTH: *(bending over the oven)* I've roasted that moose you caught, Davie.

DAVE bends over and squeezes her

Oh, don't . . .

DAVE: I can't keep my hands off you. You're the best wife a man could have.

RUTH: *(turns to him, beaming)* I'm the happiest person in the world.

DAVE: My woman!

RUTH's fantasy ends

RUTH: You must have to work awful hard to have a cottage and a car and a boat.

DAVE: No. You get them for signing up. *(laughs)*

RUTH: You're pulling my leg.

DAVE: Scared it'll come off in my hand? *(touches her leg)* Think it'll stand a dance?

RUTH: Where?

669

DAVE: Here.

RUTH: On the promenade?

DAVE: Aren't you hip to the jive?

RUTH: Nobody's dancing.

(DAVE pulls her to her feet)

Ooooh!

DAVE and RUTH jitterbug

ACT ONE SCENE FOURTEEN

The train, fall, 1945.

DIANA: (calling into the corridor) Say there . . . wake me up at seven will you? Seven sharp. I don't want to miss Lake Superior. You won't forget. (to herself) Conductor. I must get it right, he's a conductor, not a guard. Incredible accents. Will my children speak like that? Imagine turning up at the tennis club . . . (fake American accent) "Hi, how's it going? Come on, do you wanna hit a couple of balls around or not?" They'd laugh me off the court! Must remember not to say "knock up" — he was very insistent. Hope I don't have to spend too much time with his horrible old father. Conductor. Do you tip in this country? (calls out) Conductor! You'd better remember — Lake Superior. Oh, hurry up.

ACT ONE SCENE FIFTEEN

CHUCK and LUCE's room, Halifax, 1947. LUCE is staring out the window. CHUCK enters.

CHUCK: Come away from that window — d'you wanna get killed? If they break the glass! . . .

(LUCE sits down.)

They don't mean it. Well, it's not against you . . . It's against me too. If I catch the sons of . . . Look . . . I been in two fights today already over you. *(shows his wounds)* Don't you care? *(pushes his hand at her)* Sangue!

(LUCE stares at him miserably, picks up her rosary. Silence.)

Oh put that thing away. You know you don't go for that stuff. It's gonna kill Mama, you know that? She was so proud when I married you — and now this. Bastards! *(shakes his fist at the window)* Well, you could just talk to her couldn't you? What's the matter with you? Why couldn't you have just talked to the neighbours when they came 'round? Who do you think you are anyway?

LUCE: Paisani!

CHUCK: Peasants! It's no wonder they turn on you. It's no wonder our own people call you a fascist and break our —

LUCE: How they know who I am? I not go outside. . .

CHUCK: It's *because* you don't go outside. If they got to know you . . . If you just talked with them . . . Parla, yes? Tell them . . . See, they're getting called fascists themselves — fascisti — every day. They're getting attacked and you . . . you just stay home and act the lady —

LUCE: *(interrupts)* O . . . lascia stare . . . lascia stare . . .

CHUCK: They figure if anyone 'round here's a fascist it's gonna be you — or me, for bringing you back from Italy. They don't understand!

LUCE: They are Calabresi!

CHUCK: You're a goddamn snob! I suppose you think my father's a peasant. Is everyone from Naples a peasant too?

LUCE: *(shrugs)* Che miseria! Che miseria!

CHUCK: Well, at least he stays in touch with me. Not like yours. Ach! Naples, Calabria, spaghetti, baloney, whatever way you slice it, it's still Italy. Italy. You know, before the war my old man had my mother embroider a poem to hang over the bed —

"Open my heart and you will see,
'Graved inside it, Italy."

Used to bring people in to look at it, 'til he found out it was written by an Englishman. Took it down. Italy! Goddammit, why couldn't they be on the right side from the start?

(Pause)

Then we wouldn't have met, right?

(LUCE begins to cry, quietly)

Oh, Loose, come on. We got each other, haven't we? You've always got me. It don't matter what they say you are. I know it's not true.

CHUCK could have said this with more certainty. He hugs her. She clings to him.

ACT ONE SCENE SIXTEEN

PAUL is waiting for DIANA at Regina Station, 1945.

PAUL: Twelve forty-five. They said twelve forty-five. *(looks at his watch)* Quarter after ten. I should have coffee, what if it comes in while I'm gone? I wish the old man had a phone. I'd'a called him . . .

(Pause. PAUL fantasizes. In his fantasy, he plays alternately himself and his father)

(as his father) Canada is good to you, son — you must be good to her. You go and fight. *(as himself)* The war's over, Papa. If you'd only buy a radio you'd. . . *(as his father)* Over? Thank God. *(as himself)* Papa . . . I want you to meet Diana Manning — sorry Tomachuk — must get it

right — my wife — your name, my wife. Wife. *(as his father)* O moya ridna donichka. Tea ya krasna te shoa ya hotchu . . .* *(as himself)* Okay, okay, she's my wife, not yours! *(as his father)* O, moya donichka. *(weeps)*

(PAUL's fantasy ends. He is back at the station)

Maybe we should just go straight to Lethbridge. The way he eats! He'll probably fart at the table! Say's he's taught the dog to bark in Ukrainian. Jeez!

ACT ONE SCENE SEVENTEEN

The train, fall, 1945. LUCE is in her room, Halifax, alone on the couch, nursing her rosary.

DIANA: *(drying her eyes)* I'm such an idiot, Paul. I've cried half the journey . . . Whatever will you think of me? Enough to flood Lake Superior. I know you told me it was the biggest lake in the world, but I just thought you were boasting. Oh, I do love you. You're such an extraordinary person, so single-minded. I really admire that. I'll help you to be a great writer. I should be writing everything down for you. I've forgotten so much already. It's so easy to forget. Things — even the most traumatic — places . . . faces . . . Winnipeg? Oh, we've got five hours here. *(gets up and leaves the train)*

LUCE: Mama. Mama. Mama.

ACT ONE SCENE EIGHTEEN

Hamilton Station, fall, 1945. DAVE is still waiting for RUTH.

DAVE: I'll give her another hour . . . That train can't be that late. . . *(takes a folded pin-up from his breast pocket, looks at it lovingly)* You better not let me down, Rita, you saw me

---

*(Translation: Oh my darling little daughter, you're exactly what I wanted . . .)

through before, you better not let me down now. Well, we've been together for six years, haven't we?

DAVE fantasizes. Music, "Put the Blame on Me". RUTH comes on. She has become Rita Hayworth. She comes straight to him. A dramatic embrace.

DAVE: *(murmurs)* Rita. Rita Hayworth.

RITA: What a war you had, James!

DAVE: I've had a few stories to tell since I got back.

RITA: They'll never really know what you went through.

DAVE: Me — ah, come on — all I did was drive a truck.

RITA: Men would've died without supplies.

DAVE: *(cocky)* Spent half the war in the lockup. *(laughs)* I'd fight for my girl anytime.

RITA: Tiger! You can't keep those fists to yourself, can you?

DAVE: Keeping us sitting around in the Limey mud for three years. We weren't over there to sit on our knuckles.

RITA: Oh Dave! *(throws herself on him)*

DAVE: *(stopping her)* You're still a virgin?

RITA: Of course.

DAVE: I'd leave you standing here — you know that? I don't go in no place where other men've been before.

RITA: Come on. I can't wait any longer.

DAVE: Not here — wait a minute.

RITA: Behind the train.

DAVE: But it's gonna move any minute.

RITA: Who cares?

DAVE: I love you, Rita. *(stands staring straight ahead)*

ACT ONE SCENE NINETEEN

An Italian café, 1944. There should be a map of Italy on the wall. CHUCK is at a piano. He plays "Sentimental Journey". DIANA is on the train, fall, 1946. During DIANA's speech, LUCE enters the café, and, standing, sips espresso.

DIANA: Well, that was Winnipeg, Paul. Thank goodness we won't be living there — Lethbridge will be much nicer. Maybe I didn't see the right bit — you'll have to show it to me. I looked for Portage and Main but I couldn't find it, so I sat on a wall and ate oranges like a tramp. Oh Paul, I'm almost in your court — it's as if you were sitting right there. *(across from her)* It's been so long — I can only think of you in your uniform — what will you be wearing? Grey flannels and a nice cravat? And that fairisle pullover mummy knitted you for Christmas? *(looks out the window)* Portage la Prairie, Carberry, Brandon, Verden . . .

Action changes to the café. At the piano, CHUCK has changed the melody to "It's a Long Way to Tipperary". He is drinking brandy

CHUCK: *(calls out)* Fingers stiff as triggers.

(LUCE pretends not to hear him)

Not done, eh? Playing on the management's instrument. Well, you tell them I been playing soldiers all this last year just so they could keep this place open. *(tries out a few more notes of "Tipperary")* You know, the last time I played? In a church in Ortona — honest — the Tin Hats were in town. You know them? Bunch of Canadians — great entertainers when they're sober. I got to play with them — listen. *(plays "O sole mio", taking the romance out of it)*

LUCE: No, no, no. *(laughs)*

CHUCK: You can do better?

LUCE shakes her head

CHUCK: O sole mio. Italian for you are my sunshine —
know the words? Come on, sing.

LUCE: *(tongue-tied)* Is for man to sing. Is man's song.

CHUCK: Oh . . . you talk English? Well, teach it to me then
. . . come on, I'll sing it . . . *(offers to let her sit down)*

(LUCE refuses the offer, shyly)

Oh, it's okay — my dad's Italian, Malecarne, that's me —
bad meat — that's what it means, doesn't it? Malecarne.

(LUCE laughs)

Musta been lousy butchers when they were over here,
that's why they came to Canada — see, over there they
can't tell the difference! *(laughs)* See, not all of us Italians
throw in the towel. Some of us keep fighting. *(holds out his
hand)* Chuck.

LUCE: Luce.

CHUCK: Come again? Here, write that down. *(holds out a
napkin for her to write on)* Oh — Loose.

LUCE: Loo-chay.

CHUCK: *(writing)* Chuck — Charles — see — Carlo. Carlo
and Loose. *(draws a heart)* Heart. *(pats his heart)*

LUCE: Cuore.

CHUCK: Cuore.

(Pause)

Bella ragazza. *(kisses his fingers Italian style)* Here — *(pats
the stool beside him)*

LUCE wants to sit, but does not

You know the last time I was in Florence? About three
months ago. Bang, bang, bang . . .

(CHUCK acts out snipers for LUCE's benefit. LUCE nods)

Italians — not Krauts — snipers — trying to get us — ungrateful bastards, goddamnit . . . All my life I been thinking of the time when I'd come to Italy and when I get here — *(drinks)* it does nothing but rain.

LUCE: Tocca.

CHUCK: I am talking. Here — here, look — Canadian, that's me. *(traces the campaign route up from Sicily on the map)* We liberate you, right? Sicily, see, Potenza, Maple Leaf City. . . . I was about here when your side threw in the towel — Ortona — you heard about Ortona? I won't forget Ortona. Florence, Rimini. This is my second time around in Florence, and it's still raining.

LUCE: Tocca. *(shows him that she means "play")*

CHUCK: Come on, sing.

LUCE: *(smiles, suddenly sings out in a clear, tuneful voice)*

O mio babbino caro,
Mi piace bello bello —

CHUCK: *(listens, amazed, then grabs her)* Hey, siddown!

LUCE: *(sits)* I will to be cantatrice.

(Pause.)
Sing.

CHUCK: You don't say? Hey, we'll sing together — we'll get the Tin Hats to take us on . . . Why not? *(clowns, a bit drunk)*

Hitler, has only got one ball;
Goeering has two but they are small;
Himmler, has something sim'lar;
And poor Goebbels has no balls at all!

(LUCE laughs, delighted)

I go see your papa, yes? Some kinda crazy man letting you out on the street when the Canadians are in town, Loose. Know where Canada is? Canada . . . me . . .

LUCE: America.

CHUCK: America? That's on the outskirts of Halifax, isn't it?

LUCE: Yes? You Yank?

CHUCK: Canada's where it's happening. You better believe it. I'll show it to you, listen, I'll go and see your papa. Listen — you're gonna sing. You better do it over there. No one does it, see — over here you get competition — over there they all got frost on the lung. *(coughs)*

LUCE: Canada.

(Pause)

Suona, Canada.

CHUCK: So you'll come? The one I asked in Ortona slapped my face — she thought I was after something else. *(winks)* You know what my old man says — papa? "You marry nice Italian girl, Carlo, you never have to clean your own shoes again." I laughed at him, 'til I got sent over here and found out what mud was.

(He shows her his dirty boots, LUCE laughs)

(putting his arm around LUCE) I like you, you know that? You've got a sense of humour. I like that. You're a nice quiet girl, with a sense of humour. You're a beautiful girl, you know that?

LUCE: I sing.

(LUCE hums the tune of "I'll Never Smile Again". CHUCK picks the tune out. She sings a parrotted version, not understanding the words. CHUCK fantasizes. Big band swells. CHUCK is in the spotlight conducting. LUCE stands shyly in the background, singing. CHUCK's fantasy ends. LUCE sings the last line of the song, stops suddenly, and smiles)

I learn radio.

CHUCK: Very good. Listen . . . you know this? . . . *(plays the first line of "You Are My Sunshine" and sings it)* Go on, you. Yes, you.

LUCE: *(pointing to herself)* You —

CHUCK: You are my sunshine.

LUCE: You are mine . . . sun . . .

CHUCK: Shine. My only sunshine. Solo sunshine. Here, we'll make a duo. . . You make me happy, when skies are grey.

LUCE: Felice.

CHUCK: Felice.

(They laugh.)

Molto felice.

LUCE: Mister Canada. Canada.

(CHUCK hugs LUCE. She jumps up)

I must to go. Is not allowed I am here.

CHUCK: Here — wait a minute. You got five days to try me on for size. That's how long my leave lasts.

CHUCK takes LUCE in his arms and kisses her. They remain like this until the end of Act One

ACT ONE SCENE TWENTY

A field, 1943. DAVE and RUTH wander on to have a picnic. RUTH has a basket.

RUTH: It was terrible. I thought you'd stood me up. I went a bit crazy — I ran away from the farm — I don't know where I thought I was going — home most likely — I stole an old lady's knickers off a clothesline.

DAVE: *(laughs)* If I'd known that when I was inside I'd've felt a whole lot better.

RUTH: I thought they'd sent you to Dieppe.

DAVE: Didn't even know it was happening. I was in the lockup like I told you.

RUTH: I went to your base — they said they'd never heard of you.

DAVE: They wished they hadn't.

RUTH: Then I got arrested by this sourpuss policewoman. She was asking what you were like. I told her you looked like Cary Grant — she wanted to meet you —

DAVE: Yeah? What's she look like?

RUTH: Oh . . . she was about eighty. Do you know Dave, Jenny Dodds is getting married.

DAVE: Let's sit down.

RUTH: You know about her — she's on the farm. That makes five of them married and two widows. There's only me and Mary Meadows left and she never washes herself.

DAVE: You wanna be a widow?

RUTH: No . . . but it's better than being on the shelf. They all say it's easier to catch another one if you've already had one.

DAVE: Is that what they say?

RUTH: Jenny Dodds's got an uncle in Canada. She says it's lovely there — there isn't even a war on.

(DAVE looks around, a bit restless.)

Don't you like it here?

DAVE: Yeah. You can see the sea.

RUTH: She wishes her Mick was a Canadian. I borrowed an egg from the farm . . . oh, and I swapped my wellingtons for some butter coupons, so it's real butter on the bread. Who needs boots in summer anyway?

DAVE: Hmmm?

680

RUTH: Are there places like this in Canada? . . .

DAVE: No. We don't have the sea — I like the smell.

RUTH: D'you miss it? Canada?

DAVE: Sure.

RUTH: What do you miss?

DAVE: I dunno. The bush maybe. There's a kinda quiet there — down on the Indian trail, yeah. You can hear the animals moving around, you know . . . like cracking the twigs and moving their jaws, yeah . . . and you can hear the fish jump, out at the lake, and when the ducks fly out over the water . . . *(lapses into silence)*

RUTH: What do you do?

DAVE: *(laughs suddenly)* Shoot 'em. *(fires)*

RUTH: Don't!

DAVE: I go hunting sometimes.

RUTH: Do you shoot the animals? Like the sassenachs do when they come up to Scotland?

DAVE: Sure. Everyone does . . .

RUTH: Everyone?

DAVE: Sure. Or sometimes you can go down the store and get meat for nothing.

RUTH: Free?

DAVE: Well . . . I mean . . . you don't have to shoot it. You can buy as much as you like.

RUTH: It sounds wonderful.

DAVE: Would you? . . . Would you mind if I kissed you?

RUTH: How come you asked?

DAVE kisses RUTH very gently. She wants to continue. He pulls back.

681

DAVE: Loose lips sink ships. That means you don't kiss in public.

(Pause)

Can't we go someplace more private?

RUTH: This is private.

DAVE: There might be someone watching.

RUTH: It doesn't matter. We do it in the streets . . . at the bus stop . . .

DAVE: You? . . .

RUTH: *(hastily)* Well, not me.

DAVE: I . . . I think I respect you.

(Pause)

What's that on your face?

RUTH: *(embarrassed)* Powder. Why? Don't you like it?

DAVE: It smells.

RUTH: Oh, I'll take it off. *(licks her handkerchief and washes her face)* Is that better? *(offers him her cheek)*

DAVE: *(not accepting the offer)* I don't like that stuff.

(Long silence)

You should be able to be with someone and not have to say anything.

(Pause)

I feel like I want to spend all my time with you.

(Pause)

Do you think we're lovers?

RUTH: Do you?

DAVE: Hey, come on. *(drags her to her feet)* Dance . . .

682

RUTH: Here?

DAVE: Why not? You said there wasn't anybody looking —

RUTH: All right.

They dance

DAVE: Ruthie . . . I like you better than anyone I ever liked before.

(*RUTH gazes at him, waiting*)

Do you like Canada?

RUTH: I don't know.

DAVE: Do you want to go?

(*RUTH looks at him*)

With me? Like . . . do you wanna get married or something?

RUTH: Oh Dave . . .

They kiss. They remain like this until the end of Act One

ACT ONE SCENE TWENTY-ONE

PAUL and DIANA are facing each other again at the same English café three years later, in early 1944.

PAUL: Smoke?

DIANA: No thanks. You didn't smoke before did you?

PAUL: Beats chewing your fingers. So. How's the police?

DIANA: Oh fine . . . fine. The American soldiers are a bit of a pain in the neck. They're so . . . boisterous. But I'm getting used to people having nervous breakdowns all over the place — it'll be fine as long as no one drops a bomb on my head. D'you still go to bed with Karl Marx under your pillow?

PAUL: Marx?

DIANA: I thought you were a comm —

PAUL: Oh, that.

DIANA: Well?

PAUL: Sure. *(he is not sure)*

DIANA: I met a Fabian last month. He'd been beaten up. He was a conscientious objector — but of course that's not the same thing, is it?

PAUL: I volunteered.

DIANA: I'm glad. *(takes his hand)*

PAUL: I guess I was just a kid. You gotta believe in something, isn't that right?

(Pause)

Did you think about me?

DIANA: When?

PAUL: Any time.

DIANA: I was going out with an Australian for a while. My father hated him.

PAUL: Did you eat the chocolate?

DIANA: What chocolate?

PAUL: I gave it to you.

DIANA: That was two years ago.

PAUL: I've been thinking about you.

DIANA: Me?

PAUL: When we got posted back here I just hung around all the police stations figuring I'd meet you.

DIANA: It's a wonder you weren't arrested.

PAUL: I was careful.

DIANA: Why me? You must've met dozens of girls.

PAUL: I figured I . . . I owed you an apology.

DIANA: What for?

PAUL: I insulted you. I don't go 'round insulting women. I'm sorry.

DIANA: What did you say?

PAUL: I said you were English.

DIANA erupts in a peal of laughter, then stops, realizing PAUL is serious

DIANA: Oh . . . it's forgotten.

PAUL: Will you marry me?

DIANA: What?

PAUL: We'll be in France next week.

DIANA: What did you say?

PAUL: Well will you? . . . I won't guarantee I'll stay alive . . . but if I do I'm gonna make things happen. This war's opened everything up, you must see that? Well?

DIANA: Oh, you're such a . . .

Pause.

DIANA: You're not serious?

(Pause)

What a hoot.

(Pause)

What can I say?

PAUL: Yes.

DIANA: I'm stunned. I mean . . . you don't know a thing about me.

PAUL: We can write. It's been done before.

DIANA: My parents . . . you don't know them.

PAUL: So? What is there to know about them? I've just been thinking about you all the time. I think of you every night. . .

DIANA: My father's going to be mayor next year — he's a captain in the home guard. My brother Hugh's a squadron leader — I don't think they'd find you very — suitable. Neither would you.

PAUL: What's that got to do with anything?

DIANA: Well if they were to meet you —

PAUL: Fine, when do you want me to come over?

DIANA: Oh Paul, you're so incredibly serious. It's so funny. . .

(PAUL looks down into his lap, distraught)

Look . . . I don't know how I feel about you — I'm totally confused, I mean — out of the blue — I mean it's very flattering, but . . .

PAUL: Don't you want to get married?

DIANA: I didn't say that but . . . I don't know you —

PAUL: Yes you do, we've known each other for two years. I'm an okay person — I'm as good as any Australian. I don't want to go overseas without . . . without something to come back to —

DIANA: But you'll go back to Canada.

PAUL: We can go together.

DIANA: Canada? Oh, I've never even considered — I mean, whatever would my parents say? Not that it's any business of theirs. You are a hoot.

PAUL: I've been writing — I've written a lot of poetry since — I've never shown it to anyone. I write about home a lot. It's the greatest country on earth — after England of course. I've written about you.

DIANA: Paul, I . . .

PAUL: I'll wait outside the police station every night. I'll go AWOL.

DIANA: No . . . I have to think.

PAUL: You don't — there's no time for that.

DIANA: But Paul, I . . .

PAUL: Please. Didn't I say please?

DIANA: You don't just ask somebody something like that, out of the blue, and expect an answer.

PAUL: I'll keep asking it. I'll keep asking you 'til you say yes. Listen — "The eternal in woman draws us on . . ."

DIANA: Das Ewig-Weibliche, Zieht uns hinan.

PAUL: (shouts, joyfully) You see . . . it's meant to be. It's —

DIANA: Ssssh! We studied Goethe for matric, that's all.

PAUL: I love you Diana.

DIANA: I can't. You don't understand. They'd never forgive me. My parents . . . I could never come back here.

PAUL gets up suddenly and kisses DIANA full on the lips. All three couples are now happily in each other's arms.

ACT TWO SCENE ONE

Hamilton Station, 1945. RUTH is searching for DAVE on the crowded platform. She carries a bunch of flowers.

RUTH: Yoo-hoo!

She spots DAVE, puts her carry-cot and bag down, and rushes over to him

DAVE: Hey!

Pause. They look at each other, then hug

RUTH: I thought you weren't here.

DAVE: Would I not be here?

RUTH: Oh Dave.

(They hug. He is squashing the flowers.)

Mind . . . Someone gave them to me . . . Oh, it's all right, everyone's getting them — over there, look, by the train. You look . . . different without your uniform. *(lies)* I like your hat.

DAVE: You're looking . . .

RUTH: I've put on a bit of weight.

DAVE: Have you?

RUTH: You noticed, didn't you?

DAVE: Well, it's kinda . . . noticeable. *(looking at her fur)* Where'd you trap the rat?

RUTH: It's not a rat, Dave. It's real.

DAVE: Hm. It's a wonder they let you in with it. It's probably got rabies. *(pretends that it bites him, clowns)*

RUTH: Rita's right behind you.

(DAVE jumps around)

No . . . there — *(gestures to the carry-cot)*

DAVE: Rita?

RUTH: That's her name. I told you — well don't you still like
Rita Hayworth?

DAVE: Who's she?

RUTH: Oh Dave. Go on. Pick her up.

DAVE: *(not touching the baby)* Yeah but . . . we promised to
call it after my mom.

RUTH: Who did?

DAVE: Cissy. I told you . . . you can call her Rita for a
second name if you like, but my mom . . .

RUTH: Cissy Rita?

DAVE: Well, just Cissy then.

RUTH: No, it's awful. It's not even a real name.

DAVE: It's my mom's name.

RUTH: It's what you call people who're a bit soft.

DAVE: You don't know anything.

(Pause)

Well, it's not asking much is it?

(Pause)

Your eyes are red. *(bends down)* Hello Cissy.

*RUTH gets out her powder compact and dabs at her face. DAVE
watches her*

RUTH: You don't mind?

DAVE: No . . . that's good.

RUTH: Do I look all right?

DAVE: Yeah . . . I mean, you just came from the war and all
that, didn't you?

689

RUTH: Aren't you happy?

DAVE: Yeah . . . but it takes a little while to get used to it.

RUTH: But you've been married a while.

(DAVE stares at RUTH)

You're going to look after us aren't you?

DAVE: What kinda question is that?

RUTH: I'm sorry about your dad, Dave.

(DAVE shrugs, unable to say anything)

Are we going to stand here all day?

DAVE: There's a little problem, see . . . Here's the situation — we haven't got our house yet. Oh don't worry, we'll get it. We'll live at my mother's house. . . I've got a couple of handles on a job at Stelco — something should come through any time.

RUTH: But you said in your letter —

DAVE: I know. We're just gonna stay a little while. My mom's put her double bed in my room — we can keep the baby by the bed. But we all have to be quiet. None of that grunting or groaning or anything — see, there's my brother Tom in the next room . . . and she has to get up in the morning to cook our breakfast —

RUTH: I'll do that.

DAVE: Yeah. Well . . .

RUTH picks up the baby. DAVE takes the bag. She offers him the flowers, but he refuses to carry them.

RUTH: I might call her Rita by mistake sometimes.

DAVE: Don't do that. I mean . . . she's been through a lot . . . wondering if I was gonna get killed and all . . . then losing my dad.

RUTH: (looking at the baby) You do like her, don't you?

DAVE: Yeah . . . oh, yeah. It's just that I've never seen my own baby before.

RUTH: You can pick her up if you like.

DAVE: No . . . no. I'll just leave it sit there and . . .

They start to walk off together

RUTH: She was so good on the journey. You should've seen some of them. I'll teach you to change her nappies. She has a bottle every night at three o'clock.

DAVE: Well, just as long as you do it quietly.

RUTH: Oh yes Dave . . .

DAVE puts his arm around RUTH. They walk off

ACT TWO SCENE TWO

A farm about fifty miles from Lethbridge. Late fall, 1945.

DIANA: Help! Where does it end?

PAUL: Oh . . . way over — see those hills?

DIANA: You bought all of this? You could fit the whole of Chipping Norton into . . . Wait 'till I tell them back home!

(PAUL laughs. He is a little uncomfortable)

Let's drive to the house.

PAUL: I thought we'd put a well in about here . . .

DIANA: *(jumps)* O, am I standing on a spring?

PAUL: Wait a minute — I've got a witch in the truck. Maybe you can answer that. *(exits)*

DIANA: Witch? *(stares out over the land, calls)* Bring the binoculars.

PAUL re-enters

PAUL: There. *(gives her the forked stick)*

DIANA: Show me, show me everything.

PAUL: Hold it like this — see if you've got the art.

DIANA: What art?

PAUL: We'll get a well in and then we'll . . .

DIANA: Oh who cares about silly old wells. Where do the fields start?

PAUL: You're in a field.

DIANA: Where's the house? What's it like, Paul? Oh quick . . . give me the glasses.

PAUL: You don't need them.

DIANA: But —

PAUL: Look, it's all right. I don't expect you to live in a one room shack all your life.

DIANA: What?

PAUL: We can add rooms, build on. The first thing is to get the well in — we'll have a library. There's not gonna be any problem with electricity — you can have all the light you want, but if we put the well too near where we dig the septic field — that's the outhouse over there. It twitched — you're a natural!

(DIANA throws the witch down)

I sank the VLA, but we can borrow more. It's ours —

DIANA: You've been lying to me. I can't live in a cowshed.

PAUL: Who said anything about a cowshed?

DIANA: You were going to be a great writer. You had such revolutionary ideas . . .

(DIANA fantasizes. Music, "Land of Hope and Glory")

Oh Paul, I'm so proud of you.

PAUL: *(modestly)* It's nothing.

DIANA: Nothing?

PAUL: Come on — I'm only leader of the opposition.

DIANA: But not for long — next time 'round . . .

PAUL: Let's deal with this time, darling.

DIANA: Daddy'll be so pleased. He didn't think you had it in you.

PAUL: But you believed in me. *(kisses her cheek)*

(DIANA's fantasy ends)

The land's our one hope. With a farm we can —

DIANA: This isn't a farm. It's not even as good as your father has and goodness knows that's —

PAUL: It's better. It just has to be worked, that's all.

DIANA: But your back — you can't bend — the doctors told you not to lift.

PAUL: What do they know?

He picks her up. She remains ramrod stiff, staring out

DIANA: Oh Paul, don't you love me?

PAUL: Of course I love you, what do you see?

DIANA: Put me down.

PAUL: What do you see? *(puts her down)*

DIANA: Dead grass.

PAUL: We'll make it grow.

(PAUL fantasizes. He is walking through shoulder high corn. He reaches up, shucks an ear. Music, "Oh, What a Beautiful

*Morning". DIANA is kneading dough in the kitchen. PAUL
calls out to her)*

You baked enough pies to feed an army.

DIANA: We can give them to the neighbours.

PAUL: Good smells.

DIANA: Bread. Your grandmother's recipe.

PAUL: You're even getting to look like her.

DIANA: I found this in the attic. *(meaning her apron)*

PAUL: Tea ye krasna.

PAUL's fantasy ends

DIANA: Anything else but not this — it's just wilderness.
You can't do it alone . . . Oh, Paul, be realistic. You said
farming was the last thing — you were always so down
on your father —

PAUL: He'll come around to you, it's just the English he
hates. Nothing personal. He'll come around when he sees
what you can do.

DIANA: What can I do? What? I don't know one end of a
cow from another.

PAUL: We're not having cows. The less you know the better,
then there's nothing to unlearn, right?

DIANA: Paul . . . Paul, listen to me.

PAUL: I got it all figured out — all those months when I was
in traction — politics isn't the answer — there's just one
thing that's stayed the same while everything else's gone
bad . . .

DIANA: Us.

PAUL: Us and the land. I'm talking about the land. My
father knew that all the time — I wouldn't listen. Well, I'm
listening now.

(Pause)

When you've been here a bit longer you'll see. It's the key to Canada. This is peace. I turned my back on it but it's always been here for me like a patient lover.

DIANA: What? Oh Paul, you know you don't talk like that.

PAUL: How do you know how I talk?

DIANA: Well you don't write like it.

PAUL: We start off with nothing and . . . if we don't make something of it, someone else is gonna move in and pour cement.

DIANA: Out here? *(suddenly)* I don't know you.

PAUL: I wrote and told you, goddamnit.

DIANA: Don't speak to me like that.

(Pause)

I thought you were kidding. I thought you were shell-shocked or something. In pain — pain changes people's perceptions. I mean, you always sounded so . . . anguished. I didn't believe . . . you've changed.

PAUL: *(quietly)* I'm home now. The war's over. You don't go through a war without changing, sweetie.

DIANA: Don't call me that.

PAUL: It's up to you now.

DIANA: I don't know what I'm going to do . . . please . . . please . . . I can't go back Paul. I'd never be able to hold my head up.

ACT TWO SCENE THREE

The kitchen of DAVE and RUTH's house, Hamilton, 1946-47. RUTH is eating sherbet powder, licking it out of her palm.

DAVE: Come on.

(RUTH licks)

Quick, before she gets back.

RUTH: You're awful

DAVE: Upstairs, quick.

RUTH: Wee Jamie's asl —

DAVE: Put that stuff away. It's for kids.

RUTH: I haven't had it since before the war. *(laughs)* Fizzy.

DAVE: You gotta stop eating . . . you gotta get your waist back so I can take you out and show you off to the guys.

RUTH: *(stops licking)* Are you going to take me out?

DAVE: Not 'til you stop eating. Come on. *(grabs her)*

RUTH: It's afternoon. She's only gone to the store. She was all morning in the kitchen gabbing with Mrs . . . Dave . . . it's not your pals you're hiding me from . . . it's Verna. Your mum told me —

DAVE: Verna's a bit funny, that's all. Stay out of her way and you'll be okay.

(Pause)

We don't wanna waste time on her — it's been a month since we got the place to ourselves . . . *(puts his hand down her dress)*

RUTH: I wish she'd stop calling you James.

DAVE: It's only since my dad died . . . Come on —

RUTH: She said . . .

(DAVE grabs her and picks her up. RUTH screams, delighted)

RUTH: You'll put your back out.

DAVE: Takes more than a sack of Quaker Oats to do that.

RUTH: Dave!

DAVE: I don't want no more of this squawkin', okay? Wife!

RUTH beats on him in a futile attempt to escape, enjoying the chance to bellow, laughing as he carries her out

ACT TWO SCENE FOUR

CHUCK and LUCE's room, Halifax, 1948. LUCE sits in the chair, painting her toenails. CHUCK enters.

CHUCK: So, how'd it go?

LUCE: Okay.

CHUCK: Did they like you?

LUCE: Sure.

CHUCK: 'Course they liked you. The old guys don't get too many classy Italian ladies coming in to sing to them for free.

LUCE: Many are deaf. Sordo, yes?

CHUCK: 'Course they are. You'll probably be deaf when you're eighty. But they liked you, eh? That's the main thing. Bravo. Did they ask you to come back?

LUCE: Next week.

CHUCK: So you're going?

LUCE: I guess.

CHUCK: I guess . . . Then I guess I'll come along too and play for you, how's that? If we can't do it for money, we'll do it for love, or humanity or whatever you wanna call it. Oh, I forgot. Present from Papa. *(gives it to her)*

LUCE: Pizza!

CHUCK: Okay. You don't have to eat it — he's got customers lining up . . .

LUCE: Ach! *(puts her nail polish aside, picks up a magazine and buries herself in it)*

CHUCK: You know what? He put his finger on a need. People need pizza. That's what North America's all about, Loose. He's sitting on a small fortune. You find a need and you fill it and you make a pile of dough. That's capitalism.

Pause

CHUCK: And you need me. *(takes the magazine away from her)* He loves you like a daughter. Well, he's real sorry your folks don't stay in touch. He wants to change that — pay for them to come over here.

(LUCE snorts, returns to her magazine)

Okay, so they've got a few bucks. It don't mean that we're peasants. And now that I got you singing again . . . I got you going out. Well, they've stopped calling us fascists. I told you they would, didn't I? It's gonna be all right, Loose. Trust me, everything's gonna be —

(CHUCK attempts to put his arm around LUCE. She screams)

So what do you want? Tell me that?

LUCE: I want . . . I want make something. I want work.

CHUCK: Oh, come on, Loose. Just be patient, eh? There aren't the jobs for the guys. Why don't you just settle down?

(CHUCK fantasizes. LUCE is sewing a sampler)

Come on, let's see.

LUCE: No . . . no, is a surprise.

CHUCK: Come on, what's it say? *(peers over her shoulder and reads)* There's no place like —

698

LUCE: Oh, Chuck!

CHUCK: Like what . . . like Milan, like Florence?

LUCE: Guess again.

CHUCK: You're fantastic — you know that?

(LUCE tosses the sampler aside and jumps into his arms. CHUCK's fantasy ends)

You got a nice place to live here haven't you?

(LUCE goes back to doing her nails)

C'mon, smile, Loose.

LUCE smiles obligingly

CHUCK: We won't be in one room forever. Put that thing down. You're getting to like it here — it's gonna take time to admit it, that's all.

CHUCK sits beside her, caresses her, nibbles her ear

LUCE: No!

CHUCK: You like me — you love me, eh, Loose?

LUCE: Si. Sure.

CHUCK: Well, that's what matters. If a guy's wife doesn't love him, then who does? I mean, I coulda married some girl from Halifax who didn't love me, isn't that right?

(Pause)

Let's make a baby tonight.

LUCE: No.

CHUCK: Well, now then. *(grabs her)*

LUCE: Is not room for cat here.

CHUCK: You do love me? Go on — say it, say it.

699

LUCE: *(protects her nail polish)* Sei molto caro, Chuck. Carino.

CHUCK: I love you . . . go on . . . I wanna hear it in English.

LUCE: How many times?

CHUCK: Write it out fifty times after school! Listen, me and a couple of guys I went to high school with, we're gonna put a combo together. We'll cut a record . . .

(LUCE continues to paint her nails)

You'll see — it won't be too long. You won't have to spend a lifetime in here painting your goddamn toes!

LUCE stays onstage

ACT TWO SCENE FIVE

RUTH and DAVE's kitchen, Hamilton, 1949. RUTH is knitting, a pile of children's toques and mitts beside her. She has made some effort with her appearance, looking forward to DAVE coming home.

RUTH: You know what the trouble with this country is? You spend all summer getting ready for winter.

DAVE: *(laughs, jams a child's toque on his head)* Cheer up, Christmas is coming.

(RUTH snatches the toque)

Look, I got some cigarette cards for Jamie.

RUTH: For Jamie?

DAVE: Well, you don't want them, do you?

RUTH: He's too young for cigarette cards. He'll eat them.

(Pause)

It's the fifteenth of August, Dave.

700

RUTH fantasizes. DAVE produces a huge box of chocolates, gift wrapped. RUTH opens them, reacts ecstatically, tries to decide which one to eat

DAVE: *(picking one out)* Open the stable, here comes the horse — one horse, two horses, three horses, and here's the wild one . . . *(crams the chocolates into her mouth)*

RUTH: Oh, Dave, stop it! Stop it! *(splutters and laughs)*

RUTH's fantasy ends

DAVE: Yeah. Two days to payday.

RUTH: There's a cake in there. She baked it. I presume it's for you. She wouldn't let me in the kitchen this morning.

DAVE: Where is it? I'm starving.

RUTH: On the sideboard. *(nods to inner room)* It says "Happy Anniversary to my son and his wife" in blue writing.

DAVE: Why didn't she remind me?

RUTH: Maybe she thought you wouldn't need it.

(Pause)

I got us one as well.

DAVE: Two? We don't need two.

RUTH: Mine's got cream in it. Your favourite.

DAVE: Let me at them. *(begins to leave room)* Hey . . . you can't have any. You gotta lose weight so I can get you one of those strapless gowns and take you out on the town. The New Look, eh? *(leaves)*

RUTH: *(sits for a moment, looking after him)* Lose weight? You try losing weight when you're always pregnant. *(to the door through which he left)* You don't have a girlfriend, do you Dave? Dave?

RUTH stays onstage

ACT TWO SCENE SIX

The farm in Alberta, 1947. DIANA is fixing a farm implement with dogged determination and not much flair. PAUL enters.

PAUL: You could leave that you know.

DIANA: *(automatically)* It has to be done.

PAUL: Do it tomorrow. Let's go bowling. I gotta practice up for that tournament.

DIANA: You haven't got a hope.

PAUL: You'll see, I'll get down there every night.

DIANA: I wanted to clean the truck tonight. I haven't had time to — we can't all sit around *dreaming* of the perfect farm. Somebody has to do the work!

PAUL: You're doing great. Just great. But you're too serious . . . *(puts his arm around her)*

DIANA: There are only twenty-four hours in the day, Paul!

PAUL: Yeah, and don't let's make more than half of them for work, eh? *(pats her reassuringly, begins to leave)*

DIANA: Don't go bowling tonight.

(PAUL leaves)

You do still love me, Paul? Paul?

RUTH: You're not going out with someone else are you, Dave?

DIANA: The edge of the world. The edge . . . *(buries her face in her hands)*

RUTH: Don't leave me on my own.

LUCE: Why must I always be waiting? That is not why I came here. To wait.

ACT TWO SCENE SEVEN

CHUCK is in his apartment, Halifax, 1950. He is alone, practising "The Tennessee Waltz", with guitar accompaniment, imitating a crooner. He stops.

CHUCK: They don't understand nothing here — none of them ever fought in a war. Bunch of desk cases. I'm sick of just getting to play the legions. I'm gonna make people see what we went through, then they'll have to hire me. I'm gonna drop a bomb on them, sure . . .

CHUCK continues to practise

ACT TWO SCENE EIGHT

The farm in Alberta, 1950. DIANA is pulling on her rubber boots, preparing to go outside.

PAUL: Shall I go alone?

(DIANA does not reply)

Betty and Brian need some advice — they asked me.

DIANA: I have too much to do here. Besides we don't talk the same language.

PAUL makes a dismissive motion

DIANA: I feel as though they're laughing behind my back.

PAUL: Brian thinks you're pretty. He told me so.

DIANA: He told me too.

PAUL: Good.

DIANA: Strangers don't tell you things like that — not to your face.

PAUL: Ah, behind your back, eh?

DIANA: *You* don't tell me.

PAUL: Yes I do — tea dusza krasna.

DIANA: I mean in English, you chump! Oh Paul, they laugh at you too, d'you know that? They're all sniggering at us. I see enough of those people at those dreadful socials.

PAUL: Well, you drag us there.

DIANA: We have to make some kind of showing in the community.

PAUL: Showing? What kind of showing do you make? You never even change your clothes.

DIANA: Oh, I see. You want me to primp myself up like the rest of them in their pre-war monuments to bad taste!

PAUL: They think it's you that doesn't have any style.

DIANA: Me? They've got their nerve!

PAUL: Well, why don't you get your hair done?

DIANA: If you wanted a fashion plate you shouldn't've plonked me down near Lethbridge. Have you ever looked in those shops?

PAUL: I just want them to see that you're . . . Well, everyone else manages to look —

DIANA: Everyone else? What do they know? If only somebody had a sense of humour! They're not even interested in local politics, in getting anything done. They seem to expect to suffer.

PAUL: If you'd been through the depression and the war —

DIANA: Where do you think I was?

(Pause)

Can't they put a good face on it instead of laughing at us?

PAUL: They don't laugh.

DIANA: They don't? . . . At you and your experiments? . . .

PAUL: You have to experiment — that's how you learn.

DIANA: Don't tell me, tell them. Maybe they've got a point. Maybe you only learn by repeating the old ways.

PAUL: *(overlapping her line, not listening)* You've got to try new things. This is a new land. It calls for innovative methods — well of course you believe that.

DIANA: Yes. Yes . . . I'm just tired, that's all. I just wonder if it's worth it all.

PAUL: If you don't believe in it, then . . .

DIANA: Paul.

(Pause)

Paul, I want to ask you something.

PAUL: They're worse than the old man. No confidence, no ideas.

DIANA: Paul, I think we should adopt a child.

(Pause)

Are you listening?

(PAUL shakes his head)

I've already made enquiries.

PAUL: Jesus! Can't you wait?

DIANA: If we don't then I . . . *(pause)* I don't see much point in slaving like this.

PAUL: We'll have kids of our own . . . later. When we're ready.

DIANA: You know that's impossible.

PAUL: It's not. Nothing's impossible. Nothing.

DIANA: They're coming to see us tomorrow.

PAUL: I'm going into Lethbridge tomorrow.

DIANA: You'd better be here, that's all. You'd better be here.

ACT TWO SCENE NINE

DAVE and RUTH's kitchen, Hamilton, 1951.

RUTH: I went to Gallagher's this morning. He was real nice, the young man in there.

DAVE: Shhh!

RUTH: I won't shhh!

(DAVE glances nervously at the inner room)

(loudly) She's listening anyway — and if we whisper . . . *(to door)* Aren't you?

DAVE: Okay, that's it. *(shuts his mouth)*

RUTH: Well, if you don't want to talk about it.

(DAVE motions her to go ahead with a sweeping gesture)

He said I'd be better to fly. *(waits for this to sink in)* In an aeroplane.

(DAVE doesn't reply)

You don't have to pay for kids under three. I thought maybe we could find a bit extra and I could take all four of them . . . Oh, I wish you could come too, Dave. Wouldn't she lend us the . . . *(nods to inner room)* They fly to Prestwick and we can get the train to Dundee — he'll write all the tickets here — we don't have to bother with anything, isn't that wonderful? Well, I know you've been wanting to go on an aeroplane. My dad wants to take you down the pub — they've got a snooker table now. I'll bet he never gets home 'til closing. You can help him on his allotment, Angus doesn't lift a finger, just takes all the veges. Home to Mary and the kids. Well, you read the letter . . . Dave . . .

DAVE: Look . . . *(keeping his voice down)* I don't want you going over there.

RUTH: Why not?

DAVE: I don't, that's all — not without me.

RUTH: Why not?

(DAVE doesn't reply)

Well, I don't want to go without you, you know that.

(Pause)

Are you scared, Dave? Are you scared I wouldn't come back?

DAVE: Shhh!

RUTH: You know I'd come back. You don't have to be scared. Oh, Dave . . .

DAVE: You're not going, that's all.

RUTH: It's my money. I filled the coupon in. I thought up the slogan.

DAVE: I gave you the stamp.

RUTH: I bought the marmalade.

DAVE: Whose money paid for it?

RUTH: Mine. What's yours is mine.

DAVE: Okay, so you can have half the Chevy.

RUTH: What Chevy?

DAVE: The one I put the down payment on with the prize money.

RUTH: Oh Dave, you didn't.

DAVE: Take delivery a week Tuesday. Tuesday night we can drive down to Niagara Falls.

RUTH: I . . . I don't understand.

DAVE: You don't wanna come?

RUTH: No . . . no, I don't.

DAVE: Okay, so I'll take someone else. *(glances at door)* She hasn't rode in a car since Edith Jamieson died. *(waits for an answer from his mother)* Isn't that right?

RUTH: But Dave. You always said I could take a trip when we had the money.

DAVE: Well, I'm still saying it, but we don't have the money right now. Well, what's the matter — I thought you wanted a car.

RUTH: I can't drive.

DAVE: So? I'll drive.

RUTH: It won't even be paid for. You know I don't like the hire purchase.

DAVE: Ah c'mon. You're not in Scotland now. This way we can have an extra half hour in bed in the morning. I won't have to take the bus.

RUTH: But I'll still have to get up for the kids. Does she know? Was she in on this? *(raising her voice)* She encouraged you didn't she? Told you it was your right. Her and her bloody rights.

DAVE: Keep it down!

RUTH: I'll bet she thinks she's won. Well she hasn't. I'm still going to Scotland and half of that car's mine.

DAVE: Which half?

RUTH: The bit in the middle where you sit. She can ride in the boot.

DAVE laughs. RUTH storms out. DAVE remains onstage through the beginning of the next scene

ACT TWO SCENE TEN

CHUCK and LUCE's apartment, Halifax, 1951. A pile of magazines is on the floor. LUCE is vacuuming with an old-fashioned vacuum cleaner which is not plugged in. She goes over and over the same spot, concentrating. She is singing to herself.

DAVE: Doesn't know when she's well off. *(exits)*

CHUCK: Well, it'll be better when we get a couple of carpets. I'm gonna fill all these rooms with furniture for you. None of your utility stuff . . .

LUCE stops singing. CHUCK jumps up and plugs the vacuum in. LUCE lets go of the vacuum, putting her hands over her ears

LUCE: Too much noise.

CHUCK: Look, you do it like this.

> *(CHUCK shows LUCE how to vacuum. LUCE turns her back. CHUCK laughs and unplugs the vacuum)*
>
> Okay, have it your way. Who wants a clean house, anyway? Hey, listen, I talked to Papa. He might be needing some extra help — well, you're gonna have to help pay the rent. It was you that wanted this place. What's the point of winning a couple of talent competitions? Where does that get you? We need some money . . .

LUCE switches on the vacuum cleaner. CHUCK yanks the cord out

LUCE: You want clean?

CHUCK: I could kill you!

LUCE: Come . . .

LUCE invites CHUCK to do so. CHUCK relaxes suddenly, laughs. LUCE laughs. CHUCK hugs her

CHUCK: I love you and I don't know why. *(turns away, picks up a scrapbook)* Is this how you spend your time while I'm out looking for work? Barbara Ann Scott, eh? *(whistles)*

(LUCE tries to take the book away)

Judy Garland — not bad . . . Lotte Lenya? Marlene Dietrich? They're Germans — bunch of spies.

LUCE: No . . . they are women. They are success.

CHUCK: Krauts aren't women.

LUCE: At least they are not in chains.

CHUCK: Well, zey should be.

CHUCK does a Nazi salute. LUCE throws the book at him. CHUCK starts to laugh

LUCE: Is serious. Is serious.

CHUCK: Oh Loose, you got it all wrong. You got any Italians there?

LUCE: I cannot to go back to Italy — there also they keep me in chains. I cannot to leave.

CHUCK: Wait a minute . . . who's talking about leaving? We just moved in here . . .

LUCE: *(stares at him, hating him)* Here I must always be waiting for you. Is serious!

Long pause

CHUCK: Okay . . . I'll show you serious. You want America — there's America. *(slowly and deliberately tears a page out of the book)* You want Germany — *(tears)* There's Germany . . . You want —

LUCE: Listen!

CHUCK: Listen to me for a change.

LUCE: Listen to what? To your ugly music? I was thinking you are good musician. I make mistake. Is my mistake, not yours.

CHUCK: Shut up.

710

LUCE: This terrible place — you must see —

CHUCK: I said shut up.

LUCE: Fish and fog. Fish and fog — Halifax!

CHUCK: You heard me —

LUCE: If I leave —

CHUCK: Go! Get out. Go!

LUCE: Where?

CHUCK: Just go. Just go that's all. *(puts his head in his hands)*

LUCE: *(puts her arm around him)* Oh Chuck, I am sorry —

CHUCK: Get away.

LUCE: I —

CHUCK: I'm gonna make it. I'm gonna make it, I promised you that didn't I? If I promised you nothing else — it's getting better. I'm getting more bookings —

LUCE: You must to practise.

CHUCK: Yeah . . . yeah . . . *(goes to the piano)* Listen . . . what do you think of this? *(begins to play and sing "The Tennessee Waltz" in an imitative style, stops)* We gotta find my song, that's all . . . that's all. *(continues playing)*

ACT TWO SCENE ELEVEN

The farm in Alberta, 1953. DIANA has gardening gloves, a trowel, and an assortment of seeds. She is making a plan of the flower garden. PAUL comes in and looks over her shoulder.

DIANA: *(picking up the seed catalogue)* Will camellias grow d'you think? This catalogue says . . .

PAUL doesn't answer. DIANA goes on reading

PAUL: There's no necessity to stock the ponds this year.

711

DIANA: What?

PAUL: Too uncertain.

DIANA: *(dismissive)* Paul!

PAUL: Let someone else lose their shirt.

DIANA: Oh come off it.

PAUL: Too chancy. It could be years before we see any return.

DIANA: I don't want to listen to this.

PAUL: I talked to the accountant today.

DIANA: We're going to change the economy of the region. Well, fish farming's the coming —

PAUL: We can't afford to take those kind of risks. Not now.

DIANA: You do this every time! Just when we're on the point of making a success of something — bingo! You're not doing another about-turn.

PAUL: There's Nigel to think of now.

DIANA: What's he got to do with it?

PAUL: He's gotta have something better than I did. I had to work to put myself through high school.

DIANA: This isn't you talking. What about —

PAUL: That's the end of it. I've cancelled out.

DIANA: Without consulting me?

PAUL: Finished.

DIANA: You never cease to amaze me! *(gathers her things together, furious)*

PAUL: What's this? *(picks up a package of seeds)*

DIANA: *(suddenly)* What if I go ahead on my own?

PAUL: You can't. I've cancelled. What are these?

DIANA snatches the seeds back

PAUL: Canterbury Bells?

DIANA: Oh Paul, at least let's talk about this — you can't go through life picking things up and just letting them . . . Well, where does it leave me?

PAUL: I told you. We can't afford a failure. We can't be a laughing-stock. I don't mind what they say about me, but I don't want them laughing at my son. I know what it's like. They used to laugh at me when I was a kid. It's too risky.

DIANA: They laugh because you're so . . . so stupid.

PAUL: Where did you get these?

DIANA: My mother sent them. I was planning to make a real English garden.

PAUL: You're not supposed to import seeds, you know that?

DIANA: Just a few flowers.

PAUL: It's the law. It's the law of this country . . .

DIANA: Since when were you such a great upholder of the law? It frightens me Paul, just when I think I know you . . .

(PAUL turns away, about to leave)

Well, I need flowers. They're part of my heritage. We've always had flower gardens. Over here they don't even have fences — hedges . . . There's no history. I want my son to have a sense of his past.

PAUL: Only the English would put their history behind a fence.

DIANA: That's not what I'm saying. Nigel —

PAUL: *(raising his voice)* So you think you can show him history in a package of seeds.

713

DIANA: *(angry)* Oh, you don't care . . . You don't even know what it is . . . that sense of . . . of continuity with . . . everything that's gone before . . . You don't have a history.

PAUL: What? Do you know when Kiev was founded?

DIANA: Kiev!

PAUL: Yes. Kiev — that's my history.

DIANA: That's ridiculous. You've never even been there. You know what I'm talking about . . . you brought me here and wiped out my past. Are you going to tell me you've stopped loving me now?

PAUL: What's that got to do with it? God, women! What do you want from me?

DIANA: I'd like to be able to rely on you, that's all —

PAUL: What do I have to do to convince you?

DIANA: Admit that you're wrong just once.

PAUL: Okay, okay, so I shoot for the moon sometimes.

DIANA: The moon? Half the solar system as well —

PAUL: Okay. Okay, so I admit it.

DIANA: What? What do you admit?

PAUL: Everything!

DIANA: See?

PAUL: So I've been a bastard!

DIANA: Oh, what's the use?

PAUL: Well, you knew what you were in for before you married me!

(DIANA looks at PAUL. Long pause)

I've led you a hell of a dance, haven't I?

(DIANA shrugs, choked up)

I'm sorry. I'm sorry, Di. I just . . . guess I've been selfish.

DIANA: *(stares at him, unbelieving)* That's the first time I've ever heard you actually say . . .

PAUL: I know . . .

PAUL is close to tears. They embrace

DIANA: *(laughs)* Oh, Paul, you look like a donkey, and I sound like an old fish-wife.

PAUL: You are an old fish-wife!

DIANA: Not any more! You're not going to stock the ponds!

PAUL: You always have to have the last word, don't you?

DIANA: Do I?

PAUL: Typical WASP. Why'd I marry you?

DIANA: Because you're a bohunk donkey, that's why!

ACT TWO SCENE TWELVE

CHUCK and LUCE's apartment, Halifax, 1952. CHUCK is playing and singing "Mona Lisa, Mona Lisa How I Love You". LUCE is packing a suitcase. CHUCK stops playing and looks at LUCE.

CHUCK: No mi ami.

LUCE: Speak English. I cannot stand your terrible Italian.

CHUCK: You do not love me, you bitch.

LUCE: Love?

CHUCK: Love.

LUCE: *(amused)* I took your name — only for love would I take such a terrible name.

CHUCK: You think that?

LUCE: Rotten flesh?

715

CHUCK: Basta! Ascoltate! Basta!

LUCE: Speak English.

CHUCK: I have the right to speak Italian.

LUCE: Then speak it well.

Pause

CHUCK: Why didn't you say you didn't want my name?

LUCE: Why didn't you say you intended to live all your life in Halifax?

CHUCK: There's nothing wrong with Halifax.

LUCE: No? Sure is nothing wrong. Is not even possible to drink wine in a restaurant, is possible smoke opium, but is not possible drink wine — is hypocrite town — no culture.

CHUCK: Why didn't you say what you wanted before you came?

LUCE: Many things I did not know how to say Chuck. No . . . was not language. Not English, not Italian . . . how to make you understand . . . How to make you hear when you do not know how to listen.

(Pause)

Not listen to words but . . . *(reaches down inside herself, then gives up, shrugs)* Ach — the whole what you are is . . . Canadian.

CHUCK: You think you corner the market in sensibility because you're some high class dago bitch? Mussolini was an Italian.

(LUCE shrugs)

I was ashamed, you know that? When I was in Italy, I always said I was a Maritimer. Canada may be a desert but at least we don't breed thugs. Black shirts!

LUCE: You breed only bores!

CHUCK: What's that supposed to mean?

LUCE: It means I am going to Toronto.

CHUCK: For the two hundredth time — n . . . o . . . no.

LUCE: *(quietly)* It means . . . I cannot wait for you any longer Chuck. I am more than thirty years old. Time is passing — too much time. I am older than you.

CHUCK: You never would have been a singer — you know that. That's why you came here in the first place, you were a second-rater and you knew it. That's why you'd never go off to study when I gave you your chances. That's why you made out you were going off your head.

LUCE: So this time I go. Maybe this time I do go off my head . . . this time I go as far as I can. I find out what is inside me.

CHUCK: No . . . no. I won't let you.

CHUCK empties LUCE's suitcase. She picks it up calmly

LUCE: I have already accepted to go. You cannot stop me!

Pause

CHUCK: Okay, so okay. We'll make it Toronto. You win.

LUCE: No. No. No. No. I see now —

CHUCK: What do you see?

LUCE: That you have no ambition. Only dreams. Dreams and compromises.

CHUCK: So you don't compromise eh? You refuse to talk Italian. You refuse to even acknowledge where you're from and you take a job as a hostess on an Italian radio show in a city you say you hate. That's not a compromise?

LUCE: It will not be for long. Soon I get into another show
 . . . maybe television.

CHUCK: Television? This time next year it'll be dead.

(LUCE shrugs, continues to pack. CHUCK watches, helpless)

Listen Loose. It's not too late — we could still have a kid
 . . . I'm making good money. The old man's getting old
now — he keeps asking, now that Mama's gone. He's got
money put aside — wants to make an investment — he
was talking about maybe opening up a coffee bar. Well,
you could learn to bake. We could hire someone to look
after the kid . . .

LUCE: I already have a kid. *(smiles at him)*

CHUCK: Well, what am I . . . How am I supposed to make
you stay? How long would you be gone for?

LUCE: Maybe not for long . . . *(snaps the suitcase shut)*

ACT TWO SCENE THIRTEEN

Hamilton, 1955. RUTH and DAVE are alone in the kitchen.

RUTH: *(looking up)* Oh . . . I didn't expect you.

(DAVE stands looking at RUTH)

Weren't you going down the legion?

DAVE: There's a meeting on — Remembrance Day committee.

RUTH: Oh? I thought you were on it.

DAVE: Did I see Jamie on the street?

RUTH: He can play on the street.

DAVE: He can't.

RUTH: They all do. I can't have them under my feet.

DAVE: I don't want my kids on the street, okay? What's she going to think about it? *(nods toward inner room)*

RUTH: I don't ask her.

DAVE: Well remember . . .

(DAVE walks into a chair. RUTH giggles)

Goddamnit. Can't you keep things tidy? What does it take? Do I have to do everything myself?

RUTH: It's your mother's chair, not mine.

(Pause)

I took them to the doctor's today for their jabs.

DAVE: How much did it cost?

RUTH: You told me not to take them to the free clinic.

DAVE: You coulda waited.

RUTH: Did you ask your mother about baby-sitting tonight?

(Pause)

She's in there, watching TV.

DAVE: We're not going out tonight.

RUTH: But you prom . . . Oh.

DAVE: We can't be going out every night.

RUTH: We haven't been out in six months.

DAVE: Who's fault is that? Look at you — you should make friends.

RUTH: Who with? I can't even have people in . . . She . . .

DAVE: Sssssssh.

RUTH: Well, in Scotland you can just go and knock on anyone's door and they'll go down the pub with you. You won't even dance now . . . In Scotland they're kicking up their heels 'til they're eighty. No one here even picks up a couple of spoons and clacks them. Where are your songs?

719

DAVE: No one wants to sing. Who wants to sing when? . . .

RUTH: *(sensing something)* When what?

DAVE: Nothing.

(Pause)

I quit today.

RUTH: Oh Dave!

DAVE: *(mocking)* Oh Dave!

RUTH: But why?

DAVE: They were all on my back, that's why. They gave me a week to join their lousy union.

RUTH: Who?

DAVE: The guys on the floor — the guys I work with, who else? It's a free country, isn't it?

RUTH: Oh Dave!

DAVE: Is that all you can say?

RUTH: But why? Why didn't you just join and keep quiet?

DAVE: It's the principle, isn't it? This is a free country, that's what that war was about.

RUTH: They're not gonna throw eggs at our door again are they?

DAVE: I told you, I quit. They can't call me a scab this time. I didn't come back for people to start pushing me around — pushing socialism down my throat.

RUTH: But it's not socialism Dave — it's for the workers.

DAVE: I'm a worker aren't I? And I don't want it. I done a good job . . . punching in on their lousy clock, shitting myself if I was five minutes late . . . sweating to keep their lousy machines running.

RUTH: Whose machines?

DAVE: The company's.

RUTH: But whose side are you on?

DAVE: I'm on my side that's what. I got a wife and four kids to look after —

RUTH: *(quietly, patting her stomach)* Five.

DAVE: I don't have to take orders from no one. I'll do it myself. I'll tell you this, it's the last time I work for any lousy steel company.

RUTH: Did you try at Dofasco?

DAVE: You gotta have an in.

Pause

RUTH: I could get a job if your mum'd . . . I worked before . . . in the fish market.

DAVE: No wife of mine works.

RUTH: If we got a typewriter I could learn to type. If we could afford —

DAVE: I done it right didn't I? I went over there, I fought for this country — I love this country, right? I come back — I play by the rules.

Pause

DAVE: How come other guys got all the luck? Guys who weren't even over there?

RUTH: It's just luck that's all.

RUTH holds out her hand to him. He knocks it away and swipes her drink off the table

ACT TWO SCENE FOURTEEN

Staging of this scene is dependent on costume changes. Ideally, all characters should be in position at the opening of the scene and each is spotlit as he or she speaks. However, where production logistics do not allow for this, characters should step into position whenever appropriate.

New Year's Eve, 1957. LUCE is broadcasting in Toronto. RUTH is sitting at the kitchen table, a blank sheet of paper in front of her, a drink to hand, staring straight ahead. CHUCK is playing in a bar, no audience. DAVE is in the Legion, wearing his Legion tie, sitting near the Union Jack. PAUL is at his father's farm in Saskatchewan, shovelling snow. DIANA is clearing snow in their drive in Alberta.

LUCE: Felice anno nuovo, auguri a tutti voi ascoltatori della radio Italo-Toronto. Happy New Year! L'ultimo disco del'anno cinquanta sette sarà . . . si, lo so, indovinato . . . "Che sera, sera" . . . *(puts the record on, sound fades)*

RUTH: December thirty-first, 1957. Dear Mum and Dad and everybody. Well, it's the end of another year, and I've a few minutes before I get on with Dave's tea. I wanted to write — you'll be wondering why I haven't written — well, to tell you the truth, the sixth one's on the way — Dave's real pleased, he loves children. I'm sending a picture of us all, that's me in the back. As you'll see, young Jamie's just like his dad, a regular film star, and Rita's a tomboy like I used to be, they call her Cissy here for short. The Queen came to Toronto last week. I took all the kids up on the train to see her, but we stood in the wrong place. You'll be pleased to hear that, Dad, I know what you think of all that English stuff. Everyone's giving me lots of presents for the baby, they've got lots of money here in Canada. Well, I've got to go now, I've got him a steak bigger than his plate, so love to Mary and Angus and the kids and everyone. *(takes a drink)* Tell Angus to hurry up and come up on the races so he can send me a ticket to come home. I miss you . . . no. *(drinks)* Love from Ruthie.

CHUCK: Right folks, listen to this one. Don Messer, you better watch out for me. *(plays "My Old Canadian Home" for a few bars, stops)* Okay, you guys, so where are you? It's New Year's Eve, there should be someone in here celebrating!

DAVE: It's never been the same since the war, eh? *(drinks beer)* People aren't the same these days, no values, the spirit's gone out of them. Women — they're all over the place. They're all getting like the Canadian whores they sent over in the war — had their skirts up 'round their necks before they were even off the boat. That's why I married a different kind of girl. Next year I'll bring her down here . . . yeah. Happy New Year! *(drinks)* If I'd'a let Verna marry me instead'a her marrying Tom . . . sitting around all day — air traffic control — what's he know about airplanes? I was shaking hands with Buzz Beurling when Mom was still washing behind his ears. Yeah, take it easy, Buzz old buddy — remember this one could be the last. *(drinks)* That's all people want today. Forget about the war, forget about your old mother, leave that to somebody else, forget your responsibilities. Just have the one kid and forget to send him to his first communion, or ask his uncle to be godfather. Just think about holidays in Florida under some goddamn Yankee orange tree where they never even seen a Spitfire. Let someone else stay home and look after your mother's basement when it floods. Wipe out the past. No, that's not what we fought for. They wanna flush all the old standards down the drain. I didn't go over there so's Tom could have a sailboat and a new car every year, and thumb his nose at me. *(pauses)* That was the best goddamn time of my life, and I didn't even know it.

(CHUCK sings "My Old Canadian Home". Lights up on PAUL)

PAUL: Snow. Six days of the stuff — ugh. Can't leave him alone for many more winters. He'll break his neck. Put him in a home . . . he'll die . . . must talk to her about it. How? He doesn't even think of her as a person . . .

Anglicki . . . Well, I'm not gonna keep coming out to Saskatchewan every New Year's. Deserves to break his neck. Jesus, how come with all their high-flown technology they can't look after the old folks . . . Politicians! Someone should come up with a way of straightening out their priorities. Just needs a bit of vision. Someone with overall vision. Energy. Where's it gone? Energy to start over?

DIANA: Snow to see the new year in. And for the next four months . . . endless . . . *(stares out into the distance)* It was the flatness that terrified me. It doesn't bother me now. Funny . . . I can think about all that — couldn't then — numb. I remember thinking if I talked about it — if I even thought about it — I wouldn't be able to go on. If he'd only let me have a radio — that weekly paper! I couldn't laugh about it. My jaws were frozen. Had to shut it all out . . . There are times — there were times, when I'd look at the sky and wonder if it would be the same sky that they were seeing back home, or was it some other planet? It was so flat . . . and so cold in winter — the first year was the worst. The way you could hear the wolves and coyotes. I never told him . . . I thought I was on the edge of the world — the flatness under the snow. Aqui nada. That's what they said the word "Canada" came from. When the Spaniards made a map of North America they wrote it over the top. Where we are now — aqui nada. Nothing here. The silence . . . Then when I went back home I couldn't sleep for the traffic noises . . . and we didn't even live near a main road. I was — funny how ashamed I still am of those old feelings — lonely. *(shivers, catches her arms around herself)* But this is my country now. . . . I belong here. Paul . . . *(looks around, suddenly scared)* Paul, don't stay away.

PAUL: *(still clearing snow in Saskatchewan)* Couple of hours and it'll be covered over again. Just keep shovelling. He says you gotta learn to live with it — adapt — it all takes time — yeah — generations. But my time isn't that long. Someone's gotta make the changes. Something's gotta be done. I built up a good business — I got a decent kid, I love my wife — what more is there? I'm gonna write that book now! *(pauses)* I'm nearly forty years old. Anyone can do anything. Di . . . *(pulls his arms around himself)* Diana . . . *(shivers)*

Blackout. Lights up and fade on Union Jack as maple leaf flag is brought into prominence

ACT TWO SCENE FIFTEEN

Montreal, 1966. CHUCK and LUCE have just met on St. Catherine's Street.

CHUCK: I can't get over it.

LUCE: On St. Catherine's Street, just like that.

CHUCK: So. Howdeedoodi.

LUCE: What?

CHUCK: How's it going? You're looking great.

LUCE: Oh, not bad. Yourself?

CHUCK: *(grunts twice)* So. What are you doing in Montreal?

LUCE: Learning French, among other things.

CHUCK: French?

LUCE: Sure.

CHUCK: Italian isn't enough for you?

LUCE: Not in this business. Especially not with Expo opening up next year.

CHUCK: So. How is business?

LUCE: Oh. Pretty good, you know.

CHUCK: I saw you in a commercial. Dog food or something.

LUCE: Mayonnaise.

CHUCK: That's it.

LUCE: It's going very well actually. I just cut a record.

CHUCK: You did?

LUCE: Just a small one.

CHUCK: A forty-five?

LUCE: Mainly I do voice-overs in commercials. I've started to compose my own melodies. Just for the commercials.

(Pause)

It's been a long time. It's good to see you, Chuck.

CHUCK: Likewise.

LUCE: So. What are you doing so far from Halifax?

CHUCK: Vacation. You know . . . staking out the territory. We thought we might move out here . . . but we'll probably head for Ontario. That's where the work is, right?

LUCE: We?

CHUCK: Oh . . . oh, I got married. Didn't you know?

LUCE: Who is she? The lucky lady?

CHUCK: You remember Rosemary?

(LUCE shakes her head)

She used to help my dad out. He's really expanded now, three stores . . . going great guns.

LUCE: I don't remember her.

CHUCK: Yes you do. She always did the evening shift. Anyway, it's her.

LUCE: Are you happy?

CHUCK: Sure are. Hey, you should meet her — she'd like that. She's back at the motel. First vacation we've taken in five years. With the kids and all.

LUCE: Ah.

CHUCK: Two boys.

LUCE: Congratulations. I seem to be repeating myself.

CHUCK: I got a pretty good act together. Mostly Italian numbers — really suits my style. Hey . . . are you going to be around for a while? I'm trying to arrange a couple of bookings at a place in Sherbrooke while we're here.

LUCE: No . . . no. I have to get back. We start rehearsals on Monday.

CHUCK: What for?

LUCE: Just a little show. One of those back street cabaret places, you know. Bit of dancing, bit of singing.

CHUCK: Dancing? Aren't you a bit old for that? I mean . . .

LUCE: Oh, I keep in shape.

CHUCK: Yeah.

LUCE: It's just a group of friends. We got together and wrote this thing. It'll probably bomb.

CHUCK: No way. I'm probably going to be in Toronto — maybe I'll catch it. Got a couple of people to see — Holiday Inn — you know it?

LUCE: Oh, is Gary Richter still the manager?

CHUCK: I don't remember the guy's name . . .

LUCE: Maybe I can do something for you. Here. (gives him her card) Why don't you give me a call when you get into town.

CHUCK: Yeah. Yeah, sure I will. So . . . I should be getting along now. Can't keep the little lady waiting. Good meeting you Loose. Let's keep in touch now we found each other, eh?

LUCE: Yeah. Yeah. Let's do that.

(They embrace)

Au revoir, Chuck.

CHUCK: Ci vediamo. (chucks her under the chin and leaves)

ACT TWO SCENE SIXTEEN

RUTH and DAVE's kitchen, Hamilton, 1967. RUTH is locked out, slightly tipsy, yelling at the back door.

RUTH: *(sings. Tune: "Scots Wha Hae")*

"Wha will be a traitor knave,
wha can fill a coward's grave;
wha sae base a be a slave?
Traitor, coward turn and flee . . ."

Okay, so the kids are asleep. I can shout if I like . . . I don't care if she hears — can ye hear me mother? You'd better let me in, Dave. No . . . you wouldn't dare do anything.

(expectant pause)

(sings. Tune: "Bluebells of Scotland")

"Oh it's where tell me where has my bonnie laddie gone? He's gone to bonnie Scotland where the sweet bluebells grow . . ."

I had a wee dance tonight, Dave — while you were watching your hockey . . . Well, aren't you surprised? . . . Come on out and hit me. They were singing Scottish songs . . . They asked us to come back next Friday — me and Molly McLaren. We danced . . . on the tables. We did so! Aye. *(giggles)* They don't really like us here, me and Molly. They don't like us, 'cos we're not Canadians. And I'll tell you something. *(giggles)* We don't like them either. *(sticks out her tongue childishly)*

DAVE comes to the door, pulls RUTH roughly into the room, and shoves her into a chair.

DAVE: I'm going back up to bed. And don't you dare come near those stairs!

ACT TWO SCENE SEVENTEEN

La Gondola Restaurant, Niagara Falls, 1970. CHUCK plays "I Never Promised You a Rose Garden" in an Italian version. His style is exaggeratedly Mediterranean, smooth. DIANA, PAUL, RUTH and DAVE are eating in silence at a table illuminated by a single candle. LUCE sits nearby, smartly dressed and coiffed, alone at a table.

PAUL: So . . . what would you recommed we do with our time here?

DAVE: How long do you have?

PAUL: A few days. We're going to the ballet on Tuesday night — in Toronto.

DAVE: If you'd'a timed it better you coulda taken in a home game.

DIANA: Oh yes? You have rather a good football team here don't you?

DAVE: Only the best in the country. She prefers soccer. *(meaning RUTH)*

RUTH: You like it too. Dundee's doing good this year — I still listen to the Scottish League results on Saturdays, do you? They can't pronounce the names.

DIANA: I hear it was quite something when they won the World Cup.

RUTH: Aye — that was England.

DIANA: I was never very big on sports. Paul is.

PAUL: Sure am. I like to get out there and curl. *(to DAVE)* How about you?

DAVE: Curl up in bed!

DIANA: Tell them about the bowling league. He's been King Pin for three years in a row.

PAUL: What we need is a few more hours to the day.

DIANA: It's been an enormously . . . full life.

DAVE: Full?

DIANA: (signalling PAUL to help her out) I mean . . . it still is.

PAUL: You're dead right. We hardly see each other. (to RUTH) You know this is the longest time I've spent alone with my wife since . . . for about twenty years.

RUTH: But don't you live together?

PAUL: Sure. But you try living with someone who heads up just about every goddamned committee that's going! And if there isn't one going she'll start it up.

DIANA: You speak for yourself. He's so involved in politics he hardly manages to get time for supper more than twice a week. It's a good job he has an efficient manager.

PAUL: And an efficient wife! (laughs)

DIANA: We both have to be.

PAUL and DIANA smile at each other. DAVE looks disgusted

PAUL: Come on Ruth, what about a dance?

RUTH: (looks at DAVE) Oh . . . maybe when there's a few more people . . .

PAUL: I'm a bit rusty but I'm not that bad.

RUTH: I didn't mean that!

PAUL: Come on then.

PAUL gets up and pulls RUTH's chair back. They dance. DAVE and DIANA are alone at the table.

RUTH: Are you really in politics?

PAUL: I do what I can.

DAVE: So . . . who's looking after your place then? The manager?

RUTH: Oh, I thought maybe I was talking to an MP or something.

PAUL: Strictly a policy man.

Pause.

RUTH: You're a nice dancer.

PAUL: I have two left feet.

RUTH: Do you do it often? Dance, I mean.

PAUL: Not if I can avoid it.

RUTH: You're as bad as Dave! What's she on? The committees. You said —

PAUL: Oh . . . . the library board . . . civil liberties, things like that. I'll never persuade her to give them up — says she's the only one who's ever read anything.

RUTH: She was always a bit hoity toity — oh, I shouldn't say that. Would you like to come to our house? I mean . . . maybe tomorrow? You could come for a drink — Dave can come and get you.

PAUL: We rented a car.

RUTH: Then you'll come?

PAUL: I guess so. We'd like that, yes.

RUTH: I'd ask you to supper, only . . .

PAUL: We wouldn't expect you to do anything like that.

DIANA: Yes. It's the first time we've left him — I hope it'll be all right. He's quite young — barely out of agricultural school — not much older than Nigel — our son.

Silence, then DAVE and DIANA together.

DIANA: I was thinking —

DAVE: You ever thought —

DIANA: I'm sorry.

DAVE: Go ahead.

DIANA: No, it wasn't important.

Silence.

DAVE: I was gonna say . . . whether you've ever thought how it would've been if there hadn't been a war? Well, you wouldn't be over here for a start.

DIANA: God no. I'd've been married to some stuffy stockbroker probably.

DAVE: You don't think you'd'a been better off?

DIANA: No.

DAVE: I don't know. How come you Brits always have to tell us what to do?

DIANA: Oh c'mon. You know that's not true.

(Pause)

731

RUTH: About eight o'clock?

PAUL: I'll have to confirm with the boss!

RUTH: Oh, she'll say yes.

Pause. PAUL laughs and pulls RUTH a little closer. They do a fancy step.

Well, I can't say I haven't had an exciting life. I never knew what Paul was going to throw at me next.

DAVE: *(with renewed interest)* He doesn't look the type.

DIANA: I'm speaking metaphorically.

DAVE: Oh.

(Silence)

Is he always that way?

DIANA: What way?

DAVE: With women?

PAUL and RUTH glance across at DAVE and return to the area of the table

PAUL: Loosen up the old limbs.

RUTH: Let's dance Dave.

DAVE: You shoulda married Fred Astaire. *(makes no effort to rise)*

RUTH: Ach!

PAUL: I've got an idea. What do you think of this? *(whispers to RUTH)*

RUTH: Oh yes!

PAUL goes over to CHUCK. DIANA turns and watches, curious

DIANA: He's such a silly.

RUTH sits at the table and starts to peel the label off the wine bottle

DAVE: What are you doing?

RUTH: *(whispering)* I have to remember the name.

DAVE: What for?

RUTH: They're coming for a drink on Sunday night.

DAVE: What?

RUTH: Sssh!

DAVE grabs the label and puts it back on the bottle. DIANA catches this, turns and smiles. PAUL returns to the table

DIANA: Let's dance Paul.

PAUL: No, not yet. Wait a minute.

RUTH: *(to PAUL)* Dance with me.

PAUL: We'll sit this one out. *(to DIANA)* I want you to listen —

(CHUCK switches tunes and begins to sing and play "Diana")

Well?

DIANA: Nice.

DAVE: Your song eh?

(DIANA nods)

They should get Ruthie up there.

RUTH: Me?

DAVE: *(not being sarcastic)* Sure.

DIANA: Do you sing, Ruthie?

RUTH: No.

PAUL: I'll bet you do.

DAVE: You should hear her. She should be with that White Heather show, you know that? *(to DIANA)* You sing those songs too?

DIANA: Oh no. I run the choir — we managed a full-scale "Messiah" last year. We had guest soloists from Calgary.

CHUCK stops playing and begins to speak with an assumed Italian accent

CHUCK: Good evening ladies and gentlemen and welcome to La Gondola, the ship of dreams, afloat in the honeymoon capital of the world. As usual, a special hello to all of you newlyweds out there. Some of your faces I recognize from last year, and even before that — and you know what — you still look like you're in love! Well, I got bad news for you, folks — I'm abandoning ship. Yes, last week I signed a contract with a famous hotel chain that shall be nameless. It is enough to say that from the first of next month I'll be appearing nightly in the Blue Room at a certain hotel in Toronto.

(Applause)

I have invited the lady who is responsible for the Holiday Inn's good fortune — whoops! — to be here with me for my last night. Just back from New York, let me present the very lovely Luce Marini. *(pronounces her name correctly)*

(Applause)

Luce! *(drinks to her, raises glass to the audience)* Since this is my last night at La Gondola, I offer a drink on the house to everyone.

(Applause. He begins to play and sing "Lonely is the Man Without Love" in Italian)

"Quando m'inamoro . . ."

DAVE: Love . . . why don't they sing about something else?

RUTH: Like what?

DAVE: Work. *(to PAUL)* Well why not? . . . *(nods at CHUCK)* That's woman's stuff eh?

DIANA: She's quite nice looking. I've seen her in commercials.

734

RUTH: He's good looking too. We'll have to watch out for his show. D'you think I could ask them for their autograph? Janet'd like it. Maybe they'd sign this. *(meaning the menu)*

DAVE: That goes with the furniture.

(RUTH gets up)

Hey . . . come back here . . .

RUTH takes the menu over to CHUCK

DIANA: She can't be as young as she looks.

PAUL: That's show biz eh? Look at Mae West.

DAVE: Who wants to?

CHUCK: What's your name?

RUTH: *(glancing at DAVE)* Janet.

CHUCK: *(signs with a flourish)* Ciao Janet.

RUTH goes to LUCE

LUCE: No, I don't give autographs.

RUTH: Oh . . . I'm sorry.

(Pause)

We're celebrating you see. It's their anniversary. We knew each other in the war.

LUCE: Oh? So did we . . . *(glances at CHUCK)*

RUTH: Everything . . . changes doesn't it?

(RUTH smiles shyly. LUCE relents and signs)

I'm sorry to bother you . . . thank you.

RUTH goes back to the table. LUCE picks up her jacket. CHUCK puts out his hand to stop her.

CHUCK: Don't go.

LUCE: *(smiles)* Don't worry — I'll wait.

CHUCK: One more set and we can leave.

CHUCK continues to play. LUCE sits back, smiling

PAUL: *(to DAVE)* So . . . what do you think of Mr Trudeau?

RUTH: *(warning)* Dave!

DIANA: Paul headed up our local campaign committee at the last election. We got to know Eugene Whelan personally, didn't we sweetie? *(hiccoughs)* Oh . . . I think I'm getting a bit tipsy.

RUTH: They're very nice. They're Italian. I don't think he's the owner.

DAVE: War measures . . . yeah! We need more of that strong-arm stuff.

PAUL: So you've never been back to Scotland Ruthie?

RUTH: If I'd'a gone to Scotland . . . I was afraid I . . . I just might not've come back.

DAVE: Eh? You hear that? *(laughs at the absurdity of the idea)*

RUTH: The kids want me to leave him. They have it all worked out. They're talking about renting a wee flat for me and Janet and Craigie . . . the others don't need me now.

(Pause)

Rita says it's for the best. I wonder if he's going to play again? Maybe he knows some of the old songs.

Long silence. CHUCK begins to play "La Novia"

DIANA: *(brightly)* Talking of going home, the last time I was in the old country they seemed to think I was some kind of hillbilly.

736

RUTH: My dad died. I don't think of him as dead.

DIANA: Oh, I'm sorry! Well, this is our home now isn't it. It's certainly mine. It's not that I've given up — that is — I'll always be English, but I'm Canadian as well. This is where I belong. Isn't that right?

RUTH: I'm a grandmother now. Rita got married right out of university. She graduated.

DIANA: You must be very proud.

RUTH: She married a Scotsman. His family came over with Bonnie Prince Charlie — well, not with him, bu —

DIANA: I'm rather glad Nigel's not married yet — it would make us feel so old. He still hangs around the yard. Long hair — all he reads is left-wing propaganda. If you talked to him you'd think he was illiterate. Young people today! He's a strange boy — spends all his spare time learning Ukrainian. What earthly use is that going to be to him?

DAVE stands up, as if to leave

PAUL: Where are you going?

DAVE: What's that to you?

RUTH: Sit down.

DAVE: And you . . . *(gestures at RUTH, picks up a glass)*

DIANA: How many children do you have?

RUTH: Six.

DIANA: Six? Oh, do sit down, Dave.

DAVE smashes the glass. PAUL goes around the table to stop him. DAVE pushes him roughly. DIANA rushes over to PAUL. DAVE looks around, stops, brings his fist down on the table.

DAVE: Okay, you're gonna listen to me for a change. You're gonna listen to me. There's nothing wrong with the way I am — I can't help it if I'm not a goddamned Scotsman —

RUTH: I never wanted you to —

737

DAVE: There's nothing wrong with this country either. This country is the greatest in the world.

PAUL: Here here.

DIANA: No one's arguing with you Dave.

LUCE joins CHUCK at the piano

DAVE: I'm sick of hearing you run it down. It's the best goddamned country in . . . You should be grateful to be here. All of you . . . *(shouts)* All of you. I fought for Canada. It's the greatest goddamned country in the world, so what's the matter with you all? You name one that's better. Scotland? Don't make me laugh. England? It's a joke.

RUTH: *(gets up, clutching her purse, which obviously contains a bottle)* Excuse me.

DAVE: And you don't have to go out there to take a drink. You can have one right here. We're gonna drink to our kids, and to Canada. *(pours RUTH a drink)* Where are those free drinks?

DIANA: *(raising her glass)* To us, to all of us, and to Canada.

DAVE: Where's the music? What's happened to the god-damned music?

(LUCE whispers to CHUCK. He plays the opening of "Some-where Over the Rainbow". LUCE begins to sing.)

She's been the best wife a man could have and I won't let any of you say any different.

DAVE stares at RUTH, then goes over to her slowly and kisses her hand.

RUTH: Oh Dave.

RUTH and DAVE dance, holding each other closely. LUCE and CHUCK sing in duet. DIANA and PAUL raise their glasses to each other, put them down, and dance.

The End

738

WORDS TO ITALIAN SONGS

"Rose Garden" *(chorus only, CHUCK's version)*
Mi dispiace
Non ti prometto bell rose
Ore di sole
E giornate quando piove.
C'è un momento quando dai
E oltre non fa mai
Lo so-o-o-o-o
Mi dispaice . . .

"La Novia" *(The Wedding)*
Bianch'e splendente
E la novia.
Mentre nascosta
Tra la folla
Dietr'una lacrima
Indecisa
Vedo morir le mie illusioni
Là sull' altar
Lei sta piangendo.
Tutti diranno
Che di gioia,
Mentre il suo cuor'
Sta gridando.
Ave Maria.

"Lonely is the Man Without Love" *(CHUCK's version)*
Quando m'inamoro
Sarà un tesoro
Quando trovo quella per me.
Se quel'giorno viene
Pare che non viene
Solo son'un uomo senza amor'.

Allan Stratton

Rexy!

EDITOR'S NOTE: Allan Stratton was born in Stratford, Ontario in 1951. By the time he graduated from the University of Toronto with an M.A. in drama (1974), he had already begun his career in the professional theatre with work as an actor at the Stratford Festival and the sale of scripts to the CBC. In 1977, the Vancouver Playhouse presented *72 Under the O* and in 1980 Toronto's Phoenix Theatre produced his farce *Nurse Jane Goes to Hawaii*, which has become a favourite in Canadian theatres. Starring Georgia Engel, *Nurse Jane* was staged at New York's Theatre-in-the-Park. As well as *Rexy!* and a number of scripts for radio and television, Stratton has recently written *Joggers* which was presented as a work-in-progress by Calgary's Midnight Series and then by Toronto Free Theatre in 1982. CBC television aired his special *A Flush of Toys* in spring 1983 and his adaptation and translation of Eugene Labishe's *Célimare* (titled *Friends of a Feather*) was featured at the 1984 Shaw Festival and then toured.

Rexy! was first produced by Toronto's Phoenix Theatre, opening on 10 February 1981. It won a Dora Mavor Moore Award and the Canadian Author's Association Award for best play in 1981, as well as a Chalmers Award in 1982.

AUTHOR'S NOTE: Special thanks to a special director, dramaturge and friend: Brian Rintoul.

Characters:

WILLIAM LYON MACKENZIE KING   *Prime Minister of Canada*
LESTER PEARSON
COLONEL RALSTON
JOAN PATTESON
MRS. KING
ENID SIMPSON
WILLIAM LYON MACKENZIE   *Leader of the "Farmer's Revolt" in 1837 and a champion of the fight for responsible government in Upper Canada*

LORD RIVERDALE
WINSTON CHURCHILL
FRANKLIN D. ROOSEVELT
GENERAL MCNAUGHTON

The Set:

An open space bracketed by ruins, suggesting the Parliament Buildings, Kingsmere and a crypt.

The Time:

1937 to post-war.

ACT ONE

As the house lights dim we hear an instrumental version of "Tea for Two". A light pops up on Joan.

JOAN: The day Willy King came back from his state trip to Europe I was set to burst. Dear old family friend though he was, I was tired of his Ottawa stories. But Europe! For once I'd hear tales of adventure! Tales about people who mattered! And in 1937 that meant tales about that little monster with the moustache.

Lights up on KING at table with sandwiches and tea

741

KING: And they made such a fuss over me. Enormous State Luncheons, full of Herr King this and Herr King that; the occasional Sieg Heil rippling through the crowd.

JOAN: So what about *him*. Is he like Mr. Chamberlain says?

KING: Is who like Mr. Chamberlain says?

JOAN: You know perfectly well. *Him!*

KING: Oh *Him*. Well let's just say that Herr Hitler is definitely an experience.

JOAN: Did he rant?

KING: No he didn't. We spoke quietly over sandwiches and tea as a matter of fact.

JOAN: Quite civilized for a German.

KING: Yes. Did you know he's devoted to his mother?

JOAN: Really?

KING: And was once a Catholic choir boy?

JOAN: My, my!

KING: Amazing what one discovers over sandwiches.

JOAN: Like about the odds on war?

KING: I broached the subject.

JOAN: And?

KING: Well curiously enough he smiled and asked if I listened to Wagner.

JOAN: He likes music?

KING: He likes Wagner. I said I myself was fond of "Lohengrin." He nodded, began humming and peered at his sandwich as if it were some strange distant land. There's little doubt in my mind that he's a mystic. A fellow spiritualist perhaps.

JOAN: So there's hope for him yet.

KING: Oh yes. I can't abide Nazis but Hitler himself may one day be known as the great peasant liberator of his people. Perhaps even the deliverer of Europe. A modern day Joan of Arc.

JOAN: How exciting!

KING: But something quite troubling. As I sat watching him watching his sandwich I had a very peculiar wide-awake dream. As if I was looking into a mirror. And Mother was on the other side with *him* and everything I'd do *he'd* do and everything *she'd* do *you'd* do.

JOAN: Me?

KING: You were in my dream on *my* side of the mirror. Then suddenly people were screaming and everything went black and you threw a brick at the mirror and it shattered. And for some strange reason I had to put it back together again before Mother came home or I'd be spanked. And there were all these pieces, all these peculiar reflections, staring up at me from the floor — little mirrors I had to put back together into *one*. And my dear little Pat was barking and I said, "Stay back, you'll cut your paws!" But Pat said, "I've a bone to pick with you," and stood on his hind legs and did a sword dance through those shards of mirror into my arms and . . .

KING freezes, hands outstretched on the table, "seeing" something. Lights dim quickly and a clock strikes twelve

JOAN: Rex?

(KING stares off in a trance. JOAN removes the tea things from table and places her hands opposite his, fingers touching. Backlit, the figure of MACKENZIE with cane is dimly seen)

We feel your presence. Would you like to speak to us? . . .

(Beat, then two sharp knocks)

Are you known to us?

Two knocks

743

KING: Grampa?

JOAN: Are you Rexy's grandfather?

Two knocks

KING: Will there be war, Grampa? . . .

Silence

JOAN: . . . Are you still there Mr. Mackenzie?

Two knocks

KING: Is the British policy correct? Cooperation and understanding? Is that the correct policy?

(*Two knocks*)

Good, yes, thank you.

JOAN: Is Mr. Hitler to be feared?

(*One knock*)

Mr. Hitler is *not* to be feared?

Two knocks

KING: Go on Grampa.

JOAN: *(to MACKENZIE)* Do you have a message for your
grandson? . . . Mr. Mackenzie? . . .

MACKENZIE: The fate of Europe depends on Great Britain.

KING: The fate of Europe depends on Great Britain.

MACKENZIE & KING: *(together)* The fate of Great Britain
depends on Canada. The fate of Canada is in my grandson's hands. He was predestined to be prime minister at
this time. Long ago I saw that he would be a peacemaker.
Long ago I knew God had chosen him for this purpose.
Long ago . . .

(*Silence. Suddenly KING's body begins trembling*)

Rex? . . . Rexy??

KING: *(trembling increasing)* Yes Grandfather, yes. Yes!

JOAN: REX? REX??

KING: Oh Joan it's going to be all right. Everything's going to be all right.

(Lights down on KING and JOAN. We hear Big Ben. Lights up on RIVERDALE)

RIVERDALE: Prime Minister King was an absolute bastard. Difficult, dangerous and maddeningly obtuse. 1939 — we all knew war was about to break — but Mr. King? He knew better. Still favoured the old appeasement approach, of all things. As chief British liaison officer I had cause to meet him two months before the unpleasantness began.

Lights up on KING and RIVERDALE

KING: These new treaties of yours, Riverdale. Very noble documents indeed. Stirring.

RIVERDALE: We think as much.

KING: Oh yes, no question. Britain hops to the defence of Poland should she be attacked by the swastika. Very brave.

RIVERDALE: The Kraut stands warned, what.

KING: That he does. But the Kraut listens to Wagner and do you have any idea how he reacts to warnings?

RIVERDALE: How?

KING: The way any Kraut does. With drums, trumpets, tubas and thundersheets!

RIVERDALE: Thundersheets?

KING: Warnings are the last thing we need for God's sake.

RIVERDALE: What's this about thundersheets?

KING: I'm saying you're a fool to make treaties with *those* people. I mean what's *Poland*?

745

RIVERDALE: Mr. King?!

KING: Forgive me, but to threaten global war on account of a country the size of New Brunswick is ridiculous. Especially with forecasts of peace.

RIVERDALE: Peace?

KING: Yes peace.

RIVERDALE: Despite the upsets in Austria and Czecho-slovakia?

KING: Even so. I have it on the highest authority. What we need is a bridge between Herr Hitler and ourselves. Détente.

RIVERDALE: I'm afraid our government disagrees.

KING: Oh it does, does it? And with whose blood does it disagree? With whose blood do you intend to pay for this Baltic adventure?

RIVERDALE: It's not so much a question of paying as a question of drawing the line.

KING: Whose line?

RIVERDALE: Ours, naturally.

KING: You threaten world peace with a treaty which requires our support. Good, bad or indifferent, you sign it without our knowledge or approval as if we're some breed of sheep, cattle, some form of lemming, some . . .

RIVERDALE: If you don't mind my saying so . . .

KING: I DO! You flesh out your foreign policy with Canadian bodies — and you expect us to praise God for the honour of dying for your cobblestones.

RIVERDALE: We were hoping . . .

KING: You were *hoping*. That's much more like it, my good Lord Riverdale. Frankly, I'm not at all sure we Canadians like your little game of "Bait the Kraut."

RIVERDALE: I say, that's rather strong.

KING: But as you say this is the time to draw lines, to graph positions. Your people assume the colonial phrase "mother country" should be taken at face value. It's an assumption which glosses, and none too discreetly, a naked thrust for power over our foreign affairs.

RIVERDALE: But no such assumption exists.

KING: Don't insult my intelligence.

RIVERDALE: I *assure* you.

KING: There was a time, Riverdale, when I thought your accent masked only stupidity. Does it house duplicity as well?

RIVERDALE: There are limits, sir!

KING: Such as Poland? Well one final thought. *If we decide to enter a war — if —* the decision will be that of Parliament: *our* Parliament and *our* Parliament alone. Is that clear?

RIVERDALE: *(beat, then a little too sweetly)* To a point. Is it true what I read of His Majesty's tour?

KING: Depends what you read.

RIVERDALE: That the country's beside itself. Civic authorities from Moncton to Victoria commissioning statues of His Majesty.

KING: Yes. And no doubt we'll also see a proliferation of renamed roads, schools and sewage plants.

RIVERDALE: Being a monarchist such popular devotion warms my heart.

KING: You must skate on the Rideau, Riverdale. It makes one very aware of thin ice.

RIVERDALE: Does it indeed.

KING: You see I quite appreciate the depth of feeling exhibited for Their Majesties by Prairie farmboys, Ontario barristers and members of the I.O.D.E. Not least I appreciate that they vote. But there are those in this country with no love for Britain, the Empire or King George. Quebec! Sixty-five seats and I've got sixty-four of them. They parler "la belle langue," Riverdale. Blood of the Crucifixion is what they understand and I'll be their Judas if I ship them off on a British "tally ho."

RIVERDALE: You won't help at all?

KING: I won't be assumed.

RIVERDALE: But if war breaks out . . .

KING: *If* war breaks out my greatest contribution to the effort might well be keeping this mess of a country *together*, English and French *united*. After all, of what help could any nation battling *itself* be to you battling *Germans*? *(he smiles)*

RIVERDALE: *(beat)* With your permission, sir, good day.

KING: Au revoir.

RIVERDALE exits. The lights dim and we hear a Presbyterian psalm in four-part harmony. During music, KING moves to a new light area and kneels on floor, facing us in long shadows

Psalm Lyric

Oh Lord I put my trust in Thee
Let nothing work me shame.
As Thou are just deliver me
And set me quite from blame.

Organ music fades under the following

KING: Grampa — Grampa you promised peace.

MACKENZIE: *(materializing)* And peace there'd be were it not for the bloody Brits. Hitler doesn't want war. He's becoming desperate.

KING: He's not becoming desperate. He's become insane. Today I spoke to Lord Riverdale. And I spoke bravely —

like a Mackenzie. But even as the words fell from my lips I saw smoke, smelt blood, felt death. In my dreams Parliament is a big brick building with stones the size of Beelzebub's teeth, spires like ivory horns and a tail that's a road across this country leading to gunboats.

MACKENZIE: Then fight. Fight goddamnit.

KING: But I can't. In the last war we fought and conscripted. It tore this country apart — riots in Montreal and a bill to secede proposed in Quebec's own Legislature. To fight and conscript again in defense of Britain.

MACKENZIE: Then resist the British buggers.

KING: But I can't. Lord Riverdale's right. I'll have English Canada at my throat. I won't be the man to break this country in two.

MACKENZIE: Make up your mind, laddie.

KING: But I can't. God I knew this day would come — war in my bones. You lied to me!

MACKENZIE: We'll hear no more of that.

KING: You lied!!

Lights fade swiftly on MACKENZIE; lights up on MRS. KING

MRS. KING: That's no way to speak to your grandfather.

KING: But Momma I'm deep in the woods and it's getting dark and I'm lost. I feel so alone. No single living soul to hold me — to comfort and strengthen me. I knew from the moment I entered this town that to enter politics was to enter battle — and that to enter battle without a wife would be unbearably lonely.

MRS. KING: That's as may be. But the Lord wills and we must abide.

KING: Why wouldn't you even meet her?

MRS. KING: Her? That nurse of yours??

KING: Mathilde Grosshert. My fiancée.

MRS. KING: I didn't meet Miss Grosshert because I loved you. Heavens child, where would you be today if you'd married *her*? A school teacher perhaps. Not a leader of men. Not a prime minister. And Grosshert. Mathilde Grosshert — the very idea — our country about to be at war with the Germans and our prime minister married to one? Oh Willy, you and this country that needs you now to be its saviour, you both should praise God I stood firm.

KING: I never met anyone else. Never anyone like Mathilde.

MRS. KING: One can live without her kind.

KING: Her kind was love and now I'm alone and so many decisions and no one to talk to . . .

MRS. KING: You've got Pat, haven't you?

KING: Pat's a wonderful dog, a little saint — but it's not the same.

MRS. KING: I see. So it's filth you're talking. Filth you wanted.

KING: No.

MRS. KING: Little dog Pat's your companion — but what you're wanting is sweating and grunting. Bodily functions. Women that move like your hand.

KING: Mother, please.

MRS. KING: And well you might be embarrassed. My little boy who gave religious services at the Sick Children's Hospital and sang "Rescue the Perishing" at the Haven.

KING: Momma — it's just that I'm alone!

MRS. KING: And I suppose I'm to blame for that.

KING: No Momma.

MRS. KING: Of course I am. Mothers are always to blame. Sometimes I think that's why we were created. To be scapegoats.

KING: No. Momma I love you more than anyone.

MRS. KING: Nothing but words — like the words you swore to Mathilde.

KING: As a Mackenzie I swear. As a MACKENZIE!

MRS. KING: As a Mackenzie! As a MACKENZIE!! Now there's my Rebel — there's my boy!! Oh Willy — Willy my only begotten son — I know how you've suffered — how sorely you've been tempted, how cruelly denied. But the Lord moves in mysterious ways — and his finger is upon you! Why else should your grandfather have escaped the many attempts on his life . . .

KING joins in

MRS. KING & KING: *(together)* . . . have suffered imprisonment, poverty and exile, if not that to him should be borne a daughter, the thirteenth and last of a large family, to in turn bear *you* — a grandchild to inherit his name — William Lyon Mackenzie.

MRS. KING: Your enemies — they don't understand that you, your grampa and I are a Trinity — our blood one blood, coursing through your veins. So be not alone! Be not afraid! Though war be declared we shall remain united. This *country*, this *vision*, *you* the Rebel's grandson by *me* — you've a meeting with *destiny*!

Lights fade on her

KING: Momma? Momma don't leave me!

MRS. KING: You are a Mackenzie, my son. Be strong!

KING prays, lights fading on him. We hear a psalm, with the same harmonies as at the beginning of the scene

Psalm Lyric

Confound them quite and put to shame
That seek my Soul so Furiously:
Let them be turnèd back with blame
That wish me harm without cause why.

Lights pop up on PEARSON

PEARSON: *(wearing a red polka dot bow-tie, speaking with a slight lisp. To us)* W. L. M. King. He called me Pearson, and occasionally Lester, but he never called me Mike. He predicted I'd be prime minister you know. Said a little bird told him. But at *that* time, 1939, I was with External — operating out of London, England. Quite an exciting place to be when Hitler invaded Poland.

(Bomb sounds)

I was in charge of evacuating the Canadian Embassy. The plan was to move it someplace out of the way. We chose a pub. The Bull Inn.

(Air raid siren starts in background, bomb sounds swell)

The advance party had just set foot by taxi when —

(Phone rings. PEARSON answers)

(on phone) Hello? Pearson here.

Lights up on KING on phone. What with bombs, sirens, and phone static he and PEARSON are forced to talk like two deaf men

KING: *(on phone)* Hello. King here.

PEARSON: *(on phone)* Hello. Pearson, sir.

KING: *(on phone)* Hello. Parliament's given the green light. I've declared a state of apprehended insurrection.

PEARSON: *(on phone)* Apprehended insurrection?

KING: *(on phone)* We're in the fray too.

(Bomb sounds)

Hello?

PEARSON: *(on phone)* Hello?

KING: *(on phone)* Hello we seem to have a bad connection.

PEARSON: *(on phone)* We're evacuating.

KING: *(on phone)* Yes I know. Glad to catch you in.

(Bomb sounds)

An historic moment, Pearson.

(Second phone in PEARSON's area rings)

Absolutely historic.

PEARSON: *(on second phone)* Hello?

KING: *(on phone)* Hello?

PEARSON: *(on first phone, to KING)* Hello. Hang on.

KING: *(on phone)* Hang on? We're at war, Pearson. Apprehended insurrection!

PEARSON: *(on second phone)* What do you mean there's no Bull Inn?

KING: *(on phone)* Pearson?

PEARSON: *(on second phone)* It's been bombed? For gracious sake. A good thing we weren't there.

KING: *(on phone)* HELLO?

PEARSON: *(on second phone)* No don't come back here.

KING: Hello?

PEARSON: *(on second phone)* Hang on. *(on first phone, to KING)* Yes?

KING: *(on phone)* I said it's apprehended insurrection.

PEARSON: *(on first phone, to KING)* Pardon?

KING: *(on phone)* We're at war!

PEARSON: *(on first phone, to KING)* That's nice. Hang on.

KING: *(on phone)* Pearson?

PEARSON: *(on second phone)* Hi again. Stay where you are — the evacuation's still on and by the way we're in the war now too. Just a second. *(on first phone, to KING)* Hello, yes, war, yes sir! *(he listens abstractedly, looking for something)*

KING: *(on phone)* The important thing Pearson — mark this — we declared war *ourselves* in our *own* Parliament and in our *own* time.

PEARSON: *(on first phone, to KING)* Hooray for our side!

KING: *(on phone)* Yes we volunteered. We're no British puppet and I want that fully understood. Especially in Quebec.

PEARSON: *(on first phone, to KING)* Yes.

KING: *(on phone)* Speaking of which I'm not sure quite how to play those Frenchmen. But I've made an important start. No plans for conscription.

PEARSON: *(on first phone, to KING)* Good, yes, they'll like that.

KING: *(on phone)* Indeed I've made a solemn pledge against it.

PEARSON: *(on first phone, to KING)* Well done sir.

KING: *(on phone)* Thank you, yes. Big push for volunteers. "Volunteers For Victory." For home defence, mind. Our top priority is home defence.

Bomb sounds rise

PEARSON: *(on first phone, to KING)* Oh my yes.

KING: *(on phone)* Yes.

PEARSON: *(at last finding what he was looking for)* AHA!!

KING: *(on phone)* Hello?

PEARSON: *(on second phone)* Found it! Evacuation Plan Contingency A! If no Bull Inn evacuate to the Ladies College at Malvern.

KING: *(on phone)* Is everything all right?

PEARSON: *(on first phone, to KING)* I'm with you.

KING: *(on phone)* Good. Hold on a minute, would you? *(he leaves phone and lit area)*

PEARSON: *(on second phone)* Right. Full speed to the Ladies College at Malvern. And don't get any ideas. *(he hangs up second phone and returns to first phone)* I'm back again . . . Hello? . . . Sir? . . . Hello? . . . Goodbye?

He hangs up as KING returns to phone. Lights down on PEARSON. Bomb sounds out

KING: *(on phone)* Just checked the clock, Pearson — the grandfather clock that belonged to my grandfather and Pearson it's 8:10. The hands are in line like the wings of a bomber. This call's been propitious, don't you think? We've been guided, Pearson. But all depends on Quebec. Let us learn from the past. Beware conscription!

(Beat)

Pearson?

Blackout. We hear "Colonel Bogie." Light scene shift. KING and RALSTON

RALSTON: Frankly I don't give a damn what Quebec thinks of conscription.

KING: You've something against Quebec?

RALSTON: I've nothing against Quebec — so long as it's in uniform. Volunteers are simply not sufficient. As minister of defence I can't press the point strongly enough.

KING: Fools jump in where angels fear to tread, Ralston.

RALSTON: Again?

KING: At the moment those who *want* to fight *are* and those who don't *aren't*. The country's at war and it's happy. What more do you want?

RALSTON: Reserves! Our troops are adequate for the moment but should an emergency develop . . .

KING: I admire your foresight. But you must think of the national perspective.

RALSTON: For God's sake this isn't domestic politics! It's world war! And should it explode . . .

KING: So far it hasn't.

RALSTON: But when it does?

KING: It may not.

RALSTON: But if? *If* it does what do we do for reserves?

KING: The Lord provides.

RALSTON: Yes and Heaven helps those who help themselves.

KING: At any rate the question is hypothetical.

RALSTON: Conscription?

KING: For overseas?

RALSTON: Yes.

KING: No.

RALSTON: Ever?

KING: No. I pledged Quebec and that's final.

RALSTON: *(beat)* I see. *(beat. He takes a letter from his inside suit pocket)* I hereby tender my letter of resignation.

KING: Your what?

RALSTON: My letter of resignation.

KING: *(beat)* Don't overplay your hand, Ralston.

RALSTON: No bluff.

KING: But a minister of defence resigning in wartime — you put our government in considerable peril.

RALSTON: I suppose I do.

KING: But . . .

RALSTON: I'm not prepared to discuss it. You see I'm afraid words like integrity and honesty matter to me.

KING: Well aren't *we* the preacher's son.

RALSTON: Look King, we've made a commitment to this war and I'm not prepared to serve in a government that refuses to honour it.

KING: It's being honoured.

RALSTON: With talk. We're under-manned.

KING: Things will improve.

RALSTON: We need conscription, King.

KING: That's one alternative, yes.

RALSTON: Which you refuse to consider.

KING: Nonsense. I've never refused to consider it.

RALSTON: You told me just now your position was final.

KING: And it is. For the moment. But positions change with circumstance. It's the result that counts — not the figure you cut while getting there. You see I suspect, Ralston, that our differences have more to do with timing than substance. Don't doubt my commitment to the war for a second. Trust me. It's just that a united front is vital — particularly when beginning a campaign — particularly with Quebec — and *especially* as our contribution to the war will be far more than manpower. *(taps his nose)* Money, Ralston, money. Lord Riverdale figures heavily in tomorrow's agenda.

RALSTON: But as for men . . .

KING: As for bodies, yes. Full steam ahead on a recruitment campaign for home defence.

RALSTON: That's not enough.

KING: What more do you want?

RALSTON: Britain must be free to use those volunteers *overseas*.

KING: Overseas? Some of those British generals would ship them off to France in canoes!

RALSTON: What we need are fighters. In the Great War, King, I was in the trenches. I understand that terror. Strip a man of that, tell him the only action he'll see is a few ice floes off Labrador, and instead of a fighter you'll have a young man wondering what his girl's doing back in Regina! You'll have a Zombie!

KING: *(pause)* Well if it's only *volunteers* for overseas, recruit away.

RALSTON: *(beat)* Then with your agreement I withdraw my resignation.

KING: By all means. You're needed, Ralston. *I* need you. The *country* needs you. And so does the *Liberal party*.

KING is about to deposit RALSTON's resignation letter in his jacket

RALSTON: *(indicating letter)* About my letter . . .

KING: Oh sorry. Do you mind? I'd like to glue it in my diary if you've no objection.

RALSTON: I suppose not.

KING: We'll have such a laugh about this letter in years to come. "Ralston Resigns" indeed. The very idea. Without you the government would fall. Then Heaven help the country. Without us Liberals it would be a shambles.

RALSTON: Indeed. Good day, sir.

KING nods and RALSTON exits

KING: This letter will be remembered, you mark my words.

Lights shift to RIVERDALE

RIVERDALE: I confess we were hopelessly unprepared for war. But we've regrouped. We'll bowl their wickets ass-over-teakettle, what? Especially with you and Colonel Ralston seeing eye to eye.

KING: *(staring off)* Why we've always seen eye to eye.

RIVERDALE: Yes, a stable government. We're grateful for that . . . We're also grateful for this training scheme of yours.

KING: *Your* scheme I believe. No need to be modest.

RIVERDALE: Yes. Speaking personally, training our pilots on your soil would be a worthy contribution to the British effort.

KING: The *Canadian* effort. Should we decide to make it.

RIVERDALE: Naturally it's to your discretion. But it's such a far-reaching project — a project of such significance . . .

KING: It has its possibilities, yes.

RIVERDALE: The possibilities are enormous. For that very reason I thought it might strike *your* imagination in particular.

KING: *(pause)* We've great reservations about foreign military installations on our soil.

RIVERDALE: *(beat)* Your answer to the project is "no"?

KING: Not necessarily. *(beat)* Have you any idea how much this training plan will cost?

RIVERDALE: The concept is presented in theory only.

KING: I see. Well our people have figured it out. Not that it was their *job*, not that it was their *idea*, their —

RIVERDALE: What would it cost you?

KING: More than our total pre-war budget.

RIVERDALE: But the scope of the plan — it may prove the difference between victory and defeat.

KING: That's as may be.

RIVERDALE: That's as may be? THAT'S AS MAY BE?? We're looking at the apocalypse and all you can see is a bank balance??

KING: I appreciate your concern. But you seem to forget — this isn't *our* war.

RIVERDALE: What??

KING: Germany never threatened *us*; and we were certainly clever enough not to make treaties with Poland.

RIVERDALE: We've already apologized.

KING: AND THAT SOLVES EVERYTHING DOES IT? *(pause, then quietly)* This training plan unquestionably has merit. But before we can give it serious consideration we've got to take a hard look at financing, I'm afraid. It strikes me as passing strange that after Dunkirk you're not more in the market for Canadian guns, tanks, and what-not. And where are your orders for wheat? I suggest you substantially increase your rather spotty commissions of our goods — to help defray our expenses in this extra-vaganza of yours, you understand.

RIVERDALE: I'm sure we'll be more than happy to contribute to your effort.

KING: Excuse me, but insofar as there are *contributions* it's the other way around. We to you. We're not in your debt one penny.

RIVERDALE: Sorry.

KING: Quite all right. But yes, should you increase your orders for our goods, then this air training plan of yours just might interest us.

RIVERDALE: Good day, sir. *(smiles tightly, nods and turns to leave)*

KING: Not so fast Riverdale. One other thing. A trifle, really.

RIVERDALE: Yes?

KING: I want a statement from your government that these financial commitments of ours, vis-à-vis this training scheme, matter more to you than our manpower. Indeed that our volunteers are more than sufficient for the days ahead.

RIVERDALE: "*More* than sufficient"??

KING: (*smiling sweetly*) See what you can do.

RIVERDALE: Which statement made you'll guarantee the training programme?

KING: It will take some manoeuvring but yes.

RIVERDALE: In that event I'm sure my government will find your volunteers "more than sufficient."

KING: Good. And don't forget those commissions.

RIVERDALE: How could I forget.

Lights down on RIVERDALE. A drumroll. New light area. RALSTON enters

RALSTON: The recruitment campaign is not going well.

KING: Nonsense, Ralston. Like a typical Canadian you underestimate your success. Why even the British say our manpower is "more than sufficient." (*shows him letter*)

RALSTON: What?

KING: Yes. And our factories are humming — can't keep up with the new British commissions they've received. In the words of General McNaughton, "Until Britain has cannons she has no use for more cannon fodder."

RALSTON: McNaughton. I've been meaning to speak to you about the general.

KING: Oh?

RALSTON: Interference. Since his promotion he's been impossible.

KING: Head of our troops overseas — certainly some preening's in order.

RALSTON: Preening? He spends all his time doing Montgomery impersonations — walks around with a swagger stick, one hip higher than the other, defying gravity.

KING: He has a large following in Quebec, Ralston: important if we want to get those beggars into the war.

RALSTON: Don't try softening me on McNaughton. He won't even let the British War Office use what few men we have. Insists they stay in one national unit under his command.

KING: All as it should be. We're Canadians, not surrogate Brits. He's defending our independence.

RALSTON: Bullshit. He's a two-bit bureaucrat. A little empire-builder.

KING: He also happens to be a leader. An organizer.

RALSTON: An organizer? McNaughton couldn't organize a Girl Guide cookie drive.

KING: Let's not be intemperate.

RALSTON: Not only does he —

KING: ENOUGH! I'll deal with McNaughton.

RALSTON: As for our manpower crisis?

KING: I'll deal with that too. But for the moment political controversy is the last thing we need. I'm about to be engaged in rather delicate negotiations with Mr. Roosevelt. Speak to me later if you must.

Lights down on RALSTON. KING adjusts his tie, clothing, hair, etcetera, and generally primps as we hear a calypso song. The lyrics are adapted from the song "Roosevelt in Trinidad" by Fitz Maclean

Calypso Lyric

Wíllie Kíng he glád to wélcome F́.D.Ŕ.,
Ĥe de réigning Amérícan polítícál star.
Tálk a líttle whéat, tálk a líttle tráde,
Tálk a líttle Tráns-Atlántic fóreign aíd.
Wíllie Kíng knoẃ thére be nó doúbt
F́.D.Ŕ. can bé polítícál oút.
Thát whý Wíllie Kíng he só glád
To wélcóme Róosevelt tó Cánadád!

ROOSEVELT wheels himself in, briefcase on his lap

ROOSEVELT: Mackenzie, Mackenzie . . . *(extending hand for shake)* You don't mind if I call you Mackenzie?

KING: *(shaking his hand)* Not at all Mr. President.

ROOSEVELT: Good. So let's cut the red tape and get to it. This man Hitler — he's got to be stopped. No two ways about it. Denmark, Norway, Holland, Hungary, Bulgaria, Austria, Poland, France. In short, it looks like war.

KING: It already is for us.

ROOSEVELT: Yes and I'd like to join you.

KING: Hallelujah!

ROOSEVELT: Trouble is my congress doesn't. They seem to think he's just cleaning up Communists. Amazing how very bright people can't see what's staring them straight in the face.

KING: I appreciate the sentiment.

ROOSEVELT: Of course you do. I like to think we share mutual sentiments and concerns, the two of us. Like two peas in a pod.

KING: Thank you.

ROOSEVELT: And there's a third pea in our pod. Britain. Now I'm not one for metaphor, but I'm telling you

Mackenzie — you're the pea in the middle. The lynchpin. My Congress being what it is I can't very well talk to Britain. But I can surely be seen talking to our great Canadian neighbour to the north. So what I propose is to talk to Britain through you, if you catch my drift.

KING: I'm the lynchpin.

ROOSEVELT: Precisely. Mackenzie — we can make history together.

KING: You flatter me.

ROOSEVELT: What's history among friends? But to the point. Britain will fall.

KING: A somewhat bleak assessment.

ROOSEVELT: And a frightening one. Terrifying. Before it happens we must plan our future, shore up our mutual defences. And that's where you fit in, you lynchpin.

KING: What do you propose?

ROOSEVELT: I want you to get in touch with Whitehall. Impress upon them that the British government must fight to the end though it mean the abandonment of the British Isles, the flight of King George and the transference of the Royal Navy to the United States.

Pause

KING: The transference of the Royal Navy to the United States?

ROOSEVELT: *(nods)* Bring it up as your own suggestion.

KING: Why?

ROOSEVELT: They don't trust me. Makes it difficult for us to help them — and help is America's middle name.

(The phone rings)

But they'll listen to you. Never underestimate the lynchpin.

KING: Indeed not.

(The phone rings again. KING answers)

Yes? . . . Put him on immediately.

A light comes up on a telephone and the back of a large plush chair, cigar smoke rising from behind it. During the following phone conversation, ROOSEVELT takes a map from his briefcase and makes a few doodles on it

CHURCHILL: *(who is indeed the man behind the chair; on phone)* King?

KING: *(on phone)* Hello?

CHURCHILL: *(on phone)* Churchill here. I understand you're entertaining that Roosevelt fellow this afternoon.

KING: *(on phone)* You could say that.

CHURCHILL: *(on phone)* Well tell that Yankee swindler we're not dead yet! He's after the British fleet, King. And more! He's after the British Empire minus Britain!

KING: *(on phone)* The thought had crossed my mind.

CHURCHILL: *(on phone) Should* we fall because of America's benign neglect, we may choose to give our ships to no one at all. We *may* choose to smash them all on a grand suicide assault on the continent.

KING: *(on phone)* Did I hear you correctly?

CHURCHILL: *(on phone)* Yes indeed. Should tragedy strike, a roaring dénouement might be just the ticket. Communicate *that* to our friend. *(he hangs up)*

Lights down on CHURCHILL

KING: *(on phone)* Hello? *(he hangs up)* Back to our discussion of the fleet — your proposal for disposal. To contemplate plundering Britain for arms in her hour of need simply won't do.

ROOSEVELT: The thought hadn't crossed my mind.

KING: Forgive me.

ROOSEVELT: Not at all. I appreciate the subtlety of your mind. It's a veritable beaver trap.

KING: *(nods)* You see should Britain so much as suspect such a thing it would only strengthen her resolve.

ROOSEVELT: To do what?

KING: Smash her fleet against the continent.

ROOSEVELT: WHAT?

KING: Mr. Churchill has a theatrical turn of mind.

ROOSEVELT: Then full speed to my second proposal: I plan to lend Britain fifty destroyers.

KING: Fifty?!

ROOSEVELT: Free gratis. They're old, I'm afraid but —

KING: Very generous.

ROOSEVELT: Yes. Now in exchange, and as a token of appreciation — a bone I can throw my Congress — I want Britain to give me some control over the Atlantic approaches to our continent. Take a look at this map. She has territorial assets here, here and here — Bermuda, the West Indies and Newfoundland. For my fifty destroyers I want a ninety-nine year lease for military installations. America lends, Britain leases. Sound fair to you?

KING: *(beat)* I have a slight problem with Newfoundland. We've always had it in mind that one day she'd join Confederation.

ROOSEVELT: Expansionism — more power to you.

KING: But with American colonization . . .

ROOSEVELT: Mackenzie, Mackenzie, Mackenzie — I want military bases, not colonies. I'm not out to purchase headaches for America.

KING: There's also the problem of these destroyers. These *old* destroyers. Won't be worth much in a few years but the value of this real estate on the other hand . . . You seem to come out a good deal ahead on the bargain.

ROOSEVELT: True, true. But my Congress is troublesome on this war issue. I'm afraid without a good swap the deal won't go through. And we both know how badly Britain needs that equipment, don't we? Penny wise, pound foolish?

KING: *(beat)* Under the circumstances your proposal seems as generous as conditions allow.

ROOSEVELT: I'm glad you approve.

KING: Yes, well. I'll communicate our discussion to Whitehall.

ROOSEVELT: That's my boy. You're the lynchpin, Mackenzie. Don't ever forget it.

KING: I won't. Glad to assist.

ROOSEVELT: Assist? For God's sake Mackenzie, the fate of the world is in your hands!

As the lights shift to the JOAN and KING scene, ROOSEVELT wheels out and we hear the following song

Calypso Lyric

Yés Máckénzie Kíng he bé glád
To wélcóme Róosevelt tó Cánadád!

Lights up on JOAN and KING who are at a table on which are sandwiches and a phone

JOAN: "The fate of the world is in your hands"? "The fate of the world"?

KING: That's what he said.

JOAN: The president of the United States said that to *you*?

KING: Well you needn't sound so surprised.

JOAN: I'm not. It's just the PRESIDENT — I mean he doesn't just go around saying that to everybody.

KING: Of course not.

JOAN: You must have felt honoured.

KING: It did my heart good.

JOAN: I'm so proud.

KING: But best of all Joan — best of all — Ralston has been belled like old Tabby. That sword in my flesh blunted, that vinegar in my mouth turned to fresh spring water, my own crown of thorns removed! God's will be done!!

JOAN: Rexy?

KING: (as RALSTON) "Our recruitment campaign is under quota, King. What do you have to say to that?" (as himself) What I have to say to that, Ralston, is "piffle" with a capital P. We are none other than the "Lynchpin of the Allies." Oh Ralston, let he who would endanger the unity of the "lynchpin" for the sake of a few pounds of blood and guts carry the burden of defeat and Nazi domination with him to his grave. I'll give him such an earful his head will be ringing for months. I'll trumpet my case to every hamlet in the land — and mark my words, Joan, before I'm done every God-for-Harry-England-and-St.-George conscriptionist will be running for cover, tails between his legs. God's will be done! I can't wait.

JOAN: Neither can I.

KING: But first things first.

JOAN: Exactly. Tuna?

KING: Thanks.

(Using tongs, she passes him a sandwich)

Britain, Joan. In three days I plan to be off to Britain to confer with Mr. Churchill on behalf of the president of the United States. In my capacity as "lynchpin" you understand. Top secret.

JOAN: With lots of photographers? Press people?

KING: You catch my drift.

JOAN: How exciting. One lump?

KING: Two.

JOAN: Oh my!

KING: Mr. Howe has a four-engine refitted for passengers.

JOAN: Refitted?

KING: Yes.

JOAN: Not really comfy enough for a prime minister, is it?

KING: My sentiments exactly. Mr. McConnell however has made the tempting suggestion of a Boeing clipper.

JOAN: Much more like it.

KING: Yes. Only problem is if I take the clipper I can't fly direct. I'll have to fly via Baltimore and then transfer at Newfoundland.

JOAN: A bit colonial for a lynchpin.

KING: Quite. Indeed I've decided against *both* the Boeing clipper *and* the refitted four-engine.

JOAN: So how will you go?

KING: *(gravely)* I intended to arrive on board a Canadian bomber!

JOAN: That way if you fly over any U-boats you can bomb them en route.

KING: Yes. The image *is* rather heroic, isn't it? Fitting Grampa Mackenzie on his horse and me in my bo

JOAN: And the press!

KING: Reporters for days. And full of the

mendations from Messieurs Churchill and Roosevelt.

JOAN: It sounds wonderful.

KING: And prophetic. Oh Joan — it fulfills the words Mother repeats time and time again — "You the Rebel's grandson by me — you've a meeting with destiny." And so it has come to pass. God has seen fit to call his poor servant.

The phone rings

JOAN: Just a minute.

(JOAN answers the phone)

(on phone) Hello? . . . Why O.D. what a surprise . . . Yes he's here . . . Just a sec. *(to KING, handing him the phone)* It's External Affairs.

KING: *(on phone)* King here . . . Why O.D. what a coincidence — I was just about to call *you*. About my trip to Britain — I'm using *neither* the Boeing clipper nor the refitted four-engine . . . "So I've heard" what? . . . I see . . . No, no I'm not surprised. I've known for some time — surprised you people at External didn't . . . Not at all. I appreciate your calling. *(hangs up and slumps in his chair)*

JOAN: Rexy, are you all right?

KING: I'm . . . I'm fine.

JOAN: What did O.D. have to say?

KING: Oh nothing . . . nothing.

JOAN: That's a pretty long face for "nothing".

KING: It's nothing. Really. It's just that . . . well External's just received a call from Pearson and it seems that . . . it would appear that Mr. Roosevelt and Mr. Churchill are at this very moment in conversation on board ship off Placentia Bay. Placentia Bay, Newfoundland — British owned, American leased — a lease I myself negotiated, an Adventure Holiday if there ever was one.

JOAN: And they didn't invite you?

KING: *(as calmly as possible)* No they did not invite me.

A deadly silence which JOAN, wanting to be helpful, unfortunately interrupts

JOAN: Have a tuna? *(passes sandwiches)*

KING: No I do not want a tuna.

JOAN: You're sure?

KING: *(exploding, pounding table with his fist)* HOW DARE THEY ABUSE ME LIKE THIS! HOW DARE THEY?? I'M THE LYNCHPIN, DON'T THEY UNDERSTAND THAT? CAN'T THEY GET THAT THROUGH THEIR THICK HEADS?? WHAT DO THEY TAKE ME FOR? A COLONIAL? WELL I'M NOT! I'M A CANADIAN! AND THIS COUNTRY IS CANADA! IT'S NOT A COLONY! IT'S THE LYNCHPIN AND IT'S ABOUT TIME THEY UNDERSTOOD THAT!! *(suddenly quiet, but just as intense)* But beyond that, beyond all that, beyond all else the idea of meeting on board ship off Placentia Bay is madness. Good Lord, the risks, the perils — with German submarines known to be operating within a hundred and fifty miles of Newfoundland. Within a hundred and fifty miles? For God's sake one's been blown out of the water eighteen miles from Halifax. It's taking a gambler's risk with the free world at stake.

JOAN: Cheer up.

KING: Cheer up? Should some disaster overtake the gamble —

JOAN: It can't be that bad.

KING: Oh can't it.

JOAN: Of course not. I mean how would the Germans know where Roosevelt and Churchill are when *you* didn't?

KING: Spies, Joan. The Nazis *do* have *spies.*

JOAN: And you don't?

771

KING: Not on Roosevelt and Churchill, for Heaven's sake.

JOAN: Why not?

KING: BECAUSE I'M AN ALLIED PRIME MINISTER, THAT'S WHY NOT! I'M SUPPOSED TO KNOW *WITHOUT* SPIES!!

JOAN: Well don't yell at *me*.

KING: I'm sorry.

JOAN: That's okay. Have a tuna.

JOAN passes the sandwiches. KING takes one, munches it with ever-increasing fury. He takes another and another

KING: *(finally, intensely quiet, his mouth full of sandwiches)* At the bottom of this whole fiasco is vanity, pure and simple. It is absurd for Churchill, Roosevelt or any of us to leave his respective country at this time.

JOAN: *(pause, curious but not wanting to start anything)* But you were planning to leave Canada for Britain, weren't you?

KING: Yes and I am more satisfied than ever that I was right in holding out against going until now. I have fears. Grave fears. For it's all of a piece with my dream.

JOAN: I wish you wouldn't sound so prophetic.

KING: I dreamed I was in some building, some factory, high up and near an elevator shaft. I opened the shaft and a great quantity of silt fell down it. It seemed to fall to a great depth and I thought how easily one would be killed if one were to fall. Then I woke up. *(ominously)* That was this morning.

JOAN: *(scared, whispering)* What do you make of it?

KING: I saw danger to those in high positions. Danger from a depth charge!

JOAN: Roosevelt, Churchill . . . ?

KING: Oh Joan, it is contemptible the manner in which they have treated me. Contemptible. But you're with me, Mother and Grampa are with me, my little saint terrier Pat — and I have not the slightest doubt that I shall bring them all to bay who treat me so. For I have a rendezvous with destiny. I *am* the lynchpin . . . I *AM* The Lynchpin!! I . . . AM . . . THE . . . THE . . . *(he sinks onto seat)*

JOAN rushes to him

JOAN: Rex?

KING: *(clutching her around waist)* Oh Joan — what's Ralston going to say?

Light up on RALSTON

RALSTON: *(to audience)* The lynchpin, eh? Some lynch. Some pin.

Blackout. Drumroll.

ACT TWO

RALSTON and KING.

RALSTON: *(sarcastically)* With the collapse of our status as "Lynchpin of the Atlantic," and the recent fiasco in North Africa, are you yet of the opinion that times and circumstances have changed? I refer, of course, to the vexing little problem of conscription.

KING: Spare me your sarcasm.

RALSTON: And spare me your evasions.

KING: I need time to decide.

RALSTON: You've *had* time.

773

KING: Ralston . . .

RALSTON: No. I need a decision, King.

KING: *(beat, sizing RALSTON up)* We do it.

RALSTON: *(beat)* You commit the government to conscription?

KING: That's what you want, isn't it?

RALSTON: Your comrade in arms, sir. *(turns to go)*

KING: But Ralston — conscription for *home defence only.*

RALSTON: The war's being fought in Europe, King.

KING: If we're starved for manpower, as you claim, our *own* defence is surely the first priority.

RALSTON: *(as calmly as possible)* Do you know what our men at the front hear when they turn on their radios? That Nazi Lord Haw-Haw saying, "There are two armies in Canada: one fighting to *get* home, the other fighting to *stay* there."

KING: Nothing but cheap German propaganda.

RALSTON: Cheap or not — consider morale!

KING: Our boys are made of sterner stuff than that. Sticks and stones, Ralston.

RALSTON: Sticks and stones?? For Christ's sake it's war!! Don't you care??

KING: Mr. Ralston, Canadians are dying in this war. I am sending death by telegram, blood and guts in press releases, and you dare ask me if I care??

RALSTON: Yes!!

KING: Death's as cold as linotype to you, is it? You're beneath contempt.

RALSTON: Our men are dying, you won't reinforce them because of Quebec — and *I'm* beneath contempt?

KING: I WILL NOT SACRIFICE CANADA TO PRESERVE EUROPE! Priorities, Ralston, priorities. I'm afraid they come before principles!

RALSTON: Priorities, eh? Well with the free world facing collapse and Nazi domination must we be quite so sensitive to the eccentricities of Quebec?

KING: My concerns are those of *this nation*.

RALSTON: Or of the Liberal party?

KING: I'm going as far as I can. I'm going as *fast* as I can! I've promised conscription and I stand by my word. For the moment, and *just* for the moment, it's only for home defence. But it's a beginning. Have faith Ralston. A step-by-step approach.

RALSTON: Soon, King, I shall expect to see these steps turn into a quick forward march.

RALSTON exits. Drum in march tempo. Lights change

ROOSEVELT: *(wheeling on)* Mackenzie you little devil.

KING: *(acidly)* How was Placentia Bay?

ROOSEVELT: Newfoundland's splendid. Couldn't have been better. We've leased us a fine piece of rock.

KING: Glad you enjoyed it.

ROOSEVELT: Yes there was only one thing wrong. You weren't there. "Oh," I said to myself, "wouldn't Mackenzie get a kick out of this." God help us but there was more press than we knew what to do with.

KING: So I noticed.

ROOSEVELT: Now Mackenzie, do I hear a sulk coming on?

KING: Mr. President would you please get to the point?

ROOSEVELT: We're going to enter the war.

KING: What?

ROOSEVELT: Keep this under your hat but we're about to be attacked by the Japanese.

KING: WHAT?

ROOSEVELT: Yes. Tomorrow if nothing goes awry. Pearl Harbour. And when that happens, watch out — we'll be hell-bent for leather to join this little war of yours.

KING: Good.

ROOSEVELT: Yes, yes. The grand struggle for democracy. We shall fight them in the stock exchanges; we shall fight them in the boardrooms; etcetera etcetera — that Churchill has a mouth on him, hasn't he? But to business.

KING: Yes?

ROOSEVELT: Churchill and I will be needing conference sites and so forth. Being the egotist he is, Churchill won't grovel in America. At least not yet. And I'm certainly not prepared to trundle across the globe to visit *that* mangy bulldog. Neutral territory, that's what we're looking for. And it crossed my mind, "You really do owe your old friend Mackenzie a favour after Placentia Bay." In short — how would you like to host a series of them?

KING: Would I care to host a series of conferences?

ROOSEVELT: Anglo-American on Canadian soil.

KING: I'll have to explore the possibility. I would, of course, have to be present at all such conferences, be a party to all documents and communiqués, have a prominent role in all group photographs . . .

ROOSEVELT: No problem.

KING: Good. Because, and I speak purely hypothetically, should there be a breach of those understandings I'm afraid mysterious forces might conspire to have the talks cancelled. A dreadful shame, terrible embarrassment to Churchill and yourself.

ROOSEVELT: I understand.

KING: Yes, we certainly don't want another "little oversight" do we?

ROOSEVELT: Right. Now then about the details, planning . . .

KING: Leave it to me.

ROOSEVELT: That's my lynchpin. See you in conference. *(he exits)*

KING: Bye bye. *(beams, does a little tap-dance for joy)* Mackenzie King Entertains The World. *(another little dance)* All the world's my stage! Oh Mother-Mother-Mother-Mother-Mother I love you and — AND — LORD FORGIVE THEM THOUGH THEY KNOW NOT WHAT THEY DO!!

Blackout. A few bars of "I'm a Yankee Doodle Dandy." Spotlight up on JOAN

JOAN: Lord forgive them though they know not what they do. How many times Rex said that before the war was over. And he always had that sympathetic listener, Pat. How Rex loved to teach him tricks. "Salute," he'd say and little Pat would raise a paw. Or he'd put him in the hall, hide a cookie in the den, then call him in, crying "Find the enemy!" But Rex' favourite parlour trick was to sit in a chair and stretch out his legs. "Into the trenches, into the trenches," he'd cry and Pat would leap over his legs and flop on his belly. "Into the trenches, into the trenches — a military dog," Rex would laugh.

Lights up dimly on the back of a large rocking chair. KING is rocking under the following

JOAN: He loved that dog, talked to it about everything under the sun. In fact I daresay Pat heard more about war strategy than the Cabinet. But finally he was old and finally he was ill and finally he died. Rex stayed up all night rocking him in his arms, singing hymns and praying. Some people smile when they hear that but they don't

know what it is to believe in God and they don't understand what it is to love a dog like your own child.

Spotlight down on JOAN

KING: *(softly)* We'll meet again. On the other side, we'll meet
again.

*Lights fade down on KING as we hear "Abide With Me". Spotlight
pops up on PEARSON*

PEARSON: After Pat's death there was an incident that made
me wonder if the prime minister might be losing his grip.
It was during one of the conferences he arranged between
Roosevelt and Churchill with him popping in for the
photos — in the department he was known as "The
Flasher."

(Bomb sounds, air raid sirens)

At any rate Britain was being blitzed, Westminster lay in
ruins, and in the middle of it all —

*(The phone rings. PEARSON picks it up. Lights up on KING
on phone. Bomb sounds continue in background with phone
static added)*

(on phone) Pearson here.

KING: *(on phone)* Hello Pearson. King here. I'm bored,
Pearson.

PEARSON: *(on phone)* Sir?

KING: *(on phone)* I've had it to here with tripartite conferences. Roosevelt and Churchill, my but they go on.
Nothing but catfights.

PEARSON: *(on phone)* "Blessed be the peacemakers," sir.

KING: *(on phone)* Exactly what Mother says, said. Prophetic.
Because that's what I am: a peacemaker between prima-
donnas.

PEARSON: *(on phone)* Yes sir.

Bomb sounds

KING: *(on phone)* And how are things with you?

PEARSON: *(on phone)* In England?

KING: *(on phone)* Yes, having a good time?

PEARSON: *(on phone)* Within limits.

KING: *(on phone)* Limits? For Heaven's sake, Pearson, you're in the Old Country and we're stuck here.

PEARSON: *(on phone)* Pardon?

KING: *(on phone, louder)* We were talking about limits.

PEARSON: *(on phone)* Well the bombing's been rather intense. Last night Westminster destroyed.

KING: *(on phone)* I know. That's why I phoned, actually.

PEARSON: *(on phone)* Sir?

KING: *(on phone)* I was busy mediating when it suddenly struck me — my God, Westminster's nothing but rubble. They'll sweep those poor broken stones into the dump or the Thames or God knows where.

PEARSON: *(on phone)* I'm not sure I follow you.

KING: *(on phone)* Well you remember Kingsmere, don't you?

PEARSON: *(on phone)* Your estate, yes.

KING: *(on phone)* Of course. And you know how terribly it's landscaped?

PEARSON: *(on phone)* Landscaped??

KING: *(on phone)* Apart from the house all I've got is a thicket and a sundial. And then it struck me — a vision — clear as day — it needs a ruins!

PEARSON: *(on phone)* A ruins?

779

KING: *(on phone)* I want a ruins for Kingsmere! So naturally when I heard Westminster had been bombed I thought of you.

PEARSON: Oh?

KING: Get in touch with the British Office of Works, would you? Inform them I'd like an arch or two.

PEARSON: *(on phone)* WHAT??

KING: *(on phone)* I SAID — HAVE THEM PACKAGE A FEW CRATES OF RUBBLE FOR ME! PREFERABLY ARCHES!

PEARSON: *(on phone)* THE OFFICE OF WORKS??

KING: *(on phone)* YYEESS!!

PEARSON: *(on phone)* I hear you. But I'm afraid — look they're really rather busy. London's a mess. Sewer mains are broken, violent fires, transit in disarray . . .

KING: *(on phone)* Well see what you can do.

RIVERDALE enters the KING area with documents

PEARSON: *(on phone)* Given the situation I'm not sure how to put the request.

RIVERDALE coughs discreetly

KING: *(nods; on phone)* That's the diplomat in you talking. Try being a politician. If there aren't ways, create them. It's a skill you'll need when you're prime minister.

PEARSON: *(on phone)* PRIME MINISTER??

KING: *(on phone)* Bye bye. *(hangs up)*

Lights down on PEARSON

RIVERDALE: *(slightly sarcastically)* Sorry to have disturbed.

KING: Are you really, Riverdale?

RIVERDALE: Here is the statement worked out between the two leaders. Your signature to be applied here.

KING: *Perhaps* to be applied.

RIVERDALE: We've only ten minutes till the press conference and photographs.

KING: I won't be pressured.

RIVERDALE: Suit yourself. *(takes documents and prepares to exit)*

KING: Where's Churchill?

RIVERDALE: I'm afraid he and the president are still in private conference.

KING: Then I'll wait till they're through.

RIVERDALE: Afraid they plan to move directly from private conference to the press.

KING: *(beat)* I'll read it.

RIVERDALE: Nothing's to be changed. Not even the bad grammar.

KING: *(reads)* "Declaration of the United Nations."

RIVERDALE: A sweeping document full of American syntax.

KING: Permit me to read.

RIVERDALE: I'd love to but I've a pressing engagement with my American counterpart.

KING: My signature will not be assumed!

RIVERDALE: We British have assumed nothing for some time, Mr. King. Now, with America in the war, we assume less. Will you be wanting your photograph taken with the two leaders?

KING: *(silence. He signs, hands the document to RIVERDALE)* Let it never be said I shirked my duty.

RIVERDALE: *(smiling triumphantly)* We'll see you at the official handshakes. *(nods curtly and exits)*

The lights move down to a solo spot on KING. KING is wary, wild. He stands still, driven, a hunted look in his eyes

KING: Appearances are *all*. Appearances *are* all.

(The lights begin to change to dim blue and brown patches — ghost lights)

And I am a piece of Victorian bric-à-brac left to sit on a crowded mantel. Like a hideous china parrot left to collect dust. I am ugly. A rumpled grey man in a pudgy suit dropped by the likes of . . . waiting to be smashed by the likes of — No! No!! "Into the trenches, into the trenches."

(The sound of a barking dog, distant, in an echo chamber)

Yes that's a good boy, my little soldier, my little saint, it's all a game to you, isn't it? All a game.

(Sound of barking dog)

KING: Yes I know but to me — oh Pat — teach me the secret of heroism. Teach me? . . . Pat? . . . Pat?

MRS. KING: *(materializing)* Heroism?

KING: Momma. Oh Momma.

MRS. KING: Wipe your eyes, Willy. Did I raise a crybaby?

KING: What's happening to me, Momma?

MRS. KING: I said wipe your eyes. It shames me to look at you. You disgrace the fierce name of Mackenzie. Every kiss you ever gave me — I spit them back in your face. You betray me — you betray your grandfather, the way you let them walk all over you.

KING: I tried to be strong.

MRS. KING: But you failed: with Riverdale, with Ralston, with all of them.

MACKENZIE: *(materializing)* Dinnae be too hard on the boy.

MRS. KING: *(fading)* I hadn't even begun.

KING: Momma? Momma don't leave me!

(She is gone)

If only I could be worthy of her, of you. Oh Grampa — teach me the secret of heroism.

MACKENZIE: Heroism?

KING: You didn't tolerate the Riverdales and Ralstons of this world.

MACKENZIE: No. I just leapt on my horse and raised my sword.

KING: But it's hard to leap on a horse and wield a sword when you have power.

MACKENZIE: Aye, power corrupts the will.

KING: So what am I to do? Humiliated by errand boys, my government threatened from within — how am I to face my enemies?

MACKENZIE: Be brave, honest and forthright. Just leap on your horse and raise your sword.

KING: But with power . . .

MACKENZIE: Renounce it like the devil. Flee from temptation nor let the shadow of it draw nigh. *(he begins to fade)*

KING: Don't leave me Grampa. I can't be alone. Please.

MACKENZIE: Flee from temptation . . .

KING: I can't be alone. Not tonight.

MACKENZIE: . . . nor let the shadow of it draw nigh. *(he is gone)*

KING: Grampa . . .

Lights up full on KING and ENID, the whore

ENID: Evening.

KING: Good evening Miss . . . ?

ENID: Simpson. Enid Simpson. My but aren't you a sight.
You'd think you'd just seen a ghost.

KING: I have a lot on my mind.

ENID: *(trying to remove his jacket)* In five minutes you won't.

KING: Please, can't we just talk?

ENID: Aw come on. I know where you're ticklish. I know
where you're ticklish.

KING: Miss Simpson, you're a charming, thoughtful girl but
. . . Look here's a dollar and forget I was ever here.

ENID: How am I supposed to live on a dollar?

KING: Well I . . .

ENID: I mean you got your nerve, you know that buster?
You come up here and — hey don't I know you from
someplace?

KING: No.

ENID: You sure look awful familiar. Good Lord I've seen
you in the pictures! At the Odeon! *News On The March!*
You're Prime Minister what's-his-name!!

KING: Shhhhh.

ENID: I saw you open a bridge once. How's the war doing?
My brother's a volunteer.

KING: Good for him.

ENID: Yeah. He's over in Britain now and he's the bravest
person I know. Nobody scares him. Not even Hitler. Do
you think the Nazis will bomb Ottawa?

KING: No.

ENID: You're brave *too*. Can't I take your coat?

KING: Well . . . I . . .

ENID: *(takes it without resistance)* Good. An honest-to-God prime minister. It sure beats making friends with senators. Anyway my brother said how he heard the Nazis were planning to have a whole battalion of submarines sail up the St. Clair River, if that's of any help.

KING: To be sure. What division is he with?

ENID: First Division, what else? With General McNaughton.

KING: A fine general.

ENID: Don't I know it. I don't bother with the papers cause they're nothing but news, but down at the hairdresser's he's all they talk about. "McNaughton did this, McNaughton did that" — and guess what? My brother's shaken his hand!

KING: Really?

ENID: Of course he's very important, my brother. Maybe you've heard of him? Private Eric Simpson?

KING: I'm afraid not.

ENID: He's real good. I think he should be a sergeant. Of course I haven't heard from him since I left home. He sort of stopped writing me but . . . Oh my but you ripple power. Can you make him a sergeant?

KING: No.

ENID: Please? It wouldn't take much from someone like you. Just a few words and a wink.

KING: I'm afraid I'm not in control of advancements.

ENID: But you're the prime minister. You can do anything, get anything you want.

KING: I'm afraid it's not that easy. Not even for prime ministers.

ENID: Make him a sergeant and you can hold my breasts for free.

KING: Miss Simpson . . .

ENID: But I love him so much, and like maybe if you and me were friends, you know, well maybe we could help him and he wouldn't hate me so much and . . . and . . . *(she bursts into tears)*

KING: Please don't cry.

ENID: But he may be at the front by now. He may even be dead.

KING: Miss Simpson . . .

ENID: Enid.

KING: Enid . . . *(puts his hand on her shoulder)*

ENID: Oh stop it. What do you care? I'm nothing to you but a piece of toilet paper. I'm a nobody and my brother's a nobody and we're all nobodys and nobody cares.

KING: I care.

ENID: Huh. When were you ever in uniform? When was the last time you were ever in Europe except to go to some swanky "do" in somebody's castle? When have you even seen the troops?

KING: Well I . . .

ENID: See? My brother — he may even be dead and who even goes to *see* him? He's just a piece of paper *too*. A piece of paper on some pen-pusher's desk waiting for the wastebasket.

KING: *I'll* see him!

ENID: That's what they all say.

KING: *Really. (putting on his vest)* Thank you Enid.

ENID: What for?

KING: For the card I was looking for. Now come, Enid, dry your eyes. Dry your eyes.

ENID: I love my brother. We used to go to the movies together. He really *should* be a sergeant, you know.

The lights change to KING and RALSTON

RALSTON: We've got problems in Sicily.

KING: I read the papers *too*, Ralston.

RALSTON: Conscription —

KING: Ralston, you really do have a one-track mind.

(KING holds up his hand, RALSTON is about to speak)

Say no more. Overseas conscription may indeed be necessary. And that, my friend, is what I'm about to find out for myself.

RALSTON: Pardon?

KING: I'm going overseas to say hello to the boys, bring a few words of comfort and investigate our alleged shortages for myself.

RALSTON: *(suspicious)* Why?

KING: Duty, Ralston. Duty.

RALSTON: Crap.

KING: Nothing hurts more than when situations become personal and one's own position misrepresented.

RALSTON: No doubt. Well as you're off for Britain you'd better know about McNaughton.

KING: How *is* the general?

RALSTON: *(hands him a telegram)* Received this today.

KING: The British War Office — what do they want?

RALSTON: His head.

787

KING reads

KING: Montgomery threatened to arrest a Canadian general?

RALSTON: McNaughton and the War Office don't get on.

KING: So what do you propose?

RALSTON: Retire him from active duty.

KING: He *does* seem to have outlived his usefulness.

RALSTON: You're agreed?

KING: I leave it to your discretion.

RALSTON: He was one of your favourites, wasn't he?

KING: Times change. But Ralston, our reporters have made him into a hero. I understand even hairdressers are routinely comparing him to God. If you bring him home, and I don't question the decision, take care to praise him or the people will ask questions. Write him something along the lines of: "The decision was a long and painful one, involving as it did your years of ceaseless labour borne without complaint. Your return to Ottawa is a loss to our war effort. But no doubt there will be future glories and rewards, future mountains to climb . . . "

RALSTON: That's somewhat "rich," isn't it?

KING: Salt and pepper to taste. But Ralston — one can slide a long way on a little grease.

RALSTON: I've noticed.

KING: Beg pardon?

RALSTON: With regard to our manpower crisis . . .

KING: I've told you. I'm investigating the problem personally.

RALSTON: *(smiles thinly)* Yes, well you do that. Because the day of judgement is at hand, King. There'll come a time when I *will* leave and your government will fall.

KING: You think you're the indispensable man, do you?

RALSTON: Some do. Others will. Have a nice trip.

Lights down on RALSTON, up in another area. KING goes to it. He has a closed umbrella and paces as we hear an airplane, and a few lines of "Don't Fence Me In." Rain sounds. The music fades out, the rain continues

PEARSON: *(off)* The troops are lining up in formation, sir.

KING: For Heaven's sake Pearson, get in here out of the rain. You'll catch your death of pneumonia.

PEARSON: Yes sir.

(PEARSON enters with opened umbrella as KING lets out a great sneeze)

Gezundheit. Pardon me, bless you.

KING: Damn rain.

PEARSON: *(shaking his hand)* Welcome to Britain. Good of you to come.

KING: My duty, Pearson.

PEARSON: *(lowering his umbrella)* The troops have been looking forward to this. I understand they've been saying, "Can't wait to see King" and "Just wait till I see King" for weeks.

KING: I trust I won't disappoint them.

PEARSON: Oh no sir.

KING: And how did they take the news about McNaughton?

PEARSON: He was a favourite with the troops.

KING: Ah well I'm afraid Ralston was adamant. Loathed the man. Couldn't wait to have done with him.

PEARSON: I'm afraid I've never met the colonel.

KING: He has a mind like a fist.

VOICE: *(off)* Mr. Prime Minister, the troops are in place.

KING: Thank you. *(to PEARSON)* You've seen to the photographers? The press?

PEARSON: They're out in force. It will be a triumph for you sir.

VOICE: *(off)* Mr. Prime Minister, the troops are at your discretion.

PEARSON raises his umbrella

KING: *(to PEARSON)* My tie's straight?

PEARSON: It's fine.

KING: But is it straight?

PEARSON: Yes.

KING: *(to VOICE)* I'm ready.

PEARSON: *(exiting)* See you out there.

VOICE: *(off)* TTEEEENNNN-SHUN!

A drumroll. KING clears his throat, checks fly, opens his umbrella, mumbling "Don't worry, you'll be fine"

PEARSON: *(off, over microphone)* It gives me great pleasure to introduce to you the Right Honourable William Lyon Mackenzie King!

As the band strikes up "God Save the King" and KING exits to the troops, we hear a deafening chorus of boos and catcalls that last through a brief blackout. Lights up on RALSTON with a newspaper, greeting KING back home

RALSTON: *(with barely concealed glee)* I gather your tour was a triumph?

790

KING: *(tossing the newspaper into garbage can)* Well what would you expect? They all had colds. I'd have been irritable too.

RALSTON: Morale was low?

KING: As you said it would be.

RALSTON: Troop strength?

KING: As you said.

RALSTON: You're convinced, then.

KING: Yes.

RALSTON: We'll need a special sitting of Parliament.

KING: No, Ralston, the issue of conscription is bigger than Parliament.

RALSTON: What are you driving at?

KING: A plebiscite, Ralston.

RALSTON: A what??

KING: We were swept to power on the basis of our seats in Quebec. And we won those seats on a firm commitment against overseas conscription.

RALSTON: But Parliament —

KING: Let us not tarnish the good name of the Liberal party with broken promises. If we Liberals have anything, Ralston, it is honour! What we need is a plebiscite — will the people release us from that pledge.

RALSTON: More delay.

KING: Are you afraid of defeat?

RALSTON: Not in English Canada.

KING: Then leave Quebec to me.

RALSTON: What makes you think they'll vote with us?

KING: Because we're Liberals, Ralston. Besides, we're not asking them to vote *for* conscription, just to release us from our promise. Not *necessarily* conscription. . .

RALSTON: . . . but conscription if *necessary*.

KING: Exactly.

(Lights down on RALSTON, who freezes. Spotlight on KING, wiping his brow with handkerchief. A drumroll)

Not necessarily conscription but conscription if necessary. Conscription if necessary but not necessarily conscription.

(Drumroll louder. KING drops to his knees, eyes raised in prayer)

OH GOD, TELL THOSE PRIESTS OF YOURS I NEED MORE THAN THEIR PRAYERS OR I'M IN ONE HELL OF A MESS!

VOICE OF LORNE GREEN: "THAT THE GOVERNMENT BE RELEASED FROM ITS PLEDGE NOT TO INTRODUCE CONSCRIPTION FOR OVERSEAS SERVICE:" IN FAVOUR, 2,950,000; OPPOSED, 1,640,000.

KING: YIPPEE!!

VOICE OF LORNE GREEN: English Canada "Yes" four to one; Quebec "Non" four to one.

KING slumps. Lights up on RALSTON, out of freeze

RALSTON: So now we proceed.

KING: *(angry)* NO WE DO NOT PROCEED. WE DON'T DO ANYTHING. WE CAN'T.

RALSTON: We won an overwhelming victory.

KING: WE WON A FIASCO! Quebec on one side, the rest on the other.

RALSTON: Then let Quebec bend.

KING: It's not that simple.

RALSTON: It's very simple. You're afraid of them.

KING: I'm afraid for this country.

RALSTON: Damnit we have a moral obligation.

KING: We have a moral nothing. This was *not* a *referendum*, Ralston. It was a plebiscite. A mere consultation.

RALSTON: A MERE CONSULTATION?

KING: THAT IS CORRECT!

RALSTON: You have until tomorrow to change your mind. Tomorrow, King, or I leave. And I won't be leaving the Cabinet alone.

KING: Please . . .

RALSTON: Ilsley will follow me. And so will Mulock and Crerar . . .

KING: The Mobilization Act, I'll . . .

RALSTON: Power and Gibson as well . . .

KING: We'll strike the clause restricting . . .

RALSTON: Macdonald and Howe.

KING: A little time, Ralston.

RALSTON: It's run out.

KING: But . . .

RALSTON: It's conscription or a Cabinet revolt that will topple you from power. Tomorrow in Cabinet — I'll see you there.

KING: RALSTON!

(But RALSTON has gone. Suddenly KING gasps, the horror of his predicament fully realized. He paces like a caged animal. The clock strikes twelve. He freezes, in a brief moment of

inspiration, then goes to the phone and dials. Clock continues chiming)

(on phone) General McNaughton? King here . . . No time for questions or talk. I must see you immediately . . . At home, that's right . . . And hurry. No time to lose. *(he hangs up, ferrets a small sheaf of files from his desk, and begins quietly singing "Abide With Me")* "Abide with me, fast falls the eventide . . ." *(he breaks off)* Oh Laurier, I am making the march to Calvary with you tonight. We have drunk from the same bitter cup.

(McNAUGHTON enters, unseen by KING)

They hounded you in the Great War as they hound me now — the dogs of war.

McNAUGHTON: *(quietly)* Mr King?

KING: *(still facing away from McNAUGHTON)* They don't understand that more is accomplished by preventing bad action than by doing good.

McNAUGHTON: *(clears throat)* Sir?

KING: *(beat, back still to him)* Is that you McNaughton?

McNAUGHTON: The maid said to come straight up.

KING: Quite so. Sorry about the time. Good of you to come.

McNAUGHTON: I assumed it was urgent.

KING: I need your advice. Sound advice from a sound man.

McNAUGHTON: Thank you, sir.

KING: Do you think . . . in your opinion . . . is an election in wartime desirable?

McNAUGHTON: Not if it can be avoided, sir.

KING: Would a sudden election *now* be desirable?

McNAUGHTON: No sir.

KING: *(measured)* Which do you think — in government and in war, and government *is* war, General — which do you think more important: The whole or a part of the whole?

McNAUGHTON: The whole, sir.

KING: Do you think any minister in this government is indispensable?

McNAUGHTON: *(pause, then taking great care)* No more than I was overseas, sir.

KING: You have a fine mind, General. A fine mind.

McNAUGHTON: I appreciate your assessment.

KING: I never did understand why they fired you.

McNAUGHTON: I was retired, sir.

KING: *(eyes him)* It was Ralston. Wasn't it?

McNAUGHTON: I've had my differences with the colonel.

KING: McNaughton, the meek shall inherit the earth. That having been said, you're talking to the prime minister.

McNAUGHTON: Yes sir.

KING: He wronged you.

McNAUGHTON: I believe so.

KING: Yes, you were a victim. He was afraid of you, you know.

McNAUGHTON: Afraid of me?

KING: Yes.

McNAUGHTON: I don't recall giving him cause.

KING: Of course you didn't. All in his mind. His ego. As you know we've had a few difficulties getting volunteers for overseas. Ralston, being in charge of the recruitment campaign couldn't accept his own failure. "If they won't come for me they won't come for anyone," he said.

McNAUGHTON: Vanity!

KING: "Least of all for McNaughton."

McNAUGHTON: WHAT!

KING: And Lieutenant Stuart, always with an eye to advancement, fed him just the sort of reports he wanted to see.

McNAUGHTON: Stuart?

KING: *(nods)* Oh McNaughton, if there is one thing I cannot abide it is petty injustice inflicted by those of mean spirit and small mind. This is all hush-hush you understand. *(hands McNAUGHTON sheaf of files)* Lieutenant Stuart's reports to the government and the War Office.

McNAUGHTON: They're marked "secret", sir.

KING: Tell me what you think.

McNAUGHTON bites — he reads quickly and furiously

McNAUGHTON: Lieutenant Stuart is a horse's ass! Sorry, sir.

KING: Not at all. I've suspected as much.

McNAUGHTON: I never understood my *firing* either. Even Ralston in his letter — well you'd have thought I was being promoted.

KING: Ralston wrote you a letter, did he?

McNAUGHTON: Yes.

KING: What, if I may ask, did he have to say?

McNAUGHTON: He waxed eloquent about my abilities to inspire the troops and concluded that my return to Ottawa would be a loss to the war effort. Did everything but decorate me, the hypocritical son of a bitch.

KING: *(smiles, unseen by McNAUGHTON)* You wouldn't by any chance have a copy of that letter, would you?

McNAUGHTON: Sir?

KING: I want it on my desk tomorrow. First thing.

McNAUGHTON: Sir.

KING: And now, General, I think it is time to ask you to become minister of defence.

McNAUGHTON: But Colonel Ralston . . .

KING: The colonel will be resigning this afternoon, I'm afraid.

McNAUGHTON: But I . . . uh . . .

KING: Will you accept the posting?

McNAUGHTON: I, this is all so sudden.

KING: I need you, McNaughton. My government needs you. But more important the *country* needs you. Will you do your duty to God and king?

McNAUGHTON: Yes. But . . .

KING: What?

McNAUGHTON: I won't be a lackey of bureaucrats. If I'm to come to your aid I *must* be minister of defence in more than name only.

KING: You have my word, General.

McNAUGHTON: *(puffing)* I want the power to take a stiff broom to the entire department. Sweep it out. Lieutenant Stuart will be the first to go. And I want a review of all defence positions to date. A full review — including the issues of conscription and recruits.

KING: I couldn't agree more.

McNAUGHTON: Naturally the review of past policy will take time. But it's time I demand if I'm to accept your request.

KING: Rest assured, General, you can have all the time in the world. *(he beams)*

(McNAUGHTON exits as lights change. Sound of chatter, gavel. Two spotlights rise on opposite sides of the stage. KING is in one, RALSTON in the other, both seated. The scene is the Cabinet room. The space occupied by the other Cabinet members is in black. They are heard but not seen.)

Gentlemen, this Cabinet meeting will come to order. As you are no doubt aware I have been contemplating a new recruitment campaign. But Mr Ralston has assured me that this is not sufficient. He has assured me that he can do no more than he has done and that other, more drastic measures are now in order. After much painful reflection, I am forced to the conclusion that he is correct.

A few rumblings from the other Cabinet members

RALSTON: Thank you sir.

KING: Yes, I would be loath to force any of you, my ministers, into a course of action to which you felt unable or opposed. With that in mind I have decided to surrender my opposition to his conscience.

RALSTON: *(rises, beaming, it's too good to be true)* Thank you, sir.

KING: I have accepted his letter of resignation.

RALSTON: My letter of . . .

KING pulls RALSTON's Act One resignation letter from his coat

KING: Mr Ralston tendered his resignation some time ago and sadly I have been forced to act on it. It is always hard to part with a colleague, especially one who has been so close, for whom one has such high respect, indeed affection. But these are times of war. The situation is extremely dangerous and conscience is all. Mr Ralston, you are henceforth relieved of all duties.

RALSTON: *(still standing, in shock)* I . . . I have done what I could.

KING: And for that we are grateful. Not least in the counsel you gave concerning your choice of successor.

RALSTON: Counsel I —

KING: General McNaughton. *(to the others)* Mr Ralston has been lavish with praise. To McNaughton himself he wrote: *(reads from RALSTON's letter)* "Your return to Ottawa is a loss to our war effort. But surely the future will bring more glories and rewards and greater mountains to climb. Sincerely, Colonel J. Layton Ralston." I couldn't have said it better myself. And now, Colonel Ralston, you may leave. We wish you well from the bottom of our hearts.

RALSTON: I . . . *(pause, he salutes, turns on his heel and exits)*

KING: *(eyeing the others around the table with a cold smile)* And now, gentlemen, have we another Judas in our midst? I thought not. Let us proceed with business.

Blackout on the two spotlights. Lights up on PEARSON

PEARSON: I was flabbergasted. Not just that it was Ralston gone and not King, but that he'd been replaced by McNaughton! The British War Office had taken such pains to have him removed and here King turns around and makes him his minister of defence. Still the nuts and bolts were that we needed fifteen thousand recruits and were only getting twenty-four a day. And after McNaughton's much ballyhooed campaign we were only getting twenty-four point six. Still it was all time. But when the Army Council threatened to resign enmasse if he didn't introduce overseas conscription he had nowhere to go if he didn't want to lose Ontario, and the West and his government. And so on November twenty-third, 1944, he rose in the House.

(A light up on KING. He rises, his back to us)

But a curious thing. Instead of addressing his speech to the Opposition, he turned and faced his own members —

faced the very French Canadians he feared. Faced his personal terror and said —

KING has faced us

KING: If there is anything to which I have devoted my political life, it is to try and promote unity, harmony and amity between the diverse elements of this country. My friends, you may desert me. You can remove your confidence from me. You can withdraw the trust you have placed in my hands — but I shall never deviate from that line of policy. Whatever may be the consequences, I know I am in the right; and a time will come when every man, woman and child will render me full justice on that score.

KING nods gravely, turns and resumes his seat. As his light dims out, desk thumping is heard. Over this sound we hear "Pack Up Your Troubles in Your Old Kit Bag." Lights up on JOAN

JOAN: Surprise, surprise, they thumped till their hands had bruises: the English because he'd brought in conscription and the French because he'd won so much time for himself that now it was only a hop, skip and a jump to peace. He'd guided us through war and he'd kept us together and they loved him for it. And sure enough next election he won one final term before retiring, and this at a time when other war leaders like Churchill were getting dumped all over the place. It seemed he could escape from anything.

A shadowy light rises on KING in his housecoat, staring off

KING: In a coffin, Joan, there's no escape. Nowhere to move. It's hard, hard wood. And there's the earth all over you, pressing you down. The undertaker plants you like a seed that will never grow. And you'll be there forever. Alone in the ground.

JOAN: No, Rexy, no. Your mother, your grandfather, Laurier, little Pat — they travel, they speak to us. They live.

KING: I hope to God they really do. What *else* is there to dream? Nothing from this world. Oh Joan, when they write me down they'll treat me like a Vancouver winter: I'll be so much drizzle and mist they won't even see the mountains.

JOAN: Now stop it Rex. That's morbid talk.

KING: They won't even *look* for the mountains. If there *are* any . . . Ralston.

JOAN: You did right.

KING: But he was a good man. Brave. Served in the trenches. What did I ever do?

JOAN: You kept us united.

KING: No Joan, I constructed a ruins. Kingsmere. I took blocks of rubble from Westminster and created ruins with fresh mortar. I turned history into the shape of my mind. *(he lies on the bed, he coughs)* Water.

(The fit subsides as JOAN exits. The clock strikes twelve and general lights dim. KING is wrapped in a blanket)

Oh Momma, sometimes I wake up and I think I'm dead. I think I've been suffocated by War Bonds, cigar smoke — smothered by quilting bees for the Liberal party. I realize then that all my power ever amounted to was Liberal fundraising raffles in towns of five hundred for quilts stitched by my loyal supporters. In my dreams I see God quilting history, and I am a scrap of material in his hands. My place is uncertain and I . . . I —

MRS. KING and MACKENZIE enter.

MRS KING: Trust His handiwork, Willy. He will not forget his poor servant.

KING: I want so much to believe.

MRS KING: Then come with me. Now.

KING: No Momma.

MRS KING: My boy doesn't miss his poor mother?

KING: Yes but I'm frightened. I hear the recess bells the Peace Tower bells and I love those bells because they tell me I'm alive and — Momma, what is it like to be dead? I know we talk but I can't touch you and I don't know where you are — sometimes I don't even know *if* you are —

MRS KING: Willy —

KING: No. And to die without leaving memoirs. I can't. I have to discover the peaks. I have to prove they were there I —

(Sound of a dog)

Pat? . . . Pat?

MRS KING: "High up in the courts of Heaven today
A little dog angel waits;
With the other dog angels he will not play
But he sits alone at the gates . . ."

KING: ". . . 'For I know that my master will come,' says he
'And when he comes he will call for me.' "

MRS KING: You taped that poem in your diaries.

KING: Yes.

MRS KING: It's all in your diaries. You've no need for memoirs.

KING: Pat. Oh Pat — my poor dear little saint.

MRS KING: He misses you. I miss you. Your grampa misses you. And so will the country.

Pause

KING: Stay with me? Be with me?

MRS KING: You, the Rebel's grandson by me — through my blood shall we be united forever. Come.

(MRS KING and MACKENZIE move away from KING's bed)

"And his master, far on the earth below,
As he sits in his easy chair"

MRS KING & MACKENZIE: "Forgets sometimes and he whistles
low
For the dog that is not there,
And the little dog angel cocks his ears
And dreams that his master's call he hears."

*KING rises from bed and moves toward them holding out his
arms*

MRS KING, MACKENZIE & KING: "And I know when at length
his master waits
Outside in the dark and cold
For the hand of Death to ope the gates
That lead to those courts of gold"

KING: "That the little dog angel's eager bark
Will comfort his soul in the shivering dark."

*(KING grips their hands, they form a circle. Lightning and
thunder. Gentle rain as KING breaks away, faces us)*

This country — these clumps of rock and dirt that make
us poets of geography — this country was mine. I will be
remembered like an old photograph in a cardboard box.
But I will be remembered. William Lyon Mackenzie King!
My grandfather was a Rebel! And I was a Prime Minister!
Once upon a time.

Smiling, KING exits with his family as lights fade to black.

The End

Gwen Pharis Ringwood
Garage Sale

EDITOR'S NOTE: Gwen Pharis Ringwood's distinguished career spanned more than fifty years. She was born in Anatone, Washington, U.S.A. in 1910, but lived almost her entire life in Canada. As early as 1935, the Banff School of Fine Arts produced "The Dragons of Kent". After a number of radio plays, she won a playwriting scholarship to the University of North Carolina where she studied with Frederic Koch and worked with the Carolina Playmakers who staged her *Still Stands the House*. A one-act folk play, it has become a classic of Canadian drama. The next four decades saw her writing nearly thirty plays for the stage, sixteen radio scripts, a number of short stories, a novel and miscellaneous pieces, while raising a family with her doctor husband. Always closely linked with community theatre and radio, she gained new prominence in the 1970s in a nation beginning to recognize its theatre pioneers. But she hardly became an historical artifact. Instead, she wrote with renewed vigour. Among her latest works has been *Mirage*, a documentary tale of the settling of the west which premiered in 1979. She died on 24 May 1984.

Garage Sale, one of the most recent of Ringwood's plays, opened in a production by the New Play Centre at Vancouver's Water Front Theatre on 14 April 1981. It had a subsequent staging at the University of Guelph in June 1984. *Garage Sale* was first published in 1982.

Characters:

RACHEL
REUBEN

PLACE: The Back Yard.
TIME: The Present.

The verandah and a portion of the small garden of an old fashioned little house on a city street. A door to the house opens on to the porch. Two old fashioned chairs are placed on the verandah. There is a bench in the garden as well as a bird bath and a bird feeder.

In the original production the plum tree, the old fence, the lane were imagined to be in the audience area and were not shown.

The time is April and there is spring in the air. A home-made tool box or small bench on the porch may be useful.

A crocheted afghan covers one of the chairs and a crocheted cushion in the same pattern is on the other chair.

RACHEL comes out the door carrying a basket of wool and a partially completed Afghan (probably Granny squares pattern.) In the basket too is a container carrying sunflower seeds and she also has a jug of water for the bird bath. She closes the screen door carefully, places the basket of wool and afghan on the chair at right, moves to the bird feeder. She is humming softly to the tune of "Lulla lulla Lulla Bye Bye."

RACHEL: "Lulla lulla lulla lulla bye bye
Do you want the moon to play with?
A star to run away with . . .?"

(She breaks off to talk to her familiar visitors that hover just out of sight.)

There. That's all you get today. You'll eat us out of house and home if we don't watch out. Is that how you get to the feeder, you naughty thing? We'll have to cut the branch back. Oh, you silly squirrel. Come on down. I won't hurt you. Who do you think puts these sunflower seeds out every day? Mind you leave some for the chickadees. Don't be greedy.

(She moves to the plum tree.)

So! You're all in bud this morning. Good for you. Mind you, you're a little slow. The tree across the lane burst all its buds out yesterday. Of course it gets more sun. But they neglect it. They've never pruned it once. I want you to be in full blossom when Daphne comes home next week. Like a bride in a wedding veil. Daphne looked so beautiful walking down that aisle. Radiant. But somehow that all fell apart. I don't know why. I never did know why. *(Indignant, as if tree had replied.)* Of course I asked. *(Moving away)* You hurry up now. The tree across the lane is in full bloom. *(She moves to stage right to look out at the tree across the lane.)* For goodness sakes! Would you look at that now? They must be going to . . . Oh, that's sad. Those poor young people. Hmmm. That's very sad. *(She turns away, moving towards chair left on porch.)* Mind you, I'm not surprised. But still, it makes me feel — sad. *(Bemused, she sits down and begins crocheting.)* Poor people. *(Pause.)* Poor Everybody.

REUBEN comes out the door, closes it, moves onto porch.

REUBEN: Well, Rachel. You're out here. I wondered. Who were you talking to?

RACHEL: Oh, just the squirrel. The plum tree.

REUBEN: Hmm. Well, they say it makes them grow.

RACHEL: That's right.

REUBEN: I wish you'd stop talking to that jade tree in the house though. It's threatening us. Taking over.

RACHEL: The jade tree is a horticultural triumph, Reuben.

REUBEN: Who says so?

RACHEL: The Avon lady. She called once.

REUBEN: Oh yes.

RACHEL: Those were her very words — a horticultural triumph.

REUBEN: Whatever she said, you shouldn't go on encouraging that jade tree. Couldn't you . . .

RACHEL: Couldn't I what?

REUBEN: Well, couldn't you . . . just bow?

He bows elaborately. RACHEL ignores this sally.

RACHEL: I put your bran flakes out.

REUBEN: I ate them. And the avocado.

RACHEL: For breakfast? *(Crossly)* I was saving it, for a salad.

REUBEN: I've always wanted to eat an avocado for breakfast and today I did. It's going to be a nice day.

RACHEL: Occasional showers. Sunny periods.

REUBEN: Sun's burning through now. I'll get my journal and write it up out here. I've got behind on my journal what with all that pruning and painting and refurbishing.

RACHEL: Well, we're doing it for Daphne.

REUBEN: *(Moving to the door)* All on the chance she's coming.

RACHEL: This time she'll come. The end of April, she said. And that's next week. Don't hold the screen door open, Reuben. We don't want mice in the house.

REUBEN: If there was a mouse around I'd see it.

RACHEL: You might not see it. Mice move fast.

REUBEN: We've lived in this house for five years, Rachel, and every time I open this door you tell me to watch out for mice.

RACHEL: There was one . . .

REUBEN: You've blown mice up out of all proportion. Mice are not the enemy.

RACHEL: They are to me.

REUBEN: Do you know what's the enemy? Oxen.

RACHEL: Oh, you and your black oxen.

REUBEN: "The years like great black oxen tread the world, And I am trampled by their passing feet." There's your enemy.

RACHEL: Maybe I feel trampled by mice. Can I help that?

REUBEN: Yes, you can. You can refuse to allow yourself to be trampled.

RACHEL: It's not that simple. Not for everybody.

REUBEN: You have to fight back. I fight back. *(He turns to go into the house)* What was it I was going to get?

RACHEL: Your journal.

REUBEN: Oh, right.

He goes in. RACHEL moves down stage and looks across.

RACHEL: Not that simple.

She returns to her crocheting. REUBEN returns with journal, carefully closing the door behind him. He sits on the edge of the porch and begins entries in journal.

REUBEN: Let's see. April 25th. Up at 7:30; shaved; dressed. Ate bran flakes, and a whole avocado. *(He glances at RACHEL who ignores this.)* Rae in garden . . . singing. *(Looking at her)* Well, how's it coming?

RACHEL: How's what coming?

REUBEN: The Work. The Ultimate. Definitive. The Afghan.

RACHEL: It doesn't come. I fabricate it. Hand and eye.

REUBEN: What about the wool? You don't fabricate it. That's the sheep's job.

RACHEL: This wool's acrylic.

REUBEN: Oh.

RACHEL: Sheep's wool shrinks. Who wants that?

REUBEN: I do. I hate acrylic.

RACHEL: It's my afghan. I'm the one crocheting.

REUBEN: I used to think that word was pronounced "crochet" to rhyme with "watch it." *(Writing.)* Rae's crotcheting an afghan, square by square, breath other breath, each square identical to the one before, same pattern, color, size. On to infinity she spreads the crotchet afghan.

RACHEL: You said you'd hook a rug. You promised.

REUBEN: I will. I'm going to.

RACHEL: Five years now. No rug.

REUBEN: You'll see. I'll get around to it.

RACHEL: I bought you a rug kit when you — when you had that little — warning.

REUBEN: The heart attack.

RACHEL: Yes. An expensive rug kit.

REUBEN: It's a poodle pattern. If I make a rug, I'm not spending my time hooking poodles.

RACHEL: I thought you liked dogs.

REUBEN: I like dogs all right. I just don't like dogs on rugs. Besides, I plan to make my own pattern.

RACHEL: For a first rug? That's dangerous.

REUBEN: So? I'll take my chances. I'll teeter on the edge. Now I'll get this journal up to date. Remember yesterday, note down today. What's happening. Where I'm at. Who called. Did anybody call?

RACHEL: Not yet.

REUBEN: I thought I heard —

RACHEL: Heard what?

REUBEN: Heard someone calling. Would we answer?

RACHEL: We always answer. *(Pause)* Reb, did anybody call? Did anyone really call?

REUBEN: Oh yes, Rachel.

RACHEL: When?

REUBEN: At Christmas. The children. If they can get through, they always call at Christmas.

RACHEL: Sometimes when the phone rings I think it might be Doris calling. I know it couldn't be, Reb, but just for a moment I . . .

REUBEN: I know the feeling.

RACHEL: Do you? *(He nods.)* Doris was always so thoughtful.

REUBEN: *(Getting up to show her)* See, here's the Christmas entry. John and Daphne called. Rae's brother George dropped in, having strong drink taken. Aunt Selina phoned. And we saw Mary . . . looks like Poppins. Who's she?

RACHEL: Someone on the television.

REUBEN: There, you see. It pays to keep a journal.

RACHEL: I suppose they called. Lately all I seem to hear is that buzz saw. All day yesterday.

REUBEN: I told you, it's not a buzz saw, Rachel. It's a bull dozer.

RACHEL: Oh.

REUBEN: They're bulldozing down the old church to make way for a high rise.

RACHEL: The old church falling. One wouldn't expect it to be so loud.

810

REUBEN: It was a strong old church, well built. Besides, the sound reverberates against that old fence, the same as a bullet ricochets.

RACHEL: That fence is not so old. I think the Longs put it up. Then the Prentergasts painted it. And now it's the . . . the . . .

REUBEN: The Crangs.

RACHEL: Oh yes, he's Crang. She's Simla. They're on their way out now.

REUBEN: Moving?

RACHEL: Not just moving. They're terminating the relationship.

REUBEN: How do you know that?

RACHEL: Look across the lane. Through the gap in the Virginia Creeper. Everything's out there.

REUBEN: You're right. It could be they're house cleaning. It's spring.

RACHEL: They're not house cleaning, Reb. They're having their garage sale.

REUBEN: Don't jump to conclusions, Rachel. If it were a garage sale there'd be customers.

RACHEL: If you'd wear your glasses you could see the sign. Garage Sale, 10 o'clock.

REUBEN: Those glasses hurt my ears. Besides I like the way things look without them. Soft around the edges.

RACHEL: Blurry!

REUBEN: All right. I like things blurry. No one's come yet. So far there's just odds and ends piled helter skelter. Chain saw. Sofa . . . or is that a hideabed . . . or what? I'll get the field glasses.

RACHEL: Reuben.

REUBEN: They won't know. I'm interested. I might want to pick something up.

Telephone rings

RACHEL: Listen.

REUBEN: The telephone. I'll get it. Coming. Hold on, I'm coming.

He rushes into the house.

RACHEL: If it's John or Daphne I'll come so keep them on the line, Reb. *(looking at watch)* It must be John or Daphne. Who else could phone so early? I'm coming! *(She becomes tangled in the afghan)* Oh damn it. Don't hang up, Reb. I'll be right in. *(The sound of a trail bike starting next door is heard.)* Do you hear me. Reuben? I just have to . . . Oh, that noisy trail bike. I'll be glad to hear the last of it.

RACHEL starts towards the door. REUBEN comes out. He has the field glasses with him.

RACHEL: What was it, Reb?

REUBEN: Daphne. Daphne was on the phone.

RACHEL: And you didn't call me? Is she all right?

REUBEN: She's fine. Just fine.

RACHEL: You know I wanted to speak to her. I was just coming.

REUBEN: She had no time, Rae. She was waiting to board a plane.

RACHEL: Oh, she's on her way then? She's leaving London now . . . today!

REUBEN: Yes, Rae but . . .

RACHEL: But what?

REUBEN: Rae, the plane was going to Italy. To Milan.

RACHEL: Oh. So she's not coming home.

REUBEN: Well, no. She's got this good offer. She's doing the costumes for a film they're making in northern Italy. She couldn't refuse such a good offer, Rae.

RACHEL: I see.

REUBEN: She hopes we'll come visit her when she gets back to London.

RACHEL: She knows we won't do that.

REUBEN: Why not?

RACHEL: With your heart condition we can hardly go traipsing off.

REUBEN: Excuses. Excuses. You know the doctor said . . .

RACHEL: How did she sound?

REUBEN: Fine. Happy. She sends her love. She couldn't stay while I called you . . . her flight was waiting . . .

RACHEL: Well, that's that. John won't be coming. Daphne won't be coming.

REUBEN: John can't come Rae. He's bound by contract.

RACHEL: We might as well not have children. Oh, Reb.

REUBEN: *(moving to her, comforting her)* It's all right, Rae. They're grown up. My God, John's forty years old.

RACHEL: Forty-one. Why did he have to go to Nigeria? And Daphne's never even seen this house. Now if we'd stayed in the old house where they grew up, like I wanted to, if we hadn't moved. . .

REUBEN: We went back, remember. Everything was changed.

RACHEL: Where in Italy? Where will Daphne be?

REUBEN: Lake Gardona. That's where they make the pirate films. I read about it in the Geographic. I'll bring out the Globe. We'll find it on the Globe. You wait here.

He moves to the house

RACHEL: That Globe's all out of date.

REUBEN: *(as he goes in, carefully closing the door behind him)* I don't think Italy has changed that much.

RACHEL: *(At bench, gazes forlornly at the plum tree)* You don't have to hurry. She's not coming. You might as well take your time.

REUBEN returns with large globe.

REUBEN: Well, here we are . . . our turning Globe.

RACHEL: Don't leave the . . .

REUBEN: I know. Watch out! Mice!

He closes the door elaborately.

RACHEL: How did she sound, Reb? How did Daphne sound?

REUBEN: Fine. Excited. Remember when you gave me this Globe? Our 10th anniversary.

RACHEL: Fifth. Our fifth.

REUBEN: Here it is. Right here, near Milan. Now if I could find that Geographic, we'd have the whole picture. We can pretend we're there.

RACHEL: All last night I was thinking of the children. Especially Doris. She seems so alive to me, Reb. Sometimes it's as if she's closer than the others. Finally I got up and looked through all the photographs.

REUBEN: You were asleep at five. I was up at five and when I came back to bed, you were asleep, all warm and cosy.

RACHEL: I was awake. I felt your cold feet on me.

REUBEN: We could manage a trip to Italy, Rae, if you want to.

RACHEL: How?

REUBEN: Encroach on capital. We'd get a room at Lake Gardona . . .

RACHEL: No. We'd be in the way.

REUBEN: We wouldn't need to stay long. We could take Daphne out to dinner. Hail and Farewell. Then go on to Rome or Alexandria — traverse the turning globe.

RACHEL: We'd have to get used to a new globe, Reuben. And I warn you, everything's changed.

REUBEN: You don't suppose they'd be getting rid of a Globe? Crangs, I mean. Theirs would be recent. I'll take a look. *(using glasses)* Chain saw, cross country skis, pressure cooker, blender, pair of skates — those would be his.

RACHEL: The dressing table's hers. Pretty, isn't it?

REUBEN: I don't see any Globe out there. *(sound of trail bike off)* Hey, here he comes back. I hope he's not selling his trail bike. He'll need that. Hmm. He is selling it. Leaving it out with all the rest. He's just walking away from it into the house. That's terrible! I wonder how much he'd want for . . .

RACHEL: *(Moving to him in indignation)* Reuben, what on earth would you do with a trail bike?

REUBEN: *(Angrily)* I'd . . . I'd . . . What does anybody do? I'd explore! *(Turning it into a joke)* It rides two. We'd hit the trail together.

RACHEL: *(Sitting to crochet)* We'd hit the ditch together and end up in jail.

REUBEN: He looked gloomy. Poor kids. I can see them now.

He moves to other chair and sits down.

RACHEL: How can you see them if they're in the house?

REUBEN: In my mind. I see them in my mind. Don't you?

RACHEL: No. No, I don't.

REUBEN: He'll be at the stereo, fingering all those records they collected. She's standing on a chair reaching the back of cupboards, pulling down the unused wedding gifts.

RACHEL: I don't think they were married. Twice the postman left letters here addressed to Ms Rosanne Simla. I returned them.

REUBEN: To her?

RACHEL: Of course not. To the Postman. He's the one responsible.

REUBEN: We could go over. We might pick up a few things. We bought the bird bath at the Long's garage sale.

RACHEL: At least the Longs nodded to us.

REUBEN: Crang ducked his head at me. Twice. When I was mowing.

RACHEL: I took mint jelly over.

REUBEN: You did?

RACHEL: I went across the lane right into their back yard and offered her the jelly.

REUBEN: She refused it?

RACHEL: She thanked me but she said she already had mint jelly.

REUBEN: You never told me.

RACHEL: I was embarrassed. I felt like a fool.

REUBEN: She was just being honest, Rae. After all, a person can only use so much mint jelly. We know that.

RACHEL: She's very wasteful. She only uses the tips of the asparagus. The stalks go in the garbage. A lot of good in them just wasted.

REUBEN: *(looking across the lane)* Hey, here they come. She's carrying the baby. He's putting out a laundry basket. She's just putting the baby down in the basket. Rae, you don't suppose. . .

RACHEL: Of course not.

REUBEN: Last year I heard a radio program. All about a black market . . . in babies.

RACHEL: Oh, Reuben. *(Unbelieving)*

REUBEN: A true program. Documented.

RACHEL: Not in Canada.

REUBEN: This was in Canada. A flourishing black market.

RACHEL: That's awful. How could anybody . . .

REUBEN: Have you seen their baby?

RACHEL: Just from here. I made some bootees for it, but I never took them over.

REUBEN: Why not? You should have.

RACHEL: After the mint jelly?

REUBEN: Pink blanket. The baby must be a girl.

RACHEL: They don't make that distinction any more. They often use yellow. They call it Unisex. Is there a tag on that basket?

REUBEN: I can't see. The snowmobile's in the way. Oh dear, you're right, Rachel. They're breaking up. They've brought out the waterbed.

RACHEL moves to him to look across

RACHEL: So that's what they're like. It doesn't even look comfortable.

REUBEN: They've drained it, Rachel.

RACHEL: Oh, Reuben.

REUBEN: It's collapsed like a burst balloon. They're breaking up all right.

RACHEL: (returning to her chair) I didn't think it would last. I said to myself: "Rae that young couple is headed for the rocks."

REUBEN: I thought just the opposite. All that singing around the barbecue. And the smell of those steaks, sizzling over charcoal. I thought they'd make it.

RACHEL: The barbecues were a last stand. New-found friends. A raise in pay. Of course they put on a front during the barbecues. But every time I heard their singing I could foresee today.

REUBEN: How?

RACHEL: She had that gaunt look. Woman against the wall.

REUBEN: He left the good car for her. He drove the old jalopy. (Hopefully) Maybe they're just tired of their things. Want to start over — with new things.

RACHEL: No. They had a row. A lot of rows. He failed an exam. He said it was her fault he failed. He said she was too demanding.

REUBEN: Poor kid. He was trying to better himself.

RACHEL: She wanted to sing in the Civic Opera. He didn't like the way those people carry on — always kissing each other.

REUBEN: He was the one who sang at all the barbecues. I never heard her sing.

RACHEL: She used to sing. When they first moved in she sang like a fallen angel.

REUBEN: *(Irritated)* Why fallen? Why not like an angel?

RACHEL: Her song had a falling sound. They weren't angelic songs. The opposite. A falling sound.

REUBEN: Where was I when she was singing?

RACHEL: Cleaning your fish tank or down at the corner hobnobbing with old Ginger and his cronies.

REUBEN: Ginger's in hospital. Extended care.

RACHEL: His asthma?

REUBEN: Emphysema. No breath left.

RACHEL: Too bad. I wondered why you haven't been going down to get the paper.

REUBEN: I'll go tomorrow. I just have to adjust. Anyway, what have I missed? Wars, kidnappings, murders.

RACHEL: All those obituaries you read.

REUBEN: So? I have to keep up. After all, it's better to know than to ask about someone after that someone's dead. Remember you wrote that sympathy letter to Arnold Burns and his wife hadn't died at all. You listen to gossip. I wait for the obituary.

RACHEL: If you can trust the papers.

REUBEN: You can trust them when it comes to the obituary. They can't afford to misrepresent a person's death. In fact, I understand they have them all ready, waiting for you.

RACHEL: Only if you're important. *(Slight pause.)* I expect they have yours ready.

REUBEN: *(Shyly pleased)* Do you think so? Well, I suppose . . . head of repairs for the Telephone Company . . .

RACHEL: Vice chairman of the Kinsman Park committee . . .

REUBEN: So I was. I'd forgot that, Rachel. I suppose I could go down to that newspaper office and read what they have to say about me.

RACHEL: Better not, Reb. What's happening now?

REUBEN: Crang's setting up the coffee urn. They're going to serve refreshments to the customers. You know I saw him in the store last week he was buying light bulbs — 5 year warranty. *(Pause)* He must have felt secure then. She's bringing out some sort of harp.

RACHEL: *(Moving to him)* Her auto harp. Oh, I hate to see her selling that. She used to play the auto harp and sing . . . She'd sit out by the electric fountain and play and sing and her hair hung down in ringlets, like that song.

REUBEN: One of the roving kind.

RACHEL: He was the rover. Her singing drove him mad. He'd say "For God's sake, can't you sing something cheerful."

REUBEN: "Roll out the Barrel." Around the barbecue they sang "Roll out the barrel."

RACHEL: I wonder how much she wants for that auto harp?

REUBEN: Why would you want an auto harp, Rae? We've more stuff now than we need, cluttering up the place.

RACHEL: There you go again, disparaging my afghans.

She turns from him and goes back to take up the jug of water and in next sequence moves towards the bird bath with it.

REUBEN: Well, face it. We've no room for any more. *(back to glasses)* He's looking at the bird cage. It's empty! They've lost the bird.

RACHEL: She was cleaning the cage. The budgie slipped through her fingers. She tried to catch it.

REUBEN: Where would it go?

RACHEL: Away. It blew away.

REUBEN: *(Cross)* You mean it flew. It flew away.

RACHEL: I meant what I said, Reuben. The budgie blew away.

REUBEN: Oh, I don't like that.

Pause.

RACHEL: *(At bird bath)* Reuben, suppose we had one . . .

REUBEN: A budgie?

RACHEL: Just supposing. What would we sell?

REUBEN: Oh. You want a garage sale?

RACHEL: Well, it would get rid of clutter.

REUBEN: We'd be in the stream of things. We'd be keeping up.

RACHEL: What would we give over?

REUBEN: What would we keep? That's the ultimate, definitive decision?

RACHEL: Ultimate. Definitive. You're always harping on that these days. There's time enough for that.

REUBEN: The mounted deer head. I'd sell that.

RACHEL: You were proud of that six pointer. Boasted. There'd be a light place on the wall where it was hanging. They always leave a shadow on the wall.

REUBEN: I wouldn't shoot the deer now. That was my hunting stage.

RACHEL: I doubt you could shoot it now.

REUBEN: Why not? *(holding out hand)* Well, perhaps a tremor. Nothing to worry about. We'd sell those partridge feathers.

RACHEL: I always meant to do something with them. Make something.

REUBEN: A nest?

RACHEL: A fan to stir the wind. It gets close here.

REUBEN: There's a perambulator in the basement. Antique perambulators are worth a lot today.

RACHEL: No. Daphne might need that. Those years you went to war, I put John and the twins in and wheeled them all down to post those blue air mail letters. I was so afraid something would happen to the children while you were away.

REUBEN: I knew you'd manage. Hey, that China dog Aunt Connie gave me when I was on leave.

RACHEL: That China dog was a present, a good door stop.

REUBEN: I always hated it. Mean eyes, staring at me.

RACHEL: Well, if you're selling presents, what about the gold watch the telephone company gave you? You never use it.

REUBEN: I might use it. For ceremonies. It's my ceremonial watch.

RACHEL: The cowboy boots and hat John didn't want. Why have we still got them?

REUBEN: Maybe.

RACHEL: The shot gun!

REUBEN: No. Not the shot gun. A man never knows when he may have to stand up and be counted. I notice the things you want to sell are all mine. You can't play fast and loose with other people's things!

RACHEL: You make the list then.

REUBEN: The afghans. I'd get rid of them all — lock, stock and barrel.

RACHEL: I thought so.

REUBEN: We'd see the furniture again. The clean lines of the Morris chair, the sofa, the oak table, the piano.

RACHEL: We'd see the holes and scars and dints and dents.

REUBEN: You'd have your hands free. You could use your hands for — other things.

RACHEL: What?

REUBEN: Well, kneading bread. Dialing the telephone. You never use the telephone any more.

RACHEL: The lines are always busy.

Brief pause.

REUBEN: Patting. You could use your hands for patting.

RACHEL: What would I pat? The China dog? You've sold it.

REUBEN: Me? You used to pat me. You never pat me any more. Too busy crotcheting.

RACHEL: That's a silly word. Childish.

REUBEN: I pat you.

RACHEL: You slap me on the bottom. "How are you, old girl?" you say and you slap me on the bottom.

REUBEN: I won't do it again. Mark my words. Not again. Not ever.

RACHEL: Good.

REUBEN: You'll see! *(pause)* Well, what else do we get rid of?

RACHEL: My old fur coat.

REUBEN: You'd sell that? I bought you that coat when the twins were born. The daughters. I went in debt to buy that coat.

RACHEL: It's muskrat. I wanted Hudson seal.

REUBEN: Why didn't you say so?

RACHEL: You never asked. You brought the muskrat home and I was too young to tell you, but inside I was crying.

REUBEN: For Hudson seal? That's *dyed* muskrat, Rachel.

RACHEL: So? Now you know.

REUBEN: Sell it. By all means. Sell it. Don't think of my feelings in the matter.

RACHEL: The National Geographics. Forty years of them. They're probably worth a fortune now. It's not as if we ever traveled much.

REUBEN: That's why we had the Geographics. Our minds were free to travel.

RACHEL: We'd sell that Globe. It still shows Persia, Siam, Macedonia. They're gone long ago. All gone.

REUBEN: *(Upset)* Where? Where did they go? They couldn't drop into the bottom of the sea like lost Atlantis. I ask you, where did they go, Rachel?

RACHEL: They were swallowed up. Changed. Re-christened. I would have liked a coat of Persian lamb.

REUBEN: I couldn't sell the National Geographics or the Globe. It would be like selling dreams.

RACHEL: Dreams aren't worth much — not mine, anyway.

REUBEN: Day dreams, Rachel. The things you dream when you're awake. You know.

RACHEL: I'm not sure I do.

REUBEN: "A rose red city twice as old as time . . ." or was it "dawn". I'm there at the gates about to enter as the sun's rays touch the highest minaret. "My name is Ozymandias, king of kings, Look on my works, ye Mighty, and despair." I'm in the desert now — Sand everywhere you look, Sand and sky and a fallen obelisk.

RACHEL: *(Softly)* You always were one for the poetry.

REUBEN: Yes. Yes, I was.

RACHEL: In my sleep, I dream the same things often.

REUBEN: A recurrent dream. They call that a recurrent dream.

RACHEL: I dream of the missed appointment.

REUBEN: Oh?

RACHEL: It's very important that I reach this place . . . this meeting place on time. I've promised, said I'd be there, checked my watch, turned all the right corners but each time something . . . someone . . . delays me. I begin to hurry, try harder, explain I mustn't tarry. The clock's hands move on and frantically I strain to get there. Too late. Too late. I wake up trying to explain why I wasn't there for . . . that important appointment.

REUBEN: Who with? Why were you going, Rachel?

RACHEL: I don't know. It's just that I want to keep my promise . . . try. Something . . . someone delays me.

REUBEN: *(Tenderly)* You can't hurry any faster than you can, Rachel. You do your best.

RACHEL: One's best is never good enough.

REUBEN: Don't say that.

RACHEL: Well, is it?

REUBEN: I used to think it was. I think it is. I hope so. *(Pause. He touches her.)* You seemed to think it was. Isn't it.

RACHEL: Oh, that. Yes, it was. Is.

REUBEN: You're blushing.

RACHEL: Who wouldn't? The way you go on.

REUBEN: I could go and price that waterbed. Would you like me to?

RACHEL: Don't be licentious, Reuben.

REUBEN: Rabelaisian. That's a nicer word. Rabelaisian.

RACHEL: Men. One thing on their minds.

825

REUBEN: You wouldn't want me different. (*Pause. He moves away from her towards front.*) Was the missed appointment — did that have to do with us, Rachel? With me?

RACHEL: Are they still outside? Has anybody come?

REUBEN: (*Demanding*) Answer me, Rachel. Did it?

RACHEL: No. No, it was something else. Nothing to do with you, Reuben — with us. The children, perhaps. The world outside.

REUBEN: (*Moving to her.*) Remember that fall picnic and the muskrat coat? You put it down, spread it out, and we lay on it together. I never forgot that picnic. It was the best picnic we ever went on together.

RACHEL: (*Sharply*) All right. We'll keep the muskrat coat.

REUBEN: And the National Geographics. They're our life line. What about the books?

RACHEL: Those high school years' books. No one will ever look at them. And all those "how to do and how to eat and how to live" . . . let's get rid of them. We're beyond them. It's come down to that.

REUBEN: Come down to what?

RACHEL: To us and it.

REUBEN: It?

RACHEL: Whatever's outside the skin. Outside the casing. You know.

REUBEN: Yes, I know. The Whatever.

Pause.

RACHEL: We'll put the books out then.

REUBEN: The jade tree. I see they've put their tree out.

RACHEL: Yes. He should never have brought home that tree without consulting her.

REUBEN: A very exotic tree. What kind?

RACHEL: He called it a Yucca tree.

REUBEN: A touch of the tropics in his living room.

RACHEL: She hated it. She wanted something softer, not so spiny.

REUBEN: It's spiny all right. Spiny as an aardvaark. More suitable for the lobby of a zoo.

RACHEL: Those were almost her exact words, Reuben. Fancy you're saying that. Has anybody come?

REUBEN: No. But it's only a quarter to . . . Rachel, do you suppose if we put some music on the phonograph, opened the windows wide, so they had to listen . . .

RACHEL: What kind of music?

REUBEN: You know. Music to stir the heart. "Scheherazade." "The Surrey with the Fringe on Top." "Going my Way." That might give them pause. They'd remember all their days and nights and cancel the whole operation.

RACHEL: The music might wake the baby. They both get upset when the baby cries. (Moving) There's one dead branch on the plum tree.

REUBEN: I'll prune it.

RACHEL: Not now. After it blooms.

REUBEN: He's brought the mugs out. We might go over and have a cup of coffee.

RACHEL: They'd think we're prying.

REUBEN: We'll say we plan to have a garage sale of our own, want to find out how to go about it. We'll buy some little thing and we'll get talking. I'll just happen to mention the time you left me and went to Minneapolis to visit your cousin Opal. I thought I'd lost you, Rachel.

RACHEL: I was lost myself that fall. Nothing seemed right

between us. The house was never tidy. Measles, mumps. John fell off the swing and broke his arm.

REUBEN: That was my fault. I didn't put the swing up right.

RACHEL: That old stove with the oven that wouldn't heat. My cakes always fell. And you . . . you didn't seem to have any time for us — for me.

REUBEN: (Outraged) It was the other way. You shut me out. All your time went to the children. You were so pretty, and you'd turn away . . . Then one day I came home and you'd gone. You and the children.

RACHEL: You knew Opal sent the tickets, Reb.

REUBEN: I didn't think you'd use them. I didn't think you'd go.

RACHEL: I wouldn't have, but you started to help those Legion women paint the hall.

REUBEN: Rae!

RACHEL: Well, it was inconsiderate. Our every night painting away with Jane and Sophy while I'm home cleaning and washing and taking care of . . . How could you do that, Reb? That's awful.

REUBEN: Rae, Jane was old enough to be my mother. And as for Sophy . . . Oh, you're impossible. Taking off on a flimsy excuse like that!

RACHEL: It wasn't flimsy. Not to me! I wanted you to know how it feels to sit home alone.

REUBEN: You managed that all right!

Pause

RACHEL: I only meant to be gone a week, but then I found out the return ticket couldn't be used until a month was up.

REUBEN: You could have written. I would have sent money for tickets.

RACHEL: I was too proud to ask. It seems foolish now.

REUBEN: I'd come home and play the music loud so I wouldn't hear my own feet walking in an empty house.

RACHEL: I thought that month would never end.

REUBEN: You and the children came through that gate, and it was raining.

RACHEL: The door was locked. We never locked the door. I thought you'd gone.

REUBEN: I locked it. To gain time.

RACHEL: To gain time?

REUBEN: I was crying, Rachel. Men weren't allowed to cry.

RACHEL: So that was it. I always wondered. We couldn't tell them about Minneapolis, Reb. That's too personal.

REUBEN: I suppose we couldn't. What about the books? You know, that book on marriage — *Ideal Marriage*. I always thought it did *you* good. And there's another one about mirroring the anger, softening the blow. I could just casually toss them over the fence. They might help.

RACHEL: I think not, Reuben. Best not to interfere. Let things take their course.

REUBEN: They're both out now. She's fed the baby.

RACHEL: Bottle?

REUBEN: Breast.

RACHEL: That's nice.

REUBEN: Yes, she's pretty. Too thin, but pretty.

RACHEL: The baby keeps her thin.

REUBEN: Rachel, if they're breaking up, you don't think . . . They wouldn't give up the baby. Would they?

RACHEL: The Longs did. The minute their garage sale was over, they farmed out all five children, hit and miss. Couldn't get rid of them fast enough.

REUBEN: The baby's back in the laundry basket. These two keep their faces turned away from each other. Their faces are like masks. Did we do that?

RACHEL: We did. Do.

REUBEN: Punishing?

RACHEL: Protecting.

REUBEN: From each other?

RACHEL: From . . . Whatever.

(Pause)

I could finish off this Afghan. Take it over. I'd say "this is for your baby to keep it warm." No. I'd say "this is for you to keep your baby warm."

REUBEN: To protect it from Whatever. Poor baby! They haven't any right to give it up. None at all.

RACHEL: It's their garage sale, Reuben.

REUBEN: Well, if they're looking for a foster home . . . Couldn't we . . . ?

RACHEL: At our age? Social services would never allow such a thing.

REUBEN: We could lie. Say we'd found it somewhere . . . among the asparagus stalks. We could say we're the grandparents. That we're holding it in trust.

RACHEL: We'd get a puppy for it.

REUBEN: Puppy?

RACHEL: A cocker spaniel. They're the best. Remember Foxy. The twins grew up with Foxy. She protected them. Oh Reb, wouldn't it be wonderful? I'd learn to play the auto harp. I'd sing to it.

REUBEN: I'd teach it all that poetry from the Golden Treasury. "They are not long, the weeping and the laughter, Love and desire and hate . . . "

RACHEL: We'd paint the spare bedroom with flowers and little rabbits, and I'd put up a mobile. We never had one.

REUBEN: "And dreaming through the twilight
That doth not rise or set
Haply I may remember, or haply forget."
No, that's too sad. I'd have to brush up on Father William.

RACHEL: There's a high chair in the basement.

REUBEN: He's chain smoking. She's on her knees.

RACHEL: Oh, no. Begging?

REUBEN: Not her. She'd die before she'd beg. She's sorting something.

RACHEL: What?

REUBEN: I can't see. Is it important?

RACHEL: It could be.

REUBEN: Oh, it's nothing. A pile of towels marked *His* and *Hers*.

RACHEL: That used to be the style.

REUBEN: She's looking up this way.

RACHEL: Perhaps she hopes the budgie will come back. Such a beautiful blue it was . . . like a sapphire, flying. Get back!

REUBEN: She can't see me. Classical, her face I mean. Oval, with dark eyes.

RACHEL: Hmm. I hadn't noticed. *(She is jealous)*

REUBEN: *(Oblivious to Rachel's reaction)* "Is this the face that launched a thousand ships And burnt the topless towers of Ilium?" He's handing her a drink. They lift their glasses as if they're toasting one another. Hail and farewell. Ave

831

atque Vale. "I have been faithful to thee, Cynara, in my fashion."

(Sound of cars arriving next door.)

Oh dear, the rummagers are arriving! We haven't much time left!

RACHEL: Time?

REUBEN: To save them from themselves. Rachel! Suppose I bring out The Golden Treasury and pretend I'm reading that poem out loud to you, but louder so they'll hear. Do you suppose that would make a dent?

RACHEL: The one about being faithful?

REUBEN: It's worth a try. It might make them see that they're sitting among the best days of their lives. I'll get that book.

(He starts towards door)

RACHEL: *(Getting up to look across)* I think it's too late, Reb. The sale's begun. It's no time for poetry.

REUBEN: *(Returning)* You're right. They'd never hear me. The rummaging, the twisting and the turning, the hunting down the bargains. It's all begun! There's tags on everything. Oh, oh, there goes the waterbed!

RACHEL: *(Moving away from him in agitation)* I'd better finish this off, in case — you don't think it's too gaudy?

REUBEN: What.

RACHEL: This afghan. For the baby.

REUBEN: No — it's the best one you've fabricated. Far the best. It looks like they've sold the barbecue. Oh, I don't like that.

RACHEL: What!

REUBEN: Someone's taking away the crib.

RACHEL: Where's the baby?

832

REUBEN: Still in the laundry basket. Crang's putting a record on the stereo.

RACHEL: Is there a tag on the basket?

REUBEN: Yes. Yes, there is. They'll probably sell the basket right out from under the baby. Put the baby in a cardboard box. There goes the Yucca tree, thank heaven. She looks pleased.

(Sound of music)

RACHEL: Why do they play their music so loud?

REUBEN: To fill the emptiness. Oh no, no! Hold on there! Hold on.

RACHEL: What's happening?

REUBEN: Someone's looking at the baby. Measuring it. Weighing it. I feel like going over there and . . .

RACHEL: She can't give up that baby. It's not weaned! You can't wean a baby without notice!

REUBEN: They are. There's a bottle in that basket. It's true, Rae. I think it's true. They're giving up that child. A girl not more than seventeen has the baby in one arm and the basket in the other. Money's exchanging hands.

RACHEL: She's much too young. How can they be so irresponsible? Maybe we're much too old. Maybe we're not legal, but we've had experience. We know what babies need.

REUBEN: I'm going over there. I'll tell them what I think of parents who don't live up to their responsibilities.

RACHEL: We'll take it . . . if they have to give it up.

REUBEN: Right.

He starts off

RACHEL: Tell them they don't have to pay us.

REUBEN: We'll pay them.

He goes again

RACHEL: Right. Have you got your check book? In case they want a deposit?

REUBEN: I've got it.

RACHEL: Throw in the jade tree and the National Geographics, Reuben. The China dog. *(To plum tree)* Well, Tree, something important is happening, so forget what I said about not hurrying! *(Indignantly)* Of course we can look after that baby — We'll guard and protect it for them — at least until they come to their senses. There goes Reb! He's so excited. He shouldn't tear off like that, though. It can't be good for his heart. Calm down, Reb. Take it easy. Please. Take your time. He's doing it. He's making an offer!

(She looks through the field glasses.)

Waving his cheque book — telling them about the perambulator and the high chair, ready — waiting. I hope he remembers the puppy. The puppy, Reb. The puppy. Oh dear, they're . . . why, they're . . . How could they? Dear Reb, I should never have let him go and face that loud music all alone. He's looking up this way. I'll pretend I didn't see. *(She puts field glasses down.)* He looks all right, I think. Well, Tree, you can forget what I said about forgetting what I said about . . . better just stand by till I . . . I'll go to meet him. No, he wouldn't want me to. I'd better just stand by too. I'll pretend I'm . . . *(She moves to crocheting, trying to hide her agitation.)* *(REUBEN returns)* Oh, Reb. You're back! I'm just finishing this off. Are you all right?

REUBEN: Fine. I'm fine.

RACHEL: Oh, I'm glad.

REUBEN: It's not what we thought though. Over there. That girl's just a sitter they hired for the day. Until the sale is over.

RACHEL: Oh.

REUBEN: It's not your ordinary garage sale.

RACHEL: Oh.

REUBEN: Young Crang's been transferred. To Thailand.

RACHEL: I see.

REUBEN: They're both going. Taking the baby too. Divesting themselves of everything else, but taking the baby. It's a girl. Good thing I . . . Good thing we . . .

RACHEL: Found out.

REUBEN: Yes. Crang said they wouldn't dream of leaving her behind.

RACHEL: Oh, that's good. But we were standing by — in case — No reason to blame ourselves.

REUBEN: They laughed at me, Rae. When I offered to . . . They all laughed. *(He tries to hide his agitation.)*

RACHEL: That's rude. I hope you . . .

REUBEN: Oh, I carried it off. Pretended I was joking. Said I really came about the trail bike.

RACHEL: Well, you did think about buying that trail bike.

REUBEN: Rae, I went charging in there, shouting about responsibility, waving my cheque book, offering a home for a baby they never thought of giving up. I wanted to sink into the ground.

RACHEL: You couldn't know it wasn't like the Longs.

REUBEN: *(He is very upset)* I offered them money. Just like those pirates in that baby market on the radio. Old fool — meddling in other people's lives. That's what I am. An old fool.

RACHEL: *(Striving to give him back his self-esteem)* You did it for me. I got carried away.

REUBEN: She . . . she felt sorry for me, I think. She asked us to come to see the baby — after the sale. But I couldn't face them again —

RACHEL: *(Resolutely)* Why not? We'll go, Reb. We'll show them we're glad they're a family. We'll take them this afghan. . . . *(Wistfully)* I'd like to see that baby.

REUBEN: Hm. A Hail and Farewell Afghan. Suitable. Oriental word.

RACHEL: It's my last one. My last afghan.

REUBEN: No?

RACHEL: It is. It's time I have my hands free for other things.

REUBEN: Patting?

RACHEL: Men! But I wouldn't want you different, Reb. Where's Thailand?

REUBEN: It's the old Siam. It's on the globe.

RACHEL: You envy them going there.

REUBEN: Oh no. Face it, I'm too old to go traipsing off . . .

RACHEL: Not you. I'm the one. I've been sitting around waiting for a child to come home ever since . . . ever since Doris died. I'm the one, Reb.

REUBEN: You know we could go to Italy, to see Daphne, if you want to.

RACHEL: No. She's busy. But we could go somewhere else.

REUBEN: Nigeria?

RACHEL: John doesn't need us either.

REUBEN: Where then?

RACHEL: Oh, Macedonia. Peru. Wherever. You choose the first step and we'll go on from there.

REUBEN: *(Thinking she's not serious)* You really had your hopes set on that baby, didn't you.

RACHEL: Hah! I forgot about walking the floor at night, croup, measles. Go on, Reb, choose.

REUBEN: You don't think it's too late?

RACHEL: Too late?

REUBEN: Your dream. The missed appointment?

RACHEL: But we'll be together. Go on, Reb, choose.

She spins the globe.

REUBEN: Here goes then. Samothrace! Hah. The isles of Greece. "The Isles of Greece, where burning Sappho loved and sang." Let's go!

RACHEL: Well, we . . . we can't go tomorrow, Reb.

REUBEN: Oh.

RACHEL: First we have to . . . you know . . . get rid of the clutter.

REUBEN: Oh.

RACHEL: Don't we?

REUBEN: I suppose so. Right. But when?

RACHEL: What about — Saturday?

REUBEN: Next Saturday? Why not? We'll have it. We'll put up a sign. "Saturday. Ten o'clock. The Ultimate, Definitive Garage Sale."

The End

George F. Walker
The Art of War

AN ADVENTURE

EDITOR'S NOTE: George F. Walker was born in 1947 in Toronto. In 1970 he submitted his first play, *Prince of Naples*, to Toronto's Factory Theatre Lab. This began an association that has seen *Ambush at Tether's End* (1971), *Sacktown Rag* (1972), *Bagdad Saloon* (1973), *Beyond Mozambique* (1974) and *Ramona and the White Slaves* (1976), among others, produced by the Factory Theatre Lab. With *Ramona and the White Slaves* Walker successfully tried his hand at directing his own work. Others of his plays, including the highly theatrical *Zastrozzi* (1977) and *Gossip* (1977), both of which have had numerous productions outside Canada, have been staged at Toronto Free Theatre or the Tarragon Theatre. Walker directed his own *Theatre of the Film Noir* for Factory Theatre Lab to delighted audiences at the Toronto Theatre Festival (On Stage) in 1981.

The Art of War was commissioned by Simon Fraser University as the keynote address to the Conference on Art and Reality, 10 August 1982. It was first produced professionally by Factory Theatre Lab, Toronto, at Toronto Workshop Productions, in February, 1983.

AUTHOR'S NOTE: In the Toronto production we arranged to play both the Prologue and Scene Six on the patio in front of the bunker. So in fact, in the Prologue the intruder was intercepted and forced outside. And in Scene Six Jamie was caught as he was trying to figure out a way into the bunker. This was done in order to bring both scenes closer to the audience.

Characters:

TYRONE M. POWER	
JAMIE McLEAN	
JOHN HACKMAN	*Late forties*
BROWNIE BROWN	*Hackman's aide; late forties*
KARLA MENDEZ	*Hackman's guest*
HEATHER MASTERSON	*A local citizen*

The Place:

In and around a large summer estate in Nova Scotia. In the dead centre of summer.

Prologue

The murder of Paul Reinhardt.

Choreographed to heartbeat-rushing music.

Just before midnight at JOHN HACKMAN's summer estate. The house is a translucent glass bunker set into the side of a hill. We see a man looking in the front of the bunker. Then disappearing around the side. He is wearing an overcoat and a hat and he walks with a cane. The room is dimly lit, but we can make out a huge map of the world with flickering lights, some high-tech equipment and a few filing cabinets. The man enters from the side. Begins looking around. Takes out a camera and starts photographing everything. Looking through the files. In the distance we hear the voices of two men. Talking. Laughing. Getting closer. The man in the room hears them. Panics. Tries to tidy the room. Gives up. Tries to escape, but can't find an exit other than the one the voices seem to be near. Suddenly and simultaneously the two men are in the room. They are wearing evening clothes. The man in the overcoat throws himself with his arms out against the downstage wall

*of the bunker. It doesn't break and he remains splayed there. One
of the men turns the lights in the room to full. The man in the
overcoat tries to run between them. He is stopped. Thrown back.
One of the men in evening clothes produces a long, thin knife.
Advances. The man in the overcoat tries to rush out past him. He
is stopped. Stabbed. Stabbed again. He falls. The two men in
evening clothes look at each other. Then one turns away.*

Blackout.

SCENE ONE

*Midnight. The beach. Two figures approaching. HACKMAN is
carrying a flashlight. BROWN is carrying a corpse wrapped in a
blanket over his shoulder.*

HACKMAN: Is he heavy, Brown?

BROWN: No, sir. Light as a feather. A burden of love.

HACKMAN: Anywhere around here should do. Put him
down.

BROWN drops the corpse. HACKMAN starts to dig

BROWN: I'll do that, sir. You'll get yourself covered in sand.

HACKMAN: Thank you, Brown.

(*HACKMAN hands BROWN the shovel. BROWN starts to
dig*)

It's a lovely night, isn't it?

BROWN: Yes, sir. Shame to waste it in the company of
strangers.

HACKMAN: Oh he's no stranger, Brown. He's the enemy.

BROWN: He *was* the enemy . . . And not a very good one if I
may say so, sir.

HACKMAN: You killed him well, Brown. He didn't have a chance.

BROWN: Thank you, sir.

HACKMAN: Reminded me of the killing you used to do in the old days.

BROWN: Afraid I'm a little out of practice. Had to stick it in twice.

HACKMAN: Well perhaps you rushed it a bit. Didn't take time to appreciate the act fully. Nevertheless, it was an exciting thing to watch. It had an artistic touch. You're a bit of an artist in your own way, did you know that Brown.

BROWN: Never thought of it that way, sir.

HACKMAN: You can you know, from now on, if you want.

BROWN: I'm not much on art and artists, sir.

HACKMAN: Well it's all how you look at it. I suppose I'll be meeting a lot of artists in my new job. Most of them won't be very good I imagine. This dead man was an artist of sorts. A writer.

BROWN: How deep do you want this, sir?

HACKMAN: Oh not too deep. I don't suppose anyone will be looking for him. Yes. It's a lovely night. Stop for a moment, Brown. Look at it. The night.

BROWN stops. Looks around vacantly. Then looks at the corpse. Smiles

BROWN: Why you're right, sir. It is.

HACKMAN: You see, Brown. You just have to take the time to appreciate things. A lovely night. A lovely killing.

BROWN starts to dig. Blackout.

SCENE TWO

Dawn. On a nearby cliff. POWER and JAMIE. POWER is look-
ing down through a pair of binoculars. JAMIE is sitting on the
grass, chin in his palms. There is a pile of camping gear nearby.

POWER is middle-aged. Balding. With a walrus moustache.
Glasses. Wearing an overcoat. JAMIE is in his early twenties. Sort
of wiry. In jeans and a sweater.

JAMIE: What are you doing?

POWER: Looking for signs of strange behaviour.

JAMIE: Well you can look at us, Power. I'd say our behaviour is pretty strange. Sitting on top of a cliff a thousand
miles from home at five o'clock in the morning.

POWER: The guy who lives down there is a maniac.

JAMIE: You seem to be developing an obsession with him.
Why?

POWER: He's a maniac. Whatya mean, obsession. I'm not
obsessed. He's up to something, that's all. Something vile
and dangerous I'll bet. He needs to be watched.

JAMIE: Then maybe we should tell the authorities.

POWER: "Authorities"?! You make it sound like an agency of
the Lord or something. This guy down there, this John C.
Hackman, retired general, is the authority. He's an advisor to a goddamn cabinet minister in the goddamn
government. And he's a maniac. When he was advisor to
the Minister of Defence he was suspected of cooking up
bizarre arms deals with lunatic Third World politicos and
military types.

JAMIE: That's why he was fired?

POWER: He wasn't fired. They just got him off the front
pages. They shuffled him over to the Minister of Culture.

JAMIE: I didn't know we had a Minister of Culture. What
does he do.

842

POWER: It's a secret. I'm not even sure the Minister of Culture knows. It's not exactly a high-priority position. And just to prove it they make Hackman his special advisor. The guy is a career soldier. His idea of a cultural event is bombing an opera house.

JAMIE: I think your bias is screwing up your judgement, as usual. I haven't noticed anything strange about him.

POWER: You've only been working for him for a week. He's being cautious around you. Checking out your references. Did you take care of your references.

JAMIE: No problem.

POWER: Be more specific.

JAMIE: When they check they'll find that I've been a gardener at some of the best homes in the area.

POWER: How did you manage that.

JAMIE: As one private detective to another, it took some doin' but it was done.

POWER: Look. How many times do I have to tell you. We're not private detectives. I'm just a concerned citizen. And you're a punk who follows me around.

JAMIE: Well at least I'm a punk with a job. Good thing my cover on this one is to be gainfully employed because I'm starting to get the impression we don't have a client. We stand to make zippo on this case. Unless your friend Reinhardt is going to pay us.

POWER: Reinhardt is dead. Hackman killed him.

JAMIE: You know this for sure.

POWER: I sense it for sure.

JAMIE: All you know is he hasn't come home.

POWER: He told me he was coming down here because he had a tip that Hackman was up to something. Reinhardt was the kind to dig in. He'd go right into the belly of the mess and all its danger. He wasn't subtle, but he was a good newspaperman.

JAMIE: Oh Jesus. You knew this guy Reinhardt when you were a reporter. You didn't tell me that. Is he your age.

POWER: Just about. Why.

JAMIE: For chrissake, Power. He's probably a disillusioned paranoid drunk just like you were when I met you.

POWER: Shut up.

JAMIE: You're all the same. That generation of yours. Scandals in every corner. Corruption on every level. I'm going home. If Reinhardt is dead, he died of alcohol poisoning.

POWER: Reinhardt didn't drink. He was a whatyacallit.

JAMIE: A junkie?

POWER: Shut up. He was Born Again.

JAMIE: Yeah. Well I was only born once but it wasn't yesterday. And I'm not putting my life in jeopardy under these increasingly dubious circumstances. You led me to believe this was a simple job of observation and that there was a lot of money to be made.

POWER: Because that's the only way I can get you to do anything. By talking about financial profit. You're a greedy money-grabbing amoral smart-ass.

JAMIE: And you're a cause in search of an issue. Life is precious, Power. I don't want to waste it trying to reconstruct your social conscience.

POWER: The quality of life is precious. Life itself is meaningless.

JAMIE: Quality is defined by quantity. Money buys you both.

POWER: No. Money is just —

JAMIE: I don't want to talk about this on this goddamn cliff at five o'clock in the morning!

POWER: Fine. We won't. We'll just do our jobs. You will report back to work at Hackman's and keep your eyes and ears open and I'll continue my investigation.

JAMIE: Why.

POWER: Why for me. Or why for you.

JAMIE: Just why.

POWER: Why for me is I think Hackman is up to something evil, dangerous, and destructive. Why for you is because you're the smart-ass punk who has been following me around for a year and a half and is now going to do something to pay me back for letting you do it.

JAMIE: Wrong. Why for me is I'm learning a trade. Because realize it or not you're not the useless investigative reporter you used to be. You've become a pretty fair detective and I'm your partner.

POWER: All right. Look at life in your own strange brittle romantic way. You're a hard case. Just do your job. And when I show up at Hackman's try to avoid recognizing me.

JAMIE: How are you going to get in there.

POWER: I think I've got a contact in the town who can help me. I'm meeting her for breakfast. I've got to get going.

JAMIE: Why so early.

POWER: Because it's five miles and I have to walk.

JAMIE: Why didn't you rent a car.

POWER: With what. I spent almost everything I had on my camping gear.

JAMIE: We're pitiful. We're pathetic. We're poor. And why. Because you take these cases where there's no money involved.

POWER: I'm poor because I'm a freelance writer with diminishing talent. You're poor because you won't work. You just follow me around. Reality, boy. Try it out. Good-bye. *(starts off, stops)* Do me a favour. Throw my tent.

JAMIE: Where.

POWER: Right where it is.

JAMIE: Oh you mean put it up.

POWER: That's what I said.

JAMIE: The expression is "pitch the tent," Power. Not "throw it." Your grasp of contemporary idiom is scary.

POWER: Goodbye.

POWER leaves. JAMIE starts to unpack the camping gear.

JAMIE: "Reality, boy. Try it out." The man's in middle-age standing on top of a cliff talking about politicians and Third World lunatics and the quality of life and he worries about my sense of reality. He's gotta be kidding. What's this.

(From inside a duffle-bag he produces a rifle with a telescopic sight on it.)

He's gotta be kidding. Seriously.

Blackout.

SCENE THREE

Midday. The patio and garden of HACKMAN's house. HACKMAN, in shirtsleeves, is sitting in a lawn chair reading a newspaper.

KARLA MENDEZ is pacing. She is a tall, dark, angular woman in her late thirties. Tastefully, simply dressed. Wearing dark glasses. She speaks with a slight accent.

KARLA: The phone is not ringing.

HACKMAN: Be patient.

KARLA: He was to call at noon. It is now noon plus twenty.

HACKMAN: He'll call.

KARLA: I think something has happened. At the airport. It always happens at the airport.

HACKMAN: You worry too much. His papers are in order. I arranged them myself.

KARLA: You are not God.

HACKMAN: I never said I was.

KARLA: You speak sometimes like God. "I did *that*. So this is what will happen." "I made this arrangement so it is all right." Only God can make these assurances and you are not God. You are only a politician. You work for the "minister of culture." *(laughs abruptly)*

HACKMAN: How many more jokes are you going to make about that.

KARLA: I think it is funny. I think it is ridiculous.

HACKMAN: Ridiculous enough to be out of the limelight. But not too ridiculous to keep the connections that allow me to make certain arrangements.

KARLA: We'll see. If he calls. We'll see.

HACKMAN: Stop pacing.

KARLA: I'm making you nervous?

HACKMAN: It's annoying.

KARLA: Do I care. Did I ask to be sent here.

HACKMAN: I thought you did. I thought you wanted to be close to me.

KARLA: I have not wanted to be close to you for over three years. Being close to you is being close to disappointment.

HACKMAN: Remember the month we spent together in Panama City?

KARLA: No. See? I am over you. I even have no memory of you.

HACKMAN: In Panama City you were not disappointed.

KARLA: You misunderstand what I mean by disappointment. You misunderstand what I mean by everything. I should have taken my father's advice about you.

HACKMAN: What did he say.

KARLA: He said "Keep it strictly business with that man. He is good for business. Bad for everything else."

HACKMAN: Your father is a great man and he will be a great leader for your people but about things that concern you he has no judgement. He's just a father.

KARLA: Nevertheless. You soon proved him right. Several times in fact.

HACKMAN: Fidelity. That's what this is about. Loyalty to you.

KARLA: Or to anything. *(checks her watch)* Call the airport. Perhaps the flight is delayed.

HACKMAN: If it's delayed, it's delayed. Be patient. He'll call.

(JAMIE comes on, walking by, pushing a wheelbarrow full of rocks)

You. Stop. Excuse me, what's your name again?

JAMIE: Jamie. Jamie McLean.

HACKMAN: Yes. Well, Jamie. Would you mind telling me what you're doing.

JAMIE: Taking these rocks over to that flower bed.

HACKMAN: Aren't those the same rocks you removed from that flower bed yesterday.

JAMIE: No, sir. These are the rocks I took from around the shrubs out front and put around the rose bushes at the side. The rocks I took from that flower bed I put around the shrubs out front. You're probably wondering what rocks I'm going to put back around the rose bushes now that these are gone.

HACKMAN: No, I'm wondering why, since you've been employed as my gardener for over a week, all you've done is move rocks around.

JAMIE: It's my personal concept in gardening. Work from the outside in. Get the look of it before you deal with the substance.

KARLA: Typically North American.

HACKMAN: Some of the roses are dying.

JAMIE: Don't worry about it, sir. They'll be all right as soon as I get the right rocks in place. Roses are sensitive. They know they're not yet properly showcased.

HACKMAN: You're not a flake are you, Jamie. You talk like a flake.

JAMIE: Trust me, sir.

HACKMAN: You come highly recommended. But you talk like a flake and you seem to be obsessed with rocks.

JAMIE: Trust me, sir. I'm an innovator.

HACKMAN: See that's what I mean. "I'm an innovator." What kind of thing is that for a gardener to say.

JAMIE: Sorry. Would you prefer I kept my conversation more rustic.

KARLA: Really, John. So much fuss over a bunch of flowers.

HACKMAN: I'm very fond of my garden! It's a kind of passion.

(The phone rings. It is on a small table next to HACKMAN. He answers it.)

(on phone) Yes . . . Good . . . Yes . . . Goodbye. *(hangs up; to KARLA)* He's here. You should leave. He's expecting you.

KARLA: Where.

HACKMAN: The airport.

KARLA: The airport?

HACKMAN: Yes. *(to JAMIE)* Excuse me.

JAMIE: Yeah.

HACKMAN: Why are you standing there.

JAMIE: Awaiting further instructions, sir. Are there any.

HACKMAN: Yes. Stop messing around with rocks. And take care of my garden. I love my garden! Understand?

JAMIE: *(gulps)* You bet. Goodbye ma'am. Goodbye, sir.

JAMIE goes off, leaving the wheelbarrow

HACKMAN: Yes. The airport.

KARLA: Dangerous.

HACKMAN: It's arranged. I'm having him watched. I don't want him leaving there. He'll be too hard to follow.

KARLA: I don't like doing this kind of business in public places.

HACKMAN: Just go. It's arranged.

KARLA: You go.

HACKMAN: He won't talk to me. It has to be you. That's why you were sent here. Now go.

(KARLA stares at him for a moment. Then starts off)

Oh Karla.

KARLA: What.

HACKMAN reaches under his lawn chair. Produces an attaché case

HACKMAN: It's money. He'll want money.

KARLA: No he won't.

HACKMAN: He's doing this for money, Karla.

KARLA: I don't believe that. He's doing it out of loyalty to my father.

HACKMAN: Well if you're absolutely sure, don't take it.

KARLA mutters an obscenity. She grabs the attaché case. Leaves. HACKMAN returns to his newspaper. JAMIE comes back on sheepishly. Starts to push wheelbarrow off quietly. HACKMAN peers over his newspaper. JAMIE catches his eye

JAMIE: I don't have any plans for these rocks, sir. It's just that I need the wheelbarrow for . . . for . . . dirt.

HACKMAN: Dirt?

JAMIE: Soil.

HACKMAN disappears behind the newspaper. JAMIE leaves. Shaking his head. BROWN comes on. In a crisp business suit

BROWN: Heather Masterson is here to see you.

HACKMAN: Send her away.

BROWN: She claims to have an appointment.

HACKMAN: She's lying. I'm on vacation. This is my summer residence. I don't make appointments here.

BROWN: You do when you are very drunk, sir. You were at a party together last Wednesday night. You probably made the appointment then.

HACKMAN: Let her in.

BROWN goes off. JAMIE comes on carrying a small bush. Whistling. Crosses in front of HACKMAN. HACKMAN watches him leave. HEATHER MASTERSON and POWER come out of the house onto the patio. She is in her late twenties. Preppy. POWER is in shirtsleeves. His coat thrown over his shoulder. Hands in his pockets. Sweating

HEATHER: Good morning, General.

HACKMAN: Hello.

HEATHER: I'm glad you remembered I was coming. I was afraid you wouldn't. *(to POWER)* The General came to my birthday party last week. He and my daddy are old friends. My daddy got him a little bit loaded and I decided to take the opportunity to bamboozle an official appointment. *(to HACKMAN)* Oh, I'm sorry. This is Mr Power. He was just dying to meet you and I didn't think you'd mind. Do you mind?

HACKMAN: I'm not sure.

(HACKMAN looks POWER over. Then extends a hand. They shake)

Mr Power.

POWER: General. I've followed your career for many years.

HACKMAN: Idle curiosity?

HEATHER: Mr Power is a writer.

HACKMAN: Really. Of what?

HEATHER: Oh you can talk to him in a minute. I've got the official appointment, remember.

HACKMAN: Very well. Would you like to sit down.

HEATHER: No thanks.

POWER: I will if you don't mind. I had a long walk this morning. And I think I'm dying. *(sits in a lawn chair)*

HEATHER: You're about twenty pounds overweight.

POWER: It's the fresh air. They say it's like poison if you're not used to it.

HEATHER: A man your age has to be careful. My daddy is careful.

POWER: Your daddy is rich. He can afford to be careful. I'm poor. I have to take chances.

852

HEATHER: I didn't get that. *(to HACKMAN)* Did you?

HACKMAN: Heather. I thought you had something to ask me. I've got a busy day ahead of me.

HEATHER: Right. Sorry. Well as you know I am a member of the local historical board. It's great. It's local. It's historical.

(POWER looks at her.)

And we have been trying unsuccessfully for two years to open our own museum. So when we found out that you had been made an advisor to the Minister of Culture we were sure you could —

HACKMAN: Excuse me. *(picks up his phone, buzzes)* Brownie, get out here. *(hangs up)* This might save us both some time.

(BROWN comes out)

Do we have anything to do with the allocation of funds to museums.

BROWN: No sir. Minister of Education handles that.

HACKMAN: Sorry, Heather.

HEATHER: But surely the Minister of Culture —

HACKMAN: Heather. It's a new position. Just created. We don't know exactly what it means yet ourselves. *(laughs)*

POWER: When will you.

HACKMAN: I beg your pardon.

POWER: When can we expect an official statement of the Minister's responsibilities.

HACKMAN: You asked that question like a journalist, Mr. Power.

POWER: Is that good.

HEATHER: Listen, General, I promised the Historical Board that you would help.

HACKMAN: Heather. That conversation is over.

HEATHER: Well that really pisses me off. You didn't even listen, and that really is a piss-off! I'm leaving! I mean it.

(Pause, no response. She starts off)

I'll wait for you in the car Mr Power.

She leaves. BROWN starts to follow her. HACKMAN signals him to stay. BROWN stands beside HACKMAN. Arms folded.

HACKMAN: The name Power sounds familiar . . .

(BROWN whispers in HACKMAN's ear. HACKMAN smiles)

There was a T.M. Power who used to write a syndicated political column. Is that you.

POWER: Yes.

HACKMAN: I hated every word you wrote.

POWER: In my own way, so did I.

HACKMAN: Hated with a passion. Hated all journalism. Hated the media in general. Of course that was when I was advisor to the Minister of Defense. Now that I'm working for the Minister of Culture I have a different attitude.

POWER: You just don't give a damn. Politically speaking, I mean.

HACKMAN: The Minister of Culture officially supports the power of the written word. And the spoken word.

POWER: What about song lyrics.

HACKMAN: *(smiles)* Oh, he has a Deputy Minister that handles music. I'm afraid the Minister is a bit of an ignoramus in that area.

POWER: Please don't apologize for him. I mean think about it. There are only twelve notes. Musicians just move them around. What's all the fuss.

HACKMAN: I get the feeling you sometimes speak to hear your own voice, Mr Power.

POWER: It's a habit I got into when I was covering the capital. Talking to politicians. There was nothing coming my way. I had to compensate.

HACKMAN: Why did you want to meet me.

POWER: I'm working freelance now. I'm fishing around for something to write about.

HACKMAN: You think the creation of a minister of culture is a joke.

POWER: Don't you?

HACKMAN: What do you know about me.

POWER: You're a soldier.

HACKMAN: I was a soldier.

POWER: Some old soldiers never die. They just start pan-American right-wing organizations.

HACKMAN: That of course is an old and unfounded rumour.

POWER: Then why were you moved off the defence portfolio.

HACKMAN: I wanted a change. A chance for a middle-aged man to develop a new passion.

POWER: Come off it, General. Men like you have room for only one passion in their lives. And yours is not art and culture.

HACKMAN: What is it then.

POWER: Oh God. Well let's simplify it. Let's call it the communist menace.

HACKMAN: (groans) And you don't believe in the communist menace.

POWER: Actually I do. The communist menace. And the fascist menace. The menace of the church. The menace of

855

channelled information. The menace of ignorance. The menace of indifference. The menace of war. I'm sort of a menace specialist.

HACKMAN: No. You're just a liberal.

POWER: What's that supposed to mean.

HACKMAN: You think the human race is going on a journey. To peace and enlightenment. And that it's a journey everyone has the ability and the right to make.

POWER: And you don't.

HACKMAN: Let's just say I don't insist upon it. And another thing. You probably have an unholy fear of something which I take more or less for granted.

POWER: What.

HACKMAN: The vast darkness.

BROWN looks at POWER. Smiles.

POWER: The vast darkness. The existential version?

HACKMAN: No, let's simplify it. Let's call it war. The new war. The inevitable destruction of everything. Life-ending war. But even without war, it ends. Everything we build now will be ruins in, what, a thousand years, anyway.

(HACKMAN looks at BROWN. BROWN gestures a shrug with his hand)

War is a way of taking temporary control, that's all. Try thinking about war that way and it won't scare you so much. Something wrong?

POWER is rubbing his forehead

POWER: I've suddenly developed one hell of a headache.

HACKMAN signals BROWN

BROWN: Sir, it's getting late. You have several letters to dictate. And a telephone call to make. Miss Masterson is waiting in the car for this gentleman. And also . . . also . . . *(rubs his head)*

HACKMAN: *(checks his watch)* I didn't realize it was getting so late.

POWER: Time flies when you're talking about fun stuff.

BROWN is rubbing his head furiously.

HACKMAN: Are you all right, Brownie.

BROWN: Sir. In a minute sir.

POWER: What's wrong with him.

BROWN: *(advancing)* War wound!

HACKMAN: Quite serious when it flares up.

POWER: Sorry to hear that.

POWER rubs his own forehead. Stands. HACKMAN puts his arm around POWER

HACKMAN: Look, Mr Power, if you're going to be around for a few days perhaps we could talk again. Actually I'd like to insist upon it. If you're going to write anything about me, I'd like a chance to balance some of your preconceptions. Next time we'll talk about art not war. You'll see that there's more to me than most people think.

POWER: Oh I'm not sure of that.

HACKMAN: I really want to make the Department of Culture work. You could say I'm like anyone else who's new on the job and anxious to make a good impression. How can I reach you.

POWER: Through Heather.

HACKMAN: You're staying with the Mastersons?

POWER: No. But I'll be contacting her.

HACKMAN: Then where are you staying.

POWER: Around. Here and there.

HACKMAN: Why so secretive?

POWER: Habit.

(POWER frees himself from HACKMAN. Starts off. Stops.)

By the way. How did you get on with Paul Reinhardt.

HACKMAN: I'm sorry. I don't know what you mean. Who is he.

POWER: A journalist friend of mine. He was coming down here to interview you. Never showed up, eh?

HACKMAN: Not as far as I know. Brownie?

BROWN: No, sir.

POWER: Odd. *(rubs his head)*

HACKMAN: How bad is that headache.

POWER: I'll live.

HACKMAN: That's it. Think positively.

BROWN: I'll show you out. *(rubs his forehead again)*

POWER: No thanks. I can find my own way. You better get some rest.

BROWN just looks at him. POWER leaves.

HACKMAN: Three things. Find out what he's been up to since he stopped writing that ridiculous column. Find out what his connection is to Heather Masterson. Find out what he and our late friend Paul Reinhardt had in common besides the fact that they were both bad writers.

(JAMIE walks by carrying a bunch of flowers)

What are you doing with those flowers.

858

JAMIE: It's a surprise, sir. *(leaves)*

HACKMAN: One more thing. Check that kid's references out again. He's murdering my garden. I love that garden!

Blackout.

SCENE FOUR

Late evening. On the cliff. The tent is up. The area is lit by a gas lantern placed on a camping-stool.

POWER is lying unconscious on his sleeping bag, half in and half out of the tent. An empty liquor bottle beside him. Sound of someone approaching. JAMIE comes on, cautiously.

JAMIE: Power? Power, it's me. Don't shoot. *(sees POWER)* Tyrone. *(goes to him)* He's dead. *(bends down)* He's dead drunk. I knew it would come to this. The man has no self-discipline. He is doomed to a life of self-abuse. *(shakes POWER)* Power. Power, wake up, you're disgusting.

(POWER whimpers, twitches)

Don't whimper. It's really pitiful when you whimper. Wake up. *(shakes him)*

POWER raises an arm. Speaks just above a whisper

POWER: Leave me alone.

JAMIE: Wake up!

POWER: Leave me alone. Please! *(whimpers)*

JAMIE: Stop whimpering!

JAMIE shakes him violently. POWER sits up suddenly

POWER: What's going on?!

859

(JAMIE stands. Moves away.)

What were you doing. Trying to pick my pocket? Looking for loose change?

JAMIE: You were having a bad dream. I thought I'd better wake you up,

POWER: What time is it. I must have dozed off.

JAMIE: Give me a break. You were drunk. You passed out. I thought you were through with the booze. Don't you know how disgusting you are when you drink.

POWER: A temporary relapse.

JAMIE: How many times do I have to tell you. You're an alcoholic. You have a serious drinking problem.

POWER is getting up slowly

POWER: No, you have a serious drinking problem. A man has a few sips and you get all sweaty and start sermonizing. You have an unnatural fear that anyone who touches liquor will turn out like your father.

JAMIE: Leave my father out of this.

POWER: Look, Jamie. All I'm saying is that I'm not a common drunk like he was.

POWER is pouring himself a coffee from a thermos

JAMIE: Oh no. Not you. You drink for the pain in the universe and the soul of mankind. You're not a common drunk. You're a common pretentious drunk.

POWER: It was Hackman. He drove me to it.

JAMIE: Power. I was eavesdropping. I overheard your entire conversation. He sounded perfectly rational. You sounded perfectly obnoxious.

POWER: He drove me to being obnoxious. His kind always does. A knee-jerk reaction. What do you mean he sounded rational. Didn't you hear him talking about the vast darkness.

JAMIE: He was egging you on. It was a joke.

POWER: It was no joke. It was his definition of reality. He was speaking from the heart of his moral code.

JAMIE: I didn't understand a word of it.

POWER: That's because you don't have a moral code of your own to cross-reference with. He was speaking from the heart of his moral code and the heart of my moral code picked up the signals and got very, very depressed.

JAMIE: And made you go out and buy a bottle of scotch.

POWER: No. I had it with me. I had a feeling I might need it before we were through.

JAMIE: Yeah. Well, anticipation is the better part of cowardice.

POWER: I'm not afraid of him. He just depresses me.

JAMIE: Oh yeah?

(JAMIE picks up the duffle bag and takes out the rifle)

Well if you're not afraid of him what are you doing with this.

POWER: He killed Reinhardt. I know he killed him. I had a feeling about it when I was there. A kind of mental picture. And he's up to something!

JAMIE: Are you going to shoot him down, Power.

POWER: Someone has to shoot him down.

JAMIE: What?

POWER: I was speaking metaphorically.

JAMIE: Oh, so this is a metaphor. It's not a rifle. And you're not going to shoot him because you're not afraid of him even though you saw him kill your friend Reinhardt in one of your moments of psychic clarity because he's up to something which is vaguely concerned with some lunatic Third World politico and you want to find out what it is. Or maybe you don't want to find out what it is. You just want to create a mental metaphor for what it is. Then why do you have this *fucking rifle!*

POWER: Because he's dangerous!

JAMIE: And you're afraid of him!

POWER: Yes!

JAMIE: Thank you. I thank you. All of us who desperately believe in holding on to reality thank you. *(pause)* Power?

POWER: What?

JAMIE: I'm afraid of him too.

POWER: Why. What did he say.

JAMIE: It's not what he says. It's how he says it. And it's who he hangs around with. That guy Brown.

POWER: Killer eyes.

JAMIE: Yeah. You noticed them, eh. He's an ex-commando. A sergeant-major.

POWER: How'd you find that out.

JAMIE: He told me.

POWER: Exchanging pleasantries?

JAMIE: I think it was a threat. There's a room in that house full of filing cabinets and high-tech machinery that I'm not even allowed to go near. It was his way of explaining why it's not guarded. Sort of a challenge. "I'm an ex-commando and you're a skinny little kid. You want to try sneaking in that room late at night you better bring an army." I got the message. So, Power, if you're going to suggest I do some after-hours snooping, don't.

POWER: Off-limits, eh. Private chambers, eh. What did I tell you. A nefarious sneaky dangerous vile disgusting plot!

JAMIE: Calm down. Maybe it's just where he keeps his love letters.

POWER: Love? Him? Mr Vast Darkness. I can't imagine him having sex. Unless he's drilled a hole in an I.C.B.M.

JAMIE: There is a lady. She's staying there.

POWER: What's her name.

JAMIE: Karla.

POWER: Her last name.

JAMIE: Don't know.

POWER: What's she look like.

JAMIE: Terrific.

POWER: Be a little more specific.

JAMIE: Tall. Dark. Intense. Terrific.

POWER: Did she have an accent.

JAMIE: Sort of.

POWER: What kind.

JAMIE: Foreign.

POWER: You've got a mind like a computer.

JAMIE: I meant foreign in a general way. As a way of saying I couldn't pinpoint it.

POWER: Mendez. Karla Mendez. It could be her. And you think they're lovers?

JAMIE: Well there was something going on between them. I could sense it. It was kind of exciting. He's different with her. Still dangerous but also kind of warm somehow.

POWER: Shut up. You're making me sick.

JAMIE: Sure. I know. I'm sensitive to those things in a way you're not. You're good at sensing paranoid things like death and misery. That's why you won't live long. That's why you're a disgusting drunk.

POWER: And you're a romantic fool. Put any man and any woman together and you have a delirious feeling of self-projection. Have you asked her to walk on your face yet.

JAMIE: You hate women, don't you.

POWER: Look. Crawl out of my subconscious, will you. Why are you always saying things like that to me.

JAMIE: Because you've never had a successful romance and I think that has a lot to do with your problems. Besides, you started it.

POWER: I was just trying to bring you back to earth. You were falling in love with Karla Mendez or at least falling in love with the idea of falling in love which is more your style, and that could be very dangerous.

JAMIE: Why.

POWER: She's a terrorist. And a fascist. The daughter of a supreme fascist. A killer. Her father's in prison and she's wanted all over the world.

JAMIE: Sure. And she's sitting down there casually as a guest of Hackman's.

POWER: Why not? Who could see her.

JAMIE: Me. I saw her.

POWER: But you're just a gardener.

JAMIE: Yeah. But even so —

POWER: Shush. Someone's coming.

(Someone is)

Quick. The rifle. Pick it up.

JAMIE: You pick it up.

POWER: Pick it up and point it.

JAMIE: It's your rifle. You pick it up.

POWER: I hate guns. You know I hate guns. You're the one who loves guns. Now pick it up. Someone's out there.

JAMIE: I don't love guns.

POWER: Oh you do so. You love them. Playing with them. Talking about them. Being a private eye. Being tough. Using force. Except now when we might be killed. Now pick up that goddamn rifle!!

JAMIE: All right!

JAMIE picks it up. POWER gets behind JAMIE

POWER: Who's out there.

HEATHER appears from behind the tent

HEATHER: It's just me.

POWER: Oh, hello. What are you doing out here so late.

HEATHER: Tyrone, would you mind asking your friend to lower the rifle.

POWER: It's okay, Jamie . . . Jamie.

But JAMIE is in love. He is smiling like a moron. POWER looks at JAMIE. Looks at HEATHER. At JAMIE. Shakes his head. Takes the rifle from JAMIE.

JAMIE: Is she a terrorist too.

POWER: No.

JAMIE: Good.

HEATHER: What's going on here. *(to JAMIE)* You're the General's new gardener. *(to POWER)* What's he doing here.

JAMIE: Moonlighting. I thought I'd earn a few extra bucks by offering to landscape this gentleman's campsite. Now if we put a few rocks over there —

POWER: Shut up, Jamie. It's all right, Heather.

JAMIE: Is she on our side.

POWER: Yes.

JAMIE: Good.

HEATHER: I don't understand.

POWER: He works for me.

JAMIE: Actually I work *with* him. Can I get you a seat. Some coffee. How about something to eat.

POWER: Good idea, Jamie. Cook us up a three-course meal. The stove's over there.

(JAMIE goes over and starts to putter around with the stove.)

What is it, Heather?

HEATHER: Hackman called. You're invited to dinner tomorrow night.

POWER: Good.

HEATHER: He also grilled me for a while about how I knew you.

POWER: Do you think he suspects you.

HEATHER: No. He thinks I'm an airhead. That's why he bought all that crap about the local museum so easily. He suspects you though. But that might be all right. He thinks you're just down here to do a journalistic hatchet job on him.

JAMIE is approaching them

JAMIE: That's the idea. Everything is right in place. I'm in place. Tyrone's in place. And now you're in place.

HEATHER: Who is this guy, anyway.

JAMIE takes her hand.

JAMIE: Jamie McLean. I'm his partner.

HEATHER: Partner in what.

POWER: We're still working out the details.

HEATHER: Why didn't you tell me about him.

JAMIE: Hey. That's his style. Close to the vest. You gotta respect it. It gets results. He didn't tell me about you either. What's your part in this.

POWER: Heather is a friend of Paul Reinhardt's.

JAMIE: Ahhh. . . You were his girlfriend.

HEATHER: What do you mean "were"! Oh my God. You've found out that he's dead, haven't you Tyrone . . . (staggers)

POWER: Here, sit down.

(POWER helps her onto the camping-stool)

Good work, Jamie.

JAMIE: I'm sorry.

JAMIE goes behind the tent. Sits.

HEATHER: I knew. He had to be dead. He left me that night to sneak into Hackman's house. And when he didn't come back I knew. What else would Hackman do. How did you find out.

POWER: I didn't. But I'm sure he is, Heather.

HEATHER: But to get Hackman we have to prove it.

POWER: We will.

JAMIE: We will?

HEATHER: How?

JAMIE: Yeah, how?

POWER: Patience. We'll let Hackman make some moves first. I want the larger picture of what he's up to. Paul would have wanted it that way.

HEATHER: Ah come on, Tyrone. Paul was no crusader like you. He just wanted Hackman's balls on the line because it would have been a good story. He was a good reporter but he had no mission. Just get Hackman. I feel so damn guilty. It was me who tipped Paul off that Hackman was up to something.

POWER: Why didn't you tell me that before.

HEATHER: Because I thought my father might be involved. It was something I heard them talking about.

POWER: Go ahead.

HEATHER: My father. Can you leave him out of this.

POWER: Should I?

HEATHER: Jesus. I don't know. I think Hackman was after his help. I don't think my father was directly involved. Hackman just wanted money from him.

POWER: Your father shares a lot of Hackman's views.

HEATHER: Well they're from the same old world, Tyrone. But I think my father's ideas about how to sustain that world stop short of forming private armies and things like that.

JAMIE: Private armies? I don't like the sound of that.

POWER: That's why Mendez is in prison. He was forming a large illegal mercenary force. The rumour is that Hackman was a "consultant". Heather, what did Hackman want the money from your father for.

HEATHER: I can't say for sure. I could speculate.

POWER: Me too. Maybe to get someone out of prison in a foreign country? An operation like that could cost a lot of money.

HEATHER: Simón Mendez.

POWER: Simón Mendez. Yes.

HEATHER: Right. That's what Paul thought too.

POWER: Why.

HEATHER: Because he found out Karla Mendez was staying with Hackman.

POWER: For chrissake. Paul went into Hackman's place knowing that Karla Mendez was there. Was he insane.

HEATHER: You're going there tomorrow night for dinner! Are you insane.

POWER has wandered over to the cliff's edge. Is staring down

JAMIE: No he's on a mission.

POWER: Not me. Hackman's the only one with a mission. And to make it he's got to play a dicey double-edged game. He's got to stay close enough to government circles to be useful to his fascist friends and that means convincing sceptics like me that he really is nothing more now than the insignificant advisor to an insignificant minister of culture. But at the same time he's got to make his moves. This operation doesn't begin or end with setting Mendez free. They're going on to make some big insurgent move somewhere. He's afraid of me. Afraid of what I'll write. So he wants to talk cultural policy and convince me. I'll let him. And then maybe he'll think I'll write something that will convince everyone else. And then he'll make his moves with a confidence. And then I'll get him. And I'll get Mendez. And I'll get everything they both stand for.

JAMIE: But it's good to know you don't have a mission.

POWER: There's something going on down there on the beach in front of Hackman's place. Hand me the rifle.

869

JAMIE: No way. You've worked yourself into a frenzy, Power. You can't just shoot him.

POWER: The telescopic sight is infrared.

JAMIE: So what.

POWER: It sees in the dark. It was the only way I could get one. I had to buy the whole rifle. Hand it over.

JAMIE hands it to him. POWER looks through it.

JAMIE: Well? . . . Well?

POWER: It doesn't work. Nothing I buy ever works. Have you noticed that. That new typewriter I bought last month doesn't work.

JAMIE: That "new" typewriter is twelve years old.

POWER: But I bought it. And it doesn't work. I bet it worked before I bought it. Life does things like that to people like me. Why is that. Why doesn't life do things like that to people like Hackman. Think about it. I want you to think about that. I'm going down there for a closer look. *(leaves)*

HEATHER: You shouldn't let him go by himself.

JAMIE: He likes to be alone when he's like this. He likes to ask himself questions like why does life do these things to me and he likes to give himself answers like because life is stupid, Power. Life doesn't know that you're the only person alive with his own moral code. The only person who can save the whole world from destruction and spiritual emptiness.

HEATHER: It's from all those years in the newspaper business. It can do things to them. It made Paul reckless.

JAMIE is checking the telescopic sight.

JAMIE: It does work. You just have to adjust it. He's so lousy with mechanical things. I think he's in the wrong century. I'm sorry about Paul.

HEATHER: Thanks.

JAMIE: Had you been together a long time.

HEATHER: We hadn't "been together" at all.

JAMIE: But Power said —

HEATHER: No he didn't. He said I was his friend. And that's all I was. Just a good friend.

JAMIE: Oh . . . How did you meet Power.

HEATHER: Through Paul. He taught a journalism course I took. Power used to lecture us sometimes.

JAMIE: Was he tedious.

HEATHER: Well let's just say he took his subject seriously. In fact it seemed to depress him.

HEATHER takes a flask of whisky from her purse

JAMIE: Yeah, that's Power. If he knows about it, he's depressed about it. *(notices the flask)* Are you a journalist.

HEATHER: Yes. *(takes a drink)* My father owns the local newspaper. I work for it.

JAMIE: You work for your father. But you don't agree with his politics.

HEATHER: He tolerates me. Maybe because he thinks I'm stupid. Like the General does. I don't mind. I'm biding my time. Someday the paper will be mine. And its politics will be mine too.

JAMIE: And your politics are like Power's, I guess.

HEATHER: Yeah. Sort of. What are yours.

JAMIE: Ah, I don't know. All I know about politics is that it's depressing. It seems to suck the spontaneity right out of most people. And it makes others, like Power, well . . . deranged.

HEATHER: How did you meet him. Power.

871

JAMIE: I was a janitor. I used to clean offices part-time while I was going to school. I cleaned his office. Have you ever seen his office. It was a mess. Just like him. Drunk all the time. Writing this dumb novel he's been trying to finish for about a hundred years. I changed his life. I cleaned his office and infected him with my contagious spirit. Do you sense my contagious spirit.

HEATHER: It's overwhelming me.

JAMIE: I like you. We'll be close, I can tell.

HEATHER: That sounds like a threat.

JAMIE: You'll learn to love it. Just like Power did. He's alive. Sure he doesn't make sense most of the time. But he's got spirit.

HEATHER: And now he's got a mission.

JAMIE: I think he thinks it's a war. That's why he dragged us down here a thousand miles. All the way on the train his eyes were funny and he was talking about the new world fascism and the military mind. And when we got here he got worse. Like he was smelling Hackman even before he met him. Like he was sniffing in the air for the enemy. It's so ironic on top of all that, Hackman being this cultural advisor thing. Power hates art. He thinks it's "the leisurely reflection of a dying society." Those are his words, not mine. It just twists and turns, this thing between him and Hackman. And it's growing. I'm beginning to feel it myself. It would be funny if Hackman really did care about culture. You know, in the way fascists care about culture. And Power wants to destroy him. But isn't culture a fine thing, anyway. Isn't that what we're told. So it keeps twisting and turning this thing. It's got me thinking about it and I don't usually think about these things. I'm too smart. It kills you. But this is war. This is Power's war. And dammit, now I'm thinking about it too.

HEATHER: So am I.

POWER returns. Sombre-looking

JAMIE: Did you see anything down there.

POWER: Death. I saw death down there.

POWER takes a flask of whisky from a pocket. Drinks.

Blackout.

SCENE FIVE

Later. The patio. Lit by several Japanese lanterns. BROWN is looking around through a pair of binoculars. KARLA comes out.

KARLA: Where is he.

BROWN: On the beach.

   (KARLA mutters)

   How did your meeting at the airport go.

KARLA: He agreed to help us.

BROWN: You mean he agreed to let us pay him to help us. I notice you no longer have the briefcase.

KARLA: I would like a drink please.

There is a small, portable bar in a corner of the patio. BROWN leaves the binoculars on a chair, goes to the bar

BROWN: What would you like.

KARLA: I don't care.

   (BROWN makes a drink. KARLA picks up the binoculars. Looks through them)

   What's he doing down there.

BROWN: Digging.

KARLA: Why?

BROWN: You'll have to ask him.

KARLA: I'm asking you!

BROWN hands her the drink

BROWN: I'm sorry you're upset, miss. The fact that your father's old friend took money from you must be hard for you to swallow. You don't understand the mercenary mind, miss.

KARLA: Your mind, Brown?

BROWN: I'm no mercenary, miss. I have a loyalty.

KARLA: To what.

BROWN: The general.

KARLA: It's strange how he attracts certain kinds of personalities to him.

BROWN: The general will set the world right, miss. The general and men like him.

KARLA: No. Men like my father will set the world right. Men like the general are their tools.

BROWN: Beg your pardon, miss, but your father's rotting in a South American prison. I don't remember the general ever getting himself in a position anything like that.

KARLA: He has a way of looking out for himself.

BROWN: No, miss. He's just not easily beguiled.

KARLA mutters. HACKMAN comes on from the beach. Carrying a shovel.

HACKMAN: Good evening, Karla. You look upset. Didn't it go well.

KARLA: Well enough.

HACKMAN: Good. Brown, could you pour me one of those. A double.

BROWN: Sir. *(goes to the bar)*

KARLA: He said he'd have my father out within a week.

HACKMAN: Then why don't you look happy.

KARLA: I don't trust him.

HACKMAN: Because he took the money? Just because he's practical doesn't mean he can't be trusted. Relax. He'll get your father out because he knows if he doesn't I'll kill him. That's how the world works Karla. By contract. I thought you knew that. I thought that's what you believed in.

KARLA: I believe in my father.

HACKMAN: And your father believes in force. The force of contracts.

(BROWN hands HACKMAN his drink)

Thank you.

BROWN: Did you retrieve it, sir?

HACKMAN: Yes.

KARLA: Retrieve what.

HACKMAN reaches into his pocket. Produces a small notebook.

HACKMAN: This. A journalist's notebook. You know, Brown, it would have been far less unpleasant to have searched him before we buried him.

BROWN: An unforgiveable lapse, sir. I can only say that I must be out of practice.

KARLA: You killed someone.

HACKMAN: He was a trespasser. This is my property. I own it. I have a deed. A contract. People in this world must learn that certain things are inviolate. Besides, dear, he was spying on us.

KARLA: So you are suspected.

HACKMAN: It appears so.

KARLA: Are there others.

HACKMAN: There is one other. A friend of the dead journalist. That's why I retrieved the notebook. To see what he had written down and possibly passed on to his friend. Mr Power. Brownie, do me a favour. Take a quick read through this and brief me later.

BROWN: *(takes the notebook)* I won't take long, sir.

HACKMAN: Take your time. Let's not let them panic us. Let's not change our style, Brownie. They are the foolish ones, remember.

(BROWN nods. Leaves.)

You know Karla I might have to leave here. Run away. That would be sad. I like it here. I like my garden. I like the ocean. I could have even grown to like my new job. I do like artistic things, Karla. Did you know that about me.

KARLA: No.

HACKMAN: Art is the leisurely reflection of an elite society. Who said that.

KARLA: I don't know.

HACKMAN: Perhaps I just made it up then. I'm getting poetic in my old age. Karla if I have to leave, we'll go together. We'll join up with your father and work for his future success. Would you like that.

KARLA: If it was a useful merger. You can be useful. I suppose.

HACKMAN: It could be like the old days. Panama City. Madrid. Places in between. You are a woman I could love. *(touches her hair)*

KARLA: You said that once before.

HACKMAN: You see? I never repeat myself unless I mean it. I must love you. And somehow you must love me. *(touches her neck)*

KARLA: Don't . . . *(shrugs)* Of what exactly are you suspected.

HACKMAN: Of helping you. And your father. Of helping to free a charismatic right-wing lunatic who wants to change half the world. Change it to a place where contracts are honoured. And duty is done. And loyalty is kept. Change it into our kind of world. *(touches her cheek)*

KARLA: I have no loyalty to you.

HACKMAN: But I've helped your father. Put myself in danger. And I may have to run. You could comfort a man on the run.

KARLA: Comfort, maybe. But that is not love.

HACKMAN: Let me be the judge of that. *(grabs her)*

KARLA: No.

HACKMAN: Let me.

He puts his arms around her. Kisses her. She laughs.

KARLA: How do you plan to use me.

HACKMAN: How do you wish to be used.

They kiss. Blackout.

SCENE SIX

The beam of a flashlight. The sound of someone moving around, some metal clanging. Suddenly the flashlight is dropped. Darkness. A groan. A louder groan. A thud.

Pause. Lights.

We are in a small room in HACKMAN's house full of filing cabinets. BROWN is standing with his foot on JAMIE's throat. JAMIE is lying on the floor in front of him. HACKMAN stands to the rear, hands in his pockets.

BROWN: Don't move, laddie. If you move you die. Are you armed. Don't lie, laddie. If you lie you die.

JAMIE shakes his head

HACKMAN: Let him up.

BROWN removes his foot

BROWN: Up you get.

JAMIE gets up slowly

HACKMAN: Make him comfortable.

(BROWN picks JAMIE up and puts him on a filing cabinet. The filing cabinet is about four feet high. HACKMAN approaches JAMIE. JAMIE is rubbing his throat)

Let's make it simple, shall we. We know you're not a gardener. We know you're an associate of Mr. Power's. We know you've been spying on us. All we don't know is why. And you're going to tell us that right now.

JAMIE: He paid me! I'm a paid lackey. I do anything for anyone who pays me. Would you like to pay me to spy on Power. No problem. I'll do it. Trust me.

BROWN: Shut up, laddie. *(rubs his forehead)*

HACKMAN: You're telling me you don't share his political beliefs.

JAMIE: He's a washed-out liberal. Liberals, conservatives, communists, fascists. Who cares. Not me. I'm a working-class pragmatist. I believe in the politics of staying alive.

HACKMAN: Under the circumstances I would say that makes you quite idealistic.

HACKMAN nods at BROWN. BROWN pulls a stiletto from his sleeve. Places it at JAMIE's throat

BROWN: The man is telling you that you're not saying the things he wants to hear.

JAMIE: *(to HACKMAN)* I'm just trying to say I'm not interested in your political involvement.

HACKMAN: My only political involvement is as cultural advisor.

JAMIE: Right. And I can help you there too. They say this country has no real working-class art. And I think that's because it's always presented by a bunch of middle-class academics who patronize the shit out of the working-class with a lot of romantic bullshit. Now, if you pay me enough, I could set up a study, hold regional meetings, write a report on my findings and —

BROWN: Please do shut up, laddie.

BROWN is now rubbing his forehead furiously

HACKMAN: Steady, Brown.

BROWN: I'll be all right, sir. *(turns his back, goes to a corner)*

JAMIE: Why is he always doing that. Rubbing his forehead like that.

BROWN: *(advancing)* War wound!

HACKMAN gets between them. Gestures. BROWN returns to his corner

HACKMAN: Steel plate.

JAMIE: Steel plate?!

HACKMAN: Please. You'll embarrass him.

JAMIE: I'm sorry.

HACKMAN: Let's continue without him, all right?

JAMIE: Sure.

HACKMAN: Are you uncomfortable? Not too ill at ease?

JAMIE: No actually I'm starting to feel okay.

HACKMAN: Yes. Well that's a mistake.

(HACKMAN suddenly and viciously grabs JAMIE's collar and throws him off the filing cabinet across the floor and into another filing cabinet. JAMIE slowly collapses to the floor)

How are you feeling now.

JAMIE: How do you want me to feel.

HACKMAN: Scared.

JAMIE: Okay.

HACKMAN: Three questions. What were you looking for in my files. What did Power learn from Reinhardt. Has Power passed on anything he's learned to anyone else.

(JAMIE just looks at him)

Answers.

HACKMAN kicks JAMIE in the side

JAMIE: *(groans)* Okay. Stop. I've got something to say. *(groans)* But I gotta get up. *(getting up slowly)* I gotta be on my feet. *(up)* Okay, I'm up.

(He straightens, looks at HACKMAN. Inhales. Exhales.)

Go fuck yourself.

HACKMAN hits him and JAMIE falls to the floor. Unconscious. HACKMAN is standing over JAMIE. BROWN joins him

BROWN: I'm sorry you had to do that yourself, sir.

HACKMAN: It's all right, Brown. You were there in spirit.

BROWN: But a man like you shouldn't have to do things like that, sir. Those are things that a man like me should do. I've been letting you down quite a bit lately I'm afraid. It's the head. Always acts up at these times. I think it's the excitement. The promise of violence, if that doesn't sound too barbaric, sir.

HACKMAN: Not at all, Brown. You're a soldier. You have instincts. And this is war.

BROWN: Is it, sir.

HACKMAN: Oh yes, I think so.

BROWN: Have we lost it. Is that why we have to get out of the country.

HACKMAN: No that's something else. Something larger. A chance to prepare for the real war to come. This is something a bit unreal. This is a little war we have to fight before we go. A matter of conflicting points of view. This is a war between me and Mr Power.

BROWN: I hated him on sight, sir. I hated his flabby belly. I hated all the books he'd read and the schools he'd gone to. Just like that. Without even knowing him.

HACKMAN: You know him. He's the enemy. The humanist. The egalitarian. The constant appeaser. He wants to turn the world into Jello. (points to JAMIE) And that's the enemy spy. When he wakes up, do it again. And keep doing it until he talks. He has nothing to tell us but we should make him talk. It's a matter of principle. It's a battle of wills. His against ours.

BROWN: Not exactly an even battle, sir.

HACKMAN: I know. Sad, isn't it. It's a pathetic little war. But it's the only one we've got!

HACKMAN leaves. BROWN looks at JAMIE. Rubs his forehead. Advances. Blackout.

SCENE SEVEN

The patio. POWER and HEATHER. Drinks before dinner. They are dressed casually. POWER is pouring himself a glass of wine.

HEATHER: Why are they keeping us waiting.

POWER: So we'll get nervous.

HEATHER: It's working. I'm starting to sweat. I don't know if I can go through with this.

POWER: Be strong. Have a drink.

HEATHER: No thanks. I'd rather stay alert. I think it would be good if you stayed alert too.

POWER: I'm just having enough to give me a fighting edge.

HEATHER: We should have called the police.

POWER: Nah. They'd ruin everything. Besides, vengeance is mine saith the Lord and since the Lord isn't here tonight I'm standing in for him. Vengeance, therefore, is mine.

BROWN comes on. In a suit

BROWN: Are you comfortable.

POWER: Absolutely.

HEATHER smiles. Nods

BROWN: *(to HEATHER)* Would you like another cocktail.

POWER: No. I've just been helping myself to the wine.

BROWN: So I see. How unique to drink the wine before the dinner.

POWER: I was beginning to get afraid there wasn't going to be a dinner.

BROWN: Of course. Patience is the virtue of a confident man.

POWER: I don't know. I'm a confident man. And I'm just rarin' to go.

BROWN starts off. HEATHER looks at POWER

HEATHER: Oh, Brown.

BROWN: *(stopping)* Yes.

HEATHER: Is your gardener around. I thought I might ask him about the mixture in my compost heap.

BROWN: No. I'm sorry. He had a little accident. We had to send him away.

HEATHER: *(stands)* What kind of —

POWER grabs her arm

BROWN: Something wrong, miss? . . .

POWER: No. She's fine.

BROWN nods. Leaves

HEATHER: They've killed Jamie.

(POWER stares into his glass)

Tyrone. They've killed him.

(POWER doesn't respond. Just stares down)

Tyrone. Do something!

POWER: I will. *(looks up)* I will.

Suddenly the patio is filled with music. A heart-pounding, lush, symphonic march. Very loud. HEATHER and POWER have to shout over the music

HEATHER: What the hell is that?

POWER: Psychological warfare! *(grimaces)* Unbelievable! This guy is unbelievable!

HACKMAN and KARLA enter. Arm-in-arm. Pose at the door and begin a slow regal walk to the table and around it once and then stop. HACKMAN is wearing a perfectly-tailored tuxedo. Military ribbons on his chest. KARLA is wearing a black evening-gown. And a red sash with a small insignia on it. POWER and HEATHER are just staring at them. HACKMAN makes a subtle gesture and the music stops. And simultaneously BROWN is there with a camera to take a picture of KARLA and HACKMAN. BROWN leaves. Pause

HEATHER: Quite an entrance.

HACKMAN: Thank you. We were aiming for something stylish.

POWER: Unbelievable.

HACKMAN: Too much, do you think?

POWER: Oh no. It was just right. I had an orgasm. *(to HEATHER)* How about you.

HEATHER: No. Sorry.

POWER: I think she probably likes more foreplay. But for me, the earth moved. It really did.

HACKMAN: If you're finished, I'll make the introductions.

POWER: Of course, how moronically rude of me to keep the charming lady waiting. *(stands)* And she's wearing her favourite battle dress, too.

HACKMAN: Mr Power. Heather Masterson. Allow me to present Karla Mendez.

POWER: *(kisses her hand)* Daughter of Simón Mendez. Widely renowned banker and ultra-conservative patron of the political movement affectionately known as "lunatics for a better world."

KARLA: *(sits)* Are you drunk, Mr Power.

POWER: A bit, perhaps.

KARLA: Then it would be wise if you watched your tongue.

HACKMAN: *(sits)* It's all right Karla. Mr Power has what he considers to be an original conversation style. Even though to others, it may seem more like the rantings of a desperately under-equipped intellect. In any event I think we should not respond to him too hastily nor take him too seriously.

POWER: There are parts of that speech I actually agree with. You gotta guess which ones though.

KARLA and HACKMAN laugh. POWER and HEATHER frown and slump in their chairs

HACKMAN: How are you this evening, Heather.

HEATHER: What is the purpose of this dinner party, General.

HACKMAN: To eat. To make conversation.

POWER: To strike a deal.

HACKMAN: Yes. Perhaps later to even strike a deal.

HEATHER: I think it stinks. If we've got things to say let's say them.

HACKMAN: This is my house, Heather. We'll do this my way. You've changed, Heather. You're not the little girl I used to know.

HEATHER: I never was. I've hated your kind all my life.

HACKMAN: Well you've been very good at keeping it a secret. Was this so that you could spy on me.

HEATHER: Yes.

HACKMAN: For whom.

HEATHER: Friends.

HACKMAN: Like Mr Power here. No. Not Mr Power himself, of course. People like him though. Of his ilk, so to speak.

HEATHER: If that means people who believe in things like a free press and elections and . . . and . . .

885

POWER: Peace.

HEATHER: Peace. Well yeah then, yeah.

HACKMAN: You're still a child, Heather. Naive and self-righteous.

HEATHER: And you're a murdering son-of-a-bitch. And I'm not going a bit farther with this crap. *(stands)* I'm going for the police.

KARLA: I think you should sit down, little girl.

HEATHER: Don't little girl me. I know your story. You throw bombs at people to get what you want. And you've already got three million dollars in a Swiss bank. You're just a common greedy criminal.

KARLA is muttering furiously

HACKMAN: Mr Power, explain to her why she should sit down.

POWER: The general has a pistol under his jacket.

HEATHER: So what?

HACKMAN: The full sentence should have been "The general has a pistol under his jacket which he will use."

POWER: Sit down, Heather. Our time is coming.

HACKMAN: It's here now, Mr Power. I'm afraid Heather has ruined the mood for dinner. I was prepared to dazzle you with my suggestions for a cultural policy. But of course that sham will be unnecessary.

POWER: You got any other shams you want to try out?

HACKMAN: I have your friend, Mr Power. I have him and it's up to you to get him back.

POWER: He's alive?

HACKMAN: More or less.

POWER: If you've hurt him I'll —

886

HACKMAN: Oh please, Mr Power, you'll what? Lash me with your tongue? Write a nasty article about me? Put my name on a petition and send it to all your friends?

POWER: That's not a bad idea. Ban the Fascist.

HACKMAN: An unfortunate choice of words, in the modern context, I mean. I'm someone who just wants to rid the world of chaos, get the economy moving again, and restore order.

POWER: General, I've been waiting all my life to say this to someone like you. *(stands)* Any asshole can get the trains running on time!! Any asshole can do that, but it takes something more to get the people on the trains for any reason other than the fact that they're scared shitless of the asshole who got them running on time. And another thing. It's too bad you didn't get a chance to infect me with your contrived ideas on culture because I was ready for that too.

HACKMAN: Strangely enough my ideas on culture are quite sincere.

POWER: Oh I bet they are. All concerned with harmony and beauty and the glorious heart within. That piece of schlock that accompanied your musical ride into dinner was probably a good example.

HACKMAN: You would have preferred an earthy folk song, no doubt.

POWER is fuming. HEATHER is gesturing him on. KARLA and HACKMAN are shaking their heads. Muttering.

POWER: That's it. That's the point! I wouldn't have preferred. I don't *dictate*. If you'll pardon the pun. Culture, like everything else, just is. It evolves out of just being. Like everything else. Like society. A changing society. An evolving society! Oh God Almighty I want you dead and rotting in the ground!! And if I could I'd reach back into history and remove every trace of every person you have anything in common with and right all the wrong they've done in the name of all that is brutal and elitist and just plain goddamn vicious and greedy!

(In one quick move KARLA pulls a small pistol from under her dress, stands, points the gun at POWER and shoots. HEATHER yells. Pause.)

Am I shot? *(checking his body)* Am I shot? *(to HEATHER)* See any blood? I don't feel anything. Maybe I'm in shock. Maybe I'm dying.

HACKMAN: Brutal, elitist, vicious, greedy, but decisive, Mr Power. Quite decisive.

POWER: Well am I dying or not. Isn't anyone going to tell me.

KARLA: I aimed wide.

POWER: Thanks. *(sits)*

KARLA: Next time I won't. John, I think the little girl was right. Must we go on with this. This man is intolerable.

HACKMAN: But just a little bit amusing, no?

KARLA: No. Intolerable and tiring. Very tiring. And we have a long journey ahead of us tomorrow.

HEATHER: Going away for good, General.

HACKMAN: I'm afraid so. I'm afraid your friend Mr Reinhardt has probably made it impossible for me to stay.

HEATHER: You killed him. You killed him but he got you. For sure he got the word out that Miss Murder here was your guest and people will put that together with whatever you're planning to do to help her father.

HACKMAN: Well I can't be sure, but I can't take any chances either. We do have a meeting with destiny, you know.

POWER: What about us.

HACKMAN: You have a meeting with your own destiny, Mr Power.

POWER: Ah yes. The vast darkness. Chaos and death.

HACKMAN: I hope to make it a clean death, Mr Power. No chaos. Just a bullet. I was hoping to play with you some more but you're too boring. Besides, you have nothing I want and all you want from me is to listen to you rant. It really is a pathetic little war, Mr Power. No thunder. No lightning.

POWER has his hands under the table. Is leaning forward

POWER: I have a little lightning under the table, General. It's a thirty-eight calibre special. And it's pointed straight at you.

KARLA: He's lying.

POWER: Try going. Find out.

HACKMAN: It doesn't matter. Brown probably heard that shot. He'll be coming in soon, Mr Power. And no mere thirty-eight is going to stop him.

POWER: He'll just walk into it, right. He'll march into his death for you.

HACKMAN: Try him. Find out. In the meantime, perhaps it's a standoff.

HEATHER: What do we do.

POWER: I'm thinking.

Long pause

KARLA: John. He's bluffing.

HACKMAN: We'll see soon enough.

HEATHER: Tyrone.

POWER: I'm thinking.

(*Long pause. The sound of footsteps. Someone approaching. They all look. Pause. JAMIE stumbles in. His face bloodied. Limping*)

Jamie.

JAMIE: Power. He beat the shit out of me. Old Killer Eyes. He's a mean bastard . . . Power, help me . . . Power.

JAMIE falls. HACKMAN makes a move to get up, but POWER stands. POWER does have a gun. He grabs KARLA and puts the gun to her head, while almost simultaneously HACKMAN is doing the same thing to HEATHER. JAMIE is struggling to get to his feet.

HACKMAN: This looks like a standoff for sure.

POWER: Can you get up, Jamie.

JAMIE: Yeah. *(struggling up)* He hurt me. He came back to hurt me some more but . . . his head started to bother him pretty bad and I knocked him down and pushed a filing cabinet on top of him.

POWER: Don't worry, Heather. We'll get you out.

HACKMAN: Not by going to the police, Mr Power. That would mean she dies. I promise you that.

POWER: Get up, Jamie. We're leaving.

JAMIE is on his feet. Staggering

JAMIE: Yeah . . . sure . . . great idea. Old Killer Eyes is lying under a filing cabinet. He looks real stupid. But he's not dead . . . kind of wish he was. God he hurt me.

POWER: Get going. I'm right behind you.

JAMIE starts off. POWER is backing up. Holding KARLA.

POWER: Is this better, General. Is this a better quality war. I mean now we've both got prisoners. Exciting, eh.

HEATHER: For chrissake, Power. I don't much feel like sacrificing myself so you can get your rocks off.

HACKMAN: Yes. Why make the ladies suffer. How about a prisoner exchange.

890

POWER: That's not how it's done, General. Even I know that. You don't exchange prisoners in the enemy's camp. You find a neutral territory.

HACKMAN: Where.

POWER: You'll hear from me.

JAMIE: Where am I.

POWER: Just keep going.

JAMIE: Where.

POWER: Left foot. Right foot. Leave the rest to me.

JAMIE: (in a daze) Left foot. Right foot. Left . . .

JAMIE, POWER and KARLA are gone. HACKMAN lowers his gun. Lets go of HEATHER

HEATHER: He'll go to the police.

HACKMAN: I don't think so. That would spoil his fun.

HEATHER: What is this. Are you two playing some kind of game or something.

HACKMAN: He is, I think. But not me. And that's the basic difference between us which Mr Power will soon find out about.

BROWN comes on. Soiled. Walking slowly

BROWN: How did it go.

HACKMAN: More or less as planned. Your part as well, I gather.

BROWN: I think I gave a brilliant performance, if I may say so, sir.

HACKMAN: Did he hurt you.

BROWN: The fool threw an empty filing cabinet on me. Wouldn't hurt a fly. The kid thinks he's real tough.

HACKMAN: They both do, Brown. They both do.

HACKMAN laughs. Picks up a glass of wine. Drinks. Laughs again

HACKMAN: I love this!

Blackout.

SCENE EIGHT

Dawn. In different areas, eventually all merging into one. The campsite on the cliff. KARLA is sitting on a campstool. Her hands tied behind her back. POWER is kneeling next to JAMIE, washing the blood from his face.

POWER: Does it hurt?

JAMIE: Yeah.

POWER: I was right about Hackman, wasn't I. He's nuts.

JAMIE: Yeah. You were right.

POWER: *(shrugs)* Yeah. Well good for me. I guess. What possessed you to sneak in there in the first place.

JAMIE: You. Your disease. Whatever you've got I had for a while.

POWER: But you don't have it anymore.

JAMIE: Killer Eyes knocked some sense into me. Power, I think we should call the authorities.

POWER: No. This is my job.

JAMIE: Really. Who gave it to you.

POWER: Look. I'm sorry this happened to you but —

JAMIE: No you're not. You're not even here. What is it exactly you want from Hackman. I've got to know,

Power. I feel like I've been run over by a truck and I hate thinking there's no reason for it.

POWER: I want him dead.

JAMIE: Really? No metaphors? You don't mean in a larger spiritual way. You know how you usually talk? You mean really dead?

POWER: Yeah.

JAMIE: Why? Because he killed your friend Paul Reinhardt?

POWER: Sure. That's a good reason. There are others of course.

JAMIE: Of course. (shakes his head) Are you going to kill him, Power.

POWER: If I get the chance.

JAMIE: You can't. It's not in you.

POWER: Oh I think it is. I've got a feeling.

JAMIE: You've been drinking again.

POWER: Yeah. To make the feeling go away. But it won't.

POWER picks up the rifle. Wanders over to the cliff's edge

JAMIE: Is it a scary feeling?

POWER: Yeah.

KARLA: I wouldn't worry. I doubt if you'll get the chance to do anything about it.

JAMIE: I'm not in love with her anymore. (to KARLA) I used to love you from a distance. When I got closer I noticed you had serious flaws in your personality.

KARLA: That is preferable, is it not, to having no personality at all.

JAMIE: You can't insult me. You and your buddies are just about finished. My friend here is a formidable opponent. Aren't you Power.

POWER is looking through the sight, pointing the rifle down toward HACKMAN's house

JAMIE: Aren't you, Power.

POWER looks at him

POWER: I don't know.

Lights out on this area. Lights up on the patio. BROWN is sitting there. In commando gear. Loading a rifle. Looking off toward the cliff

BROWN: Come on, laddies. Come on down. Be tough. Be big tough boys. (*rubs his forehead furiously*) Oh man. I'm getting that old barbaric feeling. We're waiting, laddies. Won't you please come down.

He rubs his forehead. Then raises the rifle to check the sight. Lights out on this area. Lights up on the beach. HACKMAN is sitting on a rock. HEATHER is digging a hole with a shovel

HEATHER: What am I digging.

HACKMAN: A grave.

HEATHER: Whose?

HACKMAN: Well it's not mine.

HEATHER: It's pretty sick to make a person dig her own grave.

HACKMAN: How pessimistic, Heather. No, you're just not the same little girl I used to know. Journalism has dulled your imagination. Your friend Power is probably watching you dig. Do you suppose he's come to the same conclusion.

HEATHER: (*stops digging*) You're baiting him.

HACKMAN: (*waves his gun*) Keep digging, Heather.

HEATHER: You're a sadistic murdering bastard.

HACKMAN: Would you like to hear the speech on culture I prepared for Mr Power?

HEATHER: Not really.

HACKMAN: Well you're going to hear it anyway. I worked too hard on it for it to go to waste . . . Art. Art is the leisurely reflection of a discriminating society. Classical art is the historical reminder of earlier discrimination. The best art is the art of superficial spectacle which demonstrates the beauty of art for art's sake.

(Lights start to fade)

Give five discriminating artists enough money to create five superficial spectacles and you will have a definition of a nation's culture. Culture? Culture is . . . oh . . . Culture is . . .

Lights out on this area. Lights up on the campsite. POWER is looking through the sight, the gun pointed down at the beach

POWER: I've got to get down there. *(hands rifle to JAMIE)* Here, take this. Watch her.

JAMIE: You don't look well.

POWER: I can't win. I just realized that.

JAMIE: Then don't go.

POWER: I have to get Heather away from him. But dammit. I can't win. Even if I get him. He's the only one who can win. Violence is his way, not mine. Life is always doing things like this to me. Have you ever noticed that. Think about it.

POWER is leaving.

JAMIE: Be careful.

POWER: I don't understand. Why me. I must be doing something wrong. I wonder what it is.

POWER is gone

KARLA: He has no chance at all. *(laughs)*

JAMIE: A momentary loss of faith. A little moral crisis. He has them all the time. *(looks at the rifle)* I hate guns.

KARLA laughs. JAMIE looks at her. KARLA laughs louder. Lights out on this area. Lights up on the patio. BROWN has the rifle to his shoulder and is pointing it toward the cliff

BROWN: There once was a man called Power
Who set himself up in a tower
But when someone shot him
They all soon forgot him
And dead, Power decayed and turned sour.

(He laughs, then sings the first four lines of "Getting To Know You")

(laughs) Come on down, laddie. That's it. Here he comes. Are you ready, Sergeant. Yes sir. How do you feel Sergeant. *(rubs his forehead)* Ooh. There's a pain I can live with, sir. A real burden of love.

(The lights start to fade. He sings the first four lines of "That Old Black Magic")

Lights out on this area. Lights up on the beach

HACKMAN: Opera. Opera is an example of what I mean. Many people think opera is a wasteful and irrelevant art form. But I believe its strength lies in its wastefulness. Its arrogant belief in its own —

HEATHER: Shut up! Will you please shut up. Shoot me. Strangle me. But please don't make me listen to any more of this garbage.

HACKMAN: *(waves his gun)* Just keep digging.

Four rifle shots

HEATHER: What was that.

HACKMAN: The first two shots froze Mr Power in his tracks with fear. The third shot blew off his foot. He of course fell down. The fourth shot him in the shoulder. He is dying. Very slowly. With plenty of time to think. I have a picture of it in my head. Very finely etched. Very tasteful, in its own way. A very creative ending. Not only does he get to watch his own death, but from where he's lying he can see yours too.

HEATHER: You're insane.

HACKMAN: Please. Say something more original. Something creative. Because it will certainly be the last thing you'll ever say. (lifts his gun)

HEATHER: Mr Power has his gun pointed at your back.

HACKMAN: Well, that's creative. But it's not very original.

POWER is walking out of the darkness. Holding his gun with both hands.

POWER: I think she was going for the documentary approach.

(HACKMAN smiles)

Get his gun.

(HEATHER grabs HACKMAN's gun)

Turn around.

HACKMAN: What are you going to do now.

POWER: I'm thinking.

HEATHER: Do you know what this is, General. This is justice. You murdered Paul Reinhardt and now you're going to pay. Hooray for us, Power. I'll go call the police. (runs off)

HACKMAN: Now's your chance. All you have to do is pull the trigger.

POWER: Maybe there's another choice. I could hold you for the police.

HACKMAN: No. If you don't shoot I'm leaving. I'll be gone, out of the country before the police arrive.

POWER: Where can you go? There are international police agencies. And extradition treaties.

HACKMAN: Where I'm going I can't be touched. I'm going to burrow just beneath the surface of a foreign society. You'll know I'm around though. Occasionally you'll read something in a newspaper. A story about a return to order somewhere. The settings of things right. And you'll know I've been working . . . Well, Mr Power? Can you kill me?

POWER: I'm thinking.

Lights out on this area. Lights up on patio. BROWN is sprawled unconscious in a chair. JAMIE is standing over him. Looking in a daze at his rifle. HEATHER runs on.

HEATHER: What happened?

JAMIE: He was aiming for Power. He was going to shoot him. I saw it all through this telescopic sight. I had to stop him.

HEATHER: You killed him?

JAMIE: I tried. I missed. Three times I missed. The fourth time I hit that lantern and it fell on his head. He's unconscious. I hate violence. I really do. This is not private-eye work. Private eyes don't use rifles. They take divorce cases. And make money. There's no money in this. There's only misery in this. Where's Power.

HEATHER: On the beach. With Hackman.

JAMIE: Are you all right. I've been worried about you. I know we just met but I felt we made a psychic connection. I'm sensitive that way, you know.

HEATHER: *(touches his cheek)* I'm all right. What about you. You seem to be in a daze.

JAMIE: I am. I just tried to kill someone. I've never done that before. I think it changed my life. *(sits)*

HEATHER: You better get down to the beach. Power might need your help.

JAMIE: Helping Power makes me miserable. I just tried to kill someone to help Power. It's a habit I've got to break.

HEATHER: This is no time to go soft. This isn't defeat. This is victory. Justice. These guys killed Paul Reinhardt.

JAMIE: Politics.

HEATHER: No. Murder.

JAMIE: No. War. Yes. I'm seeing it all now. I'm seeing how it works. I'm learning. This is a battle between two men. One of them, Power, wants the world to work properly with justice and equality and all those things. The other one, Hackman, just wants the world to work. Period. I figured all that out a while ago but I couldn't figure out my part in it all. But I learned. Experience taught me. I'm a pacifist. Will you marry me?

HEATHER: What.

JAMIE: I know you like me. I want to get married? Have children. Buy a small farm someplace. Will you marry me.

HEATHER: No.

JAMIE: Is that your final answer.

HEATHER: This isn't the time. Power might be in danger. And there's something I'm supposed to be doing. I'm supposed to be calling the police. *(starts off)* Hey . . . Hey. I liked you better when you had spirit. *(leaves)*

JAMIE: Pacificists have spirit. I know. I can sense it growing inside me. A great spirit.

BROWN groans. The groan turns into the first note of "As Time Goes By". Brown sings the first four lines of the song.

JAMIE, in a daze, sings the fifth line of the song.

BROWN sits up suddenly. Sees JAMIE. Advances. JAMIE raises two sets of fingers in the peace sign. BROWN sees this. Recoils. Rubbing his head furiously, he wanders off. JAMIE is staring at his fingers, smiling. Fade out. Lights up on the beach. POWER is pointing the gun at HACKMAN. Thinking. Rubbing his head. Mumbling to himself. Gesturing. HACKMAN is looking at him curiously. KARLA appears. Walking quietly, slowly up behind POWER

HACKMAN: No, don't bother him. He's thinking.

KARLA: About what?

POWER turns. Caught between them. The gun moving from one to the other

HACKMAN: The sanctity of life, probably. The moral implications of taking action. The pros. The cons. The pros.
The cons. Ad infinitum, right, Mr Power?

POWER: How did you escape.

KARLA: I got mad. It's easy if you get mad.

HACKMAN: She's right. Perhaps you should try getting mad,
Mr Power.

POWER: I am.

And now HACKMAN and KARLA advance slowly

HACKMAN: No. You're indignant. You're outraged. You just
don't understand, do you. Anger is a weapon. Allowing
you to be brutal. Brutality is another weapon. Allowing
you to take action. In this way, you build your arsenal.
Until you have the ultimate weapon. Immorality. Which

allows you to take any action in any way at any time. Immorality is a great weapon. And you don't have it.

POWER: I don't need it. I've got a gun. See?

HACKMAN: So what.

POWER: I just thought it was a good time to remind you.

HACKMAN: The point is, you can't use it.

POWER: Just because I can't use it, doesn't mean I won't use it.

KARLA: What is he talking about.

HACKMAN: The gun is philosophically confusing to Mr Power. Perhaps you could do him a favour and take it away from him.

KARLA moves toward POWER

POWER: Stay put.

KARLA: That's impossible. To take the gun I have to be closer.

POWER: Stop right there.

KARLA: One more step.

She takes a step. Stops

POWER: Be careful.

KARLA: All right.

KARLA pulls a fancy move. Kicks the gun out of POWER's hand. Picks it up

POWER: Shit. I knew she was going to do that. I hate myself.

HACKMAN: No chance, Power. You had no chance. She hates you. She'd risk everything to beat you. You have to risk taking action! Let's go, Karla. It's over. *(starts off)*

KARLA: Almost.

She shoots POWER. POWER drops to his knees. Holding his shoulder

HACKMAN: Did you do that for me.

KARLA is walking past him

KARLA: No.

She leaves. Muttering

HACKMAN: Power . . . Power?

POWER: What?

HACKMAN: Don't die. Try to live. It would be more interesting if you lived and we met again. There's so much I could teach you.

(*POWER is trying to get to his feet*)

No. Please. No need to stand on my account. Besides, I want to remember you just as you are.

HACKMAN smiles. Pats POWER on the head. Leaves, humming an aria. POWER struggles to his feet. Turns in a circle. Falls on his rump

POWER: This is very, very depressing.

JAMIE runs on

JAMIE: Power? Power.

POWER: Over here.

JAMIE: (*rushes over*) What happened.

POWER: You tied Karla's hands, didn't you.

JAMIE: Yeah.

POWER: You did a lousy job.

JAMIE: Oh my God. You're shot.

POWER: She shot me. She got loose because you didn't tie her up properly and she came down here and shot me. Why can't you do anything properly. Why can't *we* do anything properly. It's so goddamn depressing.

JAMIE: Does it hurt.

POWER: Yes.

JAMIE: It looks bad.

POWER: I could have killed him. But I didn't. I just thought about it. You're right about me. I think too much. Thinking doesn't help.

JAMIE: Power. It looks really bad. Your wound is serious.

POWER: I'll be all right. You better get after them. Karla and Hackman. They're getting away.

JAMIE: I can't leave you. You're wounded. You may be dying.

POWER: No. I'm not. Get going. You can at least try to follow them.

JAMIE *is cradling POWER's head. Rocking back and forth*

JAMIE: I can't. You're dying.

POWER: I'm not dying.

JAMIE: Yes you are.

POWER: No I'm not. Get going. Let go of me.

JAMIE: Oh my God, Power. You're dying.

POWER: Dammit. Dammit. Dammit. I am not dying. Let me go. Get after them.

JAMIE: I'm sorry, Power. I'm so sorry. Don't die. Don't die.

POWER: I'm not. I'm not.

Lights start to fade

JAMIE: It's so bad. It's so awful. Don't die.

POWER: I can't stand it. They're getting away. We're letting them get away. We're failing again. I can't stand it. It's killing me.

JAMIE: You're dying.

POWER: No, it's killing me.

JAMIE: You're dying.

POWER: It's so depressing.

JAMIE: Please don't die.

POWER: For God's sake I'm not dying. I'm just depressed. It's just so damn depressing . . . Jamie?

JAMIE: What?

POWER: We have to do better in the future. Promise me next time you tie someone up you'll do it properly.

JAMIE: I promise.

POWER: And I promise next time I go to war I'll win . . . Or at least try to break even. I'm tired of losing. It's so . . . depressing.

JAMIE is rocking back and forth. POWER is shaking his head. HEATHER runs on. Goes to them. Kneels. Suddenly they all look up. And on the cliff KARLA, BROWN and HACKMAN are looking down. Waving.

The End

Wayne Grady, editor

THE PENGUIN BOOK OF CANADIAN SHORT STORIES

In this collection of Canadian short stories the very best Canadian writing is sampled. This vast range of stories offers something for every taste and colourfully reflects the rich diversity of one country's literary heritage.

'. . . the short story has developed into Canada's healthiest and most versatile literary genre. Several of our novelists — Morley Callaghan and Hugh Garner, for example — are better known abroad for their short stories than for their novels. And many of our best writers write virtually nothing but short stories: Mavis Gallant, Norman Levine, Alice Munro, W.D. Valgardson, and others.' — *from the preface by Wayne Grady*.

These twenty-eight stories have been carefully selected and introduced to provide both entertaining reading and an insight into the dominant themes and directions of Canadian literature from its beginnings in the early nineteenth century right up to the present day.

Wayne Grady, editor

THE PENGUIN BOOK OF MODERN CANADIAN SHORT STORIES

This anthology is presented as a companion volume to the highly acclaimed *Penguin Book of Canadian Short Stories*, and focuses on the period from the early 1960s to the present, two vital decades in the development of Canada's most important literary genre.

The twenty-four stories have been carefully selected from both published and unpublished material to reflect the broad diversity of the modern Canadian short story, as well as to provide an overview of its dominant and recurring themes. Stories by such major authors as Alice Munro, Brian Moore, Margaret Atwood, Norman Levine, Elizabeth Spencer, and Margaret Laurence are included. French-Canadian short fiction is represented by Anne Hébert, Gabrielle Roy, Gérard Bessette, and Jacques Ferron (the latter two by stories appearing here in English for the first time). Recent work by these writers is accompanied by stories from the newer generation — Sean Virgo, W.D. Valgardson, Matt Cohen, and W.P. Kinsella.

As in the *Penguin Book of Canadian Short Stories*, editor Wayne Grady has brought together stories that provide a valuable and entertaining collection for both the student of Canadian literature and the casual reader.